Lecture Notes in Computer Science 6696

Commenced Publication in 1973
Founding and Former Series Editors:
Gerhard Goos, Juris Hartmanis, and Jan van Leeuwen

Kent Lyons   Jeffrey Hightower
Elaine M. Huang (Eds.)

Pervasive Computing

9th International Conference, Pervasive 2011
San Francisco, USA, June 12-15, 2011
Proceedings

 Springer

Volume Editors

Kent Lyons
Intel Labs, Intel Corporation
2200 Mission College Blvd.
Santa Clara, CA 95052, USA,
E-mail: kent.lyons@intel.com

Jeffrey Hightower
Google, Seattle
651 N 34th Street
Seattle, WA 98103, USA
E-mail: jeffrey.hightower@gmail.com

Elaine M. Huang
University of Zurich
Department of Informatics
Binzmühlestrasse 14
8050 Zurich, Switzerland,
E-mail: huang@ifi.uzh.ch

ISSN 0302-9743   e-ISSN 1611-3349
ISBN 978-3-642-21725-8   ISBN 978-3-642-21726-5 (eBook)
DOI 10.1007/978-3-642-21726-5
Springer Heidelberg Dordrecht London New York

Library of Congress Control Number: 2011929025

CR Subject Classification (1998): C.2, H.4, D.2, H.5, H.3

LNCS Sublibrary: SL 3 – Information Systems and Application, incl. Internet/Web
and HCI

Typesetting: Camera-ready by author, data conversion by Scientific Publishing Services, Chennai, India

Printed on acid-free paper

Springer is part of Springer Science+Business Media (www.springer.com)

Preface

On behalf the Program Co-chairs as well as the entire Organizing Committee, we welcome you to the proceedings of Pervasive 2011—the 9th International Conference on Pervasive Computing. This year's conference was held in San Francisco, California, and marked the first time that this premiere forum for research in the field of pervasive and ubiquitous computing was held in the USA.

Pervasive 2011 received a total of 93 submissions to the paper track, consisting of 70 full-length paper submissions (up to 18 pages) and 23 note-length submissions (up to 8 pages). A rigorous review process was conducted by a Program Committee of 27 recognized experts in the field of pervasive computing from 10 different countries and from both academia and industry. Every submission was evaluated in a double-blind review process by at least two Program Committee(PC) members and two external reviewers. In all, 174 external reviewers participated in the process in addition to the committee. The review phase was followed by an online discussion in which both the PC members and external reviewers took part. The final discussion and subsequent selection of technical program papers and notes happened during a two-day PC meeting in December 2010 in Seattle, Washington, hosted in part by Intel Labs Seattle through the use of their facility. Ultimately, 22 submissions were selected for inclusion in the technical program, among them 19 full papers and 3 notes, for a total acceptance rate of 23.7%. The selected papers are the work of 96 different authors from 34 international industrial and academic institutions.

As in previous years, Pervasive 2011 showcased a wide range of research activities in addition to the technical program that is presented in this volume. This year's categories of participation included a full-day of workshops prior to the technical program, as well as videos, demonstrations, and posters to accommodate the presentation and discussion of research in ways appropriate to its current state. Additionally, a Doctoral Consortium for senior PhD students occurred in conjunction with ISWC 2011, the co-located 15th International Symposium on Wearable Computers. The accepted submissions in these additional categories are not published in this volume, but can be found in the adjunct proceedings for Pervasive 2011.

Pervasive 2011 was the direct result of the dedicated effort of numerous volunteers. We want to thank the Conference Committee members for their hard work and attention to detail in making sure each aspect of the conference came together. The Program Committee and reviewers worked diligently to assemble a terrific program. We also wish to thank the staff of events for their assistance with the management of the conference and our sponsors for helping make Pervasive 2011 a success.

June 2011

Kent Lyons
Jeff Hightower
Elaine M. Huang

Organization

Conference Committee

Conference Chair	Kent Lyons, Intel, USA
Program Co-chairs	Jeff Hightower, Google, USA
	Elaine M. Huang, University of Zurich, Switzerland
Demos	Tico Ballagas, Nokia Research Center, Palo Alto, USA
	Daniela Rosner, UC Berkeley, USA
Posters	Oliver Amft, TU Eindhoven, The Netherlands
	Kurt Partridge, PARC, USA
Workshops	Mirco Musolesi, University of St. Andrews, UK
	Alexander Varshavsky, AT&T Labs, USA
Videos	Daniel Roggen, ETH Zurich, Switzerland
	Gerd Kortuem, Lancaster University, UK
Publications	Fahim Kawsar, Bell Labs, Belgium and Lancaster University, UK
Publicity	Andreas Bulling, University of Cambridge, UK
Local Arrangements	Trevor Pering, Intel, USA
Web	Nirmal J. Patel, Georgia Tech, USA
Sponsorship	Thad Starner, Georgia Tech, USA

Program Committee

Andreas Bulling	University of Cambridge, UK
Alexander Varshavsky	AT&T Labs, USA
Antonio Krger	DFKI and Saarland University, Germany
Bashar Nuseibeh	Open University, UK
Chris Schmandt	MIT, USA
Daniel Avrahami	Intel Labs, USA
Florian Michahelles	ETH Zurich, Switzerland
Frank Bentley	Motorola, USA
Hao-Hua Chu	National Taiwan University, Taiwan
James Scott	Microsoft Research Cambridge, UK
Jens Grossklags	Penn State, USA
Jin Nakazawa	Keio University, Japan
John Krumm	Microsoft Research, USA
Jon Froehlich	University of Washington, USA
Judy Kay	University of Sydney, Australia
Kay Connelly	Indiana University, USA
Kurt Partridge	PARC, USA

Leila Takayama	Willow Garage, USA
Lena Mamykina	Columbia University, USA
Mike Hazas	Lancaster University, UK
Minkyong Kim	IBM T.J. Watson Research Center, USA
Nic Marquardt	University of Calgary, Canada
Patrick L. Olivier	Newcastle University, UK
Rene Mayrhofer	Upper Austria University of Applied Sciences, Austria
Shin'ichi Konomi	Tokyo Denki University, Japan
Shwetak Patel	University of Washington, USA
Tico Ballagas	Nokia Research Center, Palo Alto, USA

Steering Committee

A.J. Brush	Microsoft Research, USA
Hans Gellersen	Lancaster University, UK
Anthony LaMarca	Intel Research, USA
Marc Langheinrich	ETH Zurich, Switzerland
Aaron Quigley	University of St. Andrews, UK
Hide Tokuda	Keio University, Japan
Khai Truong	University of Toronto, Canada

Reviewers

Wael Abd-Almageed	Stephen Brewster	Sunny Consolvo
Sharad Agarwal	Gregor Broll	David Cooper
Manfred Aigner	Leah Buechley	Scott Counts
Fahd Albinali	Andreas Bulling	Landon Cox
Swamy Ananthanarayan	Tiago Camacho	Florian Daiber
Lisa Anthony	Andrew Campbell	David Evans
Lora Appel	Ricardo Chavarriaga	Eyal de Lara
Ismail Arai	Ling-jyh Chen	Dave Dearman
Daniel Avrahami	Guanling Chen	Anind Dey
Tico Ballagas	Yu-Chung Cheng	Travis Deyle
Luciano Baresi	Kunigunde Cherenack	Tawanna Dillahunt
Aaron Beach	Mauro Cherubini	Sandra Dominikus
Marek Bell	Marshini Chetty	Steven Dow
Hrvoje Benko	Keith Cheverst	Naranker Dulay
Frank Bentley	Tanzeem Choudhury	Schahram Dustdar
Alastair Beresford	Marc Christie	Nathan Eagle
Claudio Bettini	Hao-Hua Chu	David Evans
Jon Bird	Jaewoo Chung	Benjamin Fabian
Jan Borchers	Elizabeth Churchill	Benedict Fehringer
Gaetano Borriello	Anthony Collins	Steven Feiner
Nick Brachet	Kay Connelly	Mirko Fetter

Laura Forlano
Jodi Forlizzi
Adrian Friday
Jon Froehlich
Raghu Ganti
Lalya Gaye
Sven Gehring
Hans Gellersen
Joy Ghosh
Daniel Greenblatt
William Griswold
Jens Grossklags
Svenja Hagenhoff
Michael Haller
Masahiro Hamasaki
Raffay Hamid
Mike Hazas
Chantel Hazlewood
Jennifer Healey
Sumi Helal
Urs Hengartner
Steve Hodges
Jaap-Henk Hoepman
Jesse Hoey
Eve Hoggan
Paul Holleis
Lars Erik Holmquist
Gary Hsieh
Polly Huang
Bret Hull
Masugi Inoue
Stephen Intille
Shamsi Iqbal
Sibren Isaacman
Giulio Jacucci
Lee Joonhwan
Wendy Ju
Gerrit Kahl
Eunsuk Kang
Ashish Kapoor
Stephan Karpischek
Fahim Kawsar
Judy Kay
Ashraf Khalil
Danish Khan

Sunyoung Kim
Minkyong Kim
Donnie Kim
Jen King
Mikkel Baun Kjærgaard
Predrag Klasnja
Andrew Ko
Shin'ichi Konomi
Vassilis Kostakos
David Kotz
Sven Kratz
Christian Kray
John Krumm
Antonio Krüger
Tsvi Kuflik
Bob Kummerfeld
Kai Kunze
James Landay
Nicholas Lane
Marc Langheinrich
Eric Larson
Karin Leichtenstern
Jonathan Lester
Yang Li
Kevin Li
Lin Liao
Zhigang Liu
Clemens Lombriser
Hong Lu
Paul Lukowicz
Markus Löchtefeld
Julie Maitland
Lena Mamykina
Jennifer Mankoff
Natalia Marmasse
Nicolai Marquardt
Sergio Matos
Yutaka Matsuno
Rene Mayrhofer
David McDonald
Alexander
    Meschtscherjakov
Florian Michahelles
Daniel Michelis
James Mickens

Masateru Minami
Anurag Mittal
Iqbal Mohomed
Mounir Mokhtari
David Molyneaux
Meredith Ringel Morris
Ann Morrison
Floyd Mueller
Emerson Murphy-Hill
Mirco Musolesi
Jörg Müller
Tatsuo Nakajima
Jin Nakazawa
David Nguyen
Petteri Nurmi
Bashar Nuseibeh
Eamonn O'Neill
Daniel Olguin-Olguin
Patrick Olivier
Wei Tsang Ooi
Antti Oulasvirta
Joseph Paradiso
Chris Parnin
Kurt Partridge
Shwetak Patel
Sameer Patil
Don Patterson
Nick Pears
Thomas Pederson
Matthai Philipose
Andrew Phillips
Gian Pietro Picco
James Pierce
Zach Pousman
Bodhi Priyantha
Daniele Quercia
Ahmad Rahmati
Ramesh Ramadoss
Yvonne Rogers
Daniel Roggen
Stephanie Rosenthal
Romain Rouvoy
Dan Saffer
Michele Sama
Shunsuke Saruwatari

Quan Sasaki
Takeshi Sato
Andreas Savvides
Bernt Schiele
Chris Schmandt
Albrecht Schmidt
Stacey Scott
James Scott
Peter Scupelli
Julian Seifert
Mubarak Shah
Yi Shang
Pravin Shankar
Elaine Shi
Josh Smith
Timothy Sohn
Frank Stajano
Thomas Strang
Leila Takayama

Yuri Takhteyev
Poorna Talkad Sukumar
Desney Tan
Anthony Tang
Karen Tang
Nick Taylor
Thiago Teixeira
Bruce Thomas
Andrea Thomaz
Tammy Toscos
Koji Tsukada
Joe Tullio
Keisuke Uehara
Ersin Uzun
Jan Van erp
Kristof Van Laerhoven
Alexander Varshavsky
Jo Vermeulen
Nicolas Villar

Hongan Wang
Evan Welbourne
Kamin Whitehouse
Stephen Whittaker
Andy Wilson
Jake Wobbrock
Woontack Woo
Oliver Woodman
Michael Wright
Kazuo Yano
Koji Yatani
Chuang-wen You
Jaeseok Yun
Lin Zhong
Brian Ziebart
John Zimmerman

Table of Contents

Practices with Smartphones

Sensing at Home, Sensing at Work

Predicting the Future

Location Sensing

Augmenting Mobile Phone Use

Pervasive Computing in the Public Arena

Public Displays

Hands on with Sensing

Sensing on the Body

Planning, Apps, and the High-End Smartphone: Exploring the Landscape of Modern Cross-Device Reaccess

Elizabeth Bales[1], Timothy Sohn[2], and Vidya Setlur[2]

[1] University of California San Diego, 9500 Gilman Dr., La Jolla, CA 92093, USA
[2] Nokia Research Center, 955 Page Mill Road, Palo Alto, CA 94304, USA
ebales@cs.ucsd.edu,{tim.sohn,vidya.setlur}@nokia.com

Abstract. The rapid growth of mobile devices has made it challenging for users to maintain a consistent digital history among all their personal devices. Even with a variety of cloud computing solutions, users continue to redo web searches and reaccess web content that they already interacted with on another device. This paper presents insights into the cross-device reaccess habits of 15 smartphone users. We studied how they reaccessed content between their computer and smartphone through a combination of data logging, a screenshot-based diary study, and user interviews. From 1276 cross-device reaccess events we found that users reaccess content between their phone and computer with comparable frequency, and that users rarely planned ahead for their reaccess needs. Based on our findings, we present opportunities for building future mobile systems to support the unplanned activities and content reaccess needs of mobile users.

1 Introduction

In the past several years the number of personal devices a user owns and interacts with has increased. Mobile phones, laptops, desktops, slates, and in-car navigation systems are becoming increasingly popular in the daily life of a user. In a previous study of multiple device usage, Dearman and Pierce found that users interact with as many as 5 personal devices a day [13]. With multiple devices, a user's data often becomes fragmented based on the usage pattern and affordances of each device. A mobile phone will have history of phone calls, applications opened, and websites visited that are different than activity on another device. The fragmentation of digital activity creates a challenge for the user to transfer and reaccess content across their devices.

Cloud computing has offered promise to enable consistent data access on any device. Services such as Evernote [4], synchronized bookmarks, Dropbox [3], and Chrome-to-phone [2] all offer tools for users to transfer content from one device to another. These tools are designed to support planning practices, where a user recognizes information he will need later and saves it for easy reaccess. Users can sometimes forget the information they will need later, or choose not to plan ahead to preserve flexibility. These unplanned situations are often addressed by attempting to access web content by performing web query searches [24].

Web content is one of the primary sources of information today, especially as web applications that support productivity tasks are becoming increasingly popular. Both the

K. Lyons, J. Hightower, and E.M. Huang (Eds.): Pervasive 2011, LNCS 6696, pp. 1–18, 2011.
© Springer-Verlag Berlin Heidelberg 2011

computer and mobile phone are important devices in a user's ecosystem that provide access to web content. There have been a number of studies analyzing the types of web content and searches that users perform both on their desktop and mobile devices [17,18], but few have studied reaccess patterns across these devices. The explosion of mobile applications has also added a new dimension of content reaccess because the same web content can be accessed through a web browser or a dedicated mobile application.

In this paper we explore both the methods and content of web information reaccess among ones personal devices. We conducted a two week study with 15 users of high-end smartphones: iPhone, Android, N900. We used a combination of interviews, url logging, and a screenshot diary study to gather insights into cross-device reaccess patterns regardless of the method they used to access the content (e.g., web browser or mobile app). We measured cross-device reaccess by matching URLs and comparing timestamps to determine which access occurred first. This process required matching many of the URLs manually because mobile websites have different URLs than their desktop counterparts. We only considered two URLs a match if the content they referenced was the same. Our logging software captured over 123,497 web accesses on the computer and 3,574 web accesses on the mobile phone. Over the course of the study participants submitted 128 screenshots from *in situ* moments when participants noticed they were reaccessing content they had seen before. We captured over 1,200 cases where content was reaccessed on a device different from the original access device, with over 500 reaccesses originating on desktop and over 700 originating on the mobile device.

The results of our study show that:

- Cross-device reaccess, moving from computer to phone and from phone to computer, occurs with comparable frequency.
- Reaccess is often unplanned.
- Native applications are an important part of how users reaccess content.

Informed by these results, we discuss several opportunities to support content reaccess among a user's personal devices.

2   Related Work

There are three areas that researchers have explored the types of content mobile users access. These can roughly be divided into information needs, search patterns, and cross-device explorations.

2.1   Mobile Information Needs

Studies on mobile information needs have used diary study methods to gather ecologically valid data about the types of content mobile users look for. Sohn *et al.* found that mobile users attempt to address many of their information needs through web access or other online resources that may have been previously seen [24]. In a similar study, Dearman *et al.* found that mobile users would often look to online resources to address their mobile information needs, but the process could sometimes be difficult and cumbersome [12]. Church and Smyth looked at the intent behind mobile information needs and found many information needs were related to finding PIM data, hinting that the data is related to content already seen by the user [10]. These diary studies hint at mobile users relying more upon connected resources through the cloud and understanding their re-access patterns would provider further insights into assisting mobile users in limited attention environments.

2.2   Search Behavior and Revisitation Patterns

There have been a number of studies investigating web search behavior on both desktop and mobile devices. Many desktop studies have conducted query analysis on search logs reporting on query length and categorization [16,7]. Spink *et al.* conducted a longitudinal study of query behavior between 1997 and 2001 [25]. As smartphones have evolved over the years, users are accessing content through desktop and mobile web browsers. To investigate this trend, Kamvar and Baluja conducted a large-scale analysis of mobile search queries and found that mobile users with less featureful phones submitted shorter queries [17]. In a follow up study they found that iPhone users in particular behave differently than other smart phone users [18]. Their research revealed that iPhone users create search queries more like desktop computer users. We believe that this trend towards higher end smartphones being used more like computers alters how mobile users reaccess content across their devices and the type of content they reaccess.

In addition to search behavior, studies have shown that web revisitation accounts for 58% [26] to 81% [11] of all desktop web site visits. Obendorf *et al.* found that 50% of desktop web revisits occurred within 3 minutes, while the other half took place much later [22]. Adar, Teevan, and Dumais looked deeper into the intent behind revisits [6] and found a variety of revisitation patterns. When studying how users reaccess content across devices, the analysis becomes multifaceted. A single piece of content can be accessed through a desktop URL, mobile URL, or a mobile application. As far as we are aware, few researchers have studied reaccess patterns across multiple devices, specifically when the content can be accessed through a web browser or mobile application on a high end smartphone [19].

2.3   Cross-Device Interaction

Researchers have explored how users manage their life with multiple devices. Dearman and Pierce conducted a study into how users interact with all their computing devices [13]. In a study of 14 Windows Mobile phone users, Kane *et al.* found that users frequently visit websites on both their phone and laptop/desktop machine, suggesting that sharing web history among these devices could be beneficial [19]. In a later study, Karlson *et al.* looked at situational constraints that mobile users face while using their device [20]. Participants were asked to take screenshots whenever they encountered a barrier on their mobile phone. They suggest the idea of decomposing tasks into subtasks so users can complete them across their devices based on their situational context. Neither of these studies looked at the effect of web reaccess on high-end smartphones and content that can be accessed through a mobile application.

Several systems have created ways for users to plan ahead and share data between their mobile device and their desktop machine. The Context Clipboard uses a clipboard metaphor where users can place notes on the clipboard from their desktop and it is synchronized with their mobile device [15]. Gurungo uses the concept of mobile data types to identify key data that a user may want to access later on and sends the content to the device through Bluetooth [14]. There are also a number of commercial tools available today to support re-accessing content. These tools tend to support planned activities, where users knows ahead of time the content they will need later. Evernote [4] and Dropbox [3] both enable file sharing through the cloud. Googles bookmarks for maps and websites as well as the Chrome-to-phone extension let users synchronize data with their mobile device [2]. Firefox Home synchronizes bookmarks, tabs, and web history between desktop and mobile Firefox clients [5] supporting unplanned activites, where a user does not plan ahead for the content they need. The PIE system also supports unplanned activities by allowing users to search for files and documents on their devices [23].

We build upon this work by specifically exploring re-access patterns among high-end smartphone users. The high quality of smartphone interfaces and always-on connectivity have changed how phones are used today, with many phones being used more like desktops. We focus specifically on the frequency of cross-device reaccess by device type, the amount of preplanning users performed for content they reaccessed, and the role of mobile applications in content reaccess. The following sections describe our study design and results from our exploration of content re-access patterns.

3   User Study

Gathering ecologically valid data from mobile users is challenging. We wanted to gather data from the moments of reaccess on a mobile device or on a computer, but placing an observer in the field to shadow a user can be time intensive. Logging methods are useful, but as mobile applications have become much more prevalent to access web information, the content remains siloed from the data-logging processes. As a result we used a hybrid approach of logging and a diary study to capture data *in situ*. Websites represent a majority of content users may want to access on their device, so we focused mainly on studying web content reaccess through a web browser or mobile application. The following sections describe our methods for obtaining ecologically valid data about the web content that user's reaccess.

3.1   Participants

We recruited 15 smartphone participants (7 iPhone, 4 Android, and 4 N900) through an advertisement on Craigslist from a city in the United States[1]. Due to the sensitive nature of the data collected we experienced a relatively high attrition rate during our recruiting process. We also found it more difficult to recruit Android and N900 users compared to iPhone users which affected our overall recruitment numbers. Our Android users used a variety of phone models that run the Android software platform including the Nexus One, T-Mobile Cliq, and Motorola Droid. All iPhone participants used either the 3G or 3Gs models. Participants ranged in age from 22 to 50 years (μ: 35) and had

---

[1] City is anonymized for submission.

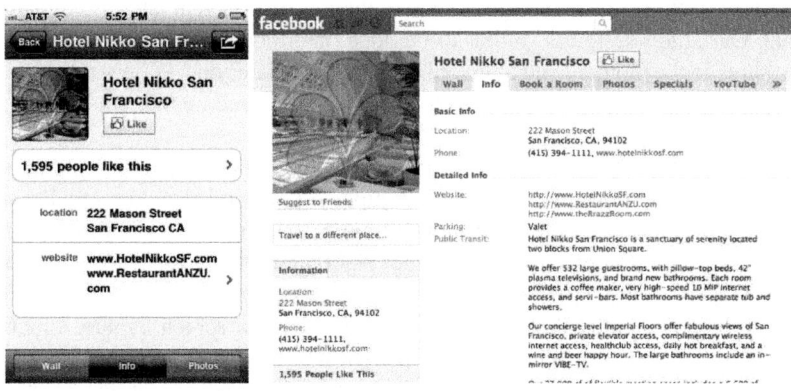

Fig. 1. Example of the same content accessed on through a native mobile application(left) and through the traditional web interface(right)

a wide variety of occupations including students, nanny, financial analyst, engineer, and freelance writer. We focused our recruiting on high-end smartphone users to understand how users of computer-like mobile phones manage content reaccess between their personal devices. Previous research found that users of high-end smartphones with computer-like capabilities behave differently than other smartphone users [18]. As a result, we chose three high-end smartphones with a modern web browser and an available set of mobile applications. All references to participants in this paper are anonymized with *i1-i7* representing iPhone owners, *a1-a4* representing Android owners, and *n1-n4* representing n900 owners.

3.2   Procedure

In order to gather in situ data from our participants, we used both a logging and screenshot capture method. The logging part of the study allowed us to observe the URLs that a participant visited on their desktop and some mobile devices. We developed a Chrome browser extension to log URL accesses on participants' laptops/desktops. The extension logged the URL, timestamp, and page title each time a participant navigated to a webpage. We did not save any content from the web page due to privacy reasons. The data collected by the extension was automatically sent to a server in our research facility. We also used device specific methods, discussed later in this section, for extracting the URL history from each user's mobile device so that it could be compared with the Chrome browser log data.

With the explosion of applications available on a mobile device, users have multiple ways to access web-based content. Many applications act as native clients to web-based content and keep content in silos from other applications. It is difficult to observe content that may be accessed on a laptop through a web browser (e.g., Facebook website) and then on a mobile device through a specialized application (e.g., Facebook application). These types of reaccesses are also important, so we asked users to take screenshots when reaccessing content on their mobile device. Participants annotated these screenshots with additional comments about their reaccess event later through a nightly journal. Our study design is similar to the idea of snippets [9,8] , where users capture screenshots in the moment and annotate them in depth later on a PC. Figure 1 illustrates an example of the same content viewed through a dedicated mobile application and on the standard web interface.

Participants attended a 1 hour in-office visit, filled out nightly online journals about their reaccess activity for the day, and participated in a semi-structured final interview two weeks after their start date. During the first in-office visit, we installed the Chrome browser and extension on the user's laptop. N900 and iPhone users were instructed to take screen shots on their mobile devices and all users were instructed to take screenshots on their computer. Android phones do not have a screen capture function, so android users were asked to use a note application to document reaccesses on their mobile devices. We sent participants daily reminders with a link to an online journal where they could elaborate on their screenshots and reaccess stories they collected throughout the day. During the initial visit we performed a detailed walkthrough of the process of creating and annotating screenshots with the participants.

We installed URL-logging software on the Android and N900 devices that uploaded the same information as the Chrome extension. This data was automatically sent to the server in our research facility. Because of device limitations on the iPhone (i.e., Mobile Safari does not allow browser extensions), we used an alternative method for collecting URL access events. iPhone participants sent us weekly phone data backups that would contain their URL history information.

At the end of the two week study we conducted an exit-interview with the participants. The interview followed a semi-structured format and asked participants about their screenshots and reaccess patterns. Participation were compensated $80 USD at the end of the study.

4   Results and Observations

We collected a total of 123,497 (μ: 6370 min: 775 max: 33892) web page visits on the computer and 3,574 (μ: 215 min: 28 max: 745) web accesses on the mobile phone. Of those webpage visits 14,642 were unique URLs on the computer and 260 unique URLs on the mobile phone. Table 1 shows a breakdown of average number of URLs accessed per user by device type. Android participants tended to browse more pages on the computer, while iPhone participants browsed more web pages on their mobile phone.

Within-device reaccess of data, defined as reaccessing data on the device of original access was observed on all device types with iPhone users averaging 98.4, Android users averaging 9.8, and N900 users averaging 79 within-device reaccesses. Within-device reaccess on the user's personal computer averaged 6683.73 over all users.

To study cross-device reaccess we matched the URL history from both devices to find access patterns. We considered two URLs a match when they accessed the same content, even if one was a mobile page and one was the full page (ex. m.cnn.com and www.cnn.com would be considered the same content even though one is the mobile URL and one is the standard URL). For password protected pages such as social

Table 1. Total number of URLs access per user by device type

Device	computer	mobile
iPhone	μ: 6370 min: 1482 max: 11667	μ: 327 min: 31 max: 745
Android	μ: 14854 min: 775 max: 33892	μ: 182 min: 28 max: 449
N900	μ: 2169 min: 2527 max: 7344	μ: 142 min: 34 max: 309

networks and email we had to rely solely on the URL to determine if the content was the same. In total there were 1276 cross-device reaccesses (μ: 35, min: 4 max: 378), with 754 starting on the phone with reaccesses on the computer, and 522 starting on the computer with reaccesses on the phone. Table 4 shows the frequency and direction of reaccess for each of the smartphone participant classes, as well as the most common content reaccessed by direction. To gain a better understanding of what type of content users reaccessed we manually analyzed all the cross-device reaccessed URLS to identify the top categories. We categorized the reaccess events from the logs into website categories based on a scheme proposed by BBC [1] . The most frequent reaccesses were related to social network (e.g., Facebook) and news websites (e.g., New York Times). Information articles were also a common category of reaccess (e.g., Wikipedia).

We also gathered temporal data about each logged reaccess event. In most cases the time to reaccess information varied between several minutes and several days (Table2). Most reaccesses were short term reaccesses, with the second access occurring on the same day as the initial access event. It is likely that the clustering of reaccesses in the short range time frame is influenced by memory, with reaccess that take place over a longer period of time being easy to forget to complete. This is especially likely when we take into account the methods participants used to remind themselves to reaccess data. WIth most participants using systems that depended on temporally affected interface,

Table 2. Temporal Information of Cross-Device Reaccesses. Percentage represents percentile error. Time is displayed in hours:minutes:seconds.

Device	Direction	25%	50%	75%	90%
iPhone	Phone to Computer	02:38:19	05:47:13	06:21:05	08:28:41
	Computer to Phone	00:45:19	07:22:27	08:18:41	10:31:17
Android	Phone to Computer	00:14:52	02:19:45	05:25:26	05:52:16
	Computer to Phone	02:33:12	04:08:23	05:31:46	06:29:27
n900	Phone to Computer	01:38:16	03:17:58	04:03:17	04:48:28
	Computer to Phone	01:12:17	03:46:24	04:29:13	05:17:57

such as email inboxes, it is likely that if they waited too long to reaccess, the email would be pushed down off the main screen and forgotten.

The following sections describe our observations around user's current methods to synchronize content among their devices, the role of planning in reaccess behaviors, and the role of native applications in content reaccess.

4.1   Current Tools Do Not Adequately Support Cross-Device Reaccess

We observed a variety of methods for sharing content among one's personal devices. Through the nightly journals and interviews, we learned that our participants use many creative, sometimes cumbersome, methods to make their devices interact with each other. Participants expressed pride when sharing their clever syncing solutions. However, even those who were proud of their solutions noted that the methods were time intensive and often reserved for tasks where they could foresee an obvious return on their invested effort.

Table 3 shows a list of the different practices employed by our participants as evidenced from their nightly journals, screenshots and interviews. The common theme among these practices was storing the information in a place for easy access later. Tools that synchronize easily across devices were used more heavily than others, but these methods were not particularly created for save and retrieval purposes (e.g., browser tabs). Email was a common place for our participants to put content they would need later. Many of our participants used a web-based email system that allowed them to access their data anywhere. In addition to emailing oneself links or files for later, users would also repurpose features to save content for reaccess. Marking an email as unread was a common example of repurposing a feature that was not necessarily meant for that purpose. One user also reported using the Facebook 'like' button to populate her 'news feed' with items she wanted to reaccess later. She knew that Facebook was easy to access from any device, and her news feed would be readily available to find the item she was looking for.

The methods shared by our participants required some amount of planning to save the needed data in a place for later access. If user's did not plan ahead, they would attempt to recreate web search queries in order to find the content they needed. Search can work effectively, but can also present additional hurdles when the technology does not behave the way the user expects. For example, *Participant a3* encountered search results on his phone that were "completely different" than the results he got on his computer, making it hard for him to find the information that he wanted to reaccess. He expected the same results he had seen before, but the search engine he used displayed different results on the computer and mobile versions.

Even if the user plans ahead, there is a high recovery cost when restarting a task or trying to find content previously seen. Bookmarks were one way to tag content to access later. However, as the number of bookmarks increases, users need to sift through large amounts of data to find their information. For some participants this lead to frustration. *"I feel like bookmarks are buried, like I have thousands of bookmarks. I have bookmarks for car stuff, I have bookmarks for vegan stuff, I have bookmarks..." (Participant a2)*

Some of these methods (e.g., browser tabs) act as a reminder tool to reaccess information later, which can be useful reinforcement. However, participants still need to

Table 3. Methods for content reaccess shared by users. Many methods require the user to plan ahead for content reaccess.

Method	Description
Email	Email applications automatically sync messages across devices. Users often depended on this feature to find content they had seen before.
Repurposing Features	Features built for other purposes were overloaded by users to identify items for reaccess later. Common examples included emailing content to themselves and using the "mark unread" feature in email to mark a read email that the user wished to return to.
Browser Tabs	Leaving browser tabs open on the mobile device as a reminder to reaccess them on another device was a common user strategy for remembering to reaccess content.
Paper	Paper for reaccess was used by several participants to help sync their devices. Informations was handwritten or printed, carried between the devices, and inputted on the second device to reaccess content.
Bookmarks	Shared bookmark systems were utilized by several users to share data between devices. Using these systems users could save a bookmark on one device and have it be available on their other device automatically.
Search	Unplanned reaccesses were frequently executed by entering search queries into another device.

manually enter the information into each device. Our participants expressed a need to overcome these challenges and have an easy method to reaccess their data.

4.2   Cross-Device Reaccess Happens in Both Directions

We found that content reaccess occurs frequently in both directions between the mobile phone and computer (Table 4). Phones and computers have different strengths that influence reaccess patterns. Computers have large screen real estate, fast processing, and a high-speed network connection. Phones are locationally aware, always on, and ubiquitously connected. Phone to computer reaccess was often driven by technical barriers and participants decomposing their tasks among their devices. Computer to phone reaccess occurred due to contextual factors including location, time, and social context. We also found that the most convenient and accessible device was a factor in deciding which device to use for reaccessing content. In the remainder of this section we analyze the different reasons for each reaccess direction.

Computer to phone: Need it at another location. Location was a prime contextual factor for motivating reaccess. Location affects the range of tasks the user can engage in, influences the external stimulus experienced by the user (which can act as a catalyst for reaccess), and often places constraints on which devices the user can interact with.

Reaccess behaviors influenced by location often began on the computer and shifted to the smartphone as users realized they needed the information while mobile. This

Table 4. Top three categories of cross-device reaccessed URLs, broken down by device and reaccess direction

Device	Top 3 Categories	Categories by direction	Phone to Comp	Comp to Phone	Total Reaccess
iPhone	News 27.6% Search/Portal 25.19% Social Networks 20.06%	Phone to comp: News 73.74% Comp to phone: Social Networks 67.34%	μ: 31 min: 3 max: 193	μ: 32 min: 1 max: 74	μ: 72 min: 4 max: 267
Android	Social Networks 49.89% Media/News 38.7% Information Articles 11.41%	Phone to comp: Social Networks 84.23% Comp to phone: Media/News 72.18%	μ: 20.5 min: 5 max: 166	μ: 10 min: 3 max: 212	μ: 28 min: 13 max: 378
N900	Social Networks 56.02% Mail 13.86% News 19.28%	Phone to comp: Social Networks 80.36% Comp to phone: Social Networks 71.93%	μ: 11.5 min: 4 max: 53	μ: 17.5 min: 7 max: 44	μ: 29 min: 11 max: 97

frequently happened with maps and directions, where turn-by-turn directions are more useful due to the mobile nature of the device. *Participant a1* shared this story of reaccess inspired by location.

"it [restaurant] had good reviews and a lot of people were talking about it, so we actually went back friday the next week. and I looked it up (on phone) to see exactly what street it was."

Location-based reaccess also occurred when users recognized that information would be more useful at another place besides the point of original access.

"Today, my girlfriend was interested in getting a new phone from sprint. I had heard about them having a few android phones, so I went online to read up on HTCs. I read a lot of information on my laptop before we left. While at the sprint store, she was curious also about HTC, but wanted different information. I went back to the same wiki and let her read, since she didn't want me basically reading 2/3 of the wiki out loud as she perused cell phones." (Participant i6)

Participant i6 knew he would need the information he looked up on his laptop, but his ability to reaccess the content a particular location is what really made it valuable.

Computer to Phone: Need it at a later time. Time was another contextual factor that motivated how users reaccessed content on their phones and computers. Participants would typically carry their phone while mobile and could rely on it being available at other times. In these types of reaccesses, users either did not have all the information they needed at the time when they started the task, the task was too long to complete at the initial access, or external events controlled the time at which they could finish the task.

"In the morning, I felt like going to Chili's for lunch so I went to the Chili's website to find locations near me. I then repeated this on my phone when it was time for lunch so that I would have the address/map with me." (Participant i4)

The participant actually had to wait until the right time, here lunchtime, before he could act on the content he accessed. He wasn't interested in knowing how to get to

Chilli's until lunchtime arrived, and waited until then to conduct his reaccess on his phone.

Time constraints were another common reason to postpone a task and reaccess it later. *Participant n3* shared an example of receiving a long email from a friend that contained a riddle. *"A friend gave me a puzzle, like a really long thing, it was going to require a really long answer and it was going to require rereading and thinking about [...] I had glanced at [it] earlier on my computer when I was at work and couldn't read it."* *(Participant n3)* When she first read the email she didn't have time to think about what the answer might be. Later when she was at the airport waiting for a plane, and consequently had a lot of time, she revisited and answered the email on her phone.

Computer to Phone: Show my Friends. Social factors was a third type of context that influenced mobile reaccess. Mobile reaccess influenced by social situations was reported 7 out of 15 participants. We define socially motivated reaccesses as any reaccess which prompted social interactions with a friend or colleague. In each of these instances, participants accessed a link, video, or picture they had seen on a device at an earlier time to share with another person. Spontaneous reaccess was common in this category, with many of the reaccesses inspired by conversations with friends. Inspired by his social context, *Participant n4* related this situation where his reaccess of a recently watched video.

"We were at a bachelor party and started playing foosball, so it kind of came up in conversation, and I was like, oh you gotta see this crazy foosball video! and I pulled it up. I googled 'Nokia foosball I had remembered that they had spelled it funny, and so I was able to recreate that funny spelling on the google search and it came right up. (Participant n4)

This reaccess was impossible for him to predict and he had to rely on his memory for the video's name and search for it on the spot. Participants noted it was especially important that the content be found quickly, otherwise the conversation flow could be negatively impacted.

Computer to Phone: Mobility Barrier. Although laptops are portable and travel frequently with their owners they are ergonomically difficult to use in settings where the user must stand or move frequently. They also have long boot up times, and are often difficult to access quickly. Participants would reach for their phone for convenience and speed depending on their current situation. Nylander *et al.* observed similar behavior in understanding the motivation for users to perform tasks on their mobile phone [21]. Participants experienced these mobility barriers, which influenced their choice of device when both were available.

"I want to access something really quickly, don't want to wait for computer to boot up [or there is] no surface to put it on OR not a safe location to reveal I have a computer that someone might want to steal OR I'm actually walking/moving somewhere [or] I'm in a situation where using a computer would be ergonomically difficult (eg. remembering something I needed to do online, but already in bed) (this sounds like a weird use case, but it happens surprisingly often..." *(Participant n3)*

Phone to Computer: Technical Barrier. When reaccessing content on the computer that was originally seen on the phone, technical barriers were the main influencing factors in a reaccess event. Although mobile phone technologies are fast approaching the capabilities of personal computers there are still some things that are impossible to do on today's mobile smart phone. For example the iPhone is incapable of rendering Flash websites, thus users were forced to view it on their desktop or laptop computer. When users came to a website that looked *"wrong"* on their phone they often would revisit it later on another device to check and see it their phone was the problem.

"I received a link to play a game and knew it would start immediately when I clicked it so I read that I got the msg but waited to get home to click the link." (Participant a2)

Although *a2* was able to receive an invitation to play an online game through his email, his phone was not capable of running the game due to technical barriers. Motivated by a desire to beat his friend's score, *a2* delayed playing the game until he knew he was on a capable device.

Phone to Computer: Decomposing Tasks. Participants would decompose tasks doing as much as they could on their mobile device and then following up later on their computer. Decomposition can occur because of barriers or mobile limitations, but can also happen when resources are more readily available at another location. *Participant i2* shared that at the grocery store she accessed a recipe on her phone so that she could buy the correct ingredients. Later at home she accessed the recipe again from her laptop to assemble the ingredients into a meal. Both of the locations in this example have a specific function, the grocery store for selling food, and the kitchen for preparing it. Accessing the same content at both locations the user was able to complete her full task.

Tasks can also be decomposed because they are ongoing over time. *Participant i7* had an ongoing task of looking for a new apartment. When she saw an apartment complex that looked reasonable while she was commuting (as a passenger on public transit) she would conduct a brief search to find the price range and amenities to see if the place peaked her interest. Later when she had more time she would use her computer to look up more in depth information on the apartments such as reviews and neighborhood information. In this example i7's physical location inspired a spontaneous access of data, however her location also imposed time and device constraints which limited her gathering of information. The cost benefits analysis of looking up basic information about the apartments on her phone was worth it, but doing more in-depth research on her phone was not. Once she determined, using her phone, to consider an apartment complex, she would wait until she was in the locational context of 'home' to peruse more details about the apartments at her leisure.

4.3   Unplanned Reaccess Behavior

Planning ahead can be one of the easiest ways to expedite reaccessing content later. Easy access to directions for an event, phone numbers in an email, printing out a map, or bookmarking a page for later are all methods and practices our participants used to access their content. Despite these methods for planning ahead, participants communicated a general preference not to plan and would rather rely on internet connectivity to reaccess information they needed. Planning ahead was mainly reserved for important items, such as the map to an interview. *Participant i5* said that she *"wouldn't preplan unless it's a big date or a longer trip."* . The typical day to day activities did not involve much planning ahead.

Unforeseen reaccess. It is often hard for users to recognize what information they will need to access later. Content was only accessed a second time if something changed in the participant's original plan. The mobile convenience of the phone serves users well in these scenarios because they can often tweak their previous search queries to get the results they need.

"what you actually need, like, when when you're right in the situation, is not just information from earlier. It's information of, like, highly contextual information if something changes. So if you try to go somewhere according to a plan or map that you had ahead of time but you get lost... and so you're pretty close to where you were supposed to be, and so you need to change it a little bit." (Participant n3)

"I had to go to a wedding and so I just said great! I had to type it the thing[phone] from the paper invite, but then it was nice, I really did like it on my phone vs. paper because when I made wrong turns I could just restart it [...] I'd get to a light and just hit recalculate." (Participant i3)

In another example of unforeseen reaccess, *Participant i6* was trying to walk his dog at a new location. *"I used a website to locate a walking trail in San Mateo country. After I chose the destination, we headed with the dogs only to discover that the place was under construction. I quickly revisited the website with my iPhone, and decided on an alternate place to roam." (Participant i6)* The participant was not planning on using his phone once he arrived at the planned location but unforeseen circumstances forced him to change his plans. Since his web history was not shared between his devices, he had to redo a search query in order to find the website.

Mobile connectivity was a crutch used by our participants to support their unforeseen reaccesses. Even if the participants had pre-planned their activities, the highly contextual nature of their circumstances and changes in plans made it difficult to anticipate the information needed later. Although it is difficult to predict what a user will need ahead of time, since user's are reaccessing web content seen before, there may be opportunity to explore shortcuts to this content.

Plan a little, find it later. Connectivity was an expectation for most of our users given their capable mobile devices. These expectations offer users the freedom to access content they might need on demand without having to completely plan ahead of time. When users would plan ahead, some would prime themselves with a small bit of information and rely on mobile connectivity to access more information while mobile. A common method for doing this was to do a search on the computer, such as visiting a website for initial ideas, but allowing final decisions to be made in a more fluid fashion as the day progressed.

I went online to yahoo movies to look for a film that I'd like to see. I chose one, but didn't select a specific time, since I was meeting someone for dinner first. When we went to the movie theater, I looked up times on my iPhone at the same website. The second search was for a different theater, so I was glad that I hadn't settled on a time - life's great when your schedule is flexible ;)". (Participant i6)

Participant i5 shared her all too familiar story of how limited preplanning and on-the-fly mobile research came together for her on a recent weekend. Although she had performed minimal pre-planning to get an idea of restaurants and clubs, she and her friends left the final decisions to the last minute, often changing their minds at the last second.

"We had done some emailing, like mostly he[boyfriend] had emailed with them, so then it was like let's meet up for dinner, and then they wanted to eat dinner while we wanted to be at the beach, so then it was like let's have drinks later. We were going to meet them at a dance club and they were like 'oh we're not really in the mood for that... maybe something more low key,' and then I was like 'ok let me look up some other bars on my phone like through yelp', and then they met us at the place." (Participant i5)

In another example, *Participant a4* shopped initially online of shoes, but visited the brick and mortar store to browse and have the in-store experience.

"She[wife] had to have these shoes and you could get them online but she wanted them today so I went out and got them for her.... I went to the store and I said 'hey I need this shoe,' and I read the description. They still asked me another question, and I said 'well I don't know, here it is, that's what I need.'" [showed clerk webpage]. (Participant a4)

Although *a4* had looked at the shoe online on his computer at home, he accessed the mobile version of the page because he was not familiar with the product details. He relied on the content he was able to access on his phone in the store, to show the store clerk what he wanted, so that he would go home with the correct item.

Plan for the long term. Proper planning was reserved for longer term activities, such as finding a job, applying for schools, finding a new apartment, or planning a big event. These longer term reaccess can be particularly difficult for users to handle because the time between the original access and the final reaccess can make it hard for the user to remember the details they need to locate the content.

Planning for travel was a common longer term reaccess behavior. Purchasing flights and accommodation usually required many visits to the same websites to check prices before a final purchase. Once tickets were purchased the confirmation emails would be reference multiple times by the user as they made their final decisions about other elements of their trip. Finally, when on the trip, webpages and previously received confirmation emails would commonly be reference to help users navigate, check-in, and remember their schedule.

"It's usually in my email (flight confirmation numbers, hotel reservations, etc.), originally viewed via computer, and I then need to access it again while in transit (on my way to the airport to figure out which terminal to go to, at the counter of the hotel, etc.) [...] what I used to do was print or write this down and carry a piece of paper with all the information in one place. With the phone and a data plan, it was possible to look it up again in transit instead." (Participant n3)

—She did note problems with this method saying *"This required logging in to my email and searching for the information, which may be spread out over several emails. I found it a bit of a frustrating experience because the internet access was always quite slow, and I needed to load many pages to get to the piece of information I needed"*. In light of the troubles she experienced while having to locate travel related documents on her phone, often months after her original access she shared her vision for a more accommodating mobile solution. *"what I really would prefer for that situation is to [...] have them all sent to my phone so that they ended up on one "page" accessible offline. Basically analogous to my printed consolidated piece of paper, only it's easier to find because it's on my phone, and the information can be collected as soon as I receive it, rather than right before the trip."*

4.4   The Role of Applications

Applications are at the center of how user's interact with and user their smartphones. These applications are typically native portals into content that could be accessed through a web browser. However, we found many of the heavily trafficked webpages from the desktop absent from the mobile phone logs when the users also had a related native application installed on their device (e.g., Bank of America application). Native applications provide numerous benefits over web pages including better performance, use of sensors and actuators, and easy access from the phone interface. In order to capture data in third party applications, we asked participants to take screenshots whenever they found themselves reaccessing content on their mobile devices. Participants sent 128 screenshots over the course of the two week study, accompanied by a story of the moment of reaccess on the phone. 30 (23.4%) of the 128 screenshots were from applications.

We expected more screenshots to be from applications given the plethora of applications that participants used. One possible reason is that frequently used applications are more conducive towards realtime content and not previously seen, static content. For example the BBC news application application for iPhone is designed towards consumption of new data, with the first screen the user is directed to presenting the most recent news stories. It may also be true that when users do engage in reaccess in these applications it is often as a subtask rather than a primary task making it harder for the user to recognize. For example, if a user goes to the Facebook application to see their friend updates and while browsing around decides to comment on a picture that she saw earlier, she may not consciously recognize this sub task as reaccess.

"I would go on Facebook and say I feel like I saw this stuff three times ... I go on physical Facebook [on the computer] a lot less than I check the phone app [...] it's probably 70-30 [iphone-computer]. (Participant i7)"

She was aware that she was revisiting content she had seen before, however she never took a screenshot on her phone of any of these encounters. It is possible that although she was reaccessing information, the fact that the content was being "pushed" to her, instead of her actively retrieving it, caused her to not recognize it as a reaccess. Self reporting is one of the difficulties with gathering data *in situ* from mobile users with a diary study method.

Participants indicated a general preference for interacting with native applications rather than mobile web pages.

"if theres an app of something I definitely will do that, like, Ill look up products on the amazon app rather than going to amazon through safari. (Participant i5)

There was also indication that the advantage native applications had over mobile web pages was slight with users others mentioning that, *"if I have Safari open, I'm not going to close it to go to an app, I'll get the mobile version anyway." (Participant i7).*

Mobile web browsers are improving with the adoption of HTML5 that gives web applications access to local storage and on-device sensors. Application-centric smartphones also allow users to save bookmarks in their application screen, letting them live side-by-side with native applications. As the debate over native versus web applications continues, our results around reaccess suggests that users want to enable data to interact among their devices regardless of how they access it.

5   Discussion

Our investigation into reaccess habits among mobile users revealed the cumbersome workarounds used to find and reaccess information. We found that users would often use features that were made for different purposes as methods to find information later. Many tools, such as Context Clipboard, Evernote, and Dropbox, have attempted to address this problem by enabling easy capture and reaccess, such as saving a link to find later [15] [4] [3]. Although these tools are seamless and easy to use, they still require planning on the part of the user. Through our interviews and discussions with participants, they communicated a general attitude of only planning ahead for big trips and not for the more common reaccess tasks that occur in their everyday life. Sometimes our participants did not know what information they needed later, thus were not able to plan ahead effectively, and other times they expressed dislike of the rigidity imposed by preplanning. Based on these observations, we offer several opportunities to support content reaccess.

First, several contextual factors were influential in computer to phone reaccess. Participants would often reaccess content previously seen on their desktop based on future location and time. This is an opportunity to identify content that a user may need later and use location and time context to present it at a relevant moment. Social context is also an opportunity to present previously seen information that can promote dialogue and help keep conversation flow moving.

Second, the general attitude among users not to plan ahead presents a large design space to create tools to assist these unplanned reaccesses. Existing tools, such as Firefox Sync, have started the process by using cloud computing to enable the sharing of bookmarks and web history across multiple devices [5] . The next opportunity is exploring how to enable just-in-time access to this data without the burden of searching for it in a mound of data. *Participant n4* said that when trying to search for information again while mobile he *"[doesn't] try very hard, if I don't find it in the first or second search then I just give up."*

Finally, breaking content free from mobile application silos can help assist with content reaccess. As applications have become the center of the mobile universe, we noticed signs that people prefer native applications. The content within the application is important, and having better reaccess tools to synchronize this content is essential. For example, after a user looks up directions on the computer, that content should automatically sync to their mobile phone. Many applications are locked in content silos that make it difficult to interact with other applications or devices. As applications continue to move forward, whether as native phone applications or web-based applications, synchronized content is the key to helping users effectively access their data and help support faster unplanned reaccess.

6   Conclusion

We presented a two-week study of high-end smartphone users exploring cross-device reaccess patterns. Our analysis of web and mobile application content through logging and screenshots revealed that reaccess occurs with comparable frequency in both directions between the phone and computer. Participants also communicated a general attitude not to plan ahead for their reaccess needs, preferring to rely on the connectivity of their device. Based on these results, we suggested several areas of opportunity to support the unplanned activities of users. As more devices are introduced into the personal ecosystem, we believe there will be even greater opportunities to support quick, easy reaccess among these devices.

References

1. BBC. The top 100 websites of the Internet,
   http://news.bbc.co.uk/2/hi/technology/8562801.stm
2. Chrome-to-phone, http://code.google.com/p/chrometophone/
3. Dropbox, http://dropbox.com
4. Evernote, http://evernote.com
5. Firefox Home, http://www.mozilla.com/en-US/mobile/home/
6. Adar, E., Teevan, J., Dumais, S.T.: Large scale analysis of web revisitation patterns. In: CHI 2008: Proceeding of the Twenty-Sixth Annual SIGCHI Conference on Human Factors in Computing Systems, pp. 1197–1206. ACM, New York (2008)
7. Beitzel, S.M., Jensen, E.C., Chowdhury, A., Grossman, D., Frieder, O.: Hourly analysis of a very large topically categorized web query log. In: SIGIR 2004: Proceedings of the 27th Annual International ACM SIGIR Conference on Research and Development in Information Retrieval, pp. 321–328. ACM, New York (2004)
8. Brandt, J., Weiss, N., Klemmer, S.R.: txt 4 l8r: lowering the burden for diary studies under mobile conditions. In: CHI 2007: Extended Abstracts on Human Factors in Computing Systems, pp. 2303–2308. ACM, New York (2007)
9. Carter, S., Mankoff, J.: When participants do the capturing: the role of media in diary studies. In: CHI 2005: Proceedings of the SIGCHI Conference on Human Factors in Computing Systems, pp. 899–908. ACM, New York (2005)
10. Church, K., Smyth, B.: Understanding mobile information needs. In: MobileHCI 2008: Proceedings of the 10th International Conference on Human Computer Interaction with Mobile Devices and Services, pp. 493–494. ACM, New York (2008)
11. Cockburn, A., Mckenzie, B.: What do web users do? an empirical analysis of web use. International Journal of Human-Computer Studies 54(6), 903–922 (2001)
12. Dearman, D., Kellar, M., Truong, K.N.: An examination of daily information needs and sharing opportunities. In: CSCW 2008: Proceedings of the 2008 ACM Conference on Computer Supported Cooperative Work, pp. 679–688. ACM, New York (2008)
13. Dearman, D., Pierce, J.S.: It's on my other computer!: computing with multiple devices. In: CHI 2008: Proceeding of the Twenty-Sixth Annual SIGCHI Conference on Human Factors in Computing Systems, pp. 767–776. ACM, New York (2008)
14. González, I.E., Hong, J.: Gurungo: coupling personal computers and mobile devices through mobile data types. In: HotMobile 2010: Proceedings of the Eleventh Workshop on Mobile Computing Systems & Applications, pp. 66–71. ACM, New York (2010)
15. Harding, M., Storz, O., Davies, N., Friday, A.: Planning ahead: techniques for simplifying mobile service use. In: HotMobile 2009: Proceedings of the 10th Workshop on Mobile Computing Systems and Applications, pp. 1–6. ACM, New York (2009)
16. Jansen, B.J., Spink, A., Bateman, J., Saracevic, T.: Real life information retrieval: a study of user queries on the web. SIGIR Forum 32(1), 5–17 (1998)
17. Kamvar, M., Baluja, S.: A large scale study of wireless search behavior: Google mobile search. In: CHI 2006: Proceedings of the SIGCHI Conference on Human Factors in Computing Systems, pp. 701–709. ACM, New York (2006)

18. Kamvar, M., Kellar, M., Patel, R., Xu, Y.: Computers and iphones and mobile phones, oh my!: a logs-based comparison of search users on different devices. In: WWW 2009: Proceedings of the 18th International Conference on World Wide Web, pp. 801–810. ACM, New York (2009)

19. Kane, S.K., Karlson, A.K., Meyers, B.R., Johns, P., Jacobs, A., Smith, G.: Exploring cross-device web use on pCs and mobile devices. In: Gross, T., Gulliksen, J., Kotzé, P., Oestreicher, L., Palanque, P., Prates, R.O., Winckler, M. (eds.) INTERACT 2009. LNCS, vol. 5726, pp. 722–735. Springer, Heidelberg (2009)

20. Karlson, A.K., Iqbal, S.T., Meyers, B., Ramos, G., Lee, K., Tang, J.C.: Mobile taskflow in context: a screenshot study of smartphone usage. In: CHI 2010: Proceedings of the 28th International Conference on Human Factors in Computing Systems, pp. 2009–2018. ACM, New York (2010)

21. Nylander, S., Lundquist, T., Brännström, A., Karlson, B.: "It's just easier with the phone" – A diary study of internet access from cell phones. In: Tokuda, H., Beigl, M., Friday, A., Brush, A.J.B., Tobe, Y. (eds.) Pervasive 2009. LNCS, vol. 5538, pp. 354–371. Springer, Heidelberg (2009)

22. Obendorf, H., Weinreich, H., Herder, E., Mayer, M.: Web page revisitation revisited: implications of a long-term click-stream study of browser usage. In: CHI 2007: Proceedings of the SIGCHI Conference on Human Factors in Computing Systems, pp. 597–606. ACM, New York (2007)

23. Pierce, J.S., Nichols, J.: An infrastructure for extending applications' user experiences across multiple personal devices. In: UIST 2008: Proceedings of the 21st Annual ACM Symposium on User Interface Software and Technology, pp. 101–110. ACM, New York (2008)

24. Sohn, T., Li, K.A., Griswold, W.G., Hollan, J.D.: A diary study of mobile information needs. In: CHI 2008: Proceeding of the Twenty-Sixth Annual SIGCHI Conference on Human Factors in Computing Systems, pp. 433–442. ACM, New York (2008)

25. Spink, A., Jansen, B.J., Wolfram, D., Saracevic, T.: From e-sex to e-commerce: Web search changes. Computer 35(3), 107–109 (2002)

26. Tauscher, L., Greenberg, S.: How people revisit web pages: empirical findings and implications for the design of history systems. International Journal of Human-Computer Studies 47(1), 97–137 (1997)

Understanding Human-Smartphone Concerns: A Study of Battery Life

Denzil Ferreira[1,2], Anind K. Dey[2], and Vassilis Kostakos[1]

[1] Madeira Interactive Technologies Institute, University of Madeira, Portugal
[2] Human-Computer Interaction Institute, Carnegie Mellon University, USA
denzil.ferreira@m-iti.org, anind@cs.cmu.edu, vk@m-iti.org

Abstract. This paper presents a large, 4-week study of more than 4000 people to assess their smartphone charging habits to identify timeslots suitable for opportunistic data uploading and power intensive operations on such devices, as well as opportunities to provide interventions to support better charging behavior. The paper provides an overview of our study and how it was conducted using an online appstore as a software deployment mechanism, and what battery information was collected. We then describe how people charge their smartphones, the implications on battery life and energy usage, and discuss how to improve users' experience with battery life.

Keywords: Large-scale study, battery life, autonomous logging, smartphones, android.

1 Introduction

Sustainability and energy reduction have emerged as important topics in the social, political and technical agendas in recent decades. The ubiquitous computing research community, with its focus on both design and development of technological systems has had to systematically face a strain between sustainability and usability. On the one hand, users express an interest in adopting more sustainable products and behavior, but on the other hand, they do not wish to do so at the expense of their comfort. Hence it is important that solutions tackling energy reduction take into accounts users' behavior and preferences before making an intervention. One area strongly related to ubiquitous computing research where substantial energy savings can be achieved by introducing more usable systems is smartphones.

Cell phones are increasingly popular and diverse, with worldwide sales approaching 1.6 billion units, just last year [8]. Thanks to the rapid development of wireless technologies, smartphones allow users to be reachable anywhere [3]. As "convergent" devices, smartphones empower users with Internet access, music, audio and video playback and recording, navigation and communication capabilities. However, the growing functionality of smartphones requires more power to support operation throughout the day. Processing power, feature-sets and sensors are bottlenecked by battery life limitations, with the typical battery capacity of smartphones today being barely above 1500 mAh [5]. This is an important limitation because smartphones are increasingly regarded as a gateway to one's daily life,

K. Lyons, J. Hightower, and E.M. Huang (Eds.): Pervasive 2011, LNCS 6696, pp. 19–33, 2011.
© Springer-Verlag Berlin Heidelberg 2011

providing networking access to email, social networking, and messaging, making the management of battery life an important task.

Despite the important limitations that battery life imposes on users, previous research has shown that existing battery interfaces present limited information, and, as a consequence, users develop inaccurate mental models about how the battery discharges and how the remaining battery percentage shown in the interface correlates to application usage [20]. In addition, users do not completely understand how they should charge their batteries to support their planned use of the phone. As a result, every year $22 million are spent in electric utility costs due to keeping cell phones plugged into outlets for more time than required, to maintain a full charge [8]. On average, cell phone power supplies use 0.2 watts when the charger is left plugged into an electrical socket and the phone is no longer attached, with less sophisticated power supply designs reaching 1 watt [8].

We argue that there exists potential in reducing the energy consumption of smartphones by better understanding users' interactions with smartphones and providing better feedback. While previous studies have focused on the shortcomings of user interfaces in relation to battery life, there is a need to assess the real-world behavior of a large number of users in terms of when, how and how long they charge their batteries. By analyzing users' battery charging behavior, we can assess the extent to which energy is being wasted, explore how often users demonstrate less than optimal charging behavior, how often they interrupt the charging cycle and when this is more likely to happen. We hypothesize that by conducting such a study we can identify design opportunities for reducing energy consumption, increasing battery life, and also predicting when intensive computational operations and long data transfers should be scheduled.

This paper starts by giving an overview of related work and current state of the art on smartphone battery management, followed by a description of how was the study deployed and conducted using the Android Marketplace, and a discussion of implementation concerns. We then present the results and a discussion of users' charging habits, how to tackle the issues of wasted energy and opportunistic processing on smartphones. We conclude with a discussion of how the results can affect the design of a future smartphone for an energy conscious world.

2   Related Work

Most smartphones offer the possibility to add new applications, through distribution channels such as the Google Marketplace for the Android platform or App Store for the iPhone platform. These applications often take advantage of the sensors available, typically GPS and Internet connectivity to develop context-aware applications [10,5], accelerometer for motion tracking [18], Bluetooth for distance measurements from the device [15] and anomaly detection [3,19].

While devices are becoming increasingly mobile, many software developers have limited experience with energy-constrained portable embedded systems such as smartphones, which leads to unnecessarily power-hungry applications that rely on the operating system for power management. In addition, users struggle to determine which applications are energy-efficient, and typically users blame the operating system or hardware platform instead of unfortunate and unintentional software design decisions [21].

Rahmati *et al.* [16] coined the term *Human-Battery Interaction* (HBI) to describe mobile phone users' interaction with their cell phones to manage the battery available. According to a survey they conducted, 80% of users take measures to increase their battery lifetime, and it can be expected that maximizing battery life will continue to be a key concern for users due to the major usability issues involved in this task. One approach to automatically deal with this issue is to rely on sensor data. For example, recent devices act proactively to reduce their power consumption, either by turning off the screen after a specific amount of time with no new interaction, switching to a lower processing speed (CPU scaling), or disabling wireless interfaces such as Bluetooth and WiFi when battery levels are low. These devices effectively take into account sensed data regarding battery levels, idle time, *etc.*

Oliver *et al.* [7] highlighted the importance of using real user data collected from the world and how it can influence application development, by introducing the Energy Emulation Toolkit (EET) that allows developers to evaluate the energy consumption requirements of their applications against the collected data. As a result, by classifying smartphone users based on their charging characteristics, the energy level can be predicted with 72% accuracy a full day in advance.

A study on the environmental impact of cell phone charging related to national energy consumption and power plant greenhouse gas emissions reveals that the energy consumed by cell phone charging has been reduced by 50% in the past years due to two technology shifts: increased usage of power management and low-power modes of battery chargers; and use of more efficient switch-mode power supplies [8]. Despite these efficiency gains, however, the US could save 300 million kWh in electricity per year, which amounts to $22 million in electric utility costs, or 216.000 tons of CO_2 emissions from power plants.

The study presented here complements Oliver's study on user charging characteristics [7] and Rahmati et al.'s [16] study on how users consume battery in their devices. It aims to identify when, how, for how long and how frequently users recharge their devices' batteries, in order to assess the extent to which energy savings can be achieved. At the same time, the collected information can be used to identify design opportunities in order to achieve such energy savings.

3   Study

We conducted a study of battery charging behaviors with 4035 participants over a period of four weeks, during which anonymous battery information was collected from Android devices running Android 1.6 or higher. In total, more than 7 million data points of battery information were collected. The Open Handset Alliance Project "Android" is a complete, free, and open mobile platform, and its API provides open access to the device hardware, abstracted from each device's manufacturer or brand [2, 13], therefore increasing the number of deployable devices. Although the study was conducted solely with Android devices, most of the results should be similar to other smartphone platforms with respect to battery information and user behavior over time [11].

There was no monetary compensation given to the participating users. The developed application, OverCharged, which was developed to help users be more aware of their battery usage, was made available for free on the Google MarketPlace.

The main function of the OverCharged application we developed is to inform participants of their smart phone's current battery level, for how long the phone was running on battery and other miscellaneous information, such as temperature and voltage. As such, the users who downloaded the application and opted in to sharing their data are already concerned with the battery life on their mobile devices. Therefore, they may in fact be atypical users, and our sample may not be representative of what all smartphone owners would do. Nonetheless, our study does serve as the first large collection of battery usage.

During the study, users had the option to opt-in to sharing their battery data anonymously in order to contribute to a better understanding of battery usage patterns.

The application captured *charging activity, battery level, device type, temperature, voltage* and *uptime*:

- *Charging activity* captured when the user charged his device, either through USB or an AC outlet.
- *Battery level* reflects the remaining battery and how long it took to discharge or charge.
- *Device type* is the manufacturer, device board, model, Android version and build and the carrier.
- *Temperature* of the battery, both Celsius and Fahrenheit.
- *Voltage* available in millivolts (mV).
- *Uptime* is the amount of time the device was on until being turned off or rebooted.

The combination of *charging activity* and *battery level* allows for the identification of events such as *"unplugged not full"*, *"charged just unplugged"*, *"finished charging"*, *"charging"* and *"running on battery"*, defined as follows:

- *Unplugged not full*: when the user stopped charging, even though the battery was not fully charged.
- *Charged just unplugged*: when the user unplugged the charger and the battery is fully charged.
- *Finished charging*: the moment when the battery is fully charged.
- *Charging*: when the battery starts charging.
- *Running on battery*: when the battery is the only power source.

3.1 Implementation

Polling a device's state can reduce battery life [10, 12]. The Android API is event-driven, hence gathering the data had a negligible impact on regular battery life. By programming a BroadcastReceiver attached to an Android Service running in the background, whenever the Android OS broadcasts ACTION_BATTERY_ CHANGED, the following battery information was recorded: battery level, battery scale (maximum level value), battery percentage, battery technology (*i.e.* Li-ion), health rating of the battery, whether the phone was plugged to AC/USB, whether the phone is charging, temperature, voltage, uptime and usage uptime, battery status (charging, discharging, full and not charging) and phone events related to battery (fully charged and user just unplugged, charging, finished charging, running on battery, unplugged when not fully charged).

As highlighted by Oliver [10], a large-scale user study distributed across the globe requires the use of UTC timestamps. We captured the UNIX timestamp on the participant's device time zone, which results in consistent times across different time zones (*i.e.*, 8pm is the same for different users at different time zones). These timestamps were used across all data collection and analysis operations.

The application was programmed to start automatically when the device was turned on or rebooted. A small icon in the notification bar at the top of the screen kept users informed that data was being collected and allowed users to view further information [Figure 1].

Fig. 1. Notification bar information

3.2 Device Distribution

Of the approximately 17000 people that were using the application at the time the study was conducted, 4035 opted in to participate on our study. After the installation of the application from the MarketPlace, if the user opted in to participate in our study, the application captured device details including device board, service carrier, manufacturer, model, Android version and Android build.

Recent Gartner worldwide mobile device sales reports [7, 19] do not place HTC as the leading sales manufacturer. Originally producing primarily Windows Mobile phones, HTC has changed their focus to Android devices, by manufacturing the Google Nexus One and EVO 4G more recently. Of the phones used by our participants, HTC devices and Sony Ericsson devices were the most popular (44.6% and 29.8% respectively). In third place were Motorola devices with 14.8%, followed by Samsung with 7.5% [Table 1]. Furthermore, Google's statistics claim that Android 2.1 is the most popular version with 41.7%, while in our study we saw that 33% of phones used this version [Table 2]. One surprise in the collected data is that Android 1.6 (Donut) is the leader with 36% of the participating devices using it.

Table 1. Most popular platforms recorded during the study

Platform	Distribution
HTC	44.6%
Sony Ericsson	29.8%
Motorola	14.8%
Samsung	7.5%

Table 2. Google's official Android distribution, as of September 1, 2010 [1]

Platform	API Level	Popularity (Source: Google)	Popularity (Source: Study)
Android 1.5	3	12.0%	-
Android 1.6	4	17.5%	36%
Android 2.1	7	41.7%	33%
Android 2.2	8	28.7%	31%

3.3   How Do Users Manage Battery Life?

Users mostly avoided lower battery levels, with the daily average of the lowest battery percentage values being 30%. This is likely due to the fact that the Android devices' battery icon turns yellow at 30%, and prompts the user with a textual notification to charge the smartphone by the time it reaches 15%.

The visualization in Figure 2 shows the average battery available at different hours of the day, across all the users, and how frequently the percentage was observed, when the battery was not being charged. Each bubble represents a different day of the study, for a given hour (with a bubble created only when there were at least 1000 datapoints for the selected day-hour combination). Hence, the visualization contains three dimensions (Percentage, Time and Frequency), with frequency (low to high) highlighted both by size (small to big) and color (light yellow to dark red). The most frequent battery averages are above the 30% battery level.

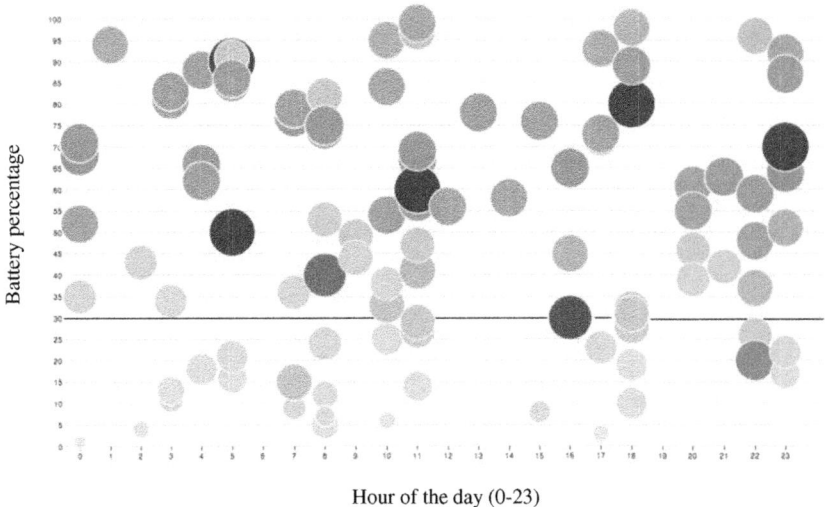

Hour of the day (0-23)

Fig. 2. Average battery levels during the day (when not charging)

On average the lowest average battery level was 65% at midnight, while the highest was 74% at 5AM. We expected that battery levels would be lowest at the end of the day, and the results confirmed it. The average battery percentage is 67% across all users throughout the day [Figure 3].

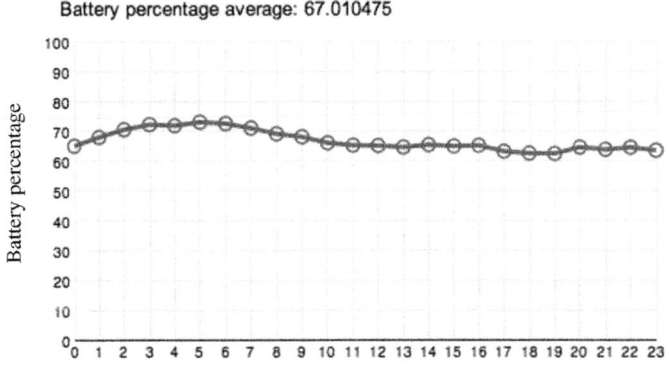

Hour of the day (0-23)

Fig. 3. Average battery levels throughout the day for the whole population

Despite the small variation of hourly battery levels across the whole population, individual users exhibited varying charging patterns. Some prefer to charge for short amounts of time throughout the day, while others allow the battery to discharge and charge it for longer periods of time until full [Figure 4].

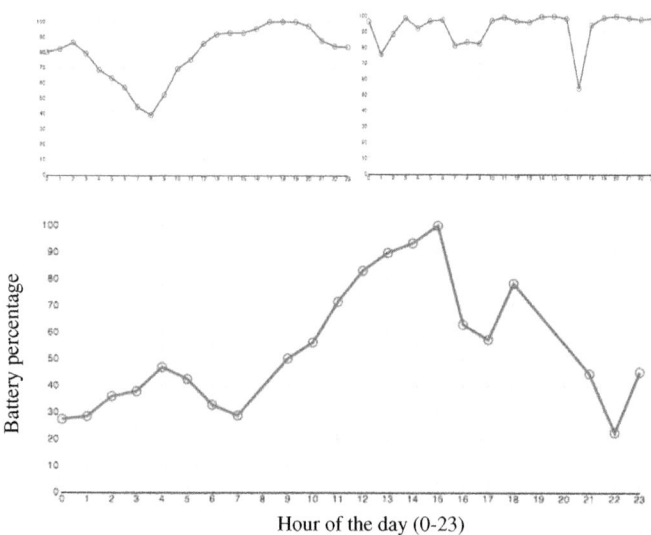

Fig. 4. Battery level during a single day for three different users

The data reveals two major charging schedules: one between 6PM and 8PM, with the majority of users initiating charging when the battery levels are at 40%, and another charging schedule between 1AM and 2AM, with a majority initiating charging when battery is at 30%. Another frequent charging event happens at 8AM, with battery levels at 80% on average [Figure 5].

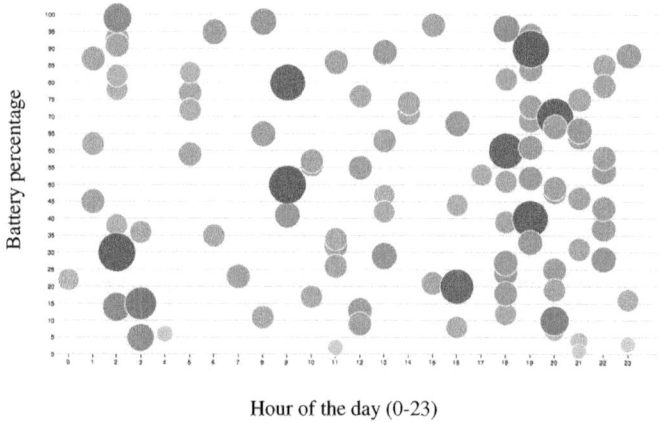

Hour of the day (0-23)

Fig. 5. Average battery levels during the day at the moment when charging begins

The majority of the charging instances occur for a very small period of time (up to thirty minutes) or between one to two hours, which is the average required time to recharge completely a battery (left side of the graph). [Figure 6].

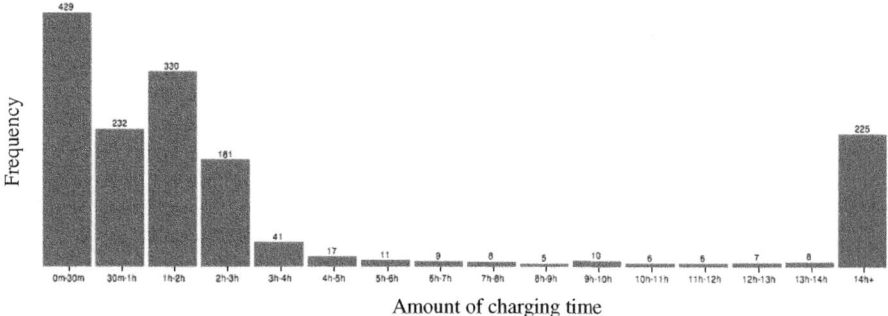

Fig. 6. Charging duration (amount of time the phone remains plugged in)

As expected, a lot of charging instances happen overnight, for 14 hours or more (right side of Figure 6). The average charging time across the whole population is approximately 3 hours and 54 minutes, but there is certainly a bimodal distribution, with the majority of charging instances lasting less than 3 hours. By charging time, we mean the time since the user plugged his device to charge until unplugged from the outlet.

Most charging instances start between 5PM and 9PM, while the least popular time to *begin charging* is from 3AM to 8AM [Figure 7], although the data in Figure 6 shows that it is likely that phones are being charged during this time.

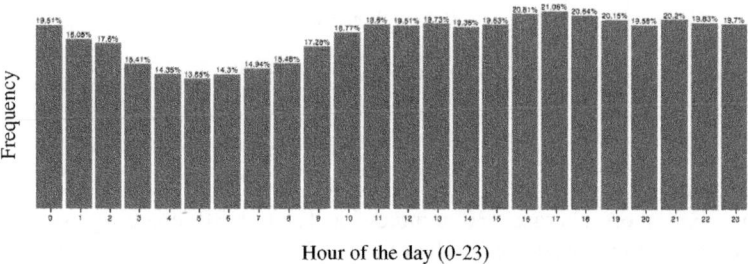

Fig. 7. Charging schedule (times when users have their phones plugged in)

3.4 How Much Energy Do Users Waste?

Overall, in 23% of the charging instances, the phone is unplugged from the charger (USB and AC) within the first 30 minutes after the battery is fully charged, while in the remaining 77%, the phone is plugged in for longer periods thus leading to energy waste. On average, users keep the phones plugged for 4 hours and 39 minutes after charging has been completed [Figure 8].

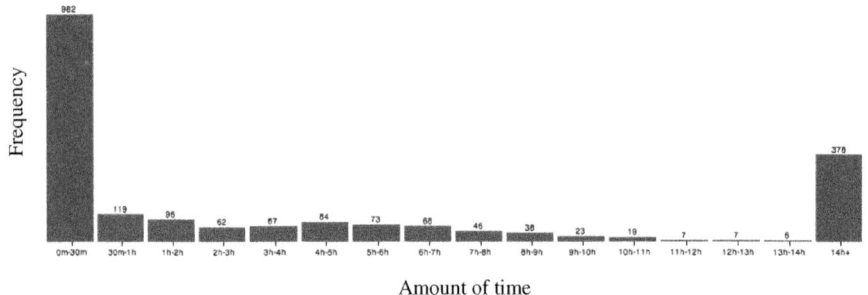

Fig. 8. Time until unplugged after the battery is full

Monitoring when the device has finished charging, we calculated how long the user took to unplug the device from the charger (USB and AC). The amount of time is greater as expected during the night, starting most often at 11PM and lasting until 8AM [Figure 9].

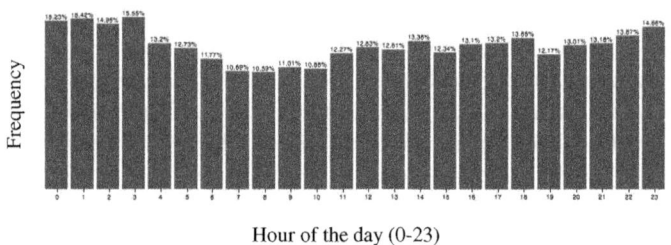

Hour of the day (0-23)

Fig. 9. Overcharging schedule

3.5 How Does Charging Happen?

As predicted, for longer charging periods AC is the preferred choice for phone charging. For short charges (30 minutes or less), USB charging is much more frequent. On average, users charge their phones 39% of the time using USB, and 61% of the time using AC [Figure 10].

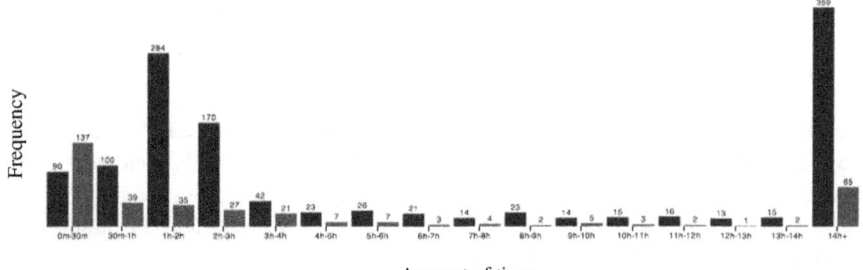

Amount of time

Fig. 10. Amount of time charging with USB (red) vs. AC (blue)

In Figure 10, blue represents AC, and red is USB charging. The initial pair on the left represents charging between 0-30 minutes, in which charging is mostly USB for this specific period of time. AC charging has two peaks, one between 1-3h of charging time and 14 hours or more for overnight charging.

3.6   How Often Is the Phone Rebooted/Turned Off?

Uptime is the time elapsed before the phone is rebooted or turned off. In our study, all participants' devices are on for at least up to a full day [Figure 11]. The results show that the likelihood of having a device on for up to two days is 33%, 18% for up to three and 11% for up to four days.

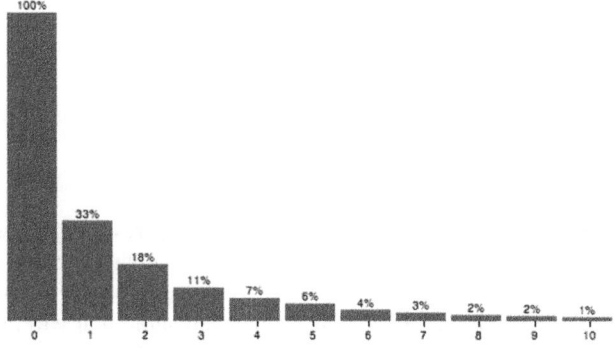

Fig. 11. Uptime in days

4   Discussion

The large-scale study described here was conducted in order to assess the extent to which energy is being wasted, explore how often users demonstrate less than optimal charging behavior, how often they interrupt the charging cycle and when this is more likely to happen. We hypothesized that by conducting such a study we could identify design opportunities for reducing energy consumption, increasing battery life, and also predicting when intensive computational operations and long data transfers should be scheduled.

Previous studies have shown that users have inadequate knowledge of smartphone power characteristics and are often unaware of power-saving settings on smartphones [16]. Users should be provided with options on how to better manage the remaining battery, and, to some extent, automated power features can also help them use the device as intended [12, 20]. Most smartphones alert the user that they need to be charged when the battery reaches critical levels [16,17], but do not notify the user when it has finished charging. For instance, explicitly notifying the user that the device is running low on battery is something Android does when the battery is at 15%.

Battery management requires user intervention in two respects: to keep track of the battery available so that users can decide how to prioritize amongst the tasks the device can perform; and to physically plug the device to the charger and surrender its mobility [17]. There is an opportunity to optimize which functionality should remain active based on the user's lifestyle and battery charging habits, improving the human-battery interface (HBI) with the user. Each user is unique and as such, the optimization system must learn and adapt to the user. The results show important differences between users' behavior and preferences, but also highlight common patterns that can be useful in understanding aggregate behavior and developing software that taps into those behaviors.

The findings of this study show that users

- demonstrate systematic but at times erratic charging behavior (mostly due to the fact that charging takes place when the phones are connected to a PC);
- mostly choose to interrupt their phones' charging cycle thus reducing battery life.
- aim to keep their battery levels above 30% due to an automatic ambient notification; and
- consistently overcharge their phones (especially during the night);

4.1   Users' Charging Habits

The study shows that users charged throughout the day resulting in erratic charging patterns and disrupted charging cycles that can reduce the lifetime of the battery [Figure 4]. A potential design opportunity exists here, whereby erratic charging behavior can be avoided by implementing a timer threshold that will prevent batteries from charging for short periods of times, e.g., for less than 5 minutes. The results [Figure 10] demonstrate that charging using USB could be triggered by command from the user (a feature already seen with some HTC Sense® devices) or if the battery percentage available is below 30%.

Interrupted charging cycles [Figure 11] leads to the necessity of battery calibration (drain the battery until depletion and fully charging it). The "memory effect", is a term loosely applied to a variety of battery ills [9]. From Corey's research [5], overcharging, over discharge, excessive charge/discharge rates and extreme temperatures of operation will cause the batteries to die prematurely. Users in this study consistently kept the battery from reaching lower levels, with an average lower percentage of 30% of battery power by charging throughout the day (e.g., plugging their devices to the car dock for navigation at 8AM [Figure 5] or charging while transferring files). Software updates and backup routines could take these moments to run power intensive operations only if the user has his phone plugged in for more than 30 minutes, since according to the results, there is a very high probability the user will charge for at least 1-2 hours.

4.2   Avoiding Energy Waste

Another problem that our study highlights in relation to charging duration is the amount of time the users keep their phones connected unnecessarily. In the past, charging a battery for a long period of time would damage the battery from overheating and overvoltage [4, 5, 21]. Modern Li-ion and Li-poly batteries come from the manufacturer prepared to interrupt charging as soon as they are fully charged

[14], but this still results in unnecessary power consumption. This study shows that this happens frequently, which suggests that manufacturers should make an effort to improve their chargers to cutoff the charging as soon as the battery is full or after some time in cases where the phone is being powered directly from the charger.

In addition, there is a design opportunity to give feedback to users the moment they plug in their phone – they usually look for confirmation that the phone is charging. At that moment feedback could be provided to change users' behavior. For example, we can predict when a "plugged in" event is likely to result in a long power consumption session, specially if it happens around 11PM. At that moment a message could inform the user that "your phone will be fully charged in X minutes", prompting them to remember to unplug it, to minimize the time when the phone is plugged in when it is already fully charged.

The combination of erratic charging and unnecessary charging observed in this study shows that users appear to have two types of charging needs: short bursts of charging to get through the day, and long charging periods during the night. One mechanism to reconcile these two distinct requirements is to allow for batteries to have a "slow-charge" mode, whereby they do not charge as fast as possible, but charge at a rate that will reduce the amount of unnecessary charging. A rule of thumb can be derived from [Figure 6], which suggests that an effective rate for "slow-charge" rate could kick-in after 30 minutes and aim for a full charge in 4 hours (the average overcharging length). A more sophisticated approach could incorporate a learning algorithm on the smartphone or even the battery itself.

4.3 Opportunistic Processing on Smartphones

In terms of identifying opportunities for intensive operations on the smartphone, the results suggest that there exists an important 30-minute threshold once charging begins. If a charging session lasts more than 30 minutes, it is very likely that it will last for a substantially longer period. Charging that uses AC is also an indicator that the user will be likely to charge for a longer period of time. Combined, the 30-minute threshold and AC power source provide a good indication as to when applications should perform power intensive operations on smartphones: large data transfers, computationally intensive activities, *etc.*

5 Conclusion

More than ever, industry and academic research have an opportunity to resolve numerous issues and conduct studies using published applications to support users' needs. Marketing and mobile phone manufacturers study a variety of user needs, focusing on the design of new handsets and/or new services [15]. Using automatic logging, in which software automatically captures user's actions for later analysis provides researchers with the opportunity to gather data continuously, regardless of location or activity the user might be performing, without being intrusive.

Asking users to anonymously collect battery information using a Google Marketplace application was a success: at the time of writing, 7 million battery information points and 4000 participating devices from all over the world were loaded into our database from which the battery charging patterns were explored.

The results provide application developers and manufacturers with information about how the batteries are being charged by a large population. The design considerations highlight how can we improve users' experience with their battery life and educate them about the limited power their devices have.

We look forward to seeing the next generation of smartphones, that learn from the user's charging routines and changes their operation and charging behavior accordingly.

Acknowledgements

We thank all the anonymous participants that contributed for the study using our application. This work was supported in part by the Portuguese Foundation for Science and Technology (FCT) grant CMU-PT/HuMach/0004/2008 (SINAIS).

References

1. Android Developer Dashboard (September 1, 2010),
   http://developer.android.com/resources/dashboard/
   platform-versions.html
2. Android OS (2011), http://www.android.com (last accessed February 24, 2011)
3. Buennemeyer, T.K., Nelson, T.M., Clagett, L.M., Dunning, J.P., Marchany, R.C., Tront, J.G.: Mobile Device Profiling and Intrusion Detection using Smart Batteries. In: Proceedings in the 41th Hawaii International Conference on System Sciences (2008)
4. Byrne, J.A.: The Proper Charging Of Stationary Lead-Acid Batteries (Your Battery Is Only As Good As How You Charge It.). In: Battcon 2010 (2010)
5. Corey, G.P.: Nine Ways To Murder Your Battery (These Are Only Some Of The Ways). In: Battcon 2010 (2010)
6. Cuervo, E., Balasubramanian, A., Cho, D., Wolman, A., Saroiu, S., Chandra, R., Bahl, P.: MAUI: Making Smartphones Last Longer with Code Offload. In: MobiSys 2010, San Francisco, California, June 15-18 (2010)
7. Gartner Research – Gartner Says Worldwide Mobile Device Sales Grew 13.8 Percent in Second Quarter of 2010, But Competition Drove Prices Down (August 12, 2010),
   http://www.gartner.com/it/page.jsp?id=1421013
8. Gartner Says Worldwide Mobile Device Sales to End Users Reached 1.6 Billion Units in 2010; Smartphone Sales Grew 72 Percent in 2010 (February 9, 2011),
   http://www.gartner.com/it/page.jsp?id=1543014
9. McDowall, J.: Memory Effect in Stationary Ni-CD Batteries? Forget about it! In: Battcon 2003 (2003)
10. Oliver, E.: The Challenges in Large-Scale Smartphone User Studies. In: International Conference On Mobile Systems, Applications And Services, Prec. 2nd ACM International Workshop on Hot Topics in Planet-scale Measurement, San Francisco, California (2010)
11. Oliver, E.: A Survey of Platforms for Mobile Networks Research. Mobile Computing and Communications Review 12(4) (2008)
12. Oliver, E., Keshav, S.: Data Driven Smartphone Energy Level Prediction. University of Waterloo Technical Report No. CS-2010-06 (April 15, 2010)

13. Open Handset Alliance, http://www.openhandsetalliance.com (last accessed February 24, 2011)
14. Ostendorp, P., Foster, S., Calwell, C.: Cellular Phones, Advancements in Energy Efficiency and Opportunities for Energy Savings. NRDC 23 (October 2004)
15. Patel, S.N., Kientz, J.A., Hayes, G.R., Bhat, S., Abowd, G.D.: Farther Than You May Think: An Empirical Investigation of the Proximity of Users to Their Mobile Phones. In: Dourish, P., Friday, A. (eds.) UbiComp 2006. LNCS, vol. 4206, pp. 123–140. Springer, Heidelberg (2006)
16. Rahmati, A., Qian, A., Zhong, L.: Understanding Human-Battery Interaction on Mobile Phones. In: MobileHCI 2007, Singapore, September 9-12 (2007)
17. Ravi, N., Scott, J., Han, L., Iftode, L.: Context-aware Battery Management for Mobile Phones. In: Sixth Annual IEEE International Conference on Pervasive Computing and Communications (2008)
18. Reddy, S., Mun, M., Burke, J., Estrin, D., Hansen, M., Srivastava, M.: Using Mobile Phones to Determine Transportation Modes. ACM Transactions on Sensor Networks 6(2), article 13 (February 2010)
19. Schmidt, A.D., Peters, F., Lamour, F., Scheel, C., Çamtepe, S.A., Albayrak, S.: Monitoring Smartphones for Anomaly Detection. Mobile Network Applications (2009)
20. Truong, K., Kientz, J., Sohn, T., Rosenzweig, A., Fonville, A., Smith, T.: The Design and Evalution of a Task-Centered Battery Interface. In: Ubicomp 2010 (2010)
21. Zhang, L., Tiwana, B., Dick, R.P., Qian, Z., Mao, Z.M., Wang, Z., Yang, L.: Accurate Online Power Estimation And Automatic Battery Behavior Based Power Model Generation for Smartphones. In: CODES+ISSS 2010, Scottsdale, Arizona, USA, October 24-29 (2010)
22. Zheng, P., Ni, L.M.: Spotlight: The Rise of the Smart Phone, vol. 7(3). IEEE Computer Society, Los Alamitos (March 2006)
23. Zhuang, Z., Kim, K., Singh, J.P.: Improving Energy Efficiency of Location Sensing on Smartphones. In: MobiSys 2010, San Francisco, California, June 15-18 (2010)

Monitoring Residential Noise for Prospective Home Owners and Renters

Thomas Zimmerman and Christine Robson

Mobile Computing Research Group
IBM Research - Almaden
650 Harry Road, San Jose CA 95120
{tzim,crobson}@us.ibm.com

Abstract. Residential noise is a leading cause of neighborhood dissatisfaction but is difficult to quantify for it varies in intensity and spectra over time. We have developed a noise model and data representation techniques that prospective homeowners and renters can use to provide quantitative and qualitative answers to the question, "is this a quiet neighborhood?" Residential noise is modeled as an ambient background punctuated by transient events. The quantitative noise model extracts noise features that are sent as SMS text messages. A device that implements the noise model has been build, calibrated and verified. The qualitative impact of sound is subjectively assessed by providing one-minute audio summaries composed of twenty 3-second sound segments that represent the loudest noise events occurring in a 24 hour sampling period. The usefulness and desirability of the noise pollution monitoring service is confirmed with pre- and post-use surveys.

Keywords: Location-based services, mobile devices, sensors.

1 Introduction

Excessive, unwanted or disturbing sound in the environment is called noise pollution. Noise affects our physical and mental health, increasing blood pressure and stress, damaging hearing and disturbing sleep [1]. Unlike chemical pollution which can be measured with a single value (e.g. parts per million) sound is difficult to quantify because it is multidimensional, varying in intensity and spectra. Similarly, the impact of noise on humans is complex. Some noises are pleasant, like flowing water, while others are annoying like car alarms, screeching breaks and people arguing.

We experience noise pollution in all aspects of our lives; at work, at home and on holiday. Noise in the workplace is regulated to protect employees against loss of hearing and other injuries [2]. The parks department is very concerned with maintaining an acceptable soundscape and uses a combination of human observers and instrumentation to measure the impact of noise pollution such as jet flyovers and recreation vehicles (e.g. snowmobiles and water craft) [3].

In this paper, we are concerned with residential noise. In annual surveys conducted by the Department of Housing and Urban Development for the past three decades, noise has been identified as the leading cause of neighborhood dissatisfaction, with

K. Lyons, J. Hightower, and E.M. Huang (Eds.): Pervasive 2011, LNCS 6696, pp. 34–49, 2011.

traffic and aircraft noise leading the list [4]. We have developed noise monitoring hardware, analysis algorithms, visual and auditory representations to help people evaluate the noise environment of a home, providing a quantitative objective answer to the question, ``is this a quiet neighborhood?''

When a person enters into a contract to purchases a house, a home inspection is performed to inform the buyer of any structural, electrical, plumbing and roofing problems. Too often, however, residents learn of unexpected noise pollution on the first night of occupancy. With this need in mind, we set out to create a device that could be used as part of a home inspection to provide an assessment of residential noise pollution.

We began with a survey to understand how noise pollution affects residents in our area and a review of current laws and literature on noise pollution. We designed and built a device to monitor noise pollution in response to these problems. Using noise samples from three representative houses, spanning the spectrum of quiet to noisy neighborhoods, we developed a noise model to characterize residential noise and a means to compress noise events of an entire day (24 hours) into a one minute auditory summary. Our design minimizes data collection, transmission and storage requirements to utilize low-cost and low-power components, while maintain sufficient measurement accuracy. We conducted a user study to measure the effectiveness of visual and auditory presentations of the collected noise data. Our results show that people prefer to compare homes by the audio summaries rather than visual representation of noise data.

2 Background

2.1 Related Work

Noise control has its US roots in the establishment of the National Environmental Policy Act of 1969 and the Noise Control Act of 1972. At that time the EPA testified before Congress that 30 million Americans are exposed to noise pollution [5]. The "Green Paper on Future Noise Policy" [6] published in 1996 set the ground work for noise policy in Europe. As more people live in cities, there are more noise sources and greater pressure from residents to control noise.

Several organizations maintain web sites with a wealth of information on noise pollution (e.g. www.nonoise.org, www.acousticecology.org, www.noisefree.org) to raise awareness and reduce noise pollution. Government agencies [7] have noise monitoring and education programs, including interactive noise maps [8, 9]. Sound meters have been combined with GPS receivers to populate a database to create sound maps of a location [10].

Airports have permanent noise monitoring equipment to measure noise produced by arriving and departing aircraft [11, 12]. The FAA is required to make noise exposure maps available to the public via the Internet [13]. Using the WebTrack tool [14] we are able to correlate the air traffic noise detected at our noise pollution study locations with departing and arriving aircraft. The site also has real time sound pressure levels from fixed location monitoring stations on the arrival and departure corridors around the airport.

Noise pollution has motivated municipalities to take an active role in monitoring and reducing noise to protect their citizens. The European Directive 2002/49/EC [15] to monitor, inform, address and develop a long term strategy to reduce offending noise, has stimulated much noise pollution research and development activity in Europe. The Directive stimulated the MADRAS project [16], creating a database of samples of noise pollution sounds used by researchers studying noise pollution. One project [17] developed an automatic noise recognition system using a hidden Markov model to classify transportation noise events (car, truck, moped, aircraft and train) with higher accuracy than human listeners.

Smart phones have been used to enable citizens to contribute to noise pollution maps [18, 19, 20, 21, 22]. Monitoring noise pollution with smart phones have several problems as reported by Santini et al. [23] including location of the phone (e.g. hand, pocket or backpack), modification of the detected sound by phone hardware and firmware (e.g. noise cancellation, low-pass filtering, automatic gain control), and power consumption limiting continuous monitoring duration. Previous works typically presents and compares noise pollution as a single number. As we will show through surveys, the impact of residential noise is too subjective and complex to be represented by a single metric. Our goal is to create a device to continuously and accurately monitor noise pollution, and data presentation methods to enable prospective home owners and renters to effectively evaluate noise pollution at several residential locations.

To achieve these goals we decided to build our own microprocessor-based audio capture system to send noise analysis results as SMS text messages. We chose to build a custom system rather than use a smart phone to control the audio performance characteristics of the device, including sample rate, dynamic range, resolution and accuracy. We developed several graphical representations and a novel audio summarization technique which we evaluated with user studies.

2.2 Noise and Hearing

The human ear detects minute changes in air pressure as sound. The ear is incredibly sensitive, with a dynamic range (the difference between the thresholds of hearing and pain) spanning 13 orders of magnitude (Table 1). To accommodate the large dynamic range, sound pressure level (SPL) is measured in logarithmic units of decibels (dB), with 0 dB defined as the threshold of hearing. A +3 dB change doubles the SPL and is the minimum increase in loudness perceivable by humans. A +10 dB increase is perceived as the doubling of loudness [24]. This implies that our noise sensor must have a large dynamic range (e.g. 30 dB to 90 dB) but with low resolution (1-3 dB).

Sound varies in amplitude and frequency. Spectrum refers to the frequency components that make up a sound. White noise has energy spread equally across all frequencies. Pink noise, also called 1/f noise, has a power spectral density inversely proportional to frequency, and is produced by flowing water and distant highway traffic (Fig 1, left). Motorcycles, propeller airplanes and helicopters are noise sources that appear prominently in our noise sampling sites and have a strong periodic component. Compressed gas emanated from the motorcycles' exhaust system and the

Table 1. Sound pressure levels (in decibels) of common loudness references

Decibels	Example
0	Threshold of hearing
20	Rustling leaves
30	Whisper, quiet library
50-70	Normal conversation at 3 to 5 feet
75	Loud Singing
80	Telephone dial tone
90	Train whistle at 500 feet, motorcycle, lawnmower
95	Subway at 200 feet
100	Diesel truck at 30 feet
110	Jack hammer, rock concert, boom box
120-140	Pain, gun blast, jet engine at 100 feet
180	Death of hearing tissue

chopping of air by propellers produce distant frequencies in the noise spectra (Fig. 1, right). While previous work uses sophisticated signal processing combined with statistical models to automatically detect and categorize these noise sources [17], our noise detection algorithm is simple enough to run on a low power 8-bit microprocessor. Instead of automatically identifying the noise source, we record short segments (e.g. 3 seconds) so humans can judge for themselves the subjective impact of noise.

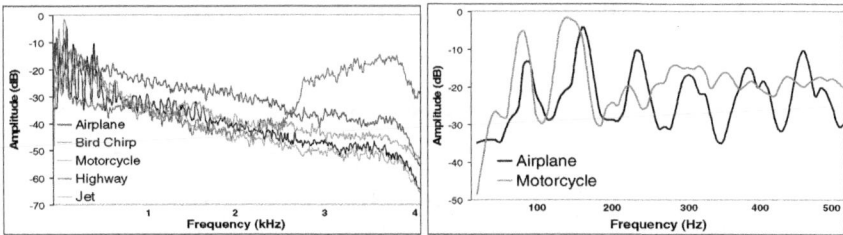

Fig. 1. Spectra of several noise sources (left), sampled at 8 kHz, covering a frequency range from 100 Hz to 4 kHz. Periodic noise sources (right) are particularly disturbing.

3 Research Methodology

The goal of our research is to develop an inexpensive, convenient and effective means of monitoring and comparing residential noise pollution. Our approach is to interview potential users to understand the significance of the problem, take some real-word measurements, build a system and verify it in the field, then test our solution with users. The paper is organized in the order we use to carry out our research:

- Conduct a survey to determine the importance of noise pollution on choosing a place to live and what noise sources are most disturbing

- Select three homes that represent a diversity of noise pollution environments and collect several days of audio recordings
- Determine a noise model that captures the salient noise features to efficiently quantify noise pollution
- Build hardware to measure salient noise features and verify in the field
- Design noise pollution data presentation methods
- Conduct a user survey to determine the effectiveness of noise pollution presentation methods.

4 Data Collection

4.1 Noise Pollution Survey

We conducted a survey of 82 people to determine if noise pollution is perceived as an important factor in choosing a place to live, and what noise pollution sources cause problems. The subjects were adult technical and administrative staff, male and female, from our research laboratory. Practically everyone (93% of respondents) indicated that a quiet neighborhood is important in selecting a place to live (55% indicated ``very important").

We classified people into ``primarily apartment or townhouse residents" and ``primarily stand-alone house residents" based on their reported residence history. People who have lived primarily in houses care more about noise then people who live in apartments (100% vs. 88%), and many feel it is ``very important": (64% vs. 49%). About 2/3 of both apartment-renters and house-dwellers remember discovering noises in a new residence that they didn't know about before hand (65%, 64%). House-dwellers are a little more likely to read and buy a noise survey (read: 77% vs. 68% ; buy:87% vs. 74%), and would pay more ($30 vs. $25 on average).

Table 2. Survey results of which noise sources annoy residents

Noise Source	Apartment or Townhouse Resident	House Resident
Loud music	55%	64%
Yard noise	43%	48%
Traffic	43%	42%
Parties	49%	24%
Children	20%	9%
Babies	31%	18%
Construction	45%	30%
Arguments	33%	42%
Pets	33%	42%

The most problematic times for noise are nights, followed by evenings and weekend mornings. The results of the relative annoyance and type of noise sources reported by survey participants are listed in Table 2. Neighbors' loud music is the biggest noise complaint for both groups, followed by yard services and traffic noise.

Traffic noise is the dominant noise pollution source detected in our monitoring since it happens every day. Leaf blowers are the biggest write-in noise complaint.

Most people (52%) do nothing in response to noise pollution. Only about 1 in 5 people have confronted a neighbor over a noise problem. One in four house-dwellers called the police over a noise incident, and the same percentage of apartment-renters has either called the police or the building superintendent/security. A further 4% have contacted the humane society over pet noises. A surprising 4% of respondents (both apartment and house dwellers) reported retaliating against loud neighbors by making noise themselves.

The variety of noise sources and the impact on individual demonstrates the subjective nature of noise pollution, and foreshadows an important lesson we learned by running our experiments and surveys; the impact of noise pollution must be evaluated subjectively by the individual.

4.2 Selection Monitoring Sites

In order to refine our understanding of what data should be collected to evaluate residential noise pollution, we made preliminary recordings at five locations. We listened to the recordings and selected three houses to represent a diversity of noise pollution environments. House A is located on a residential street far from any expressway or major road, representing a suburban location. It is a very quiet location punctuated by an occasional vehicle. House B is located in a large county park, down an unpaved road and represents a very rural setting. It is next to a creek, providing a source of pink noise (what is considered "white noise" in casual usage). We chose House A and B to study the relative impact of transient noise juxtaposed with background noise. A transient noise event (e.g. a car passing by) at house A may be perceived as more disturbing than the same magnitude event at house B since house A has a lower average sound level. However those noise events may not be as disturbing as a constant higher level of background noise. House C is located in a dense suburban development within a few blocks of two freeways, providing a variety of human activity and transportation noise sources, as would be encountered in an urban environment.

4.3 Field Recordings

For each of the three houses field recordings are made using an external electret microphone and laptop computer. The microphone has a ten foot cable, allowing it to be placed outside a window, while the laptop is located inside, plugged into the mains, to enable many hours of continuous recording. The microphone is chosen for its small size (6 mm diameter), low cost (<$1) and flat response for the bandwidth studied (100 to 4 kHz). The sampling bandwidth is determined by examining the spectra of noise sources recorded during our survey of potential monitoring sites. To avoid aliasing (acoustic artifacts), the sampling frequency must be at least twice the highest frequency detected, known as the Nyquist frequency. A low sampling rate is desired to minimize the storage used in our field recording and to minimize the speed, and hence power, of the microprocessor used in our mobile device. The highest frequency event recorded at our monitoring sights are birds chirping, which have energy between 3-4 kHz (Fig. 1, left), which agrees with published accounts [25].

From this analysis we establish 8 kHz as the sampling rate for our field recordings and the mobile device.

In order to compare sound measurements made by different instruments at different times, it is essential that each device be calibrated. We use two types of sound recording systems: a laptop with external microphone and a microprocessor-based mobile device. Each laptop runs sound recording software (http://audacity.sourceforge.net) that continuously records mono audio at 8 kHz sample rate, with 16 bits of linear amplitude resolution. The sound recordings are stored as uncompressed .wav format files to avoid any compression artifacts. The microprocessor-based mobile device samples audio at 8 kHz with 10 bits of linear amplitude resolution, with +60 dB of auto-scaling for an effective dynamic range of 20 bits.

All of our sound recording systems are calibrated with a commercial digital sound pressure meter (Extech Model 407730) which has a 2 dB accuracy and a 0.1 dB resolution. The sound pressure meter is used in A-weight filter mode, which approximates the spectral sensitivity of the human ear. To calibrate each sound recording system (microphone + amplifier + digitizer) we use radio static (tuned away from all broadcast stations) as a white noise source (equal energy at all frequencies, confirmed by spectral analysis). By varying the volume of the radio, measured with the sound pressure meter, we can produce a series of calibrated sound pressure levels.

To calibrate a field recording system, all of the system components are set in the field condition. For laptops this means specifying the gain settings of the entire audio chain (sound driver, operating system mixer and recording software) and using the exact microphone that will be used in the field. For the microprocessor-based mobile device, each gain setting (it has 4) is individually calibrated. The field recording microphone is placed next to the sound level meter microphone and in front of the radio speaker, on foam to reduce sound reflections (Fig. 2). The sound recording is started and the volume of the radio is increased in +3 dB steps. The log base-10 of the average microphone output is plotted against the sound pressure, measured with the sound pressure meter. A linear fit of this curve produces the gain and bias terms to convert microphone output into calibrated dB units.

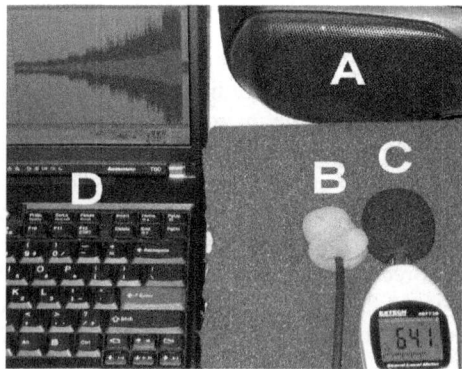

Fig. 2. Microphone calibration system. Radio (A) when tuned between stations provides white noise to calibrate microphone (B) with a reference sound level meter (C). The microphone's voltage output is recorded with a laptop (D).

4.4 Noise Monitoring Hardware

The objective of our research is to design an inexpensive mobile device that can be placed outside a residence for a day to a week to monitor noise in the environment. The device collects and processes sound samples, producing noise analysis output useful for evaluating the relative impact of noise pollution at a location. The device incorporates a mobile phone to wirelessly send the output to prospective renters and home buyers. To minimize the overall cost of the device we chose the lowest cost mobile phone we could find (Kyocera Model S2400, Radio Shack #17-3489, $9.99). To minimize the cost of mobile air time, noise analysis output is encoded and transmitted as SMS text messages.

The mobile sound monitoring device is implemented with an inexpensive 8 bit microprocessor (Zilog Z8F64200100KIT) wired to the keypad of the mobile phone through analog switches (CD4051). The hardware interface allows the microprocessor to perform any phone function a human can through the phone's keypad. The microprocessor samples sound pressure level, performs signal analysis to derive salient sound features, turns on the phone, composes a SMS text message, presses "SEND", then turns the phone off, minimizing power consumption. The text message is sent to a server as email.

The audio signal path consists of a +30 dB preamp followed by four +15 dB amplification stages. Each amplifier stage is sent to the multiplexer channels (switches) of the microprocessors' analog-to-digital converter, providing software selectable gains of 30 to 90 dB (Fig. 3). The amplitude of the selected channel is sampled at 8 KHz with 10 bits linear amplitude resolution. The samples are rectified (absolute value function), integrated over a one-second window, and the minimum sum occurring in a five-minute window is saved as the Minimum Average. If one or more samples in a one-second window exceed the previous Minimum Average by +20 dB, a Peak Counter is incremented. If the Minimum Average becomes too small or large, a different amplifier gain is selected, implementing software automatic gain control (AGC), thereby increasing the dynamic range of the system. Once an hour the microprocessor turns on the phone, composes a text message containing Minimum Average and Peak Count values and sends it to an email account, using the same key

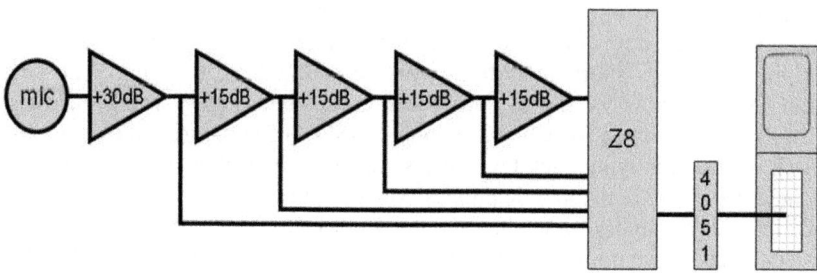

Fig. 3. Mobile noise monitoring system. A series of amplifier stages are fed to the inputs of the microprocessor's (Z8) analog-to-digital converter, providing a selectable gain from +30 dB to +90 dB. The microprocessor (Z8) performs audio analysis and sends the results as SMS text messages, using analog switches (4051) wired to the keypad to control a mobile phone.

sequence as a human composing a text message. This strategy dramatically reduces power consumption and extends battery lifetime, since the phone is only on for less a minutes every hour.

The placement of a single sensor on the residence property does present a source of variation in absolute signal strength measurement. Peppin and Probst [8] handle this variation by creating noise maps that show the average noise at multiple locations around buildings. Another approach would be to walk around the residence while measuring the instantaneous sound pressure level and locate the sensor in the area with the largest sound pressure level.

To validate the hardware, the mobile noise monitoring device is placed next to a studio-quality condenser microphone (MXL 990) connected to a laptop that has been calibrated with the method shown in Fig. 2. Over a period of 20 hours the prototype hardware automatically sends hourly SMS messages containing Minimum Averages and Peak Counts for house C, while the laptop continuously records audio. The Minimum Averages calculated from the continuous audio recordings correspond with Minimum Averages measured and transmitted by the mobile noise monitoring hardware (Fig 4), validating the mobile system.

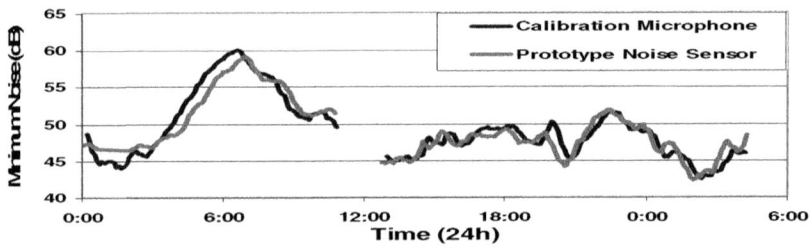

Fig. 4. Average sound pressure level sent by mobile phone as SMS text messages and average sound pressure level measured with calibrated microphone. The test was stopped for one hour to confirm calibration, resulting in the data gap between 11:00 and 12:00.

The noise analysis output sent over SMS text message (Minimum Average and Peak Counts) provides a quantitative analysis of the noise environment. To provide a qualitative representation of the noise environment we developed a method to compress one full day's of audio into a one minute "collage". The method requires multiple (e.g. 20) short recordings (e.g. 3 seconds) of audio. This can be accomplished two ways; storing the audio as analog samples using an integrated single chip solution (e.g. Nuvoton Technology ISD5008) or storing the audio digitally in flash memory. Playing back the audio samples as an analog signal would allow us to send the audio over the mobile phones' voice channel.

To test the feasibility of sending recorded noise samples over the mobile phone's voice channel, a one minute sample of noise events from house B, recorded with the laptop system, is transmitted over the mobile phone's voice channel to a WebSphere Voice Server (VoiceRite Client). The audio (line) output of a laptop is connected to the headset (mic) input of the mobile phone using a 10.3 dB attenuator and 0.1 uF capacitance coupler to match the impedance between the two devices.

Examining the amplitude of the transmitted and received signals (Fig. 5), it is clear that the combined mobile phone and network is modifying the signal in ways that defeat our purpose. We want to send and faithfully reproduce noise while the mobile phone and network is designed to fit many voice channels into a small bandwidth and minimize the transmission of noise. Therefore local flash must be used to store sound samples and can be retrieved with removable digital medium (SD card, compact flash, mini SD, etc.) or uploaded to a smart phone or laptop with a serial or wireless network. Making this easy-to-do is essential for commercial deployment.

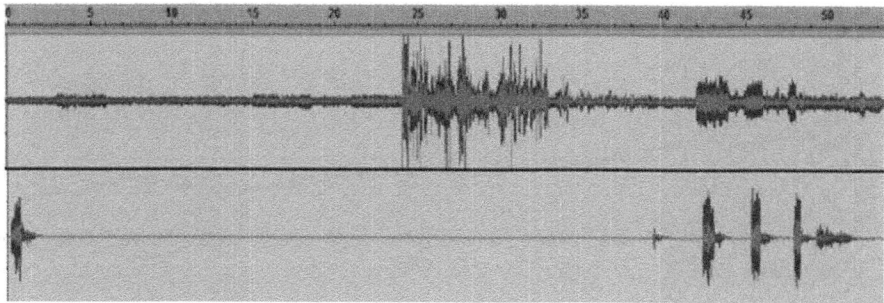

Fig. 5. Sound sample amplitude from house B before (top) and after (bottom) transmission over a mobile phone voice channel. Time scale on top of figure is in seconds.

5 Data Representation

5.1 Noise Model

In all the sound recordings, we observe the common characteristic of a slowly varying *ambient component* (caused by traffic and water) punctuated by quick *transient events* (caused primarily by vehicles) (Fig. 6, 7). The ambient component displays a cyclic

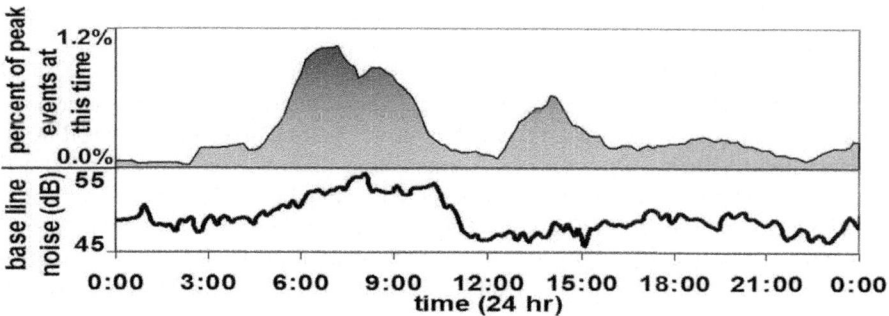

Fig. 6. Profile of House A showing average sound pressure (lower) and percent of peak events (upper), defined as an instantaneous amplitude that exceeds the average by at least 20 dB, occurring, representing the baseline noise and transient events, respectively.

variation, with a period of a day, corresponding to commuter traffic, and is most apparent in the average signal. The transient events from passing vehicles last a few seconds while aircraft flybys can last up to a minute.

We experimentally determined that a threshold of 20 dB above the minimum average is sufficient to detect a transient event. We quantify these two salient features by measuring the Minimum Average and counting the transient events (Peak Count) in a sampling window.

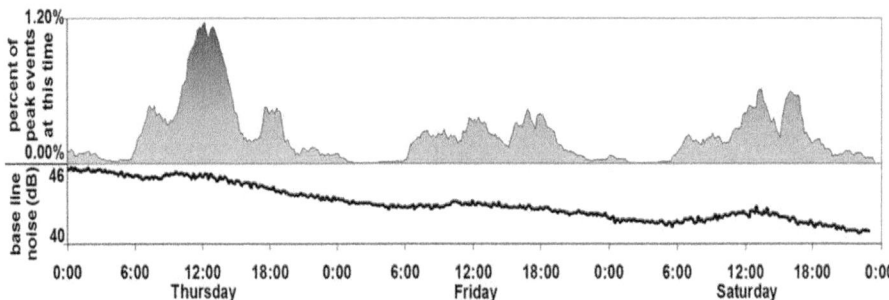

Fig. 7. Profile of house B showing peak noise events and average noise. A creek adjacent to the property creates a diminishing baseline noise caused by runoff from recent rain. Devoid of commuting traffic, transient events at this rural location are predominantly caused by airplanes, which pass overhead in the middle of the day. On Thursday a significantly increased number of airplanes were diverted over this house.

5.2   Quantitative Presentation of Noise Data

Having defined quantitative measures of the ambient component (Minimum Average) and transient component (Peak Count) of noise pollution, we prepare graphs of the measurements so users can compare houses. Three graphs are presented to users: a one day (24 hour) timeline of the Minimum Averages (Fig. 8, left), and two histograms collected over three days showing the loudest events defined as the Minimum Average at the time of a Peak Count event (Fig. 8, middle) and a histogram of the average sound pressure level (Fig. 8, right).

The urban and suburban houses A and C show peaks in the minimum noise level (Fig. 8, left graph) during morning and evening commutes. House B shows the sound of a creek adjacent to the property, which is slowly getting quieter as the swell from a recent rainfall reduces. This provides an interesting side-effect of our research; traffic levels and water flow can be indirectly observed by monitoring Minimum Averages.

The histogram of the loudest noise (Fig. 8, middle) shows the Minimum Average at the time of peak events (indicated by the increment of the Peak Count). The narrow range of noise levels on house B indicates a predominantly constant noise level (the creek), whereas the wider bands for houses A and C reflect the variable intensity of noise from vehicles near these locations. Fig. 8, right, shows that the distribution of average noise level is similar to the distribution of loud noises, albeit centered at a lower peak.

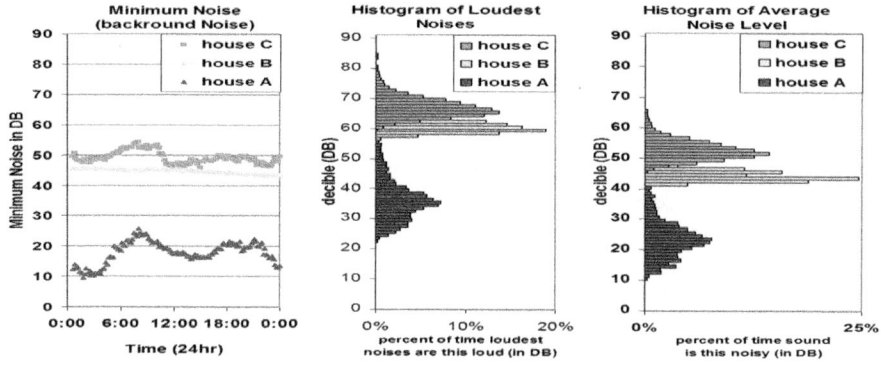

Fig. 8. Data from three sample houses (A, B and C) showing a 24 hour time period of minimum average sound in 5 minute windows (left), a histogram of the loudest noises (middle) and average noise level (right)

5.3 Qualitative Presentation of Noise Data

The temporal and statistical data presented in Fig. 8 does not identify the sound source, only the magnitude and frequency of occurrence. Instead we developed an automatic technique that saves short recording of noise events and edits them together into a single recording. Using this method we compress 24 hours of sound monitoring into a one-minute "collage" (Fig. 9). The technique works as follows: starting at 6 am through 6 am the next day, for every 72 minutes of recorded audio, a 3 second segment with the largest average amplitude is saved. The resulting 20 segments are played sequentially, providing a one-minute summary of the loudest noise events occurring in a 24 hour period.

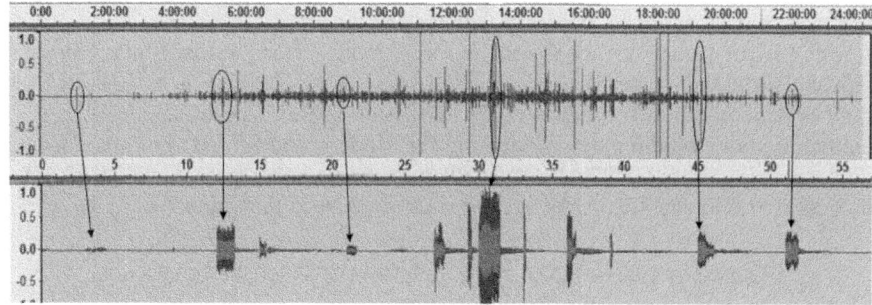

Fig. 9. Audio summary of noise for house A. One complete day (upper) (24 hours) of audio is compressed into a one-minute summary (lower) by selecting the 3 seconds of audio with the largest average amplitude, from every 72 minutes of audio. The upper scale format is hours:minutes:seconds, the lower scale is seconds.

6 Evaluation

We conducted a user study to: (1) evaluate the usefulness of the graphs representing the noise pollution data we collected, (2) explore the utility of qualitative noise samples versus quantitative summaries, and (3) see if interest in a noise monitoring service changes after trying our system. For each test site (houses A, B, and C) we create a graphical presentation of the quantitative data (shown in Fig. 8) and a one-minute audio summary (described in Fig. 9) from 24 hours of monitoring, from 6 am to 6 am on a week day.

The user study consisted of a questionnaire, three one-minute audio samples (listened with headphones), and the data graphs displayed on a laptop. Thirty five (35) participants were surveyed, drawn from the same sample group as our noise pollution survey (Section 4.1). Participants were asked to answer a few baseline questions and then rank where they would like to live based solely on viewing the graphical data and listening to the audio summaries. The test and choice orders (graphical, audio, house) were randomized to reduce any potential order-preference bias. Participants were asked which presentation method (graph or audio) they prefer, and re-asked a question from our initial survey, "How likely would you read a neighborhood noise assessment report before renting or buying a dwelling (for example, as part of a home inspection)?"

As an important validation to our system, the number of people who are "very likely" to read a noise assessment survey after trying our system jumped from 37% to 50% (Table 3). The participants preferred the one-minute audio summaries to the graphical view. When they put on their headphones, they listened intently, some pushing the headphones to there head to block out all other sound. They appeared to be mentally transported to the location, trying to figure out what it was they were hearing but could not see. Most watched a cursor move across the timeline while the audio played. As one participating commented "Having the timeline helped me think about when the noise would be disturbing." A participant said House C sounded like living in Manhattan. Another recognized the sound of someone practicing drums, an observation that cannot be discerned from any of the graphs.

Many participants were confused by the graphical view and had little experience with the significance of dB levels. In retrospect, it would have been helpful to add loudness references to the y-axis that participants could relate to, as in Table 1. The histogram views were the most confusing for users, which surprised us since many of the participants were technical people. Perhaps participants were confused because a histogram usually has frequency in the y-axis and bins in the x-axis.

Table 3. Noise assessment, audio and graphical presentation preferences

	First Survey	Second Survey
Very likely to read noise assessment	37%	50%
Likely to read noise assessment	30%	37%
Prefer audio segment	---	66%
Prefer graphical view	---	14%
Undecided	---	20%

Most people (66%) gave different rankings to the houses when listening to one-minute audio summaries then when viewing the graph. The largest variance was between houses A and B (58%). While many users identified house A as the quietest from the graphs and stated that as a preference, they had the opposite impression from the audio samples. House B has a constant background noise caused by the nearby creek which masks other sounds, whereas house A is quieter, but has occasional loud noises such as motorcycles which stand out more against the quiet background. Almost all (89% of respondents) put house C in third place after the other two, and house C was never selected as the best place to live.

Before showing users the data on these three houses, we asked users "Do you agree or disagree with the following: 'I prefer white noise such as flowing water or other continuous noise source masking other sounds, as compared to a quiet background environment with more audible sound event.'" (We didn't use the more accurate term "pink noise", since it is not commonly used or understood). Fifty seven percent (57%) agreed or strongly agreed with this statement, 14% disagreed or strongly disagreed, and 29% were neutral. There was a 24% correlation between agreement/disagreement with this statement and preferential choice of house B in the noise sample ranking (the house with the creek). This is corroborated by 17% of the participants who use wrote the term "white noise" when describing why they did or didn't like house B. This suggests that, to some extent, people are aware of their preference for "white noise" in their sound environment, and reinforces the subjectivity of noise pollution impact.

7 Conclusions

We have developed a residential noise model that quantifies ambient and transient events, producing a compact representation that can be sent over SMS text messages, and is simple enough to run on an inexpensive microprocessor. The resulting data captures the cyclic nature of noise produced by human and natural activities. We developed a novel method of compressing the noise events of an entire day (24 hours) into a one-minute summary. Evaluating the impact of residential noise is subjective for there are many noise sources whose impact varies with the individual. A majority of test subjects (66%) prefer the audio summaries over graphical presentations of noise pollution data. The audio summaries provide a direct and visceral means of exposing subjects to noise pollution, allowing them to experience the sources and make their own subjective evaluation of impact. However, this method may not be practical for screening dozens of locations with longer sampling periods (e.g. week vs. a single day). A hybrid approach may therefore be useful, where locations are first screen using noise model parameters, then top candidates are reviewed with audio summaries.

Nearly every subject in our survey said a quiet neighborhood is important in selecting a place to live, and two-thirds remember discovering noises in a new residence that they didn't know about before hand. We believe that a noise inspection device and service, as outlined in this paper, can help reduce some of the noise pollution surprises and risks encountered by new home owners and renters.

References

1. National Association of Noise Control Officials. Noise Effects Handbook,
   http://www.nonoise.org/library/handbook/handbook.htm
2. US Department of Labor Occupational Safety & Health Administration (OSHA),
   http://www.osha.gov/
3. Miller, N. US National Parks and Management of Park Soundscapes,
   http://www.hmmh.com/cmsdocuments/NMillerParksReview.pdf
4. National Association of Noise Control Officials. Noise Effects Handbook,
   http://www.nonoise.org/library/handbook/handbook.htm
5. United States Code of Federal Regulations. Noise Control Act of 1972. 42 U.S.C. 4901 to 4918 (1972)
6. European Commission. The Green Paper on Future Noise Policy (COM(96) 540) (November 1996),
   http://www.ec.europa.eu/environment/noise/greenpap.htm
7. US Environmental Protection Agency. Noise Pollution,
   http://www.epa.gov/air/noise.html
8. Peppin, R., Probst, W. An Approach to Reduce Environmental Noise: How Europe Uses Noise Mapping and Action Planning (2007),
   http://www.scantekinc.com/datasheets/PaperBanff20074rjp.pdf
9. The Scottish Government. Scottish Noise Mapping,
   http://www.scottishnoisemapping.org
10. Choa, S.: Noise mapping using measured noise and GPS data. Applied Acoustics 68(9), 1054–1061 (2007)
11. Administration de la Navitation Aerienne. Aircraft noise monitoring stations,
    http://www.aeroport.public.lu/en/environnement/bruit_avions/station_mesurage.html
12. Tout, I.: London Heathrow Airport Noise Map Briefing,
    http://www.lhrnoisemap.org/projectbriefing.html
13. Vision 100 – Century of Avaiation Reauthorization Act Public Law 108-176,
    http://www.amtech-usa.org/jpdo/VISION_100_CITATION.pdf
14. Lochard WebTrack,
    http://sjc.webtrak-lochard.com/template/index.html
15. Directive 2002/49/EC of the European Parliament and of the Council of 25 June 2002 relating to the assessment and management of environmental noise (2002)
16. Dufournet, D., Jouenne, P.: MADRAS, An Intelligent Assistant for Noise Recognition. In: INTER-NOISE, Budapest (1997)
17. Gaunard, P., Mubikangiey, C., Couvreur, C., Fontaine, V.: Automatic Classification of Environemntal Noise Events By Hidden Markov Models. Acoustics, Speech and Signal Processing 6, 3609–3612 (1998)
18. Eisenman, S., Miluzzo, E., Lane, N., Peterson, R., Ahn, G., Campbell, A.: The BikeNet Mobile Sensing System for Cyclist Experience Mapping. In: Proceedings of the 5th International Conference on Embedded Networked Sensor Systems, Sydney, Australia, pp. 87–101 (2007)
19. Maisonneuve, N., Stevens, M., Ochab, B.: Participatory noise pollution monitoring using mobile phones. Information Polity 15(1-2), 51–71 (2010)
20. Rana, R., Chou, C., Kanhere, S., Bulusu, N., Hu, W.: Ear-Phone assessment of noise pollution with mobile phones. Proc. of the 7th ACM Conference on Embedded Networked Sensor Systems (2010)

21. Kanjo, E.: NoiseSPY: A Real-Time Mobile Phone Platform for Urban Noise Monitoring and Mapping. Mobile Networks and Applications 15(4), 562–574 (2010)
22. Ballagas, R., Memon, F., Reiners, R., Borchers, J.: iStuff Mobile: Rapidly Prototyping New Mobile Phone Interfaces for Ubiquitous Computing. In: CHI (2007)
23. Santini, S., Ostermaier, B., Adelmann, R.: On the use of sensor nodes and mobile phones for the assessment of noise pollution levels in urban environments. In: Proc. of Networked Sensing Systems (2009)
24. Georgia State University. Sensitivity of Human Ear, http://hyperphysics.phy-astr.gsu.edu/HBASE/sound/earsens.html
25. http://www.wpi.edu/Pubs/E-project/Available/E-project-042910-001603/unrestricted/Bird_Call_Identification_MQP_2010.pdf

A Longitudinal Study of Pressure Sensing to Infer Real-World Water Usage Events in the Home

Jon Froehlich[1,*], Eric Larson[2,*], Elliot Saba[2], Tim Campbell[3], Les Atlas[2], James Fogarty[1], and Shwetak Patel[1,2]

[1] Computer Science and Engineering
[2] Electrical Engineering,
[3] Mechnical Engineering
University of Washington, Seattle
{jfroehli,eclarson,sabae,tcampbell,lesatlas,
jfogarty,shwetak}@uw.edu

Abstract. We present the first longitudinal study of pressure sensing to infer *real-world* water usage events in the home (e.g., dishwasher, upstairs bathroom sink, downstairs toilet). In order to study the pressure-based approach *out in the wild*, we deployed a ground truth sensor network for five weeks in three homes and two apartments that *directly monitored* valve-level water usage by *fixtures* and *appliances*. We use this data to, first, demonstrate the practical challenges in constructing water usage activity inference algorithms and, second, to inform the design of a new probabilistic-based classification approach. Inspired by algorithms in speech recognition, our novel Bayesian approach incorporates template matching, a language model, grammar, and prior probabilities. We show that with a single pressure sensor, our probabilistic algorithm can classify real-world water usage at the fixture level with 90% accuracy and at the fixture-category level with 96% accuracy. With two pressure sensors, these accuracies increase to 94% and 98%. Finally, we show how our new approach can be trained with fewer examples than a strict template-matching approach alone.

Keywords: Water sensing, activity inference, sustainability, field deployments.

1 Introduction

Low-cost and easy-to-install methods to sense and model human activity in the home have long been a focus of UbiComp research. Because water is fundamental to many activities of human life (e.g., bathing, cooking), sensing disaggregated water usage has emerged as a particularly promising area for human activity inference in the home [6, 8, 19]. In addition, these sensing systems can play a vital role in collecting highly granular consumption information for enabling eco-feedback and sustainability applications (e.g., [7]). In previous work, we introduced HydroSense [8], a pressure-based sensing solution that disaggregates water usage at the fixture level from a single installation point. HydroSense identifies the unique pressure waves generated when

---

* The first two authors contributed equally to this work.

K. Lyons, J. Hightower, and E.M. Huang (Eds.): Pervasive 2011, LNCS 6696, pp. 50–69, 2011.
© Springer-Verlag Berlin Heidelberg 2011

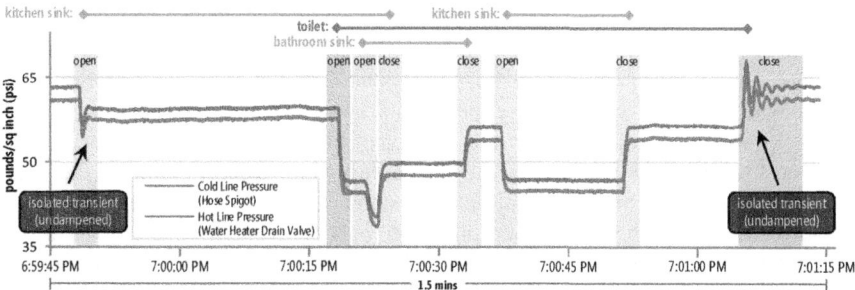

Fig. 1. A pressure stream with ground truth labels from deployment site H2. The blue line is the cold water pressure (sensed from a hose spigot) and the red line is the hot water pressure (sensed from a water heater drain valve). The pressure transients are also highlighted and colored according to fixture. Note how rapid increases and decreases in pressure correspond to opens and closes and how transient waveforms are dampened when they occur in compound.

fixtures are opened or closed. These waves propagate *throughout* a home's plumbing infrastructure, thus enabling the single-point sensing approach.

Although the original HydroSense work evaluated the pressure-based sensing approach using *staged experiments* in *controlled* home environments[8], it was unclear how well this approach would perform with *real-world* water usage. In this paper, we critically examine the feasibility of using pressure-based sensing to determine water usage activities in the home. We conduct real-world deployments in three homes and two apartments over a five-week period. In addition to installing pressure sensor sat each deployment site, we also deployed custom wireless *ground truth sensors* on individual fixtures throughout the home (*e.g.,* kitchen sink, toilet, dishwasher) to provide ground truth data on water activity events. The *ground truth sensors* were designed to track both hot *and* cold water usage at their respective fixtures. This allowed us to investigate not only whether the pressure signal could be used to infer fixture-level water activity but also whether it could be used to determine hot and/or cold water usage at each fixture. This is an important capability as water heating alone is responsible for 12.5% of residential energy consumption [17]. To our knowledge, our ground truth deployment represents the most comprehensive real-world study of hot and cold water usage in residential homes and apartments ever performed.

Over five weeks, we collected approximately 15,000 ground truth labels for the *opening* and *closing* of fixture valves (e.g., Figure 1). The scope and size of this dataset allows us to examine the practical challenges in constructing water usage activity inference algorithms and to highlight problems that any *indirect* water sensing method must address. We show, for example, that compound events (when two or more water fixtures are operating at the same time) constitute37.1% of all bathroom sink activity and nearly 20% of overall water usage activity. Such prevalence suggests that compound events should be specifically addressed and evaluated by any water disaggregation technique; however, this has rarely been the case (e.g., see [8, 9, 20]). Thus, our ground truth data serves both as a resource to inform the design of our classification algorithms as well as to evaluate their performance.

We use the ground truth labels along with the pressure stream data to design and evaluate a novel pressure-based water usage inference algorithm. Although the template matching of pressure wave transients used in our original HydroSense paper [8] worked well for controlled experiments, we show that a template-matching approach alone is insufficient for the variety of signal distortions that occur during real-world water use. For example, the speed with which a faucet handle is turned and whether an event occurs in isolation or in compound can change the shape of the pressure transient thereby rendering the naïve template matching approach inadequate. Consequently, we extend and adapt the original HydroSense algorithms to use a probabilistic model based in part on speech recognition algorithms. We show how the addition of a language model and contextual priors (e.g., fixture usage duration, and maximum flow rate) can boost classification accuracies by an average of 6% with real-world water usage data. We also show that the introduction of a language model and priors decreases the amount of training data relative to a template-based approach alone. Our current analysis provides pre-segmented pressure transients to our classification algorithm, leaving segmentation to future work. In this way, our classification results can be seen as an upper bound.

In summary, the contributions of this paper are: (1) The most comprehensive dataset of labeled real-world hot and cold water usage events ever collected in homes and apartments; (2) An analysis of our new real-world dataset to uncover challenges that any indirect sensing water disaggregation method must overcome; (3) A new probabilistic approach to water usage classification that is highly extensible and incorporates a language model, grammar, and contextual priors; (4) An evaluation showing that this new probabilistic approach performs significantly better than previous template-based methods.

2 Related Work

Automatic identification of home water usage events has largely been pursued by two non-overlapping efforts. Utilities and water resource management scientists have investigated disaggregation to inform government policy [13], plumbing codes [15], and to study the effectiveness of conservation programs [14] and low-flow fixtures [12,13]. In contrast, computing researchers have focused on human activity inference (e.g., [6, 8, 19]) and sustainability applications (e.g., [9]). We draw upon literature across both fields.

In studies by utilities and water resource management scientists, the most prevalent residential disaggregation technique is *flow-trace analysis*. Flow-trace analysis examines aggregate flow at a single *inline* water flow meter to determine the fixture *category* responsible for water usage [3]. Unlike HydroSense, flow-trace analysis only classifies at the fixture category level (i.e., it cannot determine the specific fixture or valve that was used). For example, flow-trace can determine that *a* toilet was flushed but not *which* toilet was flushed. Flow-trace analysis has been used in government- and utility- sponsored studies [3, 12, 13, 14], the largest of which included 1,188 households across North America [11]. Despite its prominence, flow-trace analysis has not been comprehensively studied. In the only known empirical investigation, Wilkes *et al.* conducted staged experiments of water usage over a five day period in one home. Flow-trace analysis correctly categorized 83% of the *isolated* water usage events at the fixture category level. When water usage overlapped (i.e., what we term *compound events*), performance dropped dramatically to 24% when two water fixtures were used in compound and 0% when three or more were used [20].

Researchers in the UbiComp and Pervasive communities have developed other water disaggregation techniques such as the Nonintrusive Autonomous Water Monitoring System [9], the original HydroSense work [8], and Sensing from the Basement [6]. In the only real-world evaluation, Fogarty *et al.*, installed microphones on water supply and sewage pipes in a single home and used temporal features in order to classify pipe noise into individual fixture usages. This work demonstrated that temporal features such as duration (e.g., a toilet flush lasts ~60 seconds) and on/off activations (e.g., a dishwasher cycles through a detectable pattern of water use) were useful in classifying water events at the fixture level. However, it also revealed the difficulty in discriminating between bathroom sink and kitchen sink uses, correctly classifying short water events (e.g., events that lasted less than 10 seconds), and correctly classifying compound events.

Our original HydroSense work was the first to show that pressure transients could be used to disaggregate water fixtures using staged experiments [8]. The experiments, however, were limited in that faucet handles were activated at approximately the same flow rate each time, and all fixtures were tested in isolation (i.e., no more than one fixture was used at a time). As we show in this paper and as could only be derived through a real-world ground truth deployment, much greater variations are common in real-world water usage. These phenomena can affect properties of the resulting pressure wave and thus the ease of classification.

3 Data Collection and Deployment

To evaluate the performance of a pressure-based approach using *real-world* data, we deployed a large ground truth water usage sensing network in three homes and two apartments. At each deployment site, we installed two pressure sensors and directly instrumented *all* water fixtures and appliances with custom wireless sensors that provided ground truth labels of water usage activity for the pressure stream. Here, we describe the ground truth data collection system and the five week study deployment.

3.1 Acquiring Ground Truth Labels in a Real-World Deployment

A key challenge in evaluating any new sensing technique is acquiring ground truth data. In the original HydroSense work [8], the team *manually* labeled the pressure stream during their staged experiments, which clearly would not work for a real-world evaluation. Thus, an automated method for labeling must be derived. An ideal labeling system would accurately detect when fixtures are turned on/off, be easy to install, work across a large variety of fixtures, and preferably provide flow and temperature information for each fixture valve. An accurate and direct approach would be to install small, wireless flow meters at each hot and cold fixture inlet (e.g., a sink would require two flow meters). Unfortunately, inline flow meters could actually distort the very phenomena we are interested in studying by impacting the

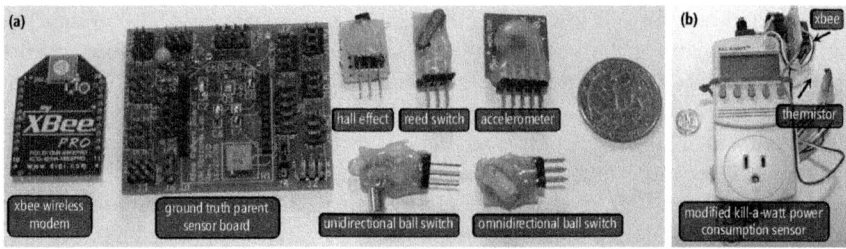

Fig. 2. The ground truth water usage sensors directly attached to (a) *fixtures* and (b) *appliances* and monitored valve *openings and closings.* This data was transmitted wirelessly in real time via the ground truth parent sensor board and aXBee wireless modem (a, left side) to a data logger.

pressure-wave signal itself. Instead, we instrumented fixtures externally, such as on faucet and toilet handles, so that we did not disturb the water stream.

We designed an array of ground truth sensors to accommodate the variety of home water fixtures: from hand operated fixtures like sinks to electromechanical appliances such as dishwashers. Even for a single fixture type, design variation affects how flow and temperature are selected and how they can be sensed. For example, some single-handle faucets move left to right for temperature and up or down for flow while dual-handle faucets select both temperature and flow by the open position of each handle.

3.2   Water Usage Activity Ground Truth Sensors

We developed seven ground truth sensors to accommodate all fixtures across our deployment sites. Each interfaced with a *parent sensor board* (wireless platform in Figure 2a, top right) to communicate water usage data in real time. At a minimum, we tracked when each valve was opened or closed and categorized temperature into *hot only*, *cold only*, and *mixed*. The parent sensor board was placed in a location protected from water and preferably next to a power outlet (5 of 33 ground truth sensor boards relied on battery power). All sensors and parent boards were weather proofed to protect against water damage. XBee Pro wireless modems (Figure 2a, top left) transmitted sensor state to a logger on a laptop installed at each deployment site. The sensor boards were configured to transmit a watchdog signal once every four minutes so failures could be quickly identified and corrected. The ground truth architecture and sensors went through several design cycles and took approximately three months to build and evaluate before being deployed in this study.

For sinks, showers, and toilets, sensors to detect handle position were affixed directly to the fixtures themselves and linked to the wireless parent board via low-voltage wires (Figure 3).We used three types of handle sensors: *reed switches* (N=34 sensors deployed), *accelerometers* (N=14), and *Hall effect sensors* (N=3). Reed switches are electrical switches that react to the presence of a magnetic field and produce binary output: on or off. They are inexpensive, robust to water exposure, and provide easily analyzable data. For toilets, we instrumented the flush handle, which only provided data on the beginning of the fill and not on the end. We discuss how this end fill information was recovered in the next section.

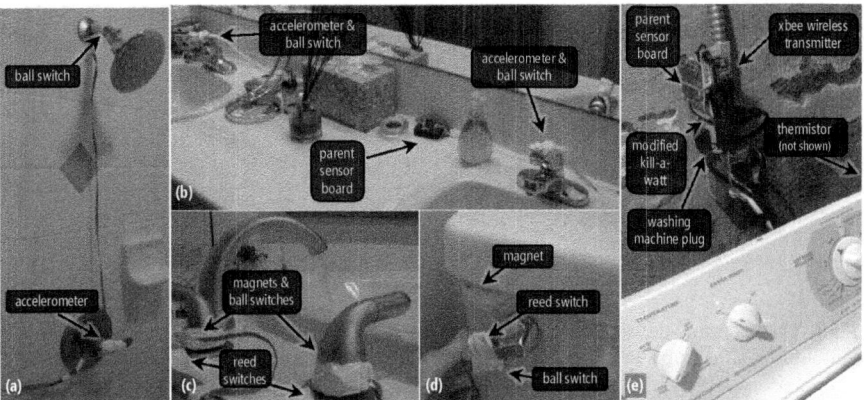

Fig. 3. A sample of instrumented fixtures from our ground truth deployments. Note how different sensors (e.g., accelerometers, reed switches) are used to accommodate the variety of fixture types.

For faucets where a single handle controls flow rate and temperature, the reed switches were insufficient. Instead, we used three-axis accelerometers (Figure 3a and 3b) to measure acceleration and interpret the handle's flow position (typically up and down movement) and temperature (typically left and right movement). Finally, we used Hall effect sensors for sensing faucets which control temperature using planar rotation but control flow through an up/down motion (i.e., where an accelerometer alone could not sense the planar motion). A Hall effect sensor provides a voltage difference representing the distance between two magnets, so we placed magnets on both sides of faucet handles and attached the Hall effect sensor to the handle itself.

Additionally, each hand-operated fixture had at least oneomni-directional *ball switch* (N=39) that acted as a vibration sensor and woke the parent board to read and transmit handle position sensor data. This allowed us to limit power consumption and unnecessary XBee wireless traffic.

For washing machines and dishwashers, we used three types of sensors: *power usage sensors* (N=7), *push buttons*(N=2), and *thermistors* (N=3). Power consumption patterns were used to reconstruct when appliances used water. We could not gain access to the power outlets in two cases (deployment site A1's washing machine and H1's dishwasher), so we used push buttons and a note reminding the resident to *"please push button when turning on <appliance>."*For sites with washing machines, we also attached thermistors to the water drain pipe to measure the temperature of the previous fill cycle and infer machine settings (e.g., Hot/Cold, Warm/Cold).

3.3 Pressure Sensors and Software Tools

The above sensor network was deployed at each deployment site to provide *ground truth labels* for our pressure sensors. For our pressure sensors, we used Pace Scientific P1600s with a resolution of 0.03 psi. Each was connected to a 16-bit Texas

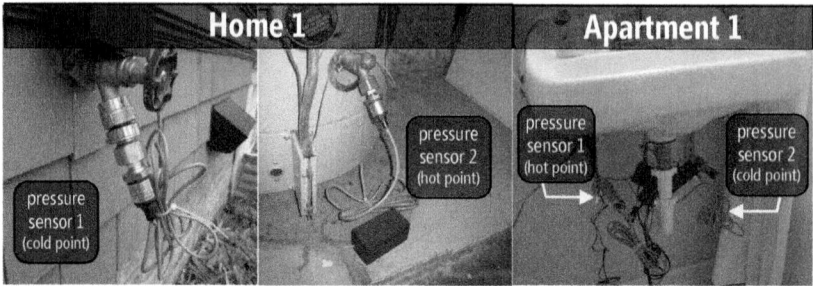

Fig. 4. Two pressure sensors were installed at each deployment site (one on a hot water access point, one on a cold) in order to study the effect of installation points on classification accuracies

Instruments ADS8344 ADC and AVR microcontroller, which interfaced with a Class 1 Bluetooth radio implementing the serial port profile with an approximate wireless range of 10m. This is the same setup as the original HydroSense study with three exceptions. First, instead of one pressure sensor, we connected *two* sensors to collect data from hot *and* cold water access points simultaneously (Figure 4). This allowed us to investigate the effect of installation point as well as the effect of two pressure streams compared to one on classification performance. Second, the original HydroSense work tested only $^3/_4$" water access points (e.g., hose spigot). We built adapters to connect to $^3/_8$" access points, which allowed us to install pressure sensors below kitchen and bathroom sinks (Figure 4, right). This was particularly important for the apartment installations, which did not have accessible $^3/_4$" access points. Finally, we used a sampling rate of 500Hz rather than 1,000Hz, as we found 500 Hz was more than sufficient to capture these pressure waves.

To communicate with the ground truth sensor network and the pressure sensors, a 2GHz Dell Inspiron 1545s laptop running Windows XP was deployed at each site. The laptops were configured with a USB XBee wireless modem and Bluetooth dongle. The laptops continuously ran a custom data logger written in C#, which received, compressed and archived data locally for backup. This was uploaded to a backend web server at 30-minute intervals. The server backend was implemented using Python and web2py. In addition to serving as a data repository, the backend automatically sent e-mail notifications when a ground truth sensor or pressure sensor was not heard from for 10 minutes or more. For analysis, we constructed a suite of tools in Matlab and C#. Because not all of the ground truth sensors provided direct labels about water usage (e.g., the power usage sensors and toilet handle sensors), we also built a custom annotation tool in C# that allowed us to quickly review the ground truth sensor streams and semi-automatically annotate the pressure stream.

3.4 Deployments

We deployed the ground truth sensor network and two pressure sensors at five sites: three houses and two apartments. Each site was a home or apartment of one of the authors. This was done because of the invasiveness of the direct sensing approach used for the ground truth data collection. There was, however, a large variation in the type, size and plumbing systems across the deployments sites (Table 1). The deployments began February 2010 and lasted for five weeks.

It took approximately two full work days per deployment site for two people to install and test the ground truth sensors. After the five-week ground truth deployments ended, we used our custom annotation tool to convert the ground truth sensor stream to labels. This was accomplished in a semi-automatic fashion—the annotation tool visualized the ground truth sensor values and the pressure streams together in a common time-series view. The ground truth sensor values could then be automatically or manually converted to labels. It took approximately 8-12 hours per week of data collected for one research assistant to convert the sensor stream to labels. These labels were then reviewed by a second research assistant for consistency, which took roughly half the time (4-6 hours per week of data).

4   Analysis of the Collected Dataset

We collected a total of 16,056 labeled events across the five deployment sites. Table 2 provides an overview. Due to ground truth sensor failures, 2.9% of this data is marked as *uncertain* and is not used in our classification experiments. Nearly 80% of the uncertainties were due to malfunctioning kitchen sink handle position sensors in H1 and H2, which were replaced within a few days of discovery. The dataset also includes *unknown* events (3.9% of our dataset), which are pressure stream transients whose origin cannot be determined because they occurred without accompanying data from the ground truth sensors. A1 has the highest proportion of unknown events (9.1%) because of water usage activity coming from other apartments. Although we do not attempt to classify uncertain or unknown events, they were not removed from the dataset and can impact classification performance when they overlap with other events. After accounting for uncertain/unknown events, we are left with 14,960 labels.

Table 1. Occupant demographics and deployment site characteristics. In A1, The toilet and shower head were replaced with low-flow equivalents ~3.5 weeks into the deployment. We discuss the effect of this change on classification performance in the results section.

	H1	H2	H3	A1	A2
# Residents	2	2	4	2	2
Gender/Age/ Profession	M/27/professor; F/29/professor	M/31/professor; F/32/office worker	4 Males/19-21/ undergrad students	M/31/grad student; F/30/post-doc	M/26/grad student; F/26/pharmacist
Fixtures/Valves	17/28	8/13	13/21	6/10 (8/13)*	8/13
Style/Built	House/2003	House/1918	House/ 1923	Apt/1920s	Apt/2000
Size/Floors	3000 sqft/ 2 floor + basement	750 sqft/ 1 floor + basement	1200 sqft / 1 floor + basement	700 sqft/ 3rd floor of 3	750 sqft/ 6th floor of 7
Expansion Tank/ Regulator	Yes/Yes	No/No	No/No	N/A	N/A
Water Heater Tank Size/ Plumbing	50 gal/ Copper	50 gal/ PEX	50 gal/ Copper	Two 100 gal tanks/ galvanized	N/A/ PEX
Pressure Sensor Install Point Hot/Cold	Main floor bathroom sink/outdoor hose spigot	Water heater drain valve/outdoor hose spigot	Downstairs bathroom sink/outdoor hose spigot	Bathroom sink hot/cold inlet	Kitchen sink hot/cold inlet

Table 3 shows valve activity at individual fixtures by temperature state (hot, cold, mixed). We use *M.* for Master and *S.* for secondary to distinguish primary and secondary bathrooms. The *M. Bath Diverter* and *S. Bath Diverter* are for the tub/shower switch that diverts water flow from the bath to the shower and vice versa; we distinguish between a shower that is turned on straightaway and a shower that is diverted from a bath. The *Other* category includes data from only one deployment site, H1, and encompasses the *Laundry Basin* and the *Refrigerator Water Dispenser*. On average across all deployment sites, there is a nearly even proportion of cold and hot events (40.7% for cold only, 39.2% for hot, and 20% for mixed). This implies that any indirect water disaggregation sensing method, such as flow-trace analysis and HydroSense, must be equally capable of sensing usage regardless of temperature. The overall frequency of fixture usage follows a power-law distribution where the first four fixtures (*kitchen sink, master bathroom sink* and *toilet,* and *secondary bathroom sink*) account for 84.7% of the events in our dataset. For purposes of human activity inference, these fixtures are thus critically important.

Table 2. High level ground truth data collection statistics. An *event* is one occurrence of either a valve open or a valve close. Uncertain and unknowns are *not* included in the totals events row.

	H1	H2	H3	A1	A2	Totals
Days of Data	33	33	30	27	33	156
Total Events	2374	3075	4754	2499	2578	14960
Avg Events/Day	71.9	93.2	158.5	92.6	78.1	95.9
Cold Only Events	855 (36.0%)	1418 (46.1%)	1637 (34.3%)	633 (25.3%)	1657 (64.3%)	6087 (40.7%)
Hot Only Events	607 (25.6%)	1329 (43.2%)	1766 (37.5%)	1818 (72.8%)	498 (19.3%)	5870 (39.2%)
Mixed Temp Events	912 (38.4%)	328 (10.7%)	1351 (28.2%)	48 (1.9%)	423 (16.4%)	3003 (20.1%)
Isolated Events	1981 (83.5%)	2477 (80.6%)	4131 (86.9%)	1914 (76.6%)	2149 (83.4%)	12393 (82.8%)
Compound Events	393 (16.6%)	598 (19.5%)	623 (13.1%)	585 (23.4%)	429 (16.6%)	2567 (17.2%)
Transient Collisions	142 (6%)	72 (2.3%)	166 (3.5%)	219 (8.8%)	120 (4.7%)	701 (4.7%)
Uncertain Events	22 (0.9%)	175 (5.3%)	189 (3.7%)	52 (1.9%)	37 (1.4%)	467 (2.9%)
Unknown Events	52 (2.1%)	79 (2.4%)	184 (3.6%)	254 (9.1%)	85 (3.1%)	629 (3.9%)

Table 3. A breakdown of valve activity by fixture, by temperature state (hot, cold, mixed) and by compound/collisions. The *Cnt* column tabulates the number of fixtures across sites.

Fixtures	Cnt	Total	Hot	Cold	Mixed	Compound	Collision	AvgDuration
KitchenSink	5	5494 (36.7%)	2438 (44.4%)	1415 (25.8%)	1641 (29.9%)	342 (6.2%)	206 (3.7%)	22.4 secs
M.Bathroom Sink	7	3934 (26.3%)	2114 (53.7%)	1294 (32.9%)	526 (13.4%)	1459 (37.1%)	185 (4.7%)	27.2 secs
M.Bathroom Toilet	5	1886 (12.6%)	0 (0.0%)	1886 (100%)	0 (0.0%)	87 (4.6%)	117 (6.2%)	43.6 secs
S.Bathroom Sink	4	1369 (9.2%)	618 (45.1%)	637 (46.5%)	114 (8.3%)	430 (31.4%)	57 (4.2%)	30.9 secs
Washing Machine	4	430 (2.9%)	93 (21.6%)	325 (75.6%)	12 (2.8%)	12 (2.8%)	66 (15.3%)	1.6 mins
M.Bathroom Bath	5	423 (2.8%)	224 (53%)	35 (8.3%)	164 (38.8%)	87 (20.6%)	20 (4.7%)	43.4 secs
S.Bathroom Toilet	3	341 (2.3%)	0 (0.0%)	341 (100%)	0 (0.0%)	11 (3.2%)	21 (6.2%)	27.2 secs
M.Bathroom Shower	5	261 (1.7%)	55 (21.1%)	4 (1.5%)	202 (77.4%)	30 (11.5%)	10 (3.8%)	8.7 mins
Dishwasher	3	261 (1.7%)	261 (100%)	0 (0.0%)	0 (0.0%)	9 (3.4%)	6 (2.3%)	1.2 mins
M.Bath Diverter	5	228 (1.5%)	17 (7.5%)	1 (0.4%)	210 (92.1%)	92 (40.4%)	5 (2.2%)	N/A
Other	1	181 (1.2%)	28 (15.5%)	149 (82.3%)	4 (2.2%)	0 (0.0%)	4 (2.2%)	8.2 secs
S.Bathroom Bath	2	59 (0.39%)	5 (8.5%)	0 (0.0%)	54 (91.5%)	2 (3.4%)	2 (3.4%)	20.7 secs
S.Bathroom Shower	2	47 (0.31%)	11 (23.4%)	0 (0.0%)	36 (76.5%)	0 (0.0%)	1 (2.1%)	9.4 mins
S.Bath Diverter	2	46 (0.31%)	6 (13%)	0 (0.0%)	40 (87%)	6 (13%)	1 (2.2%)	N/A
Totals	53	14960	5870 (39.2%)	6087 (40.7%)	3003 (20.1%)	2567 (17.2%)	701 (4.7%)	49.1 secs

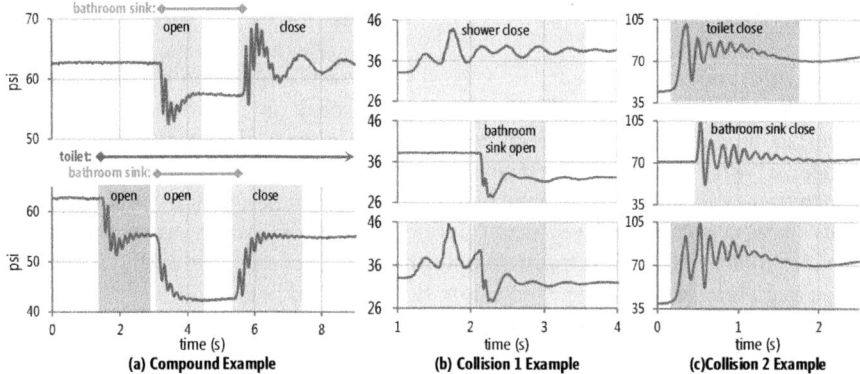

Fig. 5. (a) Bathroom sink open and close transients occurring in isolation and in compound from H2. (b) A shower close and bathroom sink close transient in isolation and colliding from A2. (c) A toilet close and a bathroom sink close transient in isolation and colliding from H3.

Although we ultimately used this data to evaluate our classification algorithms, an equally important goal was to identify potential challenges in classifying real-world water usage compared to simulated, isolated water events. A *compound valve event* is a valve event that occurs while another fixture is using water (e.g., the bathroom sink events in Figure 5a). A *collision valve event* is a valve event that occurs within *twoseconds* of one or more other valve events (Figure 5b and 5c). Previous water disaggregation sensing approaches have performed poorly in the face of compounds and collisions (e.g., [6, 20]). This is because compounds and collisions often mask or distort features used for classification. Although a collision is technically also a compound, for the purposes of our analysis we separate them to investigate the individual effect of each on classification performance. In our dataset, 17.2% of all valve events are compound while 4.7% of valve events are collisions (Table 2 and 3). The most common compound/collision events are master bathroom sink opens and closes, comprising 41.8% of all bathroom sink activity and 11% of all valve activity overall (Table 3).

With the pressure-based approach, compound valve events result in a dampening and often a severe attenuation of the high frequency component of the pressure transient. As a result, the transient signal is homogenized, making it difficult to classify. With collisions, the two colliding transient waveforms become highly distorted; although it is rarely the case that two transients occur simultaneously (more often they are offset by 200-500ms), the distortions may still render the transient unrecognizable. In Figure 5b, the shower close and bathroom sink open occur 1.1s apart. In Figure 5c, the toilet close and bathroom sink close occur 200ms apart, making it unlikely that both will be classified. For these events to be classified correctly, less emphasis may need to be placed on template matching transient signatures relative to the original HydroSense work [8]. Our new algorithm specifically addresses this issue.

5 Valve Event Classification Algorithm

To classify pressure transients as valve events, we apply a probabilistic approach using Bayesian estimation. Our particular approach is inspired by the dynamic Bayesian models used in speech recognition. Instead of recognizing *words,* we recognize *valve events*. Like many of the Bayesian approaches used in speech recognition, we incorporate a language model and grammar, which estimates the most likely *sequence of valve events* and defines permissible *valve event pairings*. This provides robustness against transient deformations that can occur during natural valve usage (e.g., brief water usage events, low-flow, and compounds).

At a high level, the classification algorithm works as follows: First, an incoming water pressure data stream is buffered and the pressure transients are segmented. This segmentation process currently uses the time series boundaries defined by the ground truth annotations but would be automated in an end-to-end system. Second, the segmented pressure transients are each compared to a library of labeled templates using a set of similarity algorithms. Third, a language model determines the likelihood of a given sequence of valve signatures and links *open* and *close* valve events into *paired tuples*. Fourth, we extract features from these paired tuples and compare them with smoothed probability distributions. For example, by pairing a *bathroom sink hot open* with a *bathroom sink hot close*, we can extract the *duration* of that event and estimate the *total flow volume* used and then obtain probabilities for those features. Finally, the probabilities from the previous three steps are multiplied together for each sequence and the sequence with the highest probability is selected.

We now formally define our Bayesian model for classifying pressure transient sequences. In eq. (1) below, let **V** denote the pressure signature template library (a vector of labeled pressure transient signatures and their transforms) and **S** denote a sequence of *unknown* segmented pressure transients. Then, using Bayes' theorem, the most likely valve sequence is defined as:

$$\hat{V} = \arg\max P(\mathbf{V} \mid \mathbf{S}) = \arg\max \frac{P(\mathbf{S} \mid \mathbf{V}) P(\mathbf{V})}{P(\mathbf{S})} \tag{1}$$

The conditional probability term $P(\mathbf{S}|\mathbf{V})$ describes the outcome of the *template*-and *feature-based comparisons*. The prior probability term $P(\mathbf{V})$ describes the likelihood of the valve sequence (using bigrams) and the likelihood of each pairing in the sequence. Note that *arg max* simply returns a specific valve sequence rather than a probability estimate, thus the normalization constant $P(\mathbf{S})$ can be discarded in practice. We can expand the numerator of eq. (1) to further highlight the four major components of our approach:

$$\overbrace{\prod_{r=0}^{R-1} f_r(\hat{\mathbf{S}}_r \mid \hat{\mathbf{V}}_r)}^{P(\mathbf{S}|\mathbf{V})} \overbrace{\prod_{n=0}^{N-1} P(v_n \mid v_{n-1}) \underbrace{\prod_{i \notin \beta} f_p(v_i)}_{\text{(iii) grammar}} \prod_{k=0}^{K-1} \prod_{\langle a,b \rangle \in \beta} f_k(\langle v_a, v_b \rangle)}^{P(\mathbf{V})} \tag{2}$$

(i) templates and signal features   (ii) bigram language model   (iii) grammar   (iv) paired valve priors

$P(\mathbf{S}|\mathbf{V})$ is now represented by the first term in eq. (2), which describes our set of R signal transformations and comparison algorithms (where f_r is the comparison algorithm for the rth transformation). $P(\mathbf{V})$ is expanded into three terms: our bigram language model, a grammar, and water usage event priors. We describe each term in the following.

Term (i): Template- and Feature-Based Comparison: Term (i) compares the segmented unknown pressure transient s with *open* and *close* valve templates in our library. Each comparison is broken into two parts: a *signal transformation* on s to achieve $\hat{s}$ and a *similarity score* calculation between $\hat{s}$ and a corresponding transformed valve template $\hat{v}$ in our template library. We use multiple signal transformations and comparison algorithms to produce a set of similarity scores for a given valve (each transformation and score is represented by f_r in term (i)). These scores are converted into probabilities and multiplied together to form a single template-match probability between s and every valve v in the template library. This is similar to our original HydroSense work which used a hierarchical classifier to prune and classify these individual pressure transients. Unlike this past work, however, these similarity scores are incorporated into a probabilistic model.

We use eight signal transformations—four filters and a Cepstral transform of each filter. Each attempts to emphasize a unique property of the pressure transient waveform. The first two filters, a 1 Hz and a 13 Hz low-pass filter, allow us to explore the temporal shape of the transient signal. The next two filters are *derivatives* of the low-pass filtered signals, which help to uncover how resonances of the transient waveform decay over time. Specifically, we use a derivative of the 13 Hz low-pass filter and a band pass derivative of the difference between the 1 and 13 Hz low-pass filters. Finally, we apply a constant-Q Cepstral transformation on *each* of the aforementioned four transforms.

The constant Q transformation uses a filter bank with overlapping and logarithmically increasing bandwidths to break apart the frequency spectrum of the transient signal. After the filter bank, we apply a magnitude and log operation to turn multiplication of two systems in the frequency domain into addition operations. This has the effect of separating the "source" (an impulse or step into the plumbing system) from the "filter" (the physical bends and pipe lengths in the plumbing system). We then take the discrete cosine transform (DCT) of the constant-Q coefficients, which compacts harmonic structures down towards lower indices of the transform (commonly known as low-time cepstral coefficients). We truncate these coefficients (known as low-time *liftering*) before applying similarity algorithms. For more information on our constant-Q transformations, see Larson *et al.* [10].

We use two similarity algorithms over the eight signal transformations: a matched filter and a Euclidean distance measure. The matched filter is an optimal similarity measure for orthogonal signals in the presence of white noise [16]. Because our signals resemble decaying sinusoids, we can expect the above transformations to result in signals that are approximately orthogonal. The matched filter is used to compare the first four signal transformations, while the Euclidean distance measure is used for the four Cepstral transformations (given that the Cepstral space is already aligned, a matched filter type approach is unnecessary). A similar set of signal transformations and comparison algorithms were used in the original HydroSense work [8]. However, to ensure the approach works robustly with real-world data, we added the 4th signal transform above (the band pass derivative) and eliminated the *mean square error* measure because it did not improve performance.

After every $\{s,v\}$ comparison has been made, we reinterpret the similarity scores as probabilities. For the matched filter comparisons, this is trivial as the matched filter already returns a similarity score between 0 and 1. For the real Cepstral transforms, we use Euclidean distance measures d_m between each transient in S and template in V, such that $f_{EucDist}(\hat{s}|\hat{v}) = e^{-|d_m|}$ (a common interpretation of Euclidean distance as a probability in log-space [18]).

At this point in the algorithm we have an unknown transient s and the results of the four matched filter comparisons and the four exponential Euclidean distance comparisons (for every template in our library). To form a single template probability score, we multiply the comparisons of each template together. These scores are then grouped by valve (i.e., all "kitchen sink open hot" scores are grouped together; all "bathroom sink close cold" are grouped, etc.). We then take the *argmax* over each valve grouping to find the probability that a particular valve is the originator of s.

Because we now have a single probability score for each valve, we can combine these with the probability of observing valve-specific features. These features are low dimensional vectors or scalars that are pre-calculated for each valve at a deployment site. In particular, we use two features: (1) stabilized pressure drop and (2) amplitude/resonance tracking; however, other features such as *damping ratio* and *time of day used* could be explored in the future. The stabilized pressure drop can be calculated by assuming that the transient is an underlying step function with three parameters: (a) time at which the step occurs, t_0, (b) magnitude of the step, A_0, and (c) region, T, where the transient has many high frequency components and cannot be modeled by a step. These parameters can be solved for (in the mean square sense) using linear regression with a "don't care" region. After regression, the stabilized pressure drop is the scalar value A_0. For resonance/amplitude tracking we assume the transient can be modeled well by a four pole system and we use an auto regressive model to estimate the pole locations. Each pole represents the strongest resonances and resonance magnitude which can vary between valves.

We train probabilities for these features by calculating the pressure drop and resonance values for all templates in our library and then using Gaussian kernel density estimation (KDE) [1] to assign probability distributions to each valve in a non-parametric way. This results in a look-up table between feature observations and valve-level probability estimates. These probabilities are multiplied with the template probabilities to complete term (i). Note that when multiple pressure sensor streams are available, such as when two installation points are used, the probabilities for each stream can be multiplied together to form term (i).If we wish to use template comparisons *only*, we can simply choose the template with the highest probability. To incorporate with a language model, we use the best valve probabilities to enumerate the state space of a trellis in a bigram graphical model(where each valve is a separate state).

Term (ii): The Language Model: The *language model* assigns probabilities for possible valve sequences. This is performed using bigrams and is represented by term (ii) in eq. (2) (N represents the length of the sequence). Bigram analysis is commonly used in the statistical analysis of text to examine co-occurrences of words or letters. Here, our bigrams are groups of two sequential valve events; for example, *toilet* *open→bathroom sink valve hot open* comprises a single bigram. The language model consists of transition probabilities for every valve pair $\langle v_{n-1}, v_n \rangle$ and is trained by counting the number of co-occurring valve pairs in our library. These counts are smoothed using Katz smoothing, which is commonly used in speech recognition and works to assign a non-zero probability to every sequence [18]. This is important for handling transition probabilities between two valves that rarely occur in our library.

Traditionally, language models use these transition probabilities to select the optimal word (valve) sequence from all possible word (valve) sequences. We maintain an *n-best list* of sequences using Viterbi-stack decoding [2]. This allows us to dynamically reorder the most probable sequences as new valve events occur. Crucially, it also allows us to reorder based on secondary knowledge sources— particularly term (iii) and term (iv) in eq. (2).

Term (iii): The Grammar: Term (iii) describes a grammar, which is typically used to define a set of structural rules that govern the composition of sentences, phrases, and words in a given language. Here, our grammar defines the possible ways in which valve sequences can be constructed. Our grammar rules are: (1) an opening of valve v_x must be followed by a closing of valve v_x; (2) a valve's closure must be preceded by its opening; (3) and the temperature state of a valve must be consistent—e.g., a *kitchen sink hot open* event cannot be closed by a *kitchen sink cold close* event. Rather than eliminating impossible valve sequences (such as a close before an open or an open with no close), we use a *soft grammar* which applies a penalty to any valve sequence that violates a rule. In this way, sequences which contain grammatical errors but have the likeliest probabilities from the other terms can still be selected as correct. The grammar is applied to each sequence in the n-best list, resulting in a set of *paired valvetuples* β. In eq. 2, the term f_p penalizes all unpaired valves (those not in β).

These paired tuples now bind together specific valve open and close events to form a full water usage event structure. For example, given the valve event sequence $v_1 \rightarrow v_2 \rightarrow v_3 \rightarrow v_4$ where v_1=*toilet open*, v_2=*bathroom sink open*, v_3=*toilet close, and* v_4=*bathroom sink close,* our pairing algorithm might link the two toilet events into $\hat{\beta}_1 = \langle w_1 | w_3 \rangle$ and the two bathroom sink events into $\hat{\beta}_2 = \langle w_2 | w_4 \rangle$. These linkages are critically important because they allow us to compute an additional feature set (described in term (iv)) that is dependent on knowing the beginning and ending of a water usage event. We note that the language model and pairing is a novel aspect of our system. The original HydroSense had no notion of either and thus could only identify individual valve events but not the relationships between those events.

Term (iv): Paired Valve Tuple Priors: By pairing valve events, we not only have the ability to link open and close transients together but also to compute classification features, such as *water usage duration* and relative *estimates of water volume*, which are not possible without a pairing methodology. For every paired valve tuple in β, we compute K features over the entire water usage event, denoted as f_k in eq. (2). Similar to the *transient features* used in term (i), a probability density is calculated using KDE and the example water usage events in our library. For example, given a particular draw length for an unknown tuple, we can use the usage durations for all kitchen sinks in our dataset to lookup the probability that the usage event is a kitchen sink.

Once all paired prior probabilities have been multiplied together, the n-best list is reordered and the likeliest valve sequence is chosen.

We use two paired valve priors selected experimentally using one week of data from each deployment site: *usage duration*, the amount of time the given valve pair is drawing water and *flow-trace max*, an estimate of the maximum amount of flow used over the duration of the event (a feature also used in flow-trace analysis [3]).

6   Analysis and Results

We compare the performance of three classification algorithms: a template classifier (term (i)); a classifier that adds a language model and grammar: *templ+LM* (terms (i, ii, iii)); and our full classifier *templ+LM+priors* (the complete eq. (2)). For baseline performance, we include *chance* and a *majority* classifier, which always selects the most likely result based purely on frequency. We were most interested in how the *templ+LM+priors* approach compares to the *template* approach. Additionally, we investigate the performance of each algorithm when using a single pressure sensor (hot or cold) versus dual pressure sensors. For the single sensor analysis, we chose the sensor (hot or cold line) that performed best. This was the cold line for all sites except for A2, where the majority of events were hot water use only.

To understand how the algorithms perform at different granularities, we conduct *valve* level, *fixture* level, and *fixture category* level classification. For valve level, the algorithm must identify the correct *fixture* responsible for the pressure transient, whether it is an *open* or a *close*, and its *temperature state* (hot, cold, or mixed). Fixture level ignores temperature state. Finally, for the fixture category level, we use the same categories as flow-trace analysis (e.g., [11]). The algorithm must correctly classify open/close events as *bath, clothes washer, dishwasher, faucet, shower* or *toilet*. Note that the same models were used to train and test all three different granularities; however, temperature errors were ignored in the case of fixture and category level.

We first focus on pre-segmented classification performance using data from a *single* pressure sensor. Figure 6 (left) displays the results of a 10-fold cross validation experiment over the full five weeks of data using the three classification algorithms and two baselines. In general, the best performing algorithm is *templ+LM+priors*, which resulted in an average overall classification accuracy of 75.5%, 89.5%, and 95.9% for valve, fixture, and fixture-category level, respectively, across the five deployment sites. The best performing home, H2, resulted in 89.4%, 94.3%, and 98.4% classification accuracies. In contrast, the worst performing home, H1, resulted in 66.6%, 79.6%, and 91.0% accuracies because of the lack of cross talk between hot and cold plumbing lines and the logarithmic pressure falloff during usage. Surprisingly, the two apartments, A1 and A2, both performed reasonably well with a single sensor: 77.3%, 89.7%, and 95% for A1 and 78.7%, 94.3% and 96.9% for A2. This is despite the pipe length distance between the hot and cold lines in an apartment being much longer than in a house.

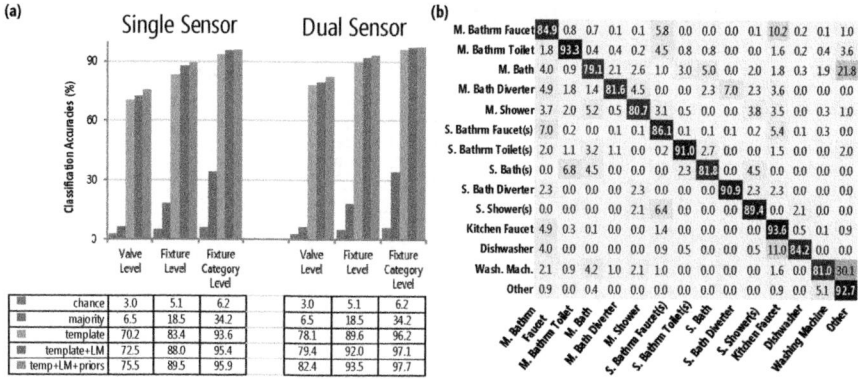

Fig. 6. (a) Average classification results across the five deployment sites comparing *algorithm*, *single* vs. *dual* sensor, and different granularities (*valve, fixture, fixture category*). (b) A confusion matrix that averages the confusions for fixture level *templ+LM+priors* classifications across deployment sites. Note that averaging makes it such that the percentages do not add to 100%.

To examine how events were misclassified, we calculated a confusion matrix for *templ+LM+priors*(Figure 6b), averaging the classification percentages at the fixture level across the five deployment sites. In general, classification accuracies are quite good—the most frequently used fixtures: kitchen sink, bathroom sinks, and bathroom toilets have an average classification accuracy of 90%. Confusions tend to occur within fixture categories (e.g., between sinks) and between fixtures that are situated close together with respect to plumbing layout. For example, the faucet in the secondary bathroom is misclassified as the master bathroom faucet 7% of the time while the dishwasher is misclassified as a kitchen sink 11% of the time (dishwashers are only a small distance from kitchen sinks). Recall from Table 3 that the *other* category involves data from only one home (H1) and is for the laundry basin and refrigerator water dispenser, which were classified correctly 86.1% and 98.6% of the time. However, the *washing machine* was confused as a laundry basin 30.1%, which is visible in Figure 6—this confusion can be attributed to their valve's proximity in the plumbing system.

With regards to compound and collision events, the two language model-based algorithms tend to perform better than the *templ* algorithm (Figure 7a). This is likely due to the transition probabilities of the language model and the paired valve priors in term (iv). Both reduce the weight placed on template-matching the distorted transient.

As expected, the addition of a second pressure sensor improves the overall classification accuracies for each algorithm and sensing resolution granularity: an average of 10% for valve level, 5.5% for fixture level and 2.1% for fixture category level across the three algorithms. The *templ* algorithm benefited the most from the addition of the second sensor. Similar to the single sensor, the *templ+LM+priors* algorithm performed the best with overall accuracies of: 82.4%, 93.5%, and 97.7% for valve, fixture, and fixture category levels. Because of the lack of cross talk between hot and cold pressure lines, H1 and the apartments benefited the most from the addition of a second sensor, especially for valve level classification (an increase of

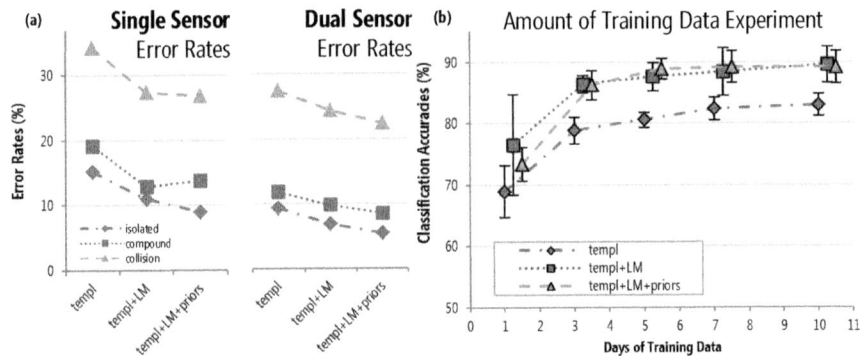

Fig. 7. (a) The error rates for fixture-level performance broken down by algorithm and whether the error occurred on an *isolated, compound,* or *collision* event. (b) The results of our amount of training data experiment; 1,3,5,7 and 10 days were used to test a two week period. Note that we offset the data points slightly for each algorithm to improve the readability of the graph. Error bars reflect one standard deviation above and one standard deviation below the mean.

9.5% vs. 3.1% for the other two sites). Two sensors also increase compound and collision accuracy by 5.3% and 4.4%. Finally, as noted in Table 1, the toilet and showerhead were replaced with low-flow equivalents in A1 approximately three and a half weeks into the deployment. After training on these new fixtures, we were able to correctly classify their usage despite being in the same fixture category and installed in the same location as the previous fixtures. For example, the new toilet was correctly classified 90.2% of the time and classified as the old toilet 8.2% of the time (we kept the old fixture templates in our database for all classification experiments).

To test whether *templ+LM+priors* offered a significant overall improvement over *templ* (the approach used by the original HydroSense work [8]), we conducted a three-way repeated measures ANOVA. We usedthe 10-fold classification accuracies as the dependent variable and *sensing resolution, number of sensors,* and *algorithm* (*templ* vs. *templ+LM+priors*) as within-subjects factors. Because we were only interested in the comparisons between the two algorithms, we report only main and interaction effects with *algorithm*. We found a significant main effect of *classification algorithm* ($F(1,4)=21.76$, $p=.010$), indicating that *templ+LM+priors* improved performance over *templ*. No interaction effects with *algorithm* were significant.

To investigate how the amount of training data impacts performance, we trained models with one, three, five, seven, and ten days of data. The amount of data is divided by days, not number of templates, as the language model requires contiguous blocks of events for training. All were then tested on 14 non-overlapping days. The results are presented in Figure 7b.Significant improvements in classification accuracy are seen with only a small number of training days. On average, *templ+LM+ priors* outperforms *templ*by 4.5%, 7.4%, 8.3%, 6.9% and 6.2%as the number of training days increases from one to ten. Note that both of the LM-based algorithms perform better throughout training though the *templ+LM* algorithm slightly outperforms *templ+LM+priors* with minimal training because it does rely on trained probability distributions for priors.

7 Discussion and Conclusion

This paper is the first to use pressure-sensing to disaggregate *real-world* water usage. Using longitudinal data collected from ground truth deployments across five residences, we showed that a single pressure sensor was sufficient to classify pressure transients with accuracies between 76% and 96% depending on granularity (i.e., valve, fixture, or fixture category). With two pressure sensors, the accuracies rose to between 82% and 98%. To achieve these results, we introduced a new type of water usage inference algorithm inspired by research in speech recognition. Unlike previous approaches [8], our algorithm is probabilistic and leverages a language model, grammar, and prior probabilities to better handle pressure transient variability and to increase robustness in the face of compound events and collisions.

Despite these advances, there are important opportunities for future work. Our current analyses used *pre-segmented* pressure transients (i.e., the start and end of waveforms are marked by the ground truth labels). Working with pre-segmented events allowed us to focus specifically on analyzing the *discriminability* and *consistency* of real-world water usage pressure transients. As such, our results demonstrate an *upper bound* of classification performance for our particular feature set and approach. Overall classification rates will likely drop once segmentation is implemented because of segmentation errors. This could be especially true for apartments which, depending on the plumbing structure, can be particularly sensitive to noise from other units in the building.

With that said, the original HydroSense work segmented staged water usage data with 100% accuracy, so segmentation of real-world data should be possible. The key challenge will be properly segmenting compound and collision events, particularly in apartments with a much noisier pressure signal. We note that our Bayesian approach is amenable to many common speech recognition detection techniques such as keyword spotting. As such, the *classification* and *segmentation* tasks could likely be combined to make the algorithm more robust to sources of ambiguity such as transient collisions. Indeed, most optimal statistical signal processing strategies become sub-optimal after separating segmentation and classification, which means the classification algorithms presented in this paper may need adjustment once incorporated with an imperfect segmentation scheme.

In terms of training, we evaluated the classification algorithms using real-world data for both training and testing. For practical end-user deployment, we might expect a small amount of *staged* training data per fixture. Future work is necessary to establish what will be the most effective staged training data for accurate classification of real-world data. For example, our current approach trains the language model and priors using data from the home where it is deployed. A more general approach could leverage usage patterns and priors (such as duration of use) across different homes, thus reducing system calibration. It may also be the case that certain fixtures, such as toilets and dishwashers, require less calibration because of more consistent transients. Furthermore, unsupervised learning approaches may allow detection of previously unknown fixtures. An interface to allow correction of misclassifications and training of the algorithm over time may also prove beneficial.

Finally, our work underscores the importance of conducting *longitudinal* evaluations *out in the wild*. Although challenging and resource-intensive, such studies are critical in providing a sound scientific basis for the sensing work that we do in the UbiComp/Pervasive communities. In our case, studying the real-world uses of water, rather than only staged experiments, uncovered crucial limitations of past approaches and allowed us to characterize general challenges for water disaggregation research.

In conclusion, this paper is the first to demonstrate that sensing pressure is a viable technique for inferring *real-world* water activity. We used *labeled* pressure stream data collected through five-week ground truth water sensor deployments across five sites to evaluate the performance of a new *probabilistic method* for inferring water usage from a single pressure sensor. To our knowledge, these ground truth deployments represent the most detailed investigation of residential hot and cold water usage ever performed.

Acknowledgements. We would like to thank: Al Dietemann, Bob Alpers, and Ray Hoffman at Seattle Public Utilities for their feedback and help; Gabe Cohn and Tien-Jui Lee for their workin designing and building the ground truth water sensors; Leah Findlater for her thoughts and feedback on early versions of this paper; and Mike Hazas for his helpful comments.

References

1. Bowman, A.W., Azzalini, A.: Applied Smoothing Techniques for Data Analysis. Oxford University Press, New York (1997)
2. Chow, Y., Schwartz, R.: The N-Best algorithm: an efficient procedure for finding top N sentence hypotheses. In: Proc. of the Workshop on Speech and Natural Language, Cape Cod, Massachusetts, October 15-18. Association for Computational Linguistics, Morristown (1989)
3. DeOreo, W.B., Heaney, J.P., Mayer, P.W.: Flow Trace Analysis to Assess Water Use. Journal of the American Water Works Association 88(1) (January 1996)
4. DeOreo, W.B., Mayer, P.W.: The End Uses of Hot Water in Single Family Homes from Flow Trace Analysis. Aquacraft, Inc., (2002)
5. Dziegielewski, B., Opitz, E., Kiefer, J., Baumann, D.: Evaluation of Urban Water Conservation Programs: A Procedures Manual. Prepared for California Urban Water Agencies by Planning and Management Consultants, Ltd., Carbondale, Illinois (February 1992)
6. Fogarty, J., Au, C., Hudson, S.E.: Sensing from the Basement: A Feasibility Study of Unobtrusive and Low-Cost Home Activity Recognition. In: Proc. of UIST 2006, pp. 91–100 (2006)
7. Froehlich, J., Findlater, L., Landay, J.: The Design of Eco-Feedback Technology. In: Proceedings of CHI 2010, Atlanta, GA, pp. 1999–2008 (2010)
8. Froehlich, J.E., Larson, E., et al.: HydroSense: infrastructure-mediated single-point sensing of whole-home water activity. In: Proc. of UbiComp 2009, Orlando, Florida, USA, pp. 235–244 (2009)
9. Kim, Y., Schmid, T., Charbiwala, Z.M., Friedman, J., Srivastava, M.B.: NAWMS: Non-Intrusive Autonomous Water Monitoring System. In: Proceedings of SenSys 2008, pp. 309–322 (2008)
10. Larson, E., et al.: Disaggregated water sensing from a single, pressure-based sensor: An extended analysis of HydroSense using staged experiments. Pervasive and Mobile Computing (in press)

11. Mayer, P.W., DeOreo, W.B., Kiefer, J., Opitz, E., Dziegieliewski, B., Nelson, J.O.: Residential End Uses of Water. American Water Works Association, Denver (1999)
12. Mayer, P.W., et al.: Great Expectations—Actual Water Savings with the Latest High-Efficiency Residential Fixtures and Appliances. In: Proc. of the Water Sources Conference, Las Vegas, NV (2002)
13. Mayer, P., DeOreo, W. B., Towler, E., Lewis, D. M.: Residential Indoor Water Conservation Study: Evaluation of High Efficiency Indoor Plumbing Fixture Retrofits in Single-Family Homes in the East Bay Municipal Utility District Service Area, Prepared for EBMUD and the US EPA (July 2003)
14. Mead, N., Aravinthan, V.: Investigation of Household Water Consumption Using A Smart Metering System. Desalination and Water Treatment 11, 1–9 (2009)
15. Navigant Consulting. Water & Heating Working Group Meeting. Residential & Multifamily: Background, Outcomes & Next Steps. ACEEE Hot Water Forum, Downey, CA (March 10, 2010)
16. North, D.O.: An analysis of the factors which determine signal/noise discrimination in pulsed carrier systems. RCA Labs, Princeton (1943)
17. US Department of Energy. US Household Electricity Report, Energy Information Administration, US DoE (2001),
    http://www.eia.doe.gov/emeu/reps/enduse/er01_us_tab1.html (last accessed October 10, 2010)
18. Chen, S.F., Rosenfeld, R.: A Survey of Smoothing Techniques for Maximum Entropy Models. IEEE Transactions on Speech and Audio Processing 8(1), 37–50 (2000)
19. Tapia, E., Intille, S.S., Larson, K.: Activity Recognition in the Home Using Simple and Ubiquitous Sensors. In: Ferscha, A., Mattern, F. (eds.) PERVASIVE 2004. LNCS, vol. 3001, pp. 158–175. Springer, Heidelberg (2004)
20. Wilkes, C., Mason, A., Niang, L., Jensen, K., Hern, S.: Evaluation of the Meter-Master Data Logger and the Trace Wizard Analysis Software. Special Appendix to Quantification of Exposure-Related Water Uses for Various U.S. Subpopulations. Prepared for US EPA (December 2005)

Exploring the Design Space for Situated Glyphs to Support Dynamic Work Environments

Fahim Kawsar[1,2], Jo Vermeulen[3], Kevin Smith[1], Kris Luyten[3], and Gerd Kortuem[1]

[1] Lancaster University, UK
{kawsar,kortuem}@comp.lancs.ac.uk, k.smith@lancaster.ac.uk
[2] Bell Labs, Belgium
fahim.kawsar@alcatel-luncet.com
[3] Hasselt University, Belgium
{jo.vermeulen,kris.luyten}@uhasselt.be

Abstract. This note offers a reflection on the design space for a situated glyph - a single, adaptive and multivariate graphical unit that provides in-situ task information in demanding work environments. Rather than presenting a concrete solution, our objective is to map out the broad design space to foster further exploration. The analysis of this design space in the context of dynamic work environments covers i) information affinity - the type of information can be presented with situated glyphs, ii) representation density - the medium and fidelity of information presentation, iii) spatial distribution - distribution granularity and placement alternatives for situated glyphs, and finally iv) temporal distribution - the timing of information provision through glyphs. Our analysis has uncovered new problem spaces that are still unexplored and could motivate further work in the field.

1 Introduction

In the field of information visualization, a *glyph* is a single graphical unit designed to convey multiple data [15]. Different parts of the representation or different visual attributes (e.g., shape, size, colour) are utilized to encode different values. One early example was shown by Chernoff [5] who represented multidimensional data through different attributes of human faces, e.g., a nose, eyes. In contemporary literature, researchers have used glyphs to represent different attributes of documents [14] or for visualising software management data [16]. Due to their intrinsic capability of representing multiple variables with a single graphical representation, we see opportunities to explore the use of glyphs for exposing salient information in a subtle fashion in dynamic work places. Recent studies have shown that there is a clear need to present task-centric information in demanding work places, such as hospitals or industrial plants [1, 2]. Consider the situation depicted in Fig. 1(a), where a nurse can choose to perform multiple activities with multiple patients and objects. She might decide to use saline water with patient one or patient three, or she might decide to support patient two instead. In each case, she needs information that matches her activity. As existing studies have shown, medical personnel would benefit most from having specific information available (e.g., guidelines) about their *current activity*, linked to *equipment* and *patients* that are relevant to this activity [2, 3].

K. Lyons, J. Hightower, and E.M. Huang (Eds.): Pervasive 2011, LNCS 6696, pp. 70–78, 2011.

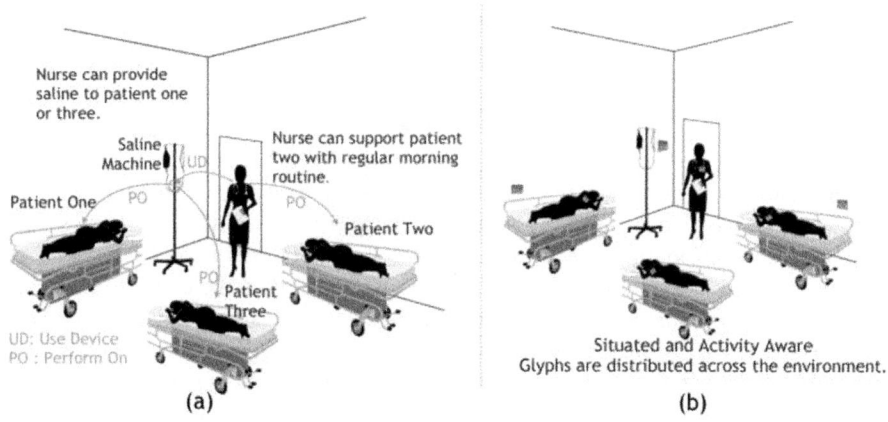

Fig. 1. A Hypothetical Nursing Home Scenario with and without Situated Glyphs

To this end, we envisage that glyphs provide an interesting design alternative to present real time in-situ information to support multiple interleaved activities involving multiple individuals and different types of equipment in complex workplaces. Accordingly, we have devised *situated glyphs* as graphical units that are situated in time and space – they are visual representations of activities, and are adaptive, mobile and replaceable. Fig. 1(b) envisions the same situation as explained above, but here the environment is augmented with multiple situated glyphs. In this case, when a nurse approaches a certain type of equipment or a patient to perform an activity, corresponding glyphs show the information that is relevant to that activity. One of the key functions of situated glyphs is to help people *discover* the activities that can be performed in a given space, at a given time with the devices and objects at hand.

There has been a lot of work on information provisioning through ambient displays – often embedded in interesting artistic objects or everyday artefacts, distributed across the environment and providing a constant stream of peripheral information [6, 10, 11]. Information presented through ambient displays is always interesting, sometimes useful but rarely vital. In contrast, our focus with situated glyphs is activity-centred. We aim to support (both cognitive and physically) demanding real-world activities, such as nursing tasks in a hospital, by mapping visual representations of activity-specific information to the physical environment using situated glyphs.

In what follows, we investigate different design cardinals for these situated glyphs which we consider as the main contribution of this note: *information affinity* (Sect. 2.1), *representation density* (Sect. 2.2), *spatial distribution* (Sect. 2.3) and *temporal distribution* (Sect. 2.4) , respectively addressing the content, appearance, placement, and timing aspects of situated glyphs. We also present an example design of a situated glyph to illustrate the concepts. Finally, we conclude by pointing to the unexplored problem space that might foster future work in this field (Sect. 3).

2 Situated Glyphs: Understanding the Design Space

Situated glyphs are visual representations of physical activities and are adaptive in a sense that they move and change their appearance to match the activity at hand. They are distributed in the environment through *place-holders*, i.e., each place holder can present different glyphs at different points in time. Typically, glyphs are mapped onto an environment by means of small embedded networked displays. Due to these characteristics, situated glyphs put forth a number of design questions. Ware [15] gives a basic background on standard glyphs emphasising on finding the right encoding mechanism to encode information into symbols. Drawing on his theory in the context of pervasive computing environments, we observe that there are four design cardinals that need to be considered for physical embodiment of these situated glyphs. These design cardinals address four basic questions - *what* information to present in situated glyphs, *how*, *where* and *when*? In the following sections, we discuss these questions and present a broad perspective on the design space of situated glyphs.

2.1 What: Information Affinity

Information Affinity describes the type of information that is substantial to maintain the operational efficiency and consistency of a dynamic work environment, i.e., it addresses the "What" aspect of situated glyphs. One way to address this information affinity is to look at the activity patterns in the work environment to expose the basic and critical information needs. Considering this paper predominantly focuses on the health care domain, in this section we will center our discussion on a nursing home scenario. Based on an initial feasibility study with nurses supporting Dementia and Alzheimer's patients at the Mainkofen Hospital in Germany, we analysed the nurses' daily routines and divided these into four generic activity patterns:

- Activity Type I: perform $action_a$, e.g., prepare injection.
- Activity Type II: perform $action_a$ with $object_o$, e.g., sterilising a scissor.
- Activity Type III: perform $action_a$ to $patient_p$, e.g., change dressing of patient one.
- Activity Type IV: perform $action_a$ with $object_o$ to $patient_p$, e.g., measure blood sugar level of $patient_p$ with a glucose meter.

Each activity is composed of an *action* and optionally an *object* (e.g. a blood pressure monitor) or a *patient*. The study results suggested that in most cases actions only involve a single object and patient. Further analysis of these activity types and discussion guided us to identify six distinct information types:

1. *Identity and Relationship*: This category of information describes the identity of a patient, medical equipment, etc. and their relationship with each other in the context of an activity. This type of information helps nurses to make informed decision regarding which equipment to use with which patient.
2. *Status*: This category of information reflects an individual's or an object's status, e.g., the operational status of an equipment (e.g., faulty, working).
3. *Instructions*: This information type provides guidelines to perform medical routines with or without specific medical equipment.

4. *Confirmation*: Feedback about the successful completion of a medical routine with or without specific medical equipment.
5. *Explanation*: This category of information provides explanations to address exceptional situations, e.g., when devices are malfunctioning.
6. *Trends*: Temporal trail or history of an equipment's status or patient's medication record.

In the next subsection, we look at how these information types can be encoded into situated glyphs.

2.2 How: Representation Density

Representation Density specifies how a glyph can be designed to present real world information using patterns, texts or pictures, in other words, it answers the "How" aspect of situated glyphs. A glyph can be abstract or very concrete depending on the situation at hand.

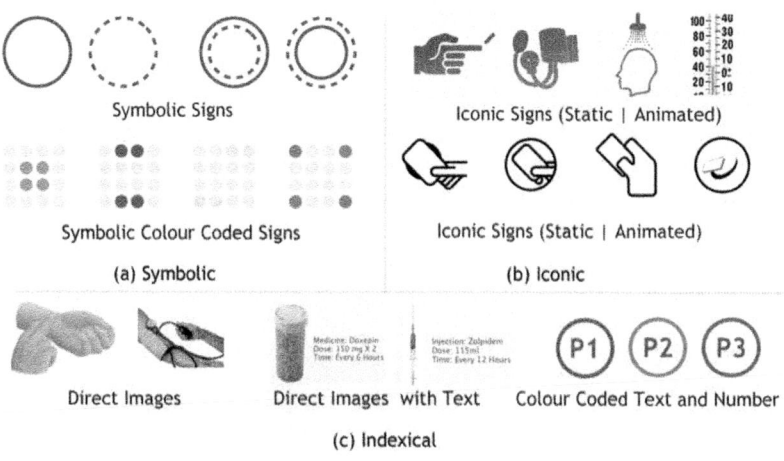

Fig. 2. Semiotics Signs: Symbolic, Iconic and Indexical

We observe that glyphs can be expressed in the language of semiotics, the branch of philosophy that deals with signs and their meanings. A semiotic sign is made up of three elements: *signified*, *signifier*, and *sense* [4]. *Signifier* signifies a *signified* (physical object) through *signs* to

		Representation Density		
		Symbolic	Iconic	Indexical
Information Affinity	Identity & Relationship	Yes (With Colour)	Yes (With Multiple Icons)	Yes (With Colour, Text and Number)
	Status	Yes (With Colour)	Yes	Yes
	Instruction	No	Yes	Yes
	Confirmation	Yes (With Colour Code)	Yes	Yes
	Explanation	No	No	Yes
	Trends	No	Yes (With Animation)	Yes

Fig. 3. Design Space of Information Affinity and Representation Density

give a sense to an observer. Semiotic signs can be Symbolic, Iconic or Indexical. Symbolic signs are completely arbitrary and abstract and need implicit domain knowledge for interpretation as shown in Fig. 2(a). Iconic signs have an intermediate degree of transparency and provide a metaphoric representation as shown in Fig. 2(b)[1]. Indexical signs are much more direct and reflect the signified object with high fidelity as shown in Fig. 2(c).

We are interested in portraying different information types into situated glyphs using semiotic signs. To this end, Fig. 3 plots various areas of representation among our identified information affinity and semiotic signs. Whilst it may be interesting to explore symbolic or iconic representations for artistic purposes especially consulting the contemporary literature on persuasive ambient displays aimed towards behaviour shaping [6, 10], looking at the design space it is clear that indexical signs are best suited for our purpose of designing situated glyphs as shown in Fig. 3. This is mainly due to the limitation of symbolic and iconic signs' capabilities in expressing instructions and explanations articulately. We are currently investigating different glyph designs using indexical signs. In this paper, we present one of the designs as an example to ground our discussion so far. Fig. 4 depicts the design of a simple glyph that utilizes colour, text and number to represent the different information types we have discussed earlier. It has a rectangular shape with multiple properties in accordance to the activity pattern introduced earlier. These properties are:

- The first property is the *colour* which is used to represent relationships : every individual and object is assigned a colour; an individual can perform an action with an object (optionally to another individual) only if their colour matches.

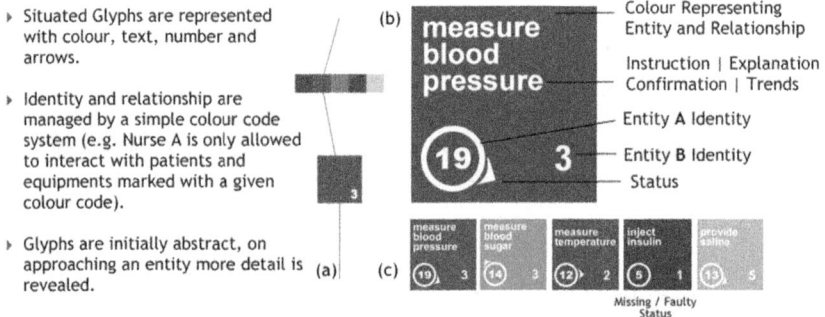

Fig. 4. An Illustrative Design of a Situated Glyph

- The second property is the *identity* which is represented by a number (lower left and lower right). Two sub properties of this identity property are a circle and a pointing arrow. The circle (lower left) represents the active component of an action (e.g., an object or a patient) as described earlier. The presence of a pointing arrow (compass metaphor) represents the status of the component (working or faulty, available or not etc) and its location direction.

---

[1] Some of these signs are collected from http://www.elasticspace.com/2005/11/graphic-language-for-touch.

– The final property is the textual description of the *action* in the form of instruction, explanation, confirmation or trends. In addition, this property is *animated* to highlight the urgency of an operation and to slide through the historical stages.

Consequently, the glyph shown in Fig. 4 (b) corresponds to a "red" coded nurse's activity of measuring blood pressure with a "red" coded patient numbered "3", using a "red" coded blood monitoring device numbered "19" which is available in the southeast direction and working fine. This glyph design is adaptive and dynamically changes its content depending on the activity at hand and the context of the activity, i.e., glyphs are initially abstract, on approaching an individual or an object more detail is revealed as shown in Fig. 4 (a).

2.3   Where: Spatial Distribution

Spatial Distribution describes the distribution granularity and placement alternatives of situated glyphs and corresponds to the "Where" aspect of the design space. One interesting point of discussion is defining the optimum number of glyphs distributed across the environment. This placement granularity reveals the design trade-off between information capacity and fragmented attention. By increasing the number of glyphs it is possible to present more fine-grained information[11]. Additionally, information can then be dispersed across these glyphs in a more situated fashion, i.e., a glyph embedded in an object shows only information about that object instead of showing about the activity as a whole. However, the caveat of increasing the number of glyphs is that it introduces fragmentation of attention due to the demanding context switches which consequently increase the cognitive load of the individuals involved in the activity.

Taking these distribution choices into account, we envisage that there are multiple possibilities for the placement of the glyphs. Delving into the "Situative Space Model" introduced by Pederson [12], we can logically distribute the glyphs into *manipulable space* and *observable space*. A third alternative is the physical embodiment of a glyph onto an entity. Accordingly we identify three design alternatives for placement of glyphs:

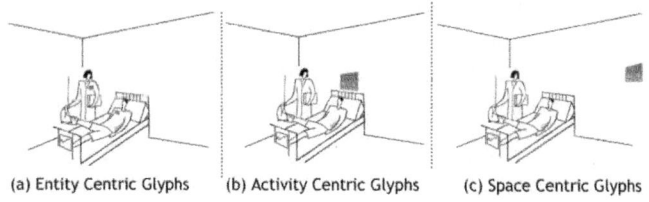

(a) Entity Centric Glyphs   (b) Activity Centric Glyphs   (c) Space Centric Glyphs

Fig. 5. Placement Possibilities for Situated Glyphs

1. *Entity Centric:* A glyph is embodied in every entity as shown in Fig. 5(a). For individuals these glyphs come in a wearable form whereas for physical objects, glyphs are embedded in them.

2. *Activity Centric:* A glyph is placed at the location of the activity climax or in the manipulable space as shown in Fig. 5(b). As an example, for an activity involving a patient and a blood pressure monitor, the glyph can be placed on the patient's bed assuming this activity will be conducted while the patient is in bed.
3. *Space Centric:* A glyph is placed in the observable space and is shared across multiple activities and entities as shown in Fig. 5(c). An example of this kind of glanceable space is the wall between two patients' beds.

Entity centric glyphs represent the extreme end of the spatial spectrum, even though they provide the finest detail of information, they introduce maximum fragmentation of attention in comparison to activity centric and space centric glyphs. In addition, entity centric glyphs require less information updates and adaptation dues to their situated nature compared to the other two alternatives.

2.4   When: Temporal Distribution

Temporal Distribution specifies the timing of information provision that a situated glyph provides and refers to the "When" aspect of the design space. This timing is directly related to the information affinity, i.e., different information requires different timing for presentation. Analysing the physical activity, we observe that there are three phases of any activity - pre-execution phase (before), execution phase (during), and post execution or evaluation phase (after).

Delving into Suchman's situated theory of action [13] and considering our identified information affinity, we have devised an information-timing matrix for situated glyphs in the context of health care domain. This is depicted in Fig. 6. The figure exposes the timing demand of each information type. As an example consider *relationship* information. It is essential for a nurse to know before performing a medical routine with an equipment that this is the right equipment for the patient in context. Furthermore, the relationship information should be maintained during the execution to ensure in-

	Before	During	After
Relationship	Yes	Yes	Yes
Status	Yes	·	·
Instruction	Yes	Yes	
Confirmation	·	·	Yes
Explanation	·	Yes	·
Trends	Yes	·	·

Temporal Distribution (columns); Information Affinity (rows)

Fig. 6. Information Affinity - Temporal Distribution Matrix

teraction consistency, and finally also be present after execution to receive the confirmation that the routine was successfully recorded for that patient. On the contrary, *status* information is only needed in the pre-execution phase to ensure that an equipment or an individual (e.g., a patient) is available. A further example is the instruction information which is only needed before and during an activity to support the action but not once the activity is completed.

3   Discussion

In the previous section, we have discussed the design space for situated and activity-aware glyphs to support dynamic work environments. Technically, such situated and activity-aware glyphs can be realised as a distributed display network. In our current prototype we have designed situated glyphs with a custom designed micro display network using Jennic JN5139 micro controllers with OLED-160-G1 displays with a resolution of 160x128 pixels at 65k colors, and running Contiki Operating System providing a TCP/IP suite on top of ZigBee wireless standard (Fig 7).

Fig. 7. Current Prototype with a Physical Size of 51mmx30mm

We feel our analysis opens up several promising directions for future research. Firstly, one caveat of our current design space is that we have not considered the interactivity aspect of situated glyphs. As it is unclear at this point that what kind of interactivity is suitable, we would like to address this in the immediate avenue of our future work. Secondly, we consider situated glyphs can be designed in many ways. In this work we have borrowed concepts from semiotics, but we feel this is an open space. In fact, many prevailing information visualisation techniques can be explored to design situated glyphs in the context of pervasive computing. Next, since situated glyphs convey what activities can be performed in a given space, at a given time, with the devices and objects at hand, they can be used to improve the intelligibility [7] of the underlying context-aware system by exposing the internal behaviour through articulated explanation and adaptive feedback. Further exploration on this area would contribute in shaping users' understanding towards such system. Finally, the analysis of spatial distribution granularity naturally prompts us to look further into the question of "how much is too much?". This is particularly important to understand the relationship between information overload and granularity of situated glyphs. As previous studies have concluded that individuals become selective and ignore large amounts of information when information supply exceeds their information processing capacity [8, 9] and this also contributes to the fragmentation of attention thus increasing the cognitive load. Unless we perform in-situ real world studies in different domains addressing different situations, it won't be possible for us to determine or approximate the upper or lower bound of the placement granularity of situated glyphs. We see opportunities for field studies that can help us in gaining further insights towards the design of situated glyphs.

References

1. Heyer, C.: Investigations of Ubicomp in the Oil and Gas Industry. In: Proc. of Ubicomp 2010, pp. 61–64 (2010)
2. Bardram, J.E.: A novel approach for creating activity-aware applications in a hospital environment. In: Gross, T., Gulliksen, J., Kotzé, P., Oestreicher, L., Palanque, P., Prates, R.O., Winckler, M. (eds.) INTERACT 2009. LNCS, vol. 5727, pp. 731–744. Springer, Heidelberg (2009)

3. Bardram, J.E., Hansen, T.R., Mogensen, M., Søgaard, M.: Experiences from real-world deployment of context-aware technologies in a hospital environment. In: Dourish, P., Friday, A. (eds.) UbiComp 2006. LNCS, vol. 4206, pp. 369–386. Springer, Heidelberg (2006)
4. Ogden, C., Richards, I.: The Meaning of Meaning. Routledge and Kegan, London, England (1923)
5. Chernoff, H.: The Use of Faces to Represent Points in k- Dimensional Space Geographically. Journal of the American Statistical Association 68, 361–368 (1973)
6. Jafarinaimi, N., Forlizzi, J., Hurst, A., Zimmerman, J.: Breakway: An ambient display designed to change human behavior. In: Proc. of CHI 2005 (2005)
7. Bellotti, V., Edwards, K.: Intelligibility and accountability: human considerations in context-aware systems. Hum.-Comput. Interact. 16(2), 193–212 (2001)
8. Eppler, M.J., Mengis, J.: The concept of information overload: A review of literature from organization science, accounting, marketing, mis, and related disciplines. The Information Society 20, 325–344 (2004)
9. Müller, J., Wilmsmann, D., Exeler, J., Buzeck, M., Schmidt, A., Jay, T., Krüger, A.: Display blindness: The effect of expectations on attention towards digital signage. In: Tokuda, H., Beigl, M., Friday, A., Brush, A.J.B., Tobe, Y. (eds.) Pervasive 2009. LNCS, vol. 5538, pp. 1–8. Springer, Heidelberg (2009)
10. Hallnas, L., Redstrom, J.: Slow technology - designing for reflection. Personal and Ubiqutious Computing 5(3) (2001)
11. Pousman, Z., Stasko, J. : A taxonomy of ambient information systems: four patterns of design. In: Proc. of AVI 2006 (2006)
12. Pederson, T.: From Conceptual Links to Causal Relations Physical-Virtual Artefacts in Mixed-Reality Space. PhD Thesis, Dept. of Computing Science, Ume University, ISBN 91-7305-556-5
13. Suchman, L.A.: Plans and Situated Actions: the problem of human machine communication. Cambridge University Press, Cambridge (1987)
14. Mann, T.: Visualization of WWW-Search Results. In. Proc. of DEXA Workshop (1999)
15. Ware, C.: Information Visualization Perception for Design. Morgan Kaufmann Publishers, San Francisco (2000)
16. Chuah, M., Eick, S.G.: Information rich glyphs for software management. IEEE Computer Graphics and Applications, 2-7 (July-August 1998)

Learning Time-Based Presence Probabilities

John Krumm and A.J. Bernheim Brush

Microsoft Research
One Microsoft Way
Redmond, WA USA 98052
{jckrumm,ajbrush}@microsoft.com

Abstract. Many potential pervasive computing applications could use predictions of when a person will be at a certain place. Using a survey and GPS data from 34 participants in 11 households, we develop and test algorithms for predicting when a person will be at home or away. We show that our participants' self-reported home/away schedules are not very accurate, and we introduce a probabilistic home/away schedule computed from observed GPS data. The computation includes smoothing and a soft schedule template. We show how the probabilistic schedule outperforms both the self-reported schedule and an algorithm based on driving time. We also show how to combine our algorithm with the best part of the drive time algorithm for a slight boost in performance.

Keywords: Location prediction, presence prediction, away prediction, energy efficiency, human routines.

1 Introduction

Predicting when a person will be at a particular location could be useful in many pervasive computing scenarios. For example, a person initiating a spoken or typed conversation may want to wait until the other party is at home or in their office if the conversation will be sensitive or long. In other situations, someone may want an impromptu, face to face meeting. Here, predicted presence would be useful to find the best time to drop in, *e.g.* "She's nearly always in her office from 8 a.m. to 9 a.m.". Another application is energy savings. Gupta *et al.* of MIT show that households could save up to 7% on their heating bill with a thermostat that knows how far the occupants are from home[1].For electric vehicles, cooling or preheating their batteries helps their performance[2], which would be aided by a prediction of when the driver will leave his or her current location. Predicted presence can also be used to detect anomalous behavior such as when a person is predicted to be somewhere but is not. Such behavior could be indicative of cognitive decline or an emergency.

This paper presents a technique for learning the probabilities, as a function of time, that a person will be at a particular place based on observations of their presence there. We concentrate on presence at home, but the technique is equally applicable to any place where a person's binary presence (*i.e.* there *vs.* not there) can be measured. In particular, we demonstrate inferences of an occupant's home/away schedule based on GPS logs of their whereabouts over time. We create a probability distribution

K. Lyons, J. Hightower, and E.M. Huang (Eds.): Pervasive 2011, LNCS 6696, pp. 79–96, 2011.

giving their probability of being away from home as a function of the time of day and the day of the week. In addition, we look at the occupant's current location as measured by GPS. We use this to override our probabilistic prediction if we discover the occupant is too far away to drive home within the prediction interval.

There is other work is aimed at making general predictions about where people will be. For instance, Ashbrook and Starner look at GPS traces to find a person's significant locations along with a Markov model to predict which one will be visited next [3]. Patterson et al. use GPS to sense activities, including making short term predictions about a person's next destination [4]. Similarly, Krumm and Horvitz look at GPS traces to predict a driver's destination based on their previous habits and general driving behaviors [5]. These efforts concentrate on predicting specific locations in the future, not the arrival or departure times that we emphasize in this paper. In particular, algorithms like this that predict destinations and routes do not predict when the trip will start. The results of this paper, instead, can be used to predict when occupancy states will change.

Previous work on time-based presence prediction is normally aimed at thermostat control. An early attempt to solve the problem of occupancy prediction for home heating was that of Mozer et al. in 1997 [6]. Mozer's Neural Network House was outfitted with sensors - including motion sensors to detect occupancy - and actuators - including one to control a central hot air furnace. They trained a neural network to predict when the home would be occupied as a function of recent occupancy observations. Gao and Whitehouse, of the University of Virginia, present a "self-programming" thermostat that is sensitive to the home/away schedule of the occupants measured, by, for instance, occupancy sensors in the home [7]. Their algorithm finds a thermostat schedule to minimize heating and cooling times given the occupant's tolerance for "miss time", which is the amount of time the house is not heated or cooled when it should be. Gupta et al.'s GPS controlled thermostat uses a driving time heuristic to conservatively predict that an occupant will be home in a given amount of time if it is possible to drive home in that amount of time [1].

One innovation in our approach is that our predictions are probabilistic, meaning that algorithms that use the predictions can tailor their behavior to the inherent uncertainty in people's future behavior. Our predictions are based on a novel way of smoothing and biasing occupancy observations. We combine our learned probabilities with the driving time heuristic of Gupta et al.[1] and show how it improves our accuracy slightly. We also show how using our algorithm significantly improves prediction over users' own ideas of their home/away schedules. While the previous work cited above used data from one (Mozer et al.[6]), two (Gao and Whitehouse [7]), and eight (Gupta et al.[1]) individuals, our results are based on surveys and GPS data from 34 individuals spread among 11 different households. The next section describes our survey and the data we gathered.

2 Household GPS Survey

In late 2009, we recruited 12 volunteer households in our area in order to gather data for our study for a period of approximately eight weeks each. These households were on a list of user study volunteers maintained by our institution, but not employed or

Table 1. Each of our participants filled out a time grid representing their typical week. In each one-hour cell, the participant could indicate sleeping, awake at home, or away from home. This is the data provided by one of our participants.

	Day of Week						
	Sunday	Monday	Tuesday	Wednesday	Thursday	Friday	Saturday
0	sleeping	sleeping	sleeping	sleeping	sleeping	sleeping	awake home
1	sleeping	sleeping	sleeping	sleeping	sleeping	sleeping	sleeping
2	sleeping	sleeping	sleeping	sleeping	sleeping	sleeping	sleeping
3	sleeping	sleeping	sleeping	sleeping	sleeping	sleeping	sleeping
4	sleeping	sleeping	sleeping	sleeping	sleeping	sleeping	sleeping
5	sleeping	sleeping	sleeping	sleeping	sleeping	awake home	sleeping
6	awake home	awake home	sleeping	sleeping	sleeping	awake home	sleeping
7	away	awake home	awake home	awake home	awake home	away	sleeping
8	away	awake home	awake home	awake home	awake home	away	sleeping
9	away	away	away	awake home	awake home	away	awake home
10	away	away	away	away	away	away	awake home
11	away	away	away	away	away	away	awake home
12	away	away	away	away	away	away	awake home
13	away	away	away	away	away	away	awake home
14	away	away	away	away	away	away	away
15	away	away	away	away	away	away	away
16	awake home	awake home	away	awake home	away	away	away
17	awake home	awake home	awake home	awake home	away	awake home	away
18	awake home	awake home	awake home	awake home	away	awake home	away
19	awake home	awake home	awake home	awake home	awake home	awake home	awake home
20	awake home	awake home	awake home	awake home	awake home	awake home	awake home
21	awake home	awake home	awake home	awake home	awake home	awake home	awake home
22	awake home	sleeping	sleeping	sleeping	awake home	awake home	awake home
23	sleeping	sleeping	sleeping	sleeping	sleeping	awake home	awake home

otherwise associated with our institution. All the households had either three or four participants each, although one participant dropped out at the beginning of the study, leaving two participants remaining in one household. Also, one household of three did not properly comply with the GPS portion of the survey (explained below), so we dropped them, leaving 11 households with a total of 34 participants. One household had two child participants, and three households had one child participant. The participants were evenly split across genders, and their ages ranged between 21 and 59, with a median age of 27. Six of the households were families with children living at home, and one was a couple without children. In return for participating in our survey, each household was offered four products of their choice from our institution (maximum value US$ 600 per product) and each participant was offered US$ 0.50 for each day of at least two hours of GPS log data.

We asked each participant to do two main tasks. One of the tasks was to fill in a time grid predicting their status among "awake at home", "sleeping at home", and "away from home" for each hour of each day of a typical week. Data from a grid for one participant is shown in Table 1. This is analogous to programming a thermostat, where a person might pick different temperatures for each of these three states. We used these participant time grids to compare against other algorithms for predicting when a person would be home or away.

The other major task of our survey participants was to carry a GPS logger with them during their waking hours. As part of our initial visit to each household, we loaned each participant a RoyalTek RBT-2300 GPS logger, equipped with an optional 1700 milliamp-hour, rechargeable battery, plus a recharger. These loggers fit conveniently in a pocket or bag, and we set them to record a time-stamped latitude/longitude every five seconds. The larger, optional battery was enough for about 18 hours of operation on one charge. We instructed the participants to carry the logger with them wherever they went and have it turned off and recharging while they were sleeping. We also asked the participants to mail their loggers to us every two weeks, switching to a second set of loggers we left with them. When we received the loggers, we uploaded and inspected the data to make sure the participants were properly complying. We then mailed back the empty loggers to serve as the replacement set after the next two-week switch, *etc.*, until the end of the survey. An example of the type of GPS data we collected is shown in Figure 1.

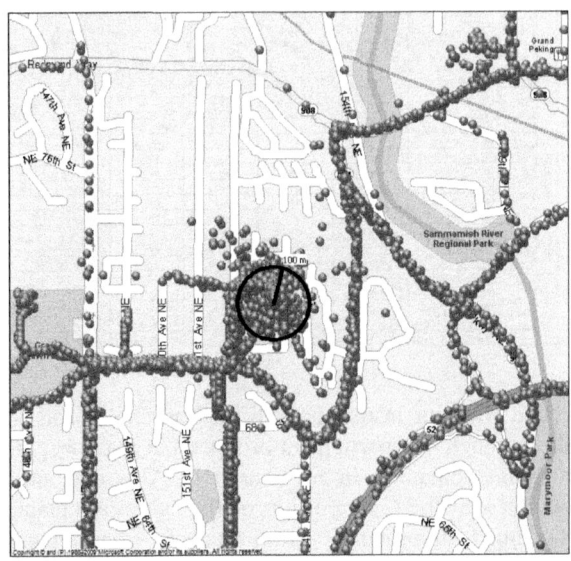

Fig. 1. This is an example of the GPS data we gathered. The black circle shows the region within 100 meters of one person's home. Due to GPS noise, points within a circle of this size around a participant's home were considered to be at home.

An analysis of the data shows that the average, minimum, and maximum number of days we observed the 34 participants were 58, 13, and 95, respectively. The participants did not have their GPS loggers on all the time, *e.g.* normally turned off overnight, and sometimes forgotten in the morning. The average, minimum, and maximum fraction of time we obtained GPS data from the participants were 38%, 18%, and 76%. Some of the lower percentages were due to loggers that failed to upload their data after two weeks of logging.

We used this GPS data to devise an algorithm for predicting when our participants would be home or away. First, however, we used their survey responses to assess how well they could predict their own home/away behavior, described in the next section.

3 Self-reported Home/Away Schedules

It may be that people are quite good at predicting their own home/away behavior. If so, there would not necessarily be a strong need to make these predictions automatically. Part of our survey asked each participant to fill out a schedule of when they are sleeping, at home, or away from home. An example schedule from one of our participants is shown in Table 1. For the purposes of this study, we designated sleeping times as being at home.

The participants' GPS data, along with knowledge of their home locations, gave us a simple way to measure their actual home/away behavior. We designated any GPS point within 100 meters of the participant's home to be at home, and designated the remaining points as away. We chose the 100 meter radius based on the observed spread of the GPS data as shown in maps such as in Figure 1. While a circle of this size could easily include many neighbors, we felt compelled to keep the circle this large to account for the occasional drift of our GPS logger.

Table 2. Participant Self-Report Confusion Matrix. The confusion matrix shows that our participants were not good at anticipating when they would be home or away, based on ground truth from GPS. They predicted they would be home much more often than they actually were.

		Inferred	
		home	away
Actual	home	76%	24%
from GPS	away	68%	32%

With the GPS home/away data as ground truth, we can assess how well our participants anticipated their own home/away behavior. We note that the quality of predictions based on a schedule like this do not vary with the look-ahead time, since each participant's predicted schedule is static. For other predictions we make below, the look-ahead time is a factor.

Table 2 shows the confusion matrix averaged over all our participants. We computed this by considering every GPS point as a ground truth point, assigning it a label of "home" or "away" depending on its location. We used the GPS point's time stamp to look up the participant's anticipated home/away state in their self-reported home/away schedule. The confusion matrix shows that when a participant was actually away (as measured by GPS), they predicted they would be home about 68% of the time. We conclude that our participants were not good at anticipating their home/away schedules, and we next consider algorithms to automatically infer home/away in hopes of improvement.

We note that the participants were likely not quite as poor at predicting their home/away status as the confusion matrix implies. We assessed their home/away prediction only when we had GPS data for ground truth, which did not include overnights, because we asked participants to turn off their GPS overnight for recharging. Thus nighttime data, when the participants were most likely home and when they likely correctly predicted they would be home, was not included in the calculations. So, we conclude that during waking hours, our participants were not good at predicting their home/away pattern. In the following sections, we use the same GPS ground truth data to assess other algorithms, so we can directly compare performance, despite the lack of nighttime data.

4 Drive Time Prediction

The work in [1] introduces thermostat control based on the location of the home's occupants. They recommend, in the absence of a programmable thermostat, to keep the house warm if the time to heat the home is more than the time it would take an occupant to drive home. Thus, this algorithm conservatively predicts that a person will always be home in the amount of time it would take him or her to drive home. We will refer to this algorithm as the "drive time" algorithm, and we will use it to measure the relative accuracy of our own presence prediction algorithm and to augment our algorithm for more accuracy.

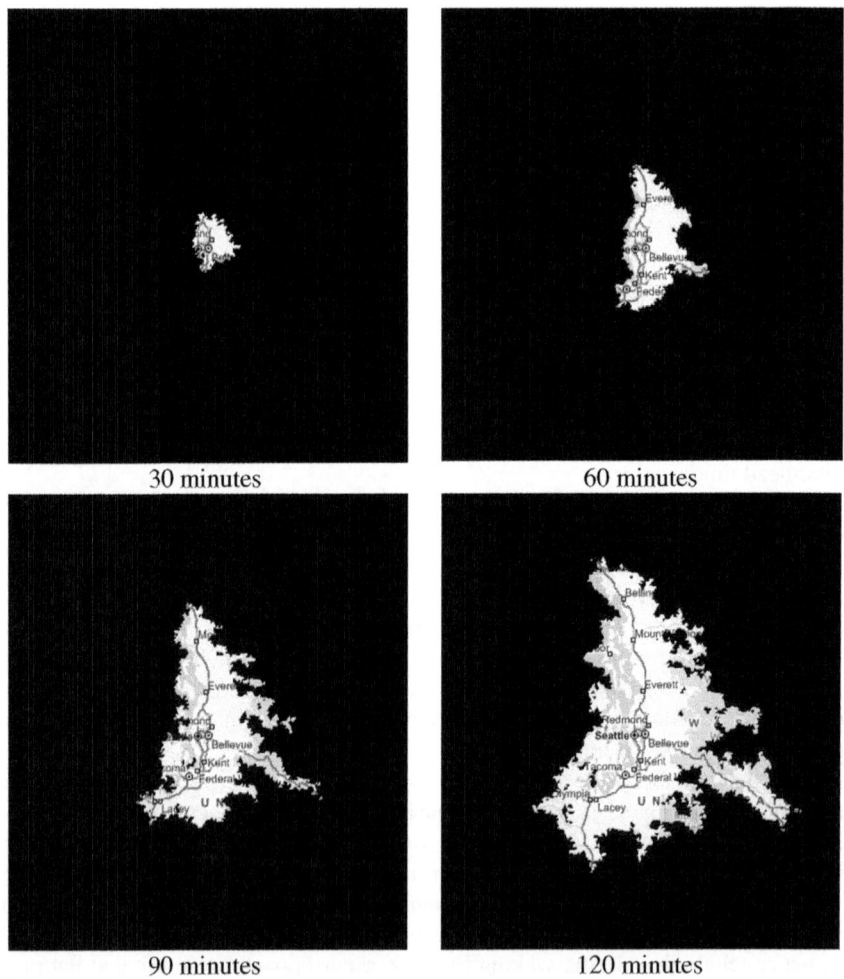

Fig. 2. These maps show precomputed drive time zones from which a person could reach their home by driving for a given amount of time

With our GPS data, we were able to assess the drive time algorithm in terms of the same type of confusion matrix presented in the last section. However, before we present the results, we describe one modification we made to the drive time algorithm for efficiency. While [1] used MapQuest to predict driving times from each GPS point, we instead computed driving times from points sampled on a map. In particular, we tessellated the map in our study region with triangles from the Hierarchical Triangular Mesh (HTM) [8]. From the available mesh resolutions, we used level 12 triangles, whose size in our study region was about 5.1 square kilometers (area) and 3.4 kilometers (length of each side). For each triangle, we computed the driving time from the triangle's center to the participant's home and stored the result. Then, given an arbitrary latitude/longitude, we found which triangle contained it and returned that triangle's driving time as an approximation of the driving time from that point. This modifica-

Table 3. Drive Time Algorithm. These confusion matrices show the performance of an algorithm that predicts the user will be home in X minutes whenever he or she is within X minutes of driving time from their home. Since most people in our study spent most of their time close to home, this algorithm almost always predicts they will be home within the prediction interval.

		Inferred	
		home	away
Actual from GPS	home	100%	0%
	away	90%	10%

30-minute drive time prediction

		Inferred	
		home	away
Actual from GPS	home	100%	0%
	away	93%	7%

60-minute drive time prediction

		Inferred	
		home	away
Actual from GPS	home	100%	0%
	away	94%	6%

90-minute drive time prediction

tion of the algorithm in [1] was not designed to increase the accuracy of the algorithm, but rather to increase the computational efficiency. Instead of computing a driving time for each query, we simply have to look up the precomputed driving time from the relevant triangle. Since the triangles are small, the loss in driving time accuracy caused by discretization is small.Thresholding the drive times in the triangles is a convenient way to show a map of the region over which a participant's home is reachable in a given amount of time, as shown in Figure 2 for an arbitrary home location.

From Figure 2 it is easy to understand the drive time algorithm. For example, if the look-ahead time for the prediction is 90 minutes, the occupant would be predicted to arrive at home in at most 90 minutes from anywhere within the 90-minute drive time region. We call this region the drive time zone.

We can apply the drive time algorithm to home/away prediction by predicting that an occupant will be home in some amount of time if they are within the drive time zone associated with that time. Otherwise we predict they will be away. We note that the schedule-based algorithm in the previous section is insensitive to the look-ahead time, because its predictions are completely determined by the time of day and day of week. The drive time, algorithm, in contrast, depends on the look-ahead time.

Applying the drive time algorithm to our participants' data, we get the confusion matrices shown in Table 3 for look-ahead times of 30, 60, and 90 minutes. The charts in Table 3, Figure 4, and Figure 5 show how the drive time algorithm compared to others we tested. The defining aspect of the drive time confusion matrices is that the algorithm almost always predicts "home" regardless of the data. This is because our participants spent the vast majority of their time near their homes. This is likely true of the general U.S. population, whose average commute time from work is about 23 minutes, and 81% of whom work within 45 minutes of home [9].

While this algorithm did not perform well on our participants' data, we show later how to combine it with a more accurate algorithm for a slight improvement in the other algorithm's accuracy.

5 Probabilistic Home/Away Schedules

Despite the fact that our participants were not good at anticipating their own home/away schedules, we suspect there is much to be gained by looking at their regular habits. This section describes how, using their GPS data, we computed the probability of them being away from home as a function of the time of day and day of week, as shown in Table 4. (We note that if the probability of being away from home is p_{away}, then $p_{home} = 1 - p_{away}$.)In this table the time slots are 30 minutes long. This is an arbitrary choice, but we found that 30 minutes worked well for our purposes.

The advantages of using a probabilistic table such as this are:

- It is based on users' actual home/away behavior, and thus is a more accurate reflection of their schedule than a self-reported one.
- The probabilities capture the fact that people are not completely predictable.
- Using probabilities means that algorithms using these predictions can explicitly account for the inherent uncertainty.
- The probabilities can be used as a prior for a more sophisticated Bayesian approach to home/away prediction.

As we did previously, we say that a participant was home when their GPS data indicated they were within 100 meters of their home latitude/longitude.

One way to build a probabilistic home/away schedule would be to create a simple histogram of normalized frequencies. For each time/day slot in the schedule, we could simply count the number of times the user was away from home, based on GPS readings, and divide by the total number of GPS readings in that slot. However, this leads to problems when there is no sample data for a slot, and it also neglects the opportunity to impose prior assumptions on the schedule.

Below we describe our procedure for building a probabilistic home/away schedule which fills in missing values, smoothes the data, and allows a soft bias in the regularity of the schedule.

Imposing a Schedule Template

We formulate the problem of finding a p_{away} schedule as a linear matrix problem, where the unknowns are the p_{away} probabilities in the time slots. Specifically, the unknowns form a vector $\boldsymbol{p}_{week}$, where each element is p_{away} for a particular time slot on a particular day of the week, *i.e.*

$$\boldsymbol{p}_{week} = (p_1 p_2 p_3 \ldots p_i \ldots p_{336})^T \tag{1}$$

This vector is 336 elements long, which is the number of 30-minute periods in 7 days. The elements are organized in day-major order, so p_1 corresponds to the first 30 minutes of Sunday after midnight, and p_{336} corresponds to the last 30 minutes of Saturday before midnight.

We suspect that people have a somewhat unvarying home/away schedule on weekdays, with more variations on weekends. Therefore, we introduce another vector of away probabilities that correspond to a generic weekday, Monday - Friday. This vector is $\boldsymbol{p}_{generic\ weekday}$, and there is one element for each 30-minute slot of a single weekday, *i.e.*

$$\boldsymbol{p}_{generic\ weekday} = (p'_1 p'_2 p'_3 \ldots p'_j \ldots p'_{48})^T \tag{2}$$

where 48 is the number of 30-minute periods in one 24-hour, generic weekday. After solving for $\boldsymbol{p}_{week}$ and $\boldsymbol{p}_{generic\ weekday}$, the final probability for a weekday slot is computed as the sum of the relevant element of $\boldsymbol{p}_{week}$ (corresponding to a time slot on a specific day of the week) and the relevant element of $\boldsymbol{p}_{generic\ weekday}$ (corresponding to the time slot on a generic weekday). The final probability for a weekend slot comes solely from $\boldsymbol{p}_{week}$.

Introducing $\boldsymbol{p}_{generic\ weekday}$ is a way to impose our bias that people have a somewhat regular schedule on weekdays. $\boldsymbol{p}_{generic\ weekday}$ represents the unvarying part of a weekday, which is summed with the elements of $\boldsymbol{p}_{week}$ that represent the variable parts of specific weekdays. There are many such possible decompositions. For instance, it may be that only daytime hours of weekdays are unvarying. We introduced the generic weekday as the intuitively most likely decomposition, but we leave for future work a verification that it improves accuracy. An interesting extension to this technique is to examine different types of probability decompositions to find which one, if any, works best for an individual. As it stands, our generic weekday decomposition is an example of how to impose these types of decompositions mathematically.

The linear matrix equation for computing the probabilities is

$$A \begin{pmatrix} \boldsymbol{p}_{week} \\ \boldsymbol{p}_{generic\ weekday} \end{pmatrix} = \boldsymbol{b} \tag{3}$$

Here A is a matrix representing constraint equations on the probabilities, with the b vector representing the constraints' constant parts. The unknown vector

$$\boldsymbol{p} = \begin{pmatrix} \boldsymbol{p}_{week} \\ \boldsymbol{p}_{generic\ weekday} \end{pmatrix}$$

contains the probabilities we want to compute. The remainder of this section discusses how we fill the elements of A and $\boldsymbol{b}$ based on data and other constraints.

Home/Away Frequencies

The main influence on the away probabilities is the home/away data itself. We create one constraint equation for each 30-minute period of collected GPS data. In these periods, we compute the proportion of GPS points outside the 100-meter radius of the home compared to the total number of GPS points measured in the time period. If one row of matrix A is represented by the row vector $\boldsymbol{a}$, and one element of vector $\boldsymbol{b}$ is represented by b, then the form of this constraint for one observed 30-minute time slot is

$$\boldsymbol{a} \cdot \boldsymbol{p} = b$$

$$(0\ 0 \dots 1 \dots 0\ 0 \mid 0\ 0 \dots 1 \dots 0\ 0) \cdot \boldsymbol{p} = \frac{n_{away}}{n_{away} + n_{home}} \tag{4}$$

Here the two 1's in $\boldsymbol{a}$ are positioned to pick up the time of day and day of week slot in $\boldsymbol{p}_{week}$ and $\boldsymbol{p}_{generic\,weekday}$ that correspond the time slot in the data. The vertical divider in $\boldsymbol{a}$ corresponds to the division between the two parts of $\boldsymbol{p}$: $\boldsymbol{p}_{week}$ and $\boldsymbol{p}_{generic\,weekday}$. If the time slot is on a weekend, the second 1 in $\boldsymbol{a}$ is replaced with a 0, because there is no generic time slot for weekends. The integers n_{home} and n_{away} are the counts of GPS points inside and outside the 100-meter circle in the data's time slot.

There is one $(\boldsymbol{a}, b)$ pair, and thus one row of matrix A, for every 30-minute time slot in the observed data. We keep appending $(\boldsymbol{a}, b)$ pairs to $A\boldsymbol{p} = \boldsymbol{b}$ until we exhaust all the participant's GPS data. With approximately eight weeks of data from each participant, there are many more 30-minute data slots than unknowns in $\boldsymbol{p}$, making the matrix equation over-constrained. We eventually use a least squares approach to find a solution.

Generic Weekday Influence

We want to adjust the magnitude of the probabilities for a generic weekday, $\boldsymbol{p}_{generic\,weekday}$, to allow for more or less variation on weekdays. To do this, we introduce a regularization factor, λ_{wd}, to potentially reduce the generic weekday probabilities. In terms of the growing $A\boldsymbol{p} = \boldsymbol{b}$ equation, we add rows to A and $\boldsymbol{b}$ that look like the following:

$$\lambda_{wd} \begin{bmatrix} 0 & \cdots & \cdots & 0 & 1 & 0 & \cdots & 0 \\ \vdots & \ddots & & \vdots & 0 & 1 & 0 & \vdots \\ \vdots & & \ddots & \vdots & \vdots & & \ddots & 0 \\ 0 & \cdots & \cdots & 0 & 0 & \cdots & 0 & 1 \end{bmatrix} \boldsymbol{p} = \begin{pmatrix} 0 \\ \vdots \\ \vdots \\ 0 \end{pmatrix} \tag{5}$$

$$[0_{48\times336} \mid \lambda_{wd} I_{48\times48}] \boldsymbol{p} = 0_{48\times1}$$

This has the effect driving all the elements of $\boldsymbol{p}_{generic\,weekday}$ to zero. This effect is moderated by λ_{wd}. We used $\lambda_{wd} = 0.0001$, and we describe subsequently how we chose this value.

Table 4. This table gives the probability of someone being away from their home as a function of the time of day and day of week. In this case, there is a high probability of being away during most normal working hours on Monday – Thursday. Also, this person appears to be often away from home on Friday nights until the first 30 minutes of Saturday. The generic weekday in the last column shows a bulge during normal work hours as expected.

Time of Day	Sunday	Monday	Tuesday	Wednesday	Thursday	Friday	Saturday	Gnrc Wkdy
12:00 AM	0.050	0.000	0.000	0.000	0.000	0.000	0.453	0.000
12:30 AM	0.000	0.000	0.000	0.000	0.000	0.000	0.000	0.000
1:00 AM	0.000	0.000	0.000	0.000	0.000	0.000	0.000	0.000
1:30 AM	0.000	0.000	0.002	0.000	0.000	0.000	0.000	0.000
2:00 AM	0.000	0.000	0.012	0.000	0.000	0.000	0.000	0.000
2:30 AM	0.000	0.000	0.035	0.000	0.000	0.000	0.000	0.000
3:00 AM	0.000	0.000	0.075	0.000	0.000	0.000	0.000	0.000
3:30 AM	0.000	0.000	0.133	0.000	0.000	0.007	0.000	0.000
4:00 AM	0.000	0.000	0.209	0.000	0.000	0.032	0.000	0.000
4:30 AM	0.000	0.000	0.300	0.000	0.000	0.084	0.000	0.000
5:00 AM	0.000	0.000	0.404	0.000	0.000	0.171	0.000	0.000
5:30 AM	0.000	0.000	0.515	0.000	0.000	0.298	0.000	0.000
6:00 AM	0.000	0.001	0.625	0.000	0.000	0.471	0.000	0.000
6:30 AM	0.000	0.807	0.728	0.371	0.001	0.692	0.000	0.001
7:00 AM	0.000	1.000	0.812	0.427	0.170	0.962	0.000	0.002
7:30 AM	0.000	1.000	0.934	0.583	0.461	0.964	0.000	0.073
8:00 AM	0.000	1.000	0.999	0.649	0.565	0.875	0.000	0.132
8:30 AM	0.000	0.833	0.294	0.797	0.587	0.875	0.000	0.061
9:00 AM	0.000	0.857	0.091	0.560	0.379	0.810	0.182	0.002
9:30 AM	0.000	0.857	0.200	0.546	0.090	0.714	0.200	0.000
10:00 AM	0.149	0.993	0.443	0.429	0.000	0.514	0.200	0.000
10:30 AM	0.376	1.000	0.833	0.637	0.341	0.571	0.011	0.219
11:00 AM	0.600	1.000	0.833	0.804	0.571	0.571	0.101	0.322
11:30 AM	0.567	1.000	0.714	0.625	0.400	0.574	0.189	0.252
12:00 PM	0.383	1.000	0.714	0.581	0.400	0.541	0.368	0.255
12:30 PM	0.400	1.000	0.714	0.714	0.703	0.400	0.375	0.325
1:00 PM	0.388	1.000	0.714	0.714	0.750	0.500	0.348	0.357
1:30 PM	0.376	1.000	0.714	0.714	0.750	0.352	0.287	0.324
2:00 PM	0.400	0.985	0.714	0.667	0.750	0.310	0.345	0.294
2:30 PM	0.721	1.000	0.714	0.667	0.714	0.315	0.143	0.283
3:00 PM	0.750	0.897	0.667	0.729	0.714	0.250	0.208	0.250
3:30 PM	0.600	0.500	0.650	0.712	0.559	0.328	0.427	0.160
4:00 PM	0.600	0.600	0.571	0.440	0.498	0.250	0.375	0.099
4:30 PM	0.600	0.368	0.709	0.336	0.429	0.151	0.148	0.043
5:00 PM	0.600	0.200	0.612	0.251	0.519	0.142	0.125	0.000
5:30 PM	0.595	0.314	0.429	0.375	0.506	0.125	0.143	0.007
6:00 PM	0.333	0.500	0.510	0.599	0.571	0.125	0.000	0.125
6:30 PM	0.333	0.429	0.532	0.429	0.460	0.125	0.143	0.085
7:00 PM	0.305	0.429	0.418	0.371	0.429	0.125	0.053	0.080
7:30 PM	0.167	0.302	0.250	0.384	0.313	0.290	0.000	0.073
8:00 PM	0.167	0.286	0.220	0.286	0.250	0.351	0.094	0.081
8:30 PM	0.167	0.172	0.125	0.286	0.290	0.375	0.143	0.083
9:00 PM	0.167	0.143	0.125	0.206	0.343	0.375	0.143	0.095
9:30 PM	0.108	0.143	0.053	0.143	0.202	0.375	0.143	0.053
10:00 PM	0.000	0.000	0.000	0.143	0.143	0.333	0.143	0.000
10:30 PM	0.000	0.000	0.000	0.200	0.143	0.400	0.143	0.000
11:00 PM	0.000	0.000	0.000	0.250	0.000	0.667	0.143	0.000
11:30 PM	0.000	0.000	0.000	0.000	0.000	0.667	0.143	0.000

Smoothing

We also allow for a degree of temporal smoothing of the away probabilities to account for vagaries in the limited observation time. Smoothing is also critical for filling in missing data, because sometimes we have no GPS data for certain nighttime time slots. For an away probability p_i from $\boldsymbol{p}_{week}$, we smooth with the probabilities of the previous and next time slots, *i.e.* we want

$$\frac{s}{2}p_{i-1} + (1-s)p_i + \frac{s}{2}p_{i+1} = p_i$$
$$\frac{s}{2}p_{i-1} - sp_i + \frac{s}{2}p_{i+1} = 0$$

(6)

where $0 \leq s \leq 0.5$ controls the amount of smoothing and p_{i-1}, p_i, and p_{i+1} are three, temporally adjacent away probabilities . This smoothing constraint is moderated by a smoothing regularization factor λ_s. For smoothing, we add rows to A and $\boldsymbol{b}$ that look like the following:

$$\lambda_s \begin{bmatrix} -s & s/2 & 0 & \cdots & 0 & s/2 \\ s/2 & -s & s/2 & 0 & \vdots & 0 \\ 0 & s/2 & -s & s/2 & 0 & \vdots \\ \vdots & & \ddots & \ddots & \ddots & 0 \\ 0 & \cdots & 0 & s/2 & -s & s/2 \\ s/2 & 0 & \cdots & 0 & s/2 & -s \end{bmatrix} \Big| 0_{336\times48} \Big] \boldsymbol{p} = \boldsymbol{0}$$

(7)

$$[\lambda_s S_{336\times336} | 0_{336\times48}]\boldsymbol{p} = 0_{336\times1}$$

Smaller values of λ_s tend to reduce the effect of smoothing on the final probabilities. Likewise, a smaller value of s means less smoothing between temporally adjacent probabilities.

Solving $A\boldsymbol{p} = \boldsymbol{b}$ and Choosing Parameters

The equation $A\boldsymbol{p} = \boldsymbol{b}$ is built from three parts: away frequencies from GPS data, moderating the effect of the generic weekday with λ_{wd}, and smoothing with s and λ_s. The equation is over-constrained, so we solve with least squares. We also require the resulting probabilities to be between zero and one, so we use a constrained solver.

To choose the parameters λ_{wd}, s, and λ_s, we used two-way cross validation on eight weeks of GPS data taken from a participant outside our study. We made a rough sweep through possible values of the parameters. For each set of parameter values, we compared the computed probabilities from half the GPS data to the ground truth computed from the other half of the GPS data. The best values of the parameters were

$$\lambda_{wd} = 0.0001$$
$$s = 0.4$$
$$\lambda_s = 0.1$$

We used these parameters to compute away probabilities for each participant. An example result for one of our participants is shown in Table 4.

Evaluation of Probabilistic Schedule

The computed away probabilities introduce a convenient parameter into prediction for presence. For presenting estimates to other people, such as the probability of a person

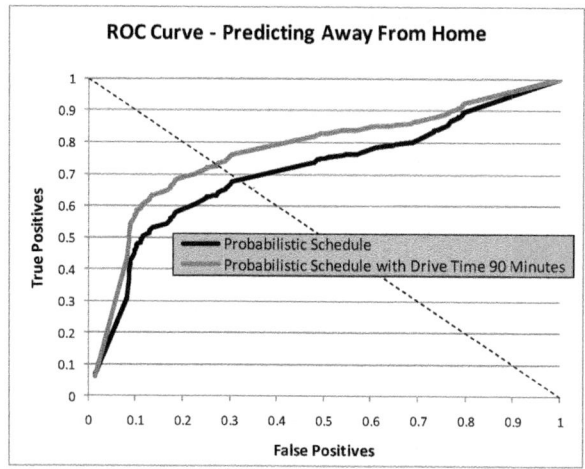

Fig. 3. This is an ROC curve for predicting "away" for one of our participants using a probabilistic home/away schedule. In this person's case, adding the drive time algorithm made a noticeable improvement in performance. The diagonal line intersects the ROC curves at the equal error rate.

being in their office, a system could simply present the computed presence probability and let the other person decide what action to take. For automatic behaviors, such as controlling a home's temperature, we can set a threshold on the away probability to decide when to trigger an action. The probability can be combined with perceived costs of incorrect predictions, giving a decision-theoretic result. For instance, a low threshold on p_{away} translates into a high threshold on p_{home}, and it means that the system would have to be more confident of an impending arrival in order to take any action. As an example, for home heating, this threshold translates into a user-adjustable tradeoff between comfort and energy savings. If comfort is more important, the user would set the threshold such that the home would be heated even if there was only a relatively small chance of arriving at home at the cost of sometimes heating an empty house. To save more energy, the user would adjust the threshold to reduce the chance of heating the home unnecessarily at the cost of sometimes arriving home to a cold house. With a probabilistic schedule like the one we produce, this tradeoff becomes possible. It is similar in spirit to the tradeoff introduced in [7] in which users set the "miss time" to control for how long the home's temperature is miscontrolled. The drive time algorithm and the self-reported schedule have no such adjustment available.

We evaluated our probabilistic schedules with 5-fold cross validation. For each participant, we split their GPS data into five equal-length parts in temporal order. For each of the five validation runs, we tested on one part and trained on the other four parts, picking a new test part for each run.

The probabilistic schedule predictor does not use a specific look-ahead time for prediction. Since it assumes that the probabilistic schedule is forever unvarying, it can be used to predict ahead any amount of time. This is manifest in our results, because

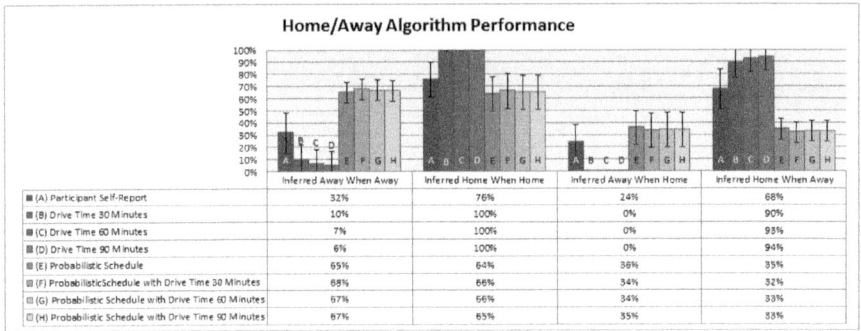

Fig. 4. This plot shows the performance of all the algorithms we tested. For each algorithm, it shows the correct rates (e.g. "inferred away when away") in the left-most two groups. Here a higher bar is better. The error rates (*e.g.* "inferred away when home") are in the right-most two groups where a lower bar is better. The error bars show +/- one standard deviation over our 34 test participants.

we show no look-ahead time for this algorithm, unlike the drive time algorithm which considers a specific amount of time for its predictions.

In evaluating the accuracy of the probabilistic schedule, we account for the adjustable probability threshold by creating an ROC curve that demonstrates the performance tradeoff at different settings of the probability threshold. An example of an ROC curve for one of our participants is shown in Figure 3. This shows the performance of predicting if the person will be away from home at different settings of the threshold on p_{away}. At high settings, the system must be very confident of an upcoming departure before it will predict an away state. This corresponds to the lower left part of the plot where the chance of a false positive is low, but where the high threshold also reduces the chance of a true positive. At the other end of the plot, the threshold is low, where the chances of a false positive and true positive are both high. Ideally there would be a threshold that gives 100% true positives and no false positives, which is the upper left corner of the plot.

One advantage of our algorithm is that it allows this adjustment, which gives higher level algorithms the flexibility to trade off one type of error for another.

To reduce the ROC curve to a confusion matrix for comparison with the other algorithms, we look at the equal error rate, which in Figure 3 is where the diagonal line intersects the ROC curve. Using the equal error rate point, the confusion matrix associated with home/away prediction using probabilistic schedules from all our participants is shown in Table 5. Figure 4 shows how this algorithm's confusion matrix numbers compare with the others. The probabilistic schedule algorithm gives a much better balance for predicting home and away compared to participant's self-reported schedules and the drive time algorithm, both of which significantly overestimate predictions that the participants will be home.

Figure 5 shows how the probabilistic dule algorithm pares to the previous algorithms in terms of accuracy, where accuracy is in our case simply the mean of the diagonal elements of the confusion matrix. The probabilistic schedule algorithm is significantly more accurate than the previous algorithms, although the accuracy figure hides the fact that the previous algorithms (participants' self-reported schedule and drive time) get most of their accuracy from over-predicting when the participant will be home. Note that the minimum accuracy in the plot in Figure 5 is ½, since this is trivially achievable by guessing "home" or "away" 100% of the time.

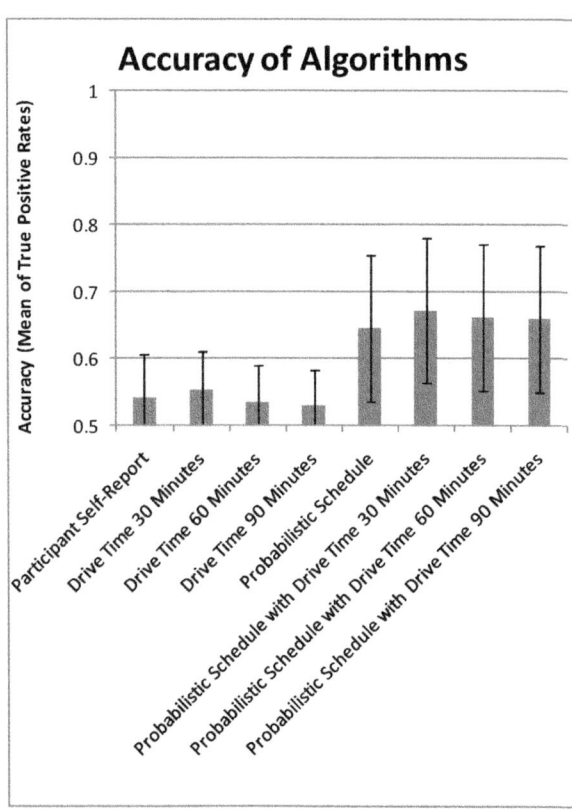

Fig. 5. This chart shows the accuracy of each algorithm, which in our case is the average of the true positive rates in the confusion matrices. The error bars show +/- one standard deviation across our 34 participants. The minimum accuracy is ½, because that is achievable by simply guessing "home" or "away" 100% of the time. The maximum possible accuracy is 1.0.

6   Combining Probabilistic Schedule and Drive Time Algorithms

There is an easy way to combine the drive time algorithm with the probabilistic schedule algorithm. The strength of the drive time algorithm is that it will never predict that a person can arrive at home in less time than it would take to drive home. Unless the person is traveling home faster than normal vehicular traffic, this heuristic will almost always be correct. Thus, we modified our probabilistic schedule algorithm to always predict "away" if the participant was outside the relevant drive time zone, regardless of the probability in the schedule. If the participant was within the drive

Table 5. Probabilistic Schedule. The confusion matrix shows the performance of prediction for the probabilistic schedule we derived from participants' GPS data

		Inferred	
		home	away
Actual from GPS	home	64%	36%
	away	35%	65%

time zone, we resorted to the probabilistic schedule instead. This combination of the algorithms takes the best part of the drive time algorithm and ignores its rule to predict "home" whenever a participant is within the drive time zone. We found that this addition improved the probabilistic schedule algorithm slightly but noticeably. The confusion matrices are shown in Table 6, and Figure 4&Figure 5show how this algorithm compares to the others. Figure 3 shows the improvement in the ROC curve for one of our participants. In all cases, there is a slight improvement.

7 Discussion and Summary

With the goal of predicting a home's occupancy for energy efficiency, this paper shows that a probabilistic home/away schedule derived from GPS data works much better than peoples' self-reported schedules and much better than making predictions based purely on the time it would take to drive home. Our study was based on approximately two months GPS data from each of 34 participants.

We introduced a matrix-based method to compute probabilistic schedules that allows for the application of a soft schedule template on the data. In our case, we used a template that emphasizes a similar schedule on weekdays. Our method also smoothes the data.

Table 6. Probabilistic Schedule + Drive Time. Adding information about the participants' distance from home slightly improves the performance of the probabilistic schedule algorithm

		Inferred	
		home	away
Actual from GPS	home	66%	34%
	away	32%	68%

30-minute drive time prediction with probabilistic schedule

		Inferred	
		home	away
Actual from GPS	home	66%	34%
	away	33%	67%

60-minute drive time prediction with probabilistic schedule

		Inferred	
		home	away
Actual from GPS	home	65%	35%
	away	33%	67%

90-minute drive time prediction with probabilistic schedule

We also showed how to increase the performance of our probabilistic schedule algorithm by adding the best part of the drive time algorithm.

Our probabilistic schedule proved much more accurate than our participants' own impression of their weekly home/away schedules. One possible objection to this result is that our participants filled out a schedule with time discretized to 1-hour pieces, while our probabilistic schedule worked with 30-minute pieces, allowing more accuracy in transition times. However, we found our participants were so poor at predicting home/away, that higher resolution discretization would not help much. For instance, as shown in Table 2, for 68% of the time when participants predicted they would be home, they were actually away. With only a few home arrivals and departures per day, adjusting these times by 30 minutes would not be enough to eliminate an error this large.

In practice, these probabilistic schedules could be kept up-to-date by processing only the most recent location traces of an individual, thus staying more current as weekly schedules inevitably change. It would be interesting to investigate more sophisticated methods for maintaining a probabilistic schedule, perhaps by assembling chunks of previous schedules. Recent work has shown that only about 38% of a family's travel activities are routine, implying that there is an opportunity for improved predictions beyond a derived schedule like ours [10]. Another promising research question is whether or not a system like ours could use a coarser, more energy efficient location system like WiFi or cell tower positioning instead of GPS.

Acknowledgments

We thank our paper's shepherd, Alexander Varshavsky, for his careful review and comments.

References

1. Gupta, M., Intille, S.S., Larson, K.: Adding GPS-Control to Traditional Thermostats: An Exploration of Potential Energy Savings and Design Challenges. In: Tokuda, H., Beigl, M., Friday, A., Brush, A.J.B., Tobe, Y. (eds.) Pervasive 2009. LNCS, vol. 5538, pp. 95–114. Springer, Heidelberg (2009)
2. Pesaran, A., Vlahinos, A., Stuart, T.: Cooling and Preheating of Batteries in Hybrid Electric Vehicles. In: 6th ASME-JSME Thermal Engineering Joint Conference (2003)
3. Ashbrook, D., Starner, T.: Using GPS to Learn Significant Locations and Predict Movement across Multiple Users. Personal and Ubiquitous Computing 7(5), 275–286 (2003)
4. Patterson, D.J., Liao, L., Fox, D., Kautz, H.: Inferring High-Level Behavior from Low-Level Sensors. In: Dey, A.K., Schmidt, A., McCarthy, J.F. (eds.) UbiComp 2003. LNCS, vol. 2864, pp. 73–89. Springer, Heidelberg (2003)
5. Krumm, J., Horvitz, E.: Predestination: Inferring Destinations from Partial Trajectories. In: Dourish, P., Friday, A. (eds.) UbiComp 2006. LNCS, vol. 4206, pp. 243–260. Springer, Heidelberg (2006)
6. Mozer, M.C., Vidmar, L., Dodier, R.M.: The Neurothermostat: Predictive Optimal Control of Residential Heating Systems. Advances in Neural Information Processing Systems 9, 953–959 (1997)

7. Gao, G., Whitehouse, K.: The Self-Programming Thermostat: Optimizing Setback Schedules based on Home Occupancy Patterns. In: First ACM Workshop On Embedded Sensing Systems For Energy-Efficiency In Buildings, Berkeley, CA USA (2009)
8. Szalay, A., et al.: Indexing the Sphere with the Hierarchical Triangular Mesh, Microsoft Research, MSR-TR-2005-123 (2005)
9. Carroll, J.: Workers' Average Commute Round-Trip Is 46 Minutes in a Typical Day (2007), (cited 2010) http://www.gallup.com/poll/28504/Workers-Average-Commute-RoundTrip-Minutes-Typical-Day.aspx
10. Davidoff, S., Zimmerman, J., Dey, A.K.: How Routine Learners can Support Family Coordination. In: 28th ACM Conference on Human Factors in Computing Systems (CHI 2010), Atlanta, Georgia, USA (2010)

n-Gram Geo-trace Modeling

Senaka Buthpitiya, Ying Zhang, Anind K. Dey, and Martin Griss

Carnegie Mellon University,
5000 Forbes Avenue, Pittsburgh, PA 15213, USA
{senaka.buthpitiya,martin.griss}@sv.cmu.edu,
{joy,anind}@cs.cmu.edu

Abstract. As location-sensing smart phones and location-based services
gain mainstream popularity, there is increased interest in developing
techniques that can detect anomalous activities. Anomaly detection capabilities can be used in theft detection, remote elder-care monitoring
systems, and many other applications. In this paper we present an n-
gram based model for modeling a user's mobility patterns. Under the
Markovian assumption that a user's location at time t depends only on
the last $n - 1$ locations until $t - 1$, we can model a user's idiosyncratic
location patterns through a collection of n-gram geo-labels, each with
estimated probabilities. We present extensive evaluations of the n-gram
model conducted on real-world data, compare it with the previous approaches of using T-Patterns and Markovian models, and show that for
anomaly detection the n-gram model outperforms existing work by approximately 10%. We also show that the model can use a hierarchical
location partitioning system that is able to obscure a user's exact location, to protect privacy, while still allowing applications to utilize the
obscured location data for modeling anomalies effectively.

1 Introduction

Over the last decade, with smart-phone and ubiquitous computing technologies
maturing, the ability to locate a user accurately has become a reality especially
in outdoor environments using the Global Positioning System (GPS). With the
ability to accurately track a user's location, it is theoretically possible to create
a model for that user's movement pattern [11]. Such a model, combined with
location-based services (and context-aware services in general), enables opportunities to provide a wide array of services using the model's ability to detect
variations from a regular routine, and its ability to predict location and variations. A comprehensive model of a user's movement patterns would be able to
detect if a user is doing something out of the ordinary. This anomaly detection
capability of the model can support context-aware applications for 1) caregivers
to monitor elderly people unobtrusively (especially those suffering from memory
ailments such as Alzheimer's Disease who are likely to wander), 2) monitoring
of young children, and 3) theft detection systems for mobile phones and cars.

In this paper we present an n-gram based model for learning a user's movement pattern using historical geo-traces (GPS tracks). Each person has a set

K. Lyons, J. Hightower, and E.M. Huang (Eds.): Pervasive 2011, LNCS 6696, pp. 97–114, 2011.
© Springer-Verlag Berlin Heidelberg 2011

of unique geo-locations and transitions (i.e., movements between those geo-locations) which act as triggers or qualifiers for the person's future locations. n-gram models are very robust at modeling relationships between a sequence of observations and outcomes dependent on the sequences. Therefore we use an n-gram model to learn a person's geo-patterns. For example, if a person visits a cafe everyday on the way to work and the person is seen at the cafe on a workday, it can be reasonably assumed that the person is on his way to work. We cluster raw GPS coordinates into geo-labels, and use sequences of geo-labels to train standard n-gram models for anomalous activity detection.

Using probabilistic methods for modeling the movement patterns of users has been attempted in previous work. These approaches have focused predominantly on using probabilistic approaches such as Markov models [30,19,1,16] and T-Pattern based models [22,10]. Yet anomaly detection using GPS traces is a novel area of research with sparse previous work. In [21], Ma proposes using generating bounding regions (with borders parallel to the longitudinal and latitudinal lines) for anomaly detection, while Binbin proposes Markov Random Fields for learning geo-tracks of people and for anomaly detection [18]. Yet, neither have as yet produced definitive results.

The work presented in this paper approaches the problem of grouping individual entries in geo-traces with a method that is distinct from previous attempts. Our method utilizes previous states (or locations) to detect anomalies in daily routines similar to using a T-Pattern or Markovian model. However, unlike those models, the n-gram based model presented here is able to skip over previous locations which are detractors (or non-contributors) to the current prediction. By skipping over location entries which are deemed to be detractors or non-contributors, the n-gram model is made more robust to noise in data caused by either GPS resolution or minor variations in a user's movements. Furthermore skipping detracting n-grams reduces the size of the model in terms of computational time and storage size (as the model has comparable performance for a lower value of n than when the model takes detracting grams into account). Therefore the work presented here is able to outperform models presented in previous work at detecting anomalies.

In this work, we make the following contributions toward the problems of mobility pattern modeling and anomaly detection in mobility patterns:

– We present an n-gram based model for modeling human mobility, which employs unsupervised learning.
– We show how this model is used for detecting anomalous behavior of a user given that user's current context.
– We present a geo-partitioning method, used by our model, that preserves a user's privacy when exposing location information to external applications by blurring GPS coordinates and, at the same time, retains enough information for mobility modeling with sufficient accuracy.
– We evaluate the model's anomaly detection capabilities with extensive real-world data, and show that it outperforms other behavior modeling approaches to anomaly detection.

This paper is organized as follows. In Section 2, we describe the properties of geo-trace data and show how our method utilizes these properties. In Section 3, we describe our approaches to quantizing geo-tags and training the n-gram model. In Section 4, we evaluate our approach with experimental results. Then, in Section 5, we discuss the experimental results and describe the class of applications enabled by anomaly detection using the n-gram model. We conclude after reviewing related work in the area of geo-trace modeling in Section 6.

2 Quantizing Geo-trace Data

Raw geo-trace information can be recorded from either a user's mobile phone (using GPS) or specialized GPS hardware. While some specialized geo-tracking devices are capable of providing a greater amount of information about the user's movements (such as velocity), we assume that the only information available to our model is raw, timestamped GPS coordinates (longitude and latitude) along with the number of visible GPS satellites. We use the satellite count to clean the data, rather than as a feature for the model [1].

In this paper, we use the term "geo-tag" to describe a tuple of raw readings consisting of a longitude-latitude pair, timestamp, and visible satellite count, and use the term "geo-label" to describe a tuple of quantized geo features derived from the raw data. The geo-trace models are built upon these geo-labels.

2.1 Location Quantization through Partition

We do not use raw GPS readings as a part of geo-labels, since the precision of the raw GPS readings is too high to generalize to a meaningful geo-trace model (i.e., the geo-trace models will attempt to learn with an unrealistic degree of granularity, resulting in many false positives/false anomaly detections). For example, knowing that the user is driving on highway I-75 close to exit 187 heading north is enough to detect his/her future location and we do not really need to know which lane he/she is at to achieve such a prediction. Essentially, in this example, we treat the left and right lanes as one location rather than two. Additionally, users may have privacy concerns over sharing precise location information with an external application (such as a server/cloud-based application utilizing geo-trace models) [15,3,16]. Therefore we abstract the raw GPS readings to reduce their precision and to generalize them to a useful geo-trace model. We now discuss two methods to perform this conversion.

Equal-sized Partition. The first method is to partition the entire surface of the earth into equal sized rectangular segments, each with a unique label. Then, all points from a geo-trace falling within a certain segment are replaced by the label of that segment. This method of partitioning is very straightforward to implement and makes comparisons between multiple users' geo-traces extremely simple. But the method also has the drawback of over- and under-granularization. In the case of over-granularization, in areas where a user rarely travels, the few geo-tags that exist (over a relatively large geographic area) are split into a large number of partitions. In the case of under-granularization, areas regularly frequented by the user will have a large number of places of interest (e.g., campus premises with different buildings of interest) and a low granularity of partitioning could lose important information regarding visits to each individual place of interest within the partition.

Density-driven Hierarchical Partition. To counter the deficiencies of the first partitioning approach, we propose a density-driven partitioning method where the granularity of partitioning varies from area to area. The granularity of partitioning for an area is determined by the frequency of visits to that area, based on observed geo-traces of a user or a group of users. The process begins by treating the entire world surface as a single partition and recursively dividing it up into child partitions by splitting it into four quadrants with a north-south line and an east-west line. Further division of a partition is halted when the number of geo-tags recorded within that partition falls below a density threshold. The resulting partition is a quad-tree. We assign a label to each leaf partition which denotes the path to the leaf node from the root node in the partitioning quad-tree. Each child partition's label is comprised of the parent partition's label as a prefix appended with a designator as to which quadrant of the parent it belongs. See Figure 1 for an example of a partitioned area on a user's route. The pseudocode for the partitioning algorithm is:

```
Create root Partition with root->region = entire world;
Assign all geo-tags to root;
PartitionSimple( root );

PartitionSimple( Partition cp ) {
    IF( cp->geo-tags <= THRESHOLD ) THEN return;

    Add 4 child partitions to cp;

    i = 1;
    FOR EACH child partition p IN cp
        Set p->region = quadrant i of cp->region;
        Set p->label = Concatenate( cp->label, i );
        FOR EACH geo-tag gt IN cp
            IF (gt lies within p) THEN Assign gt to p;
        END
        PartitionSimple( p );
        i = i + 1;
    END
}
```

While there are partitioning schemes such as Hierarchical Triangular Maps which would result in a more even spacial partitioning, these scheme require greater computational cost at run-time. Furthermore such partitioning schemes do not provide significant performance improvements.

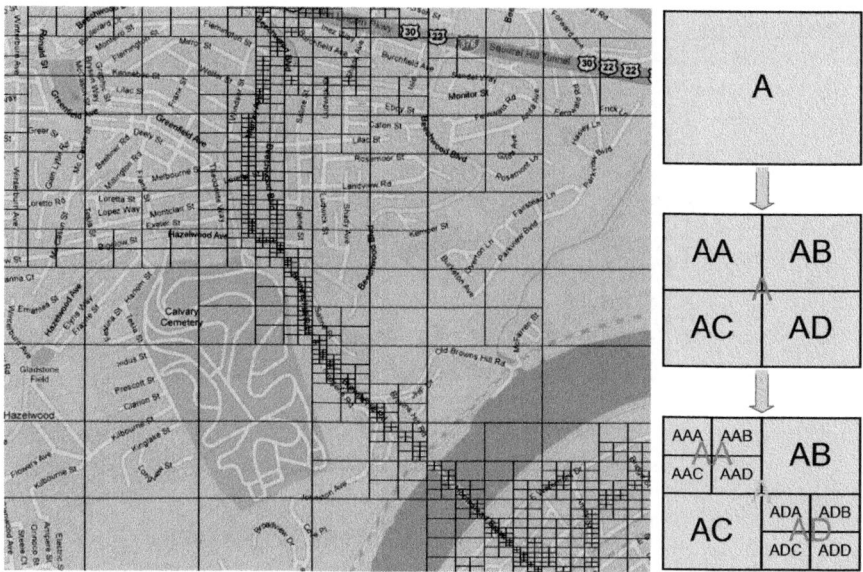

Fig. 1. The map on the left displays a partition based on the frequency of visits by the user. The image on the right shows an example of how labels are assigned to partitions in a density based partitioning scheme.

2.2   Time and Direction Features

We also extract features other than location information for geo-trace modeling.

- **direction of displacement.** The direction of displacement of a geo-tag g_i is the angle of the directional vector $g_i - g_{i-1}$, i.e., the direction the user moves from his previous location to the current location. The direction is 0 if $g_i - g_{i-1}$ points to North and 90 if East. Similar to quantizing locations, we also quantized direction of displacement into B sectors where $B << 360$.
- **time of day.** The time of day feature is extracted from the geo-tag's timestamp. We divide the 24 hour period of day into segments of equal duration (e.g., in our experiments we use 1 hour segments) and convert the actual hour:minute:second time stamp to a discrete label.
- **time spent at a location.** We replace a consecutive sequence of identical geo-tags with a single geo-tag which indicates that the user is not moving or only moving inside the current partition. The time spent at that location is converted to a discrete value similar to the "time of day" feature.

2.3   Geo-label

Different types of features are concatenated in various combinations to form a single geo-label. The combination of needed features depends on the application. For example, the location label can be combined with the time-of-day label as depicted in Figure 2.

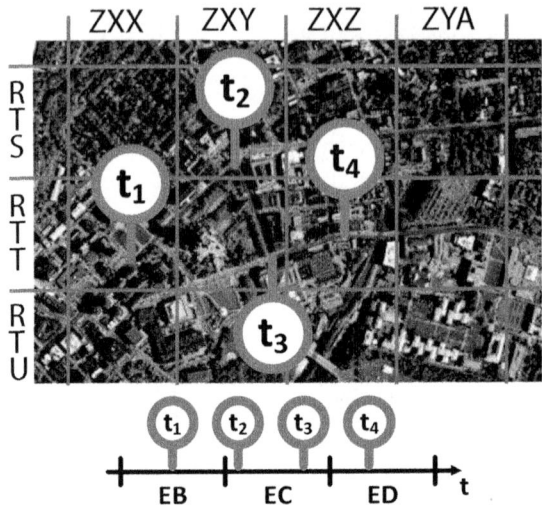

Fig. 2. Creation of geo-labels using equal-sized partition location labels and time-of-day labels. In this example, we concatenate "time spent at location" such as EB, EC, ED, with the location label such as "ZXX-RTT" and "ZXY-RTS".

3   Geo-trace Modeling

In this section, we describe the n-gram model along with two alternative methods for geo-trace modeling. We will use the alternative geo-trace modeling methods for performance comparison against the n-gram model.

3.1 n-Gram Model

Shannon established that a language could be approximated by an n-th order Markov model [26], where n may extend up to infinity. n-gram models have proven to be very robust in modeling sequences of data. Using an n-gram model trained on English text, we can estimate whether "United" or "house" is more likely to follow the phrase "the president of the" by comparing the probability $P(\text{"United"} \mid \text{"the president of the"})$ and $P(\text{"house"} \mid \text{"the president of the"})$.

In this paper, we model users' geo-trace information using the n-gram model assuming that the sequence of peoples' locations can also be approximated by n consecutive locations from the past (in essence, as a higher order Markov model). We consider a geo-label as a "word" in the language and train a similar n-gram geo-label language model on users' geo-trace data. The model can then be used to estimate the next geo-label g_i given the previous $n-1$ geo-labels from the user's geo-trace as $P(g_i|g_{i-n+1}, g_{i-n+2}, \ldots, g_{i-1})$ or in short $P(g_i|g_{i-n+1}^{i-1})$. We can also estimate the probability of a geo trace $g_1, g_2, \ldots, g_N$ as

$$P(g_1, g_2, \ldots, g_N) = \prod_{i=1}^{N} P(g_i | g_{i-n+1}^{i-1}) \qquad (1)$$

Similar to the *n*-gram language model, the *n*-gram geo-trace model is based on the Markovian assumption that a user's next location depends solely on his/her previous $n - 1$ locations. This assumption is not always true as there are many cases in which one's future location depends on locations that happened a long time ago (while the intermediate locations have little influence on the present location).

n-gram model training. The model probabilities $P(g_i | g_{i-n+1}^{i-1})$ can be estimated using the Maximum Likelihood Estimation (MLE) from the training data by counting the occurrences of geo-labels:

$$P_{\text{MLE}}(g_i | g_{i-n+1}^{i-1}) = \frac{C(g_{i-n+1}, \ldots, g_{i-1}, g_i)}{C(g_{i-n+1}, \ldots, g_{i-1})} \qquad (2)$$

MLE is problematic when a geo-trace contains *n*-grams that have never occurred in the training data before as MLE assigns probability zero to any unseen *n*-grams. Much of the prior work in GPS based user mobility modeling centers around and is limited by this assumption, that the user is highly unlikely to visit locations that he/she has not visited previously (referred to as the "close-world" assumption by Krumm and Horvitz [17]). To reject the closed-world assumption and to address this issue, we apply Good-Turing discounting and Katz backoff smoothing [29] that was developed for language modeling, in our geo-trace modeling. The key idea of smoothing (also known as discounting) is to discount the MLE probability for each observed *n*-gram in the training data to reserve some probability mass for unseen events.

Collapsing recurring geo-labels. In addition to quantizing GPS coordinates to labels, we also collapse re-occurring geo-labels into a single geo-label. This is to ensure that the *n*-gram models capture transition patterns of different locations rather than being dominated by a few locations that users spend a lot of time at. Instead, "time spent at a location" is modeled using the time-at-location feature (described in Section 2). The collapsing process is applied on both training and testing data for consistency.

Trigger bi-grams. In order to predict a user's future location, we extract discontinuous geo-label pairs from the original data to train trigger bi-gram models. A "trigger" is a geo-label pair (g_1, g_2) where g_1 and g_2 are usually not adjacent but have strong correlations. In other words, the occurrence of g_1 *triggers* the occurrence of g_2 in the future. For example, knowing that a user is at the entrance ramp of highway A close to his/her office, we can predict he/she will be at the exit of highway A close to his/her house, in the future. From the geo-trace data, we extract pairs of geo-labels that are distance d apart to train the trigger model for distance d. Conditional probabilities of seeing a "future"

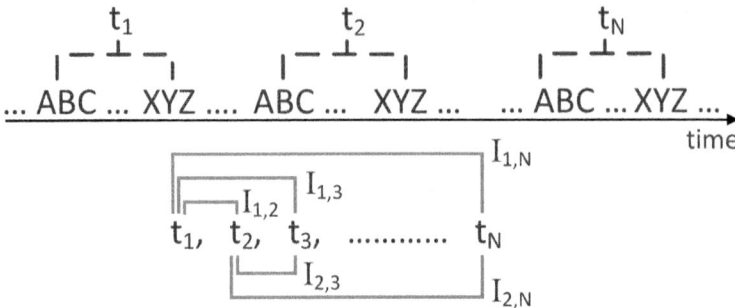

Fig. 3. Extracting a T-pattern for the geo-label combination ABC and XYZ. The interval for the ABC-XYZ t-pattern is the largest interval $I_{i,j}$ satisfying the critical interval test [22] and containing more than a threshold amount of XYZ labels in the training data.

label given the current geo-label are estimated from the extracted pairs (see Section 4.8).

The trained n-gram model is used for anomaly detection by continuously feeding the model geo-labels in real-time. The n-model then outputs a probability estimate for the current geo-label being part of the user's learned geo-trace model, given the previously seen real-time geo-labels. The probability estimate is compared against a heuristically decided threshold (see section 4.5), and if the estimate falls below the threshold it is considered an anomaly.

3.2   T-Patterns

The T-Pattern model identifies "statistically significantly" related geo-label pairs as signatures to characterize a user's movement model [22,10]. A T-Pattern is a triple of *(starting location, time interval, ending location)*, where the "starting" geo-label is followed by the "ending" geo-label within the time interval $\langle t + d_1, t + d_2 \rangle$ $(d_2 \geq d_1 \geq 0)$. The T-Pattern extraction algorithm searches through the geo-labels for the most significant pair of recurring geo-labels. Statistical significance in this case is calculated using the Critical Interval Test described by [22] (See Figure 3). This pair is collapsed as a new label and the search is repeated on the modified data until no more pairs of statistical significance can be found. The result of the iterative search is a collection of hierarchical pairs and unpaired geo-labels (similar to binary trees).

We can compare the T-patterns extracted from the testing data against those extracted from the training data to detect anomalies. In addition, when the "starting" label of a particular T-Pattern is observed in the testing data, we can predict that the user is likely to visit the corresponding "ending" location within the time interval specified by the T-Pattern.

3.3   Decaying Probabilistic Transition Network

Alternatively, we propose a Decaying Probabilistic Transition Network (DPTN) similar to [24] to model geo-traces. In DPTN, each distinct geo-label is represented as a node in a network and the network is fully connected. While traversing the DPTN following the sequence of geo-labels from a trace, the model calculates the probability of the present geo-label g_t given the preceding two geo-labels (g_{t-1}, g_{t-2}). A penalty value e_t is assigned for the present geo-label which is proportionally inverse to $P(g_t|g_{t-1}, g_{t-2})$. Denote E_t as an accumulated penalty up to time t and $E_t = e_t + \lambda E_{t-1}$, where λ is an empirically determined decay factor. When E_t exceeds an empirical threshold, we consider the geo-trace to be abnormal. The decay factor is introduced to 1) prevent the system from accumulating errors over a large amount of time, and 2) to make the model robust against sensor noise which would cause high penalties (by preventing these penalties from accumulating). The choices for the threshold value and decay factor are measures of the system's sensitivity to anomalies.

Next we compare the performance of these 3 approaches on a real-world dataset.

4   Experiments and Results

4.1   Data Collection and Preprocessing

We collected geo-trace data from 10 users living in the [anonymized] area, including a mix of students, blue-collar and white collar workers. Each user carried a QSTARZ BT-Q1000P GPS Data Logger at all times for 4 weeks (with two users using the data-logger for only two weeks). The GPS receiver had a low logging rate of approximately $8x10^{-3}$ Hz (approximately once every 2 minutes) and the battery lasted about 30 hours for each charge. We do not assume a constant capture rate for our analysis. The visible satellite count is also logged by the GPS tracker. This satellite count is used to filter out unreliable data points which have less than four satellites visible.

4.2   Anomaly Detection

In the following sub-sections we will discuss how well the n-gram model performed anomaly detection on this data. First we present experimental results of anomaly detection accuracy of the n-gram model in comparison to other models. We then analyze the impact of using different feature sets with our model. Next we discuss alternatives for tuning the parameters of the n-gram model (i.e., size of n and the model's temporal detection threshold). Then we will discuss the effect of location partitioning granularity on anomaly detection. Finally we discuss how detection accuracy varies with the amount of anomalous data seen.

The first set of experiments compares the three models described in Section 3 and a nth order Markovian model (similar to that described by Ashbrook and Starner [1]) in an anomaly detection application.

In this experiment, each model was trained using a week of a user's data. We create 4 separately trained models (of each model type) for each user. (In the case of the n-gram models, n was set to 10.) As there are 10 users, this results in 40 n-gram models for all users, 40 T-Pattern models for all users, etc. The testing phase was conducted by taking a week long geo-trace of a user and dividing it up into segments of six hours and providing each six hour segment to all training models except the model trained on the originating geo-trace. Each model provides a probability representing how likely it is that the geo-trace data is generated by the model. The owner of the model (i.e., user) that generates the highest probability is predicted to be the user that created the testing data. Table 1 shows the average accuracy of user identification using the three models described in Section 3. The n-gram model significantly out performs the T-Pattern and both Markovian models. In this experiment the anomaly we attempt to detect is whether the phone is being carried by any person other than the owner (equivalent to determining the owner of a geo-trace segment), but the anomaly detection process is capable of detecting other types of anomalous activities (such as a phone owner wandering off on unfamiliar routes).

Table 1. Comparison of owner-predicting accuracy given a segment of a geo-trace

T-Pattern	Markovian model	Decaying Probabilistic Transition Network	n-gram model
72.6%	76.8%	79.2%	86.6%

4.3   Geo-tag Feature Selection

The second anomaly detection experiment was to evaluate the use of the n-gram model with varying combinations of input features: partitioning scheme, time of day, time at location and direction of travel. The n-gram model is set to $n = 10$, while using 4 hours' testing and training data segments. The cell size for the equally spaced partitioning scheme is set to be 40 meters by 40 meters. For each of the feature combinations, the experimental procedure described in the previous experiment was applied. The various feature combinations and results from this experiment are presented in Table 2.

The results indicate that both partitioning methods have very similar impact on the performance of the model's anomaly detection. Adding additional information such as time-at-location, time-of-day, or direction-of-travel, decreases the accuracy. This is due to the fact that the model is trained on only one-week of data and adding additional information increases the dimensionality of the input, resulting in severe data sparseness.

4.4   Impact of History Length n

In this experiment, we search for the optimal value of n in the n-gram model. Increasing the order of n captures more context dependency in the nn-gram

Table 2. Prediction accuracy of the *n*-gram model with various input feature combinations

Feature Combination	Accuracy
Location label from quad-tree partitioning (density threshold = 50)	86.0%
Location label from equally spaced partitioning	86.5%
Location label from equally spaced partitioning, time of day label	73.1%
Location label from equally spaced partitioning, time at location label	57.1%
Location label from equally spaced partitioning, direction of travel label	81.6%

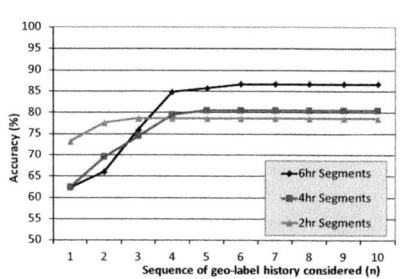

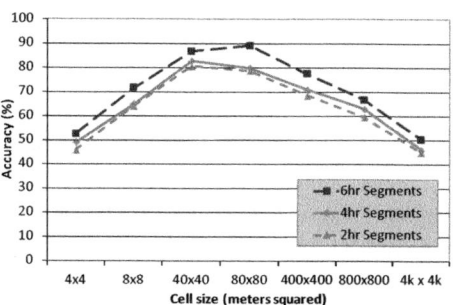

Fig. 4. Variation of anomaly detection accuracy vs. length of geo-location sequence (n)

Fig. 5. Variation of anomaly detection accuracy vs. location label cell size

model and usually increases the accuracy of the model. On the other hand, the size of resulting *n*-gram model grows fast when *n* increases which makes training and testing computationally expensive. Figure 4 shows anomaly detection accuracy vs the order of *n*-gram. This experiment is the same as described in Section 4.3 except for the varying values of *n*. Here all experiments are based on 40m-by-40m equal partitioning.

The three curves in Figure 4 represent results for the experiment repeated with testing and training data segments of 2, 4, and 6 hours respectively. The results converge for $n \geq 6$ suggesting that the current location of the user is, in the majority of the cases, dependent only on his last five locations.

4.5   ROC Curves of the *n*-Gram Model

We generate Receiver Operating Characteristic (ROC) curves for the *n*-gram model, to show how changing the model's anomaly detection threshold would affect the true positive and false positive rates for anomaly detection. The curves are generated with $n = 10$, using equally spaced partitions with granularity of 40m-by-40m. The five ROC curves displayed in Figure 6 are generated for testing segment lengths of 6 hours, 1 hour, 45 minutes, 30 minutes and 15 minutes.

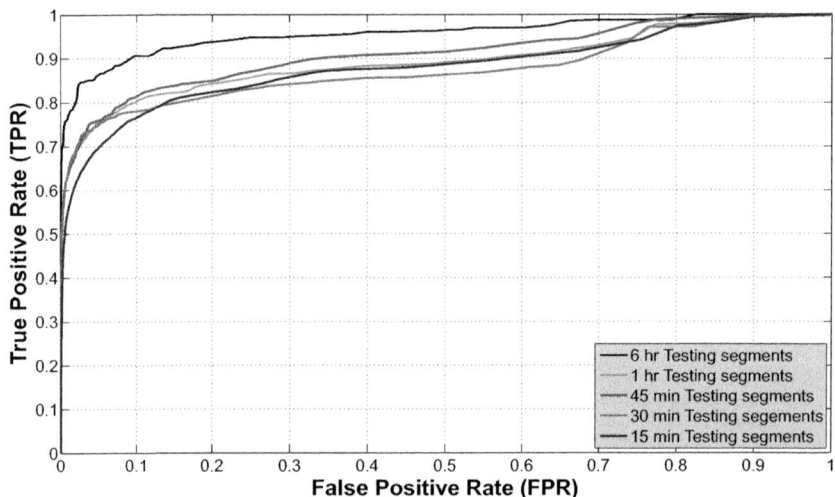

Fig. 6. Receiver Operating Characteristic (ROC) curves of the n-gram model for testing segment lengths of 4 hours, 1 hour, 45 minutes, 30 minutes and 15 minutes

On the ROC plot, the y-axis shows correct anomaly detections (as a fraction of the total number of anomalies present in the testing data), and the x-axis shows incorrect detections (as a fraction of non-anomalous test cases in the testing dataset). Points along the diagonal mean the ratio is even, and the model is performing no better than a coin flip - for every one correct detection, there is an incorrect detection. The upper left corner is a perfect anomaly detector, detecting all anomalies perfectly without any false detections. Each point on a ROC curve corresponds to a certain detection threshold. This graph makes it clear the tradeoff between segment length, true positive rates and false positive rates. We discuss this further in Section 5.

4.6   Partitioning Granularity

The fifth experiment carried out for anomaly detection was to identify the effects of geo- and temporal-partitioning granularity on the accuracy of the n-gram model's anomaly detection rate. For this experiment, the geo-partition scheme was used to partition the surface of the globe into cells of equal size, with the partition granularity varying from 4m-by-4m regions to 4km-by-4km regions. Again, we used every person-week geo-trace to train separate models and used the models to classify the owner of a segment of a geo-trace. The n-gram model uses $n = 10$. The results for this experiment are shown in Figure 5.

The three curves in Figure 5 represent results for the experiment repeated with testing and training data segments of 2, 4, and 6 hours respectively. The results indicate that the system performs best with cell sizes in the range of 40m to 80m.

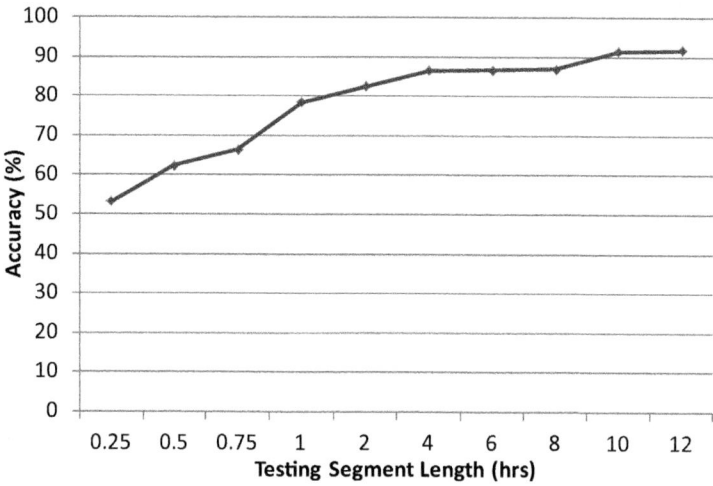

Fig. 7. Variation of anomaly detection accuracy vs. the testing segments length

4.7   Evaluating Variation of Accuracy vs. Anomalous Data Seen

An experiment was performed to estimate the amount of anomalous data that has to be seen by the *n*-gram model in order to achieve accurate detection. We used the same methodology as above; only the length of the testing data segments was varied from 15 minutes to 12 hours. Partitioning for the experiment was performed using a 40m-by-40m cell size, while *n* for the *n*-gram model is set to 10. While accuracy in detection increases with amount of anomalous data seen, only 1 hour of data is required to achieve almost 80% accuracy. We discuss this further in 5.

4.8   Effectiveness of *n*-Gram Model for Location Prediction

While not the focus of our work, the geo-trace model created for anomaly detection performed with considerable accuracy in predicting a user's future location. The *n*-gram model is capable of predicting the future location of the person after a given interval of time. Such a prediction model enables a whole new class of applications. On an individual scale, the predictive power of user movement models enables the development of applications such as 1) pre-heating a house only when a resident is homeward bound [13,25], 2) intelligent context-aware meeting/schedule organizers [6], 3) intelligent automotive navigation systems that use prediction when the user deviates from a given route [17], etc. When applied to a community, the predictive power of user movement models enables applications such as 1) intelligent call routing on cellular and other wide area networks with mobile users [20,2], 2) city wide traffic routing [9], etc.

Table 3. Percentage of correct predictions on a user's future movements based on a week of training data and the user's previous locations (only for users with four weeks of data)

Person ID	1	2	3	4	5	6	7	8
Percentage of correct predictions	61.9	82.8	96.0	55.8	31.9	83.7	82.1	93.6

To assess the n-gram model's predictive capabilities we use a week's worth of data to train a model for each person. Then using this model we attempt to predict the user's behavior for the remaining 3 weeks using the gathered data as input data and validation information. We try to predict where the user will be in the future after he/she travels for 5km. The reason that we use distance instead of time as a way to measure the "future" is because time depends on many other factors besides a user's geo-trace pattern. To answer questions such as "where is the user going to be in 20 minutes?" depends on his/her commuting method (walking, running, biking, driving, etc.) and traffic situation. A user's next location prediction output by the model is the centroid of a circle of 500m radius. The results are shown for 8 individuals in Table 3. As can be seen from the results, the model is able to predict the future locations of most people quite accurately. The prediction accuracy may drop in situations where the user's mobility patterns are quite irregular or different between the training and testing data, as is the case for the results for persons 4 and 5 in this experiment.

5   Discussion

From the experimental results in the previous section it can be seen that the n-gram model is able to perform with high accuracy even in conditions of sparse training data. In all of the above experiments the models were trained on only a week's worth of user's data, which in terms of geo-traces is a small amount of training data (e.g., a user's Saturday routine has only one example in the training set). However, with more training data, we expect the n-gram model to show further improvements in anomaly detection accuracy. With larger training datasets it is possible that incorporating additional features (such as time-of-day and time-at-location) into the model will present further performance gains.

As pointed out previously, each point on the ROC curves (Figure 6) corresponds to a certain detection threshold. Applications utilizing the n-gram model for anomaly detection will have their own unique costs for false-positives and false-negatives, and should customize the n-gram model's detection threshold so as to optimize the trade-off between false-positive and false-negative rates and overall accuracy.

We evaluated our n-gram approach with varying partition granularity size, and found that it achieved optimal performance when the size was between 40x40m and 80mx80m. This indicates that we can abstract a user's location from a very specific GPS coordinate to a much larger cell (up to 6400 sq. meters), and still achieve high performance in detecting anomalies. For applications or users that require high levels of privacy, this feature provides a significant benefit.

5.1 Applications of Geo-trace Modeling

Here, we investigate geo-trace modeling applications enabled by the ability to detect anomalies in users' mobility routines. Anomaly detection schemes using geo-traces are useful in applications such as theft detection systems for cars and mobile phones, and elder-care and child-care monitoring systems. In these applications, the user carries a phone or GPS tracking device which continuously tracks the user's location and reports the location to the anomaly detection program running on the mobile device or servers in the cloud. The model is initialized in the "observing" mode where the system only learns the geo-trace of the user and does not set off any alarms. We empirically set the "observing" time to be one week. After one week the anomaly detection function can be activated and the alarm will go off if the system believes that the mobile device is traveling on a strange route. Data points collected after the observing phase are continuously added to the training data to update the trained model.

Consider the theft detection application. The variation of accuracy of the anomaly detection system as a function of the testing data segment length is shown in Figure 7. The results indicate that the model is able to detect that the phone is stolen at an accuracy of close to 80% within an hour (approximately 30 GPS data points). The model is able to achieve an accuracy of over 60% after only 30 minutes (15 GPS readings). Alternatively, by examining the ROC curves, if a user is willing to put up with a 20% false positive rate, the model can achieve an 82% true positive rate after only 30 minutes. This is a good indicator that the *n*-gram model can be used in this real-world application.

6 Related Work

Tracking the location of mobile phone users and using tracking information to enhance user experiences have been areas of extensive research over the past decade in both industry and academia [5]. Most of these location-based systems, services and applications focus on utilizing the present location and most recent historical location information of the user [12]. There has been some research into more complex approaches that learn and model user mobility patterns. To the best of the authors' knowledge there has been very sparse previous work in detecting anomalies in a user's behavior using learned mobility models. Shi et al. [27] use GPS readings in conjunction with call-logs and mobile phone browser history to detect anomalies and test their approach with a large amount of user data, but the models used are less adaptable as they are not conditioned over prior events. Generating bounding regions of frequent travel, and Markov Random Fields for learning geo-tracks of people for anomaly detection has been proposed in [21] and [18] respectively. Both [21] or [18] are still in the proposal stage, and have not produced results that we can compare our work to.

We apply the approaches in the following previous work in user mobility modeling for comparison against the n-gram model presented in this paper. The approach employed by Salvador et al. [24] uses a state machine based probabilistic approach for anomaly detection (equivalent to the Decaying Probabilistic Transition Network in our experiments) with a different type of data which also has an important time- and sequence-dependent nature. The trajectory pattern (T-pattern) mining approach by Giannotti et al. [10] presents the notion of time dependent sequences (mined from historic data) for modeling user mobility. Ashbrook and Starner use n^{th} order Markov models to predict the next building a user will visit when observing the previous building visited by the user [1]. This model is designed to work with relatively clean location data as the preprocessing step discards or aggregates the majority of data into a few clusters. The Predestination system by Krumm and Horvitz [17] uses a partitioning method where the world is divided into equal sized cells (similar to our first partition method). They observe that a partially traveled route is usually an efficient path to the final destination. Ziebart et al. also use a Makovian model for destination prediction as well as shorter term predictions of the route to be traveled [30]. The focus of our work presented in this paper is not location prediction, but as our prediction results are promising, we propose to investigate using the n-gram model for location prediction.

While there has been little previous work in detecting anomalies in user mobility patterns, there exists some previous work in detecting anomalies in other forms of context information. For example, Duong et al. use a variant of Hidden Markov Models (HMMs), named Switching Hidden Semi-Markov Models for recognizing and detecting anomalies in human activities of daily living in smart environments [7]. There has been much work in other areas for anomaly detection, especially for security applications. An extensive survey of anomaly detection methods using machine learning approaches is provided by Hodge and Austin [14]. Xiang and Gong develop a framework for automatic behavior profiling and abnormality detection in surveillance video streams [28]. In [8], Eskin et al. describe an unsupervised anomaly detection framework for intrusion detection in network systems. A survey of work about anomaly detection in the field of intrusion detection in network security is provided by Patcha and Park [23] Chandola et al. provide a broad survey of various anomaly detection schemes and their application domains in [4].

7   Conclusion

In this paper, we present a novel method for modeling users' geo-trace patterns using n-gram models. Simple as they may be, n-gram models perform surprisingly well compared to more complicated probabilistic approaches such as T-Pattern and Markovian models for anomaly detection tasks. In this paper we also present a geo-partitioning method which can help preserve a user's privacy by blurring GPS coordinates, while retaining enough information for applications to model the user's behavior and perform anomaly detection with great accuracy.

Through initial experimentation we have seen that the *n*-gram model performs well at user location prediction. We plan to further investigate the *n*-gram model's predictive capabilities and improve its performance. We also plan to perform comparative experiments against previous work [17,30] in the area of user geo-location prediction.

We are currently investigating improvements to our *n*-gram based algorithms, such as the use of trigger *n*-grams to improve anomaly detection accuracy. We also plan to deploy and evaluate the *n*-gram model in real-world applications.

Acknowledgments. This research was supported in part by a grant from the Ericsson Research Center and by the CyLab Mobility Research Center at Carnegie Mellon under grant DAAD19-02-1-0389 and W911NF0910273 from the Army Research Office. We would like to thank Christian Köhler for helping immensely with the data collection for this work. We would also like to thank Ole Mengshoel, Patricia Collins and the blind reviewers for their comments and suggestions that helped improve this paper.

References

1. Ashbrook, D., Starner, T.: Using GPS to learn significant locations and predict movement across multiple users. Personal and Ubiquitous Computing 7(5), 275–286 (2003)
2. Bhattacharya, A., Das, S.K.: Lezi-update: an information-theoretic framework for personal mobility tracking in pcs networks. Wireless Networks 8(2/3), 121–135 (2002)
3. Brush, A.J.B., Krumm, J., Scott, J.: Exploring end user preferences for location obfuscation, location-based services, and the value of location. In: UbiComp 2010 (2010)
4. Chandola, V., Banerjee, A., Kumar, V.: Anomaly detection: A survey. ACM Comput. Surv. 41(3), 1–58 (2009)
5. Chen, G., Kotz, D.: A survey of context-aware mobile computing research. Tech. rep., Hanover, NH, USA (2000)
6. Davidoff, S., Zimmerman, J., Dey, A.K.: How routine learners can support family coordination. In: Proceedings of CHI 2010, pp. 2461–2470 (2010)
7. Duong, T.V., Bui, H.H., Phung, D.Q., Venkatesh, S.: Activity recognition and abnormality detection with the switching hidden semi-markov model. Computer Vision and Pattern Recognition 1, 838–845 (2005)
8. Eskin, E., Arnold, A., Prerau, M., Portnoy, L., Stolfo, S.: A geometric framework for unsupervised anomaly detection: Detecting intrusions in unlabeled data. In: Applications of Data Mining in Computer Security (2002)
9. Gehrke, J., Wojtusiak, J.: Traffic prediction for agent route planning. In: Bubak, M., van Albada, G., Dongarra, J., Sloot, P. (eds.) Computational Science at ICCS 2008, pp. 692–701 (2008)
10. Giannotti, F., Nanni, M., Pinelli, F., Pedreschi, D.: Trajectory pattern mining. In: KDD 2007: Proceedings of the 13th ACM SIGKDD International Conference on Knowledge Discovery and Data Mining, pp. 330–339 (2007)
11. Gonzalez, M.C., Hidalgo, C.A., Barabasi, A.L.: Understanding individual human mobility patterns. Nature 453, 779–782 (2008)
12. Gruteser, M., Grunwald, D.: Anonymous usage of location-based services through spatial and temporal cloaking. In: MobiSys 2003, pp. 31–42 (2003)

13. Gupta, M., Intille, S.S., Larson, K.: Adding GPS-control to traditional thermostats: An exploration of potential energy savings and design challenges. In: Tokuda, H., Beigl, M., Friday, A., Brush, A.J.B., Tobe, Y. (eds.) Pervasive 2009. LNCS, vol. 5538, pp. 95–114. Springer, Heidelberg (2009)
14. Hodge, V., Austin, J.: A survey of outlier detection methodologies. Artificial Intelligence Review 22, 85–126 (2004)
15. Klasnja, P., Consolvo, S., Choudhury, T., Beckwith, R., Hightower, J.: Exploring privacy concerns about personal sensing. In: Tokuda, H., Beigl, M., Friday, A., Brush, A.J.B., Tobe, Y. (eds.) Pervasive 2009. LNCS, vol. 5538, pp. 176–183. Springer, Heidelberg (2009)
16. Krumm, J.: Inference attacks on location tracks. In: LaMarca, A., Langheinrich, M., Truong, K. (eds.) Pervasive 2007. LNCS, vol. 4480, pp. 127–143. Springer, Heidelberg (2007)
17. Krumm, J., Horvitz, E.: Predestination: Inferring destinations from partial trajectories. In: Dourish, P., Friday, A. (eds.) UbiComp 2006. LNCS, vol. 4206, pp. 243–260. Springer, Heidelberg (2006)
18. Liao, B.: Anomaly detection in GPS data based on visual analytics. Master's thesis, University of Illinois at Urbana-Champaign (2010)
19. Liu, G., Maguire Jr., G.: A class of mobile motion prediction algorithms for wireless mobile computing and communication. Mobile Networks and Applications 1(2), 113–121 (1996)
20. Liu, T., Bahl, P., Chlamtac, I.: Mobility modeling, location tracking, and trajectory prediction in wireless atm networks. IEEE Journal on Selected Areas in Communications SAC 16(6), 922–936 (1998)
21. Ma, T.S.: Real-time anomaly detection for traveling individuals. In: Assets 2009. pp. 273–274 (2009)
22. Magnusson, M.S.: Discovering hidden time patterns in behavior: T-patterns and their detection. Behaviour Research Methods Instruments and Computers 32(1), 93–110 (2000)
23. Patcha, A., Park, J.M.: An overview of anomaly detection techniques: Existing solutions and latest technological trends. Computer Networks 51(12), 3448–3470 (2007)
24. Salvador, S., Philip Chan, P., Brodie, J.: Learning states and rules for time series anomaly detection. Tech. rep., Department of Computer Sciences, Florida Institute of Technology, Melbourne, FL 329012004 (2004)
25. Scott, J., Krumm, J., Meyers, B., Brush, A.J., Kapoor, A.: Home heating using gps-based arrival prediction. Tech. rep., Microsoft Research, USA (2010)
26. Shannon, C.E.: A mathematical theory of communication. Tech. rep., Bell Systems Technical Journal (1948)
27. Shi, E., Niu, Y., Jakobsson, M., Chow, R.: Implicit authentication through learning user behavior. In: Burmester, M., Tsudik, G., Magliveras, S., Ilić, I. (eds.) ISC 2010. LNCS, vol. 6531, pp. 99–113. Springer, Heidelberg (2011)
28. Xiang, T., Gong, S.: Video behaviour profiling and abnormality detection without manual labeling. In: ICCV 2005: Proceedings of the Tenth IEEE International Conference on Computer Vision, pp. 1238–1245 (2005)
29. Zhai, C., Lafferty, J.: A study of smoothing methods for language models applied to information retrieval. ACM Transactions on Information and System Security 22(2), 179–214 (2004)
30. Ziebart, B.D., Maas, A.L., Dey, A.K., Bagnell, J.A.: Navigate like a cabbie: probabilistic reasoning from observed context-aware behavior. In: UbiComp 2008, pp. 322–331 (2008)

Autonomous Construction of a WiFi Access Point Map Using Multidimensional Scaling

Jahyoung Koo and Hojung Cha

Department of Computer Science, Yonsei University,
134 Shinchon-Dong Sudaemoon-Ku, Seoul, Korea
{koojh,hjcha}@cs.yonsei.ac.kr

Abstract. To construct a WiFi positioning system, dedicated individuals usually gather radio scans with ground truth data. This laborious operation limits the widespread use of WiFi-based locating system. Off-the-shelf smartphones have the capability to scan radio signals from WiFi Access Points (APs). In this paper we propose a scheme to construct a map of WiFi AP positions autonomously without ground truth information. From radio scans, we extract dissimilarities between pairs of WiFi APs, then analyze the dissimilarities to produce a geometric configuration of WiFi APs based on a multidimensional scaling technique. To validate our scheme, we conducted experiments on five floors of an office building that has an area of 50 m by 35 m in each floor. WiFi APs were located within a 10m error range, and floors of APs are recognized without error.

Keywords: WiFi Access Point Map, Positioning, Autonomous and Unsupervised Learning, Multidimensional Scaling.

1 Introduction

Since the early 2000s, research on WiFi positioning systems [1-9] has been actively carried out, and databases for positioning systems have been constructed in various places. The databases usually consist of RF fingerprints or positions of WiFi access points (APs). A WiFi-enabled device estimates its position by matching an observed radio scan against the RF fingerprints database [1] or by estimating distances from WiFi APs within its radio range [8, 9]. Most current WiFi positioning systems build their database by inputs from dedicated operators who gather received signal strengths (RSSs) transmitted by WiFi APs, along with ground truth information where RSSs were scanned, while driving outdoors or walking indoors. It is, however, not possible for a limited number of dedicated operators to cover all locations; some places are often not open to the public. Furthermore, generating ground truth information is cumbersome and incurs a high cost.

Recently, several studies have attempted to reduce the effort needed for the database construction. Additional devices are, for instance, used to generate ground truth information [10]. Inertial sensors, such as accelerometers and gyroscopes, make it possible to estimate trajectories of a device. The performance is, however, highly dependent on the precision and mounted positions of the sensors. Hence, it is difficult

K. Lyons, J. Hightower, and E.M. Huang (Eds.): Pervasive 2011, LNCS 6696, pp. 115–132, 2011.

to produce meaningful data with a conventional device, such as a smartphone. In other studies, stochastic models were used to minimize the required amount of ground truth data [11, 12]. Generally, the initial database is constructed with a small amount of data with ground truth, then the database is expanded with more data without ground truth. The methods are devised for a particular database builder. Despite these efforts, constructing WiFi positioning systems especially in indoors that are usable by a wide variety of people in everyday lives has not yet been achieved.

Our goal is to achieve the ubiquity of WiFi positioning systems for all people at all times. To do so, a database should be built for all places that people can visit. We believe that the conventional method of data collection has limitations for reaching this goal. Hence, a scheme for ordinary people to join in building the database should be developed. Off-the-shelf smartphones have WiFi capability, and the number of these devices is dramatically increasing. Hopefully, WiFi APs can be scanned every one meter during people's daily lives. One critical problem is that most radio scans do not include information about the location of the scan.

In this paper, we propose a scheme to use radio scans gathered by smartphones to identify positions of WiFi APs. Ordinary smartphones users are not expected to move in a predefined route. Hence, ground truth information of radio scans is usually unknown. Each radio scan only includes identifiers of WiFi APs and their received signal strengths. In a scan, fortunately, radio signals from multiple APs are received. Our basic idea is to extract dissimilarities between pairs of WiFi APs from radio scans; then by analyzing the dissimilarities, produce the geometric configuration of WiFi APs. Here, we assume that we can acquire enough radio scans and that some of them are gathered in places beneficial for our scheme, for instance, a place near an AP.

To estimate the geometric configuration of WiFi APs, we adopt multidimensional scaling (MDS) techniques [13, 14, 15]. MDS has been successfully applied in the social sciences to find a spatial relationship from high dimensional data, which contains dissimilarity information between objects. In wireless sensor networks, MDS was used to estimate locations of sensor nodes through measuring all pairs of distance between nodes [16, 17, 18]. In case of WiFi AP, adopting MDS is not straightforward. Since WiFi APs cannot measure distances from other APs without changing their software, we take an approach to estimate dissimilarities between APs from radio scans gathered by smartphones. Dissimilarity does not mean exact distance. It is a measure of how close it is. Hence, a result of multidimensional scaling is relative positions of WiFi APs. Given at least three positions of APs or radio scans, relative positions can be transformed to absolute positions. In the research, we focus on accurately estimating relative positions of APs corresponding to the real geographic configuration. In addition, we expand our scheme to a multifloor environment by using three-dimensional MDS.

Knowing the positions of WiFi APs is useful in many aspects because of the following reasons: First, positions of APs are directly used to locate WiFi devices. Several systems provide positioning service based on positions of WiFi APs [3, 8]. Second, positions of APs can be used as supplementary data for constructing WiFi positioning systems [11, 19]. Third, the geometric configuration of WiFi APs provides the knowledge about the nature of networks, e.g., density, connectivity, interference properties, and models for simulations [20].

The rest of this paper is organized as follows: Section 2 presents related works. In Section 3, we propose a WiFi AP positioning algorithm using MDS. The experimental results are provided in Section 4. In Section 5, we provide information on future challenges. We conclude the paper in Section 6.

2 Related Work

According to the type of database, WiFi positioning algorithms can be categorized into two types: RF fingerprint-based and AP position-based. Some algorithms use both schemes.

In an RF fingerprint-based algorithm, a space is divided into grids. Dedicated operators gather radio scans at every grid. The gathered data from the entire grid construct an RF signal map in the space. When a mobile device scans radio signals at a position, the radio scan is searched in the signal map. The position of the best matching scan in the signal map is determined as the device's position. RADAR [1] is the representative research work on this method. Horus [2] is based on this mechanism, but the scheme uses a stochastic model to improve the performance. The commercial system Ekahau [7] also uses a similar algorithm. To achieve a high accuracy in RF fingerprint-based algorithm, we reduce the size of the grid and increase the number of scans in the grid. RSS fingerprint-based algorithm is known to be superior to AP position-based algorithm. The database construction process is, however, too laborious.

In an AP position-based algorithm, positions of APs are given a priori by a network operator; otherwise they need to be discovered through the process of wardriving. In this approach, there are several possible methods to estimate the position of a mobile device. The simplest method is to use proximity, where a mobile device takes its position from the nearest AP. The method using a Centroid or weighted centroid is also frequently adopted [3, 6]. Here, the position of a mobile device is estimated as the center of positions of APs visible to the device. If a radio propagation model is known, distances from positions of APs are calculated based on RSSs. Then, the position is estimated by multilateration [9]. Place Lab [3] and Skyhook Wireless [8] work mainly based on positions of WiFi APs. Performance of this kind is known to be relatively lower than RF fingerprint-based algorithm. Several researchers, however, tried to improve the performance of AP position-based algorithm close to the performance of RF fingerprint-based algorithm [11, 19]. Even though the performance of AP position-based algorithm is relatively low, this approach has several advantages. First, it only needs a small database, for instance, identifiers of APs and their positions. Second, system building efforts are relatively light. It does not need to survey every grid in a site; hence this algorithm is easily applied on a large scale. Third, it is more reliable in case ground truth data is inaccurate and networks frequently changes, such as addition of new APs [4, 6]. Therefore, to achieve the ubiquity of WiFi positioning system in anonymous network environments, these advantages need to be taken into consideration.

Several researchers have tried to reduce the labor in constructing a WiFi positioning system. Reducing the required number of ground truths is one approach. Wang et al. [12] devised an algorithm for a multiple floor environments. In that research, WiFi radio scans were collected with ground truth data on a floor, while on other floors, radio scans were gathered without ground truth data. They say that floor plans in a building are usually identical, and although the signals can be quite different on different floors, some correspondences exist. Hence, by aligning the position-known radio scans with position-unknown ones, signal maps of adjacent floors are constructed. However, only a few adjacent floors can be successfully processed.

In [19], AP positions were known a priori. An RF signal map was generated from scanned data by mobile nodes, which know the location of scanned radio signals. Madigan et al. [11] took a similar approach, but they did not assume that the scanned positions of mobile node were known. WiFi-SLAM [21] is an approach to build indoor radio maps with WiFi radio vectors. The scheme estimates the movement of a device and simulates the latent-space locations of unlabeled signal strength data using Gaussian process latent variable modeling. The scheme can use radio scans only gathered by one person moving at a constant speed, and its computation requirement is too expensive to be executed in a smartphone.

In contrast, Woodman et al. [10] tried to generate ground truths by using inertial sensors. They accurately estimated the moving trajectory of a person. The sensors used in the experiment are, however, too expensive and are mounted on foot, which is the best position to estimate pose and direction. Hence, this method is not practical for the average individual. Inertial sensors built in current smartphones are not accurate enough to estimate a moving trajectory. Frequent changes of positions of smart phone, for instance at hand or in a pocket, make it worse.

EZ system [22] has a similar approach to ours. The system tries to eliminate system training efforts. EZ uses radio scans gathered in unknown locations and three scans in known locations, which are essential in the algorithm. The scheme is based on an RF propagation model. From radio scans, it estimates parameters of the RF propagation model, locations of APs, and locations of radio scans. The results show that the performance is comparable to previous indoor location systems. EZ, however, requires extensive calculation, which takes a few minutes to several hours in a high-end computer, and large storage for the radio scans. In a large site, the scheme actually needs more than three scans gathered in known locations.

There have been several studies using MDS in the positioning research field. MDS-MAP [16] is the representative research work based on MDS. It estimates positions of sensor nodes by using connectivity information and finding the shortest paths between all pairs of sensor nodes. Unlike WiFi APs, sensor nodes usually have the capability to receive a radio signal or ultrasound from neighboring sensor nodes. Hence, distances are easily measured. When the average connectivity degree is larger than 9, the simulation result shows that the localization error is below the radio range of a sensor node. Xian Ji et al. [18] also applied MDS to a sensor positioning field. MDS technique was used in a distributed manner to estimate a local map for each group of neighbor sensors; these maps are then aligned together based on the alignment method. The approach is claimed to accurately estimate a sensor's position in a network with an isotropic topology.

3 WiFi AP Positioning Using MDS

Through the analysis of dissimilarities between pairs of objects, MDS makes it possible to discover a geometric configuration of the objects in a low-dimensional space, usually two- or three-dimensional, where the configuration matches the original dissimilarities between the pairs of objects [13, 14, 15]. Dissimilarity between two objects reflects how far apart an object is from the other psychologically, perceptually, or other type of sense. In various research fields, MDS has been successfully applied to identifying the spatial relationship of objects. For instance, sociologists have used MDS to obtain the structure of groups and organizations, based on members' perceptions of one another and their interaction patterns. In the case of sensor node localization, distances between pairs of sensor nodes are used as dissimilarity information. By applying MDS to distances, relative positions of the sensor nodes are estimated. The main advantage in using the MDS for positioning estimation is that even though dissimilarity information is error-prone, it can generate relatively high accurate position estimation [18].

3.1 Positioning Scheme

Consider a network of n devices, where each device is assumed to measure dissimilarities between itself and all other devices. The dissimilarity between devices i and j, when it is measured by device i, is represented by p_{ij}. X_i denotes the estimated position of device i, which is represented as (x_i, y_i, z_i) in three-dimensional spaces. The Euclidean distance between X_i and X_j is denoted as d_{ij}. The central motivating concept of multidimensional scaling is to find a configuration of devices $\{X_1, X_2, ..., X_n\}$ in some space such that Euclidean distances d_{ij} between the devices correspond to the dissimilarities p_{ij}. There are several variants to solve the problem. The basic form of the solution is to find the configuration that minimizes Equation (1).

$$\sqrt{\frac{\sum_i \sum_j [f(p_{ij}) - d_{ij}]^2}{scale\_factor}} \qquad (1)$$

In the equation, f is a continuous parametric monotonic function in metric MDS. In nonmetric MDS, f is related only on the rank order [13]. The positions of the devices that MDS estimates are relative positions, so they are always subject to rotation, translation, and scaling. Given at least three positions of the devices, the relative positions can be transformed to absolute positions. The relative positions are also important for the understanding of the network topology by themselves.

According to the method of measuring, we can define different types of dissimilarity. The simplest measure of dissimilarity is proximity, which discriminate whether two devices are within their communication ranges. We set p_{ij} as 1 in case device i receives a signal from device j. Otherwise, p_{ij} is set to any large value. The most complex measure is the Euclidean distance. Distance is known to be exponentially related to RSS according to the radio propagation characteristic. Equation (2) is frequently adopted model that shows the relationship between the received signal strength and distance.

$$P_r = P_0 - 10n \log_{10}(d/l_0) + X_\sigma, \tag{2}$$

where P_r is the RSS in dB, P_0 the signal strength at distance l_0 from the transmitter, and n is the pathloss exponent. X_σ represents the shadow noise and is modeled as a normal random variable with the standard deviation σ dB [23]. d is distance between nodes. Typically, l_0 is 1 m. If we have a priori knowledge on these parameters, we can use the distance as dissimilarity. Even though dissimilarities p_{ij} and p_{ji} are actually the same, the two values are measured differently in real environments. Hence, we need to adjust them to be symmetrical. Dissimilarity of itself, p_{ii} is set to 0. The set of dissimilarities is called a dissimilarity matrix, D=[p_{ij}].

3.2 Dissimilarity Matrix of WiFi APs

With respect to WiFi APs, there are several limitations to the method introduced in the previous section. First of all, WiFi APs usually do not have the capability of measuring distances between WiFi APs. To support this, WiFi APs' software needs to be modified. This modification is impractical in the real environment, since numerous numbers of APs are already deployed. Second, various algorithms are not applicable to WiFi APs due to the difficulty in making software changes. Hence, we need to devise a new method to obtain dissimilarities between WiFi APs without modifying already deployed WiFi APs. Our basic idea is to infer dissimilarities between WiFi APs from RSSs scanned on smartphones.

Let us assume that we have several radio scans gathered by a smartphone in a site. Each radio scan includes received signal strengths from visible APs at a position. In the case where n number of WiFi APs are scanned, a scan is represented as $scan_i = \{(AP_1, rss_1), (AP_2, rss_2), ..., (AP_n, rss_n), timestamp\}_i$, where AP_n is the identifier of n_{th} AP and rss_n is its received signal strength. The scan set is denoted as $SCAN = \{scan_1, scan_2, ..., scan_m\}$, where total m radio scans are gathered. For the dissimilarity between AP i and a smartphone, we denote p_i, which is a function of rss_i, $p_i = g(rss_i)$. The dissimilarity between AP i and AP j, which is p_{ij}, is estimated based on p_i and p_j by a certain rule, that is, $p_{ij} = f(p_i, p_j)$. g and f are functions indicating the relationship between dissimilarity and RSS. These are explained later. Here, we have two arguments. One is how to extract p_{ij} from rss_i and rss_j. The other is how to manipulate several radio scans with the same AP list.

To discuss this further, we use an example as shown in Figure 1. A smartphone scans RSSs from AP i and AP j at a position. Dissimilarities p_i and p_j are calculated based on the measured rss_i and rss_j. For the convenience of explanation, we assume that parameters of the radio propagation model are given a priori, and the Euclidean distance is calculated as dissimilarity. Here, p_i is smaller than p_j. In the scan, there is no information about directions of APs. Hence, from the viewpoint of the smartphone, the positions of APs may be points on the circles. Hence, we cannot find the exact dissimilarity p_{ij}. As seen in the figure, minimum dissimilarity between AP i and AP j is $p_i- p_j$ and maximum is p_i+p_j. Then, we may select one value between p_i-p_j and p_i+p_j as dissimilarity. Specifically, the dissimilarity is a distance between Y_i and a point of the inner circle. It is reasonable to take an average of all possible distances. For instance, when p_i equals p_j, p_{ij} is about $1.37 \times p_i$. In case $p_i \gg p_j$, p_i may be used as p_{ij}.

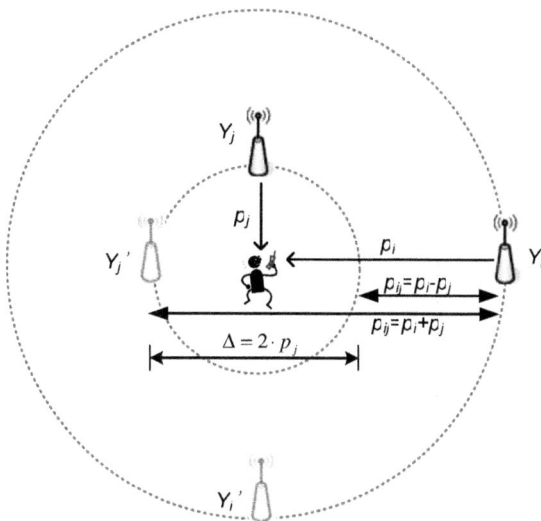

Fig. 1. At a point, a smartphone measures received signal strengths from two AP, Y_i and Y_j. The dissimilarities p_i and p_j are measured distances, and two circles show locatable positions of AP i and j, respectively. Then, the candidate of p_{ij} lies between p_i-p_j and p_i+p_j. $2 \times p_j$ is the extent of possible errors of the dissimilarity p_{ij}.

On the estimation of the dissimilarity, we can predict the extent of possible errors. In the figure, the error of an estimated dissimilarity is $2 \times p_j$ at worst. This means that error is possibly proportional to the smaller one between p_i and p_j.

In the estimation of dissimilarity, another issue should be considered. In the beginning we assumed that we could get many scans in various positions. As a result, we have several scans including the same APs. Figure 2 illustrates the situation. Four scans are gathered at positions m_1, m_2, m_3, and m_4, and their dissimilarities measured by the smartphone are $(p_{j(1)}, p_{i(1)})$, $(p_{j(2)}, p_{i(2)})$, $(p_{j(3)}, p_{i(3)})$, and $(p_{j(4)}, p_{i(4)})$, respectively. Considering we estimate dissimilarity p_{ij} from them, estimating four dissimilarities, $p_{ij(1)}$, $p_{ij(2)}$, $p_{ij(3)}$ and $p_{ij(4)}$ and averaging them is one possible solution. However, since most scans are not measured on the shortest path connecting two APs, its value is usually larger than a real distance. Hence, we select and use a radio scan that is the most proper to infer a real distance from. Measurement positions m_1 and m_3 compared, $p_{j(1)}$ is equal to $p_{j(3)}$, but $p_{i(1)}$ is larger than $p_{i(3)}$. Then, m_3 is selected as a candidate. Compared with m_2, $p_{j(2)}$+$p_{i(2)}$ is smaller than $p_{j(3)}$+$p_{i(3)}$, then m_2 is newly selected. Since m_2 and m_4 are on the shortest path, $p_{j(2)}$+$p_{i(2)}$ is similar to $p_{j(4)}$+$p_{i(4)}$. Hence, m_2 or m_4 may be equally selected. Until now we did not consider that received signal strengths are disrupted by noise. In reality, the measured signal strength is not always consistent with the expected distance. Hence, in the selection of a radio scan, we take an approach to reduce an expected error. One clue is the extent of possible errors shown in Figure 1. It is proportional to the value of the smaller one of dissimilarities between APs and a smartphone. Therefore, we finally select the radio scan with the smallest dissimilarity value, which in this case is m_2.

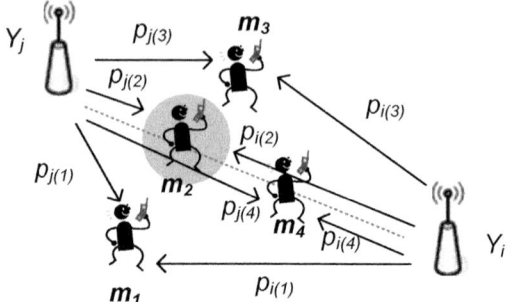

Fig. 2. At several points the received signal strengths from two APs, Y_i and Y_j are measured. The dashed line shows the shortest path between the two APs. Here, $p_{j(2)}<p_{j(1)}=p_{j(3)}<p_{j(4)}$ and $p_{i(4)}\ p_{i(3)}<p_{i(2)}<p_{i(1)}$. This shows the effect of measurement positions.

Now, we discuss the functions g and f that converts received signal strength to dissimilarity. In real environments, we do not often know parameters of the propagation model in Equation 2. Several previous researchers assumed a practical value for them. However, such assumptions are frequently fragile in many situations. Furthermore, even at the same distance, measured RSSs are different due to environmental factors including multipath fading. So, we do not try to convert received signal strength to a real distance. Instead, we quantize received signal strength into several levels. Considering the characteristic of exponential decaying of received signal strength, displacements between quantization thresholds should not be uniform. In the case where the range of received signal strength of WiFi APs is from −20dBm to −90dBm, our thresholds are −55, −70, −80, −85, and −90 in five levels, and its dissimilarities are 1, 2, 3, 4, and 5. When there is no scan including any pair of APs, we determine that they are not connected and set the dissimilarity between the two APs as any large value, for instance 9999. This quantization makes dissimilarities more robust to small variation of RSS.

In a large site, many pairs of APs are outside the communication range of the other; hence a significant portion of dissimilarities remain unmeasured. To solve this problem, we use a graph-based algorithm. Nodes in the graph represent APs, and weighted edges represent dissimilarities between two APs. In the graph, we find the shortest paths of all pairs. For the dissimilarity between unconnected APs, the distance of the shortest path is used. As the number of APs increases, we get a larger number of dissimilarities, which raises information for understanding the configuration of the APs. As a consequence, positions are more accurately estimated in a large site.

3.3 Multifloor AP Positioning

Until now, radio scans are implicitly assumed to be gathered from a single floor. In general, people live in multifloor environments. Their radio scans are actually gathered from multiple floors. In the existing studies, floors of radio scans were labeled by user intervention. To encourage grass-roots radio gathering, however, the explicit labeling should not be requested to normal users. In some radio scans, RSSs from APs on adjacent floors are included. Hence, dissimilarities between APs in different floors are also obtained. We process radio scans gathered on several floors altogether, then generate a dissimilarity matrix, which includes both dissimilarities between inter-floor APs and dissimilarities between intra-floor APs. Theoretically, MDS has no restriction on the dimension of an analysis result. One constraint is that its performance is affected by the number of dissimilarities. So, if there are enough WiFi APs in a site, applying three-dimensional MDS to multifloor dissimilarities is possible. As a rule of thumb, there should be at least twice as many dissimilarities as parameters to be estimated, to assure an adequate degree of statistical stability [13]. That is, at least 12 APs are needed for a three-dimensional MDS.

Signals from an AP reach other floors following several paths. They penetrate through floors directly or detour through outside windows. Hence, in dissimilarities between inter-floor APs, different types of attenuations are included, and this breaks the consistency between a real distance and its dissimilarity. As a result, the estimated configuration is easily distorted. To overcome this, we divide multifloor AP positioning into three steps: *three-dimensional MDS, clustering of APs* and *multiple single-floor MDS*. In the first step, all the scans gathered from multiple floors are processed together to produce dissimilarities. Three-dimensional MDS is applied to the dissimilarities, and we get the three-dimensional positions of APs. Although three-dimensional MDS estimates a distorted configuration of APs, APs from the same floor tend to be placed nearby. In the second step, we distinguish floors of APs. If the number of floors is k, we cluster APs into k clusters based on the three-dimensional positions of APs. We assume that the number of floors is given. If whole floors are scanned, it is the number of floors of a building. APs in the same cluster are considered as being placed on the same floors. In the final step, APs from the same floor are processed using two-dimensional MDS separately. The process identifies positions of APs on multiple floors from radio scans without information on which floor scans are gathered.

3.4 Autonomous Collaboration

To discover positions of WiFi APs universally, the participation of anonymous smartphone users is important; but this is not easily achieved if the technical barrier for participation is high. For instance, asking for ground truth for a scan or exact ranging to an AP hinders user participation. The proposed scheme only requires radio scan data; hence collaboration among smartphone users can be actively occurred. Here, we need to note that smartphones have different radio characteristics, which affect the dissimilarity estimation.

We discuss three cases of collaboration. In the first case, several users gather enough radio scans in a site and then estimate their own dissimilarity matrices. Each matrix reflects the different radio characteristics of smartphones. Classically, three-way MDS processes multiple dissimilarity matrices at a time. A representative three-way MDS is individual difference scaling, INDSCAL [13, 14], which aggregates the matrices based on common characteristics and produces a collaborated result. It, however, requires intensive computation. It is known that the result from INDSCAL is similar to the result from MDS for averaged data of all the dissimilarity matrices [13].

Second, users might gather enough radio scans to generate dissimilarity matrices at different sites. Then, AP positioning is performed individually and the estimated positions are patched together. In this case, radio characteristics of smartphones hardly affect the results.

Finally, it is the most concerning case that users gather radio scans sporadically in a large site, so individual scans are not sufficient to estimate a dissimilarity matrix. In this case, we estimate one dissimilarity matrix from the entire set of radio scans shared by all users. The problem is that signal strengths have different characteristics according to the device gathering them. Fortunately, this is mitigated by using a small quantization level and the fact that radio characteristics between smartphones do not differ as much as between different types of devices. In the case where we use proximity information only, this problem is almost eliminated.

4   Results

To validate the proposed algorithm, we conducted experiments in real environments and in simulation. To gather WiFi scans, we implemented software scanning WiFi signals on a smartphone, HTC Hero, running Android 1.5. With the smartphone, we gathered WiFi scans in a 20-story office building. Scans were performed for five floors, from the 10th floor to the 14th floor. As shown in Figure 3, each floor is 35 m by 50 m size and about 3 m in height. The outer wall is surrounded by glass. In the middle of each floor, there are restrooms, elevators, stairways, and meeting rooms, which are mainly constructed with concrete. The places where peoples work are divided by soft partitions. Each floor has about six WiFi APs attached on walls. The positions of WiFi APs are manually collected. The smartphone was placed on a hand or in a trouser pocket. On a scan, BSSID, SSID and RSS are stored. For analysis, some of scans were gathered with their ground truths. In experiments, only BSSIDs and RSSs are used. The strongest signals from APs are distributed from –23 dBm to –48dBm. Only two APs have signal strengths stronger than –30 dBm. The weakest signal strength was –96 dBm. In a scan, APs are listed in order of signal strengths. The AP with the strongest signal is listed first. From the scans, we found that two BSSIDs were transmitted by an AP. We gathered a total of 54,821 scans and found 57 APs in the scans whose maximum signal strength was stronger than –50 dBm. We expect that APs with maximum signal strength weaker than –50 dBm are located on other floors. Gathered scans are processed in a notebook computer running Windows XP (CPU: Intel(R) Core(TM) 2 Duo CPU 1.83 GHz; memory size: 2GB). We implemented a program to estimate dissimilarities in C. As a tool of MDS, we used the Matlab function *mdscale*, which performs nonmetric MDS by default. Results of MDS are relative configurations of WiFi APs. To evaluate accuracies of configurations, we need to match estimated configurations to the real configuration of APs. We performed this by using the Procrustes analysis, which finds the isotropic dilation, translation, reflection, and rotation that best match one configuration with another. We also used the Matlab function *procrustes*.

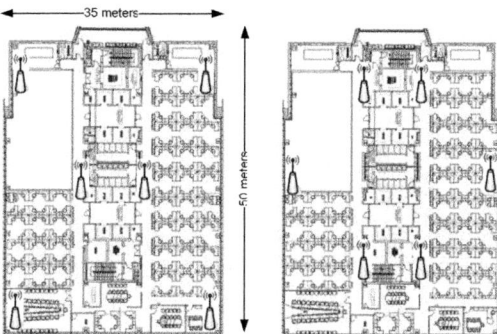

Fig. 3. Floor plans for the building. Left shows an even-numbered floor, and right shows an odd-numbered floor. Each floor has six APs setup by a network operator. Even-numbered floors have different deployments from odd-numbered floors.

4.1 Single-Floor AP Positioning

The performance of the proposed algorithm is affected by the way dissimilarities are obtained. First, we used five-level quantized RSS as dissimilarity. A brief summary of the procedure used to calculate the dissimilarity is as follows: first, whether the strongest RSS in a scan is larger than a threshold, which is –50 dBm in our implementation, is examined. Conceptually, the examination judges whether the scan is gathered near an AP. If it is satisfied, dissimilarities to all the APs in the scan are calculated. Otherwise, the scan is discarded. Dissimilarities are set as 1, 2, 3, 4, and 5 when RSS is larger than –47 dBm, –63 dBm, –75 dBm, –83 dBm, and –90 dBm, respectively. This process is repeated for all scans. If smaller dissimilarities are found in other scans, dissimilarities are updated as the new ones.

In the calculated dissimilarities, there were many mismatched pairs of p_{ij} and p_{ji}. Many factors cause this phenomenon. It is well known that symmetries of radio propagations are not guaranteed due to environmental effects, even though AP hardware is the same. In our case, dissimilarities between APs are measured indirectly by a smartphone. p_{ij} may be calculated from a scan measured nearest to AP i. In contrast, p_{ji} may be calculated from a measurement nearest to AP j. Positions of the two scans are not likely to have the same geometric conditions. One of the two scans might be closer to the line connecting two APs, and its dissimilarity has a smaller value. From this insight, we take the lower value as the dissimilarity in case the two dissimilarities are different.

Second, we used proximity information as dissimilarity. Simply, we decide a device is connected when a signal from an AP is visible. In this case, we set the dissimilarity to 1. However, this makes multidimensional scaling frequently fail to estimate positions of APs. In a small set of APs, this information is too limited to distinguish the configuration of APs. In the worst case, whole dissimilarities have the same value, for instance 1. To reduce this, we set a threshold to tighten the condition of proximity. In the experiments, we use –70 dBm as a proximity threshold. Since dissimilarities between unconnected APs are calculated by the shortest path-finding process, we obtain the effect that the amount of information increases.

Table 1. Experimental results of AP position estimation (error in meter)

	All APs (57 APs)		Duplicated APs removed (32 APs)	
	five-level quantization	Proximity only	five-level quantization	Proximity only
10th floor	9.22	8.93	5.34	8.53
11th floor	5.94	10.47	5.66	12.64
12th floor	9.49	14.64	**11.64**	13.84
13th floor	5.72	6.18	**5.48**	4.79
14th floor	8.77	12.32	10.08	12.41
Average	**7.85**	**10.50**	**7.64**	**10.44**

The results of our experiments are shown in the Table 1. In each floor, positions of 12 or 13 unique BSSIDs are estimated. The average estimation error when using a five-level quantization is 7.85 m. When proximity information is used, the average error is increased to 10.50 meters. In the case of proximity only, most of the dissimilarities have a value of 1 or 2, which is not a distinguishable condition. If the area of a site is larger, dissimilarities will have various values and the performance will be enhanced. This is proved in a simulation experiment. Among the BSSIDs, 25 are duplicated, and we removed these duplicated BSSIDs. As a result, six or seven BSSIDs remain for each floor. Again, we experimented with the refined set. The performance did not differ appreciably. From the result, we conclude that only the number of physically unique APs affects the performance. In the table, we show that performances of even-numbered floors are better than odd-numbered floors. There are two reasons for this. First, effective areas, which we define as the size of the convex hull of APs, are different. The effective area of an even-numbered floor is much smaller than the area of the odd-numbered floor. This differentiates the actual connectivity degrees, which represent how many APs are connected to an AP, and it is known that performance of MDS increases as the connectivity degree increases [16]. Second, the topology of even-numbered floor is beneficial. The topology of even numbered floors is round, but the topology of odd-numbered floors is more complex. By examining the layout of an even-numbered floor, we found many concrete walls in the middle, and concrete is difficult for radio signals to penetrate. Even though two APs in the middle are close, it is hard to identify small dissimilarities between them.

On the 13th floor, estimation performance is good (error of 5.48 m), and on the 12th floor estimation performance is poor (error of 11.64 m). Figure 4 shows the estimation results of the two floors. On the 13th floor, the configuration of estimated positions is similar to the original configuration. On the 12th floor, however, the estimated configuration is distorted compared with its original configuration. A noticeable error is that the position of AP1 moves too far inside. By analyzing the dissimilarities of the 12th floor, we found that dissimilarity between AP1 and AP4 was lower than it should have been. To identify the reason for this, we investigated all the scans gathered from the 12th floor.

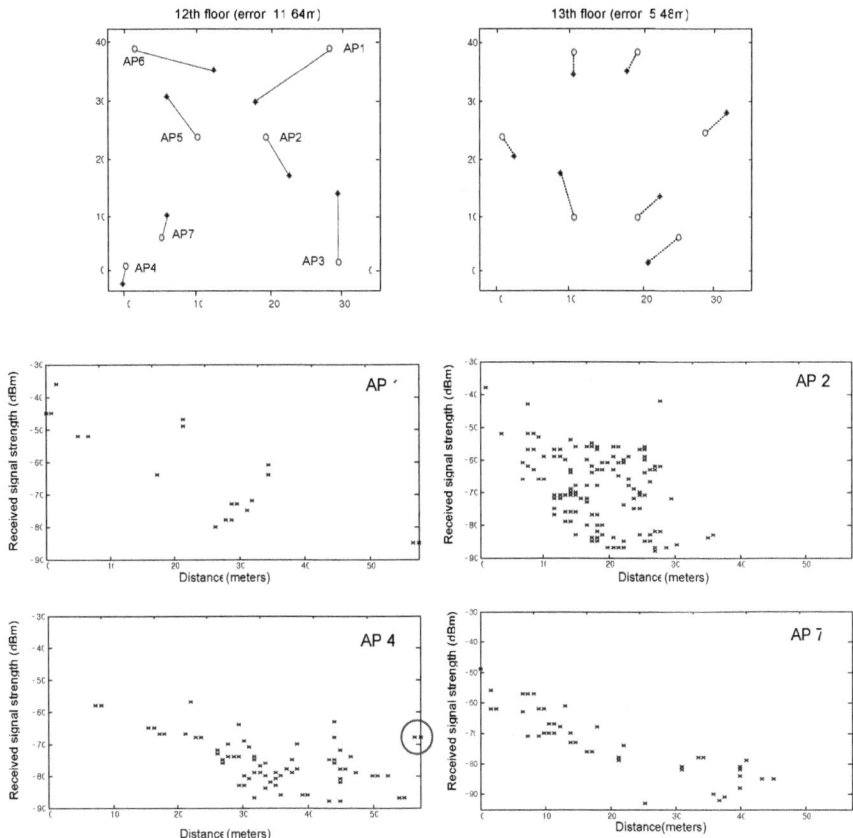

Fig. 4. The two graphs on the top show the estimation results of the 12th and 13th floors. "o" denotes the real position and * denotes the estimated position. Four graphs on the bottom depict scanned RSSs at various distances from four APs on the 12th floor, AP1, AP2, AP4, and AP7, respectively.

The four graphs on the bottom in the Figure 4 show scatter plots of scanned RSSs according to the distances from AP1, AP2, AP4, and AP7, respectively. The range of distances from the APs is from zero to 56 m. Since AP2 is located in the middle of the site, its range is only from zero to 35 m. Among signals from AP4, there are unexpected large RSSs over a long distance (circled in red). At even 56 m from AP4, RSS was –68 dBm, and was measured around AP1. This caused a decrease in the distance between AP1 and AP4. Unlike other APs, AP7 was not set up by a network operator; it was a personal AP. Its signals were relatively low and were measured only in limited areas. Hence, dissimilarities to AP7 were largely found by the shortest path algorithm.

4.2 Multi-floor AP Positioning

Even though expansions of algorithms to multifloor environments were mentioned, previous researches rarely conducted real experiments on them. In this study, we conducted a multifloor experiment. Radio scans gathered on five consecutive floors are used without floor information, but the number of floors is given.

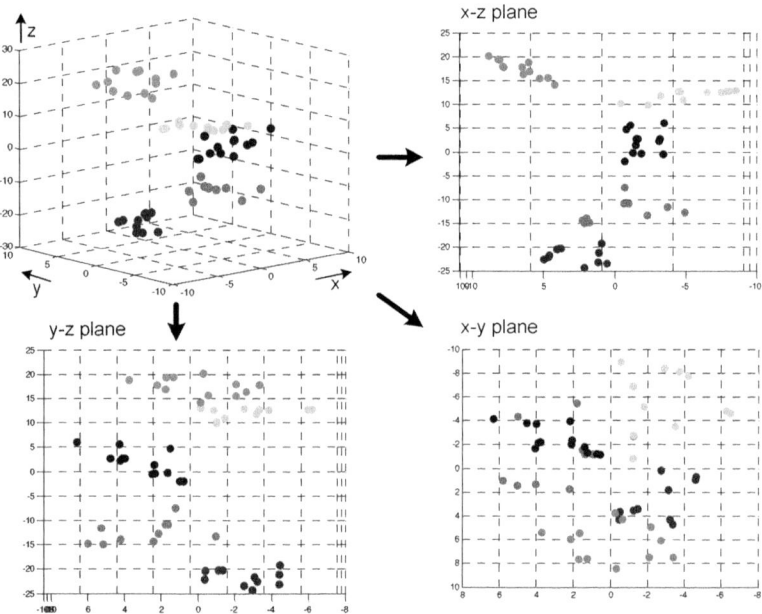

Fig. 5. A total of 57 APs on five floors are processed at the same time. Each dot shows the estimated positions of an AP. The positions are divided into five clusters. Each color shows a different floor.

All the scans are simultaneously processed to calculate dissimilarities between all pairs of APs on five floors. A total of 57×57 dissimilarities are estimated. We then applied three-dimensional MDS to the dissimilarities. The results are shown in Figure 5. Each dot denotes estimated positions of APs. We then divided the estimated positions of APs into five clusters. The Matlab function *cluster* was used for clustering. Each color in the figure shows a different cluster. In the x–z plane and y–z plane, we can see five distinctive clusters along the z-axis. To our astonishment, the clustering results show a 100% match to the real floors. This result verifies that we can identify the floor of AP with high accuracy using only radio scans collected on multiple floors.

In contrast to floor identification, two-dimensional positions on each floor are inaccurate. The x–y plane in Figure 5 depicts overlaid positions of all the floors. Each floor is biased to a different direction. When a radio signal passes through a floor, it is severely attenuated. This is frequently described by a floor attenuation factor [23].

However, since the outer wall of the building is made of glass, radio signals from other floors are easily received around the windows with only small attenuations. Even though dissimilarities are affected by these factors, they are not easily handled. Based on the clustering result, AP positioning is separately performed only with APs that are expected to be located on the same floor. This produces the same result as the single-floor experiment. The aligning problem between floors is still left, but this can be handled by radio matching methods [12].

4.3 Simulation Analysis

To analyze the proposed algorithm, we conducted simulation experiments. To generate signal maps, we used radio propagation model as shown in Equation 2. *Po* at 1 m from an AP, n the pathloss exponent and the standard deviation of shadow noise are –27dBm, 3.4, and 9 dBm, respectively. The values are extracted from the radio scans used in our real experiments by a curve-fitting method.

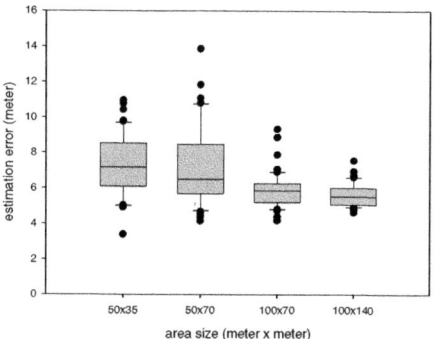

Fig. 6. While densities of APs remain the same, the size of areas is increased. The performance is enhanced as the size increases.

First, we analyzed the effect of the size of a site. We used the same density as our real experiment. In the 50×35 m² area, seven APs are used whose positions are randomly generated. In a doubled area (50×70 m²), the number of APs is doubled. In areas of 100×70 m² and 100×140 m², 28 and 56 APs are used, respectively. Figure 6 shows the results. Even though the densities of APs are the same, the performance is enhanced and stable as the size of the area increases.

As the size increases, two benefits are apparent: connectivity degrees in an AP increase, and as the total number of APs increases, the number of dissimilarities also increases. These two facts increase the amount of information about the configuration of APs.

In contrast to the previous simulation, we fixed the area of site as 100×140 m², and increased the number of APs. Figure 7 shows that as the number of APs increases, the performance is enhanced. When the number of APs is large enough, the error of using proximity information only is around 9 m, and the error of five-level quantization is around 5 m.

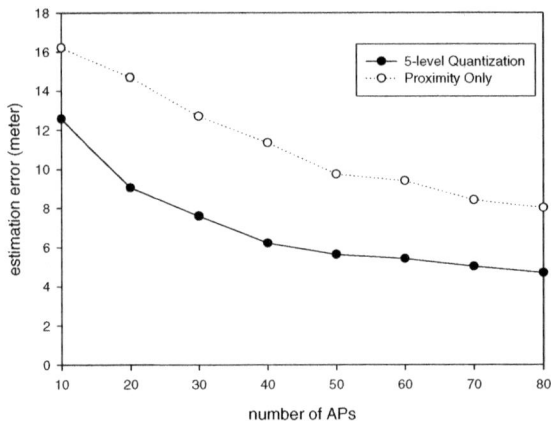

Fig. 7. Increase of connectivity degrees enhances the performance of AP positioning

5 Discussion and Future Work

We are concerned that the performance of the proposed scheme is suitable for location-based services. Outdoors, it may be enough to distinguish buildings, but indoors some location services will require more accurate results. We offer several possibilities to enhance the performance. First, performance improves as the size of an area widens. Second, an increased number of WiFi APs improves performance. In addition, a soft AP, which is a smartphone that acts like a WiFi AP temporarily, can be included to improve performance. Third, preprocessing radio scans can be applied. As shown in Figure 4, inconsistent signal strengths distort the geometric configuration of APs. We can use several stochastic methods, such as Kalman filter and Particle filter, to reduce this effect. We proposed an algorithm to estimate dissimilarities, but it can be replaced by a better method if there is one. In addition, there are many types of MDS techniques. We may use or develop a more appropriate version of an MDS technique. Despite all these variations, our overall scheme is still maintained.

In our research, we mentioned that relative positions can be transformed to absolute positions if there are at least three absolute positions of APs or radio scans. The important point is how easy it is to get three absolute positions of APs or radio scans. In general, many APs are seen outdoors where GPS signal can be received [24]. This means that we can frequently obtain absolute positions of radio scans at a boundary of a building. With the positions, absolute transformation can be performed. This is a practical situation.

The computational cost of the proposed algorithm is relatively low. In our experiment, execution of *mdscale* to 57×57 dissimilarities takes 3 s. In our opinion, the algorithm can be implemented in a smartphone or in a server. Hence, anyone can construct their own WiFi positioning system when needed.

With multifloor positioning, we distinguished floors of APs. Positions of APs are separately estimated in each floor, and then alignment of APs between adjacent floors is performed. If we can properly handle the floor attenuation factor and environmental effects across floors, we can remove all additional procedures. As our future works, we will improve the estimation algorithm of the dissimilarity matrix so that it is more robust to environmental effects including multifloor and perform an experiment of multiple users in a large site.

6 Conclusions

In this paper, we proposed an algorithm to determine a geographic configuration of WiFi APs from radio scans. Our method does not require ground truths for radio scans. Hence the assumption that we can obtain enough radio scans to build WiFi positioning system can be realized by the algorithm. We lowered the barrier of building a WiFi positioning system. Anyone using a smartphone can build their own positioning system or contribute information from their radio scans to help build a large positioning system.

To validate the feasibility of the proposed algorithm, we conducted real experiments in a 20-story office building. We gathered radio scans from five consecutive floors. On each floor, six or seven APs were found, and the average estimation error was 7.64 m. Based on the simulation result, the performance of the proposed algorithm can be enhanced as the size of the area widens. For multifloor, we are able to distinguish APs on different floors with high accuracy.

Acknowledgments. This work was supported by the National Research Foundation of Korea (NRF) grant funded by the Korea government (MEST) (No.2010-0000405).

References

1. Bahl, P., Padmanabhan, V.N.: RADAR: An in-building RF-based user location and tracking system. In: Infocom (2000)
2. Youssef, M., Agrawala, A.: The Horus WLAN Location Determination System. In: MobiSys (2005)
3. LaMarca, A., Chawathe, Y., Consolvo, S., Hightower, J., Smith, I., Scott, J., Sohn, T., Howard, J., Hughes, J., Potter, F., Tabert, J., Powledge, P., Borriello, G., Schilit, B.: Place Lab: Device Positioning Using Radio Beacons in the Wild. In: Gellersen, H.-W., Want, R., Schmidt, A. (eds.) PERVASIVE 2005. LNCS, vol. 3468, pp. 116–133. Springer, Heidelberg (2005)
4. Cheng, Y., Chawathe, Y., LaMarca, A., Krumm, J.: Accuracy characterization for metropolitan-scale wi-fi localization. In: Mobisys (2005)
5. Kim, M., Fielding, J., Kotz, D.: Risks of using AP locations discovered through war driving. In: Fishkin, K.P., Schiele, B., Nixon, P., Quigley, A. (eds.) PERVASIVE 2006. LNCS, vol. 3968, pp. 67–82. Springer, Heidelberg (2006)
6. Chen, M., Sohn, T., Chmelev, D., Haehnel, D., Hightower, J., Hughes, J., LaMarca, A., Potter, F., Smith, I., Varshavsky, A.: Practical Metropolitan-scale Positioning for GSM Phones. In: Dourish, P., Friday, A. (eds.) UbiComp 2006. LNCS, vol. 4206, pp. 225–242. Springer, Heidelberg (2006)
7. Ekahau, http://www.ekahau.com/
8. Skyhook Wireless, http://ww.skyhookwireless.com/

9. Savvides, A., Han, C.-C., Srivastava, M.B.: Dynamic fine-grained localization in Ad-Hoc networks of sensors. In: Mobicom (2001)
10. Woodman, O., Harle, R.: RF-Based Initialisation for Inertial Pedestrian Tracking. In: Tokuda, H., Beigl, M., Friday, A., Brush, A.J.B., Tobe, Y. (eds.) Pervasive 2009. LNCS, vol. 5538, pp. 238–255. Springer, Heidelberg (2009)
11. Madigan, D., Einahrawy, E., Martin, R.P., Ju, W., Krishnan, P., Krishnakumar, A.: Bayesian Indoor Positioning Systems. In: Infocom (2005)
12. Wang, H., et al.: Indoor Localization in Multi-Floor Environments with Reduced Effort. In: Percom (2010)
13. Kruskal, J.B., Wish, M.: Multidimensional Scaling. Sage Publications, Thousand Oaks (1978)
14. MAA Cox, TF Cox. Multidimensional scaling. Handbook of data visualization. Springer, Heidelberg (2008)
15. Borg, I., Groenen, P.: Modern Multidimensional Scaling, Theory and Applications. Springer, Heidelberg (1997)
16. Shang, Y., Ruml, W., Zhang, Y., Fromherz, M.: Localization from Mere Connectivity. In: MobiHoc (2003)
17. Shang, Y., Ruml, W.: Improved MDS-Based Localization. In: Infocom (2004)
18. Ji, Zha, H.: Sensor positioning in wireless ad-hoc sensor networks using multidimensional scaling. In: Infocom (2004)
19. Lim, H., Kung, L., Hou, J.C., Luo, H.: Zero-Configuration, Robust Indoor Localization: Theory and Experimentation. In: Infocom (2006)
20. Subramanian, A., Deshpande, P., Gaojgao, J., Das, S.: Drive-by localization of roadside WiFi networks. In: Infocom (2008)
21. Ferris, B., Fox, D., Lawrence, N.: Wi-Fi-SLAM Using Gaussian Process Latent Variable Models. In: IJCAI (2007)
22. Chintalapudi, K.K., et al.: Indoor Localization Without the Pain. In: Mobicom (2010)
23. Rappaport, T.: Wireless Communications — Principles and Practice. Prentice-Hall, Englewood Cliffs (1996)
24. Hoffman-Wellenhof, B., Lichteneeger, H., Collins, J.: Global Positioning System: Theory and Practice, 4th edn. Springer, New York (1997)

Identifying Important Places in People's Lives from Cellular Network Data

Sibren Isaacman[1], Richard Becker[2], Ramón Cáceres[2], Stephen Kobourov[3], Margaret Martonosi[1], James Rowland[2], and Alexander Varshavsky[2]

[1] Dept. of Electrical Engineering, Princeton University, Princeton, NJ, USA
{isaacman,mrm}@princeton.edu
[2] AT&T Labs – Research, Florham Park, NJ, USA
{rab,ramon,jrr,varshavsky}@research.att.com
[3] Dept. of Computer Science, University of Arizona, Tucson, AZ, USA
kobourov@cs.arizona.edu

Abstract. People spend most of their time at a few key locations, such as home and work. Being able to identify how the movements of people cluster around these "important places" is crucial for a range of technology and policy decisions in areas such as telecommunications and transportation infrastructure deployment. In this paper, we propose new techniques based on clustering and regression for analyzing anonymized cellular network data to identify generally important locations, and to discern semantically meaningful locations such as home and work. Starting with temporally sparse and spatially coarse location information, we propose a new algorithm to identify important locations. We test this algorithm on arbitrary cellphone users, including those with low call rates, and find that we are within 3 miles of ground truth for 88% of volunteer users. Further, after locating home and work, we achieve commute distance estimates that are within 1 mile of equivalent estimates derived from government census data. Finally, we perform carbon footprint analyses on hundreds of thousands of anonymous users as an example of how our data and algorithms can form an accurate and efficient underpinning for policy and infrastructure studies.

1 Introduction

While people travel further and faster than ever before, it is still the case that they spend much of their time at a few important places. Identifying these key locations is thus central to understanding human mobility and social patterns. Such understanding can, in turn, inform solutions to large-scale societal problems in fields as varied as telecommunications, ecology, epidemiology, and urban planning. As an example, knowing how large populations of people move about would help determine their carbon footprint and in turn help guide policies intended to reduce that footprint.

Wireless cellular networks hold great potential for providing the necessary information to identify important places in people's lives. The growing ubiquity of cellular phones means that a large percentage of people keep a phone with them most of the time. In addition, the networks need to know roughly where each phone is in order to provide the phones with voice and data services.

K. Lyons, J. Hightower, and E.M. Huang (Eds.): Pervasive 2011, LNCS 6696, pp. 133–151, 2011.

In this work, we explore the use of anonymized Call Detail Records (CDRs) from a cellular network to estimate the locations of important places in the lives of large populations of people. CDRs are routinely collected by cellular network providers to help operate their networks, for example to identify congested cells in need of additional bandwidth. Each CDR contains information such as the time a voice call was placed or a text message was received, as well as the identity of the cell tower with which the phone was associated at that time. This information can serve as sporadic samples of the approximate locations of the phone's owner.

CDRs are an attractive source of location information for two main reasons. One, they are collected for all active cellular phones, which number in the hundreds of millions in the US and in the billions worldwide. Two, they are already being collected to help operate the networks, so that additional uses of CDR data incur little marginal cost. Contrast this low cost, for example, with the expense of carrying out surveys to ask people where they spend their time. This high expense generally limits other data collection methods to orders of magnitude fewer participants.

However, CDRs have two significant limitations as a source of location information. One, they are sparse in time because they are generated only when a phone engages in a voice call or text message exchange. Two, they are coarse in space because they record location only at the granularity of a cell tower. It is an interesting research question whether CDRs can be used to identify important places in people's lives.

In this paper, we show that applying clustering and regression techniques to CDR data can indeed identify important places in people's lives. First, we present an algorithm for identifying important places. Then, we describe two other algorithms for selecting home and work locations from among those important places. We validate all three algorithms by comparing their results to ground truth provided by a group of volunteers. We then apply these algorithms to much larger anonymous populations in the Los Angeles (LA) and New York City (NY) areas. Our LA and NY dataset spans two months of activity for hundreds of thousands of phones, yielding hundreds of millions of location samples.

Finally, we present two example applications of these techniques. We start by using the home and work locations identified by our algorithms to calculate the distribution of commute distances per postal code in our Los Angeles and New York dataset. We then estimate the carbon footprints of those commutes, also aggregated by postal code.

Overall, the contributions of our work are as follows.

- We propose and evaluate a model based on logistic regression of volunteers' locations for *Important Places* analysis. In our first algorithm, we demonstrate an accurate and efficient method for identifying *Important Places* from CDRs. Our algorithm is the first to operate on the majority of cellular phone users, rather than relying either on more continuous and fine-grained tracking (e.g. GPS) or focusing on high-call-rate users whose mobility is easier to analyze.
- We propose and evaluate two other algorithms for applying semantic meaning to important locations, namely *Home* and *Work*, using other models also derived via logistic regression. Our algorithms identify these key sites with median errors under one mile.

- We test our approaches on a dataset that is more universal than prior work in several ways. First, it is simply larger than prior work in terms of CDRs and number of users. Second, it covers multiple distinct geographic areas. Third, it considers users with a wide variety of call/text rates, from as low as a few calls/texts per week up to dozens of calls/texts per day.
- Finally, we provide examples of how technology providers and policy makers might use our data and algorithms in their work. In particular, we calculate home-to-work commute distances and combine them with publicly available data to estimate the carbon footprints of those commutes in two major metropolitan areas. Our average commute distances for the LA and NY areas are within 1 mile of the equivalent averages computed from US Census data.

In summary, our work extends prior research in location identification and cellphone mobility to create effective algorithms and solid foundations for technological and societal problem-solving. The rest of this paper is organized as follows. Section 2 describes the data we obtained from volunteers as well as the much larger set of anonymous CDRs, including the measures we have taken to preserve individual privacy. Section 3 presents our algorithm for identifying important locations, Section 4 our algorithms for selecting home and work locations, and Section 5 our estimates of commuting distances and carbon footprints. Section 6 discusses related work, and Section 7 offers conclusions.

2 Data Collection Methodology and Characteristics

2.1 Anonymized Call Detail Records

We collected anonymized Call Detail Records (CDRs) from a random set of cellular phones whose billing addresses lie within specific geographic regions.

Defining Geographic Regions of Interest: We first developed a target set of 891 postal (ZIP) codes located in the Los Angeles and New York metropolitan areas. In the LA area, the ZIP codes cover the counties of Los Angeles, Orange, and Ventura. In the NY area, these ZIP codes cover the five New York City boroughs (Manhattan, Brooklyn, Bronx, Queens, and Staten Island) and ten New Jersey counties that are close to New York City (Essex, Union, Morris, Hudson, Bergen, Somerset, Passaic, Middlesex, Sussex, and Warren). Figure 7 shows maps of the regions studied as part of carbon footprint results presented in Section 5. Our selected ZIP codes cover similarly sized areas in LA and NY.

Anonymized CDR Contents: We then obtained anonymized CDRs for a random sample of phones in each ZIP code. The CDRs contain information about two types of events involving these phones: voice calls and text messages. In place of the phone number, each CDR contains an anonymous identifier consisting of the 5-digit billing ZIP code and a unique integer. Each CDR also contains the starting time of the voice or text event, the duration of the event, the locations of the starting and ending cell towers associated with the event, and an indicator of whether the phone was registered to an individual or a business. It is important to note that we collect CDRs for these phones wherever in the US they travel, not only when they contact cell towers within their billing ZIP codes.

Excluded Categories of Phones: Our goal is to understand aggregate mobility patterns of people in particular regions of the country, and to compare them analytically where possible. As such, our study omits from consideration two sets of phones from the original CDRs.

First, we omitted phones registered to businesses, retaining only phones registered to individuals. This step avoids, for example, the situation where a cellular service reseller based in a ZIP code of interest would cause us to study large numbers of phones that are not representative of that ZIP code.

Second, we removed from our sample those phones that appeared in their base ZIP code fewer than half the days they had voice or text activity. We assumed that the owners of such phones now live in other parts of the country but have retained their old billing addresses (e.g., they are college students). Therefore, their daily travel patterns may not be representative of the geographical areas we are interested in.

After these two filtering steps, our CDRs are a useful representation of mobility and telephone usage in the regions of interest. While there will always be some people using personal phones for business (and vice versa), we have compared our filtered CDRs against US Census data for the regions of interest [22] and found a strong correlation between the expected and actual number of users in each ZIP code.

Dataset Characteristics: Our data collection methodology resulted in location data for hundreds of thousands of phones split roughly evenly between LA and NY, with the number of phones in each ZIP code proportional to the population in that ZIP code. We collected data for 78 consecutive days from November 15, 2009, to January 31, 2010. Table 1 offers some general characteristics of this dataset. As shown, it contains hundreds of millions of location samples, with on the order of 10 location samples per phone per day.

Table 1. General characteristics of our Call Detail Record dataset

Metric	LA	NY
Total Unique Phones	97K	71K
Total Unique CDRs	247M	161M
Median Calls Per Day	8	9
Median Texts per Day	4	3

Privacy Measures: Given the sensitivity of the data, we took several steps to ensure the privacy of individuals represented in our CDR dataset.

First, only anonymous records were used in this study. In particular, personally identifying characteristics were removed from our CDRs. CDRs for the same phone are linked using an anonymous unique identifier, rather than a telephone number. No demographic data is linked to any user or CDR.

Second, all our results are presented as aggregates. That is, no individual anonymous identifier was singled out for the study. By observing and reporting only on the aggregates, we protect the privacy of individuals.

Finally, each CDR only included location information for the cellular towers with which a phone was associated at the beginning and end of a voice call or at the time of a text message. The phones were effectively invisible to us aside from these events. In addition, we could estimate the phone locations only to the granularity of the cell tower coverage radius. Although the effective radius depends upon tower height, radio power, antenna angle, and terrain, these radii average about a mile, giving an uncertainty of about 3 square miles for any event [21].

2.2 Ground Truth Data from Volunteers

In order to validate our work, we recruited a group of 37 volunteers who provided us the true locations of important places in their lives, as well as permission to inspect their CDRs for the purposes of this study. The group is composed of graduate students and professionals, all of which are personal or professional acquaintances of the authors. Of the 37 volunteers, 29 are male and 8 are female. Geographically, 31 recruits live in the states of New York or New Jersey and the remaining 6 live in Ohio, Georgia, or Arizona. The majority of the volunteers work at high-tech jobs.

Each volunteer filled out a survey on a website. The survey form asked them to list up to 10 important places in their lives, defined as places where they had spent a significant amount of time and/or visited frequently in the previous 60 days. It specifically requested that they include home and work in the list, and expressed the hope that they would list additional places such as a gym or the destination of an overnight trip.

The volunteers also provided us with the latitude and longitude of each place they listed. The survey website included a tool to help them find this information. Volunteers could either enter a street address, or drop a pin on a map after panning and zooming the map to the appropriate location. The tool would convert this input into a latitude-longitude pair that the volunteer could cut and paste into the survey form.

In the work described in the rest of this paper, we used the ground truth data from 18 of our volunteers as a training set for our algorithms, and data from the remaining 19 volunteers as a testing set. The 18 training volunteers were chosen arbitrarily and without regard for their mobility or calling patterns. For both our training and testing volunteers, we collected CDRs for the same 60 days covered by their survey responses.

3 Identifying Important Places

Intuitively, we know that human mobility involves moving to and from a set of places, some of which are recurringly important to us and some of which are visited less often or only fleetingly. Being able to discern significant places in people's lives is an important aspect of characterizing human mobility. Identifying important places can be used to support location-based services, improve understanding of general human movement patterns, and support the creation of realistic and practical models of human mobility. We define an *important place* as a geographic location where a person spends a significant amount of time and/or which she visits frequently. Examples of important places include: home, work, gym, grocery store, and a house of worship.

In this section, we show how mobile network events can be used to identify important places in people's lives. We identify important places based on the mobile network *events* that correspond to CDR entries. Thus, making or receiving a phone call or send-ing or receiving a text message generates an *event*. For each event (CDR), we know its time of occurrence and the location of the first and last cell towers associated with it. We refer to the list of events that were generated by a user's phone as the user's *trace*. If a cell tower appears in the user's trace on a given day, we say that the cell tower was *contacted* on that day.

Our algorithm for identifying important places has two stages. In the first stage, we spatially cluster the cell towers that appear in a user's trace. In the second stage, we identify which of the clusters are important using a model derived from a logistic regression of volunteers' CDRs. In the rest of this section, we describe these two stages in detail, present our validation results based on the important locations of our 19 testing volunteers, and compare the results characteristics for our NY and LA populations.

While in this paper we use cellular phone activity collected in the form of CDRs, our algorithms for identifying important locations, and for assigning semantic meaning to these locations such as "home" or "work", are quite general. They could also be applied to location traces collected via GPS, WiFi, or other techniques.

3.1 Clustering Cell Towers

Clustering cell towers that appear in a user's trace has two steps. In the first step, we sort the cell towers in descending order based on the total number of days they were contacted. Thus, the cell tower that was contacted on the most days will be ranked first. Sorting the cell towers serves as a modest optimization but is not required. An on-line algorithm could easily be developed by removing the sorting phase, resulting in an average change in error of less than 0.1 miles. However, sorting by the number of days the cell tower was contacted ("call-days") rather than by the total number of events associated with the cell tower is both important and novel. In particular, sorting by call-days rather than total calls helps to decrease the influence of cell towers that were contacted only on a few days, but that had a burst of events on those days. A flurry of calls from one location on a single day is not as indicative of location importance as a similar number of calls spread over many days at a location that recurs. Consider, for example, work travel to a distant location. Though the trip may be short in duration, one might make many calls back home to family and friends. These calls would then unduly increase the perceived importance of the location. This distinction helps us to maintain good location accuracy for users across a wide range of calls-per-day.

In the second step, the sorted list of cell towers is clustered according to Hartigan's leader algorithm [10]. We chose the leader algorithm because it doesn't require pre-specifying the desired number of clusters and because it works in a single pass, which is important for practical use on very large datasets such as ours (4GB, compressed).

The leader algorithm starts with the first cell tower in the sorted list and makes this tower the centroid of the first cluster. Then, for each subsequent cell tower, it checks to see whether the tower falls within a threshold radius of the centroid of any existing cluster. If it does not, the tower becomes the centroid of a new cluster. If it does fall within the threshold radius of an existing cluster, the algorithm adds the tower to the cluster and moves the centroid of the cluster to be the weighted average of the locations of all the cell towers in the cluster. The cell tower locations, in our case, are weighted

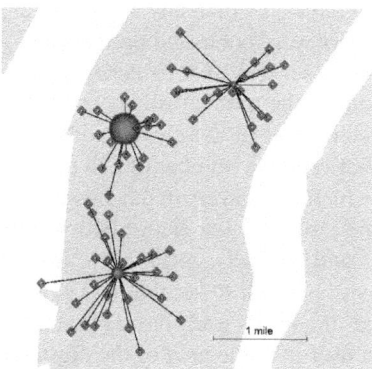

Fig. 1. Our clustering algorithm applied to a volunteer. Cell towers are clustered into groups according to Hartigan's leader algorithm. Cell towers are added to a cluster if they are within a mile of the cluster's centroid. Clusters are depicted as circles and cell towers as diamonds. A line connects each cell tower to the centroid of its cluster. Circle size is proportional to the number of days on which any cell tower in the cluster was contacted.

by the number of call-days. The algorithm completes once every cell tower has been assigned to a cluster.

Choosing a particular threshold radius around cell towers helps equalize for the fact that in urban areas towers might be as dense as 200 meters apart, while in suburban areas, spacings of 1-3 miles are more common. We experimented with a range of radii and found that 1 mile works well in practice.

Figure 1 illustrates the result of running the clustering algorithm on a volunteer's trace with a threshold radius of 1 mile. We can see that although the volunteer connected to the network through many cell towers, there are only three clusters. Note again that the size of a cluster is proportional to the number of days on which any cell tower in the cluster was contacted, and not necessarily proportional to the number of cell towers that belong to the cluster. For instance, the middle cluster in Figure 1 is the largest even though it contains fewer cell towers than the southernmost cluster. Although for this volunteer there are many cell towers belonging to each of the clusters, it is common for people to have clusters comprising only one or two cell towers.

3.2 Determining Importance

Clustering cell towers typically results in dozens to hundreds of clusters, most of which may have little importance to the user. In this section, we describe how our algorithm determines which clusters are important.

We developed an algorithm for identifying important clusters by studying the behavior of our 18 training volunteers and then testing the algorithm on a set of 19 testing volunteers. Studying the data of our training volunteers revealed the following five observable factors that are considered in determining whether a cluster is important:

– *Days*: The number of days on which any cell tower in the cluster was contacted. If two or more cell towers were contacted on the same day, the day is counted only once. This factor gives a sense of the regularity of activity in the cluster.
– *Tower Days*: The sum of the number of days cell towers in the cluster were contacted. Thus, each cell tower in the cluster adds its *Days* value to the sum. This factor gives a sense of both the number of cell towers in the cluster as well as the number of days on which cell towers in the cluster were contacted.
– *Duration*: The number of days that elapse between the first contact with any cell tower in the cluster and the last contact with any cell tower in the cluster. (For example, a cluster with one cell tower that was contacted only on the first day and on the seventh day of the user's trace has a duration value of 6.) *Duration* gives a sense of how long a user is in the area of the cluster, even if network events were not generated from this cluster on a daily basis.
– *Work Hour Events* : The number of times any cell tower in the cluster was contacted on weekdays between 1pm and 5pm. We experimented with various ranges of hours and found that 1pm to 5pm works well in practice because it is a core set of hours for both early and late workers.
– *Home Hour Events* : The number of times any cell tower in the cluster was contacted on weekends or weekdays between 7pm and 7am.

The algorithm identifies a cluster as important if the cluster satisfies each of the following three conditions. First, cell towers in the cluster should have been contacted on more than 5% of the total days in the study. In our case, this translates to the *Days* factor being higher than 2. This condition filters out transitional clusters that are rarely contacted. Second, the cluster should have a *Duration* of more than 14. This helps to remove vacations and other locations that may generate a large number of events in a short period of time but that are not consistently used throughout the trace. Third, the cluster should have a higher than 20% chance of being important according to the regression analysis discussed below. While we derived all the thresholds experimentally based on the data from the 18 training volunteers, our tests on other volunteers and on the larger dataset point to their general applicability.

To determine the likelihood of a cluster being important, we use logistic regression. We considered the five observable factors described above as well as several derived variables. Specifically, we added the rank and the percentage of each of the observable factors. Rank is calculated by ordering the clusters based on the observable factor and then assigning each cluster a sequential number. For example, the cluster with the largest *Duration* gets a ranking of 1 and the cluster with the second largest *Duration* gets a ranking of 2. Percentage is calculated by dividing the value of a given observable factor of a cluster by the sum of these values in all clusters. For instance, if the *Days* value of the current cluster is 5 and there are two more clusters with *Days* values of 20 and 25, the percentage of the *Days* factor of the current cluster is 5 divided by 50, or 0.1. In total, we ended up with 15 observable and derived factors.

$$Prob(x_1, ..., x_n) = \frac{1}{(1 + e^{\beta_0 + \beta_1 x_1 + \cdots + \beta_n x_n})} \tag{1}$$

Equation 1 shows the general form of the logistic regression formula that we use to estimate the likelihood of the importance of a cluster. In this formula, $Prob(x_1, ..., x_n)$

is the probability that a cluster with factors x_i is the closest cluster to an important location and β_js are coefficients that are discovered during the regression.

To discover the coefficients, we used the important locations of our 18 training volunteers. First, we marked clusters of each of the volunteers as either being important or not. A cluster is marked as being important if its centroid is the closest to any of the important locations specified by the volunteer. The importance of a cluster is the dependent binary variable in our regression analysis and the 15 observable and derived factors are the independent variables. Once the statistically insignificant factors were eliminated, only three factors were left: the percentage of *Tower Days*, the *Duration*, and the ranking of a cluster based on *Days*. The percentage of *Tower Days* and the ranking based on *Days* prefers clusters with many cell towers contacted on many days. The *Duration* indicates that for a cluster to be considered important its cell towers must be contacted during a large fraction of the trace. Including the *Duration* feature reduces the importance of transitionary calls made during travel by giving a higher weight to the locations where a user made phone calls many days apart. We conjecture that Duration was selected as one of the main features because people tend to return to places that are important to them often and tend to visit transitionary places infrequently. Once the training is complete, we estimate the importance of a new cluster by feeding these three statistically significant factors of the cluster into the regression formula.

Figure 2 plots the true important locations and the discovered important clusters of four volunteers. The figure confirms that the discovered important clusters match well with the volunteer-provided important locations. However, one important location in the bottom right figure was not matched by any discovered important cluster. This is because the volunteer made almost no calls from that location. It is worth noting that the algorithm performed well despite the significant difference in patterns of of important locations for different volunteers (e.g., different number of important locations, different spatial distributions, different rate of calls, etc.)

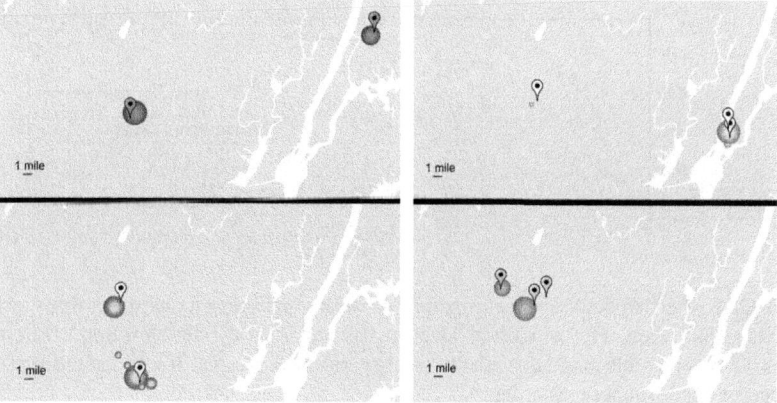

Fig. 2. True important locations vs. discovered important clusters for four volunteers. Paddles represent the important locations provided by the volunteers. Circles represent the important clusters discovered by our algorithm, with their radii signifying days of use. The four examples are drawn to the same scale.

3.3 Validation of Important Places Algorithm

We further validate our algorithm for determining important places by comparing to other approaches. Recall that each important cluster contains one or more cell towers. The location of an important place is then the weighted centroid of the geographic locations of these cell towers. To measure how well our *Important Places* algorithm works we calculate the error between each important location provided to us by our 19 testing volunteers and the nearest important place identified by our algorithm. We also compare our results to two additional algorithms: *Nearest Cluster* and *Nearest Tower*. The *Nearest Cluster* algorithm considers all clusters identified in Section 3.1 and identifies an important place as the weighted centroid of a cluster that is the nearest to an actual important location. This algorithm acts as an upper bound on our *Important Places* algorithm since it operates on all discovered clusters, without restricting the pool of clusters to choose from. The *Nearest Tower* algorithm determines an important place at the location of the cell tower that is the closest to the actual important location. This algorithm shows the limit of the accuracy we can achieve if we limit our clusters to just a single cell tower.

Figure 3 plots a CDF of the error between the actual important locations and the identified important places for the *Important Places, Nearest Cluster* and *Nearest Tower* algorithms. The figure shows that the *Important Places* algorithm performs very well, even though it reduces the total number of identified clusters by up to 90% for some volunteers. The median error of the *Important Places* algorithm is 0.9 miles, which is close to the performance of the upper bound algorithms. *Nearest Cluster* and *Nearest Tower* achieve 0.62 and 0.5 miles median error, respectively. The reason for the slightly higher error for the *Important Places* algorithm is that some people do not use their cell phone frequently at their important locations. Viewing the results more broadly, we find our approach maintains within-3-miles accuracy for 88% of the users, which suffices for the types of policy and planning applications we envision.

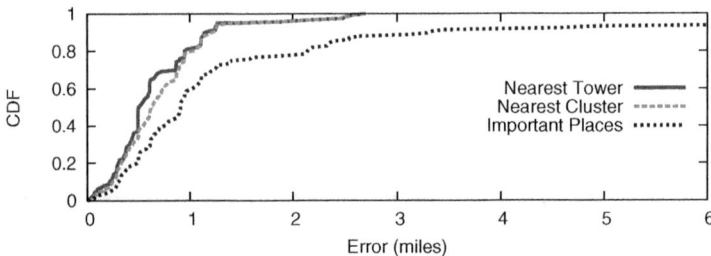

Fig. 3. CDF of errors between true important locations and those found using three techniques. Important Places refers to the clusters identified as important by our algorithm. Nearest Cluster shows the best possible outcome with clustering performed. Nearest Tower demonstrates the best that can be done without clustering.

3.4 Important Places in Los Angeles and New York

In this section, we use our full CDR data set to compare the number of important places of Angelenos and New Yorkers, as identified by our *Important Places* algorithm.

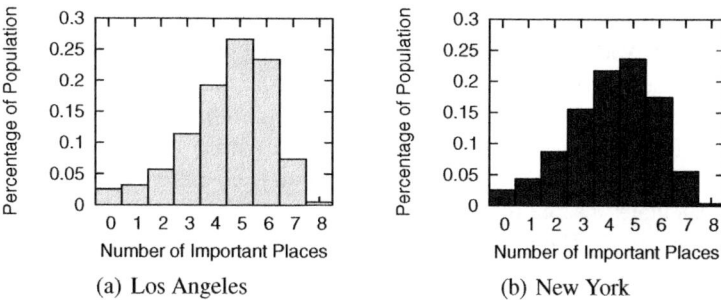

Fig. 4. Histogram of the number of important places of people in Los Angeles and New York

Without user-provided surveys, we do not know the actual number of important places of people in the LA and NY dataset, but our results allow us to roughly compare the behavior of people in the two areas. Figure 4 plots the histograms of the number of important places for the two populations. We draw three conclusions from our results. First, our algorithm succeeds in finding important locations for 97.5% of the user population, which is a very high percentage. For the remaining 2.5%, our algorithm cannot find any important places, mostly due to people not using their cell phones frequently enough for our algorithm to work. Second, about a quarter of people in both areas have exactly 5 important places and more than three quarters of people have between 3 to 6 important places. This is similar to results found in other work [2,9]. Third, New Yorkers have a higher percentage of people with 1 to 4 important places, whereas Angelenos have a higher percentage of people with 5 to 8 places. Overall, the implications are that although typical cellphone users have dozens or hundreds of towers contacted in a multi-month event trace, their main locus of mobility is concentrated on a much smaller set of places.

4 Identifying Home and Work

In this section, we move beyond identifying generally important places in people's lives, to inferring where people live and work. The knowledge of where people live and work can be used for a detailed analysis of mobility prediction models, workday patterns, commuter carbon footprints, and a variety of context-aware applications, such as location-based reminders [20].

We developed algorithms that compute estimates of where a cellphone user lives and works, given a list of important clusters identified in Section 3.2. We call these estimated locations *Home* and *Work*, respectively. Of course, not everyone will have distinct home and work locations: some people work at home, others have no fixed work site, and still others may not use their cell phones at home and/or work. Nevertheless, our validation work confirms that our algorithms produce good approximations of the true home and work locations of volunteers.

4.1 Home and Work Algorithms

Our Home and Work algorithms select, among all important clusters identified by the Important Places algorithm described in Section 3.2, the clusters that correspond to where a person lives and works, respectively. The algorithms are independent and may end up selecting the same cluster as both Home and Work.

To select Home or Work, the relevant algorithm (i.e., either the Home or Work algorithm) calculates a score for each important cluster using coefficients obtained from a logistic regression. The algorithm then assigns the cluster with the highest score to be Home or Work. To calculate a score for a cluster, we use the logistic regression formula shown in Equation 1. In this case, $Prob(x_1, ..., x_n)$ is the score calculated for each cluster, x_i is the value of the ith factor and β_js are regression coefficients fitted during training. To train our regression formulae, we repeated the procedure described in Section 3.2 using the reported home and work locations of the 18 training volunteers. Home and Work, then, are chosen as the clusters with the highest probability as computed by the coefficients given by the logistic regression.

Recall that in this study we define "home" hours to be weekends and weekdays between 7PM and 7AM, whereas "work" hours are weekdays between 1pm and 5pm. For the Home algorithm, the single most dominating factor was the *Home Hour Events*. That is, the cluster with the largest number of events during the "home" hours is selected as Home. For the Work algorithm, there are two dominating factors. The first factor is the rank of the *Work Hour Events*. In other words, after ranking all clusters based on the number of events occurring during "work" hours, a cluster with a higher ranking is assigned a higher score than a cluster with a lower ranking. The second factor is the percentage of the *Home Hour Events*. Recall that this percentage is calculated as the number of events occurring during "home" hours in the cluster, divided by the total number of events occurring during "home" hours in all clusters. A cluster is assigned a higher score by the Work algorithm if the percentage of the *Home Hour Events* in the cluster is low.

4.2 Validation of Home and Work Algorithms

Table 2 shows the 25th, 50th, 75th and 95th percentile errors between the Home and Work locations as estimated by our Home and Work algorithms and the actual home and work locations as reported by our 19 testing volunteers. Both algorithms perform well, achieving *median* errors of 0.9 miles and 0.83 miles, respectively. We also calculated the distance between the actual home and work locations and the nearest cell tower, finding them to be 0.61 miles (home) and 0.5 miles (work). Moving out to the 95th percentile, the Home algorithm continued to work well, with 3.86 miles of error, whereas

Table 2. Errors in miles from true home and work locations to those found using our Home and Work algorithms

Percentile	25th	50th	75th	95th
Home Error	0.53	0.90	1.28	3.86
Work Error	0.62	0.83	2.30	21.23

the "best-case" algorithm that chooses the cell tower nearest to the user-provided latitude/longitude has 1.12 miles of error. At the 95th percentile error, the Work algorithm's error increases to 21.2 miles, and studying these few cases in more detail revealed that the errors were due to our volunteers not using their cell phone much at work. Given that the majority of our volunteers did use their cell phones at work and given the increasing trend of dropping landlines at both home and work locations, we believe that our Home and Work algorithms are an increasingly useful tool for estimating home and work locations for the general population at large.

5   Example Applications: Commute Distances and Carbon Footprints

In this section, we show how we can apply our algorithms to larger-scale data analysis and policy planning. In one example, we compute home-to-work commute distances for populations of cell phone users aggregated by ZIP code. In another example, we combine cellular network data with US Census data to estimate the commuting carbon footprints of the same populations.

5.1   Calculating Commute Distances

We define *commute distance* as the geographic distance between a person's home and work locations. Our *HomeWork* algorithm estimates commute distance by calculating the distance between the two locations identified by the Home and Work algorithms described in Section 4.1. Here we evaluate our HomeWork algorithm by comparing its results to those of three other approaches for estimating commute distance: Oracle, TopTwo, and TimeBased.

The Oracle algorithm, given a set of important-location clusters identified by the Important Locations algorithm described in Section 3.2, estimates a volunteer's commute distance as the distance between the two clusters closest to the true home and work locations reported by that volunteer. The Oracle algorithm represents an upper bound on the accuracy of the HomeWork algorithm and is not realizable. We include the remaining two algorithms, TopTwo and TimeBased, to show HomeWork's accuracy relative to simpler algorithms. TopTwo estimates commute distance as the distance between the two important locations with the largest number of network events. The TimeBased algorithm estimates where a person lives as the cluster with the largest number of events on weekends and weekdays between 7PM and 7AM, and it estimates where a person works as the cluster with the largest number of events on weekdays between 1PM and 5PM. To estimate commute distance, TimeBased then calculates the distance between these home and work clusters.

Figure 5 plots the CDF of the commute distance error in miles for the Oracle, HomeWork, TopTwo and TimeBased algorithms. The HomeWork algorithm performs very well, estimating the commute distance within 3 miles for 82% of the volunteers. HomeWork not only significantly outperforms both the TopTwo and TimeBased algorithms, which achieve 19.9 miles and 14.2 miles for 82%, respectively, but also is close to Oracle, which achieves 1.23 miles error. The median errors for Oracle, HomeWork, TopTwo and TimeBased are 0.67, 1.16, 2.10 and 1.24 miles, respectively.

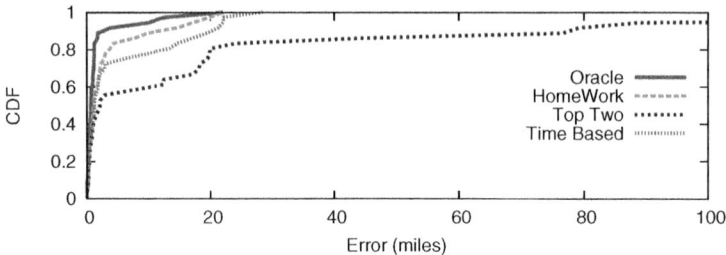

Fig. 5. Error in commute distance for volunteers. The plot is cut at 100 miles for clarity, but the extreme errors for TopTwo extends beyond 200 miles.

5.2   Commute Distances in Los Angeles and New York

As an additional check on our work, we compare commute distances as calculated by our HomeWork algorithm to those derived from US Census statistics. In particular, HomeWork estimates the average commute distance for residents of the 891 ZIP codes in our CDR dataset to be 21 and 20 miles for the Los Angeles and New York areas, respectively. Using tables of where people live and work published by the US Bureau of Transportation Statistics [4], we calculate the average commute for residents of the same ZIP codes to be 21 and 19 miles for the Los Angeles and New York areas, respectively. This very close match between HomeWork and census results further validates our approach. It is also important to note that the low cost of our approach makes it practical to regenerate current statistics much more frequently than with a census, for example every few months instead of every ten years.

We now summarize our commute-distance results with the help of boxplots. Boxplots depict five-number summaries of the complete empirical distributions of interest. The "box" represents the 25th, 50th, and 75th percentiles, while the "whiskers" indicate the 5th and 95th percentiles. The horizontal axes show miles on a logarithmic scale. Nearly any difference between our medians is statistically significant due to our large sample sizes.

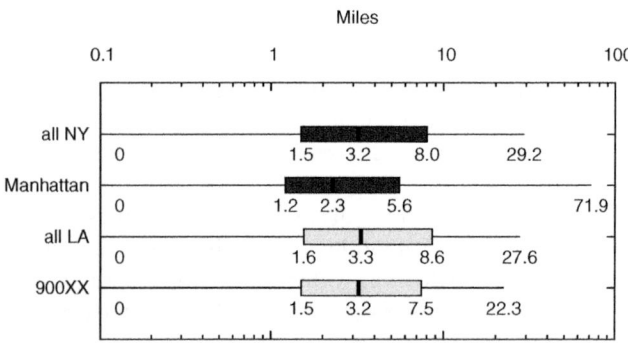

Fig. 6. Box plots of commute distances for Los Angeles and New York

Figure 6 plots the daily commute distances for Angelenos and New Yorkers. For the greater NY and LA regions, the commute distances are similar, with the median commutes at 3.2 and 3.3 miles, respectively. We also looked in detail at the data from city centers, namely Manhattan (ZIP codes 100xx) and downtown LA (ZIP codes 900xx). We make two observations from the data. First, although the commute distances of city center residents are shorter than that of the general population in both areas, the Manhattanites have a significantly shorter median commute distance compared to all NY (28% smaller) than residents of downtown LA compared to all LA (3% smaller). This is likely because the Los Angeles area is more evenly spread out than NY area. As a result, people who live in the downtown LA commute farther more often than residents of Manhattan. Second, although the median commute distance of Manhattanites is shorter than that of downtown LA residents, 2.3 miles in Manhattan vs. 3.2 miles in downtown LA, the 95th percentile commute distance of Manhattanites is 222% larger at 71.9 miles. These numbers show that when Manhattanites commute far, they commute much farther than Angelenos. Such long commutes may be due in part to the extensive commuter rail network radiating from Manhattan, which may make such long commutes more feasible.

5.3   Carbon Footprint Estimation

Our final example application makes the extension from commute estimates to carbon footprints. To accurately calculate the carbon footprint of a person's commute, we need to know the length of the commute and the mode of transportation the person uses. Although we can estimate the commute distance of a person using the HomeWork algorithm, the sparsity of our data does not allow us to determine a commuter's mode of transportation. Instead, we determine the mode of transportation of commuters at the ZIP code level using US census data. Specifically, we used Table P30 from the 2000 US census (Summary File 3): "Means of Transportation to Work for Workers 16+ Years." [22] to calculate the percentage of commuters that uses a particular mode of transportation per ZIP code.

The next step is to assign each commuter a mode of transportation that fits her commute pattern best. The intuition behind our approach is that walkers and bikers in each ZIP code are likely to be the people with the shortest commutes. To assign a mode of transportation to each commuter, we first sort the users in each ZIP code according to the length of their commute. If the census reports that P% of commuters in the ZIP code walk or bike to work, then the lowest P% of ranked users in that ZIP code are treated as walkers/bikers with zero carbon emissions. The remaining commuters are assigned the average of the remaining modes of transportation in that ZIP code. For example, assume that we have two commuters in a ZIP code with 50% walkers, 25% drivers, and 25% train passengers. In this example, the commuter with the shorter commute distance is assigned to be a walker and the other user is assigned as driving half the time and taking a train the other half.

Finally, combining this information with the amount of carbon dioxide emitted per person by each mode of transportation [3] allows us to compute the rough amount of carbon dioxide emitted per commuter. Aggregating commuters at the ZIP code level

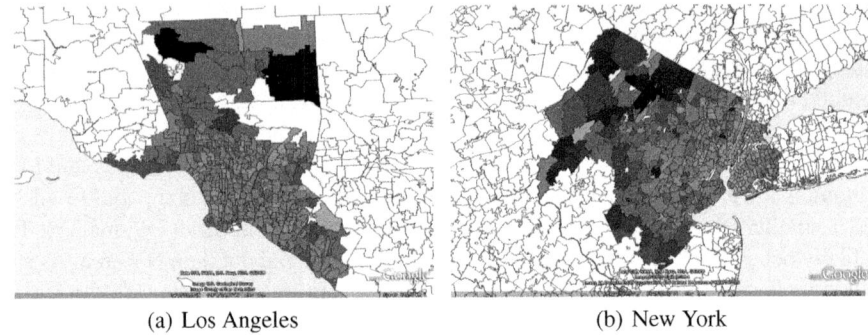

(a) Los Angeles   (b) New York

Fig. 7. Heat maps of median carbon emitted per person for each direction of a commute in the ZIP codes in our study. Darker ZIP codes denote larger carbon footprint. Note that all NY and LA ZIP codes are colored according to the same scale.

allows us to generate a distribution of carbon dioxide emissions per commuter in each ZIP code.

Figure 7 shows heat maps of LA and NY, where shading corresponds to the median carbon emission per person in each ZIP code in each direction of a commute. In the New York area, increasing distance from Manhattan correlates with increasing carbon footprint. In contrast, Los Angeles is fairly uniform throughout, with the exception of certain parts of Antelope Valley (in the northeast part of the map), which are separated from downtown LA by a mountain range that must be driven around. These patterns match well with what would be expected from both cities. Popular knowledge indicates that in New York, many people commute into the city center, while in Los Angeles, there is no specific region where people live or work. Manhattan ZIP codes have the lowest carbon footprints of all ZIP codes studied. Specifically, a median amount of carbon dioxide emitted per person is 0.5 kg per trip in Manhattan, 1.07 kg per trip in downtown LA, and 3.7 kg per trip in Antelope Valley.

Generating carbon footprint estimates is a good example of how our technique for computing commuting distances can be combined with already available data to produce new and previously difficult to obtain information.

6   Related Work

There are two broad categories of work closely related to ours. One, there is a body of work that seeks to determine people's important locations based on GPS traces or WiFi beacons. Two, there have been a number of efforts to use cellular network data to find patterns of human mobility. We next survey these two categories of work and contrast them with our own.

Recently, Hightower et al. [11] and then Kim et al. [14] presented algorithms for determining semantically meaningful places based on continuous tracking of GSM and WiFi beacons. Kang et al. [13] explored how clustering locations obtained through WiFi beacons can be used for identifying places people visit. Previous work [1,16,17,18] has also explored how semantically meaningful places can be discovered based on series of GPS coordinates. Similarly, Mun et al. [19] estimate the environmental impact of individual travel using GPS traces. Although accurate, these efforts require much finer granularity of data than is available from Call Detail Records. In contrast, we operate on a much larger data set composed of relatively sparse and coarse location samples, which requires a different approach to determining important places in people's lives. In addition, these other approaches collect data using software running on users' devices, which consumes power on those devices and may inhibit large-scale data collection. In contrast, our data is collected by the network for all devices, and does not consume any power on those devices beyond what is consumed by normal use.

There is also a growing body of work attempting to discover patterns of human mobility from cellular network data. González et al. [9] used cellphone records from an unnamed European country to create models of people's movement patterns. Our own recent work [12] characterized the daily range of movement of people in two cities in the United States. Other work has developed algorithms for predicting where a user will travel next [2,5,15]. In contrast to the work presented in this paper, that earlier body of work did not seek to attribute importance to any particular location.

Previous attempts to measure the predictability of cell phone users restrict their datasets to highly active users [21] or force phones to provide more frequent location updates than would normally occur [23]. We demonstrate in our work that these steps are not necessary. We show that we are able to accurately determine important locations across a wide range of usage modes, from highly connected individuals to users that make only a few calls a week.

Finally, Girardin et al. used cell phone usage within cities to determine locations of users in Rome [6], New York City [8], and Florence [7]. They were able to find where people clustered in these cities and the major paths people tended to take. In a sense, they explored the converse of our question. While we ask "to how many locations does this person travel?", they ask "how many people travel to this location?". Furthermore, their work is restricted to a view of a single city, while our work captures travel over a whole country for the subjects in our dataset.

7 Conclusions

This paper has described our work to identify important personal places and movement patterns based on cellular network data. As the central focus of our research, we have proposed and evaluated three algorithms derived from a logistic regression-based analysis of volunteers. The first of these algorithms identifies *Important Places* based on call and text message records. The other two, *Home* and *Work*, narrow down these important places to identify the most likely home and work locations, allowing for the case when they may be one and the same. We validated our algorithms by comparing our results to ground truth from volunteers and to US census data.

Estimating and modeling human mobility is important for many technical and policy reasons. Previously, however, significant challenges have lain in gathering large-scale, comprehensive, and accurate data on which to base such estimates and models. Our work demonstrates that call and text records from cellular networks represent an unobtrusive and accurate way to gather large-scale mobility data. Furthermore, the large degree of aggregation and anonymization allows us to usefully employ this data without unduly impinging on the privacy of any individual.

Viewed broadly, our clustering and location algorithms form a foundation for a range of accurate, low-overhead analyses of human movement and social patterns. As specific examples, this paper demonstrates how we can use home and work identification to perform analyses of commute distances and estimates of commuting carbon footprints. We demonstrate that we can find users' important locations to within 3 miles 88% of the time. We further estimate commute distances within 3 miles of ground truth 82% of the time. In fact, our commute distance estimation errors are quite close to that of an oracle technique, with a median difference from the oracle of only 0.5 miles. Our work is the first to show accurate home and work location estimates and apply them to find carbon emissions from traces that include not just heavy daily cellular phone users, but a nearly universal sample of the user population.

Acknowledgments

We thank our shepherd, John Krumm, and the anonymous reviewers for their feedback. Parts of this work were supported by the National Science Foundation under Grant Nos. CNS- 0614949, CNS-0627650, and CNS-0916246. Parts of this work were also supported by a Princeton Engineering fund for Technology for Developing Regions, a research gift from Intel Corporation, and a research internship from AT&T Labs.

References

1. Ashbrook, D., Starner, T.: Using GPS to learn significant locations and predict movement across multiple users. Personal and Ubiquitous Computing 7 (2003)
2. Bayir, M.A., Demirbas, M., Eagle, N.: Discovering spatiotemporal mobility profiles of cell-phone users. In: World of Wireless, Mobile and Multimedia Networks and Workshops (2009)
3. Bradley, M.J., and Associates: Comparison of energy use & CO_2 emissions from different transportation modes. Report to American Bus Association (2007)
4. US Bureau of Transportation Statistics, http://www.transtats.bts.gov
5. Dufková, K., Le Boudec, J.-Y., Kencl, L., Bjelica, M.: Predicting user-cell association in cellular networks from tracked data. In: Fuller, R., Koutsoukos, X.D. (eds.) MELT 2009. LNCS, vol. 5801, pp. 19–33. Springer, Heidelberg (2009)
6. Girardin, F., Calabrese, F., Dal Fiorre, F., Biderman, A., Ratti, C., Blat, J.: Uncovering the presence and movements of tourists from user-generated content. In: Intn'l Forum on Tourism Statistics (2008)
7. Girardin, F., Dal Fiore, F., Blat, J., Ratti, C.: Understanding of tourist dynamics from explicitly disclosed location information. In: Symposium on LBS and Telecartography (2007)
8. Girardin, F., Vaccari, A., Gerber, A., Biderman, A., Ratti, C.: Towards estimating the presence of visitors from the aggragate mobile phone network activity they generate. In: Intl. Conference on Computers in Urban Planning and Urban Management (2009)
9. González, M.C., Hidalgo, C.A., Barabási, A.-L.: Understanding individual human mobility patterns. Nature 453 (2008)
10. Hartigan, J.A.: Clustering Algorithms. John Wiley & Sons, New York (1975)
11. Hightower, J., Consolvo, S., LaMarca, A., Smith, I., Hughes, J.: Learning and recognizing the places we go. In: Intl. Conference on Ubiquitous Computing (2005)

12. Isaacman, S., Becker, R., Cáceres, R., Kobourov, S., Rowland, J., Vasharsvky, A.: A tale of two cities. In: Workshop on Mobile Computing Systems and Applications (HotMobile) (2010)
13. Kang, J., Welbourne, W., Stewart, B., Borriello, G.: Extracting places from traces of locations. In: Workshop on Wireless Mobile Applications and Services on WLAN Hotspots (2004)
14. Kim, D., Hightower, J., Govindan, R., Estrin, D.: Discovering semantically meaningful places from pervasive RF-beacons. In: Intl. Conference on Ubiquitous Computing (2009)
15. Laasonen, K.: Mining Cell Transition Data. PhD thesis, University of Helsinki, Finland (2009)
16. Li, Q., Zheng, Y., Xie, X., Chen, Y., Liu, W., Ma, W.-Y.: Mining user similarity based on location history. In: Intl. Conference on Advances in Geographic Information Systems (2008)
17. Liao, L., Fox, D., Kautz, H.: Extracting places and activities from GPS traces using hierarchical conditional random fields. Intl. Journal of Robotics Research 26
18. Marmasse, N., Schmandt, C.: Location-aware information delivery with comMotion. In: Intl. Symposium on Handheld and Ubiquitous Computing (2000)
19. Mun, M., Reddy, S., Shilton, K., Yau, N., Burke, J., Estrin, D., Hansen, M., Howard, E., West, R., Boda, P.: PEIR, the personal environmental impact report, as a platform for participatory sensing systems research. In: Intl. Conference on Mobile Systems, Applications and Services (2009)
20. Sohn, T., Li, K., Lee, G., Smith, I., Scott, J., Griswold, W.G.: Place-Its: A study of location-based reminders on mobile phones. In: Intl. Conference on Ubiquitous Computing (2005)
21. Song, C., Qu, Z., Blumm, N., Barabási, A.-L.: Limits of predictability in human mobility. Science 327 (2010)
22. US Census Data, http://www.census.gov
23. Zang, H., Bolot, J.C.: Mining call and mobility data to improve paging efficiency in cellular networks. In: Intl. Conference on Mobile Computing and Networking (2007)

NextPlace: A Spatio-temporal Prediction Framework for Pervasive Systems

Salvatore Scellato[1], Mirco Musolesi[2], Cecilia Mascolo[1],
Vito Latora[3], and Andrew T. Campbell[4]

[1] Computer Laboratory, University of Cambridge, UK
[2] School of Computer Science, University of St. Andrews, UK
[3] Dipartimento di Fisica, University of Catania, Italy
[4] Department of Computer Science, Dartmouth College, USA

Abstract. Accurate and fine-grained prediction of future user location and geographical profile has interesting and promising applications including targeted content service, advertisement dissemination for mobile users, and recreational social networking tools for smart-phones. Existing techniques based on linear and probabilistic models are not able to provide accurate prediction of the location patterns from a spatio-temporal perspective, especially for long-term estimation. More specifically, they are able to only forecast the next location of a user, but not his/her *arrival time* and *residence time*, i.e., the interval of time spent in that location. Moreover, these techniques are often based on prediction models that are not able to extend predictions further in the future.

In this paper we present NextPlace, a novel approach to location prediction based on nonlinear time series analysis of the arrival and residence times of users in relevant places. NextPlace focuses on the predictability of single users when they visit their most important places, rather than on the transitions between different locations. We report about our evaluation using four different datasets and we compare our forecasting results to those obtained by means of the prediction techniques proposed in the literature. We show how we achieve higher performance compared to other predictors and also more stability over time, with an overall prediction precision of up to 90% and a performance increment of at least 50% with respect to the state of the art.

1 Introduction

The ability to predict future locations of people allows for a rich set of novel pervasive applications and systems: accurate content dissemination of location related information such as advertisement, leisure events reports and notifications [20, 1] could be implemented in a more effective way, avoiding the delivery of information to uninterested users, and, therefore providing, a better user experience. For example, by exploiting the availability of future location information, Web search engines such as Google, Bing or Yahoo! and location-based social network services such as Facebook Places and Foursquare may provide "location-aware" sponsored advertisements together with search results that are relevant to the predicted user movement patterns.

K. Lyons, J. Hightower, and E.M. Huang (Eds.): Pervasive 2011, LNCS 6696, pp. 152–169, 2011.
© Springer-Verlag Berlin Heidelberg 2011

The increasing popularity of smart-phones equipped with GPS sensors makes location-aware computing a reality. Even in the case of devices where this information is not currently available, location can be roughly estimated by means of triangulation and cell estimation techniques or by profiling places through the analysis of the MAC addresses advertised by nearby devices and 802.11 access points [17]. In addition, these devices are increasingly always connected to the Internet, at least in areas where GPRS/EDGE or WiFi connectivity is present. Therefore, information about the current positions of users can be transmitted to a back-end server, where analysis of the data can be performed at run-time in order to predict future location patterns.

In this paper we propose NextPlace, a new prediction framework based on *nonlinear* time series analysis [12] for forecasting user behavior in different locations from a *spatio-temporal* point of view. NextPlace focuses on the temporal predictability of users presence when they visit their most important places. We do not focus on the transitions between different locations: instead, we focus on the estimation of the duration of a visit to a certain location and of the intervals between two subsequent visits. The existing techniques are able to forecast the next location of a user, but *not* his/her *arrival* and *residence time*, i.e., the interval of time spent in that location. Moreover, these techniques are often based on prediction models that are not able to extend predictions further in the future, since they mainly focus on the next movement of a user [19, 26, 23, 14, 2, 16].

We focus instead on patterns of residence in the set of locations that are more frequently visited by users. We show that, at least in the datasets under analysis, human presence in important places is characterized by a behavior that, even if at first glance seems apparently random, can be effectively captured by nonlinear models. Predictions are based on the collection of movement data that can be of different types: sets of GPS coordinates, registration patterns to access points or also information about presence in locations by means of passive and active transponders (such as badges). In addition, check-ins performed in location-based social networking services can be exploited to acquire movement data.

The proposed prediction technique consists of two steps. Firstly, we need to identify significant locations among which users move more frequently. Secondly, we apply a model able to predict user presence within these locations and relative residence time by means of techniques drawn from nonlinear time series analysis [12]. More specifically, the contribution of this paper can be summarized as follows:

- We describe NextPlace, a novel approach to user location prediction based on nonlinear time series analysis of visits that users pay to their most significant locations. NextPlace estimates the time of the future visits and expected residence time in those locations.
- We analyze four datasets of human movements: two GPS-based (representing respectively the positions of the users involved in the deployment of the CenceMe application at Dartmouth College [21] and the locations of cabs in San Francisco [24]) and two containing registration patterns of WiFi access points (at Dartmouth College [15] and within the Ile Sans Fils wireless network in Montreal, Canada [18]). We identify regularity and, more specifically, some previously uncaptured degree of determinism in patterns of user visits to their significant places by means of nonlinear analysis.

– We evaluate NextPlace comparing it with a probabilistic technique based on spatio-temporal Markov predictors [26] and with a linear model [6]. We report an overall prediction precision over the four datasets of up to 90%, with precision of up to 65% even after a number of hours, and a performance increment of at least 50% over Markov-based predictors. We show how the adoption of a nonlinear prediction framework can improve forecasting precision with respect to other techniques even for long-term predictions.

The rest of this paper is organized as follows: Section 2 describes NextPlace and its novel approach to prediction based on nonlinear time series analysis as well as illustrates the techniques we use for the extraction of significant places. Section 3 presents the implementation issues and the validation of our approach using real-world measurements, also reporting the results of the evaluation of our method against other predictors. Section 4 discusses related work and Section 5 concludes the paper illustrating potential future work.

2   Predicting Spatio-temporal Properties of Mobile Users

Any prediction of future user behavior is based on the assumption of determinism. From a practical point of view, determinism simply means that future events are determined by past events, so that every time a particular configuration or situation is observed, the same (or a similar) outcome will follow. Since in human societies daily and weekly routines are well-established, human activities are characterized by a certain degree of regularity and predictability [8].

The intuition behind NextPlace is that the sequence of important locations that an individual visits every day is more or less fixed, with only minor variations that are also usually deterministically defined. As an example, if a woman periodically goes to the gym on Mondays and Thursdays, she may change her routine for those days, but the changed routine will be more or less the same over different weeks. Therefore, the sequence of events may still be predictable.

From a formal point of view, let us consider a certain number of mobile users, where user i freely moves among different locations. For the moment, we do not explicitly focus on how these locations can be identified, and only assume that the start time and the duration of each visit of a user to a given location can be determined. A visit of a user is simply defined by the tuple (u, l, t, d), where t and d are respectively the time of arrival and the residence time of user u in location l. It is worth noting that this approach does not model movements but, rather, residence time in some locations, hence, it can also be adopted in systems without any spatial or geographical information about locations, i.e., access points in 802.11 WLANs.

We now introduce the two steps of NextPlace and the basic theory behind them. We first describe how we isolate the user's significant places, exploiting the technique proposed by Kim et al. in [14]. Then, we describe our novel method for the estimation of future times of arrival and residence times in the different significant places and how we exploit this prediction to compute accurate estimation of where the user will be after a given time interval. Finally, we describe the mathematical details of the prediction techniques behind our approach.

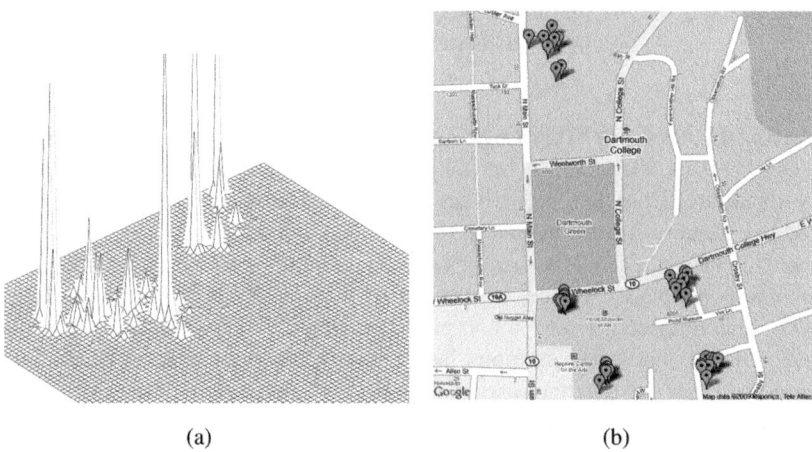

(a)   (b)

Fig. 1. Example of frequency map using GPS traces. Higher peaks in (a) reveal places where user spent most of their time and which represent its significant locations: in (b) we show some visits to these significant places reported on a geographical map.

2.1 Significant Places Extraction

In this section we present two methods we use to extract significant locations from both GPS information and WiFi association logs, the two most commonly available sources of data about user movements.

Extracting Places from GPS Data. Many solutions for the extraction of significant places from GPS measurements have been presented in the literature [11, 28, 2]. We choose one that is based on the residence time of a user to quantify the importance of a place for him/her: the intuition being that permanence at a place is directly proportional to the importance that is attributed to it by the user.

As proposed in [14], we apply a 2-D Gaussian distribution weighted by the residence time at each GPS point. This means that at each point the Gaussian distribution uniformly contributes also to nearby points, smoothing out values that are close together. The value of the variance for the Gaussian distributions that we choose is $\sigma = 10$ meters, which is related to the average GPS accuracy[1]. The resulting *frequency map* contains peaks which give information about the position of popular locations: we consider regions that are above a certain threshold T as significant places. The threshold T can be chosen as a fraction of the maximum value of the frequency map. We will show the application of this technique and how the value of the threshold T can be selected using two GPS-based datasets in Section 3.

In Figure 1(a) a close-up of a frequency map is shown: when a threshold is applied to the map, only higher peaks are selected and each peak generates an area defined

---

[1] http://www.gps.gov/

by a continuous boundary. All GPS points within that area result in visits to the same significant place. As an example, if we choose a threshold equal to 15% of the highest peak of the map, we obtain the visits to significant places shown over the area map in Figure 1(b).

Extracting Places from WiFi Logs. Alternatively, we can derive significant places from user registrations to 802.11 access points. Since these access points are fixed and easily identifiable from their globally unique MAC address, this information can be exploited to extract visit patterns to a set of locations in a straightforward manner. From this point of view, the most frequently seen access points are natural candidates to represent significant places. Hence, we can define as popular places for a user the access points he/she connects to more often, providing that a sufficient number of visits has been recorded to a given access point. More specifically, we define an access point as a significant place for a certain user if this user has a sequence of at least n visits to the access point, in order to filter out all the access points that are seldom visited and to have a sufficient number of observations from a statistical point of view. For the analysis presented in this paper, we select n equal to 20.

2.2 Predicting User Behavior

We now describe NextPlace's location prediction algorithm: in order to obtain an estimation of the future behavior, the history of visits of a user to each of its significant locations is considered. Then, for each location we try to predict when the next visits will take place and for how long they will last. After this estimation, the predictions obtained for different locations is analyzed, in order to produce a unique prediction of where the user will be at a given future instant of time. A theoretical foundation of this technique is described in Section 2.3.

For each user we keep track of all previous visits to a set of locations, that is, for each visit we consider the instant when it started and how long it lasted. The algorithm predicts the next visits to a given location by means of the previous history of visits $((t_1, d_1), (t_2, d_2), \ldots, (t_n, d_n))$:

1. two time series are created from the sequence of previous visits: the time series of the visit daily start times C and the time series of the visit durations D defined as follows:

$$C = (c_1, c_2, \ldots, c_n)$$
$$D = (d_1, d_2, \ldots, d_n)$$

   where c_i is the time of the day in seconds corresponding to the time instant t_i (i.e., c_i is in the range $[0, 86400]$);
2. we search in the time series C sequences of m consecutive values $(c_{i-m+1}, \ldots, c_i)$ that are closely similar to the last m values $(c_{n-m+1}, \ldots, c_n)^2$;
3. the next value of time series C is estimated by averaging all the values c_{i+1} that follow each found sequence;

---

[2] We will discuss the choice of parameter m in the next section.

4. at the same time, in time series D the corresponding sequences $(d_{i-m+1}, \ldots, d_i)$ are selected; the sequences have to be located exactly at the same indexes as those in C;
5. the next value of time series D is then estimated by averaging all the values d_{i+1} that follow these sequences.

As an example, if the last three visits of a certain user to a location are Monday at 6:30pm, Monday at 10:00pm and Tuesday at 8:15am, we analyze the history of visits in order to find sequences that are numerically close to (6:30pm, 10:00pm, 8:15am), i.e. (6:10pm, 9:50pm, 8:35am) and (6:35pm, 10:10pm, 8:00am): then, assuming that the next visits that follow these subsequences start at 1:10pm and 12:40pm and last for 40 and 30 minutes respectively, we estimate the next visit at 12:55pm for 35 minutes, averaging both arrival times and duration times.

The main idea behind this algorithm is the assumption that human behavior is strongly determined by daily patterns: the sequence of visit start times is therefore mapped to a 24-hour time interval, focusing only on the start time of each visit. The choice of the value m has an impact on the accuracy of the prediction: in fact, this can be improved by taking into account more visits in order to identify particular patterns that may be present only in certain intervals of time such as specific days.

We can generalize this algorithm to predict not only the next visit to a location, but also successive visits in the future: in fact, we can choose to average together not only the next values of each subsequences but also values that are 2 or more steps ahead. However, the prediction of time series can become inaccurate when adopted to calculate further values in the future [12].

Since we can predict when the future visits to all significant locations will start and for how long they will last, we can design a simple method to predict the location where the user will be at a given time in the future. Let us suppose that at time T we want to predict in which significant location user i will be after ΔT seconds. Then, the following steps are performed:

1. for each location the sequence of the next k visits (starting with $k = 1$) are predicted and a global sequence of all predicted visits $(loc_1, t_1, d_1), \ldots, (loc_n, t_n, d_n)$ is created, with $t_1 \leq \cdots \leq t_n$;
2. if there is a prediction (loc_i, t_i, d_i) which satisfies $t_i \leq T + \Delta T \leq t_i + d_i$, then loc_i is returned as predicted location (in case several predictions exist which satisfy the predicate, we choose at random between them);
3. if no prediction satisfies the condition stated above, there are two cases: if the minimum start time t_1 of the current predicted visits is smaller than $T + \Delta T$, then prediction needs to be extended further in the future in order to find a suitable visit, thus the parameter k is doubled and the algorithm is repeated considering new predicted visits. Otherwise, extending the prediction provides visits which start after $T + \Delta T$ and which cannot be exploited for prediction: thus, the algorithm terminates returning that the user will not be in any significant location.

Note that it is realistic for a user to be predicted as being outside the set of significant places (e.g., maybe transitioning from one to another) and that our technique is also able to predict this state.

2.3   Nonlinear Prediction Framework: Key Concepts and Practical Implementation Issues

In this section we provide a brief overview of the key concepts at the basis of the forecasting framework and we discuss the practical issues in implementing it.

In this work we adopt a prediction technique inspired by *nonlinear time series analysis* [12]. A time series can be seen as a collection of scalar observations of a given system made sequentially in time and spaced at uniform time intervals, albeit this last assumption can be relaxed to allow any kind of temporal measurement pattern [6].

While the scalar sequence of values contained in a time series may appear completely unrelated to the underlying system, it is possible to uncover the characteristics of its dynamic evolution by analyzing sub-sequences of the time series itself. In order to investigate the structure of the original system, the time series values must be transformed in a sequence of vectors with a technique called *delay embedding*.

More formally, a time series $(s_0, s_1, \ldots, s_N)$ can be embedded in a m-dimensional space by defining an appropriate delay ν and then creating a *delay vector reconstruction* for the time series value s_n as follows:

$$\beta_n = [s_{n-(m-1)\nu}, s_{n-(m-2)\nu}, \ldots, s_{n-\nu}, s_n]$$

where all vectors β_n have m components and are defined in a so called *embedding space*. Note that m is the parameter used in the algorithm described in Section 2.2.

The values of the parameters m and ν greatly affect the accuracy of the representation. Nonetheless, a fundamental mathematical result (the so-called *embedding theorem* [12]) ensures that a suitable value for m does exist and is related to the complexity of the underlying system. At the same time, ν might be chosen to represent a suitable time scale of the phenomenon, since consecutive values in the time series should not be too strongly correlated to each other.

An effective predictive model can be generated directly from time series data through the delay embedding. Let us suppose that a prediction for the value $s_{N+\Delta n}$, a time Δn ahead of N, must be made for the time series $(s_0, s_1, \ldots, s_N)$. The steps of the prediction process are as follows:

1. The time series is embedded in a m-dimensional space by defining an appropriate time delay ν and then creating the related embedding space;
2. The embedding space is searched for all the vectors that are close, with respect to some given metric distance, to vector β_N: more formally, a neighborhood $U_\epsilon(\beta_N)$ of radius ϵ around the vector β_N is created;
3. Since determinism involves that future events are set causally by past events, and since all vectors $\beta_n \in U_\epsilon(\beta_N)$ describe past events similar to the past events of β_N, the prediction $p_{N+\Delta n}$ is taken as the average of all the values $s_{n+\Delta n}$

$$p_{N+\Delta n} = \frac{1}{|U_\epsilon(\beta_N)|} \sum_{\beta_n \in U_\epsilon(\beta_N)} s_{n+\Delta n}$$

where $|U_\epsilon(\beta_N)|$ denotes the number of elements of the neighborhood $U_\epsilon(\beta_N)$. The value of ϵ should be chosen in order to obtain a sufficient number of vectors for the prediction.

Intuitively, this algorithm searches the past history to find sequences of values that are very similar to the recent history: assuming that the evolution is ruled by deterministic patterns, a given state will always be followed by the same outcome.

In our implementation we have chosen $\nu = 1$, since we do not have to deal with particular time scales which require to skip some values of our time series. As suggested in [12], the radius ϵ of the vector neighborhood is chosen in order to be 10% of the standard deviation of each time series: this value allows us to obtain enough vectors to perform prediction and, at the same time, filters out vectors that are not close to β_N.

We note that for each prediction all vectors in the embedding space have to be considered and searched. For this reason, it is wise to use an efficient method to find nearest neighbors in the embedding space: the main computational burden is the calculation of the neighborhood $U_\epsilon(\beta_N)$ and the asymptotic complexity $O(N^2)$ can be reduced to $O(N \log N)$ with binary trees or even to $O(N)$ with a box-assisted search algorithm [25], which is the method we implement.

3   Validation of the Prediction Framework Using Real-World Measurements

In this section we introduce the datasets used in our analysis and we describe how we process them in order to extract significant places. Then, we investigate the predictability of the time series extracted from sequences of visits of each user to his/her significant locations, using standard metrics adopted in time series analysis. Finally, we compare NextPlace prediction performance against other prediction methods.

3.1   Datasets

For the evaluation of our approach we choose four different datasets of human movements:

1. **Cabspotting.** This dataset is composed of movement traces of taxi cabs in San Francisco, USA, with GPS coordinates of approximately 500 taxis collected over 30 days in the San Francisco Bay Area. Each vehicle is equipped with a GPS tracking device that is used by dispatchers to efficiently reach customers [24]. The average time interval between two consecutive GPS measurements is less than 60 seconds.
2. **CenceMe GPS.** This dataset was collected during the deployment of CenceMe [21], a system for recreational personal sensing, at Dartmouth College. The GPS data was collected by means of 20 Nokia N95 phones carried by postgraduate students and staff members from the Department of Computer Science and the Department of Biology.
3. **Dartmouth WiFi.** This dataset was extracted from the SNMP logs of the WiFi LAN of the Dartmouth College campus. The compact nature of the campus means that the signal range of interior APs extends to most of the campus outdoor areas. Between 2001 and 2004 data about traffic in the access points was collected through three techniques: syslog events, SNMP polls, and network sniffers [9, 15].

Table 1. Properties of the different datasets: total number of users N, total number of visits V, total number of significant places P, average number of significant places per user p, average number of visits per user v, average residence time in a place D (seconds), total trace length and average proportion of time spent by each user in significant places

Dataset	N	V	P	p	v	D [s]	Trace length	Significant time
Cabspotting	252	150612	6122	24.29	597	231	23 days	7.27%
CenceMe GPS	19	3832	225	11.84	201	696	12 days	14.74%
Dartmouth WiFi	2043	772217	539	17.87	377	2094	60 days	11.24%
Ile Sans Fils	804	142407	173	3.61	177	5296	370 days	0.18%

4. **Ile Sans Fils.** Ile Sans Fils [18] is a non-profit organization which operates a network of free WiFi hotspots in Montreal, Canada. It now counts over 45,000 users with 140 hotspots located in publicly accessible spaces. These hotspots are deployed mostly in cafes, restaurants and bars, libraries, but also outdoor to cover parks and sections of popular commercial streets.

We choose a subset of regularly active users for each original dataset, filtering out all the users that appear only a few times and for which prediction may be worthless. In Table 1 we report some important characteristics and metrics of the resulting datasets.

3.2 Practical Issues

In order to extract significant places for each user in the Cabspotting and CenceMe GPS datasets, which are composed of GPS measurements, we need to choose a suitable threshold T for the frequency map. Thus, we investigate how the average number of significant places per user changes as a function of the threshold itself. As reported in Figure 2(a), the average number of places decreases as the threshold increases: for the Cabspotting dataset a suitable choice is $T = 0.10$, where the curve changes its slope, which denotes the transition from a situation with many unimportant significant areas to a situation with less but probably more important places. However, in the case of the CenceMe GPS dataset such transition does not occur: hence, we investigate how the percentage of time spent in significant locations changes with T, as reported in Figure 2(b): this percentage quickly decreases with T but the steepness of the curve changes at $T = 0.15$. Hence, we choose the value of $T = 0.15$ for this dataset. These values of T result in an average number of about 24 and 12 places per user for the Cabspotting and CenceMe GPS datasets, respectively.

When dealing with GPS measurements, the duration of a visit can be computed as the difference between two consecutive GPS samples. However, the GPS measurement process usually involves a periodic sampling of the location. When the user is located for a long time interval inside the same region, this results in several successive short visits being recorded, whose length depends on the adopted sampling interval. The same problem may occur with WiFi association logs: since WiFi connectivity may be intermittently available and handoff mechanisms are in place in this type of network infrastructure, a long residence time may be split in several shorter sessions.

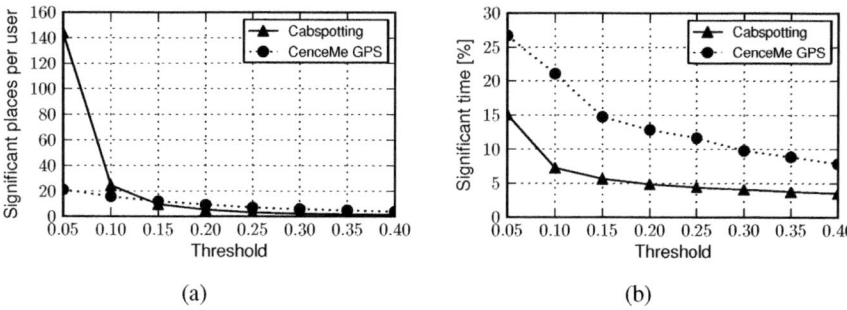

Fig. 2. Average number of significant places per user (a) and percentage of time spent in significant locations (b) as a function of the threshold T of the frequency map for the Cabspotting dataset and the CenceMe GPS dataset

In order to infer a more accurate residence time of the user in a certain region, we apply a merging procedure to the dataset of the sequence of visits. Given a sequence of visits to the same location $(t_1, d_1), (t_2, d_2), \ldots (t_n, d_n)$, if the end time of a visit is close to the start time of the next one, that is if $t_{i+1} - (t_i + d_i) \leq \delta$, we merge them in a new visit starting at t_i and ending at $t_{i+1} + d_{i+1}$. In this way the visits obtained are more likely to mimic the real patterns of presence of users, thus improving prediction. We adopted the value of $\delta = 60$ seconds for the Cabspotting dataset and $\delta = 180$ seconds for the CenceMe GPS dataset, since these are the values of the scanning period for the GPS data acquisition. On the other hand, we apply the same merging procedure to WiFi association logs in the Dartmouth and Ile Sans Fils datasets with a value of $\delta = 300$ seconds, in order to filter out casual disconnections from the access point which may last for few minutes.

From a statistical point of view, these datasets show different characteristics, as reported in Table 1: while Cabspotting, Dartmouth WiFi and Ile Sans Fils contain measurements for hundreds or thousands of users, CenceMe GPS consists of data related to a smaller group of moving users. On average about 12 significant locations have been recorded for each user in the CenceMe GPS dataset. In the Dartmouth WiFi and Cabspotting datasets the number of significant places is 18 and 24, respectively. On the other hand, in the Ile Sans Fils dataset we have less than 4 significant locations per user. This is due to the fact that the Ile Sans Fils dataset contains association logs with access points located in public spaces, thus, a large portion of individuals are seen just in few locations. In fact, public access point are not likely to capture some important places for a given user, such as his/her home and working place. There are also differences in the residence time of users in their significant locations: while for Ile Sans Fils and Dartmouth WiFi the average residence time is about 90 and 30 minutes, in the Cabspotting and CenceMe GPS datasets it is about 5 and 10 minutes.

Finally, the amount of time spent in significant locations is crucial to the investigation of the performance of the location prediction technique. While in the CenceMe GPS and in the Dartmouth WiFi datasets each user spends on average 14.74% and 11.24% of their time in a significant location, this value drops to 7.27% in the Cabspotting dataset

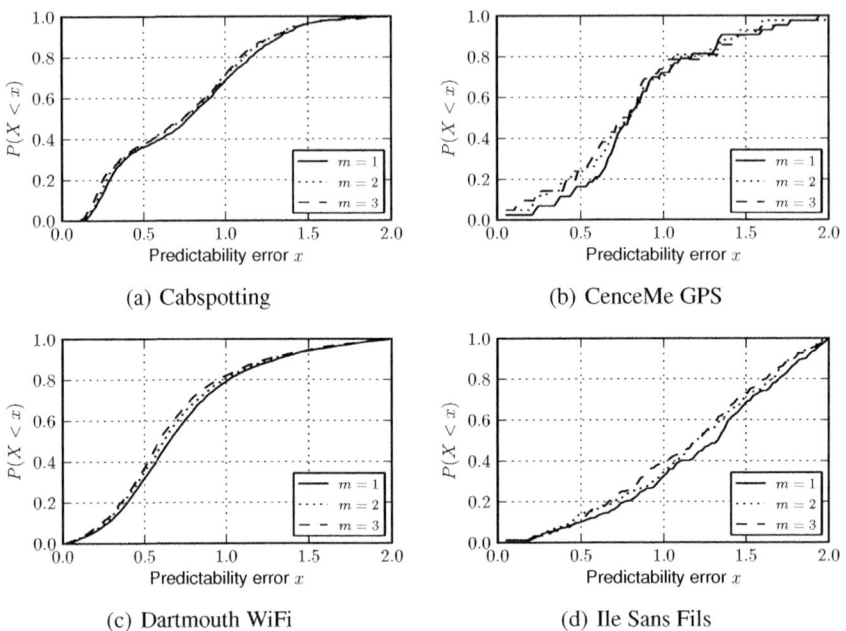

Fig. 3. Cumulative Distribution Function of the predictability error of the time series of the start instants extracted from the various datasets. We report the results for different values of the embedding dimension m adopted in the prediction method.

and to 0.18% in the Ile Sans Fils dataset, since it covers a longer period of time (more than one year) and many of its users are present less regularly than in the other datasets.

3.3 Time Series Predictability Test

In order to exploit time series techniques to predict user behavior, we first need to investigate if determinism is present in the extracted time series. In other words, we want to evaluate the *predictability* of these time series.

Let us consider a time series $(s_0, s_1, \ldots, s_N)$. If a real measurement for s_{N+1} is given, the prediction error is the difference between s_{N+1} and the predicted value p_{N+1}. Given a prediction technique, it is possible to obtain predicted values $(p_0, p_1, \ldots, p_N)$ for the whole time series. Then, the *mean quadratic prediction error* can be evaluated as $\varepsilon = \frac{1}{N} \sum_{n=1}^{N} (s_n - p_n)^2$. Large values of ε indicate that the prediction is not accurate and the time series is not predictable.

The evaluation of ε is based on the comparison to the variance σ^2 of the time series: thus, a convenient way of deciding whether ε is small or large is to take the ratio $\frac{\varepsilon}{\sigma^2}$, which is the *predictability error*: if this ratio is close to 1, then, the mean quadratic prediction error is large, while if it is close to 0, the mean quadratic prediction error is small. We refer to this ratio as the *predictability error* of a prediction algorithm. The absolute error value ε may be meaningless if not compared to the average amount of fluctuations a time series exhibits: by dividing by the variance of the series we can normalize the error and compare the prediction accuracy for different time series.

We exploit this metric to evaluate whether the time series extracted from user visits in the different datasets are predictable. We divide each dataset in two halves: we use the first half to build the model and we compute predicted values of the second half and vice versa. A value equal to 1 means that no determinism is present in the time series, since in this case the predictor has the same accuracy of the simple average value, whereas a value closer to 0 indicates a high degree of determinism.

In Figure 3 we show the Cumulative Distribution Function of the predictability error for the time series of the visit start times for different values of the embedding dimension m. We have also investigated the predictability error for the time series of visit end times, obtaining similar results, which we do not show due to space limitations. On average, a large proportion of users exhibit predictability: in the Dartmouth WiFi dataset 80% of the time series show predictability error smaller than 1, whereas in the CenceMe GPS and Cabspotting datasets the same figure is 70% and it drops to 40% in the Ile Sans Fils dataset, which show less predictability than the others. This is due to the fact that visits may not occur every day with the same pattern for access points in public places, since different individuals are likely to show less regularity in public space than in more personal locations as living or working places, which are not present in this dataset. Moreover, in all datasets the predictability error is lower for higher values of the embedding dimension m: this confirms that nonlinear methods improve prediction quality, since they are able to capture and recognise specific patterns of visits and to estimate when the next visit will be. However, we have noticed that values of $m \geq 4$ show worse performance because we do not have sufficient statistics in order to make a correct prediction.

Interestingly, we expected to observe a lower degree of regularity in the Cabspotting traces, since the movements of a taxi are related to the destinations of the different customers and these destinations can be hardly predictable. Nonetheless, we were able to identify a set of places among which taxis move with more regular patterns. These places correspond to areas where taxi drivers periodically go and wait for new customers, such as touristic locations, shopping malls, cinemas, and they tend to exhibit regular and predictable patterns.

3.4 Evaluating Prediction Accuracy

We compare the performance of NextPlace with those of other two methods: a state-of-the-art Markov-based spatio-temporal predictor and a modified version of NextPlace, where time series of visits are predicted with linear methods rather than with nonlinear algorithms.

Methodology. Firstly, we compare NextPlace with a more sophisticated *spatio-temporal Markov predictor* derived by extending the techniques presented in [26]. To the best of our knowledge, this is the most accurate algorithm that has been presented in the literature for this class of prediction problems, because it combines spatial and temporal dimensions to estimate both next location and handover time for users in a cellular network.

Consider a user visit history among several locations $H = (t_1, d_1, l_1), \dots, (t_n, d_n, l_n)$, where t_i is the time when the user arrived at location l_i and d_i is the residence time in that location. Then, from H we extract the location history $L = l_1, \dots, l_n$ and the order-k location context $L_k = L(n - k + 1, n) = l_{n-k+1}, \dots, l_{n-1}, l_n$. The history L is searched for instances of the context L_k and, for each destination that follows an instance, we examine the duration of the previous residence time. More formally, we extract the following set of inter-arrival times A_x and set of durations D_x for each possible destination x:

$$A_x = \{t_{i+1} - t_i \quad \text{if} \quad L(i - k + 1, i + 1) = (L_k, x)\}$$
$$D_x = \{d_{i+1} \quad \text{if} \quad L(i - k + 1, i + 1) = (L_k, x)\}$$

Then, we compute the estimated time when the user will move to location x and the estimated residence time in x by using a CDF predictor with probability $p = 0.8$ [26]. Moreover, a Markov predictor of order k is used to assign the probability of transition between the current location and the possible destinations. Finally, spatial and temporal information are combined to obtain the predicted location. In order to predict not only the next location but also the subsequent ones, we extend this approach taking the predicted location as the current one and computing again the next movement. We refer the interested reader to the original paper for further details [26].

To understand how largely NextPlace relies on the performance of the nonlinear time series predictor, we can design a linear version of our prediction technique. We use an *order-k running average predictor* instead of a nonlinear method to estimate the future values of a time series: given the sequence of previous visits of a user to a location, the last k visit duration times and k intervals between visits are averaged to obtain a prediction of future visits. Then, the future location is chosen among several predicted locations according to the same algorithm at the basis of the nonlinear predictor (presented in Section 2.2). However, this simplistic time series predictor ignores how user behavior changes over time, since high heterogeneity can be observed in visits occurring during different times of the day. Focusing only on recent data and not investigating these temporal aspects may not be sufficient to obtain accurate estimates.

Results. We now evaluate the performance of NextPlace with the nonlinear predictor presented in Section 2.2 compared to the other predictors previously described.

We use the following definition of correctness: if we predict, at time T, that the user i will be at location l at time $T_P = T + \Delta T$, the prediction is considered correct only if the user is at l at any time during the interval $[T_P - \theta, T_P + \theta]$, where θ is the error margin. It is important to note that each prediction algorithm can also estimate if the user will not be in any of her significant places: thus, a prediction may be correct whether the user is predicted to be in a particular location l and then he/she is in l or if the user is predicted not to be in any significant location and then, in fact, she is not. However, as reported in Table 1, the fraction of time that on average users spend in their significant locations ranges between 14.74% in the CenceMe GPS dataset and only 0.18% in the Ile Sans Fils dataset. Hence, it is not easy to understand if predictions are accurate because a method is performing well or because, on average, it is just easier to predict the user outside of all her significant locations.

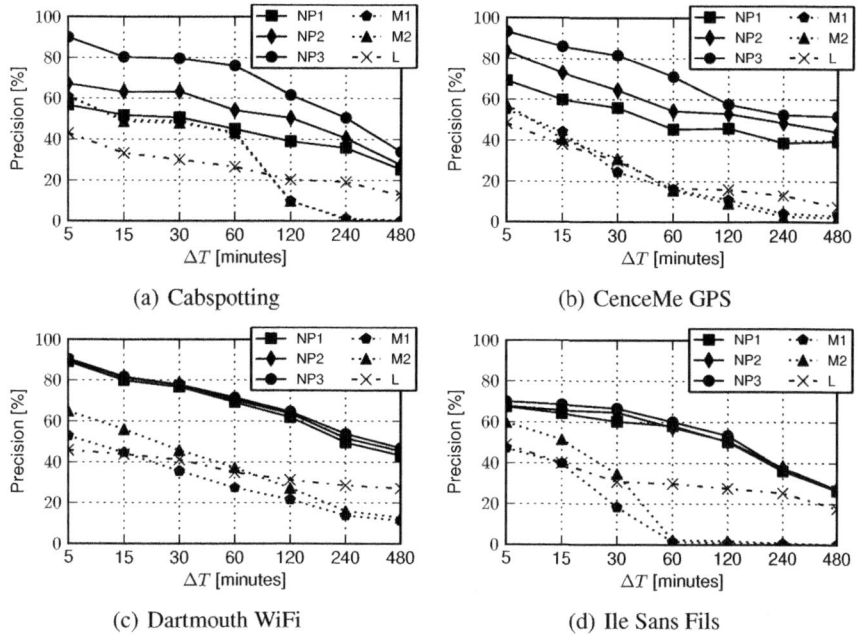

Fig. 4. Prediction precision as a function of time interval ΔT for the different datasets and for different predictors: NextPlace with nonlinear predictor for different values of embedding dimension $m = 1, 2, 3$ (NL1-NL2-NL3), first-order and second-order Markov-based (M1-M2) and NextPlace with linear predictor (L). Error margin is $\theta = 900$ seconds.

Therefore, we introduce an accuracy metric that takes into account this issue. We define the *prediction precision* as the ratio between the number of correct predictions and the number of all attempted predictions which forecast the user to be in a significant location. We do not consider for the evaluation any predictions which forecast the user outside her significant locations.

We report the performance of different predictors: we test NextPlace with different values of the embedding parameter $m = 1, 2, 3$, two order-1 and order-2 Markov-based predictors and the linear version of NextPlace with a running average predictor considering the last $m = 4$ values. For each dataset, we use the first half to build a prediction model and then we compute predictions during the second half and, for each user, we make 1000 predictions at uniformly distributed random instants. Finally, prediction precision is computed and we investigate how it changes with ΔT, using an error margin $\theta = 900$ seconds. All results are averaged over 20 runs with different random seeds.

We see in Figure 4 that for all datasets, NextPlace with its nonlinear predictor is always outperforming the other methods. We also note that using a higher value of m improves prediction quality, as it can be appreciated especially in the GPS-based Cabspotting and CenceMe GPS datasets. Similarly, Markov models are able to provide correct predictions when ΔT is smaller than 1 hour: however, except for the Ile Sans Fils dataset, the performance of the nonlinear NextPlace are at least about 50% better of the Markov-based predictors, since they reach a maximum precision of 60% while NextPlace achieves a precision higher than 90%. Moreover, when ΔT increases, the precision of Markov predictors decreases rapidly and the performance gap with the nonlinear approach widens. This can be explained by the fact that Markov predictors are generally employed to predict the next movement and, thus, when predictions are extended in the future, movement after movement, a large error is accumulated.

If we substitute the nonlinear predictor in NextPlace with a linear one, we observe a similar trend but precision is considerably lower, since errors on time series prediction are larger and, hence, affect the location prediction. However, NextPlace with both nonlinear and linear predictors is less dependent on ΔT than Markov models, which show a lower precision when predictions are extended in the future. Again, this demonstrates how NextPlace, which focuses only on temporal information of visits in significant places, is more robust for long-term predictions.

As discussed in Section 3, the Ile Sans Fils dataset exhibits less predictability. This is confirmed by the analysis of prediction precision, which shows the lowest figures among all the datasets. The other datasets score a precision equal to about 90% for $\Delta T = 5$ minutes and around 70% for $\Delta T = 60$ minutes. We also investigate the impact of the error margin θ on prediction results: prediction precision is lower for smaller error margins, but it shows the same trends for all predictors and for all the datasets. In Figure 5 we report how prediction precision of our nonlinear approach with $m = 3$ is affected by different error margins for some values of ΔT. Even with $\theta = 0$, which represents the worst case scenario, prediction precision is between 50% and 60% after $\Delta T = 60$ minutes for all datasets except Ile Sans Fils, where it is below 50%.

From a general point of view, our evaluation shows how NextPlace achieves high prediction accuracy, even for long-term predictions made some hours in advance. Furthermore, these results also show how focusing on spatial movements, as Markov models do, may be useful only for short-term predictions. Instead, focusing just on temporal information about recurrent patterns in significant places proves to be more robust both for short-term and long-term predictions, since NextPlace outperforms Markov models even for small values of ΔT.

4   Related Work

Pioneering work [3,4] has focused on the analysis of mobility traces in order to gain insight about human mobility patterns. Key papers in this area include studies on mobility and connectivity patterns, such as [5, 13]. The main findings are that contact duration and inter-contacts time between individuals can be represented by means of power-law distributions and that these patterns may be used to develop more efficient opportunistic protocols [10]. In addition, temporal rhythms of human behavior have been studied and modeled to discover daily activity patterns, to infer relationships and to determine significant locations [7]. This related body of work concentrates on the *statistical characterization* of temporal behavioral patterns of groups of users, whereas we concentrate on prediction of single users.

The evaluation of prediction techniques applied to the problem of forecasting the next location (but not the arrival time to that location and the corresponding residence

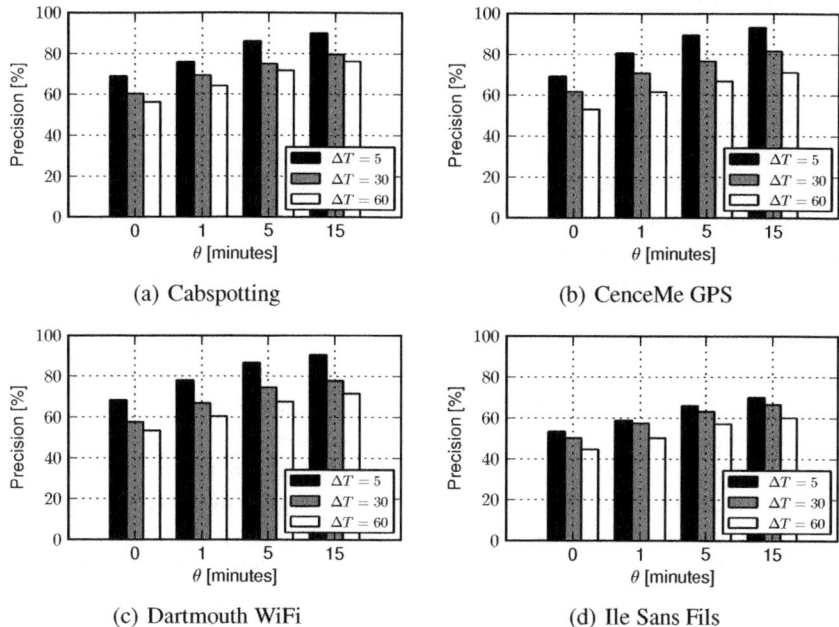

Fig. 5. Prediction precision of NextPlace with nonlinear predictor with $m = 3$ as a function of error margin θ and for different values of ΔT

time) are presented in [27]. A prediction framework based on spatio-temporal patterns in collective mobility trajectories has been presented in [22]: this method attempts to predict the next location of a moving object by matching a new trajectory to a corpus of global frequent ones. While this prediction technique is more general, as it captures dependencies between visits at different places, our method includes time-of-day information and does not rely on global patterns, allowing prediction to be made also for users who deviate from collective behavior. In [2] the authors present a model of user location prediction from GPS data. A simple first-order Markov model to predict the transitions between significant places is used, albeit in this work temporal aspects are not taken into consideration. In [19] the significant places are extracted by means of a discriminative relational Markov network; then, a generative dynamic Bayesian network is used to learn transportation routines. Another system for the prediction of future network connectivity based on a second-order Markov model is BreadCrumbs [23]. Again, this system is able to predict only the next location of the user and not the time of the transitions and the interval of time during which users reside in that specific location. Similarly, Markov based techniques have also been applied to the prediction of the destinations (geographical locations) of vehicles using for example partial trajectories [16]. As we have shown in the evaluation section, this class of models is able to provide precise predictions only for instants of time close in the future, given the inherent memorylessness of Markov predictors.

5   Conclusions

In this paper we have presented NextPlace, a new approach to spatio-temporal user location prediction based on nonlinear analysis of the time series of start times and duration times of visits to significant locations. To the best to our knowledge, this is the first approach that not only allows to forecast the next location of a user, but also his/her *arrival* and *residence time*, i.e., the interval of time spent in that location. Moreover, existing models are not able to extend predictions further in the future, since they mainly focus on the next movement of a user.

We have evaluated NextPlace comparing it with a version based on a linear predictor and a probabilistic technique based on spatio-temporal Markov predictors over four different datasets. We have reported an overall prediction precision up to 90% and a performance increment of at least 50% over the state of the art. We have showed how the adoption of a nonlinear prediction framework can improve prediction precision with respect to other techniques even for long-term predictions.

As future work, there is a number of potential improvements that can be pursued. Regular collective human rhythms can be exploited to refine the prediction and a probabilistic framework can be used to choose between equally promising next locations, giving more flexibility to applications. Finally, we are interested in the investigation of prediction models which take into account human rhythms on a weekly basis, in order to better capture regular human behavior on a longer time scale.

References

1. Aalto, L., Göthlin, N., Korhonen, J., Ojala, T.: Bluetooth and WAP Push Based Location-aware Mobile Advertising System. In: Proceedings of MobiSys 2004, pp. 49–58 (2004)
2. Ashbrook, D., Starner, T.: Using GPS to Learn Significant Locations and Predict Movement Across Multiple Users. Journal of Personal and Ubiquitous Computing 7(5), 275–286 (2003)
3. Balachandran, A., Voelker, G.M., Bahl, P., Rangan, P.V.: Characterizing User Behavior and Network Performance in a Public Wireless LAN. In: Proceedings of SIGMETRICS 2002 (2002)
4. Balazinska, M., Castro, P.: Characterizing Mobility and Network Usage in a Corporate Wireless Local-Area Network. In: Proceedings of MobiSys 2003, San Francisco, CA (May 2003)
5. Chaintreau, A., Hui, P., Crowcroft, J., Diot, C., Gass, R., Scott, J.: Impact of Human Mobility on Opportunistic Forwarding Algorithms. IEEE Transactions on Mobile Computing 6(6), 606–620 (2007)
6. Chatfield, C.: The Analysis of Time Series: An Introduction, 5th edn. Chapman & Hall/CRC, London (July 1995)
7. Eagle, N., Pentland, A.S.: Reality Mining: Sensing Complex Social Systems. Personal Ubiquitous Comput. 10(4), 255–268 (2006)
8. Gonzalez, M.C., Hidalgo, C.A., Barabasi, A.-L.: Understanding Individual Human Mobility Patterns. Nature 453(7196), 779–782 (2008)
9. Henderson, T., Kotz, D., Abyzov, I.: The Changing Usage of a Mature Campus-wide Wireless Network. In: Proceedings of MobiCom 2004, New York, NY, USA, pp. 187–201 (2004)
10. Jain, S., Fall, K., Patra, R.: Routing in a Delay Tolerant Network. In: Proceedings of SIGCOMM 2004 (2004)
11. Kang, J.H., Welbourne, W., Stewart, B., Borriello, G.: Extracting Places from Traces of Locations. SIGMOBILE Mobile Computing Communication Review 9(3), 58–68 (2005)

12. Kantz, H., Schreiber, T.: Nonlinear Time Series Analysis. Cambridge University Press, Cambridge (2004)
13. Karagiannis, T., Le Boudec, J.-Y., Vojnovic, M.: Power Law and Exponential Decay of Intercontact Times Between Mobile Devices. In: Proceedings of MobiCom 2007, pp. 183–194 (2007)
14. Kim, M., Kotz, D., Kim, S.: Extracting a Mobility Model from Real User Traces. In: Proceedings of INFOCOM 2006 (April 2006)
15. Kotz, D., Henderson, T., Abyzov, I.: CRAWDAD trace dartmouth/campus/movement/01_04 (v. 2005-03-08) (March 2005), http://crawdad.cs.dartmouth.edu/
16. Krumm, J., Horvitz, E.: Predestination: Inferring Destinations from Partial Trajectories. In: Dourish, P., Friday, A. (eds.) UbiComp 2006. LNCS, vol. 4206, pp. 243–260. Springer, Heidelberg (2006)
17. LaMarca, A., Chawathe, Y., Consolvo, S., Hightower, J., Smith, I., Scott, J., Sohn, T., Howard, J., Hughes, J., Potter, F., Tabert, J., Powledge, P., Borriello, G., Schilit, B.: Place Lab: Device Positioning Using Radio Beacons in the Wild. In: Gellersen, H.-W., Want, R., Schmidt, A. (eds.) PERVASIVE 2005. LNCS, vol. 3468, pp. 116–133. Springer, Heidelberg (2005)
18. Lenczner, M., Gregoire, B., Roulx, F.: CRAWDAD data set ilesansfil/wifidog (v. 2007-08-27) (August 2007),
    http://www.crawdad.cs.dartmouth.edu/ilesansfil/wifidog
19. Liao, L., Patterson, D.J., Fox, D., Kautz, H.: Building Personal Maps from GPS Data. In: Proceedings of IJCAI Workshop on Modeling Others from Observation (2005)
20. Marmasse, N., Schmandt, C.: Location-Aware Information Delivery with ComMotion. In: Thomas, P., Gellersen, H.-W. (eds.) HUC 2000. LNCS, vol. 1927, pp. 157–171. Springer, Heidelberg (2000)
21. Miluzzo, E., Lane, N.D., Fodor, K., Peterson, R., Lu, H., Musolesi, M., Eisenman, S.B., Zheng, X., Campbell, A.T.: Sensing Meets Mobile Social Networks: the Design, Implementation and Evaluation of the CenceMe Application. In: Proceedings of SenSys 2008, pp. 337–350. ACM, New York (2008)
22. Monreale, A., Pinelli, F., Trasarti, R., Giannotti, F.: WhereNext: a location predictor on trajectory pattern mining. In: Proceedings of SIGKDD 2009, pp. 637–646. ACM, New York (2009)
23. Nicholson, A.J., Noble, B.D.: BreadCrumbs: Forecasting Mobile Connectivity. In: Proceedings of MobiCom 2008, pp. 46–57. ACM, New York (2008)
24. Piorkowski, M., Sarafijanovic-Djukic, N., Grossglauser, M.: CRAWDAD trace set epfl/mobility/cab (v. 2009-02-24) (February 2009),
    http://crawdad.cs.dartmouth.edu/epfl/mobility/cab
25. Schreiber, T.: Efficient Neighbor Searching in Nonlinear Time Series. International Journal on Bifurcations and Chaos 5, 349–358 (1995)
26. Song, L., Deshpande, U., Kozat, U.C., Kotz, D., Jain, R.: Predictability of WLAN Mobility and its Effects on Bandwidth Provisioning. In: Proceedings of INFOCOM 2006 (April 2006)
27. Song, L., Kotz, D.: Evaluating Location Predictors with Extensive Wi-Fi Mobility Data. In: Proceedings of INFOCOM 2004, pp. 1414–1424 (2004)
28. Zhou, C., Frankowski, D., Ludford, P., Shekhar, S., Terveen, L.: Discovering Personally Meaningful Places: An Interactive Clustering Approach. ACM Trans. Inf. Syst. 25(3), 12 (2007)

Using Decision-Theoretic Experience Sampling to Build Personalized Mobile Phone Interruption Models

Stephanie Rosenthal, Anind K. Dey, and Manuela Veloso

Carnegie Mellon University
{srosenth,anind,veloso}@cs.cmu.edu

Abstract. We contribute a method for approximating users' interruptibility costs to use for experience sampling and validate the method in an application that learns when to automatically turn off and on the phone volume to avoid embarrassing phone interruptions. We demonstrate that users have varying costs associated with interruptions which indicates the need for personalized cost approximations. We compare different experience sampling techniques to learn users' volume preferences and show those that ask when our cost approximation is low reduce the number of embarrassing interruptions and result in more accurate volume classifiers when deployed for long-term use.

Keywords: interruptibility, preference elicitation, mobile devices, machine learning.

1 Introduction

As mobile devices become increasingly ubiquitous in our environments, they increasingly ring or beep at inappropriate times or in inappropriate contexts such as in meetings or in movies. While we receive reminders to turn off our phones or put them in silent mode in these contexts, we often forget to do so which can result in embarrassing situations. Even when we do remember, we then forget to turn the ringer on afterwards resulting in missed calls [21] or missed notifications about SMS messages and calendar events. In this work, we are interested in learning users' *preferences* for receiving audible notification preferences in order to enable an application we built to automatically change the volume of users' phones.

Because users often forget to change their phone volumes themselves, we cannot automatically train a machine learning classifier using their volume settingsas they are not an accurate indication of their actual volume preferences. Because we expect these preference rules to be complex, it is not feasible for users to define volume rules before using our application. Instead, our application elicits volume preferences from the user through experience sampling while they are using the phone [14, 24, 27]. However, the experience sampling itself may interrupt and embarrass the user in the same situations as the original notifications. In order to reduce these interruption *costs* associated with asking, Kapoor and Horvitz have proposed and demonstrated the success of a decision-theoretic experience sampling technique that builds accurate classifiers by asking for preferences only when the potential cost of misclassifying

K. Lyons, J. Hightower, and E.M. Huang (Eds.): Pervasive 2011, LNCS 6696, pp. 170–187, 2011.

that preference outweighs the interruption cost of asking now [13]. Our work builds upon this previous work to model user-specific costs (rather than an average cost for all users) while maintaining a high level of accuracy for all users.

In particular, while the previous work assigns constant costs for asking at an inappropriate time and for misclassifying preferences for all users and all situations, we show that different users have different costs and these costs vary for each user in different situations. One user may not want to be interrupted during work, another may not want to be interrupted during meetings at work but would answer if necessary, and another may have no problem being interrupted at work. A constant model cannot capture this complexity and the wrong model could severely impact the usability of the model for users who have high costs for interruption. We aim to address these potential usability problems by creating personalized cost models for each user. Although users may not be able to predefine their interruption costs for all situations (just as they cannot predefine preferences for a classifier), we assume they can approximate this cost for a broad set of situations that we survey them about. We propose that these approximations can be used to determine times to ask for notification preferences that reduce the interruption cost from asking while maintaining the high accuracy that Kapoor has shown previously.

We recruited participants to test the usability of our experience sampling technique against other commonly used techniques and to test the accuracy of the resulting classifiers' volume prediction. Prior to testing the on-phone application, participants filled out surveys about their predicted phone volume preferences in a variety of situations. Additionally, we asked for participants' predicted costs of being asked questions and the potential costs of an application misclassifying their preferences in each situation. Then, for two weeks, the application learned the users' preferences through one of three experience sampling techniques (random sampling, uncertainty sampling, and our augmented decision-theoretic sampling). For participants in our experience sampling condition, we used the survey costs to approximate, and to determine when to ask for, their preferences. Then, users tested the accuracy of their classifiers for an additional two weeks.

In this work, we make the following contributions. First, we contribute a method for approximating interruptibility costs and show that it improves the timeliness of questions asked during experience sampling. Second, we find that 7 out of 10 participants in the decision-theoretic condition reported very high accuracy (near 100%) with few or no errors while testing their classifier for two weeks. Third, we find that the user-specific cost models, while effective at improving usability for all users, reduced accuracy for the remaining 3 decision-theoretic participants as it asked too few questions and thus we caution using this technique for users with high asking costs. Finally, for these high cost users, we show that their initial preferences from the surveys can be used to create more accurate classifiers without sampling.

2 Related Work

As mobile phones are so ubiquitous and we increasingly have them available with us, it is becoming more important to understand when it is appropriate for them to interrupt us through rings and beeps. While users can characterize their own interruptibility *preferences* by changing phone modes (*e.g.*, ring, vibrate, silent) to avoid unwanted phone calls [27], they often forget to set and reset their phone modes, resulting in unwanted interruptions or potentially missing important calls, or SMS or calendar notifications due to silent notifications [21]. With a model of interruptibility, a phone could automatically set its volume to avoid inappropriate interruptions and important missed calls.

Phones today offer a variety of sensors such as accelerometers, microphones, and GPS that can be leveraged to classify a user's context and interruptibility preferences. Studies have shown that human interruption in offices can be captured accurately by simple sensors such as these [6, 9], and other studies have found that users decide whether to answer their phones based on their activity, location, and who is calling – all of which are becoming more observable using current phone sensors [7, 15, 16]. With new applications to classify interruption preferences and react based on these predictions, it is not clear what accuracy level is acceptable for users. Kern and Schiele found that interruption classifiers generated by users predefining rules resulted in 80-85% accuracy (the highest of all classifiers they tested) [14]. In a simulated phone experiment, Khalil and Connelly found that users rated their simulated volume changer highly even though it incorrectly changed phone volume 9% of the time, but that different users had very different satisfaction levels with the classifier accuracy [15]. It is important to test machine learning classifiers to understand whether users find their accuracy tolerable for real world use.

While it is possible for machine learning researchers to collect data and build classifiers that apply to all users in some applications, it is infeasible for creating personalized preference models such as those for interruption because different people have different preferences. Additionally, because users often forget to change their phone volumes, their current volume settings are not an accurate indication of their actual volume preferences and the labels cannot be captured automatically as in [5] to learn email classifiers. However, Kern and Schiele argue that if the mobile device could use experience sampling [2, 23] to elicit preferences while the user is using the device, the resulting classifiers would be more accurate [14].

Many different experience sampling techniques have been proposed to accurately elicit data labels from users in order to build classifiers including diary studies [3], device-initiated questions at different intervals of time [10, 20], and based on context-awareness [11] and previous labels [26]. The active learning literature have also proposed a variety of ways to choose which data should be labeled [1, 12, 17, 18]. However, it has been shown that the frequency and repetition of questions can affect the accuracy and compliance with experience sampling [22]. Horvitz has argued [8] and attempts have been made in both the machine learning and experience sampling communities [4, 12, 13, 14] to take into account users' interruption *costs* to determine when to ask. Kapoor and Horvitz propose a decision-theoretic sampling approach that trades off an interruption cost of asking and a future cost of misclassification to limit the number of questions but these costs are not personalized for each user [13]. For example, one user may be more willing to answer even when they are busy in favor of producing a higher accuracy classifier while another wants to receive as few questions as possible. Additionally, Kapoor and Horvitz's resulting preference classifiers were not deployed to users so it is unclear whether their 70% accuracy obtained during the experience sampling is tolerable for users. For clarity in our paper, we differentiate *interruptibility preferences* that are learned by the classifier from *interruption costs* of asking used to determine when to ask for preferences.

In this work, we aim to approximate users' individual interruption costs to improve the usability of an experience sampler by limiting the questions that are asked when each particular user is busy. In particular, we build upon Kapoor's decision-theoretic experience sampling technique to include our personalized cost of asking models that we approximate with users' survey responses. We use the interruptibility preference data collected via experience sampling to build a classifier to determine when users want their phone to ring (*i.e.*, when they are interruptible). We compare decision-theoretic sampling using our personalized cost models to more traditional experience sampling approaches and show that our personalized cost models lead to more timely questions for users and often led to nearly 100% accurate interruptibility preference classifiers. Additionally, we test our classifiers over two weeks to understand not only the costs of collecting personalized data but also the required accuracy of classifiers deployed to users in the real world.

3 Domain: Mobile Phone Interruptibility Preferences

We designed an Android application that learned users' volume preferences for phone calls, SMS messages, and calendar alarms. The application ran as a background process on the phone and listened for notifications (phone calls, incoming SMS messages, and calendar alarms). When a new notification arrived (*e.g.*, when the phone is about to ring), the application collected a variety of sensor and user-generated features and ran a classifier on those features to determine if the phone volume should be loud or silent. We did not turn on or off the vibration for this study.

Phone Interruption Features
We collected a variety of features based on sensor and other data that we can actively collect and have been shown to be effective at determining mobile interruptibility (*e.g.*, [7, 25, 27]) (Table 1). Examples of these features include GPS longitude, latitude, the time of day, and whether the user is talking on the phone. Additionally, the Android API provides information about the notification itself, which we will call the *reason* for the notification (in bold in Table 1). For phone calls and SMS messages, this includes information about the type of person who was contacting the user (*e.g.*, if they were in the user's favorites list, contact list, or neither) and the frequency of contact by this contactor. Calendar notification reasons included information about whether the calendar event was repeating versus a one-time event.

Due to the high battery cost of collecting this information on the phone, we only collected it when a new notification arrived with the exception of GPS coordinates. GPS coordinates were collected once per minute when the accelerometer values were above a certain threshold. Otherwise, it was assumed that the user was not moving and the GPS was turned off. As a result, the application had to quickly analyze the features and run the classifier to change the volume before the first ring or beep occurs, in case it was necessary to suppress it – in approximately ½ second.

Table 1. Features used in our personalized cost models - *bold* indicate the notification context, while the rest describe the participants' situations

GPS: Longitude, Latitude, Speed	Accelerometer X, Y, Z axes	Time until Next Meeting
User in Meeting	Noise (in dB)	Hour of Day
Day of Week	User on Phone	Count of Times On-Phone Caller has Contacted User
User on Phone with Someone in Contact List	User on Phone with Someone in Favorite List	**Next Meeting is a Repeated Meeting**
Contactor is in Contact List	**Contactor is in Favorites List**	**Count of Times Contactor Has Contacted User**

Interruptibility Classification Model

In this work, we use logistic regression (LR) classifiers because of the computational speed and efficiency on small platforms such as phones. The LR model distinguishes between two "classes" of interruption preferences – those in which the phone should audibly ring (LOUD = 1) and those in which it should not (SILENT = 0) – using the features F defined in Table 1. In particular, for a new situation with features F, LR calculates the probability of those features being labeled as LOUD as:

$$P(LOUD|F) = \frac{1}{1 + exp(w_0 + \sum_{i=1}^{|F|} w_i F_i)}$$

If P(LOUD|F) is greater than 0.5, then the prediction is LOUD. Otherwise, the prediction is SILENT. The classifier defines the weights w_i by minimizing differences (errors) between the labels y^j that the user provides through experience sampling (training data) and the classifier's predicted label Y^j for each training example j:

$$\text{while } \sum_i \Delta(w_i) > \epsilon : \forall_i, w_i \leftarrow w_i + \eta \sum_j f_i^j [y^j - P(Y^j = LOUD|f^j, w)]$$

We use experience sampling techniques to generate the training preference data that is used to learn to a classifier that distinguishes users' interruption preferences – when they want audible notifications. Each time a user responds to the experience sampler's question, the features of the current notification and the user's response are given to the LR classifier as training data to update the weights. Additionally, two of the experience sampling techniques - uncertainty and decision-theoretic sampling - use the classifier to determine whether to sample for preferences on new notifications.

Study Overview

Our study contains 3 parts. First, we surveyed users of mobile phones to understand their interruption preferences and interruption cost to learn those preferences in a variety of situations: at work, in the movies, at home. We will show that they not only had different preferences (as found in previous work) but also that they have different costs of asking. We then recruited participants to train a preference classifier for two weeks to understand the usability and accuracy of different sampling techniques.

Finally, we tested the model of their personalized classifiers for an additional two weeks to understand whether the final accuracy is tolerable for the participants.

4 Experience Sampling to Acquire Training Data

Experience sampling was originally introduced to intentionally interrupt study participants in order to have them make notes about their current situations [2]. These interruptions could happen at regular or random intervals with the expectation that participants would be more accurate in describing their current situations in the moment rather than later during interviews. Rather than depend on users to define their preferences before our study or recall them each evening, we use this approach to collect user preferences for training our classifiers.

We want to use experience sampling to build and train personalized preference classifiers for mobile phone users without affecting the usability of our application. Unlike traditional experience sampling techniques in which the participant should be interrupted, we are interested in minimizing this interruption so that users are more likely to answer the questions over time [22]. Several techniques have been proposed for when to collect accurate data from users. However while some focused on minimizing the questions, they do not guarantee that questions minimize interruption.

Random Sampling
In *random sampling*, the decision to elicit the user's preferences is made irrespective of the classifier that is being built with the user's responses. It is likely that a preference may be asked for the same or very similar situations multiple times, making some of the elicitations extraneous. However, this sampler ensures that the there is a broad set of data to train a classifier with. In our work, we assume that a user's phone rings on average 3 times per day (participants were screened for this) and we want the phone to ask at least once per day so our random sampler elicits preferences approximately 1/3 of the time when the phone rings. To decide when to ask, the sampler generates a random number p between 0 and 1 and asks if $p < 0.3$.

Uncertainty-Based Sampling
Unlike random sampling, *uncertainty sampling* builds the preference classifier using the data collected so far and then decides whether to ask for a new preference based on the classifier prediction [1, 17]. The goal of uncertainty-based sampling is to reduce the number of labeled preferences by only asking in situations that have not previously been encountered. If a new situation is encountered, it may benefit the classifier to get the user's preferences in order to classify it correctly in the future. However, if a similar situation was already encountered, the user should not have to provide their preferences again.

Specifically, classifiers such as LR, output a real value p between 0 and 1 rather than the binary 0/1 classification with the rule that if $p <$ threshold of 0.5, then predict 0, otherwise predict 1. We use P(LOUD|F), defined above, as our uncertainty measure p, where LOUD is defined as 1. The closer to 0.5, the *less certain* the classifier is of the user's actual preference and the less likely it is that there is a previously labeled situation that is similar to the current one. Uncertainty sampling asks for the user's preference for the notification if the current classifier outputs a p between 0.3 and 0.7.

Decision-Theoretic Sampling
Recently, Kapoor and Horvitz introduced *decision-theoretic* sampling to limit the number of labels the sampler requests about the user's interruptibility by taking into account the p value from uncertainty sampling and other interruption cost information about the user [13]. When the uncertainty is high, this technique trades off a prede-fined cost of asking A (a user's cost of interruption for a question) with the cost of misclassification M (user's preference for accuracy) with the aim of collecting equal amounts of data when the user was busy and when the user was available. If the cost of asking is higher than the cost of misclassification, the assumption is that the user is busy. If the cost of misclassification is higher, the assumption is that he is more will-ing to answer. The decision-theoretic sampler asks for a user's volume preference if $M > A$, where M is defined in terms of the change in the prediction uncertainty (Δp) if the new data is added (details in [12]).

In Kapoor's work, the costs of asking and misclassification were kept constant across all users and equal – 1 each. However, some recent work has indicated that different users may deal with misclassifications differently [15]. Some users may have very high cost of misclassification and therefore may be much more willing to answer questions to train an accurate classifier or vice versa. By more accurately estimating these costs for each user, we argue that it is possible to create a more per-sonalized asking mechanism that is more usable for each user. Like phone notifica-tions themselves, it is difficult for users to predefine the situations in which they are willing to be asked questions. In order to approximate the cost of interruption to de-termine when to ask, we propose to survey users' interruption preferences with a set of concrete situations and use linear regression to interpolate to other situations that the user encounters during normal daily phone use. We will compare the usability and accuracy of our augmented decision-theoretic experience sampling approach against the other experience sampling techniques.

5 Approximating Cost Models with Surveys

In order to understand phone users' predicted volume preferences and interruption and misclassification costs across a variety of situations, we surveyed users of smart phones who receive several phone calls, SMS messages, and calendar alarms daily. Participants were asked to rate their preferences for receiving audible notifications in a variety of hypothetical, but real world, situations and their expected costs to train the classifier. We analyzed the differences in preferences and cost ratings between participants in the same situation as well as differences that a single participant pro-vided across multiple situations to determine if a single approximation (as found in [15]) is sufficient or if personalized approximations are also needed.

Method
Before the survey began, participants were first asked a series of questions about their work schedule and common modes of transportation, which might affect their survey

Table 2. Eight questions were asked about whether the user's phone should ring in a meeting at work. Prior to taking the survey, participants were given definitions of the notification contexts to help them answer the questions.

Notification Type	Notification Context	Question
Phone	Favorite List, Contact List, Frequently Calls	If you were at work in a meeting and someone in your **favorites list** called, would you want your phone to ring aloud?
Phone	Not in Favorite, Contact List, Occasionally Calls	If you were at work in a meeting and someone in your **contact list** called, would you want your phone to ring aloud?
Phone	Not in Favorite, Not in Contact List, Few (if any) Calls	If you were at work in a meeting and someone **not in your contact list** called, would you want your phone to ring aloud?
SMS	Favorite List, Contact List, Frequently Texts	If you were at work in a meeting and someone in your **favorites list** texted you, would you want your phone to beep aloud?
SMS	Not in Favorite, Contact List, Occasionally Texts	If you were at work in a meeting and someone in your **contact list** texted, would you want your phone to beep aloud?
SMS	Not in Favorite, Not in Contact List, Few (if any) Texts	If you were at work in a meeting and someone **not in your contact list** texted, would you want your phone to beep aloud?
Calendar	Repeating Meeting	If you were at work in a meeting and a **repeating meeting** was about to start, would you want your phone to beep aloud to remind you?
Calendar	Non-repeating Meeting	If you were at work in a meeting and a **non-repeating meeting** was about to start, would you want your phone to beep aloud to remind you?

responses about situations in which they want audible notifications. Participants were then given 20 hypothetical situations when their phone might display a notification for each notification type. These situations were drawn from the sensor features in Table 1 and described participants' environments (*e.g.*, work or movie theater) or activities at the time of the interruption (*e.g.*, driving a car or relaxing at home).

Participants were given a short description of each of the situations and notification reason for the interruption, and were asked 1) if they would want audible notifications in that situation (interruption preference). Then they were asked to rate 2) their expected annoyance if the phone has the wrong volume setting (cost of misclassification) and 3) their expected annoyance if the phone asked which volume it should use (cost of asking). The questions were as follows:

1) In this situation, would you want your phone to ring out loud? Answer: Yes/No
2) How upset would you be if the phone did the opposite (rang when it should have been silent or *vice-versa*)? Answer: Likert scale 1 (no problem) to 7 (I would be very upset).

3)   In this situation, how upset would you be if your phone asked what it should do if it didn't know? Answer: Likert scale 1 (no problem) to 7 (I would be very upset).

An example of the questions for a situation where a user is in a meeting at work is found in Table 2, Additionally, participants were able to list exceptions to their interruption preferences for each situation.

All combinations of situations, notification reasons and notification types (phone call, SMS message, or calendar alarm) were presented to participants. Because of the number of situations that would be necessary to train a classifier, we split the survey into twelve parts. Each participant was given the option of answering all questions through all 12 surveys, but was not required to complete them all. Before each survey, participants confirmed that they did receive each notification type the survey focused on (*e.g.*, only those who received calendar alarms filled out the calendar surveys).

Participants

Participants were recruited through a Carnegie Mellon participant recruiting website to complete the online surveys. We are interested in both within-subject differences across notification types, as well as between-subject differences for each situation. In total 44 participants took all 12 surveys and 50 more participants took subsets of the surveys for an average of 69.25 participants per survey. Sixty-five out of 94 participants reported that they were students. The rest reported jobs such as cashier, machine shop manager, photographer, and administrative assistant. The average age of the participants was 25.27 with standard deviation 6.3.

Approximating Participants' Costs

We received a total of 9219 responses to our surveyed situations questions and analyzed the proportion of participants who wanted audible notifications for each notification type (calls, SMS messages, or calendar alarms), situation, and notification reason to understand interruption preferences. We found that participants had *very* different interruption preferences for each type of notification, which is contrary to current phone settings that only allow a single phone volume for all notification types. For example, at work, 45% of participants wanted calendar notifications during meetings compared to 7% on average who wanted phone calls or text messages in the same situation (Figure 1). Only 35% of participants wanted to receive phone calls at work, but more wanted text messages, especially from those on their favorites list.

Participants noted that, currently, they often kept their phone on vibrate rather than silent or loud volume because of these situational and notification type differences. One participant said that they prefer to err on the side of caution when it comes to phone volume and "I can find the time to check the onscreen message if I'm not too busy" rather than listening for an audible notification. When they had to decide on a loud or silent volume setting, participants often responded that they would not want their phone to ring "unless it was a family emergency" or "unless I'm getting a ride from that person." These exceptions are hard to enumerate and predefine and indicate a need to use experience sampling to capture preferences *in situ*.

In order to be able to collect these *in situ* responses, we use their surveyed costs of misclassification and asking. Participants reported varying costs of misclassification responses on the Likert scale from 1-7 (mean 4.3, s.d. 2.1). Participants responded

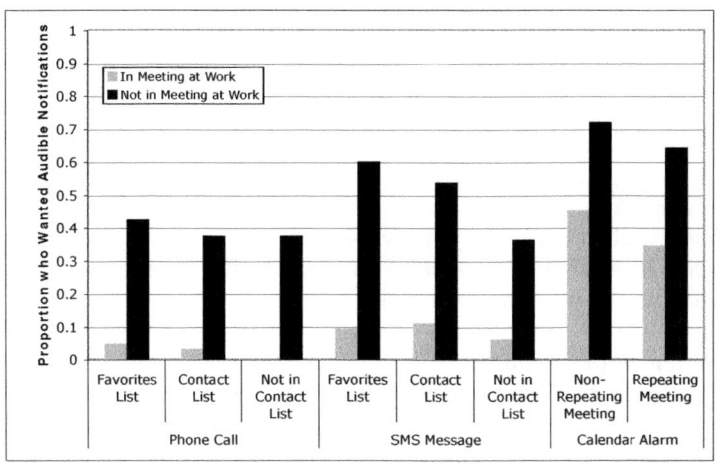

Fig. 1. Participants varied greatly in their preferences for audible notifications at work when they were not in meetings, but mostly agreed that they should not receive calls or text messages during meetings

nearly half of the time (4436/9219 responses) that they would have "No Problem" if their phone asked them for their preference (mean 2.6, s.d. 1.95). There was no particular situation where a majority of participants indicated that they would not be willing to answer. In fact, some participants indicated that they would always be willing to answer questions while others indicated there were situations when they never wanted to answer questions. These results show that a single cost model for all situations and/or all participants (from [13]) would likely interrupt many participants who indicated they did not want questions.

In order to approximate the costs for all situations in our phone app, we created artificial but plausible sensor values for each of the features in our application. Then, we used those sensor values to train a linear regression (easily computable on a phone) with the surveyed Likert ratings. For example, in order to model situations in the car, we averaged sampled accelerometer, microphone, and GPS values collected while driving with phones and labeled it with the corresponding Likert rating. For any new sensor data, the linear regression model will predict the cost of asking and misclassifying. Our linear regression models varied in their ability to capture each participant's predicted asking costs, as measured by the R^2 test, but overall was successful for such a simplistic model. Because we used only the features in Table 1 and did not use complex features, our cost approximations are easy to calculate on phones but may not always be predictive. Some of our linear regressions had R^2 values near 1; others were only about 0.3 (mean 0.65, s.d. 0.15).

Based on these findings and analysis, our phone volume application will need to learn a separate preference classifier (and use a personalized cost model) for each notification type and each participant.

6 Learning Interruption Preferences Using Experience Sampling

In order to understand the impact of personalized cost models on the usability of experience sampling and the accuracy of the resulting preference models, we designed a four-week experiment. Participants in the study were given our phone application, which learned their volume preferences and *actually* changed the volume of the phone based on learned classifiers. The application used one of three experience sampling algorithms - random, uncertainty, or decision-theoretic sampling – which asked them about their interruptibility preferences for each of the notification types, and used those preferences to build the volume classifiers.

Study Design and Procedure
Twenty of the survey participants who filled out all 12 surveys and had Android version 2.0 or higher phones were recruited to participate in our study to learn their phone volume preferences. Participants were asked to train their application, providing their volume preferences when asked, for two weeks and then test the resulting models for another two weeks, each night filling out surveys about the accuracy of the application and their current annoyance with either the questions or the volume changer itself. Participants were randomly but evenly assigned to one of four conditions – including two for decision-theoretic sampling – which determined when to ask for their preferences for phone volume when new notifications arrived:

- Random Sampling
- Uncertainty Sampling
- Decision-Theoretic Sampling
- Decision-Theoretic Sampling with Notification Reason

Because user preferences varied so greatly across participants, we did not test Decision-Theoretic (DT) sampling with a single cost model. Additionally, we do not test Kapoor's DT-dynamic condition (shown to be most accurate in highly changing domains) because we assume that users' preferences remain constant over the four weeks of the study. However, we did find in our surveys that the *reason* for the notification (*e.g.*, who is calling or whether the meeting is regularly scheduled) is a feature that users often use to determine whether they want an audible notification. We test the accuracy of preference classifiers that use this additional feature versus ones that do not, but do not test its use in experience sampling because the identity of the caller should not affect the cost of answering a question. The two DT techniques asked using the same algorithm.

Our volume changing application was loaded on each participant's phone, with a parameter file indicating which experience sampling technique to use and the linear regression cost models that were calculated from the participant surveys. Participants were told about the features that the application monitored and that it logged the features of each incoming notification, the classifier's prediction, and labels into a text file that we would collect once the study was complete. In addition to answering the application's questions, they were asked to fill out nightly online surveys on their phone about the accuracy of the model each day as well as the application's usability.

Participants were asked to keep the application running at all times during the 4 weeks of the study and were notified via email if the application quit at any time.

After two weeks, the application automatically switched from training mode, which asked users for preferences but did not change the phone volume, to testing mode, which used the prediction to turn on or off the volume of the phone for each type of notification. One participant left the study after the training phase because of a family emergency that required her to hear her phone all the time. After four weeks, researchers paid the participants $80, removed the application and collected the logs that were written to the phone over the course of the study.

Measures and Analysis
We measure four dependent variables: the number of questions asked, the accuracy of the classifier (collected each night over the 4 weeks) and the annoyance of both the asking and misclassification. The classifier accuracy is measured by comparing the classifier's predictions and the user's actual preferences collected from nightly surveys. We compare the experience samplingtechniques using a repeated measures ANOVA of the accuracy, number and timeliness of responsesover time. We collected annoyance ratings in the nightly surveys, but because participants did not have any other condition to compare to, they all rated their application as usable. Instead, we asked participants during their final interviews to recall specific situations when their application interrupted them, when the volume was incorrect as well as any other general impressions that they had about the application. We used these findings to distinguish the different sampling techniques.

Results
Overall, we found our approximated cost models had a significant effect on the number of questions that participants were asked and the usability and accuracy of the application. Participants in both decision-theoretic conditions reported that they were overall very satisfied with the timeliness of their questions and the resulting models were more accurate for most of the participants compared to the participants in random and uncertainty sampling conditions. We find that decision-theoretic participants who predicted they would have high interruption costs had lower accuracy because they were asked fewer questions, but that we can use participants' survey results to add more training examples and increase the accuracy.

Number and Timeliness of Questions
Participants received an average of 285 (min 32, max 717) phone calls, SMS notifications, and calendar alarms during the 14-day training period and received an average of 13 (s.d. 9.1), 41 (s.d. 59), and 3.2 (s.d. 5.8) questions respectively over the same period of time. Participants received far more SMS messages than phone calls and calendar alarms and the number of questions about them reflects this difference.

We compared the number of questions that participants received in each condition of the study for each type of notification (phone call, SMS message, calendar alarm) using a repeated measures test to understand whether the number of questions decreased over time and differed between conditions. We found that, for phone calls, both day of training ($F[13,195] = 4.67$, $p < 0.01$) and condition ($F[3,15] = 4.95$, $p = 0.01$) played a role in the number of questions participants received, but there was no interaction effect ($F[39,195] = 1.0$, $p > 0.05$). For SMS messages, there was high

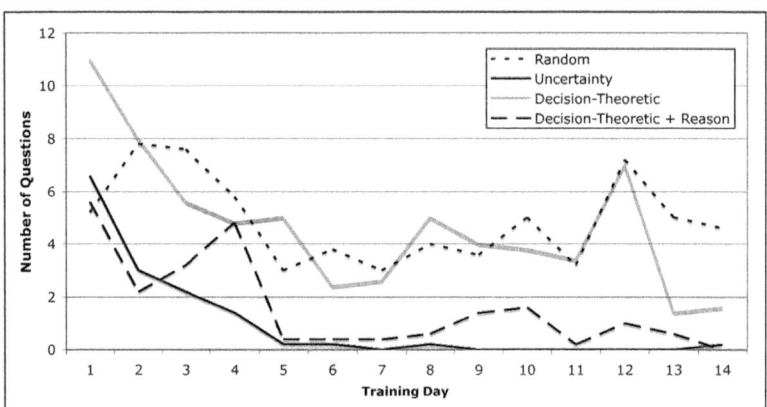

Fig. 2. As the classifier uncertainty decreased through training, the number of questions decreased for Uncertainty and both Decision-Theoretic conditions. However, it did not decrease for Decision-Theoretic participants who said they were willing to answer more questions to increase accuracy

variability in thenumber of questions by participant mainly because some participants received many more text messages than others so we found that there was only a significant effect of day of training on the number of questions ($F[13,195] = 3.55$, $p < 0.01$). There were no significant effects on the calendar alarms as all participants received very few questions to learn an accurate classifier. Next, we analyzed the specific effects that the training day and experimental condition had on the number of questions.

A Tukey HSD test on the day of training for each of the phone and SMS messages showed that participants received statistically significantly more questions on days 1 and 2 (mean phone 2.33, SMS 6.96) compared to each of days 5-14 (all phone means less than 1.0 questions per day, SMS means less than 2.5). After day 2, the number of questions decreased for both phone and SMS notifications (Figure 2). The drop in notifications in the random condition is not significant.

Interestingly, a Tukey HSD test on the experimental condition for phone calls showed that the Decision-Theoretic Sampling resulted in a statistically higher number of questions (mean 1.6 questions per day) compared to Uncertainty sampling (mean .47 questions) and Decision-Theoretic with Notification Reason (mean 0.65 questions). There was no statistical difference between Random sampling (mean 0.96) and any other condition. Because we expected the two Decision-Theoretic sampling conditions to have similar results, we investigated this anomaly further. We found that 4/5 participants in the Decision-Theoretic condition reported low estimated costs of asking - each had an average cost of less than 4 out of 7 – compared to only 2/5 with low costs of asking in the DT + reason condition. When we add an extra independent variable representing a binary high or low cost of asking in our analysis, we find (as expected) that participants in both Decision-Theoretic conditions who indicated they had a low cost of asking were asked statistically significantly more questions per day compared to those with a high cost - on average 1.45 compared to 0.52 ($F[1,6] = 6.51$, $p < 0.05$). This cost accounts for the differences in the Decision-Theoretic conditions.

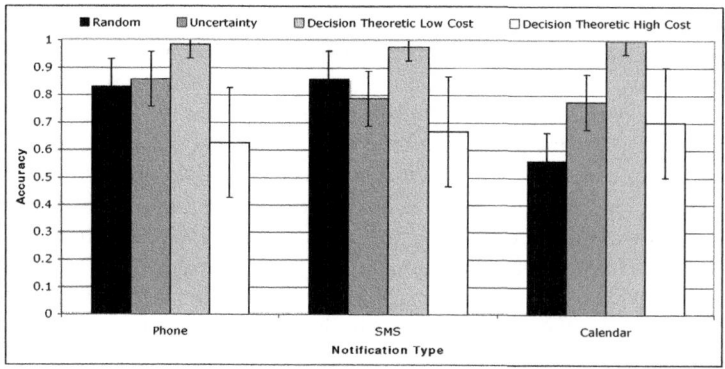

Fig. 3. Participants with low costs of asking in Decision-Theoretic conditions had the highest accuracy classifiers for each notification type (mean 0.99, 0.97, 1.00 respectively). Three participants in the two Decision-Theoretic conditions had high costs of asking because they were not asked enough questions to create accurate classifiers.

Despite the higher number of questions for 6 out of 10 of the decision-theoretic condition participants, all participants in both DT conditions reported that they were very satisfied with the timeliness of the experience sampling questions. Many participants in the random and uncertainty sampling conditions said they "eventually got used to the questions" but were annoyed by them before that. This indicates that our personalized models had the effect we intended, in reducing the number of questions when users had high interruption costs and asking at more appropriate times for all participants including those who received questions everyday.

Accuracy
Thirteen out of nineteen participants reported at the end of the study that they were happy with the accuracy of their application. Three requested to see the application in the Android app store to download again. The accuracies of the conditions were 0.83 (s.d. 0.1) for random sampling, 0.85 (s.d. 0.1) for uncertainty, 0.85 (s.d. 0.23) and 0.9 (s.d. 0.21) for decision-theoretic without and with notification reason respectively. The difference in accuracy between conditions is not statistically significant. Although participants indicated that notification reasons were important in determining their volume preferences, classifiers trained with these extra features had the same accuracy as those trained without them.

We combine the decision-theoretic conditions to show the differences in accuracy between the 6 participants with low costs of asking compared to the 4 with high costs (Figure 3). Three of the four high cost participants in the decision-theoretic conditions had accuracy lower than 0.8 for phone calls and text messages (mean 0.66, s.d. 0.16) compared to an average accuracy of 0.98 for participants with low cost of asking. Our decision theoretic samplers with approximated cost models are capable of very high accuracy when users are willing to answer questions. The experience samplers with high costs could not identify enough situations to ask but maintain usability, and the lack of labeled training data resulted in low accuracy for these classifiers.

In an effort to create more accurate classifiers for these 3 participants with high costs of asking, we examined the participants' survey responses to understand if their predictions were accurate. One participant's schedule and corresponding volume preferences changed after providing survey responses and the training period. Because the participant did not anticipate these changes, a classifier trained on these survey responses could not have been accurate. For the two other participants, however, the survey responses would have increased the classifier accuracy. For example, one participant's classifier turned the volume off in the evenings when he was relaxing causing him to miss many phone calls and text messages. The decision-theoretic experience sampler never asked for his preferences in this situation in order to preserve usability. If the classifier had used his single response to the survey – that he did want his phone to ring and beep - his accuracy would have increased from 75% to over 92%. We conclude that we can use participants' survey responses as additional training data for inaccurate classifiers.

In summary, participants in both decision-theoretic conditions reported that they were very satisfied with the timeliness of the questions they were asked compared to the participants who received random and uncertainty sampling. The resulting models were more accurate for most of the participants in these conditions as well. However, some decision-theoretic condition participants received fewer questions than others due to their high cost models and this affected the accuracy of their classifiers. We find that in most cases we can use participants' survey responses to increase the accuracy of the classifiers when they have high interruption costs.

7   Discussion

We have compared the accuracy and usability of three different experience sampling algorithms and found that our decision-theoretic sampling with personalized cost models was most accurate and asked questions at the most appropriate times. Next we address some of the participants' difficulties and suggestions that they made after using our application for four weeks.

Survey Responses as Approximate Interruption Models

Our main assumption in using experience sampling was that participants have difficulty predicting their preferences in advance, but that we could use these predictions to approximate interruptibility. We found that overall, this approach was very successful in maintaining very high accuracy while limiting the interruptions at inappropriate times. Thirteen participants also preferred answering questions over time and thought their *in situ* responses were more accurate than their survey predictions, and three thought a combination of surveys and experience sampling would be most accurate. Participants who preferred the questions reported that they liked that "it prompted me because it made me think of what I'm doing now" and that is hard to do before using it. This finding mirrors other experience sampling findings that participants answer more accurately in the moment, but contradict other HCI arguments that users should not be interrupted to train classifiers [5].

Participants who received few questions resulting in poor accuracy said that they would have been willing to answer more questions if they were told that their costs affected the classifier accuracy. A visualization showing the costs of interruption and the average resulting accuracy could allow participants to see the results of their tradeoffs concretely before using the application. Future work is needed to evaluate whether such visualizations are understandable and affect users' predicted interruption costs.

Volume Preferences Change over Time

We also found that participants' volume preferences changed throughout the study. Participants started new routines in the middle of the study – either starting classes or their kids started new activities. Because they had already started or even completed the training of their classifier, they could not reverse or change the previous responses and their classification accuracy suffered. Participants reported at the end of the study that they wanted to change or start the training over because they had such different preferences. As a result, we argue that applications should be able to employ lifelong learning techniques such as forgetting [12] or at least allow users to change their preferences to maintain accuracy as they drift or schedules change over time.

Some participants reported that there were sometimes unexpected circumstances that their classifiers could not handle. For example, some students were willing to receive audible text message notifications in class, but they did not want them on days when they had exams. Participants were not thinking about exams during their classes when they answered questions during training but had no way of changing the classifier's prediction on that particular day. For circumstances like these, we suggest the use of an override button to force the phone volume to be at a set level for a set amount of time. This button could also give users a better sense of control about their phone notifications if they are uncertain about what their classifier will predict.

Need for Intelligibility

Intelligibility became a big issue for our participants as their phone applications transitioned to testing mode. Uncertain of what their classifiers had learned, many participants emailed the authors asking how to find out what they should do if their classifiers learned the wrong thing. We argue that offering a "what if" interface (in which participants could have set different features to see the resulting prediction[19]) could have reduced some of the uncertainty and lack of control that users felt during testing mode in our study. Users could check that their classifiers make accurate predictions and provide extra examples for those situations in which it does not.

Participants also requested an interface in which they could see and change the rules that were generated for their classifier, especially if it was consistently wrong about a set of situations. We found that the classifiers were most overconfident in the uncertainty sampling condition and if users could adjust the classifiers during both training and testing phases, it could have reduced the potential errors and helped identify opportunities for the sampler to request more preference data. One student participant, for example, said that his classifier learned to turn his ringer off too early in the evening and this could have been easily resolved if he could have set the time feature. However, it is often difficult to show the rules of a classifier in a simplified way. More work is needed in order to understand what information users really want to know about their classifiers and what is too complicated or not important to show.

8 Conclusion

In this work, we have presented a phone volume application that classifies users' interruptibility and adjusts the volume accordingly. Because users have difficulty predicting their interruption level when they are not actually in the asked-about situation, we introduce an experience sampling technique that asks users to predict their costs of interruption and uses these predictions to approximate a cost model and determine when to actually ask for preferences. We deployed our volume application to learn users' preferences over 2 weeks and test the resulting classifier for 2weeks, comparing the usability and accuracy of our experience sampling technique against other traditional techniques.

We find that our method for approximating interruptibility improves the timeliness of questions asked during experience sampling. Additionally, we find that 7 out of 10 participants in the decision-theoretic condition reported very high accuracy with few or no errors while testing their classifier for two weeks. However, we find that the cost models, while effective at improving usability for all users, actually harmed accuracy for the remaining three Decision-Theoretic participants by asking too few questions and thus we caution using this technique for users with high asking costs. Finally, for these high asking cost users, we show that their initial predictions from the surveys can be used to create more accurate classifiers than the experience sampling could. Future work is needed to increase the intelligibility of the classifiers and the cost models to give users more control over their phone. Additionally, more work is needed to understand how phone preferences change over time and how we can develop classifiers to maintain high accuracy during through lifelong learning.

References

1. Cohn, D., Atlas, L., Ladner, R.: Improving Generalization with Active Learning. Machine Learning 15(2), 201–221 (1994)
2. Csikszentmihalyi, M., Larson, R.: Validity and Reliability of the Experience Sampling Method. Journal of Nervous and Mental Disease 175(9), 526–536 (1987)
3. Czerwinski, M., Horvitz, E., Wilhite, S.: A Diary Study of Task Switching and Interruptions. In: Proc. of CHI 2004, pp. 175–182 (2004)
4. Donmez, P., Carbonell, J.G.: Proactive learning: cost- sensitive active learning with multiple imperfect oracles. In: Proc. of the Conference on Information and Knowledge Management (CIKM), pp. 619–628, 2008.
5. Faulring, A., Myers, B., Mohnkern, K., Schmerl, B., Steinfeld, A., Zimmerman, J., Smailagic, A., Hansen, J., Siewiorek, D.: Agent-assisted Task Management that Reduces Email Overload. In: Proc. of IUI 2010, pp. 61–70 (2010)
6. Fogarty, J., Hudson, S.E., Atkeson, C.G., Avrahami, D., Forlizzi, J., Kiesler, S., Lee, J.C., Yang, J.: Predicting Human Interruptibility with Sensors. ACM Trans. Computer-Human Interaction 12(1), 119–146 (2005)
7. Ho, J., Intille, S.S.: Using Context-Aware Computing to Reduce the Perceived Burden of Interruptions from Mobile Devices. In: Proc. of CHI 2005, pp. 909–918 (2005)
8. Horvitz, E.: Principles of Mixed-Initiative User Interfaces. In: Proc. of CHI 1999, pp. 159–166 (1999)

9. Horvitz, E., Apacible, J.: Learning and Reasoning about Interruption. In: Proc. of the International Conference on Multimodal Interfaces (ICMI), pp. 20–27 (2003)

10. Horvitz, E., Koch, P., Apacible, J.: BusyBody: Creating and Fielding Personalized Models of the Cost of Interruption. In: Proc. of Conference on Computer Supported Cooperative Work (CSCW), pp. 507–510 (2004)

11. Intille, S.S., Rondoni, J., Kukla, C., Anacona, I., Bao, L.: A Context-Aware Experience Sampling Tool. Extended Abstract in Proceedings of CHI, pp. 972–973 (2003)

12. Kapoor, A., Horvitz, E.: On Discarding, Caching, and Recalling Samples in Active Learning. In: Proc. of Uncertainty in Artificial Intelligence (UAI), pp. 209–216 (2007)

13. Kapoor, A., Horvitz, E.: Experience Sampling for Building Predictive User Models: a Comparative Study. In: Proc. of CHI 2008, pp. 657–666 (2008)

14. Kern, N., Schiele, B.: Towards Personalized Mobile Interruptibility Estimation. In: Hazas, M., Krumm, J., Strang, T. (eds.) LoCA 2006. LNCS, vol. 3987, pp. 134–150. Springer, Heidelberg (2006)

15. Khalil, A., Connelly, K.: Improving cell phone awareness by using calendar information. In: Costabile, M.F., Paternó, F. (eds.) INTERACT 2005. LNCS, vol. 3585, pp. 588–600. Springer, Heidelberg (2005)

16. Krishnan, M.V.: Availability and Mobile Phone Interruptions: Examining the Role of Technology in Coordinating Mobile Calls. Masters Thesis MCS-2008:18, Blekinge Institute of Technology (March 2008)

17. Lewis, D.D., Catlett, J.: Heterogeneous Uncertainty Sampling for Supervised Learning. In: Proc. of the International Conference on Machine Learning (ICML), pp. 148–156 (1994)

18. Lewis, D.D., Gale, W.A.: A Sequential Algorithm for Training Text Classifiers. In: Proc of the Conference on Research and Development in Information Retrieval (SIGIR), pp. 3–12 (1994)

19. Lim, B.Y., Dey, A.K., Avrahami, D.: Why and Why Not Explanations Improve the Intelligibility of Context-Aware Intelligent Systems. In: Proc. of CHI 2009, pp. 2119–2128 (2009)

20. McFarlane, D.: Coordinating the interruption of people in human-computer interaction. In: Proc. of International Conference on Human-Computer Interaction (INTERACT), pp. 295–303 (1999)

21. Milewski, A.E., Smith, T.M.: Providing Presence Cues to Telephone Users. In: Proc. of the Conference on Computer Supported Cooperative Work (CSCW), pp. 89–96 (2000)

22. Scollon, C., Kim-Prieto, C., Diener, E.: Experience Sampling: Promise and Pitfalls, Strengths and Weaknesses. Journal of Happiness Studies 4, 5–34 (2003)

23. Shadbolt, N., Burton, A.M.: The Empirical Study of Knowledge Elicitation Techniques. SIGART Bulletin 108, 15–18 (1989)

24. Schmidt, A., Takaluoma, A., Mäntyjärvi, J.: Context-Aware Telephony Over WAP. Personal and Ubiquitous Computing 4(4), 225–229 (2000)

25. Siewiorek, D.P., Smailagic, A., Furukawa, J., Krause, A., Moraveji, N., Reiger, K., Shaffer, J., Wong, F.L.: SenSay: a Context-Aware Mobile Phone. In: Proc. of the International Symposium on Wearable Computers, pp. 248–249 (2003)

26. Stumpf, S., Rajaram, V., Li, L., Burnett, M., Dietterich, T., Sullivan, E., Drummond, R., Herlocker, J.: Toward harnessing user feedback for machine learning. In: Proc of IUI 2007, pp. 82–91 (2007)

27. Toninelli, A., Khushraj, D., Lassila, O., Montanari, R.: Towards Socially Aware Mobile Phones. In: Proc. of the Social Data on the Web Workshop (2008)

SpeakerSense: Energy Efficient Unobtrusive Speaker Identification on Mobile Phones

Hong Lu[*], A.J. Bernheim Brush, Bodhi Priyantha, Amy K. Karlson, and Jie Liu

Microsoft Research, One Microsoft Way, Redmond, WA, 98052, USA
hong@cs.dartmouth.edu,
{ajbrush,bodhip,karlson,liuj}@microsoft.com

Abstract. Automatically identifying the person you are talking with using continuous audio sensing has the potential to enable many pervasive computing applications from memory assistance to annotating life logging data. However, a number of challenges, including energy efficiency and training data acquisition, must be addressed before unobtrusive audio sensing is practical on mobile devices. We built SpeakerSense, a speaker identification prototype that uses a heterogeneous multi-processor hardware architecture that splits computation between a low power processor and the phone's application processor to enable continuous background sensing with minimal power requirements. Using SpeakerSense, we benchmarked several system parameters (sampling rate, GMM complexity, smoothing window size, and amount of training data needed) to identify thresholds that balance computation cost with performance. We also investigated channel compensation methods that make it feasible to acquire training data from phone calls and an automatic segmentation method for training speaker models based on one-to-one conversations.

Keywords: Continuous audio sensing, mobile phones, speaker identification, energy efficiency, heterogeneous multi-processor hardware.

1 Introduction

Forgetting the name of the person you are talking with can be an awkward and uncomfortable experience. Imagine being able to glance unobtrusively at a mobile device to see the name of the person who is speaking and perhaps a few other details about them. Several research projects, most notably SenseCam [2] have explored aiding people's memory using technology. However, these systems provide memory support *retrospectively*, by recording information (e.g., lifelogging) automatically and allowing the user to review events at a later time. With the advances in sensing and processing power, today's mobile phones offer the potential to provide memory assistance to the user in real time when a memory problem occurs.

Using audio sensing for memory assistance is particularly attractive because all phones have built-in microphones and audio data is less sensitive to the location and orientation of the phone as compared with other common sensors such as cameras and

---

[*] Current address: Dept. of Computer Science, Dartmouth College, Hanover NH, 03755, USA

K. Lyons, J. Hightower, and E.M. Huang (Eds.): Pervasive 2011, LNCS 6696, pp. 188–205, 2011.
© Springer-Verlag Berlin Heidelberg 2011

accelerometers. In addition to memory assistance, identifying a co-located speaker has a number of other possible uses including allowing people to set "person-based reminders" (e.g., "remind me the next time I speak to John to ask him about his vacation"), filtering social networking status feeds presented to a user based on the people they interact with face to face, or tagging life-logging data artifacts (e.g., photos) to facilitate retrieval at a later point.

Several previous prototypes have studied capturing audio to support retrospective memory assistance [e.g., 1, 5, 17] and have explored speaker identification using additional sensors [12] or multiple phones [7]. However, two key challenges must be addressed before continuous audio sensing for speaker identification is practical:

- Energy efficiency. To be useful for memory assistance and other scenarios, speaker identification must run continuously and unobtrusively in the background and be ready when needed. However, as we show in Section 4, although microphones use very little energy, *on an off-the-shelf smart phone* sampling audio data requires the phone's application processer to run and the ~335mW power consumption of continuous recording will quickly drain a phone's battery.

- Training data acquisition. Training data quality is a key factor in determining the performance of a speaker identification system. For most prototypes, researchers manually gather voice data, label them, and train a speaker model for each participant. Yet, in practice users are unlikely to be willing or able to manually train a system.

In this paper, we present the design and implementation of *SpeakerSense*, a practical, energy efficient, and unobtrusive speaker identification system. SpeakerSense tackles the above challenges by using a heterogeneous multi-processor (HMP) based mobile phone architecture, a set of robust speaker identification methods, and a novel training data collection mechanism via phone calls.

Our experiments show that using an HMP architecture to sample audio, detect high-quality voice data on a low-powered secondary processor and engage the speaker identification pipeline on a phone's processor only when necessary makes continuous audio sensing very efficient. Our system uses ~4.29mW when sensing in the background, and ~771mW on a phone when actively performing speaker identification. Using SpeakerSense, we also benchmarked several system parameters (sampling rate, GMM complexity, smoothing window size, and amount of training data needed) to identify thresholds that balance computation cost with performance. For example, our data show that 3 minutes of audio is a reasonable minimum for the amount of training data needed to train robust speaker models.

To address the challenge of acquiring training data, we investigated several unobtrusive data acquisition methods including using phone calls, one-to-one conversations, and sharing models across phones. We identify the appropriate channel compensation methods that make it feasible to train speaker models using audio data from phones calls, and an automatic segmentation method that can be used for training based on one-to-one conversations. We also validate the feasibility of sharing speaker models trained on one phone with another phone. While work remains to develop SpeakerSense into a system that can be studied with people with memory deficits, our contributions address technical challenges for speaker identification on mobile phones and move continuous audio sensing another step closer to reality.

2 Related Work

In our project, we were inspired by the use of technology to help people with memory deficits. Kapur [4]'s survey of memory aids describes the wide variety in common use which span both technological (e.g., reminders on watch alarms, mobile phones or pillboxes) and non-technological (e.g., wall calendars, notebooks) solutions, and highlights the potential for advances in technology on mobile phones, cameras and location detection devices to provide further memory assistance. Research using the SenseCam [e.g., 2, 5] has shown the potential of lifelogging to help people with memory impairments retrospectively review captured information to assist them in recalling events. Looking specifically at retrospective aids based on audio logging, Vemuri*et al.*developed iRemember [17], a memory retrieval prototype which recorded and transcribed everyday conversations so they could be later searched.

In addition to supporting retrospection, the computing power available in smartphones makes it possible to provide assistance in real time based on sensed events. The Personal Audio Loop (PAL) system [1] is a near-term audio-based memory aid that continuously records audio into a buffer; when users need assistance recalling something they recently heard (e.g., the name of the person they were just introduced to), the buffer can be played back on-demand. SoundSense [6] explores using audio beyond memory assistance, continuously sensing and classifying audio events to recognize general sound types heard by users (e.g., voice or music) and specific activities (e.g., walking, driving cars, riding elevators). These classifications enable a number of different applications including an audio daily diary and music detection service, which were both prototyped by the authors.

SoundSense and other continuously sensing applications raise concerns about battery efficiency which have been identified and studied. A variety of duty-cycling schemes have been proposed to alleviate battery life issues by samplingintermittently [e.g., 8, 19]. We take a complementary hardware-based approach to enable low power continuous sensing by offloading the initial speech detection task to a low power co-processor and using the main processor on the phone only when needed.

Most related to our interest in on-the-go speaker identification, two systems, Darwin [7] and EmotionSense [12], have recently explored speaker identification using mobile phones. Similar to both of these systems, our goal is not to design new speaker identification algorithms. Instead we leverage well-established techniques such as the MFCCs feature set[20], pitch tracking[11], and GMM classifiers [e.g., 13, 14], which have been proven effective for speaker identification. Our focus is on adapting these techniques to a mobile platform and addressing challenges that arise when using speaker identification on energy constrained mobile phones.

EmotionSense is a platform for social psychology research that aims to continuously sense the emotions of the mobile phone owner. EmotionSense includes a speaker recognition sub-system and silence detector that was used to select non-silent audio for the speaker recognition sub-system. Our work complements theEmotionSense research by exploring different approaches to address challenges in continuous audio sensing. For example, EmotionSense gathers training data offline in an explicit setup phase, while we have focused on gathering training data during everyday use. To extend battery life, EmotionSense offloads computation to a remote server, while we explore using an on-board low power processor. Finally, EmotionSense uses Bluetooth identifiers from other phones to narrow down the number of possible speakers, while in SpeakerSense we focus on the case where the user's phone must work independently without relying on anyone else to be running the same program.

Darwin [7] uses speaker identification as the example application to demonstrate a collaborative sensing platform that uses data collected across many phones to evolve classifiers, share them across multiple phones, and then collaboratively infer state (e.g., who is speaking). The authors demonstrate the potential for speaker identification using multiple phones in three experimental scenarios. Again our work is related but complementary; we focus on improving speaker recognition on a phone running independently, which does not need or assume many phones running the same system. Our research to improve speaker recognition on a single phone could contribute to overall improvements in Darwin-style collaborative approaches.

3   SpeakerSense

To unobtrusively identify the people a user interacts with face to face, SpeakerSense must run continuously on the phone, sampling and processing audio to detect human speech from other sounds, and attempt speaker identification when speech is detected. A naïve continuous speaker identification algorithm would place a heavy burden on the battery and computational resources of the phone, since the high audio sampling rate prevents the phone from going into the sleep mode, and the speaker identification process is itself computationally expensive. For example, based on our measurements, running speaker identification continuously on an HTC Touch Pro 2 (TP2) phone consumes ~771mW, which is considerably larger than the phone's idle power consumption (~11mW)when the phone is asleep and no application is running. In this section, we first introduce a heterogeneous multi-processor mobile phone architecture that can support low power continuous sensing, and then show how we can build a speaker identification system on it.

3.1 SpeakerSense Architecture

We designed SpeakerSense so that we can continuously run speaker identification without significantly impacting the phone's battery life. On current phones, individual sensor energy consumption is generally very low, but the process by which the data is *read* requires the phone's main processor to be active, which has high energy requirements. Furthermore, the high sampling frequencies (e.g 8~16KHz) required for continuous sensing do not allow enough time for the phone's main processor to sleep between sampling cycles, leading to a state of continual high-energy consumption. Recent work has shown that energy requirements for continuous background sensing can be significantly reduced using an HMP architecture, where sampling and processing of sensor data is offloaded to a low-power processor [10]. The power consumption of a modern low-power processor is similar to that of a typical sensor; and due to the simple architecture, a low power processor can make transitions between sleep and active modes very quickly.

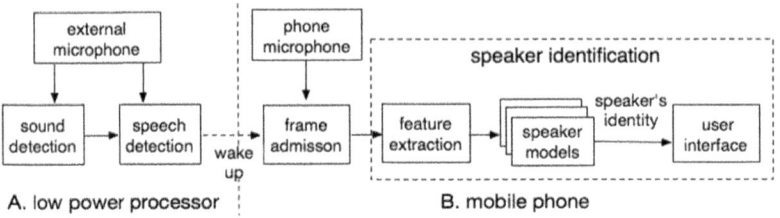

Fig. 1. The SpeakerSense architecture

SpeakerSense uses an HMP architecture where the phone's main processor is augmented with a low power MSP430F5438 processor. This processor consumes 15mW and 6μW when active (18MHz) and sleeping respectively, and has a 5μs wakeup time. We attach a typical mobile phone microphone (Knowles Acoustics model SPM0408HD5H) and an amplifier to this processor for sampling audio signals. To further reduce energy consumption, we use a hardware threshold detection circuit to detect the presence of sound, where a signal is activated when the audio level goes above 14% of the full audio scale.

The low-power continuous audio sensing feature of the HMP allows SpeakerSense to leverage the fact that a phone's owner is likely engaged in conversations only a small fraction of the day. Thus, to reduce overall power and computing resource requirements, we designed SpeakerSense as a sequence of 4 stages that have increasing power requirements, and assigned each to the processor most appropriate for the energy consumption required (Figure1). Each stage activates the higher power stage "on demand." Using the low-power processor, the Sound Detection stage first detects the presence of audio. Next, Speech Detection detects the presence of speech and wakes the phone when needed. On the phone, the Frame Admission stage identifies blocks of audio samples that contain high quality speech frames, which are sent to the Speaker Identification stage. We next describe the functional components of SpeakerSense.

3.2 Sound and Speech Detection

In SpeakerSense, the Sound and Speech detection stages run on a low-power processor. Sound Detection periodically examines the threshold detector output to determine the presence of a strong audio signal. If a strong audio signal is detected more than 50 out of 1000 times within a 0.5s period, the Sound Detection stage assumes the presence of a strong audio signal, and starts the Speech Detection stage on the microcontroller to detect the presence of voice.

The Speech Detection stage samples the audio signal at 8kHz and divide sit into frames. Each frame has 256 samples, corresponding to 32ms of data. For each frame, two lightweight time domain features that summarize the sound characteristics are extracted: zero crossing rate (ZCR) [15] and root mean square (RMS) [16].ZCR, defined as the number of zero-crossings within a frame, is an approximation for the pitch of the voice. Non-speech frames have no inherent pitch, resulting in high ZCR values, while frames with speech, particularly with vowels, typically have low ZCR values. The equation for computing ZCR is:

$$ZCR = \frac{\sum_{i=2}^{N} |sign(s_i) - sign(s_{i-1})|}{2}$$

where $s_{(i = 1 \dots N)}$ represents the samples in the frame and N is the length of the frame,(256 in this example). The value of $sign(x)$ is +1 or -1 depending on whether $(x >0)$ or $(x <0)$. For example, if two consecutive samples have opposite signs, indicating a zero crossing, ZCR increases by 1. RMS represents the energy of the sound signal, and is defined as:

$$RMS = \sqrt{\frac{\sum_{i=1}^{N} s_i^2}{N}}$$

Since floating point calculations incur high processing overhead on most low power CPUs, we use a simple integer approximation as an alternative given by:

$$RMS_{approx} = \frac{\sum_{i=1}^{N} |s_i|}{N}$$

For every window of 64 frames (approximately 2 seconds of data), Speech Detection extracts window-based features and performs classification procedures. Human speech is characterized by rapidly changing fluctuations resulting from the interleaving of consonants and vowels, which other types of sound are less likely to exhibit [15]. Using the ZCR and RMS features for each frame, we calculate four window-level features to capture the sound patterns in a window: the mean of ZCR, the variances of ZCR RMS, and the Low Energy Frame Rate, which is defined as the number of frames within the window that have an RMS value less than 50% of the mean RMS for the entire window[16]. For efficiency, we approximate the variances of ZCR and RMS as follows:

$$VAR_{approx} = \frac{\sum_{i=1}^{N} |s_i - \mu|}{N}$$

Once the features are extracted, an offline-trained decision tree classifier decides whether the sound is human speech. If speech is detected, the Speech Detection stage wakes up the phone to run the final two stages that we describe next.

3.3 Frame Admission and Speaker Identification on the Phone

SpeakerSense runs frame admission and speaker identification on the phone.

Frame admission. The role of the frame admission stage is to pick high quality speech frames from the sampled audio and discard low quality speech frames as well as silence frames that occur naturally from brief pauses in human speech. Human speech can be divided into voiced speech and unvoiced speech [15]. Voiced speech is defined as speech generated from vibrations of the vocal chords, and includes all the vowel sounds. In contrast, unvoiced speech does not involve the vocal chords, and generally includes the consonant sounds. Because there is more energy in voiced speech than in unvoiced speech, voiced speech tends to be more resilient to background noise. Thus to increase robustness within the phone context and to improve overall system efficiency, we use a frame admission policy in SpeakerSense that only forwards voiced speech for speaker analysis, skipping pauses(silence) and unvoiced frames.

Frame admission is accomplished using thresholds on two metrics, ZCR, which we also use in the Speech Detection stage, and spectral entropy [3].In the frequency domain, voiced frames have a series of strong peaks in the spectrum, corresponding to the pitch and formant of the voice, which results in low spectral entropy. On the other hand, the spectrum of unvoiced frames or non-speech frames is fairly flat, and yield relatively high spectrum entropy. Unlike standard speech processing systems, we do not adopt any commonly used energy features here, such as RMS[16], because the energy of the sampled audio is sensitive to the context of use (e.g., distance from the speaker, orientation of microphone etc.), while frequency-related features are relatively robust to environment conditions.

Speaker Identification. The speaker identification stage is based on a Gaussian Mixture Model (GMM) classifier [13] with some modifications to improve robustness and computation efficiency for use on the mobile phone. We use as our feature vector pitch[11] and the Mel-frequency cepstral coefficients (MFCCs)[20] computed for each admitted frame. SpeakerSense computes 20-dimensional MFCCs, and then ignores the first coefficient, which represents the energy of the frame, and instead focuses on the spectral shape, represented by the 2nd through 20th coefficients. While most traditional speaker identification systems use frames that overlap by 50% in order to capture subtle changes in the voice, this approach leads to sections of frames being analyzed multiple times. Given the resource constraints of the phone, we use non-overlapping frames to reduce the amount of computation required.

As is typical, we use a smoothing window, a fixed-length of successive frames, to improve system performance. In theory, a longer smoothing window increases the system performance. However, we have found that in practice, the smoothing window needs to be less than 10s, due to the latency introduced by the smoothing window and the uncertainty of turn-takings in conversations. The speaker identification algorithm attempts to identify a speaker by matching GMM speaker models to each smoothing window. Each speaker's GMM model estimates the log likelihood of the speaker, given every frame's feature vector. Assuming independence of frames, the speaker identified as the one talking during the window is the one whose speaker model gives the highest sum of log likelihood across the smoothing window. We train the GMM speaker models offline on a server. We use a universal background GMM to represent all unknown speakers [13]. To reduce the impact of noisy training data, the variance limiting technique[14] is applied with a standard expectation maximization (EM) algorithm [13] to train the GMM speaker models.

We have our low-powered processor attached to a prototype phone, so we decided to validate Frame Admission and Speech Detection on off-the-shelf phones for a better indication of feasibility and performance on currently available hardware. We implemented prototypes on an HTC Touch Pro 2(TP2) and an Apple iPhone 3Gs. The HTC TP2 runs Microsoft Window Mobile 6.5; the iPhone 3Gs runs Apple iOS 3.1.3. All signal processing and classification algorithms are implemented in approximately 1000 lines of C code to achieve high efficiency and portability between different platforms. Other system components (e.g., UI, communication, etc.) are written in the default languages for each phone, C# for the TP2 and Objective C for the iPhone 3Gs. The offline server side training code is implemented primarily in Matlab.

In our implementation, the prototype pipeline is optimized for lower CPU usage at the cost of a larger memory usage. Whenever applicable, we pre-compute parameters offline, serialize them into configuration files, and load them into the memory when the application initializes. For example, in our prototype implementations, the GMM models directly use the pre-computed inverse and determinant of the covariance matrix as the model parameters rather than the covariance matrix itself.

4   Evaluation

We evaluated several aspects of SpeakerSense including efficiency and trade-offs between computational cost and performance for system parameters. We first describe our data collection methodology and then our experiments.

4.1 Data Collection

For the evaluations we collected voice data from 17 speakers (10 males, 7 females) using the two mobile phones on which we implemented our prototype(TP2 and iPhone 3Gs). We were motivated to seek participants with a range of ages due to our interest in memory assistance applications where people would likely be interacting with family members of many different ages. The age distribution of our participants included four participants older than 45, four between 30-45, seven between 15 and 30, and two under 15. The median age was 29 and mean was 34.

For each speaker, we collected approximately 10 minutes of voice both locally and remotely though a phone call. The local recording was done by the two mobile phones simultaneously in both 8kHz 16bit mono and 16kHz 16bit mono formats. The phone call was recorded only in 8kHz, the phone channel standard. All the speech was collected in a normal office/home environment where the participant's voice was the dominant signal and there was modest background noise, such as air conditioning, desktop computer fan, or people talking remotely. All phones were placed within 1.5 meters from the subject's head. For each of the adult participants, we also collected 5 minutes of conversation with the researcher. This gave us a 15-person (eight male, seven female) one-to-one conversation database.

To train the Sound and Speech Detection stages on the low-powered processor, we also collected common ambient noises found in office and home settings. These sounds included the rubbing sound made by a phone in a pocket, the sound of walking, keyboard typing, mouse clicking, printers, copy machines, different types of fan noise, air conditioners, flowing water, street traffic, vacuuming, and various types of music. This ambient noise dataset contained approximately 250 minutes of audio.

4.2 Trade-offs between Computational Cost and Accuracy

For continuous audio sensing and speaker identification on mobile phones there are a number of possible trade-offs for system parameters that affect computational cost and accuracy. With SpeakerSense we investigated: the sampling rate and length of the smoothing window, the amount of training data needed, and number of GMM components to use.

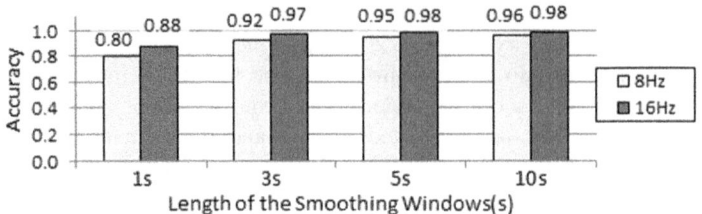

Fig. 2. SpeakerSense accuracy based on sampling rate and length of the smoothing windows

Sampling rate and length of smoothing window. A higher sampling rate captures more high frequency characteristics of the speaker's voice, improving the speaker identification accuracy at the cost of computation overhead. In Figure 2, we compare two audio sampling rates, 8kHz and 16kHz with different smoothing lengths. In this experiment, we use 10-fold cross validation. For each of the 17 speakers, the original 10-minute voice sample is partitioned into 10 subsets, nine of which are used for training and one for testing. The cross-validation process is repeated 10 times and then the average accuracy is calculated, with each of the 10 subsets used exactly once as the test data.

The benefit of a higher sampling rate is shown clearly in Figure 2. The accuracy on the 16kHz samples is consistently better than the 8kHz samples, although it doubles the amount of data to be processed. The performance difference between the two sampling rates is most apparent when the smoothing window is small, and the advantage of the higher sampling rate decreases as the length of the smoothing window increases. We therefore observe that the accuracy of speaker identification is less sensitive to sampling rate when longer smoothing windows are used. The choice of the window length dictates how fast the system responds to   changes in conversations (e.g., onset of the voice and speaker turn-taking). Considering the turn-taking patterns of everyday conversation, we believe that3s or 5s smoothing windows represent a good balance between delay and accuracy. Therefore for applications that require quick response and high accuracy, for example real time memory assistance, a higher sampling rate with smaller smoothing window setup would be preferred. In contrast, for applications that are insensitive to latency or require higher efficiency, such as life logging, an 8kHz sampling rate with longer smoothing window would be more appropriate.

Amount of training data. Intuitively, identification accuracy increases as the amount of training data increases, because the speaker model can likely encode more information. However, collecting properly labeled training data is generally expensive and cumbersome (we discuss ways to minimize this burden in Section 5). In this experiment, we investigate the minimum amount of data needed for reliable performance. Figure 3 shows the accuracy results for the 8kHz and 16kHz dataset respectively. The training data samples were sequentially taken from our voice datasets for training. For both datasets, the accuracy for 1,3,5, and 10 second smoothing windows are given for training data up to 360 seconds.

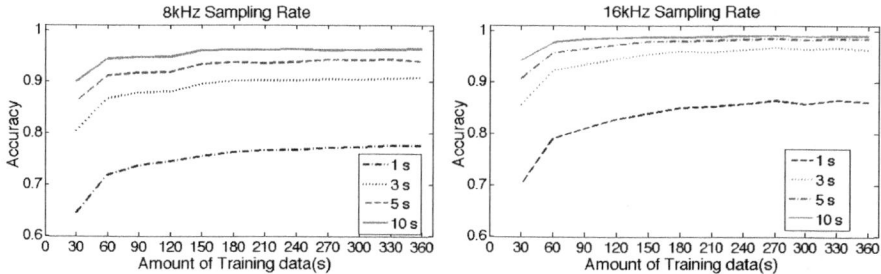

Fig. 3. Accuracy vs. amount of training data for the 8kHz (left) and 16kHz (right) datasets

We can make several observations based on the results. First, there is a sharp increase of accuracy between 30s to 60s of training data and then accuracy levels off above 120sfor 8kHz and 180s for 16kHz. These values are likely lower bounds on the amount of training data necessary to adequately model the speakers in our mobile phone setting. Second, the performance of smaller smoothing windows shows the fastest improvement. Longer smoothing windows are less sensitive to the increase of training data. Lastly, the 16 kHz system seems to benefit from more training data as accuracy increases up through 180 seconds. The reason may be that the training phase needs to model a wider frequency range, so it benefits from more data to learn from. Our experiments suggest for both 8 kHz and 16 kHz, 180 seconds (3 minutes) is a good minimum amount of training data.

The number of GMM mixture components. There is no well-established way to determine the optimal number of GMM components to model a speaker adequately. Using too few components results in an oversimplified speaker model, that is not sufficient to encode the characteristics of a speaker's voice. On the other hand, using too many components leads to a complicated speaker model with a large number of parameters, which requires a large amount of data and computation to train and makes the classification on the phone costly. Our goal is to choose the minimum number of components necessary to adequately model the speakers. Shown in Figure 4, we investigated5 different model complexities: 4, 8, 16, 32, and 64 component GMMs with 1, 3, and 5 second smoothing windows. We used 180 seconds of training data based on evaluation of the amount of training data necessary.

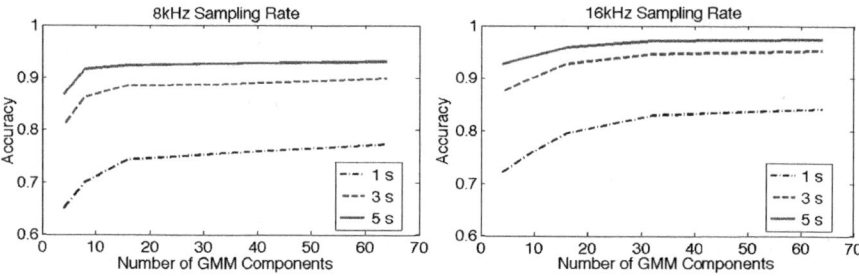

Fig. 4. Accuracy vs. number of GMM components for 8kHz (left) and 16kHz (right) datasets

With more GMM components, identification accuracy improves as expected. The accuracy for shorter smoothing windows has bigger performance gains. The greatest increase in performance occurs for all smoothing window sizes when the number of GMM components grows from 4 to 16. Above 32 GMM components, the accuracy gain levels off. Since the computation cost of identifying the speaker is proportional to the number of GMM component, we believe 32 components is a good choice to balance accuracy and efficiency.

4.3   Efficiency of SpeakerSense

We now evaluate the processing overhead and power consumption of SpeakerSense as well as the accuracy of speech detection on the MSP430 low-powered processor.

SpeakerSense Processing Overhead. On the low-powered processor, Sound and Speech Detection consume very little processing resources. Sound Detection runs as a periodic task with a 1.5µs processing time every 500µs, using only 0.3% of the processing cycles. The Speech Detection stage takes 90.9ms to process 2s of audio data, resulting in only 4.4% processor utilization.

On the phone, we evaluated the processing overhead of Frame Admission and Speaker Identification using the speaker models of the 17 participants. In the experiments, we ran 18 GMMs in parallel (17 speakers plus 1 universal speaker model for unknown speakers) to perform speaker identification. All experiments sample at 16kHz, 16-bit, mono audio from the phone's built-in microphone. Based on the experiments described in the previous sub-section, we use a 32-component GMM and a 3s smoothing window.

The TP2 uses 24.8ms to process a 32ms frame of voice data when the full pipeline is engaged (i.e., processing voiced frames). The iPhone 3Gs, which has a slightly faster processor, takes 21.7ms to process a frame. Using the profiling tool provided in the iPhone SDK, we benchmarked the resource usage of different processing stages, shown in Table 1. The memory usage stays at about 8.25 MB, including the user interface that displays the current speaker, since we preload all the models and pre-allocate the memory required for processing. We can see that when the pipeline is fully engaged, SpeakerSense uses less than 50% of the CPU, which leaves enough resources for other applications to run concurrently.

In summary, we see the full advantage of using a HMP architecture. The Sound and Speech detection stages, which likely dominate the execution time in typical usages, consume very little processor resources on the low-power processor. Frame Admission and Speaker Identification on the phone, which run only when active conversations are detected, require more resources, but still leave computing resource for other concurrent applications.

Table 1. CPU usage for Speaker Identification on the iPhone 3Gs prototype

Pipeline Stage:	Idle	Silence	Feature Extraction	SpeakerModelEvaluation
CPU Usage:	<1%	<3%	5.6% ~ 11.3%	35.1% ~ 44.9%

Table 2. HTC TP2 Power Consumption

Pipeline Stage:	Sampling Audio	Frame Admission	Speaker ID	Total
Average Power (mW):	335	21	415	771

SpeakerSense Power Consumption. Energy life is a scarce resource on mobile phones so the power consumption of SpeakerSense must be small for continuous speaker identification to be practical. First, we measured the power consumption of Sound and Speech detection stages on the low-power processor. We found that the Sound Detection stage consumes 0.73mW on average, which is an order of magnitude smaller than the 11mW idle power consumption of TP2.So, when the environment is quiet, SpeakerSense does not add noticeable burden to the battery. The Speech Detection stage consumes 4.29mW, which is still much less than TP2's idle power.

To evaluate the power consumption of the Frame Admission and Speaker Identification stages, we measure the power consumption of TP2 using the Power Monitor tool [9] (the iPhone hardware does not allow this type of measurement). Table 2 shows the total power consumption under different operating conditions with a dimmed backlight. We first observe that just continuously sampling the audio on TP2 consumes 335mW, which highlights the advantage of using a low-power processor for sampling audio for sound and speech detection. The Frame Admission stage adds 21mW, which is much smaller than the overhead due to audio sampling. The infrequently invoked Speaker Identification routine adds 415mW to the average power consumption for a total of 771mW.

Accuracy of Speech Detection on Low-Powered Processor. We have shown that introducing the low-power processor results in considerable energy savings compared to using the current mobile phone architecture. However, we also need to validate that the Speech Detection on the low-powered processor is reasonably accurate, since an efficient but incorrect detection is useless. Table 3 shows the confusion matrix for Speech Detection on the low-powered processor (these numbers implicitly evaluate both Sound and Speech Detection since Sound Detection triggers Speech Detection).

The precision of the Speech Detection stage—a decision tree classifier with depth 7—is fairly high, around 93%, at the expense of a low recall at 85%. The latter is due to the fact that during pruning, the classifier is tuned to keep the false positive rate low in order to reduce the chance of waking up the phone unnecessarily. Although more sophisticated and demanding voice detectors can achieve better performance [e.g.,3, 16], we prefer the current design that has very low resource consumption.

Table 3. Confusion matrix of the accuracy of the voice and ambient noise classifiers

Ground Truth \ Classified As	Voice	Ambient Noise
Voice	85.36%	14.64%
Ambient Noise	7.28%	92.72%

5 Training Speaker Models

Speaker recognition requires training a speaker model for each individual who needs to be recognized. Acquiring the necessary training data is a practical challenge that is often ignored in research prototypes, where researchers collect the data required for training. Collecting training data directly from participants, typically by recording a single participant's voice in a quiet environment, yields the best speaker models because the audio data is of high quality and contains data from a single known person. However, this method is labor intensive and requires participants to contribute their voice and time to train a model. While people might be willing to provide explicit training data to help a loved one with memory assistance (e.g., a grandparent or parent), this explicit training step is unappealing in general.

In Section 4.2 we showed that to build a robust speaker model, SpeakerSense needs at least 3 minutes of voice data from the speaker. In this section, we explore three additional ways beyond an explicit training phase to acquire training data for the people that a user interacts with in everyday life: using phone calls, one-to-one conversation, and by sharing speaker models across phones. We discuss the advantages and disadvantages of each method, as well as additional processing required, and compare performance to the "gold standard" of user contributed data for the 17 participants we collected data from.

5.1 Using a Phone Call to Train a Model

Using data collected during phone calls to train speaker models has many potential advantages. First, the identity of the person talking on the phone is typically known using caller identification. Second, the audio generated by the phone's owner and the caller is automatically segmented because the voices pass through two different audio channels: the owner's voice is received by the local microphone while the caller's voice is received over the telephone network.

There is no question that phone calls are an excellent way to train the speaker model for the phone's owner. The user's own voice is recorded locally by the mobile phone's microphone and can be used directly for training without any additional processing. The most striking difference between audio recorded during a phone call and user contributed data is that speech from phone calls will exhibit large segments of silence or background noise when the caller is talking. However, because SpeakerSense is already designed to select only those segments that contain voiced speech for training, breaks in the dialog are handled automatically.

Training speaker models for the caller is more challenging. The caller's voice is sampled by the phone and transmitted through the phone network where it undergoes band limit filtering and some spectral shaping because the telephone line is a narrowband communication channel. This makes it problematic to directly use the audio recording from another caller as input to the speaker model training since there is a mismatch between the narrowband speech data gathered from the phone line and the wideband testing data recorded by the phone's microphone. To determine if it is feasible to recover useful training data for a caller from a phone call, we investigated three lightweight channel compensation techniques to address the acoustic distortion produced by the telephone network: phone frequency warping [14], mean normalization[18], and the delta MFCCs features[13].

The average speaker identification accuracy for all 17 participants using the different compensation techniques is shown in Figure 5. Assuming the phone is able to provide precise caller identification information, in the experiment we manually labeled the speaker's identity for each of the mobile phone call recordings. We trained the speaker models using 5-minute call recordings and tested on 5 minutes of clean locally recorded voice data from our 8kHz dataset to match the phone channel standard. We used a 32-component GMM and the variance limiting was set to 0.1 in order to be more robust to the noisy channel. For the frequency warping method, the typical phone channel bandwidth of 300~3300 Hz was linearly warped to the full bandwidth 0~4000Hz. When using delta MFCCs features, 19 difference coefficients from a 32ms interval around the current frame are used. This introduces a 32ms delay, but is negligible compared to the smoothing window delay.

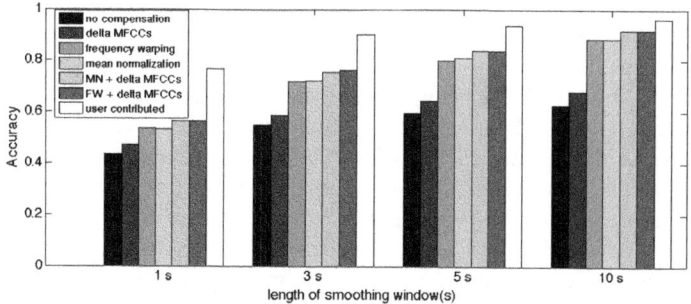

Fig. 5. Comparisons of channel compensation methods for different length smoothing windows

It is clear from Figure 5 that without further processing, the performance of speaker identification was vastly reduced by using recorded telephone speech directly for training. Even with a 10s smoothing window, the accuracy is still poor, coming in at only 63% accuracy as compared to greater than 94% when using user contributed data. When used individually, frequency warping and mean normalization are nearly equally effective, with both contributing more than a 20% accuracy gain when the smoothing window is 3s or greater. Adding delta MFCCs to the feature vector produced a moderate5% increase in accuracy when used alone. However, when Delta MFCCs was combined with frequency warping or mean normalization, it contributed an additional 4% performance gain. Because combining mean normalization with frequency warping provided no significant improvement over the use of each method individually, we omitted this combined condition from the figure. Although our experiments found frequency warping and mean normalization to be equally effective, we recommend using frequency warping over mean normalization for mobile applications because frequency warping is applied to each frame independently, which avoids maintaining a running average that introduces delay into the pipeline.

Based on this analysis, our prototype system uses frequency warping and delta MFCCs together when handling phone recorded speech. Given the ease of collecting training data using phone calls, the trade-off of slightly reduced accuracy rates compared to user contributed data seems worthwhile. It is important to note that while we have addressed the technical feasibility of gathering training data from phone calls, the cultural and legal acceptability of training speaker models based on phone calls requires further investigation.

5.2 Using One-to-One Conversations to Train Speaker Models

Another possibility for training speaker models is to collect voice data from everyday conversations, particularly those between the phone owner and one other person. While more practical than asking people to explicitly contribute training data, using data recorded during a one-to-one conversation is more complicated than using phone calls because the audio collected is not automatically labeled with the person speaking, and the recorded data likely includes speech from both the phone owner and the unknown speaker.

To process data recorded in one-to-one conversations, SpeakerSense requires the phone owner to manually mark the start and end of the (entire) conversation and enter the name of the other speaker. SpeakerSense then applies an automatic segmentation method that runs the phone owner's speaker model and the universal model on all the voiced frames. Intuitively, the user's own voice will be identified correctly, and the other speaker's voice will be marked as an unknown speaker. Once enough data from the other speaker has been accumulated, the system can train a model accordingly.

To analyze the effectiveness of this automatic segmenting approach for harvesting training voice data from one-to-one conversations we used the conversations that we collected with each of the 15 adult participants. Each conversation was sampled at 16kHz by the phone, and the start and end was marked by the researcher whose speaker model was pre-obtained. Informed by our previous experiments we used 32-component GMMs. Figure 6 compares the accuracy of speaker models trained using 5 minutes of conversation data and 5 minutes of user contributed data.

As expected, the speaker models trained from user contributed data has better accuracy, since it starts with perfectly segmented voice data containing only one speaker. In contrast, we expected that our algorithm for automatically selecting audio segments for a second speaker would not be able to perfectly segment the conversation and thus that some number of the audio segments used in training the speaker model may contain voiced data from the phone owner or both speakers.

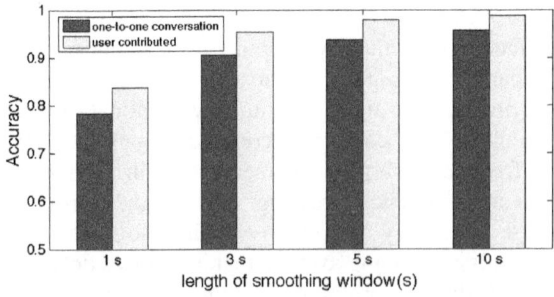

Fig. 6. Speaker models trained on one-to-one conversations compared to user contributed data

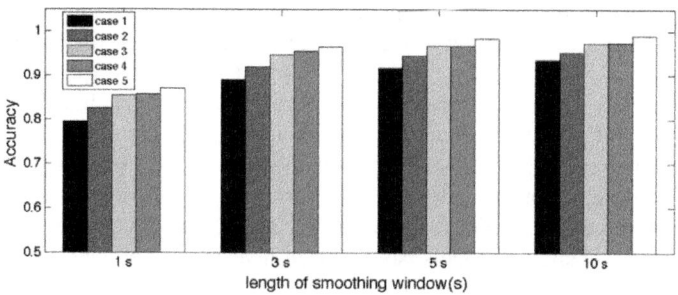

Fig. 7. Performance of sharing models between phones. Case 1: training with iPhone and testing with TP2. Case 2: training with TP2 and testing with iPhone. Case 3: training with iPhone and testing with TP2 with delta MFCCs features. Case 4: training with TP2 and testing with iPhone with delta MFCCs features. Case 5: training and testing with the same phone.

However, as Figure 6 shows, accuracy for the speaker models trained using the conversation data only marginally lag behind the speaker models trained on user contributed data. The difference is consistently less than 5% for all smoothing lengths. This shows that using automatically segmented conversation data could be a reliable and practical source for training data, especially given the reduced user effort necessary compared to getting user contributed data.

5.3   Sharing Speaker Models between Phones to Train Speaker Models

The final speaker model training solution that we explored was sharing speaker models between phones. This approach was suggested by Darwin [7], one of the only other systems we are aware of that considers the challenge of collecting training data. In Darwin's speaker identification prototype, each phone learns a speaker model for its owner and then exchanges its model with other phones, in a process termed 'model pooling.' We were intrigued by the feasibility of exchanging speaker models across different types of devices and how well speaker models trained on one device would work on another device, which was not described by [7]. If possible, sharing speaker models would greatly reduce the training effort because each person would only need to train their own speaker model.

The main challenges in sharing speaker models are the differences between the microphones on the devices used to capture the original audio. Although the built-in microphones on mobile phones are usually optimized for human voice, their frequency responses can differ. We hypothesized that using a channel normalization technique, such as using delta MFCCs features, could reduce the effect that different microphones have on the data. Using the 16kHz iPhone and HTC TP2 datasets, we conducted experiments to explore the impact of microphone variation when sharing speaker models between different phones and the effectiveness of applying delta MFCCs features to reduce the effect of the differences.

As Figure 7 shows, the mismatch between the training and testing microphone when sharing models between the two phones decreased the system accuracy by about 7%. However, using a longer smoothing window helps reduce the negative impact of using different microphones. Furthermore, adding the delta MFCCs features, which are insensitive to the microphone differences, improves the accuracy by about 4%. Thus our results from the TP2 and iPhone suggest that combining delta MFCCs features with models trained on different phones yields in an overall accuracy loss of only 3%. While it would be worth validating this small loss across more phones, we believe it is likely that speaker models can be shared across phones with only a negligible performance loss. It is important to note that while we have evidence that it is technically feasible to share speaker models across phones, user acceptance of sharing or exchanging models has not been investigated by Darwin or our research and is important to consider moving forward.

6 Conclusions and Future Work

Our research with SpeakerSense has addressed two challenges for using continuous audio sensing for speaker identification: efficient performance that enables continuous audio sensing and scalable methods for gathering the training data needed for speaker models. Through our experiments with data gathered from 17 participants in an indoor office environment, we have identified trade-offs between computational cost and performance that enable robust speaker identification on mobile phones by evaluating sampling rate options (8 kHz vs. 16 kHz), the length of the smoothing window, the number of GMM components needed to model a speaker adequately, and identified lower-bounds on the amount of training data needed to construct robust speaker models for the phone.

To address efficiency we prototyped SpeakerSense using HMP hardware. We demonstrate that splitting computation across a dedicated low-power processor that detects sound and voice and using the phone's main processor to run the computationally intensive speaker identification pipeline only when necessary enables continuous and efficient speaker identification. We believe other continuous sensing applications could benefit from a similar hardware-based approach. Lastly, we presented and evaluated methods for gathering the training data necessary for constructing speaker models during everyday activities, identifying channel compensation methods that make it feasible to gather training data from phone calls, and an automatic segmentation method for training speaker models using one-to-one conversations. Furthermore, we validate the feasibility of sharing speaker models between different phone platforms.

Our research has addressed many technical issues necessary to make continuous audio sensing and speaker identification practical, enabling the future work needed to study SpeakerSense, and similar continuous sensing applications, in day-to-day use. Field deployments will be valuable to test our approaches for gathering training data in real use, to gather data about the performance of SpeakerSense across a variety of environments, and to evaluate whether the information provided by SpeakerSense can provide memory assistance for people with memory impairment in practice. We are excited about the potential pervasive computing applications that we believe are enabled by our research.

References

1. Hayes, G., Patel, S., Truong, K., Iachello, G., Kientz, J., Farmer, R., Abowd, G.: The Personal Audio Loop: Designing a Ubiquitous Audio-Based Memory Aid. In: Proc. Mobile HCI 2004 (2004)
2. Hodges, S., Williams, L., Berry, E., Izadi, S., Srinivasan, J., Butler, A., Smyth, G., Kapur, N., Wood, K.: SenseCam: A Retrospective Memory Aid. In: Dourish, P., Friday, A. (eds.) UbiComp 2006. LNCS, vol. 4206, pp. 177–193. Springer, Heidelberg (2006)
3. Huang, L., Yang, C.: A Novel Approach to Robust Speech Endpoint Detection in Car Environments. In: ICASSP 2000, Istambul, Turkey, vol. 3, pp. 1751–1754 (May 2000)
4. Kapur, N.: Compensating for Memory Deficits with Memory Aids. In: Wilson, B. (ed.) Memory Rehabilitation Integrating Theory and Practice, pp. 52–73. Guilford Press, New York
5. Lee, M., Dey, A.: Lifelogging Memory Appliance for People with Episodic Memory Impairment. In: Proc. UbiComp, pp. 44–53 (2008)
6. Lu, H., Pan, W., Lane, W., Choudhury, T., Campbell, A.: SoundSense: scalable sound sensing for people-centric applications on mobile phones. In: Proc. MobiSys 2009, pp. 165–178 (2009)
7. Miluzzo, E., Cornelius, C., Ramaswamy, A., Choudhury, T., Liu, Z., Campbell, A.: Darwin Phones: the Evolution of Sensing and Inference on Mobile Phones. In: Proc. MobiSys 2010, pp. 5–20 (2010)
8. Miluzzo, E., Lane, N., Fodor, K., Peterson, R., Lu, H., Musolesi, M., Eisenman, S., Zheng, X., Campbell, A.: Sensing meets mobile social networks: The design, implementation and evaluation of the CenceMe application. In: Proc. SenSys 2008, pp. 337–350 (2008)
9. Power Monitor, http://www.msoon.com/LabEquipment/PowerMonitor/
10. Priyantha, B., Lymberopoulos, D., Liu, J.: LittleRock: Enabling Energy Effcient Continuous Sensing on Mobile Phones. IEEE Pervasive Computing Magazine (April-June 2011)
11. Rabiner, L.R., Cheng, M.J., Rosenberg, A.E., McGonegal, C.A.: Acomparative performance study of several pitchdetection algorithms. IEEE Trans. Acoust., Speech, and Signal Processing, 399–418 (October 1976)
12. Rachuri, K., Musolesi, M., Mascolo, C., Rentfrow, P., Longworth, C., Aucinas, A.: EmotionSense: A Mobile Phone based Adaptive Platform for Experimental Social Psychology Research. In: Proc. UbiComp 2010, pp. 281–290 (2010)
13. Reynolds, D.A.: An Overview of Automatic Speaker Recognition Technology. In: Proc. Int. Conf. Acoustics, Speech, and Signal Processing, vol. 4, pp. 4072–4075 (2002)
14. Reynolds, D.A., Rose, R.C.: Robust text-independent speaker identification using Gaussian mixture speaker models. IEEE Trans. Speech Audio Process. 3, 72–83 (1995)
15. Saunders, J.: Real time discrimination of broadcast speech/music. In: Proc. Int. Conf. Acoustics, Speech, Signal Processing (ICASSP), pp. 993–996 (1996)
16. Scheirer, E., Slaney, M.: Construction and evaluation of a robust multifeature speech/music discriminator. In: Proc. ICASSP 1998 (May 1998)
17. Vemuri, S., Schmandt, C., Bender, W.: iRemember: a Personal, Long-term Memory Prosthesis. In: Proc. CARPE 2006 (2006)
18. Viikki, O., Laurila, K.: Cepstral domain segmental feature vector normalization for noise robust speech recognition. Speech Communication 25, 133–147 (1998)
19. Wang, Y., Lin, J., Annavaram, M., Jacobson, Q., Hong, J., Krishnamachari, B., Sadeh, N.: A framework of energy efficient mobile sensing for automatic user state recognition. In: Proc. MobiSys, pp. 179–192
20. Zheng, F., Zhang, G., Song, Z.: Comparison of different implementations of MFCC. J. Computer Science & Technology 16(6), 582–589 (2001)

Text Text Revolution: A Game That Improves Text Entry on Mobile Touchscreen Keyboards

Dmitry Rudchenko, Tim Paek[1], and Eric Badger

[1]Microsoft Research and Microsoft Corporation,
One Microsoft Way, Redmond, WA 98052 USA
{dmrudche,timpaek,ebadger}@microsoft.com

Abstract. Mobile devices often utilize touchscreen keyboards for text input. However, due to the lack of tactile feedback and generally small key sizes, users often produce typing errors. Key-target resizing, which dynamically adjusts the underlying target areas of the keys based on their probabilities, can significantly reduce errors, but requires training data in the form of touch points for intended keys. In this paper, we introduce Text Text Revolution (TTR), a game that helps users improve their typing experience on mobile touchscreen keyboards in three ways: first, by providing targeting practice, second, by highlighting areas for improvement, and third, by generating ideal training data for key-target resizing as a side effect of playing the game. In a user study, participants who played 20 rounds of TTR not only improved in accuracy over time, but also generated useful data for key-target resizing. To demonstrate usefulness, we trained key-target resizing on touch points collected from the first 10 rounds, and simulated how participants would have performed had personalized key-target resizing been used in the second 10 rounds. Key-target resizing reduced errors by 21.4%.

Keywords: Game, key-target resizing, text entry, touchscreen keyboard.

1 Introduction

Mobile devices with capacitive or resistive touch sensors often utilize an on-screen, virtual keyboard(see [10] for a survey), or *touchscreen keyboard*, for text input. Without the need for dedicated hardware, touchscreen keyboards facilitate larger displays for videos, web pages, email, etc. [11]. As software, touchscreen keyboards can easily accommodate different languages, screen orientation, and key layouts. On the other hand, touchscreen keyboards lack the tactile affordances of a physical keyboard, which have been shown to be critical for touch typing [15]. Due to the lack of tactile feedback and generally small key sizes, users often produce typing errors. To reduce noisy input, researchers have developed algorithms for dynamically adjusting the underlying target areas of keys based on probabilities, a technique called *key-target resizing*. As shown in previous research [8,9], key-target resizing can significantly reduce typing errors, but requires labeled training data in the form of touch points for intended keys. In this paper, we introduce *Text Text Revolution* (TTR), a game that helps users improve their typing experience on mobile

K. Lyons, J. Hightower, and E.M. Huang (Eds.): Pervasive 2011, LNCS 6696, pp. 206–213, 2011.
© Springer-Verlag Berlin Heidelberg 2011

touchscreen keyboards in three ways: first, by providing targeting practice, second, by highlighting areas for improvement, and third, by generating ideal training data for key-target resizing as a side effect of playing the game. This paper is organized as follows. In Section 2, we describe how we designed the game to address specific text entry goals. In Section 3, we discuss how TTR relates to prior research on leveraging human computation. Finally, in Section 4, we evaluate how well TTR accomplishes its text entry goals through a user study and simulation experiment.

2 Game Design and Text Entry Goals

Because text entry on mobile touchscreen keyboards can be quite challenging, a small market has opened up for mobile typing apps, such as *SpeedType* [17] for the iPhone. In most typing apps, users are prompted with text they are required to type. When users mistype a character, they are typically notified through auditory and visual feedback, such as beeps and squiggly underlines. In some cases, the feedback can be more implied. For example, in *Turbo Type* [18], a race car representing the user slows down with typing errors. When users are finished typing, they typically receive information about their text entry speed and accuracy, but not information highlighting areas for improvement. Instead, users are typically encouraged to practice and to beat their personal best scores.

Inspired by this market for typing apps, we endeavored to design a text entry game with three goals in mind. First, like all typing applications, we sought to provide users with lots of practice targeting the keys of a mobile touchscreen keyboard. After all, the rendered keys can be quite small. For example, on the iPhone, most adult fingers easily cover two to three keys. Second, unlike most typing apps, we sought to provide users with concrete means to improve their typing by visually highlighting keys they tend to mistype. Third, we sought to obtain "ideal" training data for key-target resizing. As formalized in [8], key-target resizing employs a probabilistic approach to decoding noisy touch input. It combines probabilities from both a *language model* for predicting the likelihood of a next character given previous characters and a *touch model* for predicting the likelihood of observing a touch point (e.g., pixel coordinate or ellipsoid) given the intention to hit various keys.

Unfortunately, most of the time, it is not possible to know without inference what keys users are intending to hit, *unless*, of course, we instruct them to hit those keys. This is the hidden treasure of typing apps. By giving users text they are supposed to type, these apps are acquiring a wealth of labeled touch point data which can be leveraged immediately to learn a touch model for every key. For example, if, whenever users are instructed to type 'g', they correctly hit 'g' with some frequency and 'v' with some other frequency, we are essentially learning a probability distribution over likely touch points (mapped to keys) given the intention to type 'g'. Furthermore, if we can train touch models on the fly using data from the game, then the more users play the game, the more robust key-target resizing will be – which translates into reduced typing errors on the soft keyboard (we empirically demonstrate this in Section 4). Besides real-time adaptation, we could also aggregate user touch data in the cloud (i.e., on web servers) and leverage collaborative filtering to learn touch models for similar patterns of touch points for keys. The cloud could then push these touch models down to the mobile device. In short, by having a game that allows us to collect touch points for intended keys, we can explore opportunities for real-time adaptation and collaborative filtering.

In terms of implementation, we developed TTR using the XNA game development language and the Windows Phone 7 SDK [21]. The game runs on any Windows Phone 7 device and is available for free in the Windows Phone Marketplace.

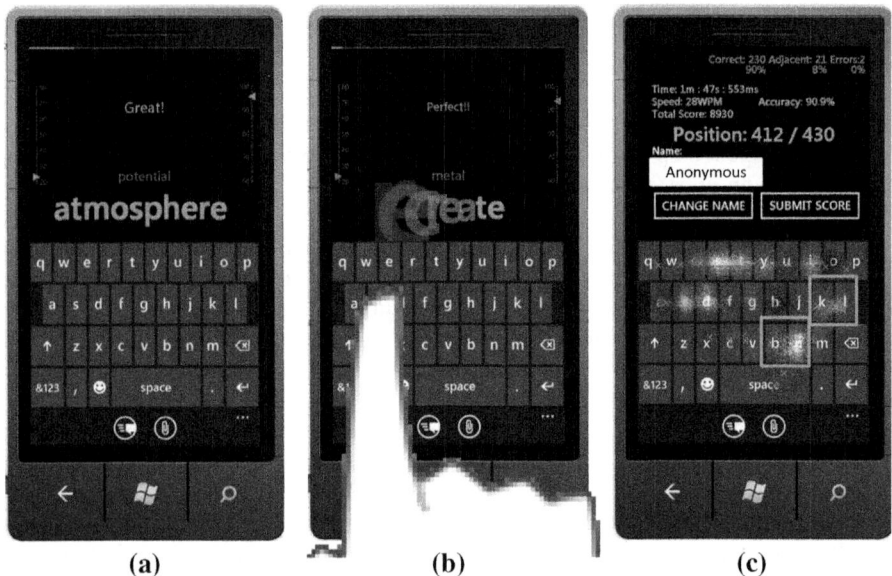

Fig. 1. Screenshots of Text Text Revolution: (a) Sample text users are instructed to type; (b) Letters exploding when users touch an expected or adjacent key; (c) End screen highlighting areas for improvement.

2.1 Game Play

With the above goals in mind, the game play of TTR proceeds as follows. As shown in Figure 1(a), users are prompted with words they are instructed to type. The words are randomly selected from a corpus of 10,000 words. Following [15], the corpus was generated by minimizing the relative entropy of character bigrams in the corpus with respect to a larger source– in our case, over 1 million email messages and transcribed voicemail messages. This allows us to provide users with consecutive characters that are representative of consecutive character sin email, a common mobile task. When users touch the keys we expect, the letters explode forward and fade out, as depicted in Figure 1(b). When users touch keys that are immediately adjacent to the keys we expect, we still explode the letters (e.g., 'q', 'w', 's', 'z' for 'a'). We did this for two reasons. First, we noticed that in typing apps where users are not permitted to move forward unless they hit the correct key, users tend to change their normal typing behavior; in particular, they tended to slow down and more carefully hunt-and-peck each key. Because we are interested in collecting "natural" touch points, we decided to relax the direct hit requirement. Second, we wanted to simulate an "ideal" typing experience. If key-target resizing could accurately infer intended keys despite the user hitting adjacent keys, then the experience of typing with unerring key-target resizing would be identical to what the game simulates. In essence, the game allows users to experience the kind of typing experience we hope to enable by collecting their labeled touch points and training key-target resizing on their data. If users hit a key that is neither the expected key nor an adjacent key, the text turns red and a beep sound is played. This immediately alerts users to their errors.

As shown in Figure 1(a) and (b), on each side of the presented text are two bars. The left bar indicates a running estimate of typing speed expressed in *words-per-minute* (WPM), and the right bar indicates a running estimate of typing accuracy. *Accuracy* is simply computed as the number of touch points that directly hit the intended key divided by the number of keystrokes. Users complete a word when they finish entering all of the word's letters. To move to subsequent words, users touch the space bar or any of the adjacent keys above the space bar. Because users sometimes miss the space bar, we can also learn a probability distribution for the space bar.

At the end of each game, we present users with a map of all of their accumulated touch points on the keyboard layout, as shown in Figure 1(c). The touch points are colored for each target key, which allows users to easily see when their touch points might be encroaching into unintended keys. For example, in Figure 1(c), most of the colored touch points for the letter 'l' are inside the boundaries of the 'l' key. However, some touch points bleed into the boundaries of the 'k'. As highlighted by the orange squares, the user in this case can immediately see areas for improvement; namely, avoid mistyping'k' for 'l', and 'b' and 'n' for the space bar. When the user presses the "Submit Score" button, the score is sent to the cloud and the user receives a screen displaying a scoreboard containing the user's best WPM and accuracy scores as well as the top scores from any user. However, even before users have the opportunity to submit their scores it is important to note that we send all of their data to the cloud for training key-target resizing. This is done with the user's permission via a privacy dialog box that is presented the first time the user launches the game.

3 Related Research

The problem of attaining touch point data to train key-target resizing can be viewed as part of the larger challenge of leveraging human computation for useful purposes. One method that has been gaining momentum in the research community is the online platform *AmazonMechanical Turk*[1], which allows developers to incorporate paid human intelligence via crowdsourcing into their applications. Indeed, due to the generally low cost of data, researchers have begun to exploitMechanical Turk for natural language processing tasks related to text entry, such as transcribing native [14] and non-native speech [6].Another method is to exchange human computation for entertainment in the context of a computer game. According to the Entertainment Software Association, 67% of American households play computer or videogames [5]. This has prompted researchers, most notably Luis Von Ahn and colleagues, to design clever *games with a purpose* (GWAP), in which human players perform tasks which computers cannot automate easily as part of the game (see [19] for a survey).

For example, in *The ESP Game* [20], players generate meaningful, accurate labels for images on the Web as they try to guess what their game partners are thinking. In essence, they are producing labeled training data for an object recognition system. Amazingly, as of July 2008, 200,000 players contributed more than 50 million labels.

While TTR falls under the rubric of a GWAP, it is also very akin to training wizards that not only teach users how to perform a task, but gather adaptation data along the way. For example, in the Windows 7 Speech Recognition Tutorial [22], users not only learn and practice voice commands for accessing features of the Windows 7 operating system by voice, but they also contribute example pronunciations for various phonemes, or segmental units of sound, that make up a language. In fact, the Tutorial has a section where users are presented with text they are instructed to read aloud. When they pronounce each word correctly, they are allowed to proceed. The acoustic data generated by the Tutorial is then used to adapt speech engine parameters. The entire setup of the Tutorial is more or less the same as what we use for TTR, except that we use a game instead of a wizard to entice users.

4 Evaluation

In order to evaluate TTR, we conducted a user study in which we recruited 6 participants, half of whom were female, to play the game. The participants played 20 rounds of TTR on a 3.5 inch WVGA, capacitive touchscreen device. Each round consisted of 250 characters, or approximately 50 words. Participants were told to use whatever posture for inputting text on the keyboard felt comfortable (e.g., two thumbs, one thumb, etc.) so long as they consistently used that posture for all subsequent rounds. Anytime participants needed a break, they could pause after completing a word during a round of TTR, or they could relax before the next round. Participants were all employees of Microsoft and were compensated for their time.

Before assessing how well TTR achieves its text entry goals, one important question to ask is whether or not the game is engaging. Since the game was released, it has been downloaded by over 25,000 unique users. 134 provided ratings [2], with an average score of 4.5/5 stars. The vast majority of raters posted positive comments about both its game play and usefulness, such as *"This is so much FUN! I can't stop playing, I think I'm addicted"*, *"The leaderboard feature makes it a lot of fun"*, and *"Very additive game. Very useful as well. My mobile typing is ten times faster now."*

With respect to text entry goals, the first goal of TTR was to provide users with targeting practice so they could improve over time by sheerrepetition. Not surprisingly, participants improved in both speed and accuracy over the 20 rounds, as shown by the trend lines in Figure 2(a) and (b). The second goal of TTR was to provide users with areas for improvement. TTR accomplishes this by visually displaying where users tended to mistype keys on a map of touch points overlaid on the keyboard. According to a post-hoc questionnaire, 4/6 participants found the touch point map to be useful. Of the 2 participants who did not find it useful, they claimed to have not even noticed the map. We are considering methods to make suggestions inherent in the touch point map more salient (e.g., written suggestions).

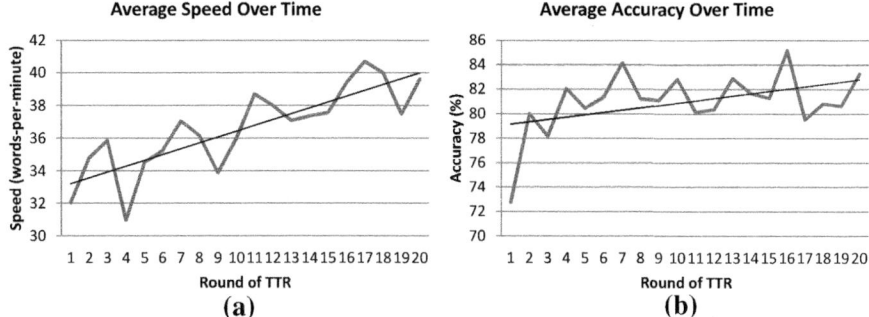

Fig. 2. Targeting practice improving (a) speed and (b) accuracy over time (multiple rounds of TTR). Trend line has been added in.

4.1 Simulation Experiment

Finally, in order to assess the third goal of TTR, generating useful training data for key-target resizing, we trained key-target resizing on touch points collected from the first 10 rounds of the participants' data, and simulated how participants would have performed had key-target resizing been used in the second 10 rounds. We are able to simulate performance by taking the touch points collected from TTR and seeing if key-target resizing would have changed the key assigned to each touch point. For example, suppose the user was attempting to type an 'a' and touched an (x,y) coordinate on the keyboard "normally" corresponding to an 's', where "normally" means using a key mapping that is based on fixed key boundaries which are equidistant in both the vertical and horizontal axis from neighboring keys. Recall that key-target resizing dynamically adjusts the key boundaries based on probabilities. It does this by simply taking an (x,y) coordinate and returning a key assignment. As long as key-target resizing is constrained to have convex target regions [9], it will assign the same key to any two touch points contained within the target region. We can now investigate whether key-target resizing would have assigned an (x,y) coordinate that was incorrectly assigned to an 's' to an 'a' instead. If key-target resizing would have assigned the (x,y) coordinate to an 'a', then the number of direct hits, and hence accuracy, would have increased. Likewise, suppose the user had touched an (x,y) coordinate normally corresponding to a direct hit. If key-target resizing would have assigned a different key to that (x,y) coordinate, then the number of direct hits, and hence accuracy, would have decreased.

Figure 3 displays the simulation results for the 6 participants. Overall, no participant would have achieved an average accuracy higher than 89% in the last 10 rounds. However, if we had applied key-target resizing, using parameters trained on general data, the average accuracy would have jumped up from 78.2% to 82.4% ($t(5)=10.0$, $p<.001$), a relative error reduction of 18.9%. In all cases, key-target resizing would have been beneficial and for some participants (viz., user 5 and 6)it would have resulted in a dramatic increase in accuracy, pushing user 5 into the 90% range. For "personalized" key-target resizing, we trained the algorithms on each user's touch points from the first 10 rounds of TTR and only that user's data. As evident in Figure 3, personalized key-target resizing consistently improves accuracy across all participants. The average accuracy of personalized key-target resizing is 82.9%, which constitutes a relative error reduction of 21.4% over key-target resizing ($t(5)$=-9.8, p<.001). Note that the personalized data we used for training was smaller than the general data for key-target resizing. As such, it is possible that with further rounds of TTR, personalized key-target resizing would continue to increase accuracy.

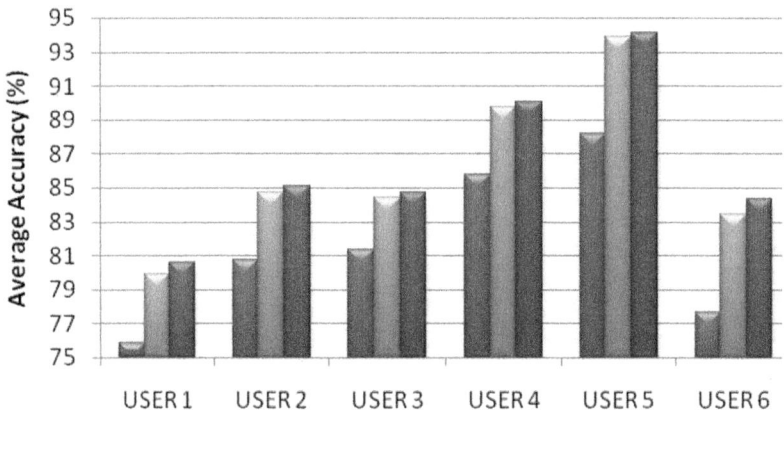

Fig. 3. Simulation results showing how well users would have done on the 11-20th rounds of TTR in accuracy had key-target resizing been on (green) and had key-target resizing been personalized to each user's data (red)

5   Conclusion and Future Directions

In this paper, we introduced TTR with three text entry goals in mind: 1. Provide beneficial targeting practice, 2. Provide useful highlighting of areas for improvement, and 3. Generate beneficial training data for key-target resizing. Through a user study and simulation experiment, we demonstrated that the game indeed achieves these three goals. As a future direction, we plan to explore using the game for real-time adaptation and collaborative filtering, as discussed in Section 2. We also plan to investigate adapting the text presented to users so that we can gather more data for areas in which our touch models have a significant amount of variance or where users simply need more practice. Finally, we are expanding the language coverage of TTR to enable widespread localization of our key-target resizing soft keyboard solution.

References

1. Amazon's Mechanical Turk, https://www.mturk.com
2. Appsfuse.com.,
   http://www.appsfuze.com/games/windowsphone.boardandclassic/
   text-text-revolution,758 (retrieved March 13, 2011)

3. Brewster, S., Chohan, F., Brown, L.: Tactile feedback for mobile interactions. In: Proc. of CHI, pp. 159–162 (2007)
4. Chao, D.: Doom as an interface for process management. In: Proc of CHI, pp. 152–157 (2001)
5. Entertainment Software Association. Industry facts,
   http://www.theesa.com/facts/index.asp (retrieved September 24, 2010)
6. Evanini, K., Higgins, D., Zechner, K.: Using Amazon MechanicalTurk for Transcription of Non-Native Speech. In: Proc. of NAACL Workshop on Creating Speech and Language Data With Amazon's MechanicalTurk (2010)
7. Games with a Purpose, http://www.gwap.com/gwap/
8. Goodman, J., Venolia, G., Steury, K., Parker, C.: Language modeling for soft keyboards. In: Proc.of AAAI, pp. 419–424 (2002)
9. Gunawardana, A., Paek, T., Meek, C.: Usability guided key-target resizing for soft keyboards. In: Proc. of IUI, pp. 111–118 (2010)
10. Kölsch, M., Turk, M.: Keyboards without keyboards: A survey of virtual keyboards. Technical Report 2002-21. University of California, Santa Barbara (2003)
11. Hoggan, E., Brewster, S., Johnston, J.: Investigating the effectiveness of tactile feedback for mobile touchscreens. In: Proc. of CHI, pp. 1573–1582 (2008)
12. MacKenzie, I.S., Tanaka-Ishii, K.: Text Entry Systems: Mobility, Accessibility, Universality. Morgan Kaufmann, San Francisco (2007)
13. Malone, T.M.: What makes things fun to learn? Heuristics for designing instructional computer games. In: Proc. of SIGSMALL, pp. 162–169 (1980)
14. Marge, M., Banerjee, S., Rudnicky, R.: Using the Amazon MechanicalTurk for transcription of spoken language. In: Proc. of ICASSP (March 2010)
15. Paek, T., Hsu, B.: Sampling representative phrase sets for text entry experiments: A procedure and public resource. In: Proc. of CHI (2011)
16. Rabin, E., Gordon, A.M.: Tactile feedback contributes to consistency of finger movements during typing. Experimental Brain Research 155(3), 1432–1106 (2004)
17. SpeedType,
   http://itunes.apple.com/us/app/speedtype/id287255484?mt=8
18. Turbo Type – The typing game to type fast,
   http://itunes.apple.com/app/turbo-type-the-typing-game/id374229839?mt=8
19. von Ahn, L.: Designing games with a purpose. Communications of the ACM 51(8), 58–67 (2005)
20. von Ahn, L., Dabbish, L.: Labeling images with a computer game. In: Proc.of CHI, pp. 319–326 (2004)
21. Windows Phone 7 Developer Tools,
   http://developer.windowsphone.com/windows-phone-7
22. Windows 7 Speech Recognition Tutorial,
   http://www.microsoft.com/enable/training/windowsvista/srtrain.aspx

Pervasive Sensing to Model Political Opinions in Face-to-Face Networks

Anmol Madan[1], Katayoun Farrahi[2,3], Daniel Gatica-Perez[2,3],
and Alex (Sandy) Pentland[1]

[1] MIT Media Laboratory, Massachusetts Institute of Technology, Cambridge, USA
[2] IDIAP Research Institute, Martigny, Switzerland
[3] Ecole Polytechnique Fédérale de Lausanne (EPFL), Lausanne, Switzerland

Abstract. Exposure and adoption of opinions in social networks are important questions in education, business, and government. We describe a novel application of pervasive computing based on using mobile phone sensors to measure and model the face-to-face interactions and subsequent opinion changes amongst undergraduates, during the 2008 US presidential election campaign. We find that self-reported political discussants have characteristic interaction patterns and can be predicted from sensor data. Mobile features can be used to estimate unique individual exposure to different opinions, and help discover surprising patterns of dynamic homophily related to external political events, such as election debates and election day. To our knowledge, this is the first time such dynamic homophily effects have been measured. Automatically estimated exposure explains individual opinions on election day. Finally, we report statistically significant differences in the daily activities of individuals that change political opinions versus those that do not, by modeling and discovering dominant activities using topic models. We find people who decrease their interest in politics are routinely exposed (face-to-face) to friends with little or no interest in politics.

1 Introduction

A central question for social science, as well as for the practical arts of education, sales, and politics, is the mechanism whereby ideas, opinions, innovations and recommendations spread through society. Diffusion is the phenomena of propagation of ideas or opinions within a social network. On the internet, the proliferation of social web applications has generated copious amounts of data about how people behave and interact with each other in online communities, and these data, are being extensively used to understand online diffusion phenomena. However, many important attributes of our lives are expressed primarily in real-world, face-to-face interactions. To model the adoption of these behaviors, we need fine-grained data about face-to-face interactions between people, i.e. who talks to whom, when, where, and how often, as well as data about exogenous variables that may affect the adoption process. Such social sensing of face-to-face interactions that explain social diffusion phenomena is a promising new area for pervasive computing.

K. Lyons, J. Hightower, and E.M. Huang (Eds.): Pervasive 2011, LNCS 6696, pp. 214–231, 2011.

Traditionally, social scientists have relied on self-report data to study social networks, but such approaches are not scaleable. It is impossible to use these methods with fine resolution, over long timescales (e.g. months or years), or for a large number of people, (e.g. hundreds or thousands). Further, while people may be reasonably accurate in their reports of long term social interaction patterns, it is clear that memory regarding particular relational episodes is quite poor. In a survey of informant accuracy literature, Bernard et.al. have shown that recall of social interactions in surveys used by social scientists is typically 30-50 % inaccurate [5,8].

A key question is how mobile sensing techniques and machine perception methods can help better model these social diffusion phenomena. This paper describes the use of mobile phone sensors at an undergraduate community to measure and model physical proximity (via bluetooth sensors), phone communication, movement patterns (via 802.11 WLAN access-points) and self-reported political opinions. Our approach provides insight about the adoption of political opinions in this community.

The contributions of this paper are as follows.

1. We devise a mobile sensing platform and observational methodology to capture social interactions and dependent variables during the last three months of the 2008 US Presidential campaigns of John McCain and President Barack Obama, amongst the residents of an undergraduate residence hall at a North American university. This dataset, first of its kind to our knowledge, consists of 132,000 hours of social interactions data and the dependent political opinions measured using monthly surveys.
2. We estimate exposure to diverse political opinions for individual residents, and propose a measure of dynamic homophily that reveals patterns at the community scale, related to external political events.
3. Pervasive-sensing based social exposure features explain individual political opinions on election day, better than self-reported social ties. We also show that 'political discussant' ties have characteristic interaction patterns, which can be used to recover such ties in the network.
4. Using an LDA-based topic modeling approach, we study the behavior differences between individuals who change opinions, and those who held their political opinions. We show statistically significant differences in the activities of people who changed their preferred party versus those that did not. People that changed preferred party often discuss face-to-face with their democrat political discussants, and their daily routines included heavy phone and SMS activity. We also find people that decrease their interest in politics often interact with people that have little or no interest in politics

2   Related Work

Sensing Human Behavior Using Mobile Devices

There has been extensive work to model various aspects of human behavior, using smartphones [16,36,1,22,15,4,17], wearable sensor badges [43,30,41], video

[46], and web-based social media data [7,48,52,33,34,3,39]. Choudhury et. al., used electronic sensor badges to detect social network structure and model turn-taking behavior in face-to-face networks [10,12]. Eagle et. al. used mobile phones as sensors to characterize social ties for a student community [16]. At larger scales, mobile location and calling data have been used to characterize temporal and spatial regularity in human mobility patterns [22], and individual communication diversity has been used to explain the economic development of cities [15]. Other examples of the use of mobile phones to map human interaction networks include the CENS participatory sensing project at UCLA [1], and the mHealth and Darwin projects at Dartmouth [4,17]. Electronic sensor badges instrumented with infrared(IR) sensors to capture the direction of face-to-face proximity, have been used by Olguin, Waber and Kim [42,41] to enhance organizational performance and productivity, for financial institutions and consultants. Vocal analysis has been used to capture nonlinguistic communication and social signaling in different contexts [11,35,43,42].

On the modeling front, Exponential Random Graph Models (ERGMs) and its extensions [45,50,24,26] have been used to understand interaction networks. Topic models have been explored for activity modeling applications [18,19,27]. New topic models have also been proposed in the context of blog post response prediction [51] and blog influence [40]. Other types of topic models, like Author-Topic [47,37] and Group-Topic [49] models have been used for social network analysis when content or contextual data is present. In this paper, we use LDA topic model [6] to better understand the behavior differences between people who changed their opinions.

Adoption of Political Opinions

In political science and sociology, an important area of study is how opinions about political candidates and parties, and voting behavior, spread through different interaction networks. Political scientists have proposed two competing models of social influence and contagion [9]. The social cohesion model suggests that influence is proportional to tie strength, while the structural equivalence model [21] proposes that influences exist across individuals with similar roles and positions in networks. Huckfeldt and Sprague [25] studied the interdependence of an individual's political opinions, their political discussant network and context and demographics during the 1984 presidential elections. They found a social dissonance effect in the propagation of political opinions, and also report an 'inverse U' relationship with tie-strength, i.e. discussant effects are stronger for less intimate relationships like acquaintances and frequent contacts than they are for close friends.

In the online context, Adamic and Glance [2] studied political blogs during the 2004 presidential elections, and found that content, discussions and news items on liberal and conservative blogs, connected primarily to separate clusters, with very few cross-links between the two major clusters. Leskovec et. al. [33] tracked the propagation of short, distinctive political phrases during the 2008 elections, and model the news cycle across both mainstream news sources and political blogs.

3   Methodology

In the past, researchers have used Call Data Records (CDRs) provided by mobile operators to better understand human behavior [22,15]. Our approach, however, is to use pervasive sensing methods for capturing social interactions, and this has several advantages. Firstly, it allows us to sample different sensors and dependent training labels, and not just calling data alone. Secondly, from a privacy perspective, this requires the user's explicit participation in data collection. Additionally, in the future, it could be used to provide the user immediate feedback on the mobile device itself.

3.1   Privacy Considerations

An important concern with long-term user data collection is securing personal privacy for the participants. This study was approved by the Institutional Review Board (IRB). As financial compensation for completing monthly surveys and using data-collection devices as their primary phones, participants were allowed to keep the devices at the end of the study. The sensing scripts used in the platform capture only hashed identifiers, and collected data is secured and anonymized before being used for aggregate analysis.

3.2   Mobile Sensing Platform

Given the above goals, the mobile phone based platform for data-collection was designed with the following long-term continuous sensing capabilities, using Windows Mobile 6.x devices. Daily captured mobile sensing data was stored on-device on read/write SD Card memory. On the server side, these logs files were merged, parsed and synced by an extensive Python post-processing infrastructure, and stored in MySQL for analysis. This sensing software platform for Windows Mobile 6.x has been released under the LGPLv3 open source license for public use [28].

Proximity Detection (Bluetooth). The software scanned for Bluetooth wireless devices in proximity every 6 minutes (a compromise between sensing short-term social interactions and battery life, [16]). The Windows Mobile phones used in our experiment were equipped with class 2 Bluetooth radio transceivers, with practical indoor sensing range of approximately 10 feet. Scan results for two devices in proximity have a high likelihood of being asymmetric, which is accounted for in our analysis. Due to API limitations of Windows Mobile 6.x, signal strength was not available during scans.

Approximate Location (802.11 WLAN). The software scanned for wireless WLAN 802.11 Access Point identifiers (hereafter referred to as WLAN APs) every 6 minutes. WLAN APs have an indoor range of approximately 125 feet and the university campus had almost complete wireless coverage. Across various locations within the undergraduate residence, over 55 different WLAN APs with varying signal strengths can be detected.

Communication (Call and SMS Records). The software logged Call and SMS details on the device every 20 minutes, including information about missed calls and calls not completed.

Battery Impact. The battery life impact of periodic scanning has been previously discussed [16]. In this study, periodic scanning of Bluetooth and WLAN APs reduced operational battery life by 10-15%, with average usable life between 14-24 hours (varying with handset models and individual usage). Windows Mobile 6.x devices have relatively poorer battery performance than other smartphones, and WLAN usage (web browsing by user) had a bigger impact on battery life than periodic scanning.

3.3   Dataset Characteristics

The mobile phone interaction dataset was collected from 67 participants and consisted of approximately 450,000 bluetooth proximity scans, 1.2 million WLAN access-point scans, 16,900 phone call records and 17,800 SMS text message events. The average duration of phone calls is approx 138 seconds, and 58 percent of phone calls were during weekdays.

3.4   Political Opinions (Dependent Variables)

The dependent political opinions were captured using three monthly web-based surveys, once each in September, October, and November 2008 (immediately following the presidential election). The monthly survey instrument was based on established political science literature, and consisted of questions shown in Table 1. The questions were identical to the survey instrument used by Lazer and Rubineau [32], who measured the monthly political opinions of students across different universities (during the same 2008 election period) and studied the co-evolution of political opinions and self-report friendship networks.

Political scientists have established that shifts in political opinions are gradual [25]. This is observed in our dataset, as approximately 30% of the 67 participants changed their opinions for each of the dependent questions during the three month observation period. Opinion changes were along 1-point or 2-points on the respective 4/7-point Likert scales. Similar variations in our dependent variables were also reported in the analysis of Lazer and Rubineau [32].

For each monthly survey, participants also identified other residents that were political discussants, close friends or social acquaintances, identical to those used here [32]. Baseline information including race, ethnicity, political opinions of the person's parents and religious affiliations was also collected from some of the participants before the start of the experiment, but is not used in our analysis.

Table 1. Political Survey Instrument used to capture different political opinions. All responses were constructed as Likert scales.

Survey Question	Possible Responses
Are you liberal or conservative?	7-point Likert scale
	Extremely conservative to extremely liberal
How interested are you in politics	4-point Likert scale
	Not interested to very interested
What is your political party preference?	7-point Likert scale
	Strong Democrat to strong Republican
Which candidate are you likely to vote for? (Sept and Oct)	Choice between leading Republican and Democrat nominees
Which candidate did you vote for? (Nov)	Choice between B. Obama and J. McCain
Are you going to vote in the upcoming election? (Sept and Oct)	4-point Likert scale
Did you vote in the election? (Nov)	Yes or No

4 Analysis

4.1 Individual Exposure to Diverse Opinions

What is an individual's social exposure to diverse ideas and opinions? Threshold and cascade models of diffusion [23,29] assume that all individuals in a population have a uniform exposure, or that the underlying distribution of exposure to different opinions is known. While exposure to different opinions is dynamic and characteristic for every individual, it has previously not been incorporated into empirical social diffusion models. Dynamic exposure to different opinions can be estimated for each participant, on a daily or hourly basis. Contact between two individuals can be given as a function of physical proximity counts (bluetooth), phone call and SMS counts, total duration of proximity, total duration of phone conversation, or other measures of tie-strength. These features represent the time spent with others having different opinions in classes, at home, and in phone communication.

Normalized exposure, N_i represents the average of all opinions a person is exposed to on a daily basis, weighted by the amount of exposure to different individuals and their self-reported opinions, where O_j represents the opinion response for person j for a particular question in Table 1, $contact_{ij}$ is the bluetooth proximity counts between i and j (tie-strength), and $Nbr(i)$ is the set of neighbors for i in the interaction network.

$$N_i = \sum_{j \in Nbr(i)} contact_{ij} \cdot O_j / \sum_j contact_{ij} \tag{1}$$

Cumulative exposure, C_i to a particular political opinion O, represents the magnitude of a particular opinion that a person is exposed to on a daily basis, and is a function of the amount of contact with different individuals and their self-reported opinion. $contact_{ij}$ can be estimated from other mobile interaction features, like counts for calling, SMS, and 802.11 WLAN co-location. In Section 4.4, N_i is used for future opinion prediction and in Section 5, C_{iO} from both bluetooth and call features are used for change of opinion modeling.

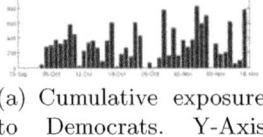 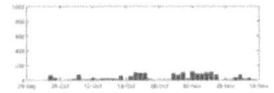 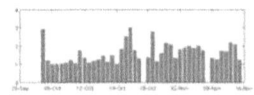

(a) Cumulative exposure to Democrats. Y-Axis is Bluetooth proximity counts

(b) Cumulative exposure to Republicans Y-Axis is Bluetooth proximity counts

(c) Normalized exposure for the Preferred party response

Fig. 1. Characteristic daily normalized and cumulative exposure for one resident during the election period (Oct-Nov 2008). Contact is Bluetooth physical proximity. X-Axis is days for all graphs. This individual had much more exposure to democratic opinions than republican during this period. Incidentally, this person did not show an opinion shift for the preferred-party response during the study (not shown).

$$C_{iO} = \delta_j \cdot \sum_{j \in Nbr(i)} contact_{ij} \qquad (2)$$

$\delta_j = 1$ only if person j holds opinion O, and 0 otherwise. Figure 1 shows cumulative and normalized exposure for one participant during the election campaign period. This individual did not have much exposure to republicans, though was often in proximity to democrats, some days much more than others.

4.2   Pervasive Reflection of Dynamic Homophily

Homophily, or the idea of "birds of a feather flock together", [31] is a fundamental and pervasive phenomenon in social networks, and refers to the tendency of individuals to form relationships with others that have similar attributes, behaviors or opinions. McPherson and Smith [38] provide an in depth review of homophily literature. The emergence of homophily during network formation has be explained using agent based models, and in economics [14] by incorporating chance, choice, and tie formation costs. In this section we define a measure of dynamic homophily based on mobile phone interaction features.

In sociological literature, homophily is estimated using the homophily index H_i, and Coleman's inbreeding homophily index, IH_i, which are a function of the relative fraction of social ties expressed between people who hold similar opinions, and those that hold different opinions. These homophily indices are explained in more detail in [14,38]. These sociological measures of homophily are useful for static networks, but do not capture the dynamics of the underlying phenomena. To overcome these limitations, we propose a measure of dynamic homophily based on social exposure features for the daily timescale, given as,

$$\Delta_i(t) = \left| O_i - \sum_{j \in Nbr(i)} contact_{ij} \cdot O_j / \sum_j contact_{ij} \right| \qquad (3)$$

$$H(t) = \sum_i \Delta_i(t)/n \qquad (4)$$

where $\Delta_i(t)$ is the difference between the individual's opinions and the opinions he/she is exposed to, $H(t)$ is a daily measure of dynamic homophily for the entire community, and O_i are an individuals political opinion responses, on the full-range of the 4 or 7-point scale, i.e., for the political interest response, O_i ranges from 1 ("Very Interested") to 4("Not at all interested") and for the preferred party response, O_i ranges from 1("Strong Democrat") to 7("Strong Republican"). Unlike the static homophily measures above, O_i is not based on the redistributed classes.

Daily variations in $H(t)$ are due to changes in mobile phone interaction features, that capture how participants interact with others. A negative slope in $H(t)$ implies that residents have more social exposure to individuals sharing similar opinions, in comparison to the previous day or week. Similarly, an upward slope implies that residents have decreasing social exposure with others having similar opinions.

This daily measure captures dynamic homophily variations during the election period, not captured using existing static measures of homophily. For a few days around the election day and final debates, participants show a higher tendency overall to interact with like-minded individuals. Statistical validation of these variations using repeated-measures ANOVA for different political opinions for three relevant conditions (periods) are given in Table 2 (plots in Figure 2).

Table 2. Statistically significant variations in Dynamic Homophily around the final election debate period (15th Oct 2008) and election day (4th Nov 2008) period. Dynamic homophily is calculated using bluetooth proximity (phone calling and SMS are not significant for any self-reported political opinions). For each period, the average dynamic homophily for the 5-day period per participant was estimated. This analysis was first done for all participants, and then repeated for freshmen-only, who had only been in the community for a month before start of the study, and where stronger effects are observed. The three experimental conditions (periods) chosen for validating the main effect were (a) Baseline Period (1st condition), i.e., 4th October to 10th October 2008 (b) Final election debate Period (2nd condition), 12th October to 18th October 2008 and (c) Election period (3rd condition): 1st November to 7th November 2008.

Opinions Evaluated for main effects over three periods (conditions)	Result Summary (plots in Figure 2)
Political Interest for all participants	Significant effect, higher tendency to interact with like-minded individuals during debate and final election period as compared to baseline period, $F-value = 8.49, p < 0.0004$
Political Interest for freshmen only	Significant effect, higher tendency to interact with like-minded individuals during debate and final election period as compared to baseline period, $F-value = 3.43, p = 0.04$
Party preference for all participants	Not a significant effect, $F-value = 0.87, p < 0.42$
Liberal-conservative tendency for all participants	Significant effect, higher tendency to interact with like-minded individuals during debate and final election period as compared to baseline period, $F-value = 6.26, p < 0.003$

Figure 2 (a) shows $H(t)$ for political interest for all participants, where daily network structure is estimated on the basis of Bluetooth proximity counts. The first dip in this graph corresponds to the period of the final election debate during the campaign, 14th Oct 2008. The difference between the three conditions is statistically significant ($F - value = 8.49, p < 0.0004$). Figure 2(b) and (c) show similar dips for the preferred-party and liberal-conservative responses. Figure 2(d) shows $H(t)$ for political interest only for freshmen, based on daily bluetooth proximity networks. The dynamic homophily effects for freshmen, who only had a month to form ties in this community at this point, are visually pronounced, and a second dip is seen around 4th November 2008 (Election day, $F - value = 3.43, p = 0.04$). We find that these behavior changes related to external events are seen in bluetooth proximity data, but not in calling and SMS interactions. This suggests that exposure to different opinions based on physical proximity plays a more important role than exposure to opinions via phone communication. Similar results are also observed for the preferred party responses and liberal-conservative responses with respect to phone calling patterns.

4.3   Inferring Political Discussants

What are the behavioral patterns of political discussants? In monthly self-reported survey responses, only 39.6% of political discussants are also close friends. Similarly, it is found that having similar political opinions does not increase the likelihood that two individuals will be political discussants in this dataset.

While these political discussants do not fit the mould of 'close friends' or individuals with similar political opinions. we find that it is possible to identify political discussants from their interaction patterns. Classification results based on mobile phone interaction features – total communication; weekend/late-night communication; total proximity; and late-night/weekend proximity, that characterize a political discussant are shown in Table 3. Two different approaches are used for comparison, an AdaboostM1 based classifier [20] and a Bayesian network classifier [13], where each input sample represents a possible tie, and both show similar results. Cost-sensitive approaches are used in both cases, to account for unbalanced classes. Political discussants are treated as unidirectional ties. Precision and recall of the discussant class are similar if self-reported the training labels are converted to bi-directional ties.

4.4   Exposure and Future Opinions

Exposure based features described in the previous section can be used as a feature to train a linear predictor of future opinions. The coefficients used in a linear model of opinion change include normalized exposure during the period, the persons opinion at the start of the study (September 2008), and a constant term that represents a linearly increasing amount of media influence as we get closer to the election date (Nov. 2008). For the various political opinion questions, regression values are in the $R^2 = 0.8, p < 0.01$ region. Using exposure

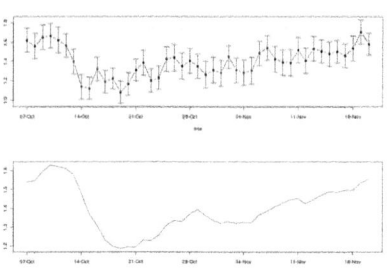

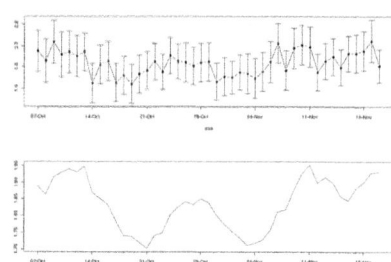

(a) Dynamic homophily of **political interest responses** (using bluetooth proximity) for all participants. Notice the decline, i.e. tendency to interact with others having similar opinions, lasting for a few days, around Oct 15th 2008, which was the last presidential debate.

(b) Dynamic homophily of **preferred party responses** (using bluetooth proximity) for all participants.

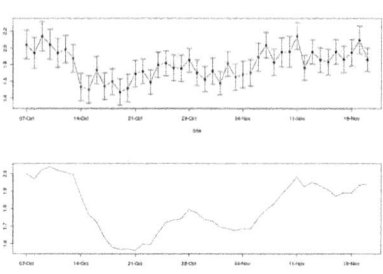

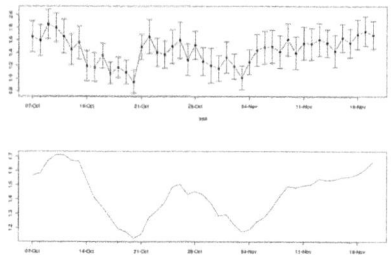

(c) Dynamic homophily of **liberal-conservative responses** (using bluetooth proximity) for all participants.

(d) Dynamic homophily of **political interest responses** (using bluetooth proximity) only for **Freshmen** . There are two periods of decline, each lasting for a few days. The first is around Oct 15th (last presidential debate) and the second is around 4th Nov, Election Day.

Fig. 2. Top: actual values of $H(t)$ with standard error bars. Bottom: Moving average.

based features explains an additional 15% - 30% variance across different political opinion questions. The effects for freshmen are approximately twice as strong as compared to the entire population, similar to the variations in dynamic homophily related to external events. In the context of social science literature, this is a relevant effect.

Table 3. Identifying Political discussants based on exposure features. Classification results using Meta-cost AdaboostM1 (individual classifiers are decision stumps), 5-fold cross validation.

Class	Precision	Recall	F-Measure
Non-discussants	0.87	0.62	0.72
Political discussants	0.35	0.67	0.46

Table 4. Identifying Political discussants based on exposure features. Classification results using cost-sensitive Bayesian Network classifier, 5-fold cross validation and K2 hill-climbing structure learning.

Class	Precision	Recall	F-Measure
Non-discussants	0.87	0.61	0.72
Political discussants	0.35	0.70	0.46

Table 5. Least squares regression results for the opinion change model. The dependent variable in all cases is the self-reported political opinion in November. The independent regression variables are averaged opinion of self-reported close friends relationships and political discussants (I), normalized bluetooth exposure (II), and normalized exposure combined with past opinion (III). As seen, automatically captured mobile phone features substantially outperform self-reported close friends or political discussants.

Political Opinion Type	I Self-reported Disc. / Close Friends	II Normalized Exp. Only	III Normalized Exp. & Sept Opinion
Preferred Party	n.s. / n.s.	0.21^{**}	0.78^{***}
Liberal or Conservative	n.s. / n.s.	0.16^{*}	0.81^{***}
Interest in Politics	n.s. / 0.07^{*}	0.24^{**}	0.74^{***}
Preferred Party (freshmen only)	n.s. / n.s.	0.46^{*}	0.83^{*}
Interest in Politics (freshmen only)	n.s. / n.s.	0.21^{**}	0.78^{***}

All values are R^2 n.s.: not significant
$^{*}: p < 0.05$ $^{**}: p < 0.01$ $^{***}: p < 0.001$

5   Modeling Opinion Change with Topic Models

An important question in sociology is 'what influences opinion change'? Is there an underlying mechanism resulting in the opinion change for some people? Can we measure this mechanism, and if so, can we predict future opinion changes from observed behavior? In this section, we propose a method for activity modeling based on the Latent Dirichlet Allocation (LDA) [6] topic model, to contrast the activities of participants that change opinions, with those that do not. We discover in an unsupervised manner, the dominating routines of people in the dataset, where routines are the most frequently co-occurring political opinion exposure patterns also referred to as topics.

5.1 Latent Dirichlet Allocation

Topic models can be used to discover a set of underlying (or latent) topics from which a corpus of M documents d is composed via unsupervised learning. They are generative models initially developed for textual content analysis. In LDA [6], a word w is generated from a convex combination of K topics z. The number of latent topics, K, must be chosen by the user. The probability of word w_t from a vocabulary of V words in document d_i is $p(w_t|d_i) = \sum_k p(w_t|z_k)p(z_k|d_i), \sum_k p(z_k|d_i) = 1$. LDA assumes a Dirichlet prior probability distribution on $\Theta = \{\{p(z_k|d_i)\}_{k=1}^K\}_{i=1}^M$ and $\Phi = \{\{p(w_t|z_k)\}_{t=1}^V\}_{k=1}^K$ to provide a complete generative model for documents. Words are considered to be exchangeable, meaning they are independent given topics. The objective of LDA inference is to obtain (1) the distribution of words given topics Φ and (2) the distribution of topics over documents Θ.

When considering behavioral data, what we refer to as 'multimodal exposure (MME) features' can be seen as analogous to text words and a user is analogous to a document. Further, latent topics are analoguous to human routines, where Φ gives an indication of how probable topics are for users, and Θ results in a distribution of exposure features given topics.

5.2 Multimodal Exposure (MME) Features and Topics

We formulate a multimodal vector of exposure features (MME features) encompassing four components: (1) time (2) political opinion (3) type + amount of interaction and (4) relationship. Overall, a MME feature captures the exposure to a particular political opinion, including details such as time and relationship. Given a survey question from Table 1, a MME feature has the following structure $(t, p_o, b, c, f, s, p_d)$. Component (1) is the time where $t \in \{10$ pm-2 am (late night $=$ LN), $2 - 8$ am (early morning $=$ EM), 8 am-5 pm (day $=$ D), $5 - 10$ pm (evening $=$ E)$\}$. These 4 time intervals in the day are specific to the overall daily activities of the users in the dataset. Component (2) is the political opinion $p_o \in o$ and o is the set of possible responses from Table 1 for the survey question chosen. Component (3) is the type and amount of interaction where b is a measure of the cumulative exposure (Equation 2) from bluetooth proximity to opinion p_o and c is the cumulative exposure from the mobile phone logs to opinion p_o. Cumulative exposure is quantized into the following bins: $b \in \{0, 1 - 2, 2 - 9, 9+\}$, $c \in \{0, 1 - 2, 3+\}$ to limit the vocabulary size. $b = 0$ implies no proximity interaction in the time interval t with political opinion p_o and $c = 3+$ implies 3 or more calls and/or SMS with political opinion p_o during time interval t. Finally, the relationship metric is defined by $f \in$ [friend, not friend], $s \in$ [socialize, do not socialize], and $p_d \in$ [political discussants, not political discussants]. Topics are essentially clusters of dominating 'opinion exposures' present over all individuals and days in the real-life data collection, described in terms of MME features.

5.3   Model Selection with Statistics

In order to choose the optimal number of topics, K, for the model, we consider statistical significance measures over the entropy of topic distributions. We chose entropy of topic distributions as it (1) enables the computation of statistical significance over a vector of probability distributions and (2) summarizes the probability distributions of user behaviors.

In Figure 3, statistical significance test results are displayed for various survey questions (Table 1) (e.g. interest in politics (I)) as a function of the number of topics (x-axis) (a) for the groups 'changed opinion' versus 'did not change' (b) considering all possible opinions and change of opinions as groups. The difference in group entropies is mostly statistically significant for the preferred party opinion when considering the 2 group case in (a), however not for all values of K. In Figure 3(a), the first two points for which statistical significance occurs are at $K = 13$ and $K = 14$ and in the case of Figure 3(b) at $K = 17$. For the opinion interest in politics (I) and the 2 group case in plot (a) at $K = 22$ the p-value reaches its minimum. We consider $K = 14$ for PP (4-point scale) and $K = 22$ for I, points which are statistically significant, in analyzing opinion change in the results.

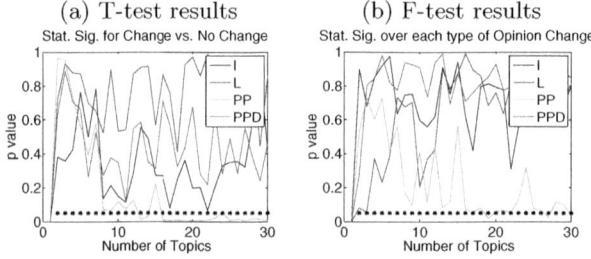

Fig. 3. Significance results (a) for 'changed opinion' versus 'did not change opinion' for interest in politics (I), liberal/conservative (L), preferred party (PP) (4-point scale) and (PPD) (7-point scale) (b) considering all possible opinions and change of opinions as groups

5.4   Results

Interaction Patterns of People who Change Opinion. The goal is to determine the difference in the interaction patterns of these two groups and we do this by comparing the most probable topics, averaged over all the users of each group. In Figure 3 for preferred party (PP) at $K = 14$, we observed the two groups 'people who changed opinion' and 'people who did not change opinion' was statistically significant with $p = 0.026$. Note, 5 users changed PP and 44 users did not. In Figure 4(a), the top plot shows the mean Φ for those that changed opinions and the bottom is for those that did not. The most probable topics (dominating routine) for users that changed opinion was topic 3, 9, and 10 visualized by (b), (c), and (d), respectively. The most dominant topic for users that did not change was topic 10, which dominated in both groups. For a given topic ((b)-(d)), we display the 3 most probable words' (top) face-to-face interaction features (middle) phone interaction features and (bottom) relationship statistics, abbreviated by FR for friends, SOC for socialize and PD for political discussants.

Looking at Topic 3 (plot (b)), we can see that users that changed opinion predominantly had face-to-face interactions with PD, that were non-friends and not people they socialize with. The preferred party of these political discussants was democrat and this interaction occurred predominantly between 10pm-5pm (LN to D time components). Further, people who changed opinion also had heavy phone call and SMS activity with democrats as well as independents, as seen by Topic 9.

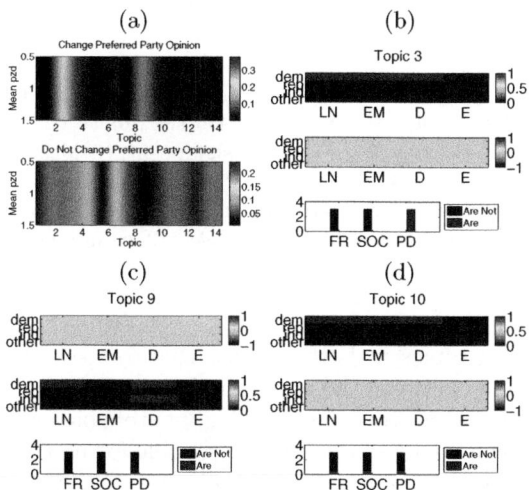

Fig. 4. (a) Mean topic distribution of users that changed opinion(top) and users that did not (bottom). Users that changed PP (4-point scale) had a high probability of topics 3, 9, 10, whereas users that did not change had a high probability of topic 10. By looking at the features of the 3 most probable words for these topics, we can see that users that changed opinion displayed (b) heavy face-to-face interactions with political discussants, and (c) they also had heavy phone call activity with non-friends.

Different Exposure for Increased vs. Decreased Interest in Politics. We considered the difference in daily routines of users which increased their interest in politics as opposed to those that decreased their interest. Figure 5(a) shows the T-test results for the entropy of topic distributions of both groups, with $p = 0.06$. Figure 5(b) is the mean probability distribution of topics given the users from the two groups with $K = 22$ topics. The mean topic distribution $p(z|d)$ is shown for (top) all users that increased their interest, and (bottom) all users that decreased their interest. Note, 14 users increased their interest and 34 users decreased their interest in politics. Plots (c)-(e) show the most probable words

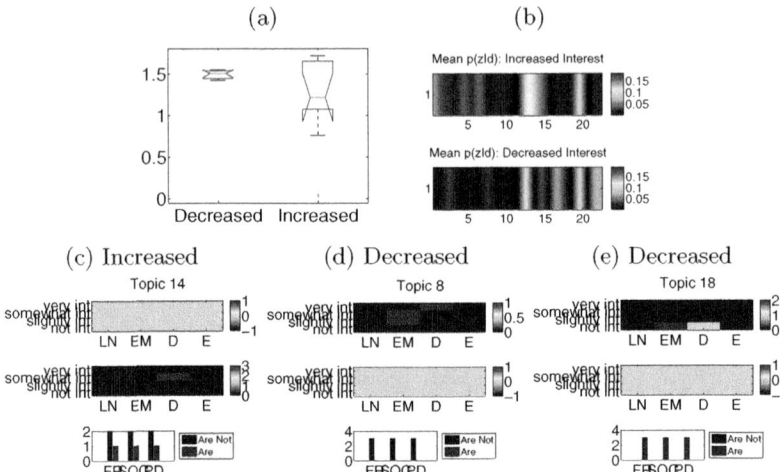

Fig. 5. Routines of people who increased their interest in politics versus those that decreased their interest. (a)T-test results reveal the difference in the entropy of topic distributions for these groups is statistically significant. (b)Mean distribution of topics for users of both groups. (c)-(e)Topics which best characterized users' daily life patterns in both groups. People who increased their interest often communicated by phone (c) and those that decreased interest had many face-to-face interactions with people with little/no interest in politics (d-e).

for the dominating topics in both groups. Due to space constraints, we show topics which differed between the groups and disregard topics which were highly probable for both groups. Topic 14 (c) is highly probable for users that increased their interest. Topic 8 and 18 are highly probable for users that decreased their interest. People who displayed increased interest were communicating most often by phone during the day. The group which decreased their interest had only face-to-face interactions (no phone communication) dominating their daily routines and it included interaction with people with little and no interest as seen by topics 8 and 18. There was heavy face-to-face interactions with friends in the early morning (EM) who had no interest in politics, for the group that decreased their interest.

6   Conclusion

In this paper we describe a novel application of pervasive sensing using mobile phones– modeling the spread of political opinions in real-world face-to-face networks. Using mobile phone sensors, we estimate exposure to different opinions for individuals, find patterns of dynamic homophily at the community scale, recover 'political discussant' ties in the network, and explain individual political opinions on election day. We use an LDA-based model to study specific behaviors of people who changed their political opinions.

There are however, several limitations of our approach. We use bluetooth sensors to identify when people are in physical proximity, but there are many cases where individuals are proximate in the same room or space, but not necessarily interacting, as discussed in [44]. Another limitation is that our dataset consists of interactions captured using mobile phone sensors, and does not account for exposure to political opinions in mass media, e.g. via television or internet blog posts. The ability to estimate future changes in political opinions would certainly improve if such data was available. Mass-media access to political information, however, has been shown to be correlated with the self-reported party preference and political interest responses of the individual. On the technical front, our Windows Mobile platform at the time did not support GPS hardware sensors.

There are several fascinating future extensions of this work. In addition to political opinions, it would be important to understand if pervasive sensing methods can help understand the propagation of other types of opinions and habits in face-to-face networks, e.g., those related to health or purchasing behavior, both in our current dataset and also in other observational data. With the constant improvement in sensing technologies, future projects could use global positioning system (GPS) or infra-red (IR) sensors for better location and proximity sensing. Overall, our quantitative analysis sheds more light on long-standing open questions in political science and other social sciences, about the diffusion mechanism for opinions and behaviors.

Acknowledgments

The authors would like to thank Dr. David Lazer, Iolanthe Chronis and various undergraduate contributors for their help with the experimental deployment. Anmol Madan and Alex Pentland were partially sponsored by the Army Research Laboratory under Cooperative Agreement Number W911NF-09-2-0053, and by AFOSR under Award Number FA9550-10-1-0122. Views and conclusions in this document are those of the authors and should not be interpreted as representing the official policies, either expressed or implied, of the Army Research Laboratory or the U.S. Government. The U.S. Government is authorized to reproduce and distribute reprints for Government purposes notwithstanding any copyright notation. Katayoun Farrahi and Daniel Gatica-Perez were supported by the Swiss National Science Foundation through the MULTI and HAI projects.

References

1. Abdelzaher, T., Anokwa, Y., Boda, P., Burke, J., Estrin, D., Guibas, L., Kansal, A., Madden, S., Reich, J.: Mobiscopes for human spaces. IEEE Pervasive Computing - Mobile and Ubiquitous Systems 6(2) (2007)
2. Adamic, L., Glance, N.: The political blogosphere and the 2004 US election: divided they blog. In: Proc. of the 3rd Intl. Workshop on Link Discovery (2005)
3. Agarwal, N., Liu, H.: Modeling and Data Mining in Blogosphere, vol. 1. Morgan & Claypool Publishers, San Francisco (2009)

4. Avancha, S., Baxi, A., Kotz, D.: Privacy in mobile technology for personal healthcare. Submitted to ACM Computing Surveys (2009)
5. Bernard, H.R., Killworth, P., Kronenfeld, D., Sailer, L.: The Problem of Informant Accuracy: The Validity of Retrospective Data. Annual Reviews in Anthropology (1984)
6. Blei, D.M., Ng, A.Y., Jordan, M.I., Lafferty, J.: Latent dirichlet allocation. JMLR 3 (2003)
7. Boyd, D., Ellison, N.: Social network sites: Definition, history, and scholarship. Journal of Computer Mediated Communication 13(1), 210 (2007)
8. Brewer, D., Webster, C.: Forgetting of friends and its effects on measuring friendship networks. Social Networks 21(4), 361–373 (2000)
9. Burt, R.: Social contagion and innovation: Cohesion versus structural equivalence. American Journal of Sociology (1987)
10. Choudhury, T.: Sensing and Modeling Human Networks. PhD thesis, M.I.T (2003)
11. Choudhury, T.: Characterizing social networks using the sociometer. Association of Computational Social and Organizational Science (2004)
12. Choudhury, T., Basu, S.: Modeling Conversational Dynamics as a Mixed Memory Markov Process. In: NIPS (2004)
13. Bishop, C.: Pattern Recognition and Machine Learning. Springer, Heidelberg (2006)
14. Currarini, S., Jackson, M., Pin, P.: An Economic Model of Friendship: Homophily, Minorities, and Segregation. Econometrica 77(4), 1003–1045 (2009)
15. Eagle, N., Macy, M., Claxton, R.: Network Diversity and Economic Development. Science 328(5981), 1029–1031 (2010)
16. Eagle, N., Pentland, A., Lazer, D.: Inferring Social Network Structure Using Mobile Phone Data. PNAS 106(36), 15274–15278 (2009)
17. Miluzzo, E., et al.: Darwin Phones: The Evolution of Sensing and Inference on Mobile Phones. In: Mobisys (2010)
18. Farrahi, K., Gatica-Perez, D.: What did you do today? discovering daily routines from large-scale mobile data. ACM MM (2008)
19. Farrahi, K., Gatica-Perez, D.: Probabilistic mining of socio-geographic routines from mobile phone data. IEEE J-STSP 4(4), 746–755 (2010)
20. Freund, Y., Schapire, R.E.: A short introduction to boosting. Japonese Society for Artificial Intelligence 5, 771–780 (1999)
21. Friedkin, N.E.: A Structural Theory of Social Influence. Cambridge University Press, Cambridge (1998)
22. Gonzalez, M., Hidalgo, C., Barabasi, A.-L.: Understanding Individual Human Mobility Patterns. Nature 453, 779–782 (2008)
23. Granovetter, M.: Threshold models of collective behavior. American Journal of Sociology 83, 1420–1443 (1978)
24. Guo, F., Hanneke, S., Fu, W., Xing, E.P.: Recovering temporally rewiring networks: A model-based approach. In: ICML (2007)
25. Huckfeldt, R., Sprague, J.: Discussant Effects on Vote Choice: Intimacy, Structure and Interdependence. The Journal of Politics 53, 122–158 (1991)
26. Hunter, D.R., Handcock, M.S.: Inference in curved exponential family models for networks. Journal of Computational and Graphical Statistics 15, 565–583 (2006)
27. Huynh, T., Fritz, M., Schiele, B.: Discovery of activity patterns using topic models. In: UbiComp, Seoul, Korea, pp. 10–19 (2008)
28. Intentionally Blank. Intentionally blank
29. Kempe, D., Kleinberg, J., Tardos, E.: Maximizing the Spread of Influence in a Social Network. In: KDD 2003, Washington DC (2003)

30. Laibowitz, M., Gips, J., Aylward, R., Pentland, A., Paradiso, J.: A sensor network for social dynamics. In: IPSN, p. 491 (2006)
31. Lazarsfeld, P., Merton, R.K.: Friendship as a Social Process: A Substantive and Methodological Analysis. Freedom and Control in Modern Society (1954)
32. Lazer, D., Rubineau, B., Katz, N., Chetkovich, C., Neblo, M.A.: Networks and political attitudes: Structure, influence, and co-evolution. Working paper series (September 2008)
33. Leskovec, J., Backstrom, L., Kleinberg, J.: Meme-tracking and the Dynamics of the News Cycle. In: ACM SIGKDD (2009)
34. Liu, H., Salerno, J., Young, M.: Social Computing, Behavioral Modeling and Prediction. Springer, Heidelberg (2008)
35. Madan, A., Pentland, A.: Vibephones: Socially aware mobile phones. In: ISWC (2006)
36. Madan, A., Pentland, A.: Modeling Social Diffusion Phenomena Using Reality Mining. In: AAAI Spring Symposium on Human Behavior Modeling (2009)
37. Mccallum, A., Corrada-emmanuel, A., Wang, X.: The author-recipient-topic model for topic and role discovery in social networks: Experiments with enron and academic email. Technical report (2004)
38. McPherson, M., Smith-Lovin, L., Cook, J.M.: Birds of a Feather: Homophily in Social Networks. Annual Review of Sociology 27, 415–444 (2001)
39. Moturu, S.: Quantifying the Trustworthiness of Social Media Content: Content Analysis for the Social Web. Lambert Academic Publishing (2010)
40. Nallapati, R., Cohen, W.: Link-plsa-lda: A new unsupervised model for topics and influence in blogs. In: ICWSM (2008)
41. Olguin Olguin, D., Gloor, P., Pentland, A.: Wearable sensors for pervasive healthcare management. PCT Healthcare (2009)
42. Olguin Olguin, D., Waber, B., Kim, T., Mohan, A., Ara, K., Pentland, A.: Sensible organizations: Technology and methodology for automatically measuring organizational behavior. IEEE Transactions on Systems, Man, and Cybernetics-B (2009)
43. Pentland, A.: Socially aware computation and communication. In: ICMI (2005)
44. Richardson, M., Domingas, P.: Markob logic networks. Machine Learning (2006)
45. Robins, G., Snijders, T., Wang, P., Handcock, M., Pattison, P.: Recent developments in exponential random graph (p*) models for social networks. Social Networks 29(2), 192–215 (2007)
46. Roy, D., Patel, R., DeCamp, P., Kubat, R., Fleischman, M., Roy, B., Mavridis, N., Tellex, S., Salata, A., Guinness, J., Levit, M., Gorniak, P.: The human speechome project. In: Vogt, P., Sugita, Y., Tuci, E., Nehaniv, C.L. (eds.) EELC 2006. LNCS (LNAI), vol. 4211, pp. 192–196. Springer, Heidelberg (2006)
47. Steyvers, M., Smyth, P., Rosen-Zvi, M., Groffiths, T.: Probabilistic author-topic models for information discovery. In: ACM SIGKDD, pp. 306–315 (2004)
48. Wang, F., Carley, K., Zeng, D., Mao, W.: Social computing: From social informatics to social intelligence. IEEE Intelligent Systems, 79–83 (2007)
49. Wang, X., Mohanty, N., Mccallum, A.: Group and topic discovery from relations and text. In: ACM SIGKDD (Workshop on Link Discovery) (2005)
50. Wyatt, D., Choudhury, T., Bilmes, J.: Discovering Long Range Properties of Social Networks with Multi-Valued Time-Inhomogeneous Models. In: AAAI (2010)
51. Yano, T., Cohen, W.W., Smith, N.A.: Predicting response to political blog posts with topic models. In: NAACL 2009, pp. 477–485 (2009)
52. Zeng, D., Wang, F., Carley, K.: Guest Editors' Introduction: Social Computing. IEEE Intelligent Systems, 20–22 (2007)

Lessons from Touring a Location-Based Experience

Leif Oppermann[1], Martin Flintham[1], Stuart Reeves[1], Steve Benford[1],
Chris Greenhalgh[1], Joe Marshall[1], Matt Adams[2], Ju Row Farr[2],
and Nick Tandavanitj[2]

[1] Mixed Reality Lab, University of Nottingham, UK
{lxo,mdf,str,sdb,cmg,jqm}@cs.nott.ac.uk
[2] Blast Theory, Unit 5, 20 Wellington Road, Portslade, Brighton, UK
{matt,ju,nick}@blasttheory.co.uk

Abstract. Touring location-based experiences is challenging as both content and underlying location-services must be adapted to each new setting. A study of a touring performance called Rider Spoke as it visited three different cities reveals how professional artists developed a novel approach to these challenges in which users drove the co-evolution of content and the underlying location-service as they explored each new city. We show how the artists iteratively developed filtering, survey, visualization and simulation tools and processes to enable them to tune the experience to the local characteristics of each city. Our study reveals how by paying attention to both content and infrastructure issues in tandem the artists were able to create a powerful user experience that has since toured to many different cities.

Keywords: Location-based performance, cycling, adaptation, Wi-Fi fingerprinting, seams, user generated content.

1 Introduction

From tours and guides, to games and performances, to educational field trips, there is a growing interest in how location-based technologies can deliver engaging new forms of leisure, entertainment and learning. Early explorations have demonstrated a variety of ways in which such experiences can combine digital media with physical settings to create exciting new experiences. Guides and tours have attached digital media to historic sites in order to enhance understanding [1,2,3,4]. Computer games have been overlaid on real cities, demanding physical engagement from players as they chase one another through the streets [5,6,7,8,9,10]. Other experiences have drawn on the pleasure of physical exploration, either to find digital resources [11,12] or to find physical resources as in the popular pastime of Geocaching [13]. Educational experiences have engaged learners in simulations that appear to be overlaid on the real world [14] and have underpinned field trips to sites of special interest [15,16]. Location-based technologies have also enhanced Live Action Role Play by enabling the creation of apparently magical or paranormal artifacts [17]. Finally, artists have combined digital media with physical locations, props and players on the city streets to create performances that draw on the everyday world as a theatrical backdrop [18].

K. Lyons, J. Hightower, and E.M. Huang (Eds.): Pervasive 2011, LNCS 6696, pp. 232–249, 2011.

While these examples demonstrate the potential of location-based technologies to underpin compelling new experiences, they also raise major challenges, especially with regard to touring them to different locations. At the heart of this challenge is the extensive work involved in adapting an existing experience to each new setting in which it is to be deployed, potentially including authoring content, but also rolling out and tuning the underlying location-service and other technical infrastructure.

Although authoring content is a challenge for established digital media such as computer games, location-based experiences raise the added problem of potentially requiring re-authoring for each new setting, with digital assets such as videos, sounds, text, graphics and virtual worlds being created afresh to match local buildings, artifacts, people and other physical assets. Even when previous content is available, it needs to be tailored to fit to new locations incurring considerable additional cost.

After creating assets, the designers have to wrestle with the complexities of location and communication technologies so as to properly locate these within the physical world. Previous studies have shown how challenging this can be, requiring them to be able to reason about the fine details of coverage and accuracy of wireless communications and positioning across a given location [20]. They may even have to actually deploy some new physical infrastructure such as tags and beacons within the new environment. Nor does their work end here, as other studies have highlighted the importance of the real-time monitoring and ongoing orchestration of an experience from behind the scenes once it has gone live [5]. While game-mastering and other forms of orchestration are already practiced with current online games, location-based experiences introduce a new level of challenge to this, as participants are often widely dispersed across a physical location, difficult to identify, and may suffer from frequent disconnections [18].

Finally, these various challenges are mutually dependent, with both the authoring of content and the orchestration of experience depending on the successful adaptation of the underlying technical infrastructure, requiring designers to wrestle with a complex mix of experiential and technical issues at each new location. Unsurprisingly, it remains remarkably difficult to create an experience that benefits from a rich integration of the digital and physical and yet can be easily rolled out across many different locations. Indeed, an inherent lack of 'tourability' may be the greatest bottleneck facing the future widespread adoption of these kinds of emerging location-based experience.

This paper presents a study of a professional location-based experience called Rider Spoke that has been deliberately designed to tour to multiple cities. Our study covers the critical fifteen month period from early concept workshops through touring to three cities, by which time it had emerged as a stable product. We focus on how artists addressed the complex challenges of tourability by creating a novel structure that, with only minimal seeding, enables participants themselves to create location-based content as they explore a city, while simultaneously driving the gradual evolution of the underlying location-service. We also describe how the artists iteratively developed new software tools to support the touring process. Our study draws on multiple sources of data, from questionnaires completed by participants that give insights into their experience, to notes and observations from meetings and performances that reveal the activities of artists and technicians, in order to present a holistic account of the story of Rider Spoke from multiple perspectives.

2   From Concept to Premiere

The first half of our study takes us from creating the initial concept up to the premiere performance of Rider Spoke at London's Barbican centre in October 2007 – a detailed examination of Rider Spoke as a cycling *experience* can be found in [19].

2.1   The Design Drivers behind Rider Spoke

Prior to Rider Spoke, our artists had created several location-based experiences and through these, had acquired extensive first hand experience of the substantial costs involved in touring them to different locations. Their primary concern this time was to create an experience that was deeply engaging and yet also lightweight and flexible enough that it could be toured to many different locations worldwide. Early design workshops explored this challenge and homed in on three key design drivers that would underpin Rider Spoke and reduce the cost of touring.

A commitment to user-driven locally-relevant content. Participants would populate the experience with content by recording personal stories that others could then listen to. It was important that these stories should be deeply engaging, for example moving, charming or hilarious, but also have local relevance, that is resonate with specific locations within the city which would somehow serve as an inspiration or backdrop for them. Thus, participants would be required to explore the nooks and crannies of the city in order to record their stories and find those of others.

A lightweight and adaptable approach to location. The location mechanism would need to be sufficiently lightweight and flexible that it could be reliably deployed and adapted to different cities. Although widely available in principle, the artists' previous experiences led them to reject GPS as being too sensitive to the particular geography of built-up urban environments, especially with regard to variable coverage, and so they were keen to experiment with an alternative approach to location.

Shifting away from a dependency on real-time data connection. Unlike many earlier experiences, Rider Spoke would deliberately operate as a disconnected experience, isolating participants from immediate contact with one another so as to create a calm and contemplative atmosphere, whilst also avoiding the severe technical challenges of dealing with disconnection that had dogged previous experiences and required extensive orchestration.

From these three principles emerged the detailed design of an experience that involves individuals cycling through a city at night, recording and then listening to personal stories that are associated with particular locations. It was felt from the start that travel on foot was too spatially constraining and that some form of transport would be required to enable a sufficiently wide ranging exploration of the city. Cars were briefly considered, but cycles were soon settled on as they allow exploration, can access a wide range of territories, help isolate players and yet still deliver a visceral experience of the city. It was also decided to stage the experience at dusk and into the night so as to heighten the sense of an unusual, even otherworldly, experience of the city as an inspiration for stories. Participants would therefore cycle through the city at night. The artists themselves expressed their intention in their documentation as follows: *"As you roll through the streets your focus is outward, looking for good places to hide, speculating about the hiding places of others, becoming completely immersed into this overlaid world as the voices of strangers draw you into a new and unknown place. The streets may be familiar but you've given yourself up to the pleasure of being lost."*

2.2   A Participant's View of Rider Spoke

Participants arrive at the hosting venue, either on their own bicycle or to borrow one. They register at the reception where they sign a disclaimer and leave a deposit. They then receive a briefing that covers the nature of the experience, how to use the technology, how to cycle safely, and also tells them of an emergency paper map and phone number under their saddle. The receptionist logs their details in a database and then sends them outside where a technician mounts a mobile console (a Nokia N800) onto the handlebar of the cycle and, for loaned cycles, adjusts their seating position so that they feel comfortable and safe. Riders leave the venue individually and the experience lasts for an hour. After the first few minutes cycling, gentle music plays, setting the tone for the experience, and a narrator begins giving instructions. The female voice is calm and measured, adopting a style and tone reminiscent of a psychotherapist:

This is one of those moments when you are on your own; you might feel a little odd at first, a bit self-conscious or a bit awkward. But you're alright and it's OK. You may feel invisible tonight but as you ride this feeling will start to change. Relax, don't forget to breathe both in and out and find somewhere that you like, it might be near a particular building or road junction, it might be near a mark on a wall or a reflection in a window. When you have found somewhere give yourself a name and describe yourself.

The rider's first task is to find an appealing location, stop, and record a name and description, as shown in figure 1. This location has to be a 'new' location within the experience, meaning one that is not already occupied by an existing recording (according to the location technology that we describe below). It is the basic rule of Rider Spoke that each new recording has to be made at a new location, requiring players to continually seek out new places in the city as the volume of recordings grows. When the Rider has found a valid location the console screen displays the invitation shown in figure 2.

The interface is designed to be distinctive and yet simple, providing just a few options to record and listen to messages. After all, Riders may be using this device for the first time while engaged in an unusual experience that also involves cycling. The overall metaphor is one of hiding and finding recordings within homes. Artistically, the design draws on a combination of Mexican votive art, with religious associations of prayer and offerings, combined with images of tattoos that are emblematic of voyages of exploration. Interaction is via a touchscreen using just a few large buttons and with safety in mind, the briefing and instructions encourage riders to stop before interacting.

Fig. 1. A rider with console attached to their bicycle listening to a recording

Fig. 2. Inviting a rider to record their description

Following this initial task, riders can repeatedly choose between recording an answer to a new question or listening to others' recordings, repeating this choice until their allotted time of one hour has elapsed. To answer a question, the rider must again find a new location. They will then be asked a question (over the audio in their headphones) that encourages them to divulge a personal story of some kind. The questions, authored by the artists, ask riders to reflect on significant, evocative or hilarious moments of their life while engaging with the city. For example, they may be asked to reflect on people or events in their lives:

Please will you tell me about your father. You might want to pick a particular time in your father's life or in your life. Freeze that moment and tell me about your dad: what they looked like, how they spoke and what they meant to you. And while you

think about this I want you to find a place in the city that your father would like. Once you've found it stop there and record your message about your father at that moment in time.

Or they may be asked to use the places and strangers in the city as inspiration for their imagination:

I want you to look for a flat or a house and find a window that you would want to go through. I want you to stare into that window and tell me what you see and tell me why you want to go through that window

Riders are given the opportunity to review and record their stories and then to save them when they are satisfied. On choosing to listen to other's recordings, the rider is offered a list of the three nearest recordings to their current location. As a result, recordings are always available to be heard, although cycling through the city will continually update the list, effectively browsing a landscape of stories. When the experience is near its end the narrator gives the rider one final task: to make and record a final promise. After this, they return to base where the device is dismounted from their bike and their deposit returned.

2.3 Implementing Rider Spoke

A substantial portion of our study is concerned with how the artists adapted the technical infrastructure of Rider Spoke, and so it is necessary to delve into some details of its implementation, especially with regard to the design of the location service and database. The design team elected to exploit the prevalence of Wi-Fi in many cities as the basis of their location service as previous research had shown that Wi-Fi could provide a sound basis for a location service [21]. After some initial experimentation, the team elected to develop a bespoke Wi-Fi location service that was tailored to the particular requirements of Rider Spoke, basing this on an existing technique called Wi-Fi fingerprinting [22,23]. The rider's console periodically scans for Wi-Fi access points as they traverse the city. The resulting list generated at any moment is taken to be a distinctive fingerprint for their current location. If this fingerprint is deemed to be different from already known fingerprints held in a database then it becomes a new location. If it is very similar, it is considered to match an already known location.

As players record stories, some of these known fingerprints become associated with recordings. The database also records adjacency links between fingerprints that are created whenever one fingerprint is seen directly after another. Thus, the resulting database takes the form of a mathematical graph, with nodes being fingerprints and edges representing direct adjacencies between these. These adjacency links enable the location-service to reason about the relative proximity of locations by working out the minimum number of links that separates them. Thus, it becomes possible to work out the likely 'nearest' recordings to a given location.

Each rider begins with a preloaded version of the database on their console from the previous day. Any new locations and data that they generate during the experience as they make recordings and explore new parts of the city are offloaded back to the central database when they return (remembering that this is a disconnected experience). At the end of each day all new locations and new recordings from that day's participants are merged back into the database. This requires the artists to filter and merge the new recordings, working out which should be made available to future riders. This involves listening to all of the recordings from that day and making two key decisions. First, is a recording engaging enough to warrant it being included. Second, where two new recordings are associated with the same new location (two riders having independently discovered and used it on that day), which should be kept and which thrown away in order to resolve the conflict.

Thus, the graph structured database of known locations, adjacencies and recordings grows and evolves as the experience unfolds over many days. The strength of this approach is that the content and location information evolve from practically nothing as the experience gradually rolls out over the city. A little seed content, normally of the order of a few tens of recordings, and a small fingerprint graph that can be built from a few short test cycle rides around the venue, is all that is required to prepare the experience.

It is important to note that this approach does not deliver, or aim to deliver, the geographical position (coordinates) of a fingerprint; it is therefore not a positioning service as are some other Wi-Fi-based services. However, it does satisfy the essential requirements of Rider Spoke, namely being able to identify new and existing locations to a mobile console, associating some of these with content, and reasoning about their relative proximities. Of course, there is still a question of 'accuracy' in the sense that recordings ideally need to be heard near to any physical locations to which they refer. However, this is deliberately a relatively fuzzy association and so the experience is carefully designed not to rely on accurate positioning. Early seed messages that are deposited by the artists are carefully constructed to be engaging but also locationally-vague as these may be potentially heard from far away while the initial graph is small and sparse. As the database grows and the graph becomes ever more dense, it should be the case that the three 'nearest' recordings are increasingly from locations that are actually nearby.

2.4 Feedback from the Premiere Performance

The premiere performance of Rider Spoke took place in London in October 2007, being experienced by 548 riders over 8 days. Between them they left 1,964 audio recordings in the city (average of 3.5 per player and maximum of 10). All riders were invited to give feedback after the event via a web-based questionnaire that probed their background, overall enjoyment, and the themes of recording and listening to stories, finding locations, and cycling. Given that this was a public event, all of the participants were self-selecting, as were the 71 (13%) of these who completed the questionnaire. Responses were quite evenly distributed across the 8 days of play, with no day receiving less than 5 or more than 10. 41 respondents were female, 28 male, and two didn't say. Most were attracted by the novelty or by the artists' reputation, and some by the cycling (54 classified themselves as 'cultural/arts events visitors' and 29 as 'cyclists'). Over half cycled regularly and 31 used their own bikes. However, 2 claimed to 'never cycle'!

The overall reception to Rider Spoke was very positive. On a five point Likert scale, 70% of respondents agreed or agreed strongly that 'taking part in Rider Spoke was fun' while 67% said that they would do the experience again. While it may of course be that those who felt most positive were also the most willing to complete the questionnaire, this fits well with anecdotal feedback that we received from riders as their returned to the venue. It appears that riders appreciated several aspects of the experience.

They enjoyed recording and listening to stories which could at times be deeply personal and apparently honest, and some even cried while recounting them: "It was a very 'moving' experience for me and very memorable. To be alone in the city, holding your bike, blubbing about your father on a Sunday evening is something else....!" Others, however, invented stories: "I was much more performative. I often made things and characters up to make it interesting, both for me and the other listeners". Listening to other people's stories could also be moving, again especially when they were personal: "One about the memory of a man's father. It was extremely touching – he also described standing on a roman wall, an evocative historical location to be thinking about memories. He even vowed to bring his dad to that spot because he thought he'd like it there. Beautiful."

Respondents also remarked on the distinctive social nature of the experience, which as one put it, involved "a disconnected intimacy with a total stranger." This was amplified by the feeling of being isolated in the city: "It was a private moment strangely enough not always in a private space." This is not to say that riders were not aware of bystanders though, which for some introduced a further sensation of being exposed and even slightly vulnerable.

Location played an important role in inspiring stories, with players choosing movie-like backdrops for their recordings: "I just found places that excited me to stand in, that would be seen in a film." and "When hiding in old alleys that reminded me of what Victorian London might have looked like, I think I romanticised the answers a bit more." Ambient sound was also important and would directly appear on the recordings: "Yes - sometimes the background noise or the atmosphere of a particular place really chimed or sometimes jarred with the words I was speaking. This added a layer of richness to the testimonials." Some locations imparted a personal meaning: "I followed a route that I like and stopped at places that had personal resonance or geographic prominence.", while others were simply aesthetically pleasing in their own right: "Cos they were quiet and beautiful in their own way." Yet others were associated with a memorable landmark: "I looked for spots which were quiet and had some kind of marking point - as if it was buried treasure, so like a squirrel I could always find it again if i wanted to!"

Finally, cycling appeared to engender a sense of freedom and liberation in some that may have opened them up to recounting stories. "I love cycling and haven't cycled regularly for a while as my bike broke and i have not got round to fixing it! So it reminded me of the freedom i feel when I cycle and to cycle with no destination is wonderful - i felt physically awakened and engaged" and "Made you look, made you stare, made you investigate dark places you wouldn't normally."

This is not to say that all players had a great time and that all stories were deeply engaging by any means. Many stories were not greatly interesting, others were unintelligible, and there were clearly moments when players found themselves in a completely inappropriate location: "*I wasn't going to speak at length about my father whilst standing in a grimy back alley that stank of excrement.*" Some players got lost, while others commented on being cold, tired, uncomfortable and even in desperate need of the toilet while cycling. Perhaps the most frequent criticism, however, arose from the slow response of the interface which could take many seconds to respond on some occasions as we discuss below. However, it does seem that on balance, the distinctive combination of freedom, isolation, vulnerability, disconnected intimacy, location, physicality and of course the artists' questions provided a framework within which many riders could create powerful content.

2.5 Lessons for the Infrastructure

While the artists were generally satisfied with the overall user experience, the technical challenges involved in delivering Rider Spoke proved to be more problematic. These revolved around two issues: the overhead of filtering content and the somewhat opaque and inflexible nature of the location mechanism.

Given the high-profile and often unpredictable nature of a premiere performance, the artists were prepared to devote a large amount of their own time to the hands-on running of the experience, and had also been willing to hire a relatively large crew to support them. This had made it (just about) feasible to listen to and filter hundreds of new recordings each day ready to be merged into the database for the next day's play. However, future touring would need to rely on a smaller crew to be financially viable, and would also have to demand less time from the artists themselves as it would take place over many years to come when they would be working on new projects. Concerns were also raised about how filtering would work with overseas touring where recordings would not necessarily be in English. Improving the filtering of content was therefore identified as a key bottleneck to be addressed to support future touring.

The second issue concerned the location mechanism. Collectively our riders logged 1,236,120 distinct sightings of 3990 unique fingerprints (locations) over the 8 days. The size of the resulting graph was a major contributing factor to the poor performance of the console software. Discussions between the artists and the technical team after the first few days revealed that it was not possible to retune the mechanism to produce a new smaller graph. Even if it had been, it was unclear what density of graph would be needed anyway. A large and dense graph could clearly cause performance problems and also make it possible to appear to place many recordings at each physical location. Too sparse a graph however might not provide sufficient locations for new content and could potentially lead riders to perceive mismatches between content and location (which had not been a significant factor in user feedback from the premiere). Furthermore, it was not clear how variations in Wi-Fi density across different cities, or perhaps even across a single city, would impact on tuning the graph. Being able to tune the fingerprint graph to match the local characteristics of each new city was therefore felt to be also important to the future touring of Rider Spoke.

3   From Premiere to Touring

The second part of our study considers the work that was done to address these challenges as Rider Spoke toured through two further cities, Athens in March 2008 and Brighton in May 2008. While nearly all aspects of the experience were tweaked to some extent (questions revised, briefings updated, and the software on the console restructured to improve performance), the greatest effort was invested in developing tools and processes to support filtering of content and tuning the location mechanism.

3.1   Managing the User Generated Content

Filtering recordings needs to address three issues. First is selecting the best content so that it can be merged into the database and made available to future riders. The aim here is to both reduce the volume of content to a manageable amount, ensuring that enough locations remain free for the new players, and also to ensure that that the content is of the best possible quality in the opinion of the artists. Second, is the need to resolve conflicts where two new recordings occupy the same location. Third, is the challenge of dealing with multiple languages. Many riders in Athens wished to record their stories in Greek and the artists (who did not speak Greek) felt that the recordings would be of higher quality if this were the case. To be able to tour Rider Spoke, the artists needed to be able to outsource the task of rating content to trusted people who could be hired in as needed, including native speakers. The first step was development of the following five point rating scale and guidelines as written down in the 'Operator Manual':

1. *I can't hear this/ would never want to listen to this. Inaudible. Very long silences. Criticizing the work: "This is boring". Repeated answer: i.e. an exact copy of this answer already exists*
2. *I wouldn't want to listen to this. Boring: an observation or sentiment that is completely undistinctive or obvious "Some parts of the city are quite rough" "I went to lots of wild parties when I was young". These answers lack anything specific, precise or personal. They are often very short. An answer that is almost exactly the same as a previous answer*
3. *I wouldn't mind listening to this. Average: a typical answer but nevertheless one that has meaning to the person speaking. "I promise that tomorrow I will be kinder to my work colleagues." "I went to a party when I was 15 and tried to kiss a boy called Peter but before I could I threw up ..." The majority of answers will be 3 and, if you are not sure what score to give, mark an answer as 3*
4. *I would enjoy listening to this. Outstanding. Contains a unique or specific insight or revelation. Something that no one else has said. Makes you laugh or moves you.*
5. *I would love to listen to this. Exceptional: hilarious, moving, surprising, unique. Not necessarily long: it could be very short*

The artists also proposed the following modifiers:

If an answer is location specific (i.e. refers to a specific building or street so that another player would know what they are talking about) +1

Any answer to "describe yourself" (because these are usually short and introductory) -1

Any answer to "make a promise" (because there are so many of them and they can be very repetitive) -1

Very brief (don't forget the effort that a player will have gone to in order to hear an answer: if an answer is very short then it may seem like a big anticlimax unless it is especially strong) -1

These guidelines were then embedded in a web-based ranking tool. One of the screens in this tool presented cases where multiple new recordings conflicted with a single new location. The tool also allowed the artists to choose a ranking threshold (1-5) such that only recordings rated above this would be merged into the database. This could be raised over time as higher quality recordings became available. In each of the three performances the ranking began at 3 on the first day and had been raised to 4 by the end (retaining 10%, 13% and 20% of the recordings in London, Athens and Brighton respectively).

The work of ranking was usually shared out among the artists who could review prior rankings day-by-day to allow for ongoing artistic oversight and the review of one another's judgments, whilst keeping the task at a level that was practically manageable. Artists also became much quicker at the task as their familiarity with the content and this new tool grew. Furthermore, the use of the ranking tool and how the above gross categories and rules might get applied was something that itself evolved as the experience became more populated with content and the artists listened to more recordings. Rankings could even be pre-reviewed within the current session to get a feel of what the overall batch of recordings sounded like in advance of the final ranking at the end of the day. In this way ranking sessions and the use of the ranking tool within them became a fine-tuned and highly nuanced resource for keeping content captivating and up to date. In addition, a particular attentiveness to locally-grounded stories enabled the artists to further refine the location-specific tuning of the experience and imbue the whole event with a sensitivity to the character of the locale that it would otherwise have lacked. Finally, being web-based allowed the task to be carried out remotely, further reducing touring costs and allowing the sharing of the work across the team of artists.

3.2   The Complexities of the Location Mechanism

Tuning the location mechanism to each new city was the second major challenge for touring Rider Spoke. It also proved to be a considerably more knotty problem to resolve. Given that the artists spent considerable effort trying to understand the technical details of this mechanism, it is necessary for us to briefly consider them here too.

The location mechanism goes through several steps to decide whether the list of currently visible Wi-Fi access points represents an existing or a new fingerprint (and hence location). Wi-Fi scanning software scans every few seconds, returning a list of all currently visible access points, each represented by its MAC address (the unique address pre-programmed into the access point) along with the received signal strength with which it has been seen. Access points below a configurable signal strength threshold, are then removed from the list because they may be susceptible to transient interference and their inclusion could lead to highly unstable fingerprints. After this, only a limited number of the remaining access points are considered, according to a configurable fingerprint size parameter, with the weakest signals being discarded. The result of applying these two parameters is a manageably long list of access points, each of which is associated with a reasonable signal strength. The resulting list is then compared against the local database of known fingerprints (the fingerprint graph). If the filtered access point list "overlaps" an existing fingerprint by a sufficient amount – specified by a third overlap threshold parameter – then the new sighting is deemed to match an existing fingerprint. If not, it is deemed to be a new fingerprint and is added to the fingerprint graph along with a new edge that connects it to the most recently sighted fingerprint before this. The overlap is the proportion of access points that are in common between the two lists, for example "A,B,C" and "A,B,C,D" have a 75% overlap. Choosing a value of 100% for the overlap threshold would require that access point lists match exactly. In this case any difference in the list would produce a new fingerprint and hence a new location. Conversely, smaller values allow an existing location to be found again if a subset of the access points are not visible, for example if they have been temporarily turned off.

In summary, the three key parameters of signal strength threshold, fingerprint size, and overlap threshold control how raw lists of access points and signal strengths are mapped onto distinct fingerprints and hence locations. Collectively, they determine the density and stability of the resulting fingerprint graph. The artists can change them to produce, on the one hand, a graph with very many but possibly transient locations, and on the other, a graph with relatively few but more stable locations. The goal is to find the correct combination that produces enough locations for a given city so that riders can find new locations at which to place their stories, and yet not so many that it feels like too many stories are at each location or that it is difficult to ever find a story again after it has been recorded.

Discussions with the artists revealed that it was difficult both to understand and predict the effect of changing individual parameters (not least because they overlap to some extent in their ultimate effect). Setting them for the London performance had been largely a matter of guesswork and the result had clearly not been optimal. It also seemed highly likely that these parameters would need to be tuned to suit the particular local distribution of Wi-Fi access points across each new city so that a more principled approach was clearly needed.

3.3 Tools to Adapt the Location-Mechanism

The team therefore created a suite of three software tools to help localise Rider Spoke to each new city. A *survey tool* was used to gather some initial Wi-Fi data from the city, along with GPS data that could subsequently help georeference this to maps of the area. A *simulation tool* processed this data, enabling the artists to very rapidly create many different graphs, arising from different parameter settings, and rank and compare. Finally, a *visualisation tool* revealed the likely distribution of a given fingerprint graph across the chosen area of the city.

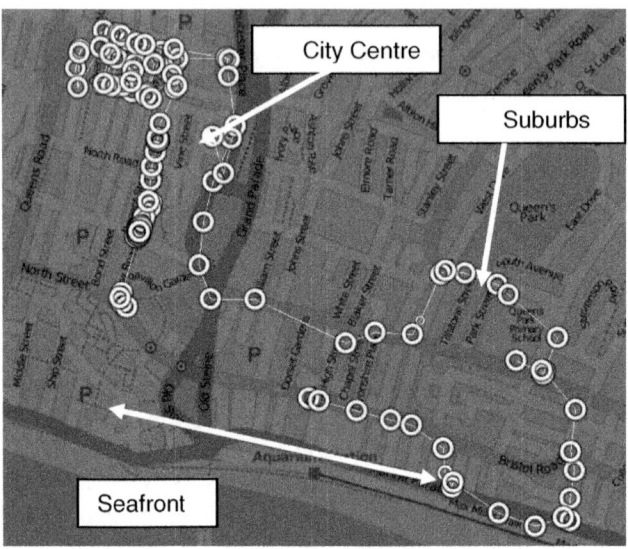

Fig. 3. Geo-referenced visualization of Brighton survey

The survey tool required someone to cycle several pre-planned routes through the city with a mobile logging device to cover likely places that riders might visit during the experience. The artists aimed to get a broad brush picture of the environment in as short a time as possible. The Athens survey was conducted by four artists in parallel and completed in about one hour. Here, the different routes were arranged so that they would cover different areas, but also contain some overlap with other routes to make connections in the fingerprint graph. The Brighton survey covered the busy city centre, the suburbs and the seafront and was completed by a single artist in about one hour. These surveys were carried out weeks in advance of the performance alongside the usual site inspection and discussions with the hosting venue and the survey data was then taken back to the studio for analysis.

The simulator tool allowed the artists to conduct a series of 'what if' experiments by feeding the survey data into the fingerprinting mechanism as if live and then stepping through ranges of values for each of the three parameters so as to automatically generate hundreds or even thousands of different fingerprint graphs. These graphs could then be sorted according to basic metrics including the number of fingerprints and edges they contained. An additional metric called 'retrievability' was introduced to capture the artists' requirement that "content and fingerprints must be easy to find". This was defined to be the total number of fingerprint sightings divided by the number of unique fingerprints generated for this graph and helped the artists find parameter settings that yield a graph whose locations might be suitably easy to find. By sorting and sifting to compare these various metrics across many graphs, the artists were able to home in on parameter settings that might hit the sweet spot of a good number of locations that were reasonably retrievable.

Finally, the visualisation tool enabled the artists to inspect selected graphs (chosen from the simulation), examining their topologies (the clustering and connectedness of fingerprints) in relation to the geography of the local area, as shown in figure 3. The graphs could be drawn as abstract visualisations to reveal their topology, but these could also be pinned onto to various geographical maps and satellite views of the local area in Google Earth.

4 Populating the City with Stories

In its varied detail, our study has revealed how Rider Spoke combines a distinctive mode of interaction (cycling through a city at night and recording and listening to personal stories) with a novel technical infrastructure (an evolving graph of locations determined through Wi-Fi fingerprinting) to create a unique experience. The ultimate success of this approach is perhaps best demonstrated by the continued popularity of Rider Spoke as a touring product. At the time of writing it has been performed in London, Athens, Brighton, Budapest, Adelaide, Sydney, Copenhagen, Bristol, Edinburgh and Linz, with further bookings pending. That Rider Spoke is both engaging for audiences (and promoters) and yet also tourable can be largely attributed to the way in which both experiental and technical issues have been addressed in tandem through a process of iterative design and testing 'in the wild' of public performance. However, beyond documenting a 'unique' experience, what more general lessons can we draw out for HCI? What can the designers of other location-based experiences and technologies take away from this study?

The co-evolution of content and infrastructure. As already mentioned, the critical feature of Rider Spoke is the way in which both the content and the underlying location database evolve in tandem over the lifetime of the experience as a result of participants exploring the city. This enables the experience to be quickly rolled out across each new city without the need for extensive pre-authoring of content, or surveying or deploying underlying infrastructure, directly addressing two major bottlenecks to touring location-based experiences.

User generated content. Web 2.0 services such as Wikipedia, YouTube and others make use of friendships, subscriptions and users' ratings to motivate 'user generated content' and ensure that the most interesting content becomes the most publicly visible (see [24] for a discussion of collaborative editing in Wikipedia for example). Rider Spoke also relies on user generated content, but in a different way. First, it provides a distinctive framing for storytelling in which anonymity and isolation, rather than friendship and discussion, are used to encourage powerful performances by members of the public. Second, the artists retain a high degree of editorial control over the final rating and filtering of content that is published back to the users. While having the artists rate content clearly limits the scalability of Rider Spoke (while ensuring high quality), it may be that other applications that employ user generated content can learn from its approach to carefully framing storytelling to enable the public to perform.

A 'placeful' experience. As a location-based experience, Rider Spoke is also able to draw on specific places in the city to provide rich and often personally meaningful backdrops for stories. Furthermore, participants are required to explore the city in order to find and create these locations for themselves rather than having the artists choose or create them in advance. In other words, in a location-based experience, creating locations can be as much a part of user generated content as recording audio or video. Rider Spoke is also distinctive in that it does not fix locations to absolute positions or demand a high degree of accuracy. One way to view it's deliberately fuzzy approach is, as Harrison and Dourish have previously argued [25], that it emphasises a sense of place rather than a consideration of the absolute geometry of the space of the city which would have arisen from adopting a more positioning-oriented approach. However, as Dourish suggests also when subsequently revisiting this argument [26], the division between place and space is sometimes less clear. We would suggest that what we see in Rider Spoke is the development and deployment of a technology that presents a 'user generated spatiality' to users with "people creating space through their movement" [27] as they cycle through the city.

Tools for flexible and adaptable location services. Finally, our study has also shown that evolution of the infrastructure requires careful management in much the same way as the user driven evolution of content. To be effective this user driven infrastructure needs to be adapted to local conditions (in our case to the local geography and variations in the distribution of Wi-Fi) and this requires careful attention and the support of dedicated tools that enable designers to survey, simulate and visualize the likely evolution of an infrastructure across a particular city and to be able to tune it as a result. This capability to reveal the nature of the technical infrastructure to the designers of location-aware experiences reflects an ongoing discussion of 'seamful design' within HCI. Previous papers have observed how the characteristics of the underlying infrastructure of positioning and wireless communications can have a major impact on the user experience and how, far from being an occasional glitch or bug, this is an ongoing aspect of such experiences that needs to be recognized by designers [20]. Lack of coverage or accuracy can be characterized as 'seams' in the infrastructure, a natural part of the fabric from which it is knitted together. Various approaches to dealing with seams have been proposed including removing, hiding, managing and even exploiting them [5]. Work on seamful games has explored the latter approach, demonstrating and studying a series of examples in which partial coverage of Wi-Fi and/or GPS becomes a resource in the game that can be exploited by players, for example, by being able to hide in the 'GPS shadows' [10]. Other work has explored the approach of revealing the infrastructure, arguing that authoring tools that allow designers to overlay digital assets onto a map or image of a physical location need to be extended with an additional infrastructure visualization layer that enable designers to take account of the availability of the underlying infrastructure across specific locations [27]. Our study has demonstrated the power of this latter approach, providing our artists with a series of tools for exposing the characteristics of its location mechanism across each new city. Part of this certainly involves overlaying visualizations of the infrastructure on maps as we see in figures 5 and 6. However, it also requires additional tools for surveying each site and for experimenting with various settings of parameters so as to explore different possible scenarios. In short, while we agree that designers do indeed need to visualize the underlying infrastructure, we recognize that this is only one part of a complex overall workflow that also involves gathering and experimenting with data and that all stages of this require support from dedicated tools.

5 Conclusion

Our study of a touring location-based experience, from its first concept to its emergence as a stable product following three performances in different cities, has revealed how professional artists worked to create an experience that was both compelling and yet also practicably tourable to different locations. We have seen how they developed a distinctive approach that involved participants exploring a city on bicycles, recording and listening to personal stories, which were then filtered and merged together into an evolving database of 'user generated content'. We have also seen how the iterative development and use of survey, simulation and visualization tools allowed this to be supported by a location service that also gradually evolved at each city and could be tuned to its local characteristics.

While Rider Spoke itself is perhaps a unique experience, we have also discussed how it embodies general principles that should be of use to the designers of future location-based services. Careful framing of the experience, drawing upon cycling as a distinctive mode of engagement with the city and deliberately isolating participants from one another, while unusual in traditional HCI terms, establishes a frame within which the public are able to create powerful user generated content. At the same time, the development of an platform that can be easily rolled out over a city with minimal seed content, supported by dedicated tools that enable adaptation to each new setting, enables the experience to be easily toured. It is through attention to detail of both content and the technology that the artists are able to deliver a successful experience.

In summary, Rider Spoke shows through its success as a touring product that there are solid, practical ways of addressing some of the core challenges that face the widespread adoption of location-based applications. Indeed, a concatenation of practical, locally-sensible strategies appears to be an inevitable aspect of managing touring location-based services where it is exactly the distinctiveness of particular locales that may trump any effort to create overly generic, standardized solutions. We hope that through the detailed study of artistic practice presented in this paper we have begun to show how some of these strategies might appear.

Acknowledgements

This work was supported by the European Commission: FP6-004457 (IPerG). Rider Spoke is featured courtesy of Blast Theory and we gratefully acknowledge all members of their team for their collaboration and kind assistance.

References

1. Abowd, G., Atkeson, C., Hong, J., Long, S., Kooper, R., Pinkerton, M.: Cyberguide: A mobile context-aware tour guide. Wireless Networks 3(5) (1997)
2. Brown, B., Chalmers, C., Bell, M., Hall, M., MacColl, I., Rudman, P.: Sharing the square: Collaborative Leisure in the City Streets. In: ECSCW 2005, Paris, pp. 427–447. Springer, Heidelberg (2005)

3. Cheverst, K., Davies, N., Mitchell, K., Friday, A., Efstratiou, E.: Developing a context-aware electronic tourist guide: some issues and experiences. In: CHI 2000, pp. 17–24. ACM, New York (2000)
4. Dow, S., Lee, J., Oezbek, C., MacIntyre, B., Bolter, J., Gandy, M.: Exploring Spatial Narratives and Mixed Reality Experiences in Oakland Cemetery. In: ACM SIGCHI Conference on Advances in Computer Entertainment (ACE 2005), Valencia, Spain (June 2005)
5. Benford, S., Crabtree, A., Flintham, M., Drozd, A., Anastasi, R., Paxton, M., Tandavanitj, N., Adams, M., Row Farr, J.: 'Can You See Me Now?'. ACM Trans. Computer Human Interaction 13(1), 100–133 (2006)
6. Boyd Davis, S., Moar, M., Jacobs, R., Watkins, M., Riddoch, C., Cooke, K.: Ere Be Dragons: heartfelt gaming. Digital Creativity 17(3), 157–162 (2006)
7. Cheok, A., Goh, K., Liu, W., Farbiz, F., Fong, S., Teo, S., Li, Y., Yang, X.: 'Human Pacman: a mobile, wide-area entertainment system based on physical, social, and ubiquitous computing'. Personal and Ubiquitous Computing 8(2) (May 2004)
8. Mitchell, K., McCaffery, D., Metaxas, G., Finney, J., Schmid, S., Scott, A.: Six in the city: introducing Real Tournament – a mobile IPv6 based context-aware multiplayer game. In: 2nd Workshop on Network and System Support for Games, CA, USA, pp. 91–100 (2003)
9. Piekarski, W., Thomas, B.: ARQuake: The outdoors augmented reality system. Communications of the ACM 45(1), 36–38 (2002)
10. Barkhuus, L., Chalmers, M., Tennent, P., Hall, M., Bell, M., Sherwood, S., Brown, B.: Picking Pockets on the Lawn: The Development of Tactics and Strategies in a Mobile Game. In: Beigl, M., Intille, S.S., Rekimoto, J., Tokuda, H. (eds.) UbiComp 2005. LNCS, vol. 3660, pp. 358–374. Springer, Heidelberg (2005)
11. Ballagas, R., Walz, S., Kratz, S., Fuhr, C., Yu, E., Tann, M., Borchers, J., Hovestadt, L.: REXplorer: A Mobile, Pervasive Spell-Casting Game for Tourists. In: CHI 2007: Extended Abstracts on Human Factors in Computing Systems, pp. 1929–1934. ACM Press, New York (2007)
12. Lindt, I., Ohlenburg, J., Pankoke-Babatz, U., Ghellal, S.: A report on the crossmedia game epidemic menace. Computers and Entertainment 5(1), 8 (2007)
13. O'Hara, K.: Understanding geocaching practices and motivations. In: CHI 2008, Florence, pp. 1177–1186. ACM, New York (2008)
14. Benford, S., Rowland, D., Flintham, M., Drozd, A., Hull, R., Reid, J., Morrison, J., Facer, K.: Life on the Edge: Supporting Collaboration in Location-based Experiences. In: CHI 2005, Portland, USA, pp. 721–730. ACM, New York (2005)
15. O'Hara, K., Kindberg, T., Glancy, M., Baptista, L., Sukumaran, B., Kahana, G., Rowbotham, J.: Collecting and Sharing Location-based Content on Mobile Phones in a Zoo Visitor Experience. In: Computer Supported Cooperative Work, vol. 16, pp. 11–44. Springer, Heidelberg (April 2007)
16. Rogers, Y., Price, S., et al.: Ambient wood: designing new forms of digital augmentation for learning outdoors. In: IDC 2004, Maryland, June 1-3, pp. 3–10 (2004)
17. Waern, A., Montola, M., Stenros, J.: The Three-sixty Illusion: Designing for Immerion in Pervasive Games. In: CHI 2009, Boston, MA, pp. 1549–1558. ACM, New York (2009)
18. Benford, S., Crabtree, A., Reeves, S., Sheridan, J., Dix, A., Flintham, M., Drozd, A.: The Frame of the game: the opportunities and risks of staging digital experiences in public settings. In: CHI 2006, pp. 427–436. ACM, New York (2006)

19. Rowland, D., Flintham, M., Oppermann, L., Marshall, J., Chamberlain, A., Koleva, B., Benford, S., Perez, C.: Ubikequitous computing: designing interactive experiences for cyclists. In: Proceedings of the 11th International Conference on Human-Computer Interaction with Mobile Devices and Services (MobileHCI 2009). ACM, New York (2009)
20. Chalmers, M., Galani, A.: Seamful interweaving: heterogeneity in the theory and design of interactive systems. In: DIS 2004, pp. 243–252. ACM, Cambridge (2004)
21. LaMarca, A., Chawathe, Y., Consolvo, S., Hightower, J., Smith, I., Scott, J., Sohn, T., Howard, J., Hughes, J., Potter, F., Tabert, J., Powledge, P.S., Borriello, G., Schilit, B.N.: Device Positioning Using Radio Beacons in the Wild. In: Gellersen, H.-W., Want, R., Schmidt, A. (eds.) PERVASIVE 2005. LNCS, vol. 3468, pp. 116–133. Springer, Heidelberg (2005)
22. Cheng, Y., Chawathe, Y., LaMarca, A., Krumm, J.: Accuracy Characterization for Metropolitan-scale Wi-Fi Localization. In: MobiSys, Seattle, Washington (2005)
23. Rekimoto, J., Miyaki, T., Ishizawa, T.: LifeTag: WiFi-based Continuous Location Logging for Life Pattern Analysis. In: Hightower, J., Schiele, B., Strang, T. (eds.) LoCA 2007. LNCS, vol. 4718, pp. 35–49. Springer, Heidelberg (2007)
24. Kittur, A., Suh, B., Pendleton, B.A., Chi, E.H.: He says, she says: conflict and coordination in Wikipedia. In: CHI 2007, pp. 453–462. ACM, New York (2007)
25. Harrison, S., Dourish, P.: Re-Place-ing Space: The Roles of Space and Place in Collaborative Systems. In: CSCW 1996, Boston, MA, pp. 67–76. ACM, New York (1996)
26. Dourish, P.: Re-Space-ing Place: Place and Space Ten Years On. In: CSCW 2006, Banff, pp. 299–308. ACM, New York (2006)
27. Oppermann, L., Broll, G., Capra, M., Benford, S.: Extending Authoring Tools for Locaion-Aware Applications with an Information Visualisation Layer. In: Dourish, P., Friday, A. (eds.) UbiComp 2006. LNCS, vol. 4206, pp. 52–68. Springer, Heidelberg (2006)

Hybrid Prototyping by Using Virtual and Miniature Simulation for Designing Spatial Interactive Information Systems

Yasuto Nakanishi, Koji Sekiguchi, Takuro Ohmori,
Soh kitahara, and Daisuke Akatsuka

Keio University, Faculty of Environment and Information Studies,
5322 Endo, Fujisawa, Kanagawa, Japan
{naka,t07412ks,ohmori,soh335,dadaa}@sfc.keio.ac.jp
http://cc.unitedfield.net/

Abstract. In this paper, we introduce CityCompiler, an integrated environment for the iteration-based development of spatial interactive systems. CityCompiler visualizes interactive systems in a virtual 3D space by combining the Processing[1] source code and the 3D model of the real space, designed with Google SketchUp. A simulation in virtual space enables us to test a spatial layout and a combination of components. In addition, the system function of smoothly switching between a virtual sensor and a real sensor realizes hybrid prototyping by means of virtual simulation and miniature simulation. These features integrate the space design with the software design and allow the smooth deployment of spatial interactive information systems into the real world.

Keywords: software design, space design, prototyping, deployment, IDE.

1   Introduction

In recent years, the use of large displays in public or commercial spaces has become increasingly popular. These displays are attractive and eye-catching, and they bring with them embodied and spatial interactions. Some notable examples of emerging applications of visual displays are sharing large-size visualized data, smart office applications, digital signage, interactive public art, and interior and exterior architectural displays. These spatial interactive systems consist of both software and real-space components. For instance, interactive digital signage or applications for urban environments mostly use software, cameras, sensors, projectors, speakers, PCs, and real spaces, such as exhibition rooms and urban buildings for projection. In order to make these systems work in the right or effective manner, developers are required to simultaneously configure software and real-space components. For example, configuring the camera/projection location, size, direction, or designing the real space is a significant process.

---

[1] http://www.processing.com/

K. Lyons, J. Hightower, and E.M. Huang (Eds.): Pervasive 2011, LNCS 6696, pp. 250–257, 2011.

Various input and output devices are available for constructing such interactive environments, spanning a large design space. The choice of devices determines modalities, which affect both the nature and the impact of the interactions of such environments with a system. They are crucial for the usability and acceptance of the system by its users, and the integration of interaction design with space design is a topic of considerable interest.

However, in general, after the input and output devices have been decided and the software for the interactive system has been developed, the problem of where to physically place these devices arises. In particular, it should be noted that optical devices such as cameras or displays have a limited field of view, which needs to be considered. Presently, it is difficult for software developers to configure such system components before the system is deployed and runs in the real space. Some developers use low-fidelity techniques, such as paper prototypes and mental walkthroughs, and others have to wait for a full-scale deployment. In other words, software developers are unable to properly test the entire system in the early stages of system development.

To solve these problems, we propose CityCompiler, which enables spatial interactive system developers to create their systems using an iteration-based development process, using iterative visualization or trial-and-error. CityCompiler simulates how an interactive system developed with Processing runs in a 3D virtual world, modeled using Google SketchUp. Simulation in the virtual 3D world allows not only collaboration between the software developer and the space designer, but also trial-and-error testing when sketching a spatial interactive system by choosing input and output devices. The objective of CityCompiler is to support the interaction design concerning the choice of sensors and actuators and their placement in the 3D world, including the assessment of their range of sensitivity and effect such as the visibility of a display.

2   Hybrid Prototyping with CityCompiler

2.1   Sketching and Prototyping

CityCompiler is composed of two modules: a Java class library and a 3D viewer. The 3D viewer is based on the jMonkeyEngine, which is a Java-based 3D game engine[2]. These modules are compressed in jar format, which allows developers to use the prototype with an integrated development environment (IDE), such as Eclipse or NetBeans. Our Java class library provides several Java classes and interfaces that support the development of spatial interactive systems, and some spatial components that work in the virtual spaces are also implemented. Figure 2 shows a part of the CityCompiler class diagram.

- The Model class loads the 3D models saved in the .obj file format created with 3D modeling tools.
- The Projector class projects the Processing application onto the 3D models.

---

[2] http://www.jmonkeyengine.org/

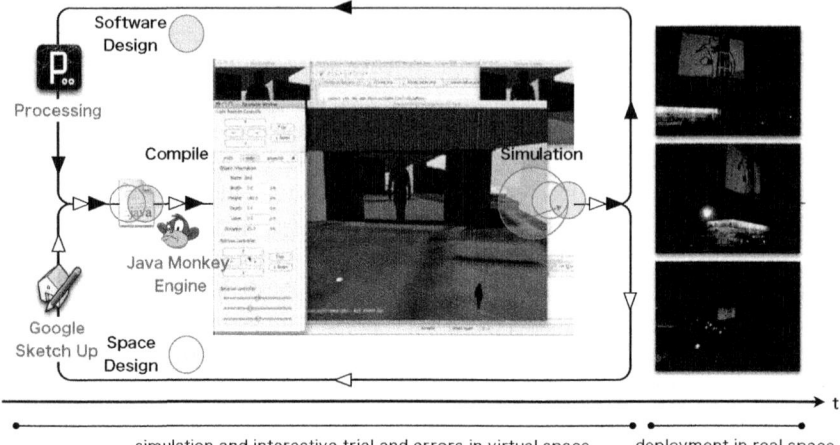

Fig. 1. Overview of CityCompiler

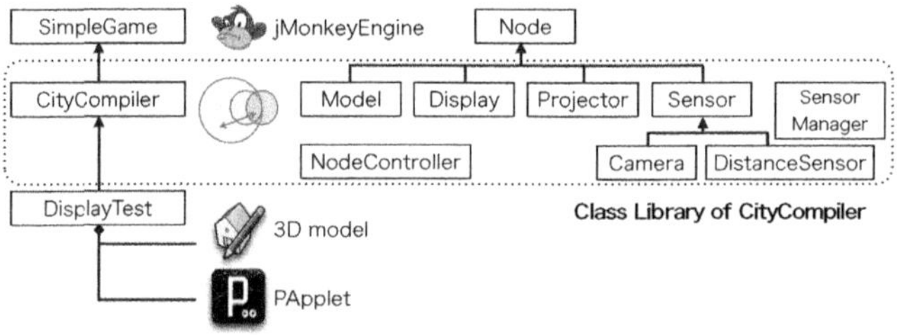

Fig. 2. Class Diagram for CityCompiler

- The Display class shows the application on the surface.
- The Camera class captures images in the virtual world and transfers them to any other Java application.
- The DistanceSensor class returns distances to other objects on the basis of collision detection in the virtual world.

The developer creates a subclass of the CityCompiler class in order to integrate 3D models, the Processing application, and input/output devices in a virtual world. These three main elements that the developer creates are as follows.

(a) Source code as a subclass of the PApplet class for a Processing application
(b) A 3D model for the surrounding environment
(c) Source code based on CityCompiler for integration of the system components

To be more specific, (a) would be installed in (b), and (c) would be used to visualize (a), which runs in (b) and supports several trial-and-error tests with regards to (a). For (c), the developer defines a class that is a subclass of the CityCompiler class, and has several instances of the Display class or Camera class together with the general Java class library.

2.2   Testing Layout and Combination of Components

Once the source code for (a) and the model for (b) are prepared, the developer then compiles (c). After compiling the source code (c), the 3D viewer is displayed along with the parameter window, the camera viewer, and the user application's window. The parameter window allows the developer to manipulate several parameters of the 3D components, such as the position and rotation during runtime. For example, the developer can use the parameter window to configure and check the elevation of the virtual cameras with realistic heights, such as 180 cm or 120 cm. This allows the developer to simultaneously compare the layout of actuators from multiple viewpoints, such as their display or projector.

After carrying out the above-mentioned processes, the developer can return to the process of coding the source (a) or (c), or both, or designing the 3D models (b), which happens in the case of iteration.

2.3   Switching Virtual Devices and Real Devices

In most cases, the space required for developing and testing these types of systems and the space required for deploying them are different. It is impossible to reliably prepare specific visual, spatial, and sensory contexts for the final deployment. Thus, when deploying a system into a real space, unexpected situations often arise, and parameters of the software logic must be adjusted in order to handle inputs from sensors. In some cases, the logic itself is even revised on the site, although such cases should be avoided as much as possible; the visualized simulation in our CityCompiler will make the software logic robust and flexible. In particular, we suppose that operating a system within both a virtual space and miniature space and comparing the corresponding source code will help developers to handle the parameters and revise codes. Obtaining different inputs from a number of sources will allow for further development. In addition, comparing operations in a virtual space and miniature space will aid the successful installation of a system in real space.

In CityCompiler, a SensorManager class is implemented for managing input devices that allow for smooth switching operations in virtual, miniature, and the real space. This class tries to gain access to a real sensor connected to the PC and selects a real sensor or a virtual sensor as the data source. For example, when a USB camera is detected, real-world images are captured and are sent to the application, otherwise, virtual-world images are captured and are sent by the system. Our current implementation can use both USB cameras and Phidgets[3] for USB sensing and control, and these devices are available as real sensors and virtual sensors. Switching virtual sensors with real sensors, and adding the number of various virtual sensors also supports the design decision of choosing between available sensors and actuators.

Figure 3 shows a system deployed into the real space after carrying out repeated simulations both in the virtual space and in the miniature space. The system comprises two distance measuring sensor units connected to a Phidgets

---

[3] http://www.phidgets.com/

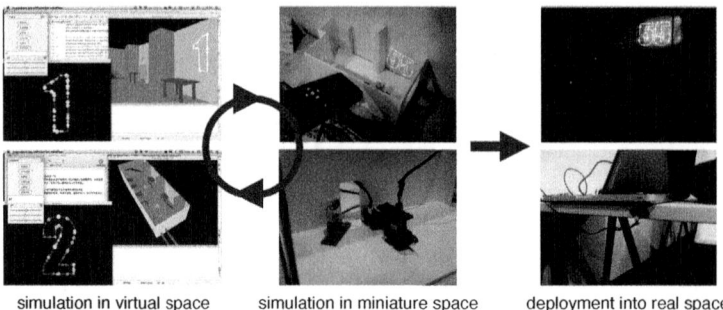

simulation in virtual space   simulation in miniature space   deployment into real space

Fig. 3. Deployment into real space after carrying out repeated simulations both in the virtual space and in the miniature space

board and a projector. It counts the number of visitors at the entrance of a room, and displays the results with motion graphics. First, we developed a system that works in the virtual space and arranged virtual sensors and a virtual projector in a model of our room. Next, we ran it in a miniature space made of white styrofoam with real sensors and a mini-projector. In the virtual space, we can arrange any numbers of projectors in any location, and it is easy to arrange them horizontally. However, in the miniature space, such an ideal placement is difficult. Therefore, in the Processing application, we added a function to change the size, angle, and location of the counted number. We also ran the distance sensors in the miniature space by using a finger to represent one person and moving it around. However this did not work as well as in the virtual space, because the values of parameters for sensing people were different. Thus, a function was added to change the thresholds of the sensing logic during runtime.

Figure 4 shows a system that displays several photos those include location information on a map. We planned to exhibit it with a screen set to the window of our room, which faces the road. First, we developed the processing application, and arranged a virtual projector in the virtual model of our room. Next, we ran it in a miniature space with a mini-projector. The miniature model was made of white styrofoam, and we used a small piece of cloth as a miniature screen. Our current system does not calculate the size of the styrofoam and the cloth automatically, so we calculated the sizes of the parts based on the 3D model and assembled them. We checked how the system worked by watching a movie sent from a wireless camera on the head of a doll, and matched the scale of the miniature to the height of the doll. We found that the size of displayed photos was too small, and so we added a function that changes the sizes of photos for the whole application during runtime. Next, we noticed that the brightness of both the room and the road were the same in the miniature space, although the room was bright and the road was dark at night. Therefore, we added a white LED in the miniature room to introduce such a brightness gap. We also found that the brightness difference between the room and the road changed the appearance of the photos. Thus, we added a function to adjust the brightness of the whole application.

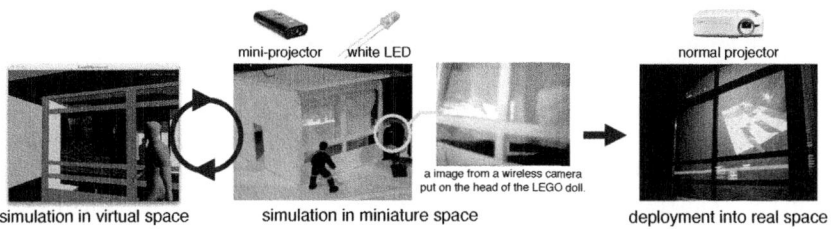

mini-projector   white LED

normal projector

a image from a wireless camera
put on the head of the LEGO doll.

simulation in virtual space   simulation in miniature space   deployment into real space

Fig. 4. Another case of hybrid prototyping

In these two cases, we obtained the required parameters and the revised points of codes by carrying out the simulation in the miniature space. Such improvements make the system more robust and flexible, and will ensure that the system is smoothly deployed in the real world.

We call this hybrid prototyping, and it is a process that can be used to integrate a space design with a software design. In order to deploy devices that match the simulation, we have to implement virtual devices that have the same specifications as the real devices. However, it is difficult to make devices the same as they are in the miniature space. In the above-mentioned cases, the differences between the virtual simulation and the miniature simulation helped us to discover parameters and brought about spiral design cycles. Running the code in several different spaces, and with different devices helps to evolve both the software and the spatial arrangement of devices, which is a benefit of hybrid prototyping. From this viewpoint, it might not necessarily be good that our system helps to automatically form an exact miniature model with a 3D printer.

There are limitations in hybrid prototyping. For example, it cannot tell all the necessary parameters, even if we repeat virtual and miniature simulations, and we might find further problems in the final deployment. However, updating the source code using hybrid prototyping would allow the flexibility to handle new problems. A further limitation is that it is time-consuming, expensive, and complicated to arrange several displays or cameras in a miniature space. In this case, it is more realistic to use a virtual simulation and a partial miniature simulation concurrently.

3   Related Works

There have been many prototyping tools for various domains. Topiary is a tool for prototyping location-enhanced applications, and enables iteration on designs by using a map that demonstrates scenarios composed of interaction sequences[8]. Papier-Mâché is a toolkit for building tangible user interfaces using computer vision, etc., and introduces a high level event model[5]. Both these systems and our system aim to make it easy to prototype, evaluate and iterate on augmented environments. Incorporating the functions of Topiary and Papier-Mâché will makes our system a better tool. Singh et al. proposed the use of immersive video as a means of rapid prototyping and an evaluation tool for mobile and ambient applications[6]. This approach uses immersive video with surround sound as a simulated infrastructure to create a realistic simulation of a ubiquitous environment for software design. The objective of CityCompiler is also to simulate for a ubiquitous computing environment. However, it aims at having both virtual and miniature simulations rather than creating just one realistic simulation. UbiREAL[3] and eHomeSimulater[1] are simulators used for developing and testing devices that run on a smart home, and their main aim is developing hardware or software. CityCompiler also simulates a smart environment, and supports not only indoor smart space environments, but also outdoor systems, such as urban areas. The objective of CityCompiler is to integrate software design and spatial design with iteration-based development. CityCompiler places great emphasis on iteration-based development, rather than accurate simulation. This is the reason why we selected Processing and SketchUp.

Firefly is a set of software tools that bridge the gap between 3D modeling software, micro-controllers and the internet[4]. It also allows near real-time data flow between virtual and model spaces, and will read/write data to/from internet feeds or sensors. However, it changes shapes made by parametric and algorithmic design, and does not target sound, video, graphics, or animation, which Processing and CityCompiler do. Nakanishi et al. proposed two multiagent-based participatory simulation methods for a large-scale socially embedded system[4]. One involves participatory simulation, in which scenario-guided agents and human-controlled avatars coexist in a shared virtual space and jointly perform simulations. The other involves an augmented experiment, in which an experiment is performed in a real space by human subjects, enhanced by a large scale multi-agent simulation. They can be Cross-Reality[2] or Augmented-Virtuality to combine a virtual space and a model space and to combine people with multi-agents. Hybrid prototyping as Cross-Reality or Augmented-Virtuality would be a promising way to design and develop spatial information systems or responsive augmented environments.

Yamashita et al. demonstrated that seating arrangements exert an important influence on video-mediated conversations; different seating arrangements yield differences in speech patterns, senses of unity, and quality of solutions[7]. The display layout allowed the participants to change their body orientations, head movements, and seating arrangements, creating different patterns of video-mediated conversations. This means that both the software design and the space design, along with the orientation and disposition of input/output devices influences the way people interact. The integration of interaction design with space design, and in particular, spatiality, is a topic of considerable interest.

4   Conclusion and Future Work

One problem in developing pervasive computing applications is the simulation of the required input/output devices in the environment in which they are to be deployed. In this paper, we introduced CityCompiler, an integrated environment

---

[4] http://www.fireflyexperiments.com/

for the iteration-based development of spatial interactive systems. CityCompiler visualizes an interactive system in a virtual 3D space by combining the Processing source code and a 3D model designed with SketchUp. In the Web interface design, graphic design is integrated with software design. In the case of the spatial information systems design, space design should be integrated with software design in the same way, and simulations using CityCompiler are studied to realize the integration. CityCompiler enables the developer to carry out interactive trial-and-error tests with the testing layout and a combination of components. Here, the developer uses both the virtual space and the miniature space before the final deployment into the real space. The simulation allows the software designer, space designer, or interaction designer to browse the intended activities, and to collaboratively highlight their context in the urban environment by considering spatial regions and the installation of input and output devices. In this paper, we introduced only two of our processes employing hybrid prototyping. In future, we will investigate the effectiveness of hybrid prototyping by analyzing more cases. We believe hybrid prototyping would be effective not only for deploying a system into the real world but also for designing a system with a new concept. We will also use both virtual and miniature simulations to come up with an idea and investigate the advantages and disadvantages of each method.

Acknowledgments. This research is supported by the JST PRESTO program.

References

1. Armac, I., Retkowitz, D.: Simulation of Smart Environments. In: Proceedings of the IEEE International Conference on Pervasive Services, pp. 257–266 (2007)
2. Lifton, J., et al.: Metaphor and Manifestation - Cross Reality with Ubiquitous Sensor/Actuator Networks. IEEE Pervasive Computing 8(3), 24–33
3. Nishikawa, H., Yamamoto, S., Tamai, M., Nishigaki, K., Kitani, T., Shibata, N., Yasumoto, K., Ito, M.: UbiREAL: Realistic Smartspace Simulator for Systematic Testing. In: Dourish, P., Friday, A. (eds.) UbiComp 2006. LNCS, vol. 4206, pp. 459–476. Springer, Heidelberg (2006)
4. Nakanishi, H., Ishida, T., Koizumi, S.: Virtual Cities for Simulating Smart Urban Public Spaces. In: Handbook of Research on Urban Informatics: The Practice and Promise of the Real-Time City, pp. 256–268. IGI Global
5. Scott, R., et al.: Papier-Mch: Toolkit Support for Tangible Input. CHI Letters, Human Factors in Computing Systems. In: CHI 2004, vol. 6(1) (2004)
6. Singh, P., et al.: Immersive video as a rapid prototyping and evaluation tool for mobile and ambient applications. In: Proceedings of Mobile HCI 2006, p. 264 (2006)
7. Yamashita, Y., et al.: Impact of Seating Positions on Group Video Communication. In: Proceedings of CSCW, pp. 177–186 (2008)
8. Li, Y., et al.: Topiary: a tool for prototyping location-enhanced applications. In: Proceedings of the 17th Annual ACM Symposium on User Interface Software and Technology (UIST 2004), pp. 217–226 (2004)

Designing Shared Public Display Networks – Implications from Today's Paper-Based Notice Areas

Florian Alt[1], Nemanja Memarovic[2], Ivan Elhart[2], Dominik Bial[1], Albrecht Schmidt[4], Marc Langheinrich[2], Gunnar Harboe[3], Elaine Huang[3], and Marcello P. Scipioni[2]

[1] University of Duisburg-Essen, Schützenbahn 70, 45117 Essen, Germany
{florian.alt,dominik.bial}@uni-due.de
[2] University of Lugano, Via G. Buffi 13, 6904 Lugano, Switzerland
{ivan.elhart,marc.langheinrich,nemanja.memarovic,
marcello.scipioni}@usi.ch
[3] University of Zürich, Binzmühlestrasse 14, 8050 Zürich, Switzerland
{harboe,huang}@ifi.uzh.ch
[4] University of Stuttgart, Pfaffenwaldring 5a, 70569 Stuttgart, Germany
albrecht.schmidt@vis.uni-stuttgart.de

Abstract. Large public displays have become a regular conceptual element in many shops and businesses, where they advertise products or highlight upcoming events. In our work, we are interested in exploring how these isolated display solutions can be interconnected to form a single large network of public displays, thus supporting novel forms of sharing access to display real estate. In order to explore the feasibility of this vision, we investigated today's practices surrounding shared notice areas, i.e. places where customers and visitors can put up event posters and classifieds, such as shop windows or notice boards. In particular, we looked at the content posted to such areas, the means for sharing it (i.e., forms of content control), and the reason for providing the shared notice area. Based on two-week long photo logs and a number of in-depth interviews with providers of such notice areas, we provide a systematic assessment of factors that inhibit or promote the shared use of public display space, ultimately leading to a set of concrete design implication for providing future digital versions of such public notice areas in the form of networked public displays.

Keywords: public display, observation, advertising.

1 Introduction

Large digital displays are rapidly permeating public spaces. The availability of suitable display technologies for outdoor use, together with decreasing prices for large screen display hardware, has led to a transformation from paper-based to digital signage and advertising. Urban landscapes are being augmented with digital signage solutions by large digital-out-of-home (DOOH) advertisers (e.g. Stroer, JC Decaux) replacing more and more traditional billboards. Apart from reducing the cost of updating their contents, these displays allow for the addition of animations and/or interlacing news content in order to make them more visible and attractive to passers-by.

K. Lyons, J. Hightower, and E.M. Huang (Eds.): Pervasive 2011, LNCS 6696, pp. 258–275, 2011.
© Springer-Verlag Berlin Heidelberg 2011

However, so far these digital displays are not globally networked and access is typically restricted to their owners.

We envision that in the future, these individual displays and isolated display solutions could be inter-connected through the Internet. Hence, a canvas across urban space can be provided that allows for distributing any type of content onto this display landscape, not only from large advertisers but instead from neighboring shops, local residents, and visitors. Technically, the challenge of such a vision is to create a suitable middleware that supports the remote exchange and programming of arbitrary content onto arbitrary displays, as well as suitable interfaces to interact with such systems. A far greater challenge, though, lies in the design and deployment of suitable control tools that can support the stakeholders' understanding of how these displays ought to be used. Without suitable incentives and means for staying in control, display owners might be reluctant to grant access to their displays and relinquish their control over what is being shown on their in-store displays. Our central research question thus is: how can we build digital public display networks that can go beyond today's isolated advertisement displays, and instead provide an open platform for posting and displaying user-generated content? Yet instead of tackling the technical challenge of such a vision directly, we begin our investigation with trying to understand the social and economical drivers to support this vision: What would motivate display owners to allow others access to their displays? And what would control interfaces and incentive structures have to look like to support widespread uptake of such systems?

We decided to ground our research in today's practices surrounding the precursors to our vision: shop-windows, notice boards, and wall hangers, where customers, community members, and visitors can use pen & paper and pins & tape to put up their messages, notices, posters, and classifieds (c.f. Figure 1). For the purpose of this paper, we collectively call such boards, walls, and hangers "Public Notice Areas", or PNAs. We began by observing the use of PNAs in 29 locations in two different countries, using photo logs to document their use and change over 4 weeks. We then performed in-depth interviews with most of the people responsible for the observed PNAs, in order to understand their current practices for controlling access to the PNAs, elicit their motivations for offering PNAs, and identify concerns they might have when relinquishing control in a fully digital public display network. The results from the observational studies and interviews were analyzed in a quantitative and qualitative fashion, using a "data walkthrough" analysis that we developed to give all team members an in-depth view of the data collected by other team members.

Fig. 1. Types of Displays. (1) Scaffolded Classifieds Display (2) Non-Scaffolded Classifieds Display (3) Information Display (4) Event Display.

After briefly discussing related work in section 2 below, we will enumerate our research questions in section 3, followed by a description of our study design in section 4. Section 5 describes the data analysis and section 6 presents our findings based on the research questions. Finally section 7 deals with inferred design implications.

2 Related Work

Public displays have been subject to research for many years. With decreasing prices, many traditional displays are being replaced with digital counterparts. Many projects have looked at the technical requirements for networking digital displays, mostly within and across offices (e.g. [1], [3]) but also in public space (e.g. [12],[15]). Also, novel interaction methods have been studied, both in terms of user behaviors (e.g. [2],[11]) and interface technology (e.g. [6],[7]). Although technical and architectural suggestions could be drawn from these studies, our initial work in this domain focuses on understanding the design implications from *existing practices* of posting on PNAs and *latent motivations* for offering and maintaining PNAs.

There have been several such studies that looked at current practices around publicly available notice boards and displays. Taylor et al. [16] looked at community notice boards in a rural village to inform the design of a digital version. Churchill et al. [4] looked at community notice boards in an urban area and in their own workspace to inform the design of their Plasma Poster Network, a system that enhances the chance to encounter interaction and awareness of different workgroups' activities. Huang et al. [8] conducted a field study to analyze various paper and digital displays and their actual placement, as well as how much people actually look at them. Based on their findings, they provided design recommendations for increasing the visibility of displays and for better matching between people's behavior and the displays' content. Although there is some overlap between previous studies and our research, our primary goal is to come up with general implications that inform the design of a public display network system that go beyond display visibility and office space and suburban area settings.

As can be seen from the previous paragraph, public displays have a large potential to foster communities. Redhead et al. [13] presented a qualitative analysis of local community interaction among its members. One of their main findings was that public displays could increase the perception of unity as well as communities' interests. Some of their findings, e.g. suggestions for content and features of such displays, support the perspective of the community and delivery of local messages. A report of their findings on the usage of a digital community notice board is available in [14].

Studies exploring the impact of digital notice boards on communities have been conducted in several settings. As mentioned previously, Taylor et al. [17] looked into notice board practices in a rural village and informed the design of the Wray Display, a community photo sharing display aimed at understanding how digital displays can help to support communities in suburban areas. Churchill et al.'s Plasma Poster Network [5] looked into how displaying social media impacts relationships among co-located colleagues in their workplace. The CoCollage [10] aimed at cultivating community in a café by showing posters and quotes and hence enhancing awareness, interaction, and relationship among people. Of particular interest is Huang et al.'s [9] finding that people spend less time learning about system capabilities when it is not supporting current use practices. The users' desire and interest to use novel system need be taken into account [11]. This emphasizes the necessity of embedding existing routines in novel system to support its use. Note that in our view, this entails not only catering to users' needs, but also reflecting on PNA providers' motivations.

3 Sharing Public Display Space

Traditional public displays are a very common way of communication and they are ubiquitous in our environment. They scale from post-it notes on an office door telling people who stop by "back in 5 minutes" to graffiti on a train making a political statement. This form of communication is very effective and observers will not be even aware of reading the signs in many cases, but they still do. Such public displays are an example of *invisible technologies* that allow transparent use, as Weiser suggests [18].

In our work we are particularly interested in public displays for information dissemination and for one-to-many communication. Spaces for these forms of communication and publicly sharing information can be found in many places, such as grocery stores, cafes, and restaurants but also in city administrations, public libraries, universities, and schools. Such places provide space that is visible, accessible, and frequented by people. Examples are notice boards and walls on which people are allowed to attach posters, and windows as well as doors where people can hang up flyers or notes. There is a huge variety of such PNAs, and many types of content can be found. Generally it can be seen that these displays have a function in their environment, and that the form factor of the display and the types of contents shared are influenced by the location, the owner, and the expected audience. In contrast to other forms of communication these displays support the following properties: (1) dissemination of content that is mainly locally relevant, (2) addressing of the receivers by selection of space, and (3) forcing information and content on people that pass through a certain space.

Traditionally, posting information in PNAs also had the function of personal communication from one individual to many receivers. However, this function of public displays has lost importance with the digital social networks and the World Wide Web. Popular forms of content include sales, housing, job and service offers, events, promotions, lost and found, and advertisements, all of which are at least showing one of the characteristics above. In order to derive an understanding of how to create digital displays that provide new flexibility and cost-effectiveness and at the same time retain the qualities of the analog PNAs, we investigate several issues further.

3.1 Value Propositions of PNAs for Stakeholders

In the optimal case, PNAs provide value to all stakeholders, including the people owning the space, people providing content, and people observing the content. First, it is important to identify stakeholders for a PNA installation, and their motivations. In many cases there is interplay between interests, incentives, and value propositions.

Consider the following scenario of a notice board for classified ads in a supermarket. The content provider (e.g. a customer who wants to sell a bike) has the opportunity to reach people in the local community. The observer (e.g. another customer looking for a used bike to buy) via PNA becomes aware of the product she is looking for. The supermarket provides customers with a further reason to visit the store.

Values have to be seen in the greater context of the PNA and its place of use. Here issues such as exercising control over what content can be placed, by defining access to the display and implementing means for restricting content placement to a certain group play a role. The following questions help to identify these issues:

- Who is allowed to post?
- Who decides what content is appropriate?
- What content can be posted?
- What is the motivation for the owner to allow posting?
- What is the motivation for content providers to post?
- What is the motivation for observers to look at the content?

3.2 Mechanism for Content Creation, Posting, Removing and Access Control

The utility of public displays depends on the fact that displayed information is useful. In general, content is posted to the display and removed or overwritten after a certain time. The mechanisms used both for posting and removing content as well as for enforcing usage policies are essential success factors. Often it is desirable that content can be created ad-hoc, without specific knowledge or tools (e.g. writing with a pen provided at the board onto pre-printed cards). Yet, the simpler the means for content provision, the more likely that spam or inappropriate content will be posted.

Many different ways can be found with which such control mechanisms for content creation and posting are restricted, ranging from having the notice board in a public area (where users posting content may be observed) to explicit approval of content. We suggest the following questions to identify and structure these mechanisms:

- How can content be placed onto the display?
- What flexibility is available for content creation?
- What tools are required to create content?
- What is the process for approval of content?
- How is content removed or overwritten?
- How is access control implemented for content providers and viewers?
- How are viewers supported to help them remember content?

3.3 Learning from Practices in the Analog World

Many different types of PNAs are in use in different places. This multitude evolved over a long time and many of their properties fulfill a certain need. Similarly, many sorts of posted content are publicly posted. Here, too, a long tradition exists for creating and designing content, ranging from artistic expression to minimalistic presentations. In this paper we aim at identifying these rich characters of different displays, content types, and related practices. For deriving design implications for digital displays, understanding practices and the rationale behind these is very valuable. In particular we are interested in the communication aspects that such displays facilitate.

A further important aspect of public displays is that they have a potential function for the community. By positing information in publicly accessible space but in a specific location, a clear addressing to the local community is made. Here it seems interesting to uncover functions that displays have that go beyond the communication of individuals or groups. To learn about the practices we ask the following questions:

- What practices have been established around sharing on a display?
- What are the reasons for these practices?

4 Study Design

To answer our research questions we ran a two-week field study during summer 2010 in four different cities in Switzerland and Germany, involving observational studies (photo logs) and subsequent interviews with the people responsible for the observed PNA, i.e. shop-owners and personnel.

4.1 Observational Studies

We aimed at observing a wide variety of locations, displays, and audiences. To do so, we looked for any kind of institutions, stores, and restaurants/eateries that displayed public notice boards. Due to the labor-intensive nature of the work, we opted for a convenience sampling of the observed sites (places were located along our work routes), allowing us to regularly visit these places over the course of four weeks. Consequently, the observed locations were within the local neighborhoods surrounding the universities and central stations of Lugano (Switzerland), Essen, Düsseldorf and Munich (all Germany). An overview of the locations can be found in Table 1.

After choosing suitable locations, we identified the persons responsible for the PNA to be observed. We introduced ourselves, explained the purpose of the study and asked for permission to take pictures of the PNA. We provided a written description of the study and explained that all data collected would be used for scientific purpose only. While most people immediately agreed to permit the study and even showed interest in the results, some of them (notably in larger stores) first had to check with central management and asked us to report to the management every time we returned. In two locations we were refused permission to conduct the study, as the management felt that this would strongly affect their customers' privacy.

After permissions had been obtained, we visited each location on consecutive working days over the course of roughly four weeks, each time taking several pictures of all postings. Pictures were mainly taken in the morning (on the way to work), during lunch break, and in the late afternoon / evening (on the way back home). We tried to make sure that pictures were taken at comparable times of the day. In total, 4 researchers were involved in the study, each one being assigned a fixed set of locations. Due to scheduling constraints it was not in all cases possible to take pictures on consecutive working days. However, we made sure that for each location at least 10 picture sets from different days were taken within no more than 4 weeks.

Table 1. Overview of study locations

ID	Name	Description	Obs. | Int.	Type	Cur.
E1	Turn Headshop (Rack)	Retail	x | x	ED	-
E2	Turn Headshop (Door)	Retail	x | x	ED	-
E3	Diocese (Office)	Church	x | x	ID	x
E4	Diocese (Entrance)	Church	x | x	ID	x
E5	Supermarket	Retail	x | x	SCD	-
E6	Supermarket	Retail	x | x	UCD	-
E7	University cafeteria	Public Bldg./Gov.	- | x	UCD	x
D1	City administration	Public Bldg./Gov.	x | x	ID	x
D2	Adult Education Center	Public Bldg./Gov.	x | x	UCD	-
D3	Public Library	Public Bldg./Gov.	x | x	ED	x
D4	Child Services	Public Bldg./Gov.	x | x	ED	-
M1	Supermarket	Retail	- | x	SCD	-
M2	Supermarket	Retail	- | x	SCD	-
M3	Supermarket	Retail	- | x	SCD	-
M4	Supermarket	Retail	- | x	SCD	-
L1	Supermarket	Retail	x | x	SCD	-
L2	University	Public Bldg./Gov.	x | x	UCD	-
L3	Bakery	Service	x | x	UCD	x
L4	Church	Church	x | -	ID	x
L5	Supermarket	Retail	x | x	SCD	-
L6	Café	Service	x | -	ED	-
L7	Hairdresser	Service	x | -	ED	-
L8	Bar	Service	x | x	ED	-
L9	Café	Service	x | x	ED	x
L10	Pharmacy	Retail	x | -	ED	-
L11	Bookstore	Retail	x | x	ED	-
L12	Red Cross	Public Bldg./Gov.	x | x	ID	x
L13	Laundry	Service	x | -	ED	-
L14	Church	Church	x | -	ID	x

Abbreviations:
Obs | Int: Observation | Interview
Cur: Curated Display

Display Types:
SCD / UCD (Scaffolded / Unscaffolded Classifieds Display), **ID** (Information Display), **ED** (Event Display)

4.2 Interviews

After finishing our observational study we conducted a number of interviews with people in charge of managing the displays. Those were not necessarily the display owners, but also store managers or regular staff. With the interviews we aimed at understanding a range of issues surrounding PNAs: the shops' motivation for having such a PNA; the practices for adding, editing, and removing content; any restrictions as to what customer were allowed to post; any problems with the displays; and whether people could imagine substituting the "analog" display with a digital version.

We conducted interviews in the locations that were covered in our observational study. However, for two locations we were not able to get hold of a responsible person. We also included additional locations with similar PNAs to gather further information.

For the interviews we returned to the location and tried to identify the person (currently) in charge of the display, asking her or him to answer a set of 10 questions. We offered to return at a convenient time in case people were too busy to talk to us. As interviews happened during business hours, the interviewee's time was in general scarce. Consequently, we limited our interviews to maximum 10 minutes. We either audio-recorded the interviews with a voice recorder (in case people felt comfortable to do so) and transcribed them later, or took hand-written notes during the interview. It should be noted that the interviews were limited to the parties who owned and "administered" the displays for reasons of accessibility. Information we gained about the perception and use of these displays by passers-by and other stakeholders in the interviews was conveyed to us by display administrators and therefore may reflect their particular interpretation of phenomena regarding the displays. For the purpose of this study, we relied primarily on our observations to gain insight into the practices and needs of passers-by and other stakeholders to complement the more direct inquiry into the practices of display owners and administrators.

5 Data Analysis

We conducted an extensive qualitative analysis of the collected photographs and interviews. Because of the large volume of data generated by the study and the distributed fashion in which the data was collected, we designed a "data walkthrough" analysis method. The goal of this method was to help team members become highly familiar with data that had been collected by other members of the team, and provide a view on that data that would afford both a comprehensive overview of all of the data from all of the sites, as well as an individual detailed view of each site.

The team printed out photos from each day of data collection for each data collection site and affixed these photos (in total 298) to walls and whiteboards in a single room. The photos were placed in chronological order, grouped by site. Additionally, interview transcripts and field notes were affixed along with the corresponding photographs. Five members of the research team then proceeded to "walk through" the data, analyzing the photographs, interviews, and notes, and writing observations on individual sticky notes that were used to annotate the collections of data (see Figure 2). As the team discovered patterns and higher-level observations, these were written on a separate whiteboard.

After this exploratory phase of analysis, the team then used an affinity diagram to identify themes in the data and associate them with our research questions (see *(3) Affinity Diagram* in Figure 2):

- Who are the stakeholders? (6.1)
- What "characters" of displays arise and what determines them? (6.2)
- What are current practices for sharing displays space? (6.3)
- What is the role of "posting displays" in a space? (6.4)
- How do the space, stakeholders and content interplay? (6.5)
- What are the needs of people who are posting and display owners, and how do the displays satisfy them? (6.6)

This was achieved by taking all of the observations and categorizing them to derive the general findings from the data. The identification of findings was done as a group, and each observation was discussed as to how it might fit with other observations.

Fig. 2. Data Walkthrough (1) Photos, field notes, and transcribed interviews were printed and affixed to walls. (2) Analysis and annotation of material by researchers. (3) Affinity Diagram to identify themes in the data.

6 Findings

Based on the data collected and analyzed, we report in this section the findings, with a focus on current practices. We first identify stakeholders, describe characteristics of displays and content, and uncover the motivation for shared public displays. During the data analysis we did not discover any obvious differences in the data gathered in both countries.

6.1 Stakeholders and Motivation

The data from observations and interviews provide a clear indication of a number of diverse stakeholders involved in operating and using public notice boards and shared public displays. On a highest level we can discriminate three different groups: *display providers and managers, content providers, and viewers.*

Display Providers and Managers

Based on interviews (L1, L2, L5, E3, E4, E5, E6, D1, M1, M2, M3, M4) we discovered that the decision to install a PNA is taken on a *higher management level,* e.g. in store chains and public authority institutions, and hence each branch or store will have a PNA as standard inventory. Also public and ecclesiastic institutions see information dissemination as a part of their mission and use them to distribute important information about their current activities. In locations where *venue and shop owners* are running the place (L3, L8, L9, L11, E3, E4, E5, M1, M2, M3, M4), interviews revealed that the decision to have a display and how to use it is in one hand.

The motivation for providing public displays is manifold: retail and service have them to increase customer satisfaction (interviews at M1, M3, M4, E6, D2), public authorities and ecclesiastic institutions mainly used them to disseminate information on their current activities (observations at L4, L14, interviews at E7, D1, D2, D3, D4), and some of them (interviews at E3, E4, E7, D1, D2, D3, D4) feel the need to have a space for third party content as long as it fits within the institution's scope and does not harm its reputation.

In interviews, we found that some venues (L3, E3, E4, M3) have a dedicated person in charge of the content approval, i.e., a *notice board manager* whereas in other places it is less formalized. In the case of public and ecclesiastic institutions there is typically a dedicated manager, whereas smaller venues, like shops and cafés are more likely to distribute this role throughout their staff, i.e., each staff member can act as a manager.

Content Providers

We can see two distinct groups of content providers: *classifieds providers and third party advertisers*. Both groups seek to *distribute information* to the target audience. People living in the vicinity of the venue or its frequent visitors can be seen as *classifieds providers*, seeking for 'matchmaking' opportunities, e.g. students exchanging books, people offering and looking for housing, or selling furniture. The content defines in many cases how long one can expect a poster to remain on the board.

While classifieds providers are mostly individuals, third party advertisers are usually affiliations: church, government, business, musicians, non-profit, or other. All of them have a common goal of reaching a large audience and advertise in the vicinity of the target community's physical center, e.g. music events have multiple posters at music-oriented bars and universities, church-related events appear within its parish's locality, and even third party advertisements on government public display are topically focused. Interestingly enough, some of the venues take on the role of the third party advertiser and try to blend in with the rest when advertising its own events (e.g., Li8).

There is an inherent tension between display owners and content providers as both rely upon each other (e.g. a PNA without content is not interesting and a person providing content cannot do so without space). The best way to minimize the risk of conflicts is to create a shared understanding about venues' *board expectations* (e.g. it is clear what content is expected on a certain display). It seems that this is quite common for PNAs as there were very few reports of abuse of the displays (interviews at L1, L5, L8, L9, L11, E1, E2, D1, D2, D3, D4).

Viewers

The motivations for *viewing* content ranges from clear information needs (e.g. someone looks actively for a place to rent among postings) to accidental reading (e.g. waiting at the bus shelter and reading the posts in lack of any other occupation). *Viewers* are typically related to the location (e.g. they work or live close by) and may act at some time as viewer and at some other times as content provider.

Many PNAs are located near high-traffic areas with guaranteed waiting time, e.g. next to printers and copiers, whereas other locations use them for decoration, e.g. bars. In cases where people are waiting, e.g. for a drink or a print job to finish, it is very likely that they browse through the PNA's content. Supporting evidence can be found in [5].

6.2 Displays and Content

During our observations and data analysis we discovered a number of different display types that are targeted to specific types of content. In the following we discuss typical groups that are commonly in use for PNAs (see also Figure 1).

Scaffolded Classifieds Displays: Our observations indicate that retail stores and supermarkets favor a well-organized arrangement of their PNA (e.g., L1, L5). These areas are highly scaffolded with preprinted cards provided at the display, which can be filled in and inserted into several rows of slots. Their content is in general informal and hand-written and sometimes includes tear-aways (e.g. name and telephone number). Content creation is very fast (on the order of a minute). Typically, content providers are asked to provide a date to later remove outdated content. Often content not fitting the scaffold is attached next to the board. Content usually has a high turnover.

Unscaffolded Classifieds Display: These displays are characterized by the absence of prescribed structure leading to flexible and ad-hoc posting practices. Typically they are not well organized. Content in any form can be placed at any position, even if it fully or partially occludes other content. Interviews showed that for most of these displays (e.g., L2, L8), there is no particular person in charge to check and remove posters placed in improper place or with unwanted content. These displays reflect the self-service nature of the postings. Content posted on such displays is in general similar to the aforementioned displays, with less structured layout, mixed sizes of posts, more colorful posts and more event-related content. We discovered such displays at university, the adult education center, and also grocery stores (L2, L8, D2).

Information Display: As part of their information duty, many institutions, churches and libraries provide curated PNAs (observations at L4, L12, L14). They are characterized by formal, mostly professional content, including ads and events. In general they have a smaller number of postings compared to the abovementioned types. Content is thematically focused (even if from third parties) and often applies to a larger vicinity. There is often a process for submitting and approving through existing/formalized organization networks. These PNAs typically have a means for prohibiting unauthorized postings (e.g. by having a glass front pane, see Figure 1c).

Event Display: Observations showed that bars and retailers offer event-focused PNAs (E1, L6, L8, L9). They are characterized by professional ads (posters, flyers), are thematically tightly scoped (e.g. techno events) and contain mostly third party content. The content is usually colorful, sometimes chaotic (depending on whether scaffolding is provided) and often provides some form of urban aesthetic.

6.3 Managing Content and Supporting Memory

Different mechanisms exist that help viewers to remember content they have seen. We came across 3 types of practices with regard to supporting memory: (1) information that is meant to stay on the board and where viewers are expected to remember essential information, (2) content that is completely taken away, and (3) content that offers parts with contact details that can be taken away. To allow for *taking away information*, current practices include providing multiple copies (e.g. flyers) or posts

Fig. 3. Taking away information – Flyers (left, E1), Posts with takeaway tabs (right, E6)

with takeaway tabs (see Figure 3). If viewers have to remember content, it is important that this is well feasible, e.g. by providing an easy-to-remember URL. With the wide availability of mobile-phone cameras we also see a further practice conceptually combining (1) and (3). As people take photos of public display content, they take the information with them and at the same time leave the content for others.

We found different practices of *post management* with regard to cleaning displays.

- **Expiration Date:** The most popular practice we discovered for cleaning content is the removal of outdated content. This can be done either with a posted expiration date (e.g. after 30 days of posting) or with an implicit expiration date (e.g. the date of an event).
- **Complete Cleanup:** Another practice is entirely erasing PNAs based on a regular schedule, e.g. monthly. We found this practice for PNAs that contained too much content for manually selecting stale content (observation and interview at L2).
- **Curated Content:** Especially in municipal and official institutions we found that displays are often curated. Content is usually submitted at the reception or sent via mail, and has to be approved by the director prior to being published. We observed that curated displays are in general very tidy and posts are not attached above each other so that they obscure other content.

6.4   The Role of Shared Displays in a Space

One function of displays is that they tend to *create a central location for community activity* (observations at E1, E2, E7). Such communities may be geographical, cultural, and also religious. Even though platforms such as Ebay or Craig's list exist, means for locally exchanging goods are still of interest. Especially items whose shipping costs outweigh their price are popular. Notice boards offer a convenient way of offering items to a local community where it is likely to find interested persons who are able to fetch items personally. Additionally, we found content that is relevant to the expected community visiting the location. E.g. in a music bar (observation at L8), PNAs mainly included promotion for music events (parties, live shows, concerts, etc.).

Further, boards are often used as *community support tools*. An example is the PNA at the adult education center, which was mainly used as a forum to exchange study-related material (e.g. people offered their course material to people in lower courses).

6.5 Interplay between Space, Stakeholders, and Content

We found that PNAs are *often placed in high traffic areas* (e.g. next to the main entrance of a location or in spots with waiting times) and that this had a strong impact on turnover in content. The same appeared to be true for *communication and information hotspots*. PNAs were often placed next to opinion boxes, store hours, space for prospects, and content from the display owner itself.

Most interesting though, *posts are very local in nature*. We found that content with no relation to a certain location (e.g. products, movies) appeared only rarely. In contrast, content seemed to be locally highly relevant. An example is posts on babysitting, as these people would usually not cover too large distances. This finding is also supported by the fact that information on local events is often posted in multiple locations in close proximity (e.g. in various stores in the pedestrian area). Similarly, *boards often seem to express the identity of a venue*. During our interviews we found that certain types of content is removed (e.g. political content, certain music events).

6.6 Needs of Content Providers and Display Owners

We observed that *PNA owners often have an agenda*. This in general correlates with their motivation for having a PNA (e.g. information obligation, dissemination of culture). Interestingly, persons in charge of managing the PNA sometimes serve as a gatekeeper, hence supporting certain events in an altruistic way as they feel that competing events are already sufficiently well publicized. As an example, the public library D4 refuses to announce Mardi Gras events but instead favors independent theatres.

Further, many places *provide support for posting*. Such support includes tables for writing posts as well as scaffolding in the form of structured cards and pens.

In addition, we found that *flexibility of content creation is supported* in many places. Whereas especially scaffolded displays provide standard cards, most of the display owners allow in parallel for customized postings. Thus, homemade posts, professionally printed or colored to make them more visible and eye-catching, can also be found. Another example we observed was that it seemed to be OK for most display owners to extend the provided display space in order to fit more content, e.g. by attaching content next to the designated posting area.

We also found many places that allow for *multiple copies of the same item of content*. This was observed for different types of PNAs. On unscaffolded displays posters are freely tiled up next to each other, making a larger area more distinguishable from other parts of the board. This practice was observed also with scaffolded displays. Multiple posts of the same ad/post appear on different PNA locations and sometimes with small or no differences that are not easy spotted: in cases of non-professional handwritten posts, multiple posts are hard to recognize. Only by reading them carefully and comparing contact details can these be noticed. Obviously, having multiple copies of a single post increases the chances of the post being seen. The motivation for the content providers to put up multiple copies of the post is that they are afraid that their post is going to be removed for some reason.

Finally, we found that there are often *difficulties of indicating a venue's expectations of the board*. When asking for problems with PNAs, several display owners reported on discussions with people in order to explain what content is / isn't allowed. Content that is removed is mainly political content, offending or provocative content, competing content, and content that does not fit the agenda of the display owner. There are very few examples where we found explicit notices that certain types of content are not allowed or have to be approved. One example was at the adult education center, where a notice stated that teaching content is to be approved first.

7 Design Implications

Our observations identified important stakeholders and some of their needs, as well as current processes and structures helping them to fulfill their goals, or that emerge as a result of their joint activities. Naturally traditional displays are not technically networked. However we could observe a connectedness on a conceptual level. Connectedness was exhibited by enforcing the same policies across a set of displays or by having the same design and structure across all displays. Our design implications assume that the stakeholders' needs will still have to be met within an open digital public display network, but that the concrete processes and features do not need to match existing solutions one-to-one. We propose 5 broad principles, and offer specific ideas for how to apply them.

A. Design for Specific Uses of Notice Boards

One of the clearest patterns in the observations was the great variety of notice boards and surfaces, depending on the purpose they were meant to fulfill, particularly the type of content they present, and on the preferences of the stakeholders. This indicates that no single design may be an appropriate replacement for all the current uses of notice boards. A system that displays large numbers of classified ads should optimally look different and work differently from one that seeks to create awareness of local events. The notice board styles, posting form factors, and content described above offer a starting point for developers to target their systems; designers should complement this general description with specific knowledge and understanding of their particular users. A digital notice board designed for a chain of coffee shops might for example draw on elements from unscaffolded classifieds and event displays, and would consider the type of clientele, the activities that take place in the shop, and the chain's design aesthetic and brand image.

The design should take into account that users interact with more than one display. In a department store they may see one at the entrance, one in the elevator, and one where they try on some shoes. The design should capitalize on the fact that users will be exposed to a network of displays. If the used technologies allow determining in which order users see the displays the presentation should utilize this, e.g. creating a story within the display content across the physical display network.

B. Respect the Neighborhood Focus of Notice Boards

Of the thousands of postings we observed across the 29 sites, every one, with almost no exception, was related to the local area or to the community that used the space. The vast majority of these were classifieds relevant to a limited area or notifications for local events. Across the very different styles of notice boards, it is clear that the neighborhood is the audience for and the source of the postings. If a digital notice board is to play the same role, it should be based on postings and ads that have a clear connection to the place or neighborhood, not on centralized ad campaigns. Especially for networked display systems, where technically there is no limitation for the distribution we recommend to design posting procedures in a way that supports locality and to restrict the content to a certain neighborhood. Such mechanisms are most likely a property of the system architecture as well as a part of the actual design.

Note that this is not simply a matter of geographical restriction, but of community identity, even more though when using display networks. The handwritten nature and tear away tabs of many classified postings create an indirect physical connection between advertiser and reader, which may lead to greater intimacy and trust. Further, the aesthetic of a concert poster both communicates the intended audience and is used by that audience to provide a shared group identity. A digital notice board might attempt to capture the direct intimacy of handwritten notes by allowing posters to record short video messages as part of postings.

C. Support the Emergent Profiling of a PNA by Owners and Users of the Space

The different styles of notice boards we observed reflect, among other things, different agendas on the part of the owners of the space. Some are considered decorative or a way to express the identity or support the image of the place, some are appreciated as providing another activity for customers to engage in, increasing the importance of the venue to the community and potentially even attracting customers. Perhaps the most important agenda, however, is in disseminating information the notice board owners have and interest in or sympathy with, such as a library posting notices for classical concerts or an adult learning center ones for trading course books.

Board owners actively use their control to promote all of these priorities. At the same time, we found that in many cases they have difficulty articulating their agendas, and when asked, many were unable to give a good explanation for why they even offered a PNA. Even more importantly, they rely on third-party posters for most of the content. These factors mean that the actual profile of the PNA is usually not predefined, but emerges from the interplay of the interests of the board owners and users.

This goes to the core of reasons why venue owners are willing to offer free advertising space and must be taken very seriously. In a globally networked digital system, the owner of the venue may no longer be the owner of the board and may have a much less direct control of the content that is posted. A digital replacement must give the venue owners overall control over the board profile, and designers must recognize that this is usually not a choice that is made once, but a day-to-day activity. Features could be provided to the managers or owners of each venue allowing them to easily choose which postings to allow or remove (and perhaps learning and automating their patterns over time) and to oversee the overall appearance of the board.

D. Design for Flexibility of Input, Low Overhead to Post

Across all locations we found an impressive variety of posts, comprising hand-written notes in various sizes and colors on a set different materials, printed notes enhanced with images or maps, and professionally designed advertisements. We recommend that digital notice boards provide means for preserving this flexibility, supporting:

- **Ad-hoc posters:** For people (coincidentally) approaching the display a mechanism has to be provided allowing for on-site creation of notes (e.g. predefined templates, standard input devices such as mouse, keyboard, or touch).

- **Sophisticated Posters:** People preparing content in advance need to be given means to easily transfer it to the board locally, e.g. via a scanner, a USB stick or Bluetooth and in networked settings remotely, e.g.. via a web interface.
- **Professional Posters:** In a similar way, people distributing professionally designed content (e.g. flyers) need to be granted easy access to the board.

As a result of the flexibility of current approaches we see that the entry barrier is kept low, hence attracting a large amount of posters. We believe that for globally networked display systems the success heavily depends upon speed and ease of use of the content creation mechanisms.

E. Support Takeaway of Information

The opportunity to take away information is a crucial prerequisite for the success of classifieds as well as for event promotions. In the design of this mechanism two basic options exist: providing a pointer for the user to take way (e.g. a URL or a phone number) or to provide a copy of the content to take away (e.g. a flyer). Traditional systems use a combination where a pointer is taken away (e.g. by tearing off a piece of paper) and this also contains a minimal summary of the content. In digitally networked systems and considering users equipped with mobile devices many mechanism exist to support users in taking content with them, including users taking photos of the content, to sending this information via SMS or Bluetooth, by providing a QR code, or simply by printing it out. Whereas the primary motivation is to preserve information such as a date, a name, an address, or a telephone number, additional implicit information is embedded with the takeaway information: the number of missing takeaways, e.g. indicates high interest. On digital displays similar information could be provided by displaying the number of poster downloads, or even by restricting the number of possible downloads.

8 Conclusion and Future Work

Traditional displays are all around us and interaction with them is a common activity. The communication characteristics we can find in traditional displays are in many ways complementary to the Internet. The importance of using public displays to address a larger number of people with general content has declined with the advent of digital social networks and the World Wide Web. However public displays play a major role in addressing groups of people that can be found in a certain location. We believe that understanding practices in the use of traditional analog displays can provide valuable insights for future generations of globally networked public displays.

Analyzing the observations of the usage of a large number of public displays situated in different context as well as based on follow-up interviews with stakeholders we collected and described various practices related to public displays. In particular we were interested in the various stakeholders and their motivation in the use of public displays. Additionally we investigated how content can be provided and removed and how access control is implemented. Based on our reflection and understanding of the data we suggested a set of design implications for digital display systems.

The central design recommendation is to take the context of a potential display into account: the people likely to pass by, the neighborhood and community in which the display is situated, and the display owners' expectations with regard to content. Beyond this flexible content creation, content posting, and content control are central to allow a broad set of people using it. To increase the effectiveness of posted content it is important that viewer have means to take the information with them – through physical tokens or digital technology.

Currently we are working on an implementation, called *Digifieds*, which supports practices that are effective in traditional signage systems and that can provide new features for creating rich communication media based on public displays. Digifieds will be deployed as a finalist of the UbiChallenge in Oulu, Finland in summer 2011.

Acknowledgement

The research leading to these results has received funding from the European Union Seventh Framework Programme (FP7/2007-2013) under grant agreement no. 244011.

References

1. Agamanolis, S.: Designing displays for human connectedness. In: Public and Situated Displays Social and Interactional Aspects of Shared Display Technologies, pp. 309–334. Kluwer Academic, Dordrecht (2003)
2. Brignull, H., Rogers, Y.: Enticing people to interact with large public displays in public spaces. In: Proceedings of INTERACT 2003, pp. 17–24. ACM, Zurich (2003)
3. Churchill, E., Nelson, L., Denoue, L., Girgensohn, A.: The Plasma Poster Network: Posting Multimedia Content in Public Places. In: Proc. INTERACT 2003, Zürich, Switzerland (2003)

4. Churchill, E.F., Nelson, L., Denoue, L.: Multimedia fliers: Information sharing with digital community bulletin boards. In: Communities and Technologies, pp. 97–117. Kluwer Academic, Deventer (2003)
5. Churchill, E.F., Nelsen, L., Denoue, L., Helfman, J., Murphy, P.: Sharing multimedia content with interactive public displays: a case study. In: Proceedings of the DIS 2004, pp. 7–16. ACM, Cambridge (2004)
6. Ferscha, A., Vogl, S.: Pervasive Web Access via Public Communication Walls. In: Mattern, F., Naghshineh, M. (eds.) PERVASIVE 2002. LNCS, vol. 2414, pp. 84–97. Springer, Heidelberg (2002)
7. Greenberg, S., Boyle, M., Laberge, J.: PDAs and shared public displays: Making personal information public, and public information personal. In: Personal and Ubiquitous Computing 1999, pp. 54–64. Springer, Heidelberg (1999)
8. Huang, E.M., Koster, A., Borchers, J.: Overcoming assumptions and uncovering practices: When does the public really look at public displays? In: Indulska, J., Patterson, D.J., Rodden, T., Ott, M. (eds.) PERVASIVE 2008. LNCS, vol. 5013, pp. 228–243. Springer, Heidelberg (2008)
9. Huang, E.M., Mynatt, E.D., Trimble, J.P.: When design just isn't enough: the unanticipated challenges of the real world for large collaborative displays. In: Personal and Ubiquitous Computing, pp. 537–547. Springer, Heidelberg (2007)
10. McCarthy, J.F., Farnham, S.D., Patel, Y., Ahuja, S., Norman, D., Hazlewood, W.R., Lind, J.: Supporting community in third places with situated social software. In: Proceedings of C&T 2009, pp. 225–234. ACM, University Park (2009)
11. Michelis, D., Müller, J.: The Audience Funnel. International Journal of HCI (2010)
12. Nakamura, M.A.: Creating a new channel for campus communication. In: Proceedings of ACM SIGUCCS 2004, pp. 56–59. ACM, Baltimore (2004)
13. Redhead, F., Brereton, M.: A qualitative analysis of local community communications. In: Proceedings of OZCHI 2006, pp. 361–364. ACM, Sydney (2006)
14. Redhead, F., Brereton, M.: Designing interaction for local communications: An urban screen study. In: Gross, T., Gulliksen, J., Kotzé, P., Oestreicher, L., Palanque, P., Prates, R.O., Winckler, M. (eds.) INTERACT 2009. LNCS, vol. 5727, pp. 457–460. Springer, Heidelberg (2009)
15. Storz, O., Friday, A., Davies, N., Finney, J., Sas, C., Sheridan, J.: Public Ubiquitous Computing Systems: Lessons from the e-Campus Display Deployments. IEEE Pervasive Computing 05(3), 40–47 (2006)
16. Taylor, N., Cheverst, K.: Exploring the Use of Non-Digital Situated Displays in a Rural Community. In: Workshop on Public and Situated Displays to Support Communities (2008)
17. Taylor, N., Cheverst, K., Fitton, D., Race, N.J., Rouncefield, M., Graham, C.: Probing communities: study of a village photo display. In: Proceedings of OZCHI 2007, pp. 17–24 (2007)
18. Weiser, M.: The computer for the 21st century. Scientific American, 65–75 (1991)

Recognizing the Use of Portable Electrical Devices with Hand-Worn Magnetic Sensors

Takuya Maekawa, Yasue Kishino, Yasushi Sakurai, and Takayuki Suyama

NTT Communication Science Laboratories
2-4 Hikaridai Seika-cho, Souraku-gun, Kyoto, Japan
{surname.name}@lab.ntt.co.jp

Abstract. The new method proposed here recognizes the use of portable electrical devices such as digital cameras, cellphones, electric shavers, and video game players with hand-worn magnetic sensors by sensing the magnetic fields emitted by these devices. Because we live surrounded by large numbers of electrical devices and frequently use these devices, we can estimate high-level daily activities by recognizing the use of electrical devices. Therefore, many studies have attempted to recognize the use of electrical devices with such approaches as ubiquitous sensing and infrastructure-mediated sensing. A feature of our method is that we can recognize the use of electrical devices that are not connected to the home infrastructure without the need for any ubiquitous sensors attached to the devices. We evaluated the performance of our recognition method in real home environments, and confirmed that we could achieve highly accurate recognition with small numbers of hand-worn magnetic sensors.

Keywords: Wearable sensing; Activity recognition; Magnetic sensor.

1 Introduction

Activity recognition is one of the most important technologies in relation to context-aware and lifelogging applications, e.g., elder care support and fitness monitoring. We can categorize activity recognition technologies into two main approaches; wearable sensing and environment augmentation. The wearable sensing approach recognizes activities by using sensor data obtained from such body-worn sensors as accelerometers and microphones [1,11,12,13]. In many cases, the environment augmentation approach uses ubiquitous sensors such as RFID tags and/or switch sensors installed in the environment [20,17,19,14]. Although the environment augmentation approach places a smaller burden on the user than the wearable sensor approach, ubiquitous sensors are expensive to deploy because we have to attach them to various indoor objects and maintain a large number of them. On the other hand, several studies have used a sensor device attached to a single point in the environment [5,16]. For example, [16] recognizes electrical device use by monitoring electrical noise on residential power lines. Many environment augmentation approaches detect the use of daily objects in the environment by using small sensors attached to the objects and/or a single point

K. Lyons, J. Hightower, and E.M. Huang (Eds.): Pervasive 2011, LNCS 6696, pp. 276–293, 2011.

device that monitors the objects and then estimates high-level daily activities using the detected information. This approach is based on the idea that objects in use relate to an activity the user is performing. For example, when a user is using a razor and preshave lotion, we can easily assume that the user is shaving.

On the other hand, because many wearable sensing approaches use body-worn accelerometers, they can recognize only simple low-level activities such as walking and running. However, unlike the environment augmentation approach, the wearable sensing approach can sense users' activities in both indoor and outdoor environments. Also, as mentioned above, its deployment cost is smaller than that of the environment augmentation approach. In this paper, we try to recognize the use of daily objects solely by employing wearable sensors that have the above advantages. That is, we recognize which object is in use by employing only wearable sensors without any sensors embedded in the user's environment. This permits us to realize a low deployment cost and place-independent high-level activity recognition. In this work, by using hand-worn magnetic sensors, we try to recognize the use of portable electrical devices such as digital cameras, cellphones, electric shavers, video game players, and music players. That is, we sense the magnetic fields that the devices emit and determine the device a wearer is using by analyzing the sensor data. In modern societies, because we are surrounded by large numbers of electrical devices, we can estimate high-level activities by recognizing the use of these devices. For example, when we recognize that a wearer is using a hair dryer, we can know that she is doing her hair. Such high-level activity recognition is a fundamental technology of context-aware systems and lifelogging. Therefore, many studies have been undertaken with the aim of recognizing the use of electrical devices. However, several approaches require a sensor node for each electrical device [8]. Also, because other approaches utilize the existing infrastructure in a home, i.e., power lines [16], they cannot recognize the use of electrical devices that are not connected to the infrastructure via power outlets. Because the new method proposed in this paper recognizes the use of portable electrical devices by employing a magnetic field emitted from magnets and ICs embedded in the devices, we can recognize the use of devices that are not connected to the infrastructure. In addition, we can recognize the use of the devices in outdoor environments. Portable electrical equipment such as digital cameras and cellphones are frequently used out of doors.

In the rest of this paper, we first introduce work related to activity recognition with sensor data, and then describe the magnetic field emitted from electrical devices and the mechanism of the magnetic sensors. After that, we describe the design and implementation of our proposed sensor device, and explain our method, which recognizes the use of portable electrical devices by employing magnetic sensor data. By using the sensor device, we collect sensor data in three actual home environments and then evaluate our method by using the data. The contributions of this paper are that we propose a new method that recognizes the use of portable electrical devices without the need to install any sensors in environments, i.e., without attaching sensor nodes to the devices. In addition, we experimentally investigate the appropriate number and locations of magnetic sensors attached to wearer's hands. To achieve this, we attempt to recognize the use of devices accurately with small numbers of sensors. This enables us to reduce the burden it places on wearers.

2   Related Work

As mentioned in section 1, activity recognition methods are categorized into environment augmentation and wearable sensing approaches. Many environment augmentation approaches employ a large number of small sensors such as switch sensors, RFID tags, and accelerometers installed in the corresponding environments [20,17,19]. Although the approach can achieve fine-grained measurements of daily lives, its deployment and maintenance costs, e.g., costs related to battery replacement, are very large. Several studies employ a single point sensor device that can monitor home infrastructures to detect the use of electricity, water, or gas in home environments [3,5,16]. However, the approach cannot monitor the use of devices and objects that are not connected to the home infrastructure such as the plumbing or electrical systems. The method proposed in this paper can recognize the use of portable electrical devices that are not connected to the home infrastructure by employing wearable sensors. However, as described below, our approach may not be able to recognize the use of many large stationary electrical devices such as washing machines and refrigerators, which are usually connected to power lines. We consider that, by combining our method with the infrastructure-based method, we can recognize the use of both portable and stationary electrical devices in both indoor and outdoor environments with small deployment costs.

Most wearable sensing approaches use multiple accelerometers attached to the wearer's body [1,18]. Although these approaches can recognize the wearer's activities in outdoor environments, they place a burden on the wearer because she has to wear several sensors. Also, unlike approaches that leverage the use of daily objects, the wearable sensing approaches recognize just simple low-level activities such as walking and running because they only use accelerometers. On the other hand, some studies can recognize high-level activities by employing such rich sensors as body-worn microphones and cameras [2,10,12,13,15]. However, the methods that employ such rich sensors as cameras and microphones may generate privacy concerns. Because the method proposed in this paper employs magnetic sensors, there is less of a privacy issue than with camera and/or microphone based methods. The magnetic sensor simply outputs a sequence of numerical values in the same way as accelerometers. In addition, rich sensors such as cameras and microphones must handle a large amount of data and/or consume a lot of energy.

3   Magnetic Field and Magnetic Sensor

Before explaining our approach, we describe the magnetic field emitted by electrical devices and the magnetic sensor mechanism.

3.1   Magnetic Field Emitted by Electrical Devices

The magnetic fields in electrical devices have two main sources. The first source is permanent magnets embedded in the devices. Because permanent magnets are widely used components of motors, speakers, and earphones, they are familiar in our daily lives. The intensity of the magnetic field emitted by a permanent magnet attenuates greatly according to the distance from the magnet. The attenuation feature depends on the form and strength of the magnet. With a horizontally-located pillar-shaped magnet 5 mm in diameter, 3 mm thick, and with a residual magnetization of 1.2 T, for example, the magnetic flux density values 5 mm and 10 mm away in the vertical direction are 36.0 and 7.1 mT, respectively. 1.2 T magnets are commonly used as speaker components. The second source is the flow of an electric current in the devices. An electric current flowing through a device produces a magnetic field, and the intensity of the magnetic field also attenuates according to the distance. Such a magnetic field is emitted by conductive wires, coils, and ICs included in electrical devices. On the other hand, to restrict the harmful effects of a time-varying magnetic field on a person's health, some organizations have established exposure guidelines [4,6]. Based on these guidelines, many electrical devices are designed to limit magnetic field leakage by surrounding the magnetic sources with such magnetic materials as iron. This effect is called the shielding effect. The intensity of magnetic fields emitted by conductive wires and ICs is much smaller than that by permanent magnets and coils, and the intensity is also smaller than that of the earth's magnetism (0.03 - 0.04 mT) in many cases. It is difficult to capture the small magnetic fields by using body-worn magnetic sensors that are affected by the earth's magnetism. Therefore, we mainly focus on permanent magnets and coils.

3.2   Magnetic Sensor

Magnetic field detection has various applications such as current sensing, orientation sensing, diagnosis of disease, and paper currency validation, and so various kinds of magnetic sensors have been developed [9]. Here, we introduce the widely used Hall effect sensors. A Hall effect sensor is a kind of magnetic sensor that utilizes the electromotive force integrated in an electrical conductor carrying a current when it is placed in a magnetic field perpendicular to the current. A Hall effect sensor outputs a voltage in proportion to the magnetic flux density that penetrates its element. Because of its simple mechanism, very small and inexpensive sensors, e.g., from about 1 to 2 mm square, have become commercially available.

4   Sensor Device Design

4.1   Manual Use of Electrical Devices

To obtain a design guideline for our sensor device, we first categorize the ways of using electrical devices into two types. The first is that the user picks up the device and uses it. The second is where the user employs a fixed static device by pushing its buttons, turning its knobs, etc. The ways of using many large devices such as refrigerators and washing machines fall into the second category. Most large devices are connected to power outlets, and so the methods that monitor power line infrastructures can recognize the use of these devices [16]. On the other hand, most of the devices employed in the first way are small because the user holds the devices in her hand when using them. Also, because these devices are portable, many of them are battery powered, which makes them impossible to recognize with the methods that monitor power line infrastructures. As mentioned in the previous section, electrical devices emit magnetic fields from their embedded magnets, coils, etc. The idea we propose in this paper is that we recognize the electrical device a user is using by employing the magnetic field. In particular, we recognize the use of portable electrical devices with hand-worn magnetic sensors. As described in the previous section, a magnetic field attenuates greatly because of its characteristics and the shielding effect. Thus, if a user holding a portable device wears a sensor on her hand, we can effectively detect the magnetic field emitted by the device. Then, we analyze the detected magnetic field and recognize which device the wearer is using. We detail the recognition method later.

Here, we examine the parts of the hands to which we should attach magnetic sensors. We consider there to be two criteria for selecting the parts. (i) Although the magnetic sensors are small, we should select locations where the attached sensors do not place a large burden on the wearer. For example, when we attach sensors to a person's fingertips, the sensors may impede the operation of buttons and keyboards. Moreover, if we attach sensors to the regions surrounding the finger joints, they will be uncomfortable when the wearer bends her fingers. (ii) We should attach sensors to locations where the sensors can effectively detect the magnetic fields emitted by portable devices held in the wearer's hands. As mentioned in the previous section, because magnetic fields attenuate greatly, we should attach sensors to locations where they can monitor devices near them.

Here, we look at the ways of holding various kinds of portable electrical devices in the hands. We found that button position and shape of a device affect the way it is held as shown in Fig. 1. For example, when holding a device with buttons as shown in Fig. 1 (a) and (c), we usually hold the device in a way that enables us to access the buttons with our fingers. Moreover, a device with a handle, as shown in Fig. 1 (c), is normally held by the handle. As above, we basically hold the devices with the fingers and palm. In addition to the shape and button position, its size affects the way it is held. We often hold small and lightweight devices with just our fingers. For example, when holding a small camera as shown in Fig. 1 (a), we can hold it using only our fingers. We hold slightly larger and heavier devices with part of the palm in addition to the fingers, e.g., when holding a relatively large smart phone as shown in Fig. 1 (b). That is, we hold devices mainly with the fingers and also with part of the palm. Based on the above facts, we decided to sense the magnetic fields from portable devices by mainly focusing on the fingers. In particular, we focus on the parts of the fingers where sensors would

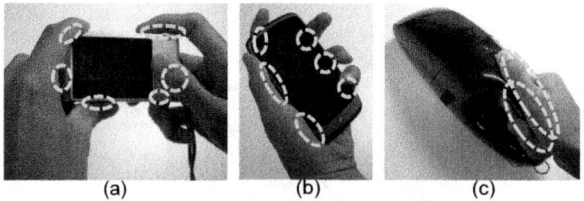

Fig. 1. Ways of handling portable devices: (a) digital camera, (b) smart phone, and (c) hand-held cleaner. Regions circled with dashed lines represent those parts of the devices that the hand touches.

not impose a large burden on the wearer, i.e., between the first and second joints and between the second joint and the base of the finger. We considered that, by embedding a magnetic sensor in a finger ring, which is usually worn between finger joints, we could achieve a low burden and convenient sensing.

In our investigation, we also found that the way a portable device is held depends on the device (or the operation of the device). As mentioned above, the ways devices are held are determined by their shape and the positions of their buttons. That is, the way a device is held is almost identical whenever the user performs a certain operation.

4.2 Basic Idea of Recognition Method

As described above, we try to distinguish which portable electrical device a user is using by analyzing time-series sensor data obtained from hand-worn magnetic sensors that sense magnetic fields emitted by various components embedded in the devices. Therefore, we should solve the multi-class recognition problem, namely we must classify sensor data at each time slice into an appropriate activity class (use of an electrical device). Here, to solve the problem, we look at two discriminative characteristics of sensor data obtained from hand-worn magnetic sensors. The first is strength of magnetic field (magnetic flux distribution). Assume that a permanent magnet is embedded at a certain position on a device. When the way of holding the device is identical whenever the wearer performs a certain operation, a magnetic sensor fixed to a certain hand position may output similar sensor values whenever the operation is performed. This is because the strength of a magnetic field depends on the intensity of the magnet and distance from the magnet. Because the intensity and positions of the embedded magnets differ from device to device, we consider that we can recognize which device a wearer is using by utilizing the strength of a magnetic field picked up by hand-worn magnetic sensors. The second discriminative feature is the temporal change in the strength of a magnetic field. For example, when the amount of current flowing in a device changes or a wearer changes the way of holding a device when operating it, the strength of the magnetic field obtained from a hand-worn magnetic sensor may change. Such characteristic temporal variations in the magnetic field can allow us to distinguish between activity classes.

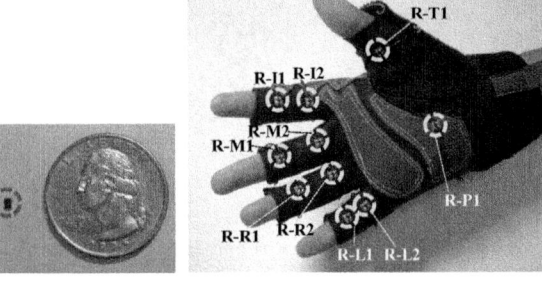

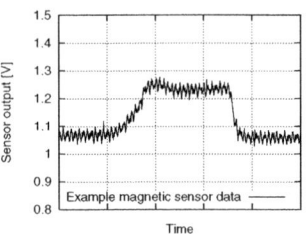

Fig. 2. A magnetic sensor shown next to a quarter dollar coin (left) and our prototype sensor glove (right). We provided each sensor on the glove with an identifier. The identifier is labeled with an initial letter indicating the left or right hand, an initial letter showing its position, and a serial number. For example, the identifier of the first sensor attached to the little finger of the right hand is R-L1.

Fig. 3. Time-series raw magnetic sensor data of R-I1 obtained when we brought a cellphone close to the sensor and then moved the phone away from the sensor. (The voltage values are shifted.)

4.3   Design and Implementation of Prototype Device

Based on the characteristics of a magnetic field mentioned in section 3.1 and the ways of using portable electrical devices mentioned in section 4.1, we design and implement a sensor device that focuses on the fingers and palm. However, it is not clear which of the finger parts that we focus on are actually effective for recognizing the use of portable devices. Moreover, it is unclear how many sensors are needed to achieve highly accurate recognition. Thus, in this paper, we first develop a sensor device that is equipped with many sensors at important locations on the hand mentioned above, and then we determine the good locations experimentally. The prototype device developed in this study is in the form of a glove with ten magnetic sensors as shown in Fig. 2. We attached magnetic sensors to the important parts of the hand mentioned in section 4.1. We also attached a magnetic sensor to the center of the palm. We used Asahi Kasei's HW105A Hall ICs as magnetic sensors, and also used a glove that fitted the hand well. As shown in Fig. 2, the sensor is sufficiently small. Because the device is a prototype, these sensors are connected to a USB port of a host PC via cables and a sensor board. The board samples the sensor data at a sampling rate of about 330 Hz. We implemented the devices for both right and left hands. If we can recognize the use of electrical devices with a small number of sensors, we can achieve convenient sensing by using a small finger ring shaped device with a magnetic sensor because we assume that the sensors will be attached between finger joints. Note that several magnetic sensor products are sensitive to temperature changes. That is, output voltage characteristics of the sensors change according to ambient temperature. When we use such sensors, we should correct sensor outputs by using temperature data.

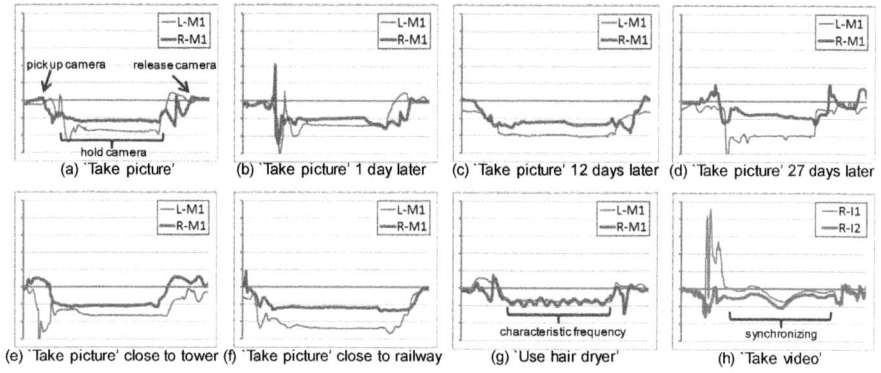

Fig. 4. Sensor data sequences obtained from our devices. Positive or negative sensor data values indicate the direction of the magnetic flux that penetrate a sensor.

4.4 Characteristics of Sensor Data

We examine sensor data obtained from our implemented sensor device. Fig. 4 (a)-(f) show time-series sensor data sequences obtained from sensors attached to the middle fingers of both hands when the wearer was performing a certain activity at different times and at different locations. (The sensor identifiers are L-M1 and R-M1 as shown in Fig. 2.) The activity consists of the wearer picking up a digital camera, turning on the camera, taking a picture, turning off the camera, and then releasing the camera. The x- and y-axes of the graphs represent time and the output voltage of the magnetic sensor, respectively. (The voltage values are amplified, smoothed, and then shifted.) From Fig. 4 (a)-(d), we can find that the sensor data values obtained on different days while holding the camera were similar. Also, Fig. 4 (e) and (f), respectively, show sensor data sequences obtained at places close to a power transmission tower and an electric train line, which may generate magnetic fields. As mentioned in section 3.1, because the magnetic field attenuates greatly, magnetic sensors were not affected by magnetic field sources located at a distance. In addition, although these data change depending on the orientation of the sensor as a result of the effect of the earth's magnetism, the amount of change was small. On the other hand, Fig. 4 (g) shows sequences of sensor data obtained when the wearer was using a hair dryer. The sequences are different from those obtained when the wearer was taking a picture.

5 Recognition Method

We attempted to recognize the use of electrical devices by using the sensor data sequences introduced above. Fig. 5 shows the architecture of our recognition method. In this architecture, we first amplify the output voltages from hand-worn magnetic sensors and then denoise them. As shown in Fig. 3, we can detect the presence of high-frequency noise in a sequence of raw output voltage signals. Therefore, we remove the noise by employing a low-pass filter (moving average).

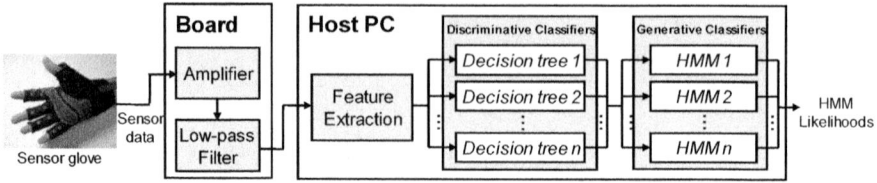

Fig. 5. Architecture of our recognition method

The charts in Fig. 4 show smoothed signals. The host PC samples the smoothed sensor data from the board at a sampling rate of 33 Hz. The host PC then extracts features from the data and classifies the extracted feature vectors at each time slice into the appropriate activity class. We describe the feature extraction and the classification method below.

5.1   Feature Extraction

We extract features from sensor data that are used to model/recognize activity classes. We compute features from each sample of sensor data. Thus, because the host PC samples sensor data from the board at a sampling rate of 33 Hz, about 30 feature vectors are generated per second and become inputs of the classification method. In addition to the smoothed output voltage values from the hand-worn magnetic sensors, we also use (i) energy, (ii) dominant frequency, and (iii) the difference between the output voltage values of different sensors as features.

The energy and dominant frequency are computed for each sensor data sequence. We extract the energy and dominant frequency features based on the FFT components of each 64-sample window because we can find a characteristic frequency in the sensor data captured during the performance of several activities as shown in Fig. 4 (g), which may be caused by motor rotation. The energy can be used to distinguish low intensity changes in sensor data from high intensity changes. The energy feature is calculated by summing the magnitudes of squared discrete FFT components. For normalization, the sum was divided by the window length. Note that the DC component of the FFT is excluded from this summation. The dominant frequency is the frequency that has the largest FFT component, and this component should be ten times larger than the average component of all the frequencies in this implementation.

We also compute the difference between the output voltage values of two different sensors sampled at the same time. We compute the differences for all combinations of two sensors attached to the same hand, and then use them as features. As mentioned in section 4.4, magnetic sensors are affected by the earth's magnetism. Fig. 4 (h) shows sequences of sensor data obtained during digital camcorder use. We found temporal changes in the sensor data sequences and the changes of these sequences were synchronized. This was caused by changes in the wearer's orientation when using the camcorder. That is, the magnetic sensor data change according to the orientation of the sensor. Our idea is that, by using the difference between the sensor data values of two sensors, we cancel out the changes caused by earth's magnetism (the orientation change).

As described above, we use the smoothed sensor data value, energy, dominant frequency, and difference as features. When a user wears 10 sensors on the right hand and 10 sensors on the left hand, the generated feature vector consists of a total of 150 feature values $((10 + 10 + 10 + 45) \times 2)$, i.e., the vector has 150 dimensions.

5.2 Classification Methodology

We classify an extracted feature vector in an appropriate class by employing supervised machine learning techniques. That is, we first model each activity (use of a device) by using labeled training data and then recognize test data with the learned models. Note that a label includes information about the class label of its related activity and activity start and end times. Here, the classification approaches used in machine learning are divided into two groups: one group uses discriminative techniques that learn the class boundaries, and the other uses generative techniques that model the conditional density functions of the data classes. The classification performance of the discriminative techniques, which find the discriminant boundaries of the classes, often outperform those of generative techniques. By contrast, handling missing data is often easier with the generative techniques. State of the art activity recognition studies achieve high accuracy by employing a hybrid discriminative/generative approach that can combine the advantages of the two techniques [7,10,11,13].

These facts provide our motivation for using the hybrid discriminative/generative approach shown in Fig. 5. Our classification method employs two main modules: discriminative classifiers and generative classifiers. The input of the first module is the extracted feature vector sequence. The first module consists of some decision tree based binary classifiers trained with feature vectors. We build each decision tree to recognize its corresponding activity class. That is, the number of decision trees n corresponds to the number of activities the method learns. Each decision tree computes its associated class probability for each feature vector in the feature vector sequence. That is, each decision tree outputs the class probability sequence. For example, a decision tree for the 'vacuum activity' class outputs the probability of the class for each feature vector. The input of the second module consists of n-dimensional class probability sequences computed by the n decision trees. The second module also comprises n HMM classifiers [21], which can be used to recognize signals with temporal patterns, trained with a sequence of output class probabilities of the discriminative classifiers. We also build each HMM to recognize its corresponding activity class, that is, each HMM also outputs the likelihood of its corresponding activity. The class with the highest likelihood is the classified class.

6 Evaluation

In this section, we evaluate our activity recognition approach by using sensor data obtained in real environments. We also investigate how many magnetic

Table 1. Information about experimental environments and participants

Houses	House A	House B	House C
Type	house	house	apartment
#rooms	7	5	2
#days	8	4	7
#sessions	10	6	12
#residents	3	3	1
Age	60	35	32
Gender	male	male	male

Table 2. Activities performed in our experiment

	Activities			Activities
A	talk on cellphone		H	vacuum
B	operate cellphone		I	watch TV
C	use smart phone		J	play video game
D	listen to music		K	listen to radio
E	shave		L	use flashlight
F	use hair dryer		M	take picture
G	brush teeth		N	take video

sensors are required and to which parts of the hands we should attach them to achieve highly accurate activity recognition that imposes the minimum burden on the wearer.

6.1   Data Set

We collected sensor data in three different dwellings; one seven-room house (house A), one five-room house (house B), and one two-room apartment (house C). One resident (an experimental participant) in each house wore our prototype devices on both hands and collected sensor data. Our devices were connected to a laptop PC in a backpack via cables. To annotate the collected sensor data, each participant also wore a head-mounted camera that captured the region in front of the participant's body. Table 1 shows an overview of the experimental conditions. During the experimental periods, the participants collected sensor data without being supervised by researchers.

Here, the most natural data would be acquired from the normal daily lives of the participants. However, obtaining sufficient samples of such data is very costly. We collect sensor data by using a semi-naturalistic collection protocol [1] that permits greater variability in participant behavior than laboratory data. In the protocol, participants perform a random sequence of activities (obstacles) following instructions on a worksheet. The participants are relatively free as regards how they perform each activity because the instructions on the worksheet are not very strict, e.g., "shave your face" and "vacuum the room with a hand-held cleaner." During the experimental period, the participants completed data collection sessions that included the random sequence of activities (use of portable electrical devices) listed in Table 2. We selected these portable devices (activities) from those frequently found in appliance stores and online stores.

Here we describe how these activities were performed in detail. In activity B, each participant operated his cellphone, i.e., texting and dialing. In activity C, we instructed the participants to browse an arbitrary web page on a smart phone. In activity E, each participant shaved his face with an electric shaver. In activity G, each participant brushed his teeth with an electric toothbrush. In activity H, we instructed the participants to vacuum their house with a hand-held cleaner. In activity I, we instructed the participants to operate a TV with a remote control, e.g., control its volume and switch channels. In activity J, each participant operated a video-game console such as Nintendo DS or Wii in his house. In activity K, we instructed the participants to listen to a radio program on a portable radio. In activity M, we instructed the participants to take a picture with a digital camera. In activity N, we instructed the participants to take a video with a (digital) camcorder. Here, the electrical devices used in the experiment were located in their appropriate places in each house. For example, an electric toothbrush was placed on a wash stand. Note that, with respect to devices that are usually used in various places such as cellphones and digital cameras, we instructed the participants to use the devices in various places both in and outside the house. Also, when a participant did not have a device, we asked him to buy the device. (We paid for it.)

6.2   Evaluation Results

We evaluated the performance of our approach by using the collected and annotated sensor data. We conducted a 'leave-one-session-out' cross validation evaluation. That is, we tested one session obtained in a house by using classifiers trained on other sessions obtained in the same house. To evaluate the performance of our method, we used the precision and recall calculated based on the results for the estimated class at each time slice.

Performance of our method. The left part of Table 3 shows the precision and recall of our recognition method in each house when we used sensor data obtained from all 20 magnetic sensors. As shown in the table, our method achieved very high recognition accuracy simply by using wearable sensors. We achieved about 80% average precision and recall in each house. The accuracies for houses A and C were higher than that for house B. This may be because the amounts of training data in houses A and C were sufficient. With large amounts of training data, we can capture various ways of using electrical devices. However, in house A, the precision of the 'take picture' activity was not good. As shown in the confusion matrix of house A in Table 4, other activities such as 'use smart phone' and 'watch TV' were mistakenly classified in the 'take picture' class. This may be because we could not model the 'take picture' class well. When the participant in house A took a picture, he changed the way he held the camera slightly depending on the type of photograph he was taking, e.g., closeup photograph or telephotograph. Although the changes were very small, the data values obtained from the sensors were very different as shown in Fig. 6 (a) and (b). The time-series sensor data sequences in Fig. 6 (a) were obtained when the participant in house A took a picture of the landscape in front of him. The time-series sensor data sequences in Fig. 6 (b) were obtained when the participant took a picture of an object by pointing the camera directly at it. Although the data values obtained with the R-M2 sensor were similar to each other, those obtained with the L-M1 sensor were different. This was caused by the magnetic field, which attenuates greatly with distance, as mentioned in section 3.1. Depending on the sensor position, the sensor data values change considerably. This phenomenon

Table 3. Accuracies (precision / recall) of the recognition method in each house. The values are percentages. The left portion of this table shows the accuracies when we use the sensor data from all 20 sensors. The right portion shows the accuracies when we use the sensor data of only the top-4 contributing sensors.

	All 20 sensors			Only top-4 sensors		
	House A	House B	House C	House A	House B	House C
A: talk on cellphone	95.1/82.2	25.2/80.2	27.2/89.9	89.6/88.8	58.5/43.1	43.7/75.0
B: operate cellphone	89.5/84.9	89.4/73.3	98.2/80.4	70.0/79.9	58.1/73.5	91.9/89.7
C: use smart phone	92.5/76.0	91.4/85.5	91.6/83.6	68.0/64.9	77.4/61.7	98.4/93.4
D: listen to music	87.2/71.0	63.4/65.5	73.0/89.5	75.1/72.8	59.6/37.2	81.3/89.5
E: shave	78.8/78.8	99.9/100.0	93.9/68.8	84.9/84.9	86.4/71.8	81.1/67.1
F: use hair dryer	95.9/99.4	94.4/89.9	91.2/89.3	91.4/93.7	96.1/95.5	97.2/94.0
G: brush teeth	95.4/95.5	79.6/51.2	79.2/67.4	65.7/79.0	50.8/81.0	55.7/72.0
H: vacuum	90.0/83.3	99.4/66.0	98.0/85.4	82.8/79.6	26.6/58.5	93.6/86.2
I: watch TV	79.4/78.9	84.3/73.8	89.3/69.4	76.8/74.1	72.3/69.5	95.2/83.5
J: play video game	95.5/97.7	99.3/99.5	95.9/85.8	88.8/96.0	99.1/100.0	88.8/89.8
K: listen to radio	89.0/73.6	92.9/81.2	69.8/70.1	59.3/41.5	74.9/78.9	72.7/73.2
L: use flashlight	86.9/90.7	95.2/80.0	98.3/71.6	58.3/80.8	22.7/21.6	80.9/73.2
M: take picture	35.3/77.2	98.4/92.0	90.8/99.9	82.5/82.8	99.0/88.8	73.8/75.2
N: take video	91.4/78.7	53.3/28.7	99.3/92.2	96.7/82.2	40.6/29.0	98.0/80.9
Average	85.9/83.4	83.3/76.2	85.4/81.7	77.9/78.7	65.9/65.0	82.3/81.6
Overall	83.3/83.3	79.6/79.6	81.2/81.2	77.6/77.6	68.8/68.8	82.7/82.7

was also observed for 'talk on cellphone' in houses B and C. However, this result indicates that, when we have sufficient amounts of training data, we may be able to achieve very fine-grained recognition of electrical device operation, e.g., distinguish a closeup photograph from a telephotograph. As above, the various ways of holding the electrical devices reduced the accuracy in our experiment.

We found another reason for recognition failure, namely the positions of the components in electrical devices. The accuracies of 'brush teeth' and 'take video' in house B were poor because the intensities of magnetic fields that the hand-worn sensors sensed in these activities were very small. That is, the magnetic components included in the devices that were used in these activities may have been located far from these sensors when the devices were used. It is very difficult to recognize the use of such devices with our approach because our approach employs the intensity of the magnetic field. This problem occurred with 'brush teeth' and 'take video' in house B, and 'watch TV' in house C. However, although the hand-worn sensors could not sense the high intensity magnetic field emitted by the electric toothbrush in house B, the accuracy of 'brush teeth' in house B was not very bad. When the participant in house B brushed his teeth, he controlled the toothbrush so that it brushed his front teeth, back teeth, upper teeth, and lower teeth. That is, he moved his hand to control the toothbrush and then the posture of his hand changed. In section 4.4, we mentioned that magnetic sensors are slightly affected by the earth's magnetism. When the posture of the hand changes, sensor data obtained from hand-worn sensors also change

Table 4. Confusion matrix in house A when we use sensor data of all 20 sensors. The values are percentages.

	A: talk on cellphone	B: operate cellphone	C: use smart phone	D: listen to music	E: shave	F: use hair dryer	G: brush teeth	H: vacuum	I: watch TV	J: play video game	K: listen to radio	L: use flashlight	M: take picture	N: take video
A	82.2	0.0	2.2	0.0	0.0	0.0	4.7	0.0	9.1	0.0	0.0	0.9	0.8	0.0
B	0.0	84.9	0.0	0.7	0.4	0.0	0.2	0.1	0.2	0.0	0.4	2.4	9.4	1.3
C	0.0	0.7	76.0	0.0	0.3	0.0	0.0	0.0	3.7	5.6	0.0	1.1	12.2	0.4
D	0.5	4.2	0.6	71.0	5.1	0.3	0.6	0.6	1.1	0.8	6.0	0.6	6.4	2.0
E	0.2	3.0	0.0	0.9	78.8	0.3	0.1	2.2	0.9	0.0	0.4	0.0	12.5	0.6
F	0.3	0.0	0.0	0.0	0.0	99.4	0.0	0.0	0.0	0.0	0.0	0.0	0.0	0.3
G	0.0	0.0	0.0	0.7	0.0	0.0	95.5	0.0	1.2	0.0	0.0	0.0	0.4	2.2
H	0.0	0.8	0.0	0.1	0.0	0.0	0.0	83.3	0.0	2.2	0.1	2.6	10.6	0.3
I	0.0	0.0	2.0	0.0	0.2	0.5	0.0	0.5	78.9	0.1	1.7	0.0	15.3	0.8
J	0.0	0.2	0.1	1.1	0.0	0.0	0.0	0.1	0.2	97.7	0.0	0.0	0.5	0.0
K	0.0	2.0	1.3	4.2	2.2	0.0	0.8	1.5	4.8	0.4	73.6	0.0	9.1	0.0
L	0.0	0.2	0.0	0.0	0.0	0.0	0.0	1.8	0.8	0.2	0.0	90.7	6.3	0.0
M	0.0	0.0	0.4	2.0	10.2	0.8	0.4	0.0	3.9	1.0	1.7	1.1	77.2	1.4
N	0.0	0.1	0.0	0.1	0.0	0.1	0.0	0.0	10.9	0.0	0.5	0.6	9.1	78.7

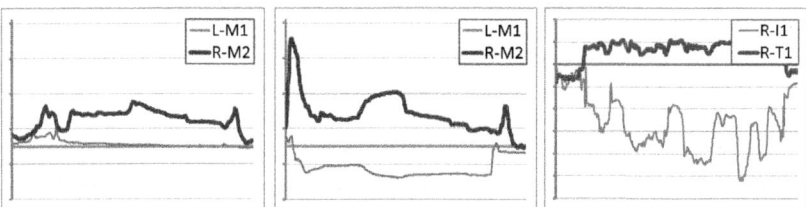

(a) `Take picture' at house A (b) Another `take picture' at house A (c) `Brush teeth' at house B

Fig. 6. Example sensor data sequences obtained in our experiment

because the orientation of the sensors changes. Fig. 6 (c) shows sensor data sequences obtained when the participant in house B brushed his teeth. We can see that the sensor data value of R-I1 suddenly changes several times. These changes were caused by changes of hand posture. We could find such sensor data changes in other 'brush teeth' activities in house B. We consider that our method modeled the 'brush teeth' activity class by using the characteristic changes of sensor data. As above, even though the hand-worn sensors cannot sense high intensity magnetic fields emitted by electrical devices, our method may be able to recognize activities that involve characteristic changes of hand posture, e.g., walking and running in addition to tooth brushing.

Recognition with small numbers of sensors. In the above evaluation, we confirmed that our approach could achieve very high accuracy activity recognition with 20 hand-worn magnetic sensors. However, it is impractical to wear a large number of sensors on the hands continuously in our usual daily environment. To reduce the number of required sensors, we investigated which magnetic sensors on which parts of the hand were effective for recognizing the use of electrical devices by employing our obtained data sets. That is, we find sensors that help us to recognize the use of electrical devices. More specifically, we find extracted features that help us to discriminate the feature vectors of activity classes. Once we obtain discriminative features, we then also obtain effective sensors from the features. For example, when we find that the energy feature of the L-M2 sensor data assists us to recognize many activities, we can say that the L-M2 sensor is important.

The problem of finding a discriminative feature is called the feature selection problem. Several studies have found discriminative features by employing the concept of information gain. The information gain of a feature increases the better the feature classifies the instances. For more detail, see [22]. In our case, an instance corresponds to a feature vector at a time slice. By using the information gain, we obtained the ranking of 20 magnetic sensors on hands by the contribution to the classification of instances. We employ the simple ranking method described below. (1) We compute each feature's information gain when distinguishing feature vectors of an activity class from those of other activity classes by using its feature values in the training data. This permits us to obtain the measure of the contribution, i.e., the information gain, of each feature to distinguish the activity class from other classes. We describe the information gain of the ith feature to distinguish the jth class as $gain(f_i, C_j)$. By applying this procedure to all activity classes, we can obtain the information gain of a feature for each activity class. (2) We compute the sum of the information gain of all activity classes for each feature. We regard the sum as being an overall measure of the contribution of the feature. We describe the overall measure of ith feature as $score_f(i) = \sum_j gain(f_i, C_j)$. (3) To obtain a measure of the contribution of the kth sensor, we again compute the summation of $score_f(i)$ related to the sensor. We can describe the measure of the kth sensor as $score_s(k) = \sum_{f_i \in F(k)} score_f(i)$, where $F(k)$ denotes a set of features computed from the kth sensor data. (4) We rank the 20 magnetic sensors by $score_s(k)$.

The table in Fig. 7 (a) shows the rankings of the top 8 sensors in each house computed by employing the above procedure. As described above, in the rankings, the magnetic sensors are listed in descending order of contribution to the feature vector classification. The 'all' columns in the table show the rankings of the top 8 sensors among all 20 sensors. In the rankings, we can see that the rank orders of sensors on the right are high in all three houses. This is because the participants are right-handed. They used electrical devices with their right hands in many activities, and thus the importance of the sensors on the right hand became high. Of the sensors on the right hand, the sensors on the middle finger were particularly important. This may be because the middle finger is positioned in the center of the hand. We consider that sensors in the center of the hand tend to be located nearer electrical devices held in the hand than outlying sensors such as those on the little finger. On the other hand, the 'ring'

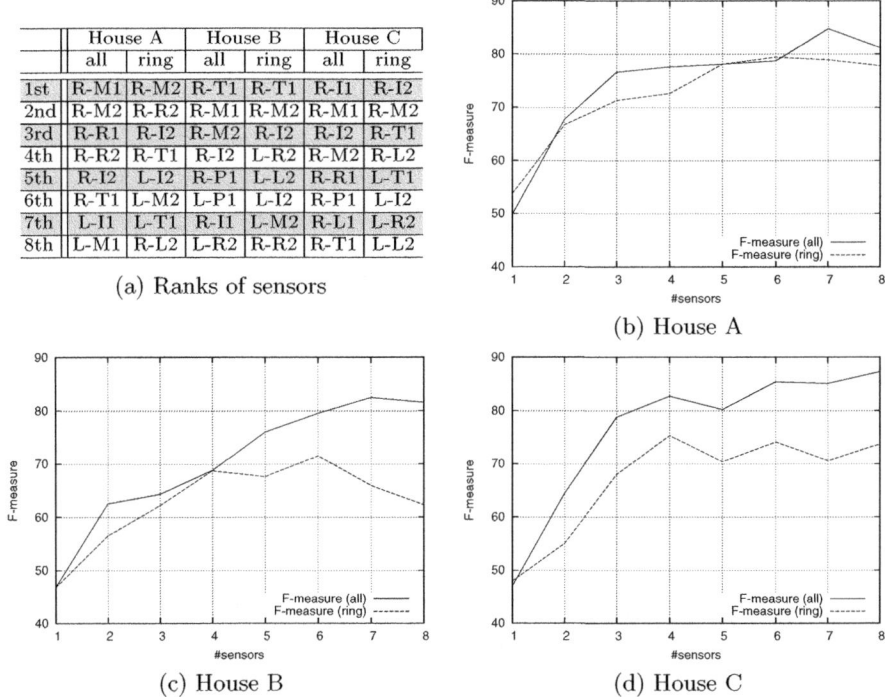

	House A		House B		House C	
	all	ring	all	ring	all	ring
1st	R-M1	R-M2	R-T1	R-T1	R-I1	R-I2
2nd	R-M2	R-R2	R-M1	R-M2	R-M1	R-M2
3rd	R-R1	R-I2	R-M2	R-I2	R-I2	R-T1
4th	R-R2	R-T1	R-I2	L-R2	R-M2	R-L2
5th	R-I2	L-I2	R-P1	L-L2	R-R1	L-T1
6th	R-T1	L-M2	L-P1	L-I2	R-P1	L-I2
7th	L-I1	L-T1	R-I1	L-M2	R-L1	L-R2
8th	L-M1	R-L2	L-R2	R-R2	R-T1	L-L2

(a) Ranks of sensors

(b) House A

(c) House B

(d) House C

Fig. 7. (a): Rankings of magnetic sensors in each house. The table shows the rankings of the top-8 sensors of all 20 sensors and the rankings of just 10 sensors on hand positions where common forms of finger rings are attached. (b), (c), (d): Transitions of the overall F-measure when we increase # sensors in descending order of the rankings in each house. ($F\text{-}measure = \frac{2 \cdot precision \cdot recall}{precision + recall}$.)

columns in the table in Fig. 7 (a) show the top 8 sensors in the ranking of just 10 sensors at hand positions where common forms of finger rings are worn, i.e., (L|R)-T1, (L|R)-I2, (L|R)-M2, (L|R)-R2, and (L|R)-L2. That is, we assume that magnetic sensors are embedded in finger ring-form devices. This is a practical condition. In these rankings, the sensors on the right hand were also important.

Fig. 7 (b), (c), and (d) show the transitions of the overall F-measure when we increased the number of sensors in descending order of the rankings in Fig. 7 (a). For example, when the number of sensors is 2 in the line chart of house A, the y-axis value of the 'F-measure (all)' line indicates the recognition accuracy computed by using sensor data obtained from only the R-M1 and R-M2 sensors, which are the top 2 sensors in house A. We use these charts to investigate the required number of sensors. From the charts, we find that we can achieve high accuracies equaling those obtained with 20 sensors with only about seven sensors. The accuracies were still high (over 75%) with only three sensors in houses A and C. The right part of Table 3 shows the detailed recognition accuracies when we used the sensor data of the top 4 sensors. Even though we used only four sensors, the average and overall accuracies decreased by only about 5 to 10% compared with those obtained when using all 20 sensors. As shown in the charts in Fig. 7 (b), (c), and (d), when we limit the sensor positions to common finger ring positions, the accuracies decreased somewhat. However, with only four or five sensors, we could achieve accuracies of over 75% in houses A and C. Here, the accuracies in house B are not stable because the amount of training data may be insufficient.

The above results show that we can achieve the highly accurate recognition of the use of portable electrical devices with small numbers of magnetic sensors. Strictly speaking, the importance of the sensor positions was different in each house as shown in the table in Fig. 7 (a). However, in any environment, by simply attaching several sensors to a dominant hand, we consider that we can achieve fairly good accuracy. (In fact, by simply using the R-M1, R-M2, R-I1, and R-I2 sensors, we could achieve 76.8, 67.6, and 82.7% overall F-measures in houses A, B, and C, respectively.) In particular, attaching sensors to the middle fingers may significantly improve the accuracy.

7   Conclusion

In this paper, we proposed a new method that recognizes the use of portable electrical devices with hand-worn magnetic sensors. In modern societies, we live with large numbers of electrical devices. Many studies have attempted to detect/recognize the use of electrical devices because this would allow us to recognize various high-level activities. The method proposed in this paper can recognize the use of portable electrical devices that are not connected to the home infrastructure without using any sensors attached to the devices in both indoor and outdoor environments. In this paper, we evaluated our recognition method in real environments and achieved very high accuracies. We also confirmed experimentally that we could achieve highly accurate recognition with small numbers of hand-worn sensors. As part of our future work, we will attempt to recognize simple low-level activities that do not involve the use of electrical devices, such as walking and running, with hand-worn magnetic sensors because we found in our experiment that our method may be able to recognize activities involving characteristic hand movements. This is because magnetic sensors are affected by the earth's magnetism, and so the hand-worn sensors can capture characteristic hand movements. This permits us to recognize both the use of electrical devices and low-level activities with only hand-worn magnetic sensors.

References

1. Bao, L., Intille, S.S.: Activity recognition from user-annotated acceleration data. In: Ferscha, A., Mattern, F. (eds.) PERVASIVE 2004. LNCS, vol. 3001, pp. 1–17. Springer, Heidelberg (2004)
2. Blum, M., Pentland, A.S., Troster, G.: Insense: Interest-based life logging. IEEE Multimedia 13(4), 40–48 (2006)
3. Cohn, G., Gupta, S., Froehlich, J., Larson, E., Patel, S.N.: GasSense: Appliance-level, single-point sensing of gas activity in the home. In: Floréen, P., Krüger, A., Spasojevic, M. (eds.) Pervasive Computing. LNCS, vol. 6030, pp. 265–282. Springer, Heidelberg (2010)

4. The Swedish Confederation for Professional Employees, http://www.tco.se/
5. Froehlich, J.E., Larson, E., Campbell, T., Haggerty, C., Fogarty, J., Patel, S.N.: Hydrosense: Infrastructure-mediated single-point sensing of whole-home water activity. In: Ubicomp 2009, pp. 235–244 (2009)
6. ICNIRP Guidelines. Guidelines for limiting exposure to timevarying electric, magnetic, and electromagnetic fields (up to 300 GHz). Health Physics 74(4), 494–522 (1998)
7. Huynh, T., Schiele, B.: Towards less supervision in activity recognition from wearable sensors. In: Int'l Symp. on Wearable Computers, pp. 3–10 (2006)
8. Kim, Y., Schmid, T., Charbiwala, Z.M., Srivastava, M.B.: ViridiScope: design and implementation of a fine grained power monitoring system for homes. In: Ubicomp 2009, pp. 245–254 (2009)
9. Lenz, J.E.: A review of magnetic sensors. Proceedings of the IEEE 78(6), 973–989 (1990)
10. Lester, J., Choudhury, T., Borriello, G.: A practical approach to recognizing physical activities. In: Fishkin, K.P., Schiele, B., Nixon, P., Quigley, A. (eds.) PERVASIVE 2006. LNCS, vol. 3968, pp. 1–16. Springer, Heidelberg (2006)
11. Lester, J., Choudhury, T., Kern, N., Borriello, G., Hannaford, B.: A hybrid discriminative/generative approach for modeling human activities. In: IJCAI 2005, pp. 766–772 (2005)
12. Lukowicz, P., Ward, J., Junker, H., Stäger, M., Tröster, G., Atrash, A., Starner, T.: Recognizing workshop activity using body worn microphones and accelerometers. In: Ferscha, A., Mattern, F. (eds.) PERVASIVE 2004. LNCS, vol. 3001, pp. 18–32. Springer, Heidelberg (2004)
13. Maekawa, T., Yanagisawa, Y., Kishino, Y., Ishiguro, K., Kamei, K., Sakurai, Y., Okadome, T.: Object-based activity recognition with heterogeneous sensors on wrist. In: Floréen, P., Krüger, A., Spasojevic, M. (eds.) Pervasive Computing. LNCS, vol. 6030, pp. 246–264. Springer, Heidelberg (2010)
14. Maekawa, T., Yanagisawa, Y., Kishino, Y., Kamei, K., Sakurai, Y., Okadome, T.: Object-blog system for environment-generated content. IEEE Pervasive Computing 7(4), 20–27 (2008)
15. Mayol, W.W., Murray, D.W.: Wearable hand activity recognition for event summarization. In: Int'l Symp. on Wearable Computers, pp. 122–129 (2005)
16. Patel, S.N., Robertson, T., Kientz, J.A., Reynolds, M.S., Abowd, G.D.: At the flick of a switch: Detecting and classifying unique electrical events on the residential power line. In: Krumm, J., Abowd, G.D., Seneviratne, A., Strang, T. (eds.) UbiComp 2007. LNCS, vol. 4717, pp. 271–288. Springer, Heidelberg (2007)
17. Philipose, M., Fishkin, K.P., Perkowitz, M.: Inferring activities from interactions with objects. IEEE Pervasive Computing 3(4), 50–57 (2004)
18. Ravi, N., Dandekar, N., Mysore, P., Littman, M.L.: Activity recognition from accelerometer data. In: IAAI 2005, vol. 20, pp. 1541–1546 (2005)
19. Tapia, E.M., Intille, S.S., Larson, K.: Activity recognition in the home using simple and ubiquitous sensors. In: Ferscha, A., Mattern, F. (eds.) PERVASIVE 2004. LNCS, vol. 3001, pp. 158–175. Springer, Heidelberg (2004)
20. van Kasteren, T., Noulas, A., Englebienne, G., Krose, B.: Accurate activity recognition in a home setting. In: Ubicomp 2008, pp. 1–9 (2008)
21. Welch, L.R.: Hidden markov models and the baum-welch algorithm. IEEE Information Theory Society Newsletter 53(4) (2003)
22. Witten, I.H., Frank, E.: Data Mining: Practical machine learning tools and techniques. Morgan Kaufmann, San Francisco (2004)

3D Gesture Recognition: An Evaluation of User and System Performance

Michael Wright, Chun-Jung Lin, Eamonn O'Neill , Darren Cosker, and Peter Johnson

Department of Computer Science,
University of Bath,
Bath, BA2 7AY, UK
{maew20,mcscjl,eamonn,d.p.cosker}@cs.bath.ac.uk,
p.johnson@bath.ac.uk

Abstract. We report a series of empirical studies investigating gesture as an interaction technique in pervasive computing. In our first study, participants generated gestures for given tasks and from these we identified archetypal common gestures. Furthermore, we discovered that many of these user-generated gestures were performed in 3D. We implemented a computer vision based 3D gesture recognition system and applied it in a further study in which participants used the common gestures generated in the first study. We investigated the trade off between system performance and human performance and preferences, deriving design recommendations. We achieved 84% recognition accuracy by our prototype 3D gesture recognition system after tuning it through the use of simple heuristics. The most popular gestures from Study 1 were regarded by participants in Study 2 as best matching the task they represented, and they produced the fewest recall errors.

Keywords: Gestural interaction, 3D gesture recognition.

1 Introduction

This paper reports an investigation of gesture as an interaction technique in a pervasive computing environment. We conducted a linked series of empirical studies and system development investigating gestural interaction in a pervasive computing environment. In phase 1 of the research, we sought to identify a candidate set of gestures that could be useful and usable across a range of devices, services and contexts. We asked participants spontaneously to generate gestures to perform given interaction tasks. The tasks were selected through a process of iterative scenario generation and refinement, and ranged from concrete tasks familiar to computer users, e.g. "Select ...", to more abstract tasks, e.g. "Show me a ...". We recorded the gestures made by each participant and categorized typical or most common gestures for the different tasks. In addition, we discovered that many of the gestures were 3-dimensional.

In the next phase, we implemented a computer vision based 3D gesture recognition system and trained it using the set of archetypal gestures derived from the study in phase 1. The system uses 3D cameras to capture a user's hand movements, and

K. Lyons, J. Hightower, and E.M. Huang (Eds.): Pervasive 2011, LNCS 6696, pp. 294–313, 2011.

Hidden Markov Models (HMMs) to recognize the gestures. Participants were trained on the gestures and then asked to perform interaction tasks using only these gestures. We collected data on user performance (recalling the correct gesture), user ratings of how well a gesture matched the task being performed and system recognition rates.

Typically there is a balance of cost or effort between the user and the system for a given performance and different approaches tend to put more of the burden on either the user or system while attempting to find an acceptable balance and adequate performance. For example, handwriting recognition systems on mobile devices, such as Graffiti on previous Palm devices, forced the user to form letters in a non-standard way, increasing the burden on the user in order to reduce the burden on the recognition system. Therefore, in the final phase of our study we performed a comparative assessment of the ability of users to remember and perform gestures, the accuracy of the system in recognizing the gestures and the balance achieved between burdening the user and burdening the system for a given level of overall performance and user satisfaction.

2 Background and Motivation

Our research is focused on exploring gesture as an interaction technique for pervasive computing environments. Our work focuses on gestural interactions that range from traditional desktop metaphor interactions (e.g. select, open, move) to more abstract or conversational interactions (e.g. "take a picture of …", "show me information about …").

Categorization of gestures allows us to explore opportunities to exploit the characteristics of different types of gesture for different types of interaction. Kendon [2] describes a set of gesture categories, (gesticulation, language-like gestures, pantomimes, emblems and sign language), which range in their formalism. For example, gesticulation is "free form gesturing which typically accompany verbal discourse" and sign language contains a complete grammatical specification. Other categorizations include those used by Efron [6] and McNeill [7].

These categorizations of gestures allows us to explore the characteristics of gesture such that they can be exploited. For example, [9] examines different categorizations of gesture in order to produce realistic interactions between humans and Artificial Intelligence agents while [13] defines a vocabulary of gestures to be used when interacting with a gesture interface.

Our ultimate aim is to allow users to interact more naturally in pervasive computing environments with more complex interactions. Exploiting the features of these different categorizations may enable these types of interactions. For example, the types of interactions that might be supported range from selecting an image on a large display (manipulative) to taking a photo (iconic), to pointing at a street sign and asking "show me where I am on a map" (gesticulation), to missing an announcement over the public address system in a railway station and cupping your hand behind your ear and pointing at your mobile phone to stream the announcement to the phone (pantomime).

However, the majority of the literature on gesture focuses on the technology used to capture gestures made by the user. Such technology includes accelerometers, infra-red tracking, data gloves, and cameras. The largest body of literature on systems for gesture recognition uses computer vision algorithms with 2D and 3D cameras. For example,

[3, 4, 8, 11, 12] describe systems which use HMM models with 2D or 3D cameras in order to capture and recognize gestures made by a user. Wu and Huang [18] provide a review of vision-based gesture recognition systems and techniques.

In each of these systems, the gestures are defined by the designer. As Wobbrock [10] articulates, although these gestures are designed skillfully, they are often designed with priority given to system recognition rates rather than to the users' requirement for gestures that they feel fit the actions being performed. Palm's Graffiti is another example of this, as is MIT's Sixth Sense [15]. Sixth Sense utilizes vision based gesture recognition techniques to enable the use of gestures to interact with a system. Users can use gestures to perform actions such as taking a photo and controlling user interfaces projected by the device on to different surfaces. These gestures are defined by the system designers and rely on physical and desktop metaphors. This is a reasonable design decision, however as Wobbrock highlights, in a technology which is maturing into commercial systems and products there is a need to explore the gestures that users find most appropriate for given tasks.

Wobbrock's observations expose a gap in the research where gestures are often not designed based on user preference or need but rather on the needs of the system. Although gestures are designed based on a principled design approach, as his study illustrates, even experienced designers cannot predict a gesture set that can fully meet user expectations of interaction.

Similar studies into user defined gesture sets have been undertaken by Fikkert [17] and Kray [5]. Fikkert describes a wizard-of-oz study in which users were asked to perform gestures to control the pan and zoom of a map interface on a large display out of reach of the user. They also conducted a user survey in which participants rated different proposed gestures for 6 different commands when interacting with a large display at a distance. Based on these studies they propose an initial gesture set for interacting at a distance with large displays, based on agreement amongst users both in the generation and in the rating of gestures.

Similarly, Kray describes a study where users were asked to perform gestures using a cell phone to interact with other cell phones, large displays and interactive tabletops. Again, they propose a gesture set based on agreement amongst participants. Further to this study they also assess the ability of cell phones to recognize the gestures in this gesture set and provide design recommendations for sensor hardware to be incorporated into future cell phones.

In all three of these studies it was observed that users produce similar gestures for tasks. Based on this observation, we explored user-generated gestures for interaction in pervasive computing environments. This extends the work done by Wobbrock, Fikkert and Kray by exploring more general interactions in an environment where there are potentially many different devices (e.g. large displays, audio, embedded sensors) and services (e.g. location tracking, travel information etc).

Additionally, we also set out to apply user generated gestures to an implementation of a gesture recognition system and to explore the trade off between the user requirement of natural gestures that fit the action being performed and the system requirement of gestures which can be effectively recognized. This extends the assessment conducted by Kray in that it applies the gestures to a working gesture recognition system and explores the requirements and adaptations needed by both the user and the system.

3   Study 1: Generation of a Common Gesture Set

Prior to running this study, we collaborated with colleagues in several academic and industrial organizations to develop a set of scenarios that explore the ways in which future users might interact with pervasive computing. The scenarios focus on the theme of Augmented Travel where multiple devices, services and users come together to enable and enhance the traveling experience from booking tickets to providing contextual information while *en route*. From these scenarios we abstracted example tasks for our study. The tasks included:

- Move a [document/image/advert] from one device to another
- Go back to the previous [page in a document/image/advert]
- Show me the location of this cafe

Study 1 was a generative empirical study in which participants proposed gestures to perform the tasks drawn from the scenarios. Tasks ranged from concrete tasks familiar to computer users, e.g. "Select ...", to more abstract, e.g. "Show me a ...".

Twenty two participants took part in the study, aged from 20 to 44 with a mean age of 29. 16 participants were male and 6 were female. All participants were recruited from around the University of Bath.

Participants were asked to imagine themselves performing the tasks in the course of interacting with a pervasive computing environment. They were asked to visualize the interfaces and objects they might be interacting with. They were deliberately not provided with 'props' or interfaces in order to focus the participants on generating gestures that would allow them to perform the task rather than focusing on the gestures that could be made to interact with a specific interface or object.

Participants were run individually. Each participant was provided with the context in which she should imagine herself performing the gestures. The experimenter read aloud each task in turn and the participant made a gesture of her own choice to perform the task. A subset of the tasks is presented in Table 1. The order of the tasks was randomized for each participant. The gestures performed by each participant were video recorded for later analysis.

Table 1. A subset of the 68 tasks presented to participants in Study 1

Task No	Task
2	Go to an image
4	Select
17	Zoom in to an image
25	Close
26	Close an application
39	Show me information about this cafe
41	Show me my location
51	Move an application from one device to another
52	Go to an image and zoom in
53	Select a piece of text and delete it
54	Open a document and select a piece of text
57	Zoom in to a map and show me my location

3.1 Results

The resulting video record was analyzed to investigate the gestures generated by participants. In analyzing the gestures, we were particularly interested in the similarity of gestures made across participants for a particular task. Here we focus on the 'verbs' in the tasks, i.e. Select, Move, Go To, as these gestures are the actions or manipulations the participant performed on an imagined interface or object.

Two researchers independently analyzed the resulting video and produced descriptions of the gestures made by participants for the verb in the task. To ensure that the resulting categorization of gestures was based on the same observed gesture we ran an inter-rater reliability test. Each researcher gave a description of the gesture made for each task. These descriptions were then compared and a Kappa statistic was produced to determine consistency between the researchers. The results of the test indicate a very high level of agreement (Kappa = 0.818, p<0.001) between the descriptions of the gestures performed by each participant.

Tables 2 to 4 respectively present the 3 top level categories we identified from our analysis of the gestures. Category A consists of tasks for which a single common gesture was used by more than 65% of participants for the given task, and the overall variance (i.e. the number of different types of gestures performed) was low. Category B consists of tasks for which the variance was low but there was not a single dominant gesture as there was in Category A. Category C consists of tasks for which the variance was high.

In Category A (Table 2) for each of the actions Select, Open, Close, Stop, Pick Up, Drop and Move, participants typically made one gesture. Furthermore, there is a low variance in the gestures made, i.e. there are few alternative gestures. In all but one case (Open) the variance is 1 if we exclude outliers, i.e. where a gesture was made by only one participant. Thus, for these tasks in the context of the study there was a high level of agreement across participants on the archetypal gesture for this task.

In Category B (Table 3) there is low variance (between 2 and 3) for each of the gestures generated for the tasks Zoom In, Zoom Out, Move Forward, Move Back and Go Back. The cause of variance in this category is primarily due to the direction in which the gesture was performed. For example, both the Zoom In and Zoom Out gestures were performed either as a movement of the hands forwards and inwards to a point or spreading apart outwards from a point. One possible explanation for this variance is the interaction metaphor used by the participant. In the Zoom examples, either gesture could be used depending on the metaphor employed by the participant, e.g. magnifying glass or stretch to zoom. In selecting an archetypal gesture for the Zoom gestures, we added together percentages from the forwards and inwards movement and the outwards and further apart movement and selected as the archetype the higher percentage. Therefore, Zoom In is defined as a movement of the hands forwards and inwards to a point as this direction was used by 48% of participants whereas the movement of the hands spreading apart outwards from a point was 35%. There is no *a priori* reason not to prefer the opposite direction for the Zoom gestures but, in this category, direction is the main distinguishing feature and so the most common direction was used to select the archetypal gesture.

Table 2. Category A: Gestures produced in Study 1 for which there is low variance and a greater than 65% concurrence by participants on the gesture for a given task

Action	Gesture Made	% used
Select	**point**	**86%**
	sideways movement	13%
	circle	1%
Open	**movement outwards like a book**	**71%**
	double tap	9%
	point	12%
	open hand/flash	5%
	upwards movement	3%
Close	**movement inwards like a book**	**73%**
	x shape	22%
	close hand	5%
Stop	**"halt!" sign**	**86%**
	cutting motion	2%
	point	11%
Pick Up	**grasp and pick up**	**80%**
	upwards movement	9%
	sideways movement	11%
Drop	**open hands and a movement down**	**66%**
	push down movement	30%
	x shape	5%
Move	**movement from side to side**	**100%**

Table 3. Category B: Gestures produced in Study 1 for which there is a low variance in the number of gestures produced but there is no single gesture which was generated by participants more than 65% of the time

Action	Gesture Made	% used
Zoom In	**movement forwards towards a point**	**42%**
	movement inwards like a book	**6%**
	movement from the user outwards	24%
	movement outwards like a book	11%
	pinch	17%
Zoom Out	**movement from the user outwards**	**47%**
	movement outwards like a book	**12%**
	movement forwards towards a point	18%
	movement inwards like a book	9%
	pinch	14%
Move Forward	right to left movement	18%
	left to right movement	**36%**
	z axis forward movement	25%
	circle	14%
	physically move forward	7%
Move Back	**right to left movement**	**36%**
	left to right movement	18%
	z axis backwards movement	25%
	circle	16%
	physically move back	7%
Go Back	left to right movement	11%
	right to left movement	**41%**
	z axis backwards movement	25%
	physically move back	7%
	circle	16%

Table 4. Category C: Gestures produced in Study 1 where there is a large variance. In addition, the point gesture is typically used as a default.

Action	Gesture Made	% used
Go To	**sideways movement**	**36%**
	physically move	11%
	point	41%
	double tap	3%
	icon of object e.g. media or tv	9%
Search	point to eye	6%
	shrug	5%
	question mark (?) icon	17%
	circle	**44%**
	side to side in a z shape	14%
	downwards or sideways movement	15%
Turn On	**turn of the wrist**	**16%**
	up movement	9%
	open hand/ flash	9%
	point	61%
	open gesture	5%
Turn Off	**turn of the wrist**	**20%**
	downward movement	11%
	eyes	5%
	x shape	11%
	two handed large cross movement	7%
	point	32%
	close gesture	14%
Play	point	48%
	open gesture	7%
	wave	5%
	circle	**16%**
	open hand(s)	2%
	right to left movement	2%
	tap	9%
	icon(thumbs up or triangle play)	11%
Show Me	point	47%
	point at eyes	8%
	shrug/hands open gesture	**22%**
	icon of object e.g. media or tv	8%
	circle	7%
	open hand(s)	9%
Delete	**draw an x shape**	**48%**
	right to left movement	9%
	throw	27%
	rip	3%
	close gesture	8%
	downward movement	5%

In Category C (Table 4) there is large variance (between 4 and 6) for each of the gestures generated for the tasks Go To, Search, Turn On, Turn Off, Play, Show Me and Delete. The point gesture was performed for almost all of the tasks. One explanation is that actions such as Turn On, Go To etc were, for our participants, considered as equivalent to selecting the object. However, in tasks such as "Show me information about this cafe" the point gesture was used as a default when the participants struggled to think of an appropriate gesture for the task. Hence, it seems more likely that pointing is in many of these cases a symptom of participants' not articulating the specific meaning of the task through the gesture, rather than the various tasks being semantically equivalent to selecting. In determining the archetypal gesture for Category C tasks, we simply chose the gesture generated the greatest number of times by the participants, disregarding the point gesture. These gestures are effectively arbitrary and it is therefore likely that they will be more difficult to learn and remember than Category B gestures where there was less variance, and Category A where there was even less.

Participants performed gestures in a variety of directions and orientations depending on how they visualized the interfaces and objects they might interact with in a pervasive computing environment. For example, the Select gesture often had a different direction depending on where the participant imagined the target object to be located and a different orientation of the hand depending on the type of task (figure 1(a) and 1(b)). Another example is the Zoom In and Zoom Out gestures where, although participants made the same gesture in terms of the direction of movement of their hands, the orientation of their hands could either be vertical towards the ground or horizontal in front of them (figure 1(c) and 1(d)). Existing gesture recognition systems typically operate only with 2D gestures, e.g. [11, 12, 15]. Given the predominance of 3D gestures in the gesture set we derived from Study 1, there would appear to be a need for gesture recognition systems that can recognize gestures in 3D.

(a) Select a TV   (b) Select a but- (c) Zoom in to a (d) Zoom in to an
                    ton   map   image

Fig. 1. Different directions and orientations performed by participants when asked to generate gestures for different tasks

In the remainder of this paper we present an implementation of a computer vision based 3D gesture recognition system followed by a further study. In this second study we trained participants on the candidate common gesture set derived from the first study and assessed the ability of the users to remember and perform the gestures, the accuracy of the 3D recognition system in recognizing the gestures, and the balance achieved between burdening the user and burdening the system for a given level of overall performance and user satisfaction.

4   Gesture Recognition System

Our 3D gesture recognition system drew on [12]. In [12] they propose a method by which hand movements can be categorized based on a topology of vectors calculated from the movement of the user's hand. We extended this topology to include the third dimension. Furthermore, in [12] only one hand is tracked; in our implementation we are able to track 2 hands and, therefore, to recognize two handed gestures.

Our gesture recognition system is comprised of two main modules: an image processing module and a HMM module. We used a Bumblebee 2 stereo camera (figure 2(a)) to capture the image of the user performing a gesture. From this image the system extracts the x, y and z coordinates of each pixel and uses color detection to locate and track the user's hands. We convert the RGB colour values for each pixel into the Y'UV444 color space to reduce the effects of changes in lighting. To increase performance and object recognition rates, we perform this conversion only if the z value of the pixel is in an active range based on the clustering of detected pixels. If an individual pixel falls outside the z value range of this cluster then it is rejected.

Following identification of the objects, we apply two more filters. The first filter treats as noise detected potential objects whose total number of pixels is not greater than a predefined threshold. The second filter treats the detected object as static if the distance the object has moved between frames is below a predefined threshold.

In the next stage the system calculates a Gesture Sequence for the movement of the user's hands between frames. This sequence is used as input to the HMM model which returns the gesture whose Gesture Sequence best matches the one performed. In order to capture both hands we produce a separate Gesture Sequence for each hand and the HMM is trained using these separate sequences. The outputs of the HMM predictions for the left and right hands are then examined together.

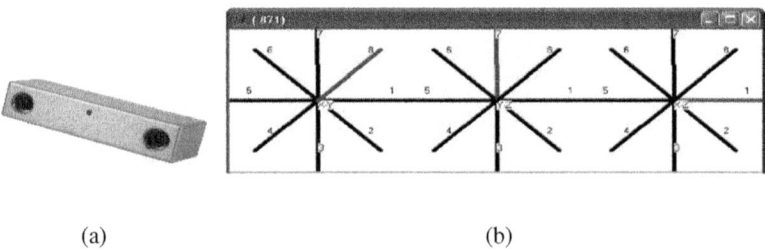

(a)   (b)

Fig. 2. The system developed used a 3D stereo camera and HMM models in order to capture and recognize gestures in 3D

In order to encode the hand movements, the system calculates the centre point of the detected object and tracks the movement of this centre point between frames. Using this movement data we divide the x,y,z values into three planes of movement, X-Y, X-Z and Y-Z, with each plane divided into eight directions (figure 2(b)). These coordinates are saved into a buffer. Using this buffer the system is able to calculate the angle between the two movements of an object. Using these angles we can build up a sequence of movements for each axis from one frame to another.

After all the angles have been converted to directions, the system combines the three directions into a number. For example, if x-y is 8, y-z is 7, x-z is 1, the system encodes those directions as 871. Figure 2 shows an example of a section of a Gesture Sequence used as input to the HMM. The HMM module provides a probability that the Gesture Sequence input is a particular gesture. We used the Accord Statistics Library API [1] in order to implement the HMM.

In training mode, the HMM module was given a training set of gesture sequences for each gesture in our candidate set of common gestures derived from Study 1. From the training set the HMM module produces a model for each gesture. In prediction mode, the HMM was given as input the Gesture Sequence derived for each gesture performed by the user. The HMM then identifies and outputs the gesture that has the best match based on the trained gesture sequences.

5   Study Two: User and System Evaluation

Study 2 applied our 3D gesture recognition system to the archetypal gestures derived from Study 1. We aimed to evaluate simultaneously both the participants' performance and experiences in recalling and performing the gestures and the performance of the system in recognizing the participants' gestures. Furthermore, as we report in section 6, we examined the balance between, on one hand, requiring a recognition system effectively to handle the inevitably diverse range of interpretations by users of even a constrained set of gestures and, on the other hand, requiring users to adapt their performance to conform to the equally inevitable constraints of a given recognition system implementation. Historically, some proponents of an 'engineering-oriented' approach have taken the line of 'optimizing' a system's performance at the cost of considerable constraints on allowable user behaviors, while most proponents of a 'human-oriented' approach have argued that the human users should be given more freedom to behave and express themselves as they want, with the system having to cope as best it can. The optimal approach to combining limited machines with diverse humans is probably somewhere between these two extremes.

5.1   Method

Study 2 builds upon Study 1 and uses the gesture recognition system described in Section 4 in order to test the accuracy of the system to recognize the gestures as well as the ability of the users to remember and perform the correct gestures. Participants were trained on a subset of gestures derived from Study 1 (Table 5) and then asked to perform given tasks using only these gestures. As in Study 1 participants were not given any physical devices on which to make a gesture and the study took place in a lab where no devices were present apart from the laptop and stereo camera comprising the gesture recognition system.

18 participants took part in the study, aged from 20 to 44 with a mean age of 30. 14 of the participants were male and 4 were female. All participants were recruited from around the University of Bath.

Participants were run individually. In the first part of Study 2, participants were trained on the set of gestures derived from Study 1 (Table 5). We deliberately removed some gestures from this set so that they could be used in an interference task between training the participants and asking them to complete the tasks.

In the training phase, the participant was asked to perform a specific gesture in front of the gesture recognition system. The participant was shown the gesture by the experimenter and asked to perform each gesture 10 times. Each repetition was recorded by the system and the experimenter made sure that the participant performed the gesture correctly by ensuring the movements made by participants were the same as those demonstrated. In line with our view that human-computer interaction is a 2-way street, it is worth noting that this process trained both the user and the recognition system on the gestures as performed by that particular user.

Following training, the participant performed an interference task in which the experimenter read aloud a task from those previously used in Study 1 (and not otherwise used in study 2), and asked the participant to generate a gesture or gestures they thought corresponded to that task. Participants were encouraged to be as creative as possible in generating these new gestures and they were not constrained to the gestures they had just been shown. Each participant generated gestures for 15 new tasks, taking a minimum of 5 minutes to complete.

Next, the experimenter again read aloud a task, but this time the participant was asked to perform the task using only gestures she had learned in the training phase of Study 2. This was repeated for all the tasks in the training set. The gestures made by the participants were video recorded. The experimenter noted correct gestures made (i.e. that the gestures were recognizable – by the experimenter! – and of the correct type), corrected any mistakes of gesture type (e.g. making a Select gesture rather than an Open gesture) and prompted participants if they could not remember the gesture.

Finally, the participants completed a questionnaire on their experience of the gestures and tasks. In addition, they were asked for their perceptions of how 'natural' they perceived the gestures to be for accomplishing the given tasks.

Table 5. Subset of gestures generated in Study One and carried forward into Study Two

Gesture	Description
Select	point
Open	movement outwards like a book
Close	movement inwards like a book
Pick Up	grasp and pick up
Drop	open hands and a movement down
Zoom In	movement forwards towards a point
Zoom Out	movement from the user outwards
Move Forward	left to right movement
Move Back	right to left movement
Search	circle
Show Me	shrug/hands open gesture
Delete	draw an x shape

5.2   Results

In keeping with our focus on both sides of the human-computer interaction, we analyzed and compared both the users' performance and the 3D gesture recognition system's performance. We first present results on the system recognition rates and then on the success of the participants in recalling and performing the correct gesture when completing the tasks. Furthermore, we report participants' qualitative preferences in terms of how well they felt the gesture matched the task in each case. In section 6 we compare system and user performance.

System Recognition Rates. In order to evaluate the performance of our 3D gesture recognition system we followed a leave-one-out testing strategy to derive an overall accuracy rate as well as a break down of the gestures that were misidentified by the system. Leave-one-out testing involved training the HMM model on all the training data of all but one participant. The omitted participant's data was then input into the system and the output was the identification of the gesture by the HMM based system, from which we were able to evaluate the accuracy of the gesture recognition system.

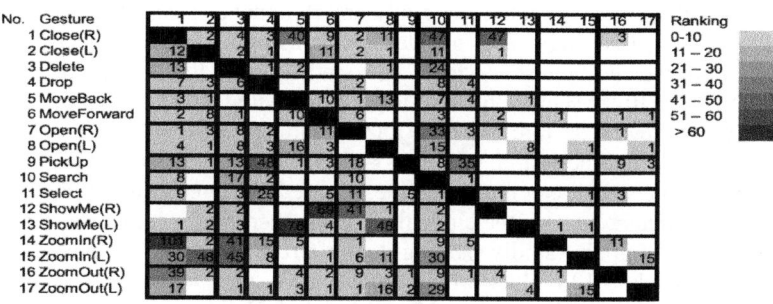

Fig. 3. Confusion Matrix – 61% accuracy: each gesture is shown relative to the gestures with which the system confused it

Using our initial implementation of the system we achieved an average recognition rate of 61%. Figure 3 shows a confusion matrix for the results of our initial leave-one-out testing. From this matrix we can see that there are a number of cases where the gesture recognition system misidentified a gesture frequently by confusing it with another similar gesture. By examining the clusters of misidentifications, i.e. where the number of errors is above 30, we can identify some common misidentifications:

1. Zoom In with Close
2. Zoom Out with Close
3. Show Me with Move Back, Move Forward and Open
4. Close with Show Me and Move Back
5. Close with Open
6. Pickup with Drop
7. Pick Up with Select
8. Search in general

To improve the accuracy of the system's gesture identification we applied heuristics to confusions 1-4 in the above list. These heuristics worked because at least one of the gestures being confused was a two-handed gesture. Our first heuristic attempts to correct the confusion between the Zoom In and Zoom Out gestures and the Close gesture. From the confusion matrix we can see that the confusion comes from the misidentification of Zoom In Right Hand with Close Right Hand (101 errors) and Zoom In Left Hand with Close Left Hand (48 errors). However, the reverse is not true, with Close Right Hand and Left Hand not being confused with Zoom In. This is a similar pattern for Zoom Out Right and Left Hand and Close Right and Left Hand. To correct this, we made the Zoom gesture dominant, e.g. if a Zoom In gesture is reported for one of the hands and a Close for the other then the gesture for both hands is assumed to be a Zoom In.

Using the same method as above, our second heuristic made the Show Me gesture dominant over the Move Back, Move Forward and Open gestures. Therefore, if a Show Me was reported for one hand then it was assumed that a Show Me gesture had been performed if the other hand reported either a Show Me, Move Back, Move Forward or Open gesture. Similarly, our third heuristic made the Close gesture dominant over the Show Me and Move Back gestures.

Finding heuristics or improvements in recognition for confusions 5-8 in the above list proved difficult as we could not apply any dominance rules since these gestures are all one handed gestures. The misidentifications in 5 came from each hand being misidentified with its opposite, which we found difficult to correct, e.g. Close Left Hand with Open Right Hand and Close Right Hand with Open Left Hand.

Finally, the Search gesture caused a lot of confusion with all of the gestures. The reason for this is that the Search gesture is a circle. The circle made by the participant, depending on the speed, can mean that the captured Gesture Sequence includes more codes on a particular edge of the circle than on another. For example starting out with the hand at 12 o'clock, rapidly moving it in a circle to 6 o'clock and then slowing down from 6 back to 12 o'clock would produce a Gesture Sequence with more codes that relate to the Gesture Sequence of Zoom Out Left Hand.

Figure 4 shows the results of applying the heuristics in the 3D gesture recognition system. Again we use a confusion matrix to illustrate where misidentification of gestures occurs. The misidentification of gestures is greatly reduced, with the overall accuracy rate increasing from 61% to 84%. As noted in Section 4, we based our system on [9] which had an overall accuracy rate of between 94.29% and 98.6% over a very small set of highly distinct 2D gestures. Our system compares favorably as our 84% accuracy rate was over a larger number and diversity of both one and two handed gestures and in 3D.

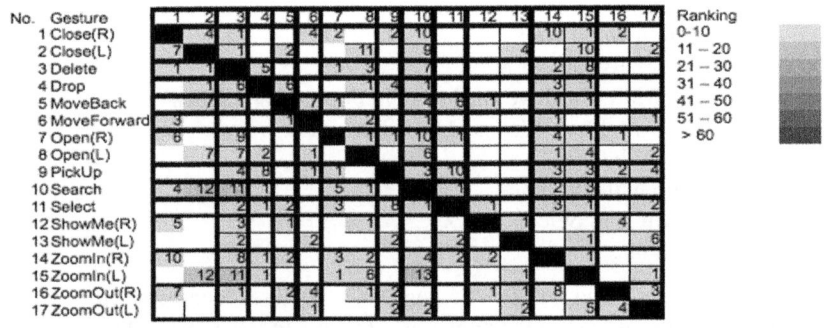

Fig. 4. Confusion Matrix – 84% accuracy: each gesture is shown relative to the gestures with which the system confused it

Participant Data. This section presents an analysis of the participants' ability to recall and perform the gestures correctly for the given tasks. In addition, we describe the participants' ranking of how well they thought the gestures matched the actions. Table 6 gives the overall accuracy rate across all participants. It is important to note again that here we are considering correctness of a gesture in terms of whether or not the gesture was of the right type, i.e. a Select gesture when the Select task was intended, rather than whether or not the gesture was recognizable by the 3D gesture recognition system. A gesture made by a participant to perform a particular task could have been of the right or wrong type in these terms. Orthogonally, it might or might not be recognizable as a particular gesture by the recognition system. Thus, the user could intend to perform the gesture for Task A, actually perform the gesture for Task B (poor user performance), and have it recognized by the system as the gesture for Task C or not recognized at all (poor system performance). Thus, accuracy in Table 6 is based on the participants' ability to recall the correct gesture and the experimenter's observation and assessment of the users' performance of the gesture. Table 6 is ordered by incorrectly performed gestures based on the percentage of gestures that participants got wrong.

Category C gestures are clearly mis-performed the largest percentage of times. However, there is a less clear distinction between the mis-performance of Category A and B gestures. The main reason for mis-performing a gesture was the user forgetting the gesture for a given task. This is the main reason for Category C gestures and is not unexpected as these gestures are more abstract than those in Categories A and B. Category B gestures were often mis-performed because participants used the incorrect direction. Again this is not surprising as the cause of variance in Category B was primarily due to the direction in which the gesture was performed.

Surprisingly, since it was a Category A gesture, the Close gesture was often mis-performed. This was often due to the correct gesture being forgotten but in several instances the Delete gesture was performed instead. The Delete gesture was to draw an 'x' shape. A similar shape is extremely commonly used to close a window in traditional desktop user interfaces and it is likely that users' previous experience with this convention overrode their relatively newly acquired gestural metaphor of closing a book. This explanation is corroborated by users' perceptions of how well the gestures matched their associated tasks.

Figure 5 shows a ranking of how participants perceived that a gesture matched its corresponding task, ordered by how well the participants rated each gesture. So, for example, 10 participants gave the Select gesture the maximum score of 20, with a cumulative score of 335 for Select. With the exception of Close, participants felt that Category A gestures matched their tasks well. This is as expected since Study 1 found little variance in the user-generated gestures for these tasks. The results of Studies 1 and 2 combined give us some confidence that these are indeed good archetypal gestures for these tasks. There was more variance in the Category B gestures and, again as expected, less agreement on how well these gestures matched their tasks in Study 2. Finally, Category C gestures had the most variance when generated by users in Study 1 and we saw no real consensus amongst the participants in Study 2 that the chosen gestures matched their tasks well. The notable exception here was Delete. Thus, as with performance accuracy, the Close and Delete gestures were the only exceptions to the predicted ranking. The Category A Close gesture was ranked very low while the Category C Delete gesture was ranked high.

Table 6. Accuracy rate of participants when performing a gesture

Gesture	Category	% Performed Incorrectly	Reason
Show Me	C	36.11%	Forgot (33.33%), Used select (2.78%)
Search	C	19.44%	Forgot (16.67%), Used move back (2.28%)
Close	A	13.89%	Forgot (11.11%), Used delete (2.78%)
Move Forward	B	11.11%	Used wrong hand (5.55%), Used two hands (2.78%), Used move back (2.78%)
Delete	C	7.41%	Did zoom in (1.85%), Forgot (5.56%)
Pick Up	A	5.56%	Used drop (2.78%), Performed incorrectly (2.78%)
Zoom In	B	3.70%	Used zoom out (3.70%)
Open	A	2.78%	Used Select (1.39%), Included a close gesture (1.38%)
Select	A	2.78%	Dragged over text (0.93%), Forgot (0.93%), Used zoom in (0.92%)
Move Back	B	2.78%	Forgot (2.78%)
Drop	A	0.00%	
Zoom Out	B	0.00%	

Gesture	Category	1	2	3	4	5	6	7	8	9	10	11	12	13	14	15	16	17	18	19	20	cumulative weighting
Select	A													1		1	1	1	2	2	10	335
Pick Up	A										1		2			3	3	3	6			77
Open	A									1			1		1	1	2	2	5	5		60
Delete	C					1					1			2		4	4	1	5			48
Drop	A													2	3	3	4	1	5			58
Move Forward	B	1					1			1	1			2	3	2	2	1	4			48
Move Back	B	1					1			1	1			3	3	2	1	1	4			42
Zoom In	B			1					3			1	1	1	3	2	1		1	4		34
Zoom Out	B			1					3			1	1	1	3	2	1		1	4		44
Close	A				1							1	1		3		5	4		3		28
Search	C	1			1		2			2	2	2	1		2	1	2	1		1		13
Show Me	C	2	1	3	1	2		1			1	1	1			1	3			1		16

Fig. 5. User ranking of how well the gesture matched the action with 20 being very strong and 1 being very weak

6   The Trade Off between System and User

In the previous section we described the results from our second study in terms of both user performance and preferences and system performance. Table 7 presents a comparison between the user ranking of gestures from Study 2 and a ranking of the recognition errors made by the 3D gesture recognition system. A user ranking of 1 represents the best perceived match to the corresponding task and a system error ranking of 1 represents the fewest errors in system recognition of the gesture.

Taken individually, these results could provide design recommendations for the form of the gestures, where the recognition algorithm needs improvement, and even whether gestures should be adopted or rejected. However, the comparison illustrated in Table 7 demonstrates some of the potential conflicts in design recommendations based solely on examining either the user or system performance. For example, the system recognition results would suggest that despite a high user preference the gesture for Pick Up should be changed because of its low system recognition rate. Conversely, the user preference results would suggest that Show Me should be changed based on user ratings that indicate the gesture was not perceived as a good match to the action being performed.

Table 7. Comparison of the user ranking of gestures and the misidentification error rate of the system (1 being the highest user ranking and producing the fewest system errors and 12 being the lowest user ranking and producing the most system errors)

User Ranking	Gesture	Gesture	System Error Ranking
1	Select	Move Forward	1
2	Pick Up	Show Me	2
3	Open	Drop	3
4	Delete	Select	4
5	Drop	Delete	5
6	Move Forward	Move Back	6
7	Move Back	Zoom Out	7
8	Zoom In	Open	8
9	Zoom Out	Zoom In	9
10	Close	Close	10
11	Search	Pick Up	11
12	Show Me	Search	12

Table 8. Generalized design recommendations derived from the direct comparison of user and system performance

System Performance vs User Performance	High	Medium	Low
High	Keep gesture and system in current form	Improve the system and keep gesture the same	Improve the system and keep gesture the same
Medium	Require the user to learn the gesture and keep the system the same	Work could be done on *either* - improving the system performance - tweaking the gesture to allow for better recognition (e.g. orientation of hands)	Work on improving the system, however, if this is not practical or the cost:benefit ratio of doing so is high then the gesture could be altered
Low	Require the user to learn the gesture and keep the system the same	Consider changing the gesture unless there is an easy way of improving the system to recognize the gesture	Change the gesture

By examining the system and user results together we can begin to explore the potential trade off between the need for gestures that are effective for humans and that are distinct enough to be recognized effectively by a given gesture recognition system. Based on this exploration we can propose a set of design recommendations that take into account this trade off (summarized in Table 8). These recommendations highlight where there is a need to improve the recognition system implementation, alter the characteristics of the gesture (e.g. specifying a particular orientation of the hands) or change the gesture entirely.

In Table 9 we map the results of our study to the general recommendations of Table 8. We then provide an enumerated list of the resulting design recommendations for our 3D gesture recognition system. Recommendations 3, 4, 5 and 6 illustrate the value of considering the trade-off between what works for the user and what works for the system. In each of these cases, simply considering either the users' experience or the system performance alone could have led to very different conclusions.

Table 9. Gestures from our study mapped to the generalized design recommendation table

System Performance (recognition rate for individual gestures from Study 2) vs User Performance (user rating of gesture in Study 2)	High (recognition accuracy between 91-100%)	Medium (recognition accuracy between 81-90%)	Low (recognition accuracy between 71-80%)
High (majority of ratings > 15)	Drop	Select Open Delete	Pick Up
Medium (ratings spread out but most > 15)	Move Forward	Move Back Zoom Out	Zoom In
Low (ratings spread out but most < 15)	Show Me		Close Search

1. **Drop:** this gesture should be retained in its current form as both the user and system performance are high.
2. **Select, Open and Delete:** these gestures are regarded by users as an excellent match to their corresponding tasks. However, the medium system recognition rates indicate that work needs to be undertaken to improve the system.
3. **Pick Up:** similarly, Pick Up should be retained due to its high user rating and work should be undertaken on improving the system.
4. **Move Forward and Show Me:** participants gave these gestures a medium and low rating respectively, indicating that these gestures were only a reasonable or low match to the task being performed. However, both these gestures have high system recognition rates. Therefore, it is recommended that these gestures should be retained and the user should be encouraged to learn the gestures. In the case of Show Me, this is further corroborated by Study 1 where, setting aside the simple Point gesture as discussed above, the Show Me gesture chosen was easily the most popular gesture generated for this task. Show Me is sufficiently abstract a task that it is unsurprising that Study 2 participants did not rank it highly. It seems likely, again corroborated

by the findings of Study 1, that they would have had similar or greater concerns with any other gesture chosen to perform this task.

5. **Move Back and Zoom Out:** the generalized design recommendations suggest that either the gesture or the system could be altered. However, based on the mirrors of these gestures (Move Forward and Zoom In) being retained in their current form, it would seem sensible to recommend that the Move Back and Zoom Out gestures should be retained in their current form and improvements made to the gesture recognition system.

6. **Zoom In:** although the system recognition rate for Zoom In was low, participants reported that the gesture was a reasonable match to the action being performed. Therefore, it is recommended that improvements are made to the system rather than altering the gesture.

7. **Close and Search:** these gestures should be rejected as participants did not regard them as matching their tasks well and the system recognition rate was poor.

7 Conclusions and Future Work

In this paper we have reported a series of empirical studies and system development undertaken to investigate the use of gestures as an interaction technique in pervasive computing environments. In phase 1, participants were asked to generate gestures that we categorized based on the degree of consensus and the number of different gestures generated by participants. Additionally, we discovered that many of the gestures generated by participants were performed in 3D.

Therefore, in phase 2, we implemented a computer vision based 3D gesture recognition system and applied it in a further study in which participants were trained on the archetypal gestures derived from phase 1. Participants were asked to perform tasks using these gestures. From this study we were able to collect data on both user performance and preferences and system performance.

Finally, we explored the trade off between the requirement for gestures to support high system performance versus the requirement for gestures to support high human performance and preference, deriving design recommendations.

Deriving user-generated gestures, as we did in phase 1, enabled us to define an archetypal gesture set for specific types of interactions in pervasive computing environments. The advantage to this approach is that we are able to define gestural interactions that are considered natural and intuitive, based on user expectations and preferences and the degree of consensus amongst participants.

However, considering only the user requirements for gestures when implementing a gesture recognition system for use in pervasive computing environments excludes from the equation the needs of the system. Therefore, we proposed a method by which we could compare both user performance and preference and system performance. The resulting general design recommendations indicate where the archetypal gestures can remain unchanged, where adjustments need to be made to the gesture performance by the user, where development effort is needed to improve a recognition implementation and where a potential gesture could be rejected.

We illustrated the application of these general recommendations to our particular gesture set and system implementation.

As part of our future work we wish to define a framework that designers can employ to add new gestural interactions to our archetypal gesture set for new tasks. This framework should not only take into account how to generate gestures for particular tasks but also the practicalities of gesture recognition and interaction. For example, the technology used to recognize gestures (e.g. computer vision with 2D or 3D cameras, accelerometers etc) and the context of the interaction.

Furthermore, we plan to identify further gestures using this framework and evaluate them with a range of gesture recognition systems for pervasive computing environments. The aim is to compare these different systems, exploring the trade off between user and system performance. From these studies, we aim to provide insights into the types of gestural interactions that work well – and poorly – for different recognition technologies in different contexts.

References

1. Accord_Statistics_Library, http://www.crsouza.com
2. Kendon, A.: Current Issues in the Study of Gesture. In: The Biological Foundations of Gestures: Motor and Semiotic Aspects, pp. 23–47. Lawrence Erlbaum, Mahwah (1986)
3. Ramamoorthy, A., Vaswani, N., Chaudhury, S., Banerjee, S.: Recognition of Dynamic Hand Gestures. Pattern Recognition 36(9), 2069–2081 (2003)
4. Keskin, C., Erkan, A., Akarun, L.: Real Time Hand Tracking and 3D Gesture Recognition for Interactive Interfaces using HMM. In: ICANN/ICONIPP 2003, pp. 26–29 (2003)
5. Kray, C., Nesbitt, D., Dawson, J., Rohs, M.: User-Defined Gestures for Connecting Mobile Phones, Public Displays and Tabletops. In: MobileHCI 2010, pp. 239–248 (2010)
6. Efron, D.: Gesture and Environment. Morningside Heights. King's Crown Press, New York (1941)
7. McNeill, D.: Hand and Mind: What Gestures Reveal about Thought. University of Chicago Press, Chicago (1992)
8. Chen, F., Fu, C., Huang, C.: Hand Gesture Recognition Using a Real-Time Tracking Method and Hidden Markov Models. Image and Vision Computing 21(8), 745–758 (2003)
9. Poggi, I.: From a Typology of Gestures to a Procedure for Gesture Production. In: International Gesture Workshop 2002, pp. 158–168 (2002)
10. Wobbrock, J.O., Morris, M.R., Wilson, A.D.: User-Defined Gestures for Surface Computing. In: CHI 2009, pp. 1083–1092 (2009)
11. Oka, K., Sato, Y., Koike, H.: Real-Time Fingertip Tracking and Gesture Recognition. IEEE Computer Graphics and Applications, 64–71 (2002)
12. Elmezain, M., Al-Hamadi, A., Appenrodt, J., Michaelis, B.: A Hidden Markov Model-Based Isolated and Meaningful Hand Gesture Recognition. Electrical, Computer, and Systems Engineering 3(3), 156–163 (2009)
13. Nielsen, M., Störring, M., Moeslund, T.B., Granum, E.: A Procedure for Developing Intuitive and Ergonomic Gesture Interfaces for HCI. In: Camurri, A., Volpe, G. (eds.) GW 2003. LNCS (LNAI), vol. 2915, pp. 409–420. Springer, Heidelberg (2004)
14. Wu, M., Balakrishnan, R.: Multi-Finger and Whole Hand Gestural Interaction Techniques for Multi-User Tabletop Displays. In: UIST 2003, pp. 193–202 (2003)
15. Mistry, P., Maes, P., Chang, L.: WUW - Wear ur World - A Wearable Gestural Interface. In: CHI 2009, pp. 4111–4116 (2009)

16. Malik, S., Ranjan, A., Balakrishnan, R.: Interacting with Large Displays from a Distance with Vision-Tracked Multi-Finger Gestural Input. In: UIST 2005, pp. 43–52 (2005)
17. Fikkert, W., van der Vet, P., van der Veer, G., Nijholt, A.: Gestures for Large Display Control. In: Kopp, S., Wachsmuth, I. (eds.) GW 2009. LNCS, vol. 5934, pp. 245–256. Springer, Heidelberg (2010)
18. Wu, Y., Huang, T.: Vision-Based Gesture Recognition: A Review. In: Braffort, A., Gibet, S., Teil, D., Gherbi, R., Richardson, J. (eds.) GW 1999. LNCS (LNAI), vol. 1739, pp. 103–115. Springer, Heidelberg (2000)

Recognition of Hearing Needs from Body and Eye Movements to Improve Hearing Instruments

Bernd Tessendorf[1], Andreas Bulling[2], Daniel Roggen[1], Thomas Stiefmeier[1], Manuela Feilner[3], Peter Derleth[3], and Gerhard Tröster[1]

[1] Wearable Computing Lab., ETH Zurich
Gloriastr. 35, 8092 Zurich, Switzerland
{lastname}@ife.ee.ethz.ch
[2] Computer Laboratory, University of Cambridge
15 JJ Thomson Avenue, Cambridge CB3 0FD, United Kingdom
{firstname.lastname}@acm.org
[3] Phonak AG, Laubisrütistrasse 28, 8712 Stäfa, Switzerland
{firstname.lastname}@phonak.com

Abstract. Hearing instruments (HIs) have emerged as true pervasive computers as they continuously adapt the hearing program to the user's context. However, current HIs are not able to distinguish different hearing needs in the same acoustic environment. In this work, we explore how information derived from body and eye movements can be used to improve the recognition of such hearing needs. We conduct an experiment to provoke an acoustic environment in which different hearing needs arise: active conversation and working while colleagues are having a conversation in a noisy office environment. We record body movements on nine body locations, eye movements using electrooculography (EOG), and sound using commercial HIs for eleven participants. Using a support vector machine (SVM) classifier and person-independent training we improve the accuracy of 77% based on sound to an accuracy of 92% using body movements. With a view to a future implementation into a HI we then perform a detailed analysis of the sensors attached to the head. We achieve the best accuracy of 86% using eye movements compared to 84% for head movements. Our work demonstrates the potential of additional sensor modalities for future HIs and motivates to investigate the wider applicability of this approach on further hearing situations and needs.

Keywords: Hearing Instrument, Assistive Technology, Activity Recognition, Electrooculography (EOG).

1 Introduction

Hearing impairment increasingly affects populations worldwide. Today, about 10% of the population in developed countries suffer from hearing problems; in the U.S. even 20% adolescents suffers from hearing loss [22]. Over the last generation, the hearing impaired population grew at a rate of 160% of U.S. population growth [13]. About 25% of these hearing impaired use a hearing instrument (HI) to support them in managing their daily lives [13].

K. Lyons, J. Hightower, and E.M. Huang (Eds.): Pervasive 2011, LNCS 6696, pp. 314–331, 2011.
© Springer-Verlag Berlin Heidelberg 2011

Over the last decade considerable advances have been achieved in HI technology. HIs are highly specialised pervasive systems that feature extensive processing capabilities, low power consumption, low internal noise, programmability, directional microphones, and digital signal processors [10]. The latest of these systems –such as the Exelia Art by Phonak– automatically select from among four hearing programs. These programs allow the HI to automatically adjust the sound processing to the users' acoustic environment and their current hearing needs. Examples of hearing need support include noise suppression and directionality for conversations in noisy environments.

Satisfying the users' hearing needs in as many different situations as possible is critical. Already a small number of unsupported listening situations causes a significant drop in overall user satisfaction [14]. Despite technological advances current HIs are limited with respect to the type and number of hearing needs they can detect. Accordingly, only 55% of the hearing impaired report of being satisfied with the overall HI performance in common day-to-day listening situations [14]. This is caused, in part, by the fact that adaption is exclusively based on sound. Sound alone does not allow to distinguish different hearing needs if the corresponding acoustic environments are similar. We call this limitation the *acoustic ambiguity problem*.

1.1   Paper Scope and Contributions

In this work we investigate the feasibility of using additional modalities, more specifically body and eye movements, to infer the hearing needs of a person. As a first step toward resolving the acoustic ambiguity problem we focus on one particular listening situation: the distinction between concentrated work while nearby persons have a conversation from active involvement of the user in a conversation. The specific contributions are: 1) the introduction of context-aware HIs that use a multi-modal sensing approach to distinguish between acoustically ambiguous hearing needs; 2) a methodology to infer the hearing need of a person using information derived from body and eye movements; 3) an experiment to systematically investigate the problem of acoustically ambiguous hearing needs in an office environment, and 4) the evaluation of this methodology for automatic hearing program selection.

1.2   Paper Organisation

We first provide an overview of the state-of-the-art in HI technology, introduce the mechanisms that allow HIs to adapt to the user's hearing needs, and discuss the limitations of current systems. We then survey related work and detail our methodology to infer the user's hearing need from body and eye movements. We describe the experiment, discuss its results, and provide a brief outlook on the technical feasibility of integrating body and eye movements into HIs.

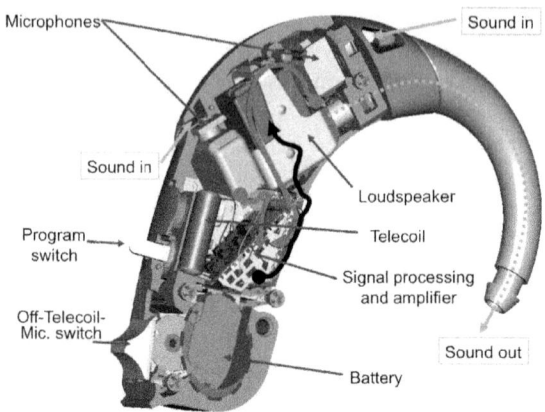

Fig. 1. Components of a modern behind-the-ear (BTE) HI [19]

2   Hearing Instrument Technology

Figure 1 shows the components of a modern behind-the-ear (BTE) HI. HIs are also available in smaller form factors. E.g., Completely-in-the-Canal (CIC) devices can be placed completely inside the user's ear canal. Current systems include a DSP, multiple microphones to enable directivity, a loudspeaker, a telecoil to access an audio induction loop, and a high-capacity battery taking up about a quarter of the HI housing. HIs may also integrate a variety of other accessories such as remote controls, Bluetooth, or FM devices as well as the user's smart phone to form wireless networks, so-called hearing instrument body area networks (HIBANs) [3]. These networking functionalities are part of a rising trend in higher-end HIs. This motivates and supports our investigation of additional sensor modalities for HIs that may eventually be included within the HI itself, or within the wireless network controlled by the HI.

A high-end HI comprises two main processing blocks as shown in Figure 2. The audio processing stages represent the commonly known part of a HI. It performs the traditional audio processing function of the HI and encompasses audio pickup, processing, amplification and playback. The second processing block is the classifier system. It estimates the user's hearing need based on the acoustic environment of the given situation, and adjusts the parameters of the audio processing stages accordingly [12]. The classification is based on spectral and temporal features extracted from the audio signal [4]. The classifier system selects the parameters of the audio processing stages from among a discrete set of parameters known as *hearing programs*. The hearing programs are optimised for different listening situations. Most current high-end HIs distinct four hearing programs: natural, comprehensive hearing (*Speech*), speech intelligibility in noisy environments (*Speech in Noise*), comfort in noisy environments (*Noise*), and listening pleasure for a source with high dynamics (*Music*). The hearing programs represent trade-offs, e.g. speech intelligibility versus naturalness of sound,

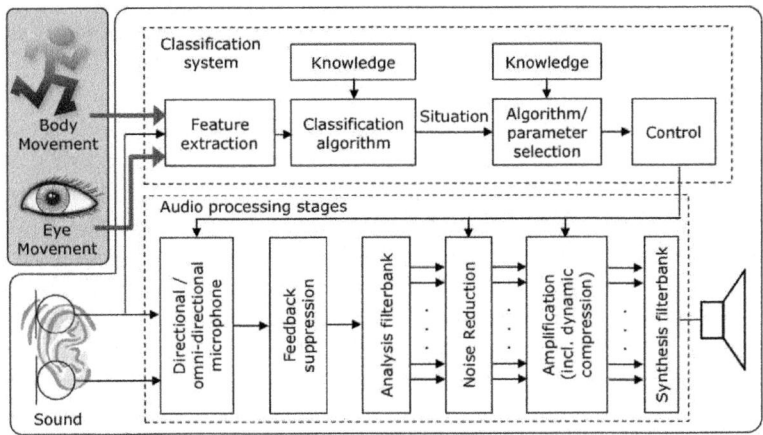

Fig. 2. Bottom: audio processing stages of the HI, from microphone pick-up to amplified and processed sound playback. Top right: classification of the acoustic environment based on sound to adjust the parameters of the audio processing stages. Top left: the extension proposed in this paper. Body and eye movement data are included in the classification system to select the appropriate hearing program. (Figure extended from [10]).

or omnidirectional listening versus directivity. The automatic program selection allows the hearing impaired to use the device with no or only a few manual interactions such as program change and volume adjustment. Adaptive HIs avoid drawing attention to the user's hearing deficits. Users consider automatic adaption mechanisms as useful [4]. Further technical details on HI technology can be found in [10, 21].

2.1 The Acoustic Ambiguity Problem

HIs select the most suitable hearing program according to the user's acoustic environment. The current acoustic environment is used as a proxy for the user's actual hearing need. This approach works well as long as the acoustic environment and hearing need are directly related. This assumption does not hold in all cases and leads to a limitation we call the *acoustic ambiguity problem*: Specifically, in the same acoustic environment a user can have different hearing needs that require different hearing programs. A sound-based adaption mechanism cannot distinguish between these different hearing needs. Therefore, it is important to not only analyze the acoustic environment but to also assess the relevance of auditory objects [23]. The challenge here is not the effectiveness of the dedicated hearing programs but rather automatically adapting the hearing program to the specific *hearing need*, rather than to the *acoustic environment*. The following story illustrates the acoustic ambiguity problem:

Alice suffers from hearing impairment and works in an open office space. Alice is focused on her assigned task when Bob enters the office space to talk to a colleague sitting next to Alice. Alice's HI senses speech in noise and optimizes for speech intelligibility. She now has a hard time focussing on her work, as the HI adapts to the distracting conversation that occurs around her. Then Bob starts talking to Alice. She now needs the HI to support her interaction with colleagues in the noisy environment. Alice doesn't like to select hearing programs manually and desires a robust automatic adaption to her current hearing need.

In the first case, the HI user takes part in a conversation, in the second case, the user could be concentrated on her work and and experiences the conversation as noise. The key challenge in this example is to assess the relevance of speech in the acoustic environment to the HI user. The HI needs to choose between a hearing program that optimizes speech intelligibility and a hearing program treating the speech as noise for user comfort. In both situations, the HI detects the same acoustic environment and thus cannot select a suitable hearing program in both of the cases. A possible strategy is a static "best guess"choice based on a predefined heuristic rule. It could favor speech intelligibility over comfort in noise as social interaction is generally considered important.

Other typical situations in which state of the art classification systems fail include listening to music from the car radio while driving or conversing in a cafe with background music [10].

2.2   Vision of a Future HI

We envision the use of additional modalities to distinguish between ambiguous hearing need requirements in the same acoustic environment. These modalities will be included within the HI itself, or within a wireless network controlled by the HI. Wireless networking functionalities are now starting to appear in higher-end HIs. These new sensors need not be specifically deployed for HIs: they may be shared with other assistive technologies, such as systems designed to detect falls or to monitor physiological parameters. Thus, we see the HI as one element included in a broader set of ambient assisted living technologies. Wearable and textile integrated sensors have become available and sensor data from a mobile phone that may be carried by an individual can be used. We believe the next step in HI technology is to utilize this infrastructure to improve HI performance.

3   Related Work

Various sensor modalities have been proposed to detect social interaction, conversation, or focus of attention from wearable sensors. In [8] body-worn IR transmitters were used to measure face-to-face interactions between people with the goal to model human networks. All partners involved in the interaction needed to wear a dedicated device.

In [11] an attentive hearing aid based on an eye-tracking device and infrared tags was proposed. Wearers should be enabled to "switch on" selected sound sources such as a person, television or radio by looking at them. The sound source needed to be attached with a device that catched the attention of the hearing aid's wearer so that only the communication coming from the sound source was heard.

In [7] different office activities were recognised from eye movements recorded using Electrooculography with an average precision of 76.1% and recall of 70.5%: copying a text between two screens, reading a printed paper, taking hand-written notes, watching a video, and browsing the web. For recognising reading activity in different mobile daily life settings the methodology was extended to combine information derived from head and eye movements [6].

In [18] a vision-based head gesture recognizer was presented. Their work was motivated by the finding that head pose and gesture offer key conversational grounding cues and are used extensively in face-to-face interaction among people. Their goal was to equip an embodied conversational agent with the ability to perform visual feedback recognition in the same way humans do. In [9] the kinematic properties of listeners' head movements were investigated. They found a relation of timing, tempo and synchrony movements of responses to conversational functions.

Several researchers investigated the problem of detecting head movements using body-worn and ambient sensors. In [1] an accelerometer was placed inside HI-shaped housing and worn behind the ear to perform gait analysis. However, the system was not utilised to improve HI behavior.

Capturing the user's auditory selective attention helps to recognise a person's current hearing need. Research in the field of electrophysiology focuses on mechanisms of auditory selective attention inside the brain [24]. Under investigation are event-related brain potentials using electroencephalography (EEG). In [17] the influence of auditory selection on the heart rate was investigated. However, the proposed methods are not robust enough yet to distinguish between hearing needs and are not ready yet for deployment in mobile settings.

All these approaches did not consider sensor modalities which may be included in HIs, or assumed the instrumentation of all participants in the social interactions. In [26], analysis of eye movements was found to be promising to distinguish between working and interaction. Head movements were found to be promising to detect whether a person is walking alone or walking while having a conversation. However, the benefit of combining modalities was not investigated. Moreover, the actual improvement in hearing program selection based on the context recognition was not shown.

4   Experiment

4.1   Procedure

The experiment in this work was designed to systematically investigate acoustically ambiguous hearing needs in a reproducible and controllable way, still remaining as naturalistic as possible. We collected data from 11 participants (six male, five female) aged between 24 and 59 years, recruited from within the lab. The participants were normal hearing and right handed without any known attributes that could impact the results.

Table 1. Experimental procedure to cover different listening situations and hearing needs. The procedure was repeated eight times with the different office activities mentioned above and with the participants being seated and standing.

Time Slot [min]	Situation	Hearing Need
1	Participant and colleague are working	work
2	Disturber and colleague converse	work
3	Disturber and participant converse	conversation
4	Disturber and colleague converse	work
5	Colleague and participant converse	conversation

The experiment took place in a real but quiet office room. The participant and an office colleague worked in this office. A third person, the disturber, entered the office from time to time to involve them in a conversation. The participants were given tasks of three typical office activities: Reading a book, writing on a sheet of paper, typing text on a computer. The participants had no active part in controlling the course of events. They were instructed to focus on carrying out their given tasks and to react naturally. This assures that the resulting body and eye movements are representative for these activities.

The experiment was split in one minute time slots each representing a different situation and hearing need (see Table 1). In the first minute, the participant worked concentrated on his task. In the second minute, the participant tried to stay concentrated while the office colleague was talking to the disturber. In the third minute, the participant was interrupted and engaged in a conversation with the disturber. In the fourth minute, the disturber talked to the colleague again. In the fifth minute, the participant and the colleague had a conversation.

This procedure was repeated eight times with the office activities mentioned above and with the participants being seated and standing. The total experiment time for each participant was about 1 hour. We then assigned each of these activities to one of the following two hearing needs.

Conversation includes situations in which the participant is having a conversation. The HI is supposed to optimize for speech intelligibility, i.e. the hearing program should be "Speech in Noise" throughout. Figure 3 shows all four combinations of sitting and standing while talking to the conversation partners.

Work includes situations in which the participant is carrying out a work task. This case covers situations in which no conversation is taking place around him and situations in which two colleagues are having a conversation the participant is not interested in. The HI is supposed to be in a noise suppression program called "Noise". Figure 4 shows the participant work sitting and standing. Figure 5 shows the participant work in speech noise for the sitting case only.

4.2   Performance Evaluation

We investigate how accurate we can distinguish the two classes *conversation* and *work*. The hearing programs we declared as optimal for each of the situations

Fig. 3. Situations with the hearing need *Conversation*, including all four combinations of sitting and standing conversation partners. The HI is supposed to be in a program optimizing for speech intelligibility (*Speech In Noise*).

Fig. 4. Situations with the hearing need *Noise* for the case *Work*. Working tasks include reading a book, writing on a sheet of paper, and typing a text on the computer. The participant works sitting and standing.

Fig. 5. Situations with the hearing need *Noise* for the case *Work in Speech Noise*. The participant tries to focus on his working task while two colleagues are having a conversation. Only the sitting case is shown here.

served as ground truth: *Speech In Noise* for conversation and *Noise* for work. It is important to note that the *Noise* program is not optimized for supporting the user with concentrated work, but is the best choice among the available hearing programs in our conversation cases. Robust detection of working situations would enable to augment existing HIs with a dedicated program and sound signal processing strategies. For evaluation we compare for each signal window whether the classification result corresponds to the ground truth. We count how often classification and ground truth match in this two-class problem to obtain an accuracy value. In addition, we obtained as a baseline the classification result based on sound. To this end, we analysed the debug output of an engineering sample of a HI[1].

4.3   Data Collection

For recording body movements we used an extended version of the Motion Jacket [25]. The system features nine MTx sensor nodes from *Xsens Technologies* each comprising a 3-axis accelerometer, a 3-axis magnetic field sensor, and a 3-axis gyroscope. The sensors were attached to the head, the left and right upper and lower arms, the back of both hands, and the left leg. The sensors were connected to two XBus Masters placed in a pocket at the participants' lower back. The sampling rate is 32 Hz.

For recording eye movements we chose Electrooculography (EOG) as an inexpensive method for mobile eye movement recordings; it is computationally light-weight and can be implemented using on-body sensors [5]. We used the Mobi system from Twente Medical Systems International (TMSI). The device records a four-channel EOG with a joint sampling rate of 128 Hz. The participant wore it on a belt around the waist as shown in Figure 6. The EOG data was collected using an array of five electrodes positioned around the right eye as shown in Figure 6. The electrodes used were the 24mm Ag/AgCl wet ARBO type from Tyco Healthcare equipped with an adhesive brim to stick them to the skin. The horizontal signal was collected using two electrodes on the edges of both eye sockets. The vertical signal was collected using one electrode above the eyebrow and another on the lower edge of the eye socket. The fifth electrode, the signal reference, was placed away from the other electrodes in the middle of the forehead. Eye movement data was saved together with body movement data on a netbook in the backpack worn by the participant.

We used two Exelia Art 2009 HIs from Phonak worn behind the left and the right ear. For the experiment we modified the HIs to use them for recording only the raw audio data rather than logging the classification output in real-time. With the raw audio data the HI behavior in the conducted experiment can be reconstructed offline. Using the same noise for overlay gives equal conditions for each participant to rule out different background noise as an effect on the resulting performance. Moreover, it is possible to simulate for different acoustic environments, e.g. by overlaying office noise. Another advantage of recording

---

[1] This work was carried out in collaboration with a hearing instrument company.

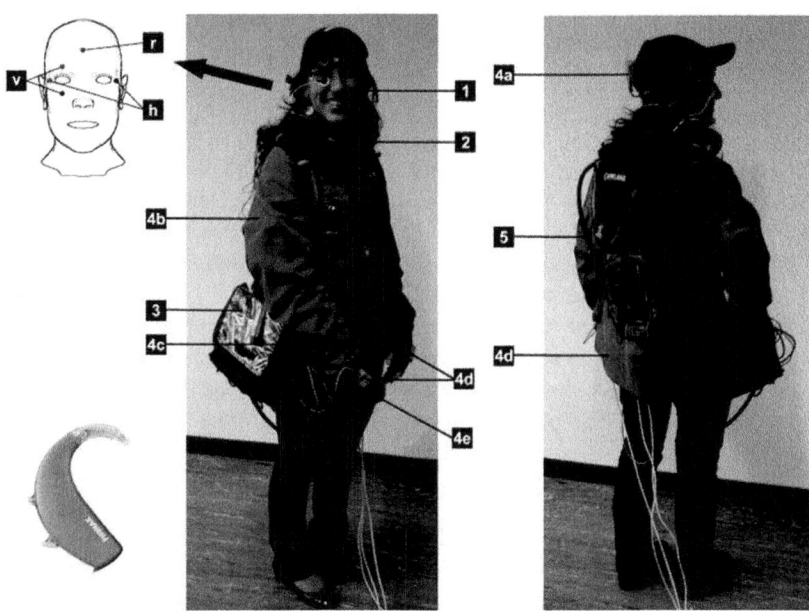

Fig. 6. Sensor setup consisting of HIs (1), a throat microphone (2), an audio recorder (3), five EOG electrodes (h: horizontal, v: vertical, r: reference), as well as the Xsens motion sensors placed on the head (4a), the upper (4b) and lower (4c) arms, the back of both hands (4d), the left leg (4e), two XBus Masters (4d), and the backpack for the netbook (5)

raw audio data is the possibility to simulate the behavior with future generation of HIs. We used a portable audio recorder from SoundDevices to capture audio data with 24 bit at 48 kHz. Although not used in this work, participants also wore a throat microphone recording a fifth audio channel with 8 bit at 8 kHz. Based on both sound recordings we investigate detection of active conversation based on own-speech detection in future research.

Data recording and synchronisation was handled using the Context Recognition Network (CRN) Toolbox [2]. We also videotaped the whole experiment to label and verify the synchronicity of the data streams.

5 Methods

5.1 Analysis of Body Movements

We extract features on a sliding window on the raw data streams from the 3-axis accelerometers, gyroscopes and magnetometers. For the magnetometer data we calculate mean, variance, mean crossing and zero crossing. For the gyroscope data we additionally extract the rate of peaks in the signal. For the accelerometers data we calculate the magnitude based on all three axes. Based on a parameter sweep we selected a window size of 3 seconds and a step size of 0.5 second for feature extraction.

5.2   Analysis of Eye Movements

EOG signals were first processed to remove baseline drift and noise that might hamper eye movement analysis. Afterwards, three different eye movement types were detected from the processed EOG signals: saccades, fixations, and blinks. All parameters of the saccade, fixation, and blink detection algorithms were fixed to values common to all participants. The eye movements returned by the detection algorithms were the basis for extracting different eye movement features using a sliding window. Based on a parameter sweep we set the window size to 10 seconds and the step size to 1 second (a more detailed description is outside the scope of this paper but can be found in [7]).

5.3   Feature Selection and Classification

The most relevant features extracted from body and eye movements were selected with the maximum relevance and minimum redundancy (mRMR) method [20]. Classification was done using a linear support vector machine (see [15] for the specific implementation we used). We set the penalty parameter to $C = 1$ and the tolerance of termination criterion to $\epsilon = 0.1$. Classification and feature selection were evaluated using a leave-one-participant-out cross-validation scheme. The resulting train and test sets were standardised to have zero mean and a standard deviation of one. Feature selection was performed solely on the training set.

5.4   Analysis of Sound

We used the classification output of commercial HIs as a baseline performance for sound based classification. We electrically fed the recorded audio stream described in section 4.3 back into HIs and obtained the selected hearing programs over time with a sampling rate of 10 Hz. To simulate a busy office situation we overlaid the recorded raw audio data with typical office background noise. In silent acoustic environments without noise, the hearing instrument remains mainly in the *Clean Speech* program for both the working and the conversation situation. We focus on the scenario with noise: The HI needs to decide wether optimizing for speech is adequate or not.

5.5   Data Fusion

To combine the unimodal information from the different motion sensors we used a fusion approach on feature-level. We built a feature vector comprising features from each of the sensors. To combine the multimodal information from body movement, eye movement, and sound we used majority voting as a standard fusion method on classifier-level. When there was no majority to make a decision we repeated the most recent decision. In this way, we suppress hearing program changes based on low confidence.

6   Results and Discussion

6.1   Analysis of the Different Modalities

We first evaluated the performance of the different modalities. Accuracies are given for the two-class classification problem comprising active conversation and working while colleagues are having a conversation. Figure 7 shows the accuracies for distinguishing the hearing needs using sound, body movements, eye movements, and combinations of these modalities averaged over all participants. The results for body movements are based on sensors attached to all nine body locations whereas the results for sound-based adaption are based on the classification output of the HIs.

The limited recognition accuracy of 77% for adaption based on sound is a consequence of the acoustic ambiguity problem that has been provoked in this scenario. The sound based analysis does not distinguish between relevant and irrelevant speech. The HI optimizes for speech in both of the cases described in section 4.1: When the participant is having a conversation and also when the colleagues are having a conversation.

As can be seen from Figure 7, recognition based on body movement data from all available movement sensors (placed at head, back, arms, hands, leg) achieves the best performance with an accuracy of 92%. Adaptation based on eye movement performs slightly worse with 86% accuracy. Looking at combinations of different modalities shows that the joint analysis of body and eye movements has an accuracy of 91%, sound and body movement results in 90% accuracy, and combination of sound and eye movements yields 85% accuracy. Complementing body movements with eye movements or sound results in a lower standard standard deviation, meaning more robustness across different users. First results suggest the inclusion of movement sensors additionally to sound into the HI.

6.2   Analysis of Body Locations

Based on these findings we selected body movements for further analysis. We investigated on which body locations the movement sensors provided the highest

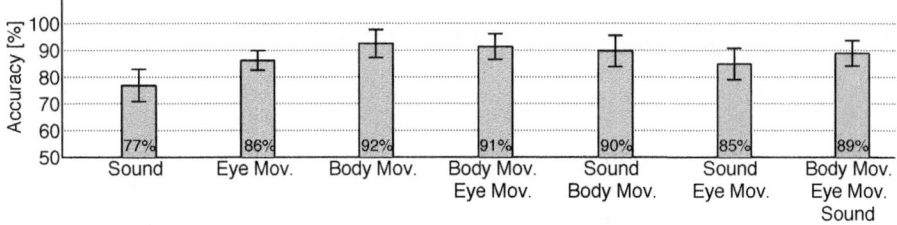

Fig. 7. Accuracies for distinguishing the hearing needs in our scenario based on sound, eye movements, body movements (placed at head, back, arms, hands, leg), and all possible combinations. Results are averaged over all participants with the standard deviation indicated with black lines.

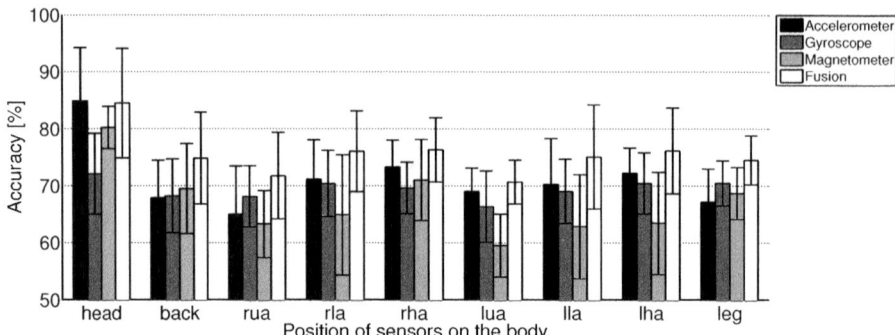

Fig. 8. Accuracies of adaption based on individual sensors (Accelerometer, Magnetometer, Gyroscope) for each of the 9 locations on the body: head, back, left upper arm (lua), left lower arm (lla), left hand (lha), right upper arm (rua), right lower arm (rla), right hand (rha), and leg. Results are averaged over all participants with the standard deviation indicated with black lines.

accuracies. Figure 8 provides the accuracies for adaption using individual sensors (Accelerometer, Magnetometer, Gyroscope) as well as using sensor fusion on feature level for each of the nine body locations averaged over all participants.

Figure 8 shows that from all individual body locations the sensor on the head yields the highest performance with accuracies between 72% for the gyroscope and 85% for the accelerometer. It is interesting to note that fusing the information derived from all three sensors types at the head does not further improve recognition performance (see first group of bars in Figure 8). For all other body location, sensor fusion consistently yields the best recognition performance. Single sensors placed on other body locations perform considerably worse with accuracies ranging from 59% (magnetometer on the left upper arm, lua) to 73% (accelerometer on the right hand, rha). These sensors may still prove beneficial if combined with other sensors located at other parts of the body. The higher utility of analyzing sensors on the right arm (rha, rla, rua) can be explained by the fact that all participants were right handed.

6.3 Further Analysis of the Head Location

As shown in the previous sections, the head is the most relevant individual body location. The sensors at this location are also the most promising with respect to a later implementation into a HI.

Figure 9 shows the accuracies for distinguishing the hearing needs based on sound, head movements, eye movements, and all possible combinations. As can be seen from Figure 9, from the three individual modalities, an accuracy of 86% was achieved using eye movements. Moreover, the standard deviation is lower than the one for head movements that yields an accuracy of 84%. From all individual modalities, eye movement analysis performs best. From all combinations

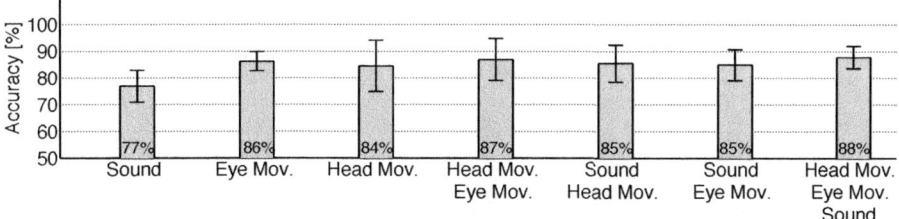

Fig. 9. Accuracies for distinguishing the hearing needs in our scenario based on sound, eye movements, head movements, and all possible combinations. Results are averaged over all participants with the standard deviation indicated with black lines.

of two modalities (bars 4–6 in Figure 9), joint analysis of head and eye movements perform with 87%. The combination of all three modalities yields the highest accuracy of 88%.

Adaption based on eye movements (86%) outperforms adaption based on head movements (84%). As described in section 5, eye movement analysis requires a three times larger data window size (10 seconds) than body movement analysis (3 seconds), leading to a larger classification latency. The joint analysis of body and eye movements combines the more long-term eye movement analysis, and more short-term body movements and yields an accuracy of (85%).

Taking into account movement from all body location corresponds to the idea of leveraging the HIBAN described in section 2. Sensing head and eye movements corresponds to the idea to eventually integrate all sensors into the HI. The HIBAN approach leads to higher than the stand-alone approach at the cost of additional locations on the body that have to be attached with a sensor. The two cases represent a trade-off between accuracy and required number of body locations attached with sensors. Hearing impaired can decide to take the burden of wearing additional sensors to benefit from better hearing comfort. Besides, smartphone and on-body sensors are more and more likely to be available. As shown, the system functions stand-alone with reduced performance.

6.4 Individual Results for Each Participant

To further investigate the large standard deviation for head movements we additionally analysed the individual recognition performance for each participant. Figure 10 shows the accuracy of choosing the correct program for adaption based on sound, head movements, eye movements, and their fusion on feature level for each individual participant. This analsyis reveals that for four participants eye movements performed best, for the remaining 7 participants head movements performed best. Eye movements provide more consistent high performances for all participants between 82% and 91%. Results for head movements were less consistent. In particular participant 9 and 10 showed reduced accuracies of 61% and 74%. A possible reason for this can be a displaced sensor, e.g. caused by the user adjusting the cap. For eye movements the variability is smaller in the given

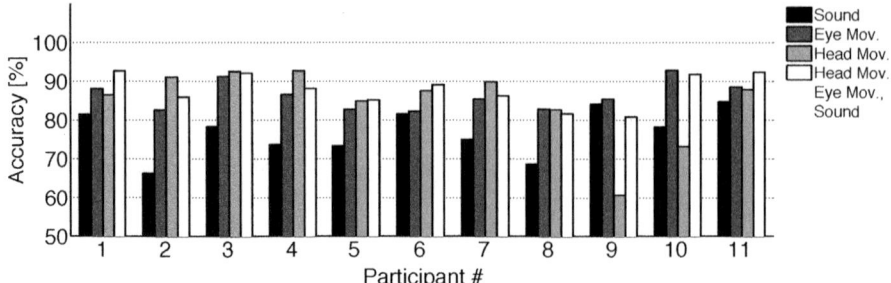

Fig. 10. Accuracy for adaption based on sound, head movements, eye movements and their combination, individually for each participant

data set. Sound adaption compares worse to body and eye movement adaption since this scenario intentionally contains acoustically ambiguous hearing needs.

6.5   Integrating Body and Eye Movement Sensing into a HI

The integration of additional sensor modalities is within reach of future HIs driven by the trend of HIBANs. HIs may in some cases be one of many deployed ambient assisted living technologies. Thus, wearable and textile integrated sensors, as well as the user's smart-phone may become part of the HIBAN. Future HIs can also take advantage of additional sensors that are already deployed for other purposes (e.g. motion sensing for fall detection). This reduces the user burden of utilizing multiple sensors while improving his auditive comfort.

Whenever HiBANs are not available, sensors could also be completely integrated into the HI itself to provide a stand-alone solution. Low power accelerometers with small footprints are available for integration into a HI. EOG is an inexpensive method for mobile eye movement recording. These characteristics are crucial for future integration of long-term eye movement data into future HIs in mobile daily life settings. EOG integration into a HI could follow integration achievements of EOG into glasses [7] or headphones [16].

6.6   Limitations

Although we significantly enhanced the distinction of two ambiguous auditory situations, our multimodal context recognition approach remains a proxy to infer what is essentially a subjective matter: the *subjective hearing need* of a person. Thus, even a perfect context recognition would not guarantee that the hearing need is detected correctly all the time. Ultimately, this would require capturing the user's auditory selective attention. Our evaluation is based on the recognition accuracy compared to the objective ground truth defined in the scenario. However, to assess the actual benefit experienced by the user, a more thorough user study with hearing impaired will need to be carried out.

We currently investigated a single ambiguous auditory situation. Nevertheless there are a large number of other ambiguous situations for current hearing instruments. Our objective is to identify the smallest subset of additional sensor modalities which can help to distinguish a wide range of currently challenging auditory situations. Thus, this work in an office scenario is an exemplary proof-of-concept approach. It still needs to be shown that the approach can be generalised and that one can resolve ambiguity in a sufficient number of other situations to justify the inclusion of additional sensor modalities within HIs.

The office scenario we chose may be a limitation. We chose a specific office work situation, but a variety of other office situations are thinkable, e.g. with more conversation partners and different activities. For this proof-of-concept study it was necessary to choose a trade-off between variety and control to collect data in a reproducible manner for multiple participants. After the experiment we went through a short questionnaire with each participant. The general feedback was, that the sensor equipment was found to be bulky, but overall the participants felt that they were not hindered to act natural.

Overlaying background noise as described in section 5.4 may be a limitation. We overlaid one typical office background noise. Many different kinds and intensities are thinkable. In some cases, the performance of the sound-based HI might be better. However, the performance based on body and eye movement is independent of the present sound. As a further potential limitation the participants may not act the same as they would if there is actual background noise.

6.7   Considerations for Future Work

There are a large number of other challenging situations that are faced by current HIs, e.g. listening to music from the car radio while driving, reading a book in a busy train, or conversing in a cafe with background music. This motivates the investigation of additional modalities, acoustic environments, and hearing situations in future work. A critical issue will be the trade-off in improving context awareness in HIs while minimising the burden caused by additional sensors. Possible additional sensor modalities are the user's current location, proximity information, or information from other HIs or the environment. Based on the promising results achieved in our proof-of-concept study, we plan to deploy our system in further real-life outdoor scenarios to study the benefit in everyday life experienced by the user.

7   Conclusion

Hearing instruments have emerged as true pervasive computers and are fully integrated into their user's daily life. In this work we have shown that multimodal fusion of information derived from body and eye movements is a promising approach to distinguish acoustic environments that are challenging for current hearing instruments. These results are particularly appealing as both modalities can potentially be miniaturised and integrated into future HIs.

Acknowledgments. This work was part funded by CTI project 10698.1 PFLS-LS "Context Recognition for Hearing Instruments Using Additional Sensor Modalities". The authors gratefully thank all participants of the experiment and the reviewers for their valuable comments.

References

1. Atallah, L., Aziz, O., Lo, B., Yang, G.Z.: Detecting walking gait impairment with an ear-worn sensor. In: International Workshop on Wearable and Implantable Body Sensor Networks, pp. 175–180 (2009)
2. Bannach, D., Amft, O., Lukowicz, P.: Rapid prototyping of activity recognition applications. IEEE Pervasive Computing 7, 22–31 (2008)
3. Biggins, A.: Benefits of wireless technology. Hearing Review (2009)
4. Büchler, M., Allegro, S., Launer, S., Dillier, N.: Sound Classification in Hearing Aids Inspired by Auditory Scene Analysis. EURASIP Journal on Applied Signal Processing 18, 2991–3002 (2005)
5. Bulling, A., Roggen, D., Tröster, G.: Wearable EOG goggles: Seamless sensing and context-awareness in everyday environments. Journal of Ambient Intelligence and Smart Environments 1(2), 157–171 (2009)
6. Bulling, A., Ward, J.A., Gellersen, H.: Multi-Modal Recognition of Reading Activity in Transit Using Body-Worn Sensors. ACM Transactions on Applied Perception (to appear, 2011)
7. Bulling, A., Ward, J.A., Gellersen, H., Tröster, G.: Eye Movement Analysis for Activity Recognition Using Electrooculography. IEEE Transactions on Pattern Analysis and Machine Intelligence 33(4), 741–753 (2011)
8. Choudhury, T., Pentland, A.: Sensing and modeling human networks using the sociometer. In: ISWC, p. 216. IEEE Computer Society, Washington, DC, USA (2003)
9. Hadar, U., Steiner, T.J., Clifford Rose, F.: Head movement during listening turns in conversation. Journal of Nonverbal Behavior 9(4), 214–228 (1985)
10. Hamacher, V., Chalupper, J., Eggers, J., Fischer, E., Kornagel, U., Puder, H., Rass, U.: Signal processing in high-end hearing aids: State of the art, challenges, and future trends. EURASIP Journal on Applied Signal Processing 18(2005), 2915–2929 (2005)
11. Hart, J., Onceanu, D., Sohn, C., Wightman, D., Vertegaal, R.: The attentive hearing aid: Eye selection of auditory sources for hearing impaired users. In: Gross, T., Gulliksen, J., Kotzé, P., Oestreicher, L., Palanque, P., Prates, R.O., Winckler, M. (eds.) INTERACT 2009. LNCS, vol. 5726, pp. 19–35. Springer, Heidelberg (2009)
12. Keidser, G.: Many factors are involved in optimizing environmentally adaptive hearing aids. The Hearing Journal 62(1), 26 (2009)
13. Kochkin, S.: MarkeTrak VIII: 25-year trends in the hearing health market. Hearing Review 16(11), 12–31 (2009)
14. Kochkin, S.: MarkeTrak VIII: Consumer satisfaction with hearing aids is slowly increasing. The Hearing Journal 63(1), 19 (2010)
15. Lin, C.J.: LIBLINEAR - a library for large linear classification (February 2008) http://www.csientuedutw/~cjlin/liblinear/
16. Manabe, H., Fukumoto, M.: Full-time wearable headphone-type gaze detector. In: Ext. Abstracts of the SIGCHI Conference on Human Factors in Computing Systems, pp. 1073–1078. ACM Press, New York (2006)

17. Molen, M., Somsen, R., Jennings, J.: Does the heart know what the ears hear? A heart rate analysis of auditory selective attention. Psychophysiology (1996)
18. Morency, L.P., Sidner, C., Lee, C., Darrell, T.: Contextual recognition of head gestures. In: ICMI 2005: Proceedings of the 7th International Conference on Multimodal Interfaces, pp. 18–24. ACM, New York (2005)
19. Naylor, G.: Modern hearing aids and future development trends, http://www.lifesci.sussex.ac.uk/home/Chris_Darwin/BSMS/Hearing%20Aids/Naylor.ppt
20. Peng, H., Long, F., Ding, C.: Feature selection based on mutual information: criteria of max-dependency, max-relevance, and min-redundancy. IEEE Transactions on Pattern Analysis and Machine Intelligence 27(8) (2005)
21. Schaub, A.: Digital Hearing Aids. Thieme Medical Pub. (2008)
22. Shargorodsky, J., Curhan, S., Curhan, G., Eavey, R.: Change in Prevalence of Hearing Loss in US Adolescents. JAMA 304(7), 772 (2010)
23. Shinn-Cunningham, B.: I want to party, but my hearing aids won't let me? Hearing Journal 62, 10–13 (2009)
24. Shinn-Cunningham, B., Best, V.: Selective attention in normal and impaired hearing. Trends in Amplification 12(4), 283 (2008)
25. Stiefmeier, T., Roggen, D., Ogris, G., Lukowicz, P., Tröster, G.: Wearable activity tracking in car manufacturing. IEEE Pervasive Computing 7(2), 42–50 (2008)
26. Tessendorf, B., Bulling, A., Roggen, D., Stiefmeier, T., Tröster, G., Feilner, M., Derleth, P.: Towards multi-modal context recognition for hearing instruments. In: Proc. of the International Symposium on Wearable Computers (ISWC) (2010)

Recognizing Whether Sensors Are on the Same Body

Cory Cornelius and David Kotz

Department of Computer Science, Dartmouth College, Hanover, NH, USA
Institute for Security, Technology, and Society, Dartmouth College, Hanover, NH, USA

Abstract. As personal health sensors become ubiquitous, we also expect them to become interoperable. That is, instead of closed, end-to-end personal health sensing systems, we envision standardized sensors wirelessly communicating their data to a device many people already carry today, the cellphone. In an open personal health sensing system, users will be able to seamlessly pair off-the-shelf sensors with their cellphone and expect the system to *just work*. However, this ubiquity of sensors creates the potential for users to accidentally wear sensors that are not necessarily paired with their own cellphone. A husband, for example, might mistakenly wear a heart-rate sensor that is actually paired with his wife's cellphone. As long as the heart-rate sensor is within communication range, the wife's cellphone will be receiving heart-rate data about her husband, data that is incorrectly entered into her own health record.

We provide a method to probabilistically detect this situation. Because accelerometers are relatively cheap and require little power, we imagine that the cellphone and each sensor will have a companion accelerometer embedded with the sensor itself. We extract standard features from these companion accelerometers, and use a pair-wise statistic – coherence, a measurement of how well two signals are related in the frequency domain – to determine how well features correlate for different locations on the body. We then use these feature coherences to train a classifier to recognize whether a pair of sensors – or a sensor and a cellphone – are on the same body. We evaluate our method over a dataset of several individuals walking around with sensors in various positions on their body and experimentally show that our method is capable of achieving an accuracies over 80%.

1   Introduction

Mobile sensing of the human body is becoming increasingly pervasive with the advent of personal devices capable of processing and storing large of amounts of data. Commercial devices like the FitBit [7] and BodyBugg [1] allow a person to collect nearly continuous data about his or her health. The FitBit, for example, allows a person to track one's own fitness and sleeping patterns by wearing an accelerometer on the waist.

Typically these devices are highly specialized, end-to-end solutions, but we imagine the sensors in these products becoming commodities and inter-operating with a device most people carry with them everyday: cellphones. A person could wear several sensors of varying types (e.g., blood pressure monitor, pulse oximeter, pedometer, blood glucose meter). Because of the physiological requirements, or comfort, these sensors will

K. Lyons, J. Hightower, and E.M. Huang (Eds.): Pervasive 2011, LNCS 6696, pp. 332–349, 2011.

necessarily be attached at different locations on the body. We imagine these sensors wirelessly communicating with a person's cellphone, which would store and aggregate all data coming from the sensors. In fact, this scenario is feasible today, and there are purchasable medical and fitness sensors capable of communicating to cellphones via Bluetooth.

There are many security issues, not to mention privacy issues, with this scheme. How does the cellphone authenticate valid sensors? How do sensors discover the presence of the cellphone, without exposing their own presence? How does the user pair sensors with the cellphone? What types of encryption are employed to maintain confidentiality and integrity? How do we balance privacy and usability? We focus our attention on one specific challenge: how can we verify that a suite of sensors are attached to the same person?

Suppose Alice and Fred, a health-conscious couple living together, each decide to buy a fitness-monitoring sensor. The instructions indicate that each should "pair" their respective sensor with their own cellphone. *Pairing* ensures, through cryptographic means, that a sensor is only able to communicate with a specific cellphone. One day, when Alice and Fred go for a run, Alice unknowingly wears Fred's sensor, and Fred wears Alice's sensor. As they run, thereby remaining in communication range, Fred's cellphone will be collecting data about Alice, but labeling the data as Fred's and placing it in Fred's health record, and vice versa. This problem, a result of the one-to-one pairing model, is even more likely as the number of sensors grows. The implicit assumption when pairing is that the sensors paired with a cellphone will not be used by anyone else but the user of the cellphone.

Our goal is to make life easier for people like Alice and Fred. Although Alice and Fred buy identical sensor devices, Alice should be able to strap on either device and have her cellphone recognize which device is attached *to her*, automatically creating the phone-device association without an explicit pairing step. Similarly, if Alice and Fred jointly own another sensor device, either may use the sensor at any time, and again the correct cellphone should detect which body is wearing the sensor and receive the data into the correct person's health record.

To achieve this vision requires two core problems to be solved. First, Alice's phone must be able to determine which sensors are attached to Alice's body, ignoring sensors that may be in radio range but not attached to Alice. Second, the phone and sensor devices must be able to agree on a shared encryption key, to secure their communications; ideally, this should require no user assistance and be more secure than in most "pairing" methods today. In this paper we specifically address the first challenge, leaving the second challenge to future work. There are existing solutions that address the second challenge, but it is unclear if those solutions can be applied for accelerometers that are not intentionally shaken together [13].

To address the first challenge, the sensor device must somehow attest (to the cellphone) which body is wearing the sensor at the current time. Ideally, the phone would analyze the data coming from the sensors to see whether it identifies the wearer by some biometric measure. However, not all types of sensors, or sensor locations, produce data that is suitable for biometric identity verification. Thus we propose the following compromise: every sensor device will include an accelerometer sensor in addition to its primary sensor (ECG, blood pressure, etc.). Accelerometers are cheap, so this is a relatively inexpensive addition; instead of biometric identity verification with a wide variety of sensor data, sensor placement, and usage conditions, we only need to find correlations for the accelerometer data that answers the question: are the devices in a given set all attached to the same body?

We recently [6] formalized this problem as the "one-body authentication problem," which asks: how can one ensure that the wireless sensors in a wireless body area network are collecting data about one individual and not several individuals? We identified two variants of this problem. The *strong* version of this problem requires identifying which person the sensors are attached to, whereas the *weak* version of this problem simply requires determining whether the sensors are on the same body. We noted how existing solutions do not necessarily solve the problem and called for further research. Thus, we now aim to provide a solution to the weak one-body authentication problem; given such as solution, one might solve the strong-body problem for one of the sensors in a set, and be able to extrapolate the verification to all of the sensors on the body.

Our paper is organized as follows. In the next section we describe our model. In the third section we briefly describe our approach and hypothesis as to why we believe our approach will work. In the fourth section we describe, in detail, our method. In the fifth section we describe the data we collected as well as our collection method. In the sixth section we evaluate our method. In the final sections, we discuss related work and distinguish our work from earlier approaches, and provide some discussion about our method's limitations and about some potential future work.

2   Model

We imagine a world where personal health sensors are ubiquitous and wirelessly connect to a user's cellphone. Thus, there are two principle components in our system:

- One **mobile node** (e.g., the user's cellphone) per user.
- Many **sensor nodes** (e.g., blood glucose, pedometer, electrocardiography).

We assume that mobile nodes communicate wirelessly with sensor nodes. Sensor nodes are also capable of communicating wirelessly with mobile nodes but have limited computational resources relative to the mobile nodes. Additionally, sensor nodes have the ability to detect when they are attached to a user (although they will not know to whom). The sensor node might contain a circuit that is completed, for example, when the user straps a sensor node onto their body and the two ends of a necklace or wrist-strap come into contact. Finally, we also assume each sensor node, and the mobile node, has an accompanying triaxial accelerometer of the same type (so that their readings may be directly compared). Since accelerometers are tiny, cheap, and require little energy to operate, this is a reasonable assumption[1].

---

[1] The Freescale MMA845xQ line of accelerometers, for example, cost $0.95 (in quantities of 100K) and consume "1.8 microamps in standby mode and as low as 6 microamps in active mode" [8].

2.1 Binding

"Binding" occurs when a user wishes to use a sensor node. The following happens:

1. The user straps the sensor node to their body, thereby turning it on.
2. The sensor node detects that it was applied, and broadcasts its presence.
3. The mobile node receives the broadcast, thereby binding it with the sensor node, and labels that sensor node as unauthenticated.

Binding is like pairing, but without the need for user intervention. In a pairing scenario, the user is usually required to enter a shared key on one of the devices. Binding does not have this requirement. When a sensor node is bound to a mobile node, the sensor node enters an unauthenticated state.

2.2 Authentication

"Authentication" is a process, initiated by the mobile node, for verifying which of the mobile node's bound sensor nodes are on the same body. Once a sensor node is authenticated, the mobile node will record sensor data from that node; until then, the data will be ignored. (As it may take some time for authentication to succeed, in some implementations the mobile node may buffer the incoming data received between the moment of binding and the moment of authentication, recording the data only once authentication is assured. This "retroactive authentication" of the early data is feasible because of our assumption that a sensor node can detect its own attachment and removal; if a sensor node is moved from one body to another before it was authenticated on the first body, the unbinding and rebinding events will clear the buffer on the first body's mobile node).

To achieve authentication, our protocol requires an algorithm that is able to decide whether two streams of data are originating from sensor nodes on the same body. That is, given a stream of accelerometer data from a sensor node, the algorithm examines the correlation between a sensor node's data stream and the mobile node's data stream, with the requirement that the two streams should correlate well only when both the mobile node and the sensor node are on the same body. The algorithm should return true if and only if the two data streams are well correlated and false otherwise. We present the details of our algorithm in Section 4.

Procedure 1 provides an overview of the process for the mobile node to authenticate sensor nodes. Because our method depends on recognizable acceleration events, our algorithm performs authentication only when the user is walking. The mobile node records acceleration data using its internal accelerometer for t seconds. Simultaneously, it asks the other sensor node to send it acceleration data for the same duration. The duration required depends on the level of confidence desired; a shorter duration may lead to more incorrect results (false positives and false negatives), but a longer duration makes the approach less responsive after the person first puts on the sensor. It then runs our algorithm, called AreCorrelated, to determine whether its internal acceleration data correlates with the sensor node's acceleration data. Only when the accelerometer data correlates well does the mobile node begin to record that sensor node's other sensor data (e.g., electrocardiography data).

Procedure 1. Authenticating sensor nodes, from the mobile node's perspective

Notation:
B: set of bound sensor nodes, initially empty
A_i: acceleration data from sensor node i, where $i = 0$ is the mobile node's acceleration data.
$\mathsf{Record}(t)$: read mobile node's accelerometer for t seconds
$\mathsf{Recv}(b, t)$: read sensor node b's accelerometer for t seconds
$\mathsf{AreCorrelated}(x, y)$: determine whether acceleration data x and y

---

1: **while** { true } **do**
2:     **if** $b := \mathsf{NewSensorNodeDetected}()$ **then**
3:         $B := B \cup b$
4:         { Mark sensor node b as unauthenticated }
5:     **end if**
6:     **for** $b \in B$ **do**
7:         **if** $\mathsf{Disconnected}(b)$ **or** $\mathsf{Timeout}(b)$ **then**
8:             $B := B \setminus b$
9:         **else if** $d := \mathsf{RecvData}(b)$ **and** $\mathsf{IsAuthenticated}(b)$ **then**
10:             $\mathsf{RecordData}(b, d)$ { Save b's data d in our health record }
11:         **end if**
12:     **end for**
13:     **if** $\mathsf{UserIsWalking}()$ **then**
14:         **for** $b \,|\, b \in B$ **and not** $\mathsf{IsAuthenticated}(b)$ **do**
15:             { The next two lines are accomplished in parallel }
16:             $A_0 := \mathsf{Record}(t)$
17:             $A_b := \mathsf{Recv}(b, t)$
18:             **if** $\mathsf{AreCorrelated}(A_0, A_b) = \text{true}$ **then**
19:                 { Mark sensor node b as authenticated }
20:                 { Tell sensor node b to send sensor data }
21:             **end if**
22:         **end for**
23:     **end if**
24: **end while**

2.3 Unbinding

Unbinding occurs when a user removes a sensor node. In the ideal case, the following happens:

1. The user unstraps the sensor node from their body.
2. The sensor node detects that it was removed and notifies the bound mobile node of this fact.
3. The mobile node acknowledges this notification, thereby unbinding it with the sensor node.
4. Upon receipt of this acknowledgement (or upon timeout), the sensor node turns off.

A sensor node may lose power or go out of range of the mobile node, during this process or prior to the user unstrapping the sensor node. Thus, the mobile node periodically pings each sensor node (not shown in Procedure 1); if the sensor node does not reply (after some timeout period), the sensor node is likely not on the same body, and the mobile node treats it as unauthenticated and unbound.

3   Approach

Our goal is to determine whether a sensor node is on the same body as a mobile node receiving the sensor node's data. That is, we provide a solution for the weak one-body authentication problem. Our solution could be used as the first step in a strong one-body authentication solution by first verifying that all the sensors are on the same body, then using some subset of the sensors to provide strong one-body authentication (i.e., via some biometric one of the sensors could determine) to all the sensors on the body. To maximize the generality of our solution, we require each sensor to have an accompanying accelerometer.

Our intuition is that if sensors are on the same body, then (at a coarse level) all of the sensors' accelerometers experience similar accelerations. If a user is seated, or lying down, then there is not much information we can extract from the accelerometer data to make the determination that a suite of sensors are on the same body. There are a variety of activities that cause bodily acceleration, but we focus on walking. When walking, a human body is largely rigid in the vertical direction. Although our limbs do bend, we hypothesize that the vertical acceleration (i.e., the acceleration relative to gravity) experienced by sensors placed anywhere on a walking body should correlate well. As one foot falls, that side of the body experiences a downward acceleration due to gravity, followed by an abrupt deceleration when the foot contacts the ground. Sensors on one side of the body should experience a similar vertical acceleration, while sensors on the other side of the body will experience the opposite. We should expect positive correlation for one side of the body, and an inverse correlation on the other side. Of course, this observation is complicated by the fact that it is difficult to extract the vertical acceleration component without knowing the orientation of the sensor. Furthermore, although the signal can be very noisy, the accelerations due to walking are likely to dominate the accelerations due to intra-body motion (such as arm swings or head turns) and we should be able to reliably make a determination that the supposed suite of sensors are on the same body.

Fortunately, there is already an existing body of work that shows how to do activity recognition given user-annotated data [2], and even on a mobile phone class device [4]; these techniques are particularly good at detecting when a user is walking. Our approach, therefore, is to detect periods when a user is walking by monitoring the accelerometer data periodically; when the data indicates the user is walking, we use Procedure 1 to collect accelerometer data from the sensors. (In Section 8 we discuss users who cannot walk).

Lester et al. [11] provide a solution the one-body authentication problem, but only for sensors that are carried in the same location on the body. They also propose using accelerometers attached to each sensor and measure the *coherence* of the accelerometer data. "Coherence measures the extent to which two signals are linearly related at each frequency, with 1 indicating that two signals are highly correlated at a given frequency and 0 indicating that two signals are uncorrelated at that frequency" [11]. By looking

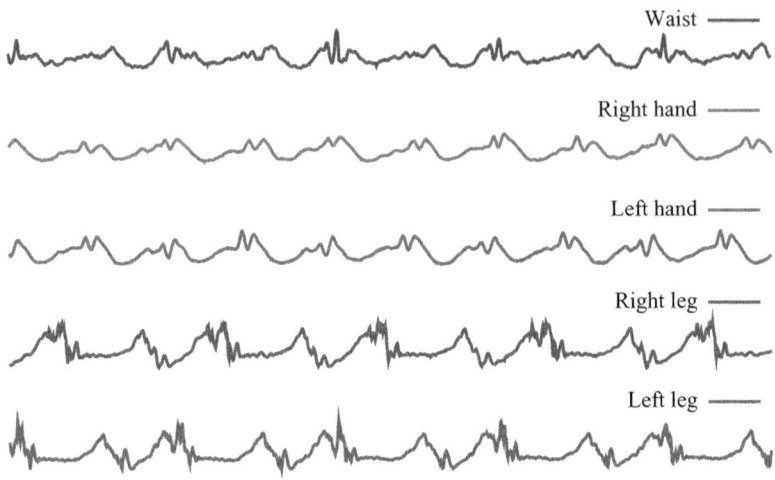

Fig. 1. Five seconds of magnitude data for each position on the body for one user

at the coherence at the 1-10Hz frequencies (the frequency range of human motion), they can experimentally determine a threshold (e.g., coherence > 0.9) at which it is appropriate to deem two sensors as located on the same body.

We extend Lester et al. [11] to sensors carried at different locations on the body – wrist, ankle, and waist – by using features often used for activity recognition. We then extract the pairwise *coherence* of features for the sensors on the same body. Given these coherences, we can train a classifier and use it to determine whether the alleged set of sensors are on the same body. We train our classifier to be as general as possible by using data collected from several individuals; the same model can then be used by all users for all sensor devices. We describe our method in more detail in the following section.

4   Method

As stated previously, we assume each sensor node has an accompanying accelerometer; our method uses only the accelerometer data. Specifically, consider a signal s sampled at some frequency such that:

$$s = \{(x_0, y_0, z_0), (x_1, y_1, z_1), \ldots\}$$

where x_i, y_i, and z_i are the three axes of the instantaneous acceleration, relative to gravity, at time i.

Because sensors might be mounted in different orientations, or might be worn in different orientations each time they are worn, we discount orientation by using the *magnitude* of the acceleration. Figure 3 shows that the magnitude exposes the overall walking motion well. Thus, we compute the magnitude of all three axes for all samples in s:

$$m_i = \sqrt{x_i^2 + y_i^2 + z_i^2}$$

This gives us the rate of change of speed over time for that particular sensor node.

4.1 Feature Computation

We partition this orientation-ignored signal $\{m_0, \ldots, \}$ into non-overlapping windows of length w. For each window j, comprising $\{m_{jw}, \ldots, m_{jw+w}\}$, we extract seven common features (mean, standard deviation, variance, mean absolute deviation, inter-quartile range, power, energy); collectively, these seven values form the *feature vector* $F_j = (f_j^1, f_j^2, \ldots, f_j^7)$.

We chose these features primarily because others [12, 14] have used these features successfully to detect physical activities, and we hypothesize they would similarly be useful for our problem. If they can capture the physical activity of walking and we examine the correlation of these features, we should expect them to correlate if and only if they are attached the same body.

4.2 Coherence

Coherence is a measure of how well two signals correlate in the frequency domain. More precisely, it is the cross-spectral density of two signals divided by the auto-spectral density of each individual signal. Like Lester et al. [11], we approximate coherence by using the magnitude-squared coherence:

$$C_{xy}(\phi) = \frac{|S_{xy}(\phi)|^2}{S_{xx}(\phi)S_{yy}(\phi)}$$

In the above, x and y are the signals, S_{xy} is the cross-spectral density between signals x and y, S_{xx} is the auto-spectral density of signal x, and ϕ is the desired frequency. Cross-spectral density is calculated by the Fourier transform of the cross-correlation function. If x and y are well correlated at some frequency ϕ, then $C_{xy}(\phi)$ should be close to 1.

To get a final measure, we compute the normalized magnitude-squared coherence up to some frequency $\phi_{\max}$:

$$N(x, y) = \frac{1}{\phi_{\max}} \int_0^{\phi_{\max}} C_{xy}(\phi) d\phi$$

We chose $\phi_{\max} = 10$ because, as Lester et al. notes, "human motion rests below the 10Hz range" [11].

In addition, to compute the cross-spectral density over different frequencies, it is necessary to window the signals x and y. We choose a Hamming window of length equal to one-half of the size of the signals with no overlap.

4.3 Feature Coherence

Given two sets of feature matrices $A = (F_1, F_2, \ldots)$ and $B = (F_1, F_2, \ldots)$ with entries F_j as described above, we want to determine how well A and B are correlated. Here, A and B represent the *feature matrices* extracted from the accelerometer data of the mobile node and sensor node respectively.

We apply coherence to the feature matrices in the following manner. For some window length c (the feature coherence window), we compute the normalized coherence of A and B as such:

$$N_k^{AB} = \left\{ N(A_{k...k+c}^1, B_{k...k+c}^1), N(A_{k...k+c}^2, B_{k...k+c}^2), \ldots, N(A_{k...k+c}^7, B_{k...k+c}^7) \right\}$$

where $A_{k...k+c}^1 = \{ f_n^1 \in A : k \le n < k + c \}$, the window of a specific feature of A. That is, we take each feature (i.e., a column of the matrix) of A and the corresponding feature of B, and compute the normalized coherence using c samples (i.e., the rows of the matrix). At this stage, we are left with a matrix of normalized coherences for each feature and window k.

Because we want to capture how the two signals are related over time, the coherence window c should be sufficiently large to capture periodicities in the features. Because the typical walk cycle is on the order of seconds, it is advisable to chose a coherence window on the order of several seconds.

4.4   Supervised Learning and Classification

To account for the many positions a sensor node might be placed on the body, we collect data from several locations. In our method, we compare the mobile node's accelerometer data to each other sensor node's accelerometer data. That is, the mobile node acts as a reference accelerometer, to which every other sensor node must correlate using the method described above. For a given set of locations and one reference location, we compute the feature coherence of each location (i.e., A in the above) relative to the reference location (i.e., B in the above). In our experiments, we compute the coherence of the right wrist and waist; left wrist and waist; left ankle and waist; and right ankle and waist. When we do this for one user, this yields feature coherences of the sensor on the same body, and we can label them as such. To yield feature coherences of sensors on different bodies, we take pairs of users and mix their locations. For example, at the waist and left hand there are two possible ways to mix up the sensors: Alice's waist and Fred's left hand, Fred's waist and Alice's left hand. By mixing locations for any pair of users, it is possible to compute an equal number of feature coherences that are and are not on the same body, labeling them as such.

Given a set of feature coherences and their respective labels, we can train a classifier to learn a model that is the coherence threshold for each feature. We employ support vector machines (SVMs) for this task since, once trained, they are good at predicting which label a given feature coherence is associated with. An SVM accomplishes this task by finding the hyperplane with the largest separation between the set of training feature coherences that are on the same body, and those that are not on the same body. In our experiments, we trained a support vector machine with a radial basis kernel using LIBSVM [5].

Given a trained SVM, we can use it to classify whether a given feature coherence is on the same body. That is, at the window the feature coherence was computed, the support vector machine can determine if the sensor node is on the same body as the mobile node. The SVM does so by determining on which side of the hyperplane the test feature coherence lies.

User	Walking Time (minutes:seconds)	Magnitude Samples	Feature Vectors
1	18:45	288017	9000
2	29:57	460047	14375
3	21:02	322962	10092
4	19:30	299553	9361
5	20:24	313215	9787
6	28:33	438484	13701
7	19:01	291974	9123

Fig. 2. Time spent walking, total acceleration samples, and number of features extracted for each user

4.5 Classification Smoothing

The classification method described above makes an instantaneous classification of a feature coherence for that particular coherence window. It is, however, possible to boost the classification rates by examining a window of classifications over time. For example, if over the course of three classifications, two classifications positive and the third classification is negative, we can use a simple voting scheme to smooth over these misclassifications. In the example, because the majority of the classifications are classified as on the same body, we assume the sensor node is on the same body for that classification window. We can empirically determine the best window by varying the window and choosing the one that yields the best classification rates.

5 Dataset

We collected a set of accelerometer data, from several test subjects wearing sensors in several locations on their body, to use as training data (for the model) and to use as test data for (for our evaluation). We used WiTilt (version 2.5) accelerometers [15]. We followed the user with a laptop as they walked around a flat, predetermined course. The laptop was used to synchronize the accelerometer readings sent via Bluetooth by the WiTilt nodes.

We collected 2.5 hours of acceleration from 5 accelerometers sampled at 255Hz from seven users for a total of 13 hours of acceleration data. The average user walked for 22 minutes while wearing 5 accelerometers (waist, left wrist, right wrist, left ankle, right ankle). We chose the waist (specifically, the right pocket), because it represents a common location for the mobile node (cellphone). Of the likely locations for medical sensors (arms, legs, chest, head) we chose the wrists and ankles for our experiments because (as extremities) we expect they would raise the most difficult challenge for our method. Figure 2 gives more detailed information about how much data was collected for each user.

6 Evaluation

We evaluate how well our method performed for each location, at the wrists only, at the ankles only, on the left side of the body, on the right side of the body, and at all locations.

For each experiment we used only the data from that location, or type of location, for training and for evaluation; for example, in the "left leg" case we train on (and test on) the accelerometer data from the left ankle in comparison to the data from the waist. In neither the learning process nor in the operation of our system was the data labeled as to which location produced the acceleration data. We varied the coherence window size from 2 to 16 seconds.

Using these datasets, we performed two types of cross-validations to evaluate the accuracy of our method. The first cross-validation we performed was a simple 10-fold cross-validation. A *k-fold cross-validation* partitions the dataset into k partitions, trains the classifier over $k - 1$ of the partitions (the training set) and classifies the remaining partition (the testing set), repeating this procedure for each partition. This type of cross-validation will tell us how well our classifier generally performs since it will classify every sample in the dataset. The second cross-validation we performed is a variant of leave-one-out cross-validation we call leave-one-user-out cross-validation. A *leave-one-user-out cross-validation* leaves an entire user's data out as the testing set and trains the classifier using the remaining data. We then test the classifier using the left-out user's data, repeating this procedure for each user. This type of cross-validation will tell us how general our classifier is. Ideally our classifier would not be user-specific, and would perform well in the case of a never-before-seen user.

We define a *true feature coherence* as a feature coherence computed from a sensor node and mobile node on the same body, and a *false feature coherence* as a feature coherence computed from a sensor node and mobile node *not* on the same body. A *positive classification* means the classifier determined that the given feature coherence indicates the sensor node and mobile node were on the same body, while a *negative classification* means the classifier determined that the given feature coherence indicates the sensor node and mobile node were *not* be on the same body. It follows, then, that a *true positive* occurs when a true feature coherence is classified as positive, and a *true negative* occurs when a false feature coherence is classified as a negative. A *false positive* occurs when a false feature coherence is classified as positive, and a *false negative* occurs when a true feature coherence is classified as negative.

We present the accuracy, precision and recall for each possible scenario. *Accuracy* is the sum of true positives and true negatives over the total number of classifications. Accuracy tells us how well our classifier is doing at classifying feature coherences. *Precision* is the number of true positives over the total number of positive classifications. Precision tells us how well our classifier is able to discriminate between true and false positives. *Recall* is the number of true positives over the sum of true positives and false negatives. Recall tells us how well our classifier classifies true features coherences.

In all of our experiments, we chose a feature window size of 17 acceleration magnitudes with no overlap so that each second may be divided evenly and thus yield 15 features per second. We present results using our dataset for both our method and the method used in Lester et al. [11] for sake of comparison.

6.1   Our Method

We ran a 10-fold cross-validation using the data from all users and for each specified location, resulting in Figures 3(a), 3(b), and 3(c). The results show how the choice of coherence window size affects the accuracy, precision and recall. A smaller window is more desirable because the coherence window size is directly proportional to the window of accelerometer data that needs to be transmitted to the mobile node, and wireless communication is typically expensive. However, a smaller window will not capture the periodicity of walking. According to Figure 3(a), a 4–6 second coherence window, or about 60–90 feature values, performed the best and minimized the communication overhead. In such cases our method was about 70–85% accurate.

In general, as the coherence window length increases the accuracy briefly climbs then settles down, precision increases steadily, and recall drops significantly. Given a longer coherence window length, this means the classifier is more likely to make negative classifications rather than positive ones. Since a longer coherence window means more walking cycles are taken into account, it also means there is more opportunity for the signals to differ due to accumulated noise and/or a change in walking style in accordance with the environment.

These plots show that the method was more accurate for the legs than for the hands, which is not surprising because the legs have more consistent motion behavior during walking than do the hands, particularly across users. The right leg (or left hand) seemed to do better than the left leg (or right hand, respectively), perhaps because the waist accelerometer was always carried in the right pocket, and most people swing their hands in opposition to their legs. When the hands and legs were combined, as in the left-body and right-body cases, this effect was cancelled out and the results of both were fairly similar to the all-body case.

In Figure 3(d), we ran a leave-one-user-out cross-validation for each user with a fixed coherence window of 6 seconds. The accuracy, precision, and recall for all users are nearly identical, thus providing some evidence that our trained model is not specific to any user, and can in fact be used to predict a never-before-seen user.

6.2 Lester et al. Method

For comparison's sake, we implemented the method described in Lester et al. [11], after extending it to use a support vector machine for determining the threshold instead of choosing an arbitrary threshold. Figure 4 shows that for any of the given locations, their method has poor classification rates, little better than random guess (0.50).

Lester et al. [11] do present results for "devices at other locations on the body, including accelerometers on the wrist, placed in one or both pockets, in a backpack, and in a fanny pack." These placements, however, are in the same relative location and therefore not comparable. Furthermore, we evaluated the scheme over longer time intervals, and averaged the results for a specified window.

6.3 Classification Smoothing

We now return to the leave-one-user-out experiments, as they most closely model how the method would be used in practice. In these experiments, for each user left out (the testing set), we used the model trained on all other users' data to predict the testing set. Now, instead of instantaneous prediction, we use a simple majority vote to smooth over classifications and plot how well this smoothing performed for a given window size of classifications.

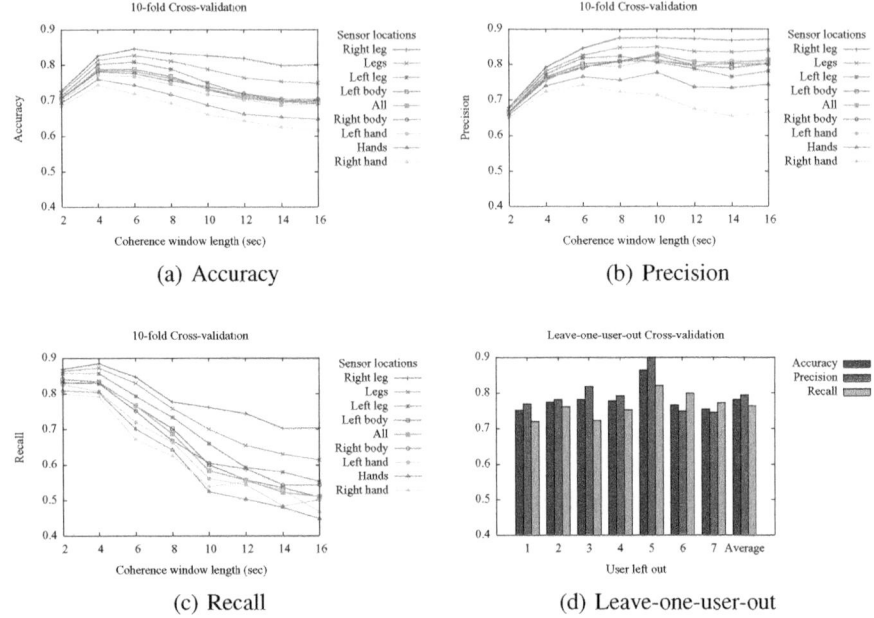

Fig. 3. Evaluation of our method. Subfigures (a), (b), and (c) were computed from a 10-fold cross-validation of all users at the specified locations and coherence windows. Subfigure (d) was computed from a leave-one-user-out cross-validation for each user with a coherence window of 6 seconds.

Figure 5 shows the average accuracy, precision, and recall over all users for varying classification windows with a fixed coherence window of 6 seconds. Our method, Figure 5(a), benefits slightly from classification smoothing as does Lester et al.'s method, Figure 5(b). This result tells us that our method makes sporadic mis-classifications that can be reduced with smoothing. Like any smoothing scheme, one must strike a balance between the size of a smoothing window and the desired classification rates. For our method, a 42 second smoothing window, or 7 feature coherences, modestly boosts our instantaneous classification rates by 8%.

7   Related Work

Mayrhofer et al. [13] provide a solution to exchange a cryptographic key between two devices by manually shaking the two devices together. They use the method described in Lester et al. [11] to determine whether two devices are being shaken together. But, as they notice, coherence "does not lend itself to directly creating cryptographic key material out of its results" [13]. To extract key material they extract quantized FFT coefficients from the accelerometer data to use as entropy for generating a key. Our problem is more difficult because the accelerometers are not being shaken together but are attached to a body and will therefore experience less-correlated accelerations.

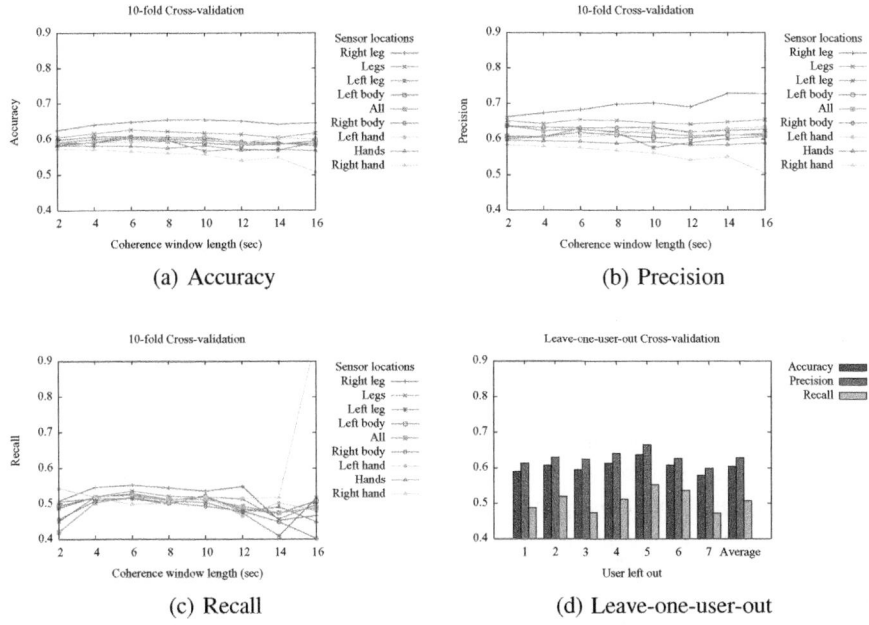

(a) Accuracy

(b) Precision

(c) Recall

(d) Leave-one-user-out

Fig. 4. Evaluation of Lester et al. method. Subfigures (a), (b), and (c) were computed from a 10-fold cross-validation over all users at the specified locations and coherence window lengths. Subfigure (d) was computed from a leave-one-user-out cross-validation for each user with a co-herence window of 6 seconds.

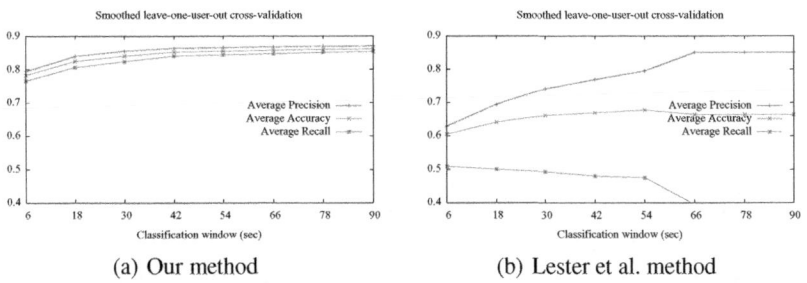

(a) Our method

(b) Lester et al. method

Fig. 5. Average accuracy, precision and recall over all users for different classification windows with a fixed coherence window of 6 seconds

Kunze et al. [10] provide a method for determining where on a body a particular sensor is located. They detect when a user is walking regardless of the location of a sensor, and by training a classifiers on a variety of features (RMS, frequency range power, frequency entropy, and the sum of the power of detail signals at different levels) on different positions on the body they can use the classifier to determine where on the body the sensor is located. We seek to provide a method that determines whether a suite of sensors is located on the same body without having to use multiple classifiers for different body locations. It might be the case that knowing the location of a sensor node could boost our classification rates, but we leave that for future work.

Kunze et al. [9] provide similar methods to account for sensor displacement on a particular body part. This problem is difficult primarily because "acceleration due to rotation is sensitive to sensor displacement within a single body part" [9]. To alleviate this problem, the authors observe that "combining a gyroscope with an accelerometer and having the accelerometer ignore all signal frames dominated by rotation can remove placement sensitivity while retaining most of the relevant information" [9]. We choose to limit our approach to accelerometers; although the inclusion of a gyroscope might increase accuracy, it would also increase the size, cost, and energy consumption on each sensor device.

Sriram et al. [16] provide a method to authenticate patients using electrocardiography and acceleration data for remote health monitoring. While electrocardiography has proven to be useful for authentication, they observe that these methods do not perform well in the real world because physical activity perturbs the electrocardiography data. By employing an accelerometer to differentiate physical activities, they can use electrocardiography data from those physical activities to authenticate patients. We both make the observation that "the monitoring system needs to make sure that the data is coming from the *right person* before any medical or financial decisions are made based on the data" [16] (emphasis ours). Our work is complementary since it is necessary to establish that accelerometer is on the same body as the sensor used to collect electrocardiography data. Their method extracts 50 features from the electrocardiography and accelerometer data and uses these features to train two types of classifiers, k-Nearest Neighbor and a Bayesian Network, whose output can be used for identification and verification. We follow a similar procedure except that we work exclusively with accelerometer data, again, to reduce the complexity and cost of the solution. We also look at the correlation between sensors, whereas they assume there is a prior profile of the patient's combined electrocardiography and accelerometer data.

8   Discussion and Future Work

There are a variety of existing technologies one could imagine using to solve the weak one-body authentication problem. For example, one could employ a wireless localization technique to ensure the sensors nodes are within some bodily distance. The body, however, might block all or some of the wireless signal thereby limiting localization, nor is it clear how these kind of techniques would provide confidence to a physician that the data is coming from one body. Similarly, one can trivially use a form of body-coupled communication [3], but the security properties these type of communication mediums provide are not well understood. If two users were to hold hands, for example, would they be considered one body?

When two people are walking together, it is a common natural phenomenon for two walkers to synchronize their walking patterns. It is unclear whether our method will be fooled by such a situation, mis-classifying Alice's and Fred's sensor devices as being on the wrong body. The first dataset we captured to test this method actually employed one user trying to mimic the gait of another user, and our first results showed our algorithm not being fooled by this. This case, however, requires exploration in a larger dataset.

Our method relies on the assumption that a user is capable of walking, which may not be true for some users. It remains as future work to determine whether we can extend the method for a person who is confined to a wheelchair, for example. Even for a user who is able to walk, there may be an extended period of time after binding a sensor node and before the user walks. It may be necessary for the mobile node to alert the user that they should walk around so that authentication can be performed. As future work, we may explore other acceleration events; for example, to ask the user for clap their hands, or perform some unique movement.

Ideally the algorithm should be tuned to produce more false negatives (i.e., the algorithm determined the sensor nodes to be on different bodies when they really were on the same body) than false positives (i.e., the algorithm determined the sensor nodes to be on the same body when they were actually not) because the consequences of a false positive (recording the wrong person's data in someone's health record) are more severe than the consequences of a false negative (losing data). It may be possible to 'bias' the SVM toward false negatives by adding a margin to its hyperplane-testing function.

Although we do not discuss encryption mechanisms, ensuring data confidentiality is paramount in any health-related scenario. If one were to optimize the authentication phase by simultaneously authenticating all bound sensor nodes, it might be necessary to encrypt the acceleration data to avoid replay attacks (in which the adversary replays one node's acceleration data in hopes that its rogue sensor node will be authenticated as being on the same body as the victim). Even if such an attack is discounted, the accelerometer data itself might be privacy sensitive because accelerometer data may be used to recognize a victim's activity. Some activities are clearly privacy sensitive, and some of those sensitive activities might be detected from accelerometer data alone.

In a practical system, one must consider energy and computational costs. In our model, the sensor node sends raw acceleration data to the mobile node. If this proves to be too expensive, then the sensor node could compute features from a window of acceleration and communicate those features instead. We leave exploring this delicate balance between extendability (allowing use of other features in the future), computability (due to limited computational capabilities on a sensor node), and energy requirements (with trade-offs specific to the technology in a sensor node) as future work. In terms of the mobile node, we assume the cellphone will be more than capable of computing correlations, but the energy costs of these functions is unknown and require more careful analysis. Should the computation prove to be too expensive or time consuming, then one may need to explore optimizations or approximations or the assistance of a back-end server, with due consideration to the trade-off of computational overhead, accuracy, and privacy.

9   Conclusion

Mobile health will play a major role in the future of healthcare. Wearable health sensors will enable physicians to monitor their patients remotely, and allow patients better access to information about their health. The method presented in this paper provides the foundation for any mobile-health system, because, in order for the data to be useful, physicians need confidence that the data supposedly collected about a patient actually came from that patient. We provide the first step in that verification process: generically authenticating that all the sensor nodes bound to a mobile node are the same body. We show that our method can achieve an accuracy of 80% when given 18 seconds of accelerometer data from different locations on the body, and our method can be generically applied regardless of the sensor type and without user-specific training data. In summary, we make the following contributions:

- We describe a novel problem in the mobile healthcare domain and provide a solution to the weak version of the one-body authentication problem.
- We extend Lester et al. [11] to sensors carried at different locations on the body – wrist, ankle, and waist – by extracting used for activity recognition.
- We provide empirical results to our solution using a dataset of seven users walking for 22 minutes to show that it is feasible.

Acknowledgements

This research results from a research program at the Institute for Security, Technology, and Society at Dartmouth College, supported by the National Science Foundation under Grant Award Number 0910842 and by the Department of Health and Human Services (SHARP program) under award number 90TR0003-01. The views and conclusions contained in this document are those of the authors and should not be interpreted as necessarily representing the official policies, either expressed or implied, of the sponsors.

We also thank the anonymous reviewers, and our colleagues in the Dartmouth TISH group, for their valuable feedback.

References

[1] Apex Fitness. BodyBugg (October 2010), http://www.bodybugg.com/
[2] Bao, L., Intille, S.S.: Activity Recognition from User-Annotated Acceleration Data. In: Ferscha, A., Mattern, F. (eds.) PERVASIVE 2004. LNCS, vol. 3001, pp. 1–17. Springer, Heidelberg (2004)
[3] Barth, A.T., Hanson, M.A., Harry, J., Powell, C., Unluer, D., Wilson, S.G., Lach, J.: Body-coupled communication for body sensor networks. In: Proceedings of the ICST 3rd International Conference on Body Area Networks, BodyNets 2008 (2008)
[4] Brezmes, T., Gorricho, J.-L., Cotrina, J.: Activity Recognition from Accelerometer Data on a Mobile Phone. In: Omatu, S., Rocha, M.P., Bravo, J., Fernández, F., Corchado, E., Bustillo, A., Corchado, J.M. (eds.) IWANN 2009. LNCS, vol. 5518, pp. 796–799. Springer, Heidelberg (2009)
[5] Chang, C.-C., Lin, C.-J.: LIBSVM: a library for support vector machines (2001), software http://www.csie.ntu.edu.tw/~cjlin/libsvm
[6] Cornelius, C., Kotz, D.: On Usable Authentication for Wireless Body Area Networks. In: Proceedings of the First USENIX Workshop on Health Security and Privacy (HealthSec) (2010)
[7] Fitbit, Inc. Fitbit (October 2010), http://www.fitbit.com/
[8] Freescale Semiconductor. Freescale Xtrinsic accelerometers optimize resolution and battery life in consumer devices (September 2010), press release http://www.media.freescale.com/phoenix.zhtml?c=196520&p=irol-newsArticle&ID=1470583

[9] Kunze, K.S., Lukowicz, P.: Dealing with sensor displacement in motion-based onbody activity recognition systems. In: Proceedings of the Tenth International Conference on Ubiquitous Computing (UbiComp), pp. 20–29 (2008)

[10] Kunze, K.S., Lukowicz, P., Junker, H., Tröster, G.: Where am I: Recognizing On-body Positions of Wearable Sensors. In: Strang, T., Linnhoff-Popien, C. (eds.) LoCA 2005. LNCS, vol. 3479, pp. 264–275. Springer, Heidelberg (2005)

[11] Lester, J., Hannaford, B., Borriello, G.: "Are You with Me?" - Using Accelerometers to Determine If Two Devices Are Carried by the Same Person. In: Ferscha, A., Mattern, F. (eds.) PERVASIVE 2004. LNCS, vol. 3001, pp. 33–50. Springer, Heidelberg (2004)

[12] Maurer, U., Smailagic, A., Siewiorek, D.P., Deisher, M.: Activity Recognition and Monitoring Using Multiple Sensors on Different Body Positions. In: Proceedings of the International Workshop on Wearable and Implantable Body Sensor Networks (BSN), pp. 113–116 (2006)

[13] Mayrhofer, R., Gellersen, H.: Shake Well Before Use: Intuitive and Secure Pairing of Mobile Devices. IEEE Transactions on Mobile Computing 8(6), 792–806 (2009)

[14] Ravi, N., Dandekar, N., Mysore, P., Littman, M.L.: Activity Recognition from Accelerometer Data. In: Proceedings of the Twentieth National Conference on Artificial Intelligence (AAAI), pp. 1541–1546 (2005)

[15] SparkFun Electronics. WiTilt v2.5 (October 2010), Data sheet
http://www.sparkfun.com/datasheets/Sensors/WiTilt_V2_5.pdf

[16] Sriram, J.C., Shin, M., Choudhury, T., Kotz, D.: Activity-aware ECG-based patient authentication for remote health monitoring. In: Proceedings of the Eleventh International Conference on Multimodal Interfaces (ICMI), pp. 297–304 (2009)

Sensing and Classifying Impairments of GPS Reception on Mobile Devices

Henrik Blunck, Mikkel Baun Kjærgaard, and Thomas Skjødeberg Toftegaard

Department of Computer Science
Aarhus University, Denmark
{blunck,mikkelbk,tst}@cs.au.dk

Abstract. Positioning using GPS receivers is a primary sensing modality in many areas of pervasive computing. However, previous work has not considered how people's body impacts the availability and accuracy of GPS positioning and for means to sense such impacts. We present results that the GPS performance degradation on modern smart phones for different hand grip styles and body placements can cause signal strength drops as high as 10-16 dB and double the positioning error. Furthermore, existing phone applications designed to help users identify sources of GPS performance impairment are restricted to show raw signal statistics. To help both users as well as application systems in understanding and mitigating body and environment-induced effects, we propose a method for sensing the current sources of GPS reception impairment in terms of body, urban and indoor conditions. We present results that show that the proposed autonomous method can identify and differentiate such sources, and thus also user environments and phone postures, with reasonable accuracy, while relying solely on GPS receiver data as it is available on most modern smart phones.

1 Introduction

Positioning using GPS receivers is a primary sensing modality in many areas of pervasive computing, such as behavior recognition (e.g., health status monitoring [20]), collaborative sensing (map generation [15] and environment impact monitoring [17]) and community applications (e.g., Micro-Blogging [4] and GeoPages [3]). In these application domains, the GPS receivers are assumed to be worn and used by people during their everyday life. However, the mentioned articles do not consider the impact of the user's body on the positioning performance. Several of the above articles mention that the applications described depend on GPS performance parameters such as availability and accuracy, but link difference and impairment in GPS performance only to the user's surrounding environments, e.g. urban or indoors.

In the first part of our paper, we study and analyze the body impacts on the performance of GPS receivers, focusing on in-phone systems, and intending to inform researchers and developers about these impacts. Our work builds on knowledge from existing studies of the body impact on in-phone GSM communication [1,19], while our methodology as well as our analysis results differ in nature from those described for GSM communication, since, first, the performance parameters of GPS differ from those of communication services, and, second, since a variety of factors, other than

K. Lyons, J. Hightower, and E.M. Huang (Eds.): Pervasive 2011, LNCS 6696, pp. 350–367, 2011.
© Springer-Verlag Berlin Heidelberg 2011

body effects, impacts GPS positioning more severely than GSM communication (due to the weakness of the GPS signals); such factors include the user's environment (e.g. urban or indoor) as well as, potentially, other simultaneous phone operations, e.g. GSM or WiFI transmissions or CPU computations [5]. Our study is also motivated by the recent body related issues with modern antenna designs in mobile phones [7] and by a recent short paper by Vaitl *et al.* [24] who quantify the GPS positioning accuracy for four on-body locations and three phone models in walking experiments.

The second part of this paper is motivated by the fact that existing mobile phone applications designed to help users identify sources of GPS performance degradation are restricted to radar views of satellites' signal strength and accuracy estimates. To help both users as well as application systems in understanding and mitigating body, urban and indoor effects, we want to provide information to the user about which effects are impacting the current performance of the GPS. For the indoor effects we build on the results of our recent study of indoor positioning using GPS presented in Kjærgaard et al. [8]. Consequently, in the second part of this paper we present a concept for how to differentiate these effects utilizing only signal quality data made available by in-phone GPS modules, enabling the GPS receiver as a new sensor modality for sensing body placement and environment. Our method calculates a number of features from the signal quality data among others it compares data to an open sky model of how strong signals should have been received given no impairments. The calculated feature values are used as an input to a standard machine learning algorithm that outputs a classification of current positioning impairments.

This concept is motivated foremost by the potential of information about GPS impairments and respective sources to improve GPS positioning quality and quality awareness: Both through GPS receiver algorithms, middleware [14] and application systems, utilizing such information, but also via informing the user directly via on-phone applications about current impairments, increasing his understanding of the position quality and help answering questions, such as "What is impacting my GPS positioning accuracy?" and "Can I improve GPS performance by changing my grip style or placement?" One might consider if the need for answering these questions could be removed by switching to other positioning means, such as WiFi or GSM positioning. But while we found body impacts to cause GPS positioning errors in the range between three to thirty meters, the WiFi or GSM positioning exhibits usually even larger errors in rural and urban areas [13].

We make the following contributions in this work: First, we argue that body related issues are significant for GPS performance and present results for different hand grip styles and body placements which show that signal strength drops as high as 10-16 dB can be experienced and double the positioning error. Finally, we propose a method for sensing and classifying GPS reception and positioning impairments in terms of body, urban and indoor conditions using a set of features calculated via a model for open-sky conditions. We present results that show that the method can estimate the correct cause with reasonable accuracies.

The remainder of this paper is structured as follows: In Section 2 we give a brief introduction and overview of research on GPS with a focus on in-phone GPS systems. In Section 3 we present our study of body-related impacts on GPS reception. In Section 4 we present the proposed method for sensing present GPS performance impairments and for identifying their sources. In Section 5 we discuss shortcomings and potential improvements and utilizations of the proposed method and provide directions for future work. Finally, Section 6 concludes the paper.

2 GPS: Operation Basics and Sources of Impairment

In this section we review basic concepts and recent advances in GPS positioning, as well as, research on how the user's environment impacts GPS performance and on how the user's body impacts other phone signal operations, specifically GSM signaling.

2.1 GPS Operation Principles

GPS satellites send signals for civilian use at the L1 frequency at 1.575 GHz; these signals are modulated with a *Pseudo-Random Noise (PRN)* code unique to each satellite. A GPS receiver tries to *acquire* each GPS satellite's signal by correlating the signal spectrum it receives at L1 with a local copy of the satellite's PRN code. An acquisition is successful, once the local copy is in sync with the received signal, which requires shifting the copy appropriately both in time and in frequency. The latter shift is due to the Doppler effect caused by the satellite's and the user's relative motion. Once a satellite's signal has been acquired, the receiver *tracks* it, that is, the receiver continuously checks the validity of the shift parameters above and updates them if necessary.

Each satellite's signal is modulated not only with its PRN code but additionally with a navigation message, which contains almanac data (for easier acquisition of further satellites) as well as its precise *ephemeris data*, that is the satellite's predicted trajectory as a function of time, allowing GPS receivers to estimate the current position of the satellite. Finally, to achieve precise 3D positioning with a standard GPS receiver via trilateration, the positions of and distances to at least 4 satellites have to be known; those distances can be computed from the time shift maintained while tracking the respective satellites. As a general rule, the more satellites can be tracked, and the wider they are spread over the sky as seen by the user, the more precise the positioning –due to the additional distance data and a satellite geometry resulting in less error-prone lateration.

A popular enhancement of GPS positioning is given by *Assisted GPS (A-GPS)* [25], which provides assistance data to GPS receivers via an additional communication channel, which for in-phone GPS operation is usually the cellular network. This assisting data contains ephemerides and often also atmospheric corrections. A-GPS eases satellite acquisition and can therefore drastically reduce the time to first fix and the initial positioning imprecision of a receiver, once the assisting data has been transmitted. Furthermore, A-GPS can improve positioning accuracy by eliminating systemic, e.g. atmospheric, error sources [16, Chapter 13.4].

2.2 Environment Impacts on GPS Performance

GPS performance degrades in terms of both coverage and accuracy when experiencing problematic signal conditions, e.g. in urban canyons and especially in indoor environments. The cause for this is termed signal *fading*, subsuming two fundamental signal processing obstacles: First, when GPS signals penetrate building materials, they are subjected to attenuation, resulting in lower *signal-to-noise ratio (SNR)*. Furthermore, the signal is subject to *multipath phenomena*: Reflection and refraction of the signal results in multiple echoes of the *line-of-sight (LOS)* signal arriving at the receiver. Low signal-to-noise ratios and multipath handicap both acquiring and tracking GPS signals and usually result in less reliable positioning due to less suitable satellite geometry and less accurate individual time shifts measurements. For investigations of GPS positioning in urban and indoor environments and its limitations, see, e.g., [8,22,27]. *High-Sensitivity GPS (HSGPS)* [12] subsumes advances in GPS receiver technology to alleviate the limitations mentioned above. HSGPS is claimed to allow tracking for received GPS signal strengths down to -190 dBW, corresponding to a nominal SNR value of 14 dB: three orders of magnitude less than the GPS signal strength to be expected in open-sky conditions [16]. These thresholds are constantly being improved using new processing techniques [25, Ch. 6].

2.3 In-Phone Signal Recption and Antenna Design Considerations

Today, most smart-phones allow for reliable and accurate GPS positioning in open-sky conditions. Van Diggelen lists the main technological advances which have led to this achievement, stating furthermore, that "we thought the main benefit of this would be indoor GPS, but perhaps even more importantly it has meant very, very cheap antennas in mobile phones" [26]. It is agreed within the GPS research community, that antenna design, placement, and utilization is key for the further improvement of in-phone GPS positioning [5,6]. Central aspects in this challenge are the cost-effectiveness of the antenna design and the limiting of interference caused by other in-phone components, such as the GSM communication module. Finally, increasing form factor minimization also increases the constraints on antenna size, suggesting cohabitation, i.e., the use of one antenna for multiple services such as GPS reception, and GSM, Bluetooth, or WiFi communication [5]. More recently, a growing focus on in phone GPS technology lies on limiting the power consumption [25] and consequently, most GPS chip manufacturers emphasize and provide details about the improved energy-efficiency of their latest products for in-phone integration.

While the in-phone GPS reception is strongly influenced by the kind of environment, e.g. urban or indoor, another source of impairment can be the user himself, more specifically the parts of the user's body, which are either i) close to or even ii) contacting with the GPS in-phone antenna, or iii) just blocking the line-of-sight between the antenna and specific GPS satellites. All these three phenomena have impacts on GPS reception, the magnitude of which depends also on the design of the smartphone used. Sokova and Forssell give indications, that in difficult positioning conditions, e.g., indoor environments even pedestrians passing by can cause severe impairment of GPS reception [21]. In general, the closer the body is to a receiving antenna and the more it shields it, the more signal power dissipates into the body, impairing the desired resonation of the antenna with the incoming signal. Such body effects have been investigated thoroughly for the sending and receiving of signals of various types, most prominently for cell phone communication signals [1,2]. The above research identified that for the quality of signal sending and reception the following (interrelated) parameters are crucial:

the antenna type, its location within the phone, and the way the user holds the phone, specifically the phone's orientation and the amount of body shielding and contact the phone's antenna is subjected to.

Furthermore, the results of these studies allow the conclusion that the body impacts on signal reception are complex to model in simulation and that the respective results often differ from the effects as observed in real-world situations. Furthermore, the effects depend in a complex manner on the signal frequency. Consequently, these studies provide an intuition about the body effects on the reception of signals at the GPS signal frequencies –but due to the GPS signals differing from GSM signals not only in frequency, but also in strength, purpose and structure, these studies don't allow for proper predictions of body effects on GPS reception in real-life use-cases, and even less so for predictions of the resulting impacts on the experienced GPS positioning performance.

3   Quantifying the Body and Phone Impact on GPS Reception

In this section we present results from measurements designed to quantify the impact of the user's presence and handling of the phone in real-world settings. More specifically, we measure impacts of various grip styles selected according to previous work; both in this and the subsequent section we will relate these impacts also to effects originating from the user's environment.

3.1   Methodology

The primary measure we used in our analysis of in-phone GPS performance are the signal strengths as they are experienced on the phones for the GPS satellites tracked by the phone. It has been observed that this set of signal strength values gives a good indication of overall GPS positioning quality including the essential performance parameters availability and accuracy, and we provide evidence for that in Section 3.2. Hence, to evaluate the impairment of GPS performance caused by a form of user interaction, e.g., a certain grip style, we measured the signal strengths in respective setups and compared the observed SNR values to those observed on a reference phone affected neither by body nor user environment impacts. To be able to draw valid conclusions from such signal strength comparisons, it is essential, that the everyday difference in observed signal strengths between two unaffected reference phones is small. To validate this assumption, we have collected sixty hours of measurements with two unaffected Google Nexus One phones placed statically in open-sky conditions, 2 meters apart from each other, with no nearby pedestrians, and running only our measurement collection software. As we measure body and user environment impacts over 10 minutes using two phones and average the GPS signal reception properties over this time span, the two assumptions we depend on are that a) the deviation in signal strength between phones within the ten minutes are small and b) that for the same phone the signal properties measured differ only slightly in consecutive measurements. Mainly to validate our measurement setups, we also investigated whether interference between close by GPS receivers [5] can impair any GPS performance measures: In several experiments in which several GPS enabled phones were placed as close as 5 centimeters apart we observed no visible degradations.

Table 1. Absolute signal strength deviations between two unaffected phones in open sky conditions for Google Nexus One phones

Scenario	Four Strongest Satellites [dB]			All Satellites [dB]		
	μ	σ	max	μ	σ	max
Between Phones	1.10	0.86	4.35	1.20	0.93	4.91
Same Phone (Consecutive)	0.62	0.47	2.29	1.01	0.81	4.04

As shown in Table 1 for the validation of our assumption, we give quantifications of signal strength differences by mean, standard deviation and maximum differences – averaged over i) the four GPS satellite signals which are received strongest on the phone and ii) over all satellite signals tracked by the phone[1]. The results in Table 1 indicate mean variations around 1 dB with standard deviations below 1 dB and maximum variations below 5 dB. It follows that for our results to deviate from the mean with more than one standard deviation (this deviation is relevant as visual inspection of the distributions supports that they are normally distributed), the signal strength would have to differ at least 1.96 dB in the case of the four strongest satellites and 2.13 for all satellites.

3.2   Measured Impacts of the User Body on GPS Reception

As reviewed in Section 2 there are results from studies of, e.g., cellular technologies that confirms that bodies negatively impact signal reception in mobile phones. We want to add to this knowledge by studying the effects on the GPS antenna. In this specific study we focus primarily on the Google Nexus One phone but also present results for the Nokia N97.

To select relevant hand and body placements we base our selection on a study by Pelosi et al. [19] who identified common hand grip styles for both data and talk mobile phone usage. Based on their study we have selected three data style grips one with 3 fingers in the bottom third of the device, a five finger style and a double hand style, and a soft and a firm talk style grip with five fingers, as depicted in Figure 1. As GPS usage is also relevant when the user does not have the phone in the hand we have also evaluated an overarm jacket pocket placement, e.g., similar to popular overarm straps for runners, a trouser pocket placement and a placement in the top of a bag carried by a person. To limit the study we did not consider special casings of the phone or special phone configurations, e.g., opening of the keyboard on the Nokia N97. We conducted the experiments outdoors in open sky conditions and collected measurements for 10 minutes with one affected phone held in the evaluated body position and a unaffected phone statically placed 1.5 meter away from the person carrying out the experiment. To compare the data we calculate the drop in signal strength as the mean signal strength difference between the measurements from the affected and the unaffected phone.

The results listed in Table 2 from the measurements with two Google Nexus One phones show that signal strength drops depending on the hand grip style and body

---

[1] We chose to give measure - i) additional to measure - ii) because the strongest satellites will also be the most important contributors to the positioning accuracy of the GPS. Therefore, a significant drop of their SNR will have a higher impact than that of the SNR of already weaker satellites that the GPS may weigh less (or not even consider) in the position computation [10].

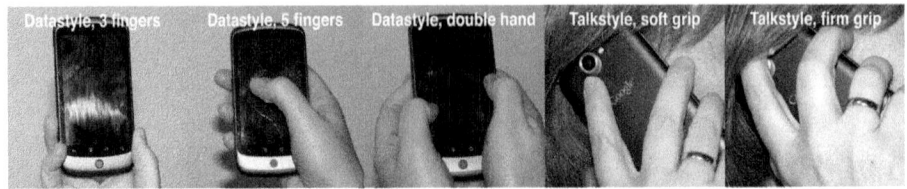

Fig. 1. Illustrations of different hand grip styles

placement. The most significant drops between 6.9 to 10.6 dB are experienced with *Talkstyle, firm grip, 5 fingers* and *Datastyle, double hand*. For comparison, Kjærgaard et al. [8] lists the following values for attenuation of glass 2.43 dB, a wooden wall 4.8 dB, a brick wall 10.38 dB and reinforced concrete 16.7 dB. Generally the drops for the four strongest and all visible satellites correlate only the *Running style, overarm jacket pocket* scenario deviates where the drop considering all satellites is 3.7 dB.

Table 2. Drops in signal strength for the four strongest and all satellites with different hand grip styles and body placements comparing pairs of Google Nexus One and Nokia N97 phones

	Google Nexus One		Nokia N97	
Scenario	Four Strongest [dB]	All [dB]	Four Strongest [dB]	All [dB]
Running style, overarm	0.3	3.7	-	-
Datastyle, 3 fingers	0.4	0.4	4.7	2.7
Everyday style, bagpack	1.5	2.0	-	-
Talkstyle, soft grip, 5 fingers	2.5	2.0	-	-
Talkstyle, firm grip, 5 fingers	6.9	7.3	17.3	14.2
Datastyle, 5 fingers	8.0	3.6	11.8	10.5
Everyday style, trouser back pocket	9.4	6.6	-	-
Datastyle, double hand	10.6	8.8	16.1	14.5

To argue that the signal strength drops are not only pertinent to the Google Nexus One phone we collected similar measurements with two Nokia N97 phones for a subset of the scenarios. The results are also listed in Table 2 and indicates even bigger drops in the range of 4.7 dB to 17.3 dB which is five dB higher than for the newer Google Nexus One for similar hand grip styles and body placements. From these measurements we can conclude that the body impact is present and in some cases amounts to the attenuation experienced in indoor environments.

To quantify the effect on positioning accuracy during everyday use measurements were collected by a person walking a 4.85 kilometer tour twice through both open-sky and urban positioning conditions carrying six phones with different placement. The data set consists of ground truth positions and 1 Hz GPS from the built-in sensors in the Google Nexus One and the Nokia N97. The ground truth was collected at 4Hz with a high accuracy u-blox LEA-5H receiver with an dedicated antenna placed on the top of a backpack carried by the collector. The ground truth measurements were manually inspected to make sure they followed the correct route of the target.

Figure 2 shows error plots for four of the Google Nexus One and Nokia N97 traces, respectively. The error is computed as the distance between the ground truth positions reported by the dedicated GPS to the positions reported by the phones. The figures depict cumulative distributions of the individual positioning errors throughout the traces. From the figures one can observe a significant difference in accuracy comparing the nearly body unaffected placements of *Upper compartment of bagpack* and *Datastyle, 3 fingers* to the affected trouser placements and the *Datastyle, 5 fingers*. Considering the median, the increase in error is for the Google Nexus One from five meters to ten meters and for the Nokia N97 from ten meters to twenty meters. One can therefore conclude that the body impact can have a strong impact on the positioning accuracy. In a study, conducted at the same time as ours and for three mobile phones Vaitl et al. [24] also identified the phone placement within trouser pockets as the worst for GPS accuracy.

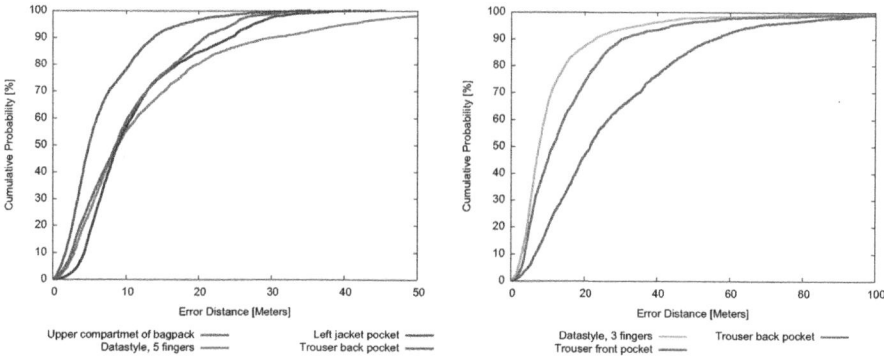

Fig. 2. Drops in positioning accuracy with different hand grip styles and body placements for Google Nexus One (left), and Nokia N97 (right)

The body effects also impact the positioning availability in the everyday measurements, but only for the Nokia N97, whereas for the Google Nexus One, which was released in early 2010, 16 months after the N97, there were no major drops. For the N97s the availability dropped from 88% during collection in the *Datastyle, 3 fingers* case to 51% for the back pocket trouser placement. Availability drops may occur also on the Nexus One, as we observed in the data set collected to evaluate the method proposed in Section 4: In four urban and five indoor data traces a Nexus One placed in a trouser pocket did not produce any fixes at all and in one urban and four indoor data traces, and a Nexus One held with the *Datastyle, 5 fingers* grip style did produce only very few. In the same traces both a phone held with grip style *Datastyle, 3 fingers* and a reference phone placed some meters away from the person collecting the data produced continuous fixes throughout the experiments. Therefore, we can conclude that body effects impact GPS availability, however, more significantly for the N97 than for the Nexus One.

4 Sensing and Classifying Impairment Sources

To assist both application systems as well as the user in understanding and mitigating body and environment-induced effects, we aim to provide information about which effects are currently impacting the GPS device's performance and to which extent. In the following, we present an approach for differentiating such effects and respective sources utilizing only GPS signal quality data, in particular SNR measurements paired with directional information about GPS satellites; note, that such data is made available by most popular last generation smart-phones. The information about sources of GPS performance impairment, that we provide, adds to existing user assistance such as radar views of satellites strengths and accuracy estimates, and can be delivered as either visual, audible or tactile feedback, assisting, e.g. in answering questions such as "What is impacting my positioning accuracy?" and "Can I improve GPS performance by changing my grip style or placement?".

4.1 Classification Concept and Procedure

The proposed concept is illustrated in Figure 3. An in-phone GPS module outputs signal quality measurements –even in conditions in which only few and very weak signals can be acquired. Therefore, our method is functional even in cases where the GPS module is not able to produce any position fixes at all. From the signal quality measurements a range of features are computed with the help of an open-sky model that estimates how strong signals would be received for a given satellite and on the device if placed in open-sky conditions and not suffering from body, indoor or urban effects.

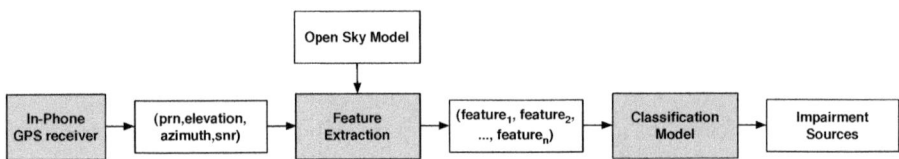

Fig. 3. Process for classifying impairment sources via analyzing in-phone signal measurements

Classification output domain. The classification model outputs information about inferred sources of GPS performance impairment. We have chosen to consider two types of GPS positioning impairments, environment- and body-induced ones. Furthermore, we considered two resulting categorizations: In the first one we distinguish twelve categories, i.e. twelve potential outcomes of the classification, corresponding to the twelve combinations of three environment types (open-sky, urban and indoor) and four phone placement and posture types (datastyle 3 fingers, datastyle 5 fingers, trouser back pocket, and no-body reference). In the coarser second categorization, we consider only six categories, combining the three environment types (open-sky, urban and indoor) with cases of no or weak body effects (datastyle 3 fingers and no-body reference) and cases of significant body effects (datastyle 5 fingers and trouser back pocket).

4.2   Feature Extraction

The aim in designing suitable features for classification is to numerically capture the occurrence of patterns which –ideally– are specific to a single environment or on-body phone placement or posture, or –more generally– allow us to separate different (combinations of) environment and body placement types. In the following, we first sketch some of these patterns we look for, then we present features designed for detecting them, after introducing a utilized reference model, which holds expected SNR values in open-sky conditions. Some of the patterns we are looking for include:

When separating environment types. Naturally, for *open-sky* environments hardly any SNR drops or deviations w.r.t the model of SNRs in open-sky conditions occur. If deviations exist, they are distributed normally over both azimuths and elevations of the satellites tracked. In *urban* environments, drops occur for low elevation satellites, while the signals of higher satellites are received stronger. *Indoors*, satellite signals are received strongest through windows and wall openings, i.e. from satellites at low elevation and within 'horizontal clusters', i.e. at specific azimuth ranges, corresponding to window areas and wall openings.

When separating phone placement types. The blocking effect of the user body shows for different on-body placements in SNR drops of a particular range of azimuth values: E.g., for the trouser back pocket-placement this range is almost hemispherical. In contrast, when the user holds the phone in hand, the attenuation is more evenly distributed with regards to azimuth. Furthermore, different grips styles can often be distinguished by the overall amount of attenuation.

An Empirical Model of Open-Sky Conditions. Our identification of GPS reception impairments is based mainly on interpreting signal degradations. An indicator of the latter, which is even more suitable than the absolute SNR values recorded, is given by the drops of SNR w.r.t. ideal conditions, i.e. when not impacted by body- or environment-induced effects. Therefore, our system is supported by an *Open Sky Model* which provides estimations of the SNR values to be currently expected on the device at the user's geographic position.

To the best of our knowledge, there does not yet exist an accurate theoretical model for open-sky GPS signal conditions. There are two main reasons for this, firstly, that SNR values depend both on properties of the antenna and the receiver chip, and secondly, that the transmission power of GPS satellites vary depending on their generation and age. Therefore, to characterize open-sky conditions we propose to use a device-specific and empirical parametrized model. This model holds for each GPS satellite a function which maps for each GPS satellite its evaluation to a Gaussian distribution of the SNR of that satellite at that elevation, as recorded by the device. The resulting function table contains less than 3000 entries, .i.e. a mere 60 kilobytes. The motivation for modeling not only average SNR values, but also error distributions is that deviations are caused by several error sources, such as atmospheric weather, ground multi-path effects and integer rounding imprecision of the elevation data. Note, that since GPS orbits repeat every sidereal day, these differences are observable from the mappings which each use only 24 hours of the recorded data. The daily SNR pattern, as well as

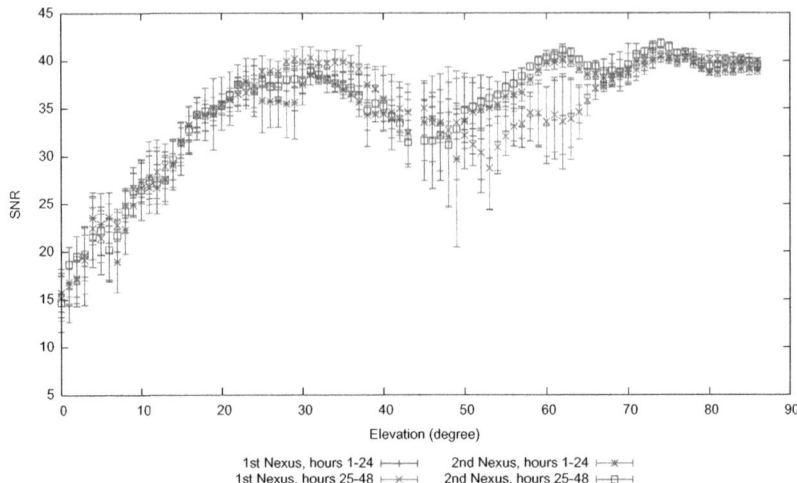

Fig. 4. SNR measurements for GPS satellite PRN 31, recorded on Google Nexuses in open-sky no-body conditions

differences in this pattern observed over two consecutive days are depicted exemplary for GPS satellite PRN 31 as recorded in Aarhus, Denmark, in Figure 4.

As our model's mappings are gained by empirical data won over 48 hours at one particular location, the accuracy of the model diminishes with the temporal and spatial distance from that recording. We will though later on present evidence that our system performs well also with less accurate or less detailed models.

Classification Features Employed. We now give an overview of the 29 features our current classification is based on, as well as discuss their suitability and limits in providing a successful classification of (combinations of) body-induced and environment-induced impairments.

Features Based on Averaged SNR Drop: One of the features used in classification considers the experienced SNR drop w.r.t. the open sky model, averaged over all satellites within the GPS constellation which were trackable according to the open sky model. This feature captures the overall level of signal attenuation experienced. Figure 5(a) illustrates the differentiation of phone postures and placements achievable by this feature: The probability distributions shown represent output of the feature, i.e. average SNR drops. Each distribution subsumes data, described in more detail in Section 4.3, from 12 five-minute measurements for each particular combination of environment and phone-body context. Note, that to achieve better visualization of the characteristica of the distribution, feature output was beforehand mapped to bins. The plot shows, that in open-sky environments almost no SNR drops occur for the grip style using only 3 fingers, while in contrast large drops occur (in any given environment), when the phone is held firmly with 5 fingers, and even significantly larger drops occur when the phone is kept in the back pocket of a trouser. Furthermore, the two distributions in Figure 5(a) showing data gathered in urban settings, show that the environmental

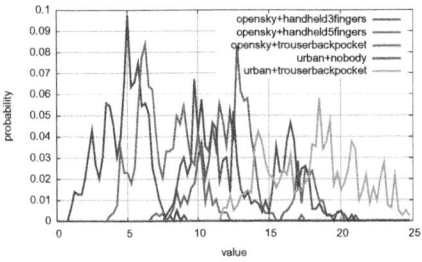 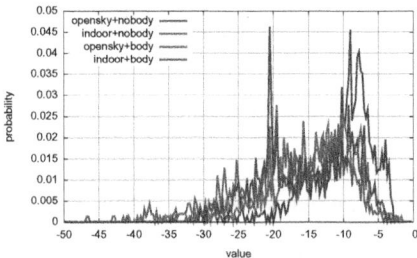

(a) SNR drop w.r.t. opensky model, averaged over all receivable satellites

(b) Maximal SNR difference between two satellites, consecutive in the increasing order of the received satellites by elevation

Fig. 5. Probability plots exemplifying two classification features

attenuation visibly 'blurs' the separation between different contexts; a fact that represents a general challenge for the body context classification: As a rule of thumb, the more attenuating and impairing the user's current environment is in itself, the harder it becomes to differentiate between different phone-body contexts.

Features Based on Elevation Order: The following feature is designed to distinguish environment types: It captures the maximally negative difference of SNR between two satellites, consecutive in the increasing order of the received satellites by elevation. Figure 5(b) shows output of this feature, originating from the measurements mentioned above. The distributions shown result from grouping measurements, undertaken in open-sky as well as in indoor areas and with various body-phone contexts, by severity of GPS impairment –following the coarser one of the categorizations described in Section 4.1. The plot shows, that for most indoor locations the feature output values are high. This is because satellites are received most strongly at low elevations, e.g. through windows, and because these satellites are ultimately followed in the elevation ordered sequence by a satellite that is highly attenuated by either walls or ceilings. In contrast, the open-sky measurements provide feature values close to zero. This again gives evidence, that if the impairment in one domain –in this case the body-induced one– is severe, it becomes harder for the feature to differentiate impairments of another domain –in this case of the user environment, .i.e. to tell apart indoor locations from open-sky ones. Another feature is obtained as a variant of the one just described: It measures the maximal positive, instead of negative, SNR difference; this allows for identifying the urban environment type, since in urban canyons usually the satellites above the 'skyline' of surrounding buildings are received significantly stronger.

Features Based on SNR Drop Order: Three of the features currently employed are computed on basis of the sequence of the tracked satellites, sorted by the SNR drop experienced for them. E.g., when averaging over the azimuth difference between satellites consecutive in that sequence, the resulting feature captures the entropy for the sequence w.r.t. azimuth; for open-sky no-body conditions this entropy is usually high, while the lowest entropy was obtained in a no-body setup in indoor locations: Satellites similar in azimuth often reach the user through the same building element and therefore exhibit also similar SNR values.

Features Based on Azimuth Order: Alternatively, if one sorts the satellites instead by azimuth, one can capture, e.g. hemispherical, body shielding effects for in-pocket setups: One of our features identifies the azimuth half-space separation, for which the difference between the averaged signal drop in the respective hemispheres is maximized. This feature naturally generalizes for angles other than 180 degree.

Further Features: Further features are extracted from already established signal quality indicators, e.g., DOP values as provided by the phone's GPS system [16]. Feature design techniques, which we consider worth of exploring in future work, we discuss in Section 5.

4.3 Classification Results

As depicted in the procedural outline given in Figure 3, the classification model has to infer present GPS positioning impairments, once provided with feature outputs, computed as described in the previous section. To implement the classification model we chose to use the Weka Machine Learning toolkit [28]. Prior to processing the feature outputs, we aggregate them by averaging over a five second window to remove outliers[2].

To evaluate the proposed classification concept, we collected a data set at three open-sky, three urban, and three indoor exemplary locations, employing different phone-body contexts in order to cover all twelve classification context categories listed in Section 4.1. At each location four consecutive measurements were collected at a fixed position, and for two opposite directions e.g. facing north and south, resp. For each location and orientation, measurements were undertaken by two users of differing stature in order to investigate the influence of body physique on the GPS reception and on our impairment classification process. In each measurement, four Google Nexus One phones were used where one was placed 2 meters away as reference, one was placed in the user's trouser back pocket and the two remaining ones were held by the user with the *Datastyle, 3 fingers* and the *Datastyle, 5 fingers* grip style, resp. In total, 144 measurement traces of five minutes each were collected. Each trace contains GPS position fixes and signal quality measurements sampled at 1 Hz. This experimental setup was designed to collect a balanced data set w.r.t. locations, users, orientations and body placement; however, since at some locations positioning availability was not 100%, some categories naturally have fewer data samples. Thus, we have applied a re-sampling filter to balance the data, so that we are able to judge the performance of the classification model directly from the classification accuracies and confusion matrices.

In Table 3 we present classification results for six and twelve categories, resp., and for two different machine learning algorithms, the basic Naive Bayes algorithm and the more accurate J48 decision tree algorithm and for three types of evaluations: firstly,

---

[2] We evaluated different window sizes: For the window size chosen the classification results benefited from the resulting noise removal, whereas for larger windows it suffered too much from the size reduction of the data set.

Table 3. Classification accuracy results for classifying GPS positioning impairments into six and twelve categories, resp.

	10 Fold Cross-Validation	Different Persons	Different Orientation
12 Categories			
Naive Bayes	59	44	46
Decision Tree	94	50	51
6 Categories			
Naive Bayes	73	71	66
Decision Tree	**96**	**75**	**73**

ten fold cross-validation on the complete data set, secondly, training with data for one person and testing the resulting classification model with data from the other person and, thirdly, training with data for the respectively first chosen orientation and testing with the data of the respective opposite orientation. The results show that the decision tree algorithm performs better than the naive Bayes algorithm with accuracy rates of 94% and 96% for twelve and six categories, respectively. However, there are indications of overfitting because separating the training and test data, either w.r.t. to person or orientation, lowers the results to 75% and 73%, respectively, for six categories and even more for twelve categories. Similarly, training with data from only half of the investigated environments and subsequent testing with the remaining data, results in a lower classification accuracy –implicating, that for accurate classification in arbitrary environments training data from a broader variety of locations would be essential, as well as further development of the proposed features.

To further analyze how the errors are distributed, Table 4 shows the confusion matrix for the results of the decision tree algorithm with six categories and when separating training and test data w.r.t. the collecting person. From the matrix one can see that data from the classes *open-sky, no body* and *urban, no body* are classified highly accurate, whereas data from *indoor, no body* and *indoor, body* is not; the poor separation performance of the algorithm in this case shows in high confusion values of 28.9% and 30.8% between the two categories. This observation is in agreement with the statement made

Table 4. Confusion matrix for the decision three algorithms for six categories and with separate training and test data depending on the collecting person

	Classified As					
	open-sky no body	urban no body	indoor no body	open-sky nody	urban body	indoor body
open-sky, no body	**92.1**	0.1	1.2	6.6	0	0
urban, no body	3.3	**88.2**	6.8	0	1.5	0.3
indoor, no body	7.9	4.7	**45.6**	9.3	1.7	*30.8*
open-sky, body	8.7	0	6.4	**70.0**	1.7	13.1
urban, body	0	0	8.5	0	**81.5**	10.0
indoor, body	0	0	28.9	0.2	0.9	**70.0**

above, that in weak signal environments it is harder to differentiate body effects: even telling none body effects situations from those with body effects becomes challenging.

The results shown in Table 4 were obtained using an open-sky model that considered each satellite independently which has the drawback that reference data ideally should be collected at many places on the globe to account for local differences in observable signal strengths. Thus, we have also evaluated our method using an alternative, simpler model that combines gathered SNR data across satellites to compute the strength of GPS reception per elevation, averaged over all satellites. When using this model instead of the proposed open-sky model, the accuracy of the classifications, using either the naive Bayes or the decision tree algorithm, did only decrease by 2 to 3 percent.

5   Discussion

The work presented shows that classification of GPS impairment sources can be done, relying only on current GPS signal quality data obtainable on most last generation smart phones. In the following, we discuss the classification concept presented, how to utilize it, as well as future research directions for refining and improving it.

The feasibility of the classification concept in terms of classification accuracy has been documented in Section 4. We expect further improvement from integrating additional features into our classification procedure. Among these will be the detection of geometric clusters (w.r.t. elevation and azimuth) of similarly strong satellites, to detect environmental features, such as window areas indoors, and street canyons in urban areas. Additionally, the consideration of the recent data history –additional to the most recent GPS signal quality data snapshot, may allow to more reliably detect and keep track of 'static' features such as windows, walls or buildings, and to tell them apart more easily from body features, which are always 'moving' with the user. Worth investigating is also the incorporation of indicators for the user's phone handling as well as his context, e.g., his transportation mode, which are provided through data from sensors other than the GPS. E.g., Vahdatpour et al. [23] propose to detect a device's on-body placement from accelerometer readings.

In terms of output semantics, an integration of further as well as more fine-grained classes of user environments, distinguishing between different building types and transportation vehicles, the user may currently be in, would be desirable, depending on user requirements and application scenarios. W.r.t. resulting classification accuracies, Table 4 illustrates the naturally poorer absolute accuracy when classifying into a higher number of classes; note, though that the majority of false classifications still determine the user environment correctly and only confuse similar phone postures and placements.

Furthermore, the issue that the diversity of the physiques of users result in drops in classification performance, as noted in Table 3, has to be addressed: First, the system should be trained through data gathered by subjects of various statures. Secondly, we plan to evaluate the benefits of providing the user with a training procedure, designed to determine the impact of the user's physique on GPS reception w.r.t., comparing the gathered data with the training data provided by users of various physiques.

The potential for application and middleware-specific benefits of the proposed on-device sensing and classifying of GPS impairments in real-time require further investigation, for improving both ad-hoc and general user behaviour, as well as for enhancing the positioning quality and quality awareness of GPS receivers. The latter can be achieved since identifying current impairment sources can inform the receiver which satellites' ranging data to trust: GPS receivers can ignore ranging information from individual satellites which are believed to be distorted or currently received only indirectly; while such selection has been shown to potentially improve GPS accuracy [11], knowing the current user environment is crucial for picking proper selection criteria: E.g., in open sky environments stronger signals usually provide preciser ranging information, whereas in indoor environments the contrary can hold, when the strongest signals are likely to be signal reflections, reaching the user through windows, but only indirectly and thus yielding large ranging distortions [8]. Furthermore, providing application developers with access to the classifications is an example of benefitial seamfull design for developers [14]: E.g., in a positioning middleware, which is designed following a seamfull design approach to provide translucency w.r.t. the positioning process, the classifications could be used as an input to adapt application logic.

To investigate to which extent the proposed classification can benefit ad-hoc and general user behaviour, we are currently considering a phone application which provides as feedback the classification results regarding reception impairments and sensed environments and phone postures. Additionally, we want to explore ways to provide visual or acoustic feedback, which not only assesses and classifies current GPS impairment sources, but which can also guide the user towards a more beneficial phone holding posture or placement, or help him identify more reception-beneficial spots within or close to his current environment, e.g., using information collected by fingerprinting GPS positioning quality [9]. Finally, the computational load and energy consumption induced by different impairment classification schemes should be investigated, to ensure that real-time processing is feasible on common smart phones –also for feature sets, larger than the currently used one. Our preliminary investigations indicate that real-time processing on common smart phones is possible for the presented system.

6   Conclusions

We presented a concept for sensing present impairments of GPS reception and positioning performance, and for classifying impairment sources in terms of body, urban and indoor context. Results obtained from a measurement campaign provided reasonable classification accuracy and a proof of concept, that both the type of environment, the user is currently in, as well as the way a user is currently holding or storing his phone can be determined with reasonable accuracy through analysis solely of GPS signal quality data as available on most modern smart phones. Finally, in Section 5 further improvements of the accuracy of the presented classification system were identified, and directions for how to bring benefits of such a classification concept to the users were illustrated.

Additionally, to assess user-body effects on GPS reception and to aid and inform existing and future research and application systems, we have empirically evaluated for different hand grip styles and body placements the respective effects on GPS positioning performance of modern GPS enabled smart-phones. The evaluation showed that GPS reception depends highly on how the phone is kept or held, and that body-effects can cause attenuation of average signal strength of up to 10-16 dB, which is more than that caused by a typical brick wall, and can lead to a doubling of the median positioning error as experienced in open-sky conditions in the absence of body effects.

Acknowledgment

We thank Lasse Haugsted Rasmussen for his help in collecting measurements, acknowledge the financial support granted by the Danish National Advanced Technology Foundation for the project "Galileo: A Platform for Pervasive Positioning" (009-2007-2) and by the Danish National Research Foundation for MADALGO - Center for Massive Data Algorithmics and acknowledge Nokia and Google for hardware grants.

References

1. Al-Mously, S.I., Abousetta, M.M.: Anticipated impact of hand-hold position on the electromagnetic interaction of different antenna types/positions and a human in cellular communications. International Journal of Antennas and Propagation 2008 (2008)
2. Alexiou, A., Kostarakis, P., Christofilakis, V., Zervos, T., Alexandridis, A., Dangakis, K., Soras, C., Petrović, V., Kolundžija, B., Dordević, A.: Interaction between gsm handset helical antenna and user's head: Theoretical analysis and experimental results. The Environmentalist 25(2), 215–221 (2005)
3. Cai, Y., Xu, T.: Design, analysis, and implementation of a large-scale real-time location-based information sharing system. In: Proceeding of the 6th International Conference on Mobile Systems, Applications, and Services, pp. 106–117. ACM, New York (2008)
4. Gaonkar, S., Li, J., Choudhury, R.R., Cox, L., Schmidt, A.: Micro-blog: sharing and querying content through mobile phones and social participation. In: Proc. of the 6th International Conference on Mobile Systems, Applications, and Services, pp. 174–186. ACM, New York (2008)
5. Haddrell, T., Ricquier, N., Phocas, M.: Mobile-phone gps antennas. GPS World 2 (2010)
6. Hurte, B., Leisten, O.: Getting into pockets and purses. GPS World 11 (2005)
7. A. Inc. Letter from apple regarding iphone 4. Press Release (July 2010)
8. Kjærgaard, M.B., Blunck, H., Godsk, T., Toftkjær, T., Christensen, D.L., Grønbæk, K.: Indoor positioning using GPS revisited. In: Floréen, P., Krüger, A., Spasojevic, M. (eds.) Pervasive Computing. LNCS, vol. 6030, pp. 38–56. Springer, Heidelberg (2010)
9. Kjærgaard, M.B., Weckemann, K.: PosQ: Unsupervised Fingerprinting and Visualization of GPS Positioning Quality. In: Proceedings of the Second International Conference on Mobile Computing, Applications, and Services (MobiCASE 2010). Springer, Heidelberg (2010)
10. Kuusniemi, H., Wieser, A., Lachapelle, G., Takala, J.: User-level reliability monitoring in urban personal satellite-navigation. IEEE Transactions on Aerospace and Electric Systems 43, 1305–1318 (2007)
11. Kuusniemi, H., Lachapelle, G.G.: GNSS signal reliability testing in urban and indoor environments. In: Proceedings of the NTM Conference (2004)
12. Lachapelle, G., Kuusniemi, H., Dao, D., MacGougan, G., Cannon, M.: HSGPS signal analysis and performance under various indoor conditions. Navigation, Inst. of Navigation 51(1), 29–43 (2004)

13. LaMarca, A., Chawathe, Y., Consolvo, S., Hightower, J., Smith, I., Scott, J., Sohn, T., Howard, J., Hughes, J., Potter, F., Tabert, J., Powledge, P., Borriello, G., Schilit, B.: Place Lab: Device Positioning Using Radio Beacons in the Wild. In: Gellersen, H.-W., Want, R., Schmidt, A. (eds.) PERVASIVE 2005. LNCS, vol. 3468, pp. 116–133. Springer, Heidelberg (2005)

14. Langdal, J., Schougaard, K.R., Kjærgaard, M.B., Toftkjær, T.: PerPos: A translucent positioning middleware supporting adaptation of internal positioning processes. In: Gupta, I., Mascolo, C. (eds.) Middleware 2010. LNCS, vol. 6452, pp. 232–251. Springer, Heidelberg (2010)

15. Minamimoto, S., Fujii, S., Yamaguchi, H., Higashino, T.: Local Map Generation using Position and Communication History of Mobile Nodes. In: Proceedings of the 2010 IEEE International Conference on Pervasive Computing and Communications, pp. 2–10 (2010)

16. Misra, P., Enge, P.: Global Positioning System: Signals, Measurements, and Performance, 2nd edn., Navtech (2006)

17. Mun, M., Reddy, S., Shilton, K., Yau, N., Burke, J., Estrin, D., Hansen, M., Howard, E., West, R., Boda, P.: Peir, the personal environmental impact report, as a platform for participatory sensing systems research. In: Proceedings of the 7th International Conference on Mobile Systems, Applications, and Services, pp. 55–68. ACM, New York (2009)

18. Kivekäs, T.L.O., Ollikainen, J., Vainikainen, P.: Bandwith, sar, and efficiency of internal mobile phone antennas. IEEE Trans. on Electromagnetic Compatibility 46(1), 71–86 (2004)

19. Pelosi, M., Franek, O., Knudsen, M., Christensen, M., Pedersen, G.: A grip study for talk and data modes in mobile phones. IEEE Transactions on Antennas and Propagation 57(4), 856–865 (2009)

20. Ryder, J., Longstaff, B., Reddy, S., Estrin, D.: Ambulation: A tool for monitoring mobility patterns over time using mobile phones. In: International Conference on Computational Science and Engineering, pp. 927–931 (2009)

21. Sokolova, N., Forssell, B.: Moderate pedestrian traffic: Indoor hsgps receiver performance. European Journal of Navigation 5(3), 2–7 (2007)

22. Teuber, A., Paonni, M., Kropp, V., Hein, G.: Galileo signal fading in an indoor environment. In: Proc. 21st Intl. Techn. Meeting Satellite Division Inst. of Navigation (ION GNSS) (2008)

23. Vahdatpour, A., Amini, N., Sarrafzadeh, M.: On-body device localization for health and medical monitoring applications. In: Proceedings of the Ninth Annual IEEE International Conference on Pervasive Computing and Communications (2011)

24. Vaitl, C., Kunze, K., Lukowicz, P.: Does on-body location of a gps receiver matter? In: Int. Workshop on Wearable and Implantable Body Sensor Networks, pp. 219–221 (2010)

25. van Diggelen, F.: A-GPS: Assisted GPS, GNSS, and SBAS. Artech House, Boston (2009)

26. van Diggelen, F.: The smartphone revolution. GPS World 12 (2009)

27. Watson, R., Lachapelle, G., Klukas, R., Turunen, S., Pietil, S., Halivaara, I.: Investigating gps signals indoors with extreme high-sensitivity detection techniques. Navigation, Inst. of Navigation 52(4), 199–213 (2006)

28. Witten, I.H., Frank, E.: Data Mining: Practical machine learning tools and techniques, 2nd edn. Morgan Kaufmann, San Francisco (2005)

Author Index

GPSR Compliance

The European Union's (EU) General Product Safety Regulation (GPSR)
is a set of rules that requires consumer products to be safe and our
obligations to ensure this.

If you have any concerns about our products, you can contact us on
ProductSafety@springernature.com

In case Publisher is established outside the EU, the EU authorized
representative is:

Springer Nature Customer Service Center GmbH
Europaplatz 3
69115 Heidelberg, Germany

Batch number: 09490872

Printed by Printforce, the Netherlands